Communications in Computer and Information Science 1161

Commenced Publication in 2007
Founding and Former Series Editors:
Phoebe Chen, Alfredo Cuzzocrea, Xiaoyong Du, Orhun Kara, Ting Liu,
Krishna M. Sivalingam, Dominik Ślęzak, Takashi Washio, Xiaokang Yang,
and Junsong Yuan

More information about this series at http://www.springer.com/series/7899

Slimane Hammoudi · Luís Ferreira Pires ·
Bran Selić (Eds.)

Model-Driven Engineering and Software Development

7th International Conference, MODELSWARD 2019
Prague, Czech Republic, February 20–22, 2019
Revised Selected Papers

 Springer

Editors
Slimane Hammoudi
Siège du Groupe ESEO
Angers, France

Luís Ferreira Pires
University of Twente
Enschede, The Netherlands

Bran Selić
Malina Software Corporation
Nepean, ON, Canada

ISSN 1865-0929　　　　　　ISSN 1865-0937　(electronic)
Communications in Computer and Information Science
ISBN 978-3-030-37872-1　　　ISBN 978-3-030-37873-8　(eBook)
https://doi.org/10.1007/978-3-030-37873-8

This Springer imprint is published by the registered company Springer Nature Switzerland AG
The registered company address is: Gewerbestrasse 11, 6330 Cham, Switzerland

Preface

The present volume contains extended versions of selected papers from the 7th International Conference on Model-Driven Engineering and Software Development (MODELSWARD 2019), held in Prague, Czech Republic, during February 20–22, 2019.

The purpose of MODELSWARD 2019 was to provide a platform for researchers, engineers, academics, as well as industrial professionals from all over the world to present their research results and development activities in using models and model-driven engineering techniques for Software Development. Model-Driven Development (MDD) is an approach to the development of IT systems in which models take a central role, not only for analysis of these systems but also for their construction. MDD has emerged from modeling initiatives, most prominently the Model-Driven Architecture (MDA) fostered by the Object Management Group (OMG). In the scope of MDA, a couple of technologies have been developed that became the cornerstones of MDD, like metamodeling and model transformations. MDD relies on languages for defining metamodels, like the Meta-Object Facility (MOF) and Ecore (developed in the scope of the Eclipse Modeling Framework), and transformation specification languages like QVT and ATL.

This volume contains 16 papers that were selected by the event chairs, based on the evaluation and comments provided by the MODELSWARD Program Committee members, the session chairs' assessments, as well as the program chairs' review of all papers included in the technical program. The authors of the selected papers were then invited to submit a revised and extended version of their papers with at least 30% additional new material. The selected papers address some of the most relevant challenges being faced by researchers and practitioners in this area, and cover topics such as language design and tooling, programming support tools, code and text generation from models, behavior modeling and analysis, model transformations and multi-view modeling, as well as applications of MDD and its related techniques to cyber-physical systems, cybersecurity, IoT, autonomous vehicles, and healthcare.

We would like to thank all the authors for their contributions, and also the reviewers, who helped ensure the high quality of this publication.

February 2019

Slimane Hammoudi
Luís Ferreira Pires
Bran Selić

Organization

Conference Chair

Bran Selić   Malina Software Corp., Canada

Program Co-chairs

Slimane Hammoudi	ESEO, ERIS, France
Luis Ferreira Pires	University of Twente, The Netherlands

Program Committee

Achilleas Achilleos	University of Cyprus, Cyprus
Bülent Adak	Aselsan, Turkey
Ludovic Apvrille	LTCI, Télécom ParisTech, Université Paris-Saclay, France
Ethem Arkin	Aselsan, Turkey
Uwe Assmann	TU Dresden, Germany
Marco Autili	University of L'Aquila, Italy
Elarbi Badidi	United Arab Emirates University, UAE
Omar Badreddin	University of Texas at El Paso, USA
Mira Balaban	Ben-Gurion University of the Negev, Israel
Antonia Bertolino	CNR, Italy
Lorenzo Bettini	Università di Firenze, Italy
Stamatia Bibi	University of Western Macedonia, Greece
Paolo Bocciarelli	University of Rome Tor Vergata, Italy
Antonio Brogi	Università di Pisa, Italy
Achim Brucker	SAP Research, Germany
Matthias Brun	ESEO Group, France
Philipp Brune	Neu-Ulm University of Applied Sciences, Germany
Christian Bunse	University of Applied Sciences Stralsund, Germany
Juan Calleros	Universidad Autónoma de Puebla, Mexico
Renata Carvalho	Eindhoven University of Technology, The Netherlands
Hassan Charaf	BME, Hungary
Olena Chebanyuk	National Aviation University, Ukraine
Yuting Chen	Shanghai Jiaotong University, China
Dan Chiorean	Babes-Bolyai University, Romania
Antonio Cicchetti	Malardalen University, Sweden
Nebut Clémentine	LIRMM, Université de Montpellier, France
Andrea D'Ambrogio	University of Rome Tor Vergata, Italy
Guglielmo De Angelis	CNR-IASI, Italy
Sergio de Cesare	University of Westminster, UK

Wolfgang Reisig	Humboldt-Universität zu Berlin, Germany
Werner Retschitzegger	Johannes Kepler University, Austria
Colette Rolland	Université De Paris1 Panthèon Sorbonne, France
Jose Raul Romero	University of Cordoba, Spain
Gustavo Rossi	Lifia, Argentina
Francesca Saglietti	University of Erlangen-Nuremberg, Germany
Comai Sara	Politecnico di Milano, Italy
Anthony Savidis	Institute of Computer Science, FORTH, Greece
Wieland Schwinger	Johannes Kepler University, Austria
Itai Segall	Nokia Bell Labs, USA
Bran Selić	Malina Software Corp., Canada
Alberto Silva	IST, INESC-ID, Portugal
John Slaby	Raytheon, USA
Stefan Sobernig	WU Vienna, Austria
Pnina Soffer	University of Haifa, Israel
Stéphane Somé	University of Ottawa, Canada
Hui Song	SINTEF, Norway
Jean-Sébastier Sottet	Luxembourg Institute for Science and Technology, Luxembourg
Romina Spalazzese	Malmö University, Sweden
Ioanna Stamatopoulou	CITY College, International Faculty of the University of Sheeld, Greece
Ioannis Stamelos	Aristotle University of Thessaloniki, Greece
Alin Stefanescu	University of Bucharest, Romania
Arnon Sturm	Ben-gurion University of the Negev, Israel
Hiroki Suguri	Miyagi University, Japan
Massimo Tivoli	University of L'Aquila, Italy
Naoyasu Ubayashi	Kyushu University, Japan
Andreas Ulrich	Siemens AG, Germany
Gianluigi Viscusi	EPFL Lausanne, Switzerland
Layne Watson	Virginia Polytechnic Institute and State University, USA
Gera Weiss	Ben Gurion University, Israel
Gereon Weiss	Fraunhofer ESK, Germany
Hao Wu	National University of Ireland, Ireland
Husnu Yenigun	Sabanci University, Turkey
Chunying Zhao	Western Illinois University, USA
Haiyan Zhao	Peking University, China
Kamil Zyla	Lublin University of Technology, Poland

Additional Reviewers

Ievgen Ivanov	National Taras Shevchenko University of Kyiv, Ukraine
Rahad Khandoker	University of Texas at El Paso, USA
Omar Masmali	University of Texas at El Paso, USA

Sylvain Vauttier   LGI2P, France
Christopher Werner   TU Dresden, Germany

Invited Speakers

Hans Vangheluwe   University of Antwerp, Belgium
Ed Seidewitz   Model Driven Solutions, USA
Bran Selić   Malina Software Corp., Canada

Contents

Integrating UML and ALF: An Approach to Overcome the Code Generation Dilemma in Model-Driven Software Engineering

Johannes Schröpfer[✉] and Thomas Buchmann

Applied Computer Science I, University of Bayreuth, 95440 Bayreuth, Germany
{johannes.schroepfer,thomas.buchmann}@uni-bayreuth.de

Abstract. The state of the art in model-driven software engineering is a combination of structural modeling and conventional programming to supply the operational behavior of the system. This fact leads to the so-called code generation dilemma when model and hand-written code evolve independently during the software development process. In this paper we present an approach of integrating two OMG standards to overcome this problem: A tight integration of UML used for structural modeling and the Action Language for Foundational UML (ALF) for behavioral modeling using a textual surface notation leads to a full-blown model-driven process which allows for the generation of fully executable source code. Supplying hand-written code fragments in the target language is no longer necessary.

Keywords: Model-driven development · Code generation · Executable models · ALF · UML · BXtend · fUML · Xtext

1 Introduction

This paper is an extended version of [20] and provides besides an extended example use case some more technical details. *Model-driven software engineering* (MDSE) [24] aims at reducing effort for developing software by specifying higher-level (executable) models, instead of lower-level hand-written source code. An initial model capturing the requirements is often the starting point from which a number of models over multiple levels of abstraction is derived, until the system is eventually implemented. In order to support model-driven software engineering in a full-fledged way, key enabling technologies are mandatory for defining modeling languages and specifying and executing model transformations.

Usually, *modeling languages* are defined with the help of *metamodels* in the context of object-oriented modeling. To this end, the *Object Management Group (OMG)* provides the *Meta Object Facility (MOF)* standard [18]. Throughout the last two decades, *UML* [19] has been established as the de-facto standard modeling language for model-driven development. In its current version, UML

© Springer Nature Switzerland AG 2020
S. Hammoudi et al. (Eds.): MODELSWARD 2019, CCIS 1161, pp. 1–26, 2020.
https://doi.org/10.1007/978-3-030-37873-8_1

comprises seven kinds of diagrams dedicated to structural modeling and seven different diagrams addressing behavioral aspects of a software system. In order to support model-driven software engineering in a full-fledged way, having models which allow for a generation of fully executable code is crucial.

However, generating executable code requires a precise and well-defined execution semantics of behavioral models. Unfortunately, not all behavioral diagrams provided by UML are equipped with such a well-defined semantics. Furthermore, some diagrams with a well-defined execution semantics, e.g., activity diagrams, are on a lower level of abstraction in terms of specifying control flow. As a consequence, the state of the art in model-driven software engineering nowadays is specifying the static structure of the software system using models from which source code is generated. This generated source code is then augmented with behavioral elements using regular programming languages.

This fact which we call the *"code generation dilemma"* [6] is problematic as the different fragments of the software system tend to evolve separately which quickly leads to inconsistencies between the model and the (generated) source code. Round-trip engineering [7] may help to keep the structural parts consistent but unfortunately there is still no adequate representation of the manually supplied behavioral fragments.

The *Action Language for Foundational UML (ALF)* [15] is also an OMG standard addressing a textual surface representation for a major part of UML model elements. Furthermore, it provides an execution semantics via a mapping of the ALF concrete syntax to the abstract syntax of the OMG standard of a *Foundational Subset for Executable UML Models*, also known as *Foundational UML* or just *fUML* [16]. The primary goal is to provide a concrete textual syntax allowing software engineers to specify executable behavior within a wider model which is represented using the usual graphical notations of UML. A simple use case is the specification of method bodies for operations contained in class diagrams. To this end, it provides a language with a procedural character whose underlying data model is UML. However, ALF also provides a concrete syntax for structural modeling within the limits of the fUML subset.

In the academic world, the *Eclipse Modeling Framework (EMF)* [22] constitutes the platform for research dedicated to model-driven software engineering. Its metamodel *Ecore* is based on a subset of MOF called *Essential MOF (EMOF)*. Following a pragmatic approach, EMF strictly focuses on principles from object-oriented modeling only providing core concepts for defining classes, attributes, and relationships between classes. Furthermore, it allows for Java code generation from these structural model definitions. EMF provides an extensible platform for the development of MDSE applications.

In this paper, we present a tight integration of the OMG standards UML and ALF to realize an integrated modeling environment which allows for structural as well as behavioral modeling. Fully executable Java source code is generated from the resulting models, allowing for "real" MDSE approaches.

The paper is structured as follows: Sect. 2 provides a conceptual overview of our solution. An example use case is presented in Sect. 3. Technical details

are given in Sect. 4, while our approach is discussed in Sect. 5. Related work is
discussed in Sect. 6 before Sect. 7 concludes the paper.

2   Overview

As stated above, the current state of the art in model-driven software engineering is modeling the structure of a software system which is used as a basis for
generating code. In a subsequent step, the generated code is augmented with
manually programmed method bodies to supply behavior as shown in Fig. 1.
In a strict waterfall-like development process, this approach is feasible. But in
iterative processes, the danger of model and code evolving separately is imma-
nent. In the past, approaches addressing this issue using round-trip engineering
between model and source code have been published [5,7,9]. However, a much
better solution would clearly separate the primary development artifacts – i.e.,
the development models – from generated ones – i.e., the generated platform-
specific source code – in order to avoid a concurrent evolution of artifacts located
on different levels of abstraction as depicted in Fig. 2.

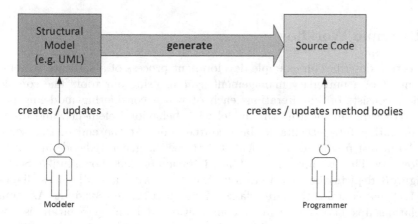

Fig. 1. A state-of-the-art MDSD process.

To this end, our work presented in this paper integrates two OMG standards
in a single tool-chain. (1) UML [19] models are used for structural modeling and
(2) ALF [15] is used to model the behavior in terms of method bodies. While
UML provides a wide range of diagrams supporting structural modeling, we limited ourselves to package diagrams for the task of modeling-in-the-large [4] and
class diagrams for modeling-in-the-small. The ALF standard primarily addresses
a textual surface representation for a subset of UML model elements. Its main
benefit is an execution semantics which allows for the generation of *executable
code* out of ALF specifications. Executable code in this context means that the
resulting source code also comprises method bodies and extending generated
source code with hand-written code fragments is no longer necessary.

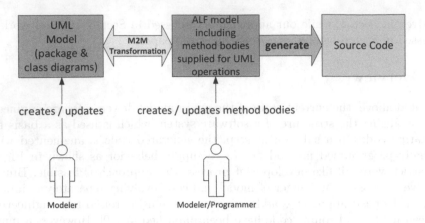

Fig. 2. MDSD process realized with our approach.

The following section introduces an example workflow which may occur in a real-life iterative development process as an interaction between design and implementation phase.

3   Example Workflow

This section describes an example development process of a software system in the context of a university management system using our tool. The complete workflow consists of four iterations each of which considering modeling parts of the structure, augmenting the model with behavioral elements, and eventually generating fully executable Java source code. At the end of this section some JUnit test fragments are provided that use the generated code and test its functionality. This example is an extended version of that shown in [20, Sect. 5].

Figure 3 depicts the first iteration. We start with a UML class diagram (step 1.1) that contains the three classes Exam, Result, and Student. As semantic relationships between them, a composition and an aggregation is used. The classes contain one operation and several properties where the property Result::note is derived; for an instance of the class Result, the value note constitutes the string representation of the numeric literal stored by Result::value, e.g., the note "excellent" for the values 1.0 and 1.3. By invoking the corresponding command, the background transformation creates the ALF model system from the UML model (step 1.2). The ALF model system consists of the main model for the structural model elements and two branch models for the created ALF operations storing the behavioral elements; one ALF operation corresponds with the UML operation and one with the derived UML property. Since derived UML properties are not contained in the fUML subset, they are approximated by ALF operations that are supposed to define the computation semantics. In addition, fUML does not support aggregations. In this case, the user is informed of this incidence and can decide whether the transformation is executed or aborted; if the transformation is not aborted, its execution results

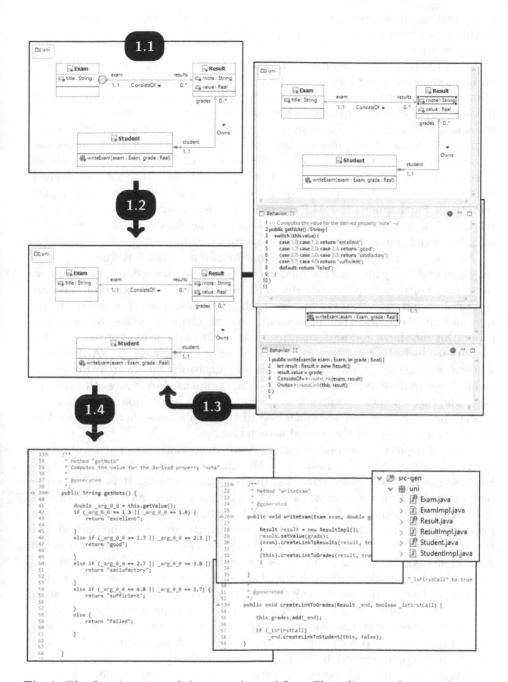

Fig. 3. The first iteration of the example workflow. Class diagram elements that are colored red are non-fUML elements that are adapted during the process. (Color figure online)

in converting the aggregation into an ordinary, fUML-compatible association. In this scenario, the user decides to accept this simplification and executes the transformation.

After the transformation has been executed, the semantics of the ALF operations is modeled (step 1.3). By clicking the related UML element – the operation or the derived property, respectively – the user gets access to the textual representation of the related branch model within an extra view providing an embedded text editor. At this moment, the operations only consist of the structural elements, i.e., the operation head and its parameters. By completing the respective operation textually, its behavior is defined. First, the ALF operation `Result::getNote()` for the derived UML property `Result::note` is defined by means of a switch statement for mapping the real values to string representations. Furthermore, the ALF operation `Student::writeExam(...)` for the related UML operation creates a new instance of the class `Result` and inserts it into the model system by means of link operation expressions for creating links.

Now, the structure as well as the behavior of our model is defined, i.e., it is fully executable. By invoking the related command, Java source code is generated (step 1.4). For the complete class diagram, one package is created that contains several Java interfaces and classes. For each UML class, there is one Java interface and one Java class that implements the respective interface; by means of generating interfaces and implementing classes, the obstacle of expressing multi-inheritance in UML with Java is overcome. Since in this case, the ALF switch statements cannot be expressed by completely analogous Java switch statements (underlying version: Java 1.8), Java if statements are used to express this semantics. The link operation expressions are mapped to invocation expressions of special Java methods that are generated in the Java classes that correspond to UML member classes of the related association.

Figure 4 depicts the second iteration. At the beginning, the structural model is extended (step 2.1). The resulting UML class diagram has a new data type `Evaluation` for storing statistical information about exams. It is used by the new operation `Exam::computeStatistics()` that returns an instance of this data type. Furthermore, the class `Student` contains two properties where the property `Student::matrNr` is set to be read-only. By executing the background transformation again, the modifications of the UML model are propagated to the ALF model system (step 2.2), i.e., it is not built up from scratch again but it is augmented by new elements such that the behavioral ALF elements that have been defined within the preceding iteration are still contained. The model system exhibits two additional ALF operations – one corresponds with the new UML operation and one with the read-only property `Student::matrNr`. Properties in fUML cannot be set to read-only and are therefore not supported by ALF. The semantics is approximated by mapping UML read-only properties to private ALF properties and ALF access operations to read the values; i.e., while the values can be modified within their respective classes by setting the property, from outside only the getter operations can be accessed since the visibility of

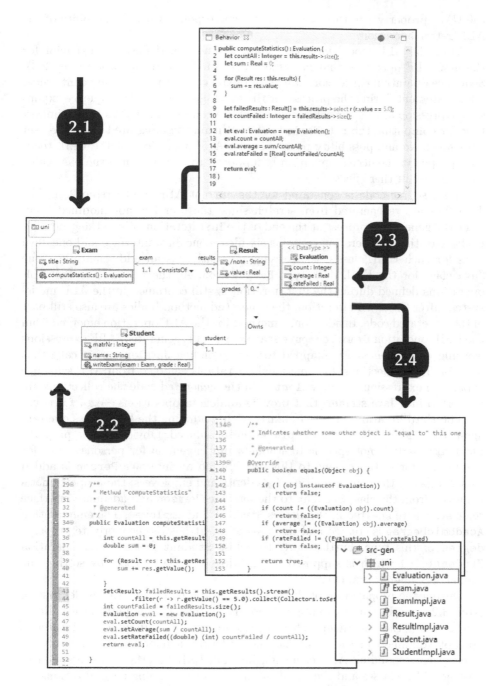

Fig. 4. The second iteration of the example workflow. Elements that are colored red are additional class diagram artifacts or source code files which are created during the second iteration. (Color figure online)

the UML property – in this case `public` – corresponds with the visibility of the ALF getter operation.

After the ALF model has been adapted, the user defines the behavior for the new ALF operation that has emerged from the UML operation (step 2.3). Sequence operation expressions are used for the computation of the `count` value, a for statement during the process for the `average` value, and a sequence expansion expression to find the correct subset of the collection `results` that is important for computing the `rateFailed` value. Within the integrated view, the user does not have any possibility to modify the ALF operation for the UML readonly property; the access operation is supposed to purely return the base value without any further effects.

Next, source code is generated for the current ALF model (step 2.4). The Java files are regenerated from scratch since the user has not modified them after the generation process at the end of the first iteration. While the generated package of the first iteration contains six files – one Java interface and one Java class for each UML class – the package currently has an additional file – one Java class for the UML data type `Evaluation`. As the behavior of the ALF operations defined during the first iteration is still contained in the ALF model system after the second iteration, the generated method bodies are also still part of the generated code. In addition, a method for the ALF operation emerged from the UML operation `Exam::computeStatistics()` is generated. ALF expressions working on sequences are mapped to corresponding Java operation calls that work on Java collections; for functional operations emerged from ALF sequence expansion expressions – e.g., `select` –, in the generated code the collections are converted into Java streams that provide analogous operations – e.g., `filter`.

The third iteration (cf. Fig. 5) starts with modifying the UML class diagram again (step 3.1). A new class `Employee` is introduced. Obviously, the property `Student::name` is not specific to students but is general for persons – also for employees, for instance. Due to this observation an interface `Person` is added that comprises the commonalities of students and employees; the property `name` is moved from the class `Student` to the interface `Person` and adequate interface realizations are inserted in the classes `Student` and `Employee`. The enumeration `AcademicDegree` is created and the class `Student` has the new private property `degree` of this type. Furthermore, the class `Student` has the new operation `Student(...)` which is supposed to initialize a student object by setting the property `Student::matrNr`.

During the propagation of the new modifications to the ALF model system (step 3.2), another approximation of non-fUML elements is performed. Within this iteration, the class diagram has been augmented with an interface. Interfaces are not contained in the fUML subset and can therefore not be mapped to directly corresponding ALF elements; instead, UML interfaces are mapped to abstract ALF classes and their realizations to corresponding generalizations.

Now, the new operation can be implemented (step 3.3); in its textual syntax, the operation can be identified to be a constructor by means of the annotation `@Create`. The constructor is supposed to assign an initial value to the

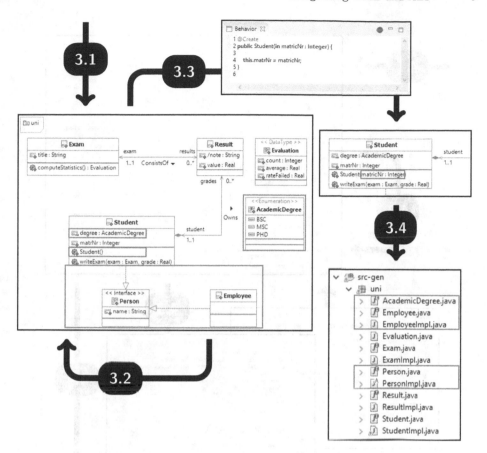

Fig. 5. The third iteration of the example workflow. Elements that are colored red are additional class diagram artifacts or source code files which are created during the third iteration. (Color figure online)

property `Student::matrNr`. At this point, the user recognizes that the constructor needs an input parameter and the signature modeled in the class diagram is not complete as there is no input parameter defined at all. Since the text editor represents the complete ALF operation – including head and in particular its parameter –, this modification can also be performed now. In the operation body, the value of the parameter is assigned to the property. While completing and saving the ALF operation modification process, the edit within the parameter list is incrementally propagated to the UML model and as a result, it is also visible in the UML diagram.

At the end of the third iteration, source code is generated (step 3.4). The source package contains five new files: one Java interface and one Java class for each of both the new UML class – that was transformed to an ALF class – and the new UML interface – that was also transformed to an ALF class – and one Java enumeration for the UML enumeration. The Java interface `Person` for the UML class `Person` is a super-interface of both the Java interfaces `Student` and

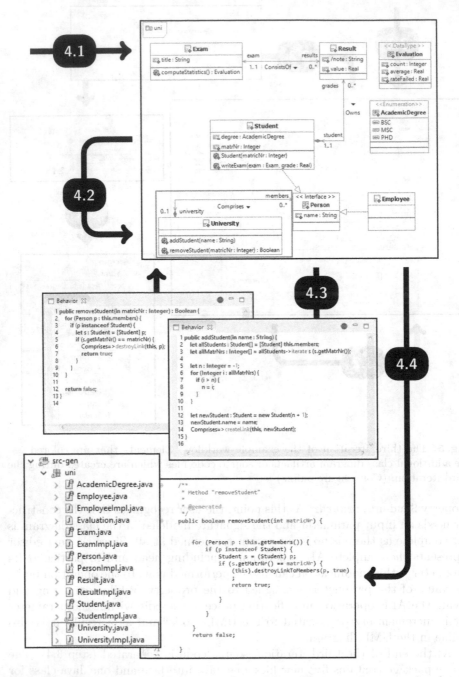

Fig. 6. The fourth iteration of the example workflow. Elements that are colored red are additional class diagram artifacts or source code files which are created during the fourth iteration. (Color figure online)

Employee. The Java class `PersonImpl` for the UML class `Person` is a super-class for both the UML classes `StudentImpl` and `EmployeeImpl`. From the ALF constructor, a Java constructor is generated that can be called to create new instances of this class.

Finally, a fourth iteration follows (cf. Fig. 6) which starts again with adding UML elements to the class diagram (step 4.1). The university itself is modeled by means of a UML class `University` that is connected to the interface `Person` by means of a composition. For the purpose of managing students, two UML properties are inserted in the new class `University`. The UML operation `addStudent(...)` adds a student with the `name` value specified as parameter. The UML operation `removeStudent(...)` removes the student with the `matrNr` value specified as parameter and returns `true` if and only if there exists an appropriate object; otherwise, `false` is returned.

During the transformation process (step 4.2), two new branch models for the two UML operations are created. The behavior is implemented (step 4.3). Both operations `addStudent(...)` and `removeStudent(...)` use for statements in order to iterate over collections. While the operation `removeStudent(...)` uses the reference `University::persons` itself as its underlying collection, the operation `addStudent(...)` converts the collection of persons to a collection of integers representing the students' matriculation numbers; for that purpose, a cast expression is used to filter the `Student` objects within the collection of `Person` objects and a sequence expansion expression (`iterate`) is used to map the collection of students to the collection of their `matrNr` values. For adding and removing the links, both operations use adequate link operation expressions. Since the `matrNr` value is supposed to be unique among all `Student` objects contained in some `University` object, the `Student` object created by the operation `addStudent(...)` gets the currently maximum value incremented by one as its `matrNr` value.

Listing 1. JUnit test cases for the generated Java code.

```
@Test public void testStudentsCreation() {
    University university = new UniversityImpl();
    assertTrue(university.getStudents().isEmpty());
    university.addStudents("Alice");
    university.addStudents("Bob");
    assertEquals(2, university.getMembers().size());
    assertTrue(university.removeStudent(1));
    assertFalse(university.removeStudent(1));
    assertTrue(university.removeStudent(0));
    assertTrue(university.getStudents().isEmpty());
}

@Test public void testStudentsCreation() {
    University university = new UniversityImpl();
    university.addStudent("Alice");
    Student s = (Student) university.getMembers().iterator().next();
    Exam exam = new ExamImpl();
    assertTrue(exam.getResults().isEmpty());
    assertTrue(s.getGrades().isEmpty());
    s.writeExam(exam, 3);
    assertTrue(!exam.getResults().isEmpty());
    assertTrue(!s.getGrades().isEmpty());
}
```

At the end of the fourth iteration, Java code is generated for the last time (step 4.4). For the new UML class, two Java files are generated. The ALF link operation expressions for creating and destroying links are mapped to invocations of special Java methods that are generated in the Java classes corresponding to the UML members classes of the new composition.

During four iterations a model has emerged that contains structural as well as behavioral elements from which fully-executable source code has been generated that does not require any further user editing in order to use it by further programs. As an application for the generated Java source code, several test cases are provided. Listing 1 depicts two JUnit test methods that check the correct semantics of the generated Java source code, in particular of the generated Java methods that have emerged from the specified ALF operations.

4   Integration of UML and ALF

This section describes the implementation background concerning the technical as well as the visual integration of the textual ALF editor and the graphical UML-based modeling tool *Valkyrie* [1]. The diagram editor within the Valkyrie environment was created using GMF; *GMF* (*Graphical Modeling Framework*)[1] generates projectional editors as this is a typical architecture for graphical editors: The underlying model – in case of Valkyrie the UML model – and the diagram that constitutes a view onto the model – in this case the class diagram – are separated into two files. When the user edits the model using editor commands – e.g., the name of a model element is modified –, the underlying model is modified and afterwards, the changes are propagated to the diagram.

In contrast to the projectional GMF-based editor, the textual ALF editor was built using *Xtext*[2] and therefore constitutes a parser-based editor: The text files are persisted and a parser creates an in-memory model representation for each text file; the resulting model is a temporary artifact and is not persisted within an additional file. The visual integration combines the projectional graphical UML class diagram editor for modeling structure and the parser-based textual ALF editor for modeling behavior as well as a bidirectional and incremental synchronization between them.

4.1   Overview of the Tool Chain

Figure 7 shows an overview of models involved in the tool chain of our approach. The graphical editor shows the UML class diagram (1) that corresponds to an underlying UML model (2). Since the graphical editor is a projectional editor, the user modifies the underlying model directly and the changes are propagated to the diagram.

The UML model is involved in the background model transformation. A bidirectional and incremental transformation (3, cf. Sect. 4.4) converts it into

---

[1] https://www.eclipse.org/modeling/gmp/.
[2] https://www.eclipse.org/Xtext/.

an ALF model system (4, cf. Sect. 4.2) – corresponding to the UML model, but containing several models – and vice versa. The ALF model system is augmented with behavioral elements by means of the textual ALF editor (5). For each UML element within the class diagram, a counterpart within the ALF model system is present. As a result, the for ALF editor functions – e.g., content assist proposals – as well as the code generation process (6, cf. Sect. 4.3) can be limited to the ALF system since no information from the UML model is required.

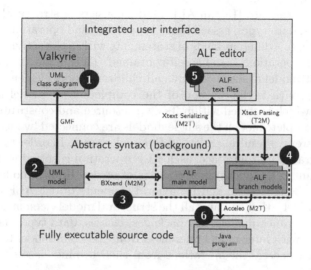

Fig. 7. An overview of the tool chain. Based on [20, Fig. 3].

The basic idea of the visual integration within an integrated user interface provides a textual editor that only shows an ALF operation and not the complete ALF model. The ALF model system comprises several models: one main model – which contains most of the structural elements corresponding to the UML model aside from operation contents as parameters – and several branch models – which comprise apart from structural artifacts of the ALF operations all the behavioral model elements which are not stored in the UML model.

From the branch models, the textual representations of the ALF operations – that are visible in the text editor – are created by means of reusing the Xtext serialization process. The serialization process works incrementally, i.e., if a textual representation of the ALF operation already exists, the body is not affected; thus, custom layout and comments are preserved. When the text files are modified, a parsing process propagates the changes to the respective branch model. Within this process, the abstract syntax tree that is build temporarily by the Xtext parser is used to store the mentioned changes permanently within the ALF model system; when this process is performed, the contents of the branch models are changed but no new resource is created such that the references between the main model and the branch models are not affected. Finally, the code generator that is implemented using Acceleo[3] creates Java files for ALF model elements. The code generator retrieves information from the main model as well as the branch models; as a result, fully executable source code is generated that contains complete method bodies without requiring any manual code extensions by a user.

4.2 The ALF Model System

According to the standard [15], an ALF model consists of structural elements – packages, classes, data types, associations, properties, and operations – as well as behavioral elements – different kinds of statements within the activity definitions of the respective operations – and is self-contained. Thus, a model resource with exactly one root model element contains all children model elements. The basic idea of this approach is the division of the complete ALF model into several models each of which is stored within its own resource and constitutes a certain portion of the complete model; the single models are connected by means of inter-model cross references resulting in an ALF model system. In order to achieve the goal of an integrated user interface, each ALF operation is stored within its own model. Hence, an ALF model system consists of several branch models – each of which contains the structural and behavioral elements of one ALF operation – and one main model – that contains all the structural model elements that are not contained in the branch models, i.e., packages, classes, data types, associations, and properties – with inter-model references from the main model to the branch models in order to access the operations from their owning classes.

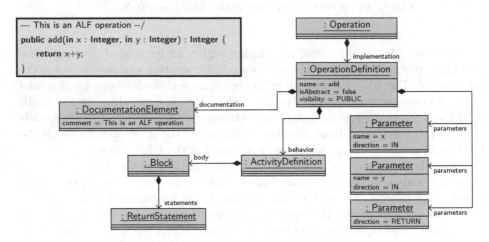

Fig. 8. A textually represented example ALF operation and its abstract syntax tree (simplified).

---

[3] https://www.eclipse.org/acceleo/.

To this end, the underlying ALF metamodel resulting from the official standard was slightly modified in order to conform to our approach. The standard provides one metaclass `Operation` for ALF operations. The access to the surrounding context – represented by the metaclass `Class` – is provided by means of a container reference – called `ownerClass` here. The adapted metamodel that is used for this approach comprises three metaclasses for representing ALF operations:

- The metaclass `OperationDefinition` contains all the information about operations that is necessary in order to serialize them within a text file. This includes attribute values – e.g., the name and the visibility –, documentation, contained formal parameters – represented by the metaclass `Parameter` –, and the contained behavior – represented by the metaclass `ActivityDefinition`.
- The metaclass `Operation` serves as the root class for the branch models. Instances of `OperationDefinition` are contained in respective instances of `Operation`. For technical reasons, not the metaclass `OperationDefinition` serves as the root class; instead, an additional metaclass was introduced. The textual representation of an `Operation` instance only comprises an initially empty text file; if the textual representation contains an ALF operation representation, this corresponds to an `OperationDefinition` instance that is contained in the `Operation` instance.
- Finally, the adapted metamodel contains the metaclass `OperationNode` that provides the container reference `ownerClass`. Its instances are contained in the main model and serve as placeholders for the operations that are contained in the branch models and accessed by means of the inter-model cross reference `operation` with the metaclass `OperationNode` as its source and `Operation` as its target.

Figure 8 depicts the textual representation of an example ALF operation and the underlying model. The root `Operation` contains the `OperationDefinition` object – represented by the whole text fragment – that contains three parameters, some documentation, and a `ReturnStatement` object as a behavioral element.

Figure 9 shows a complete ALF model system consisting of a main model – with a `Model` instance as its root – and two branch models. The main model contains the classes, enumerations, properties, and `OperationNode` instances that provide links to the root objects of the branch models – `Operation` instances. The branch models contain the operations – `OperationDefinition` instances – as well as their parameters and the respective body – represented by an `ActivityDefinition` instance.

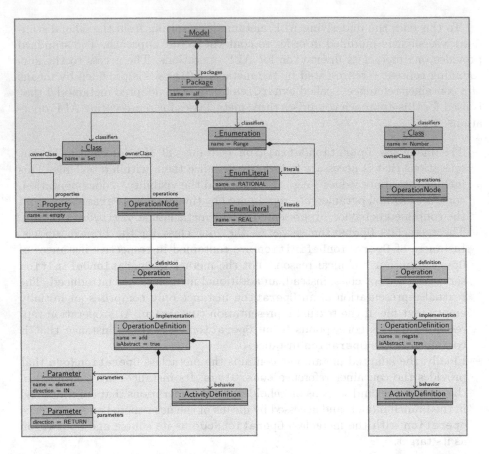

Fig. 9. An example ALF model system (simplified). Each model persisted within its own resource is surrounded by a rectangle; elements of the main model are colored blue, elements of the branch models brown. (Color figure online)

4.3 Generation of Java Source Code

In order to execute the modeled software system, Java source code is generated using a model-to-text transformation. For this purpose, we use *Acceleo*[4] that allows to express the transformation by templates and queries pretty intuitively using the *Object Constraint Language* (*OCL*) [17]. It constitutes a pragmatic implementation of the *MOF Model to Text Transformation Language* (*MOFM2T*) [14] standard. Acceleo allows for an integration of Java code: Queries can be defined by invoking Java methods besides expressing the queries exhaustively with OCL expressions. For this approach, "Java services" are used to access other parts of the implementation, e.g., the ALF type system used for the text editor.

---

[4] https://www.eclipse.org/acceleo/.

For a given ALF model system, the Acceleo templates use the main model as well as all the branch models for generating fully executable source code. The contained ALF classifiers are successively transformed to Java files – ALF classes to pairs of Java interfaces and classes, ALF data types to Java classes, and ALF enumerations to Java enumerations. By accessing the branch models, the body implementations of the ALF operations are transformed to corresponding Java method bodies. Functional ALF expressions that cannot be expressed by completely analogous Java 1.8 constructs – e.g., operations for filtering collections – are mapped to Java operation calls that work on streams. Java streams are sequences of elements supporting sequential and parallel aggregation operations as filtering and mapping methods.

4.4 The Kernel Model-to-Model Transformation

The kernel of the tool chain constitutes the model transformation between UML models and ALF model systems. It was implemented using the *BXtend* approach [3]; a physically persisted correspondence model contains objects which represent the correspondence links between UML and ALF model elements. The transformation is bidirectional: An arbitrary UML model is transformed to an ALF model system that contains ALF elements that approximately express the semantics given by the UML model and vice versa.

Since ALF only supports fUML which is a proper subset of the complete UML metamodel, some UML elements cannot be transformed into completely corresponding ALF element; using alternate mappings an approximation of the UML elements in question by several ALF elements is performed such that significant non-fUML elements often used in practice are also supported by this approach (cf. Table 1).

Table 1. Mapping significant non-fUML elements to appropriate ALF elements [20].

UML model elements	Alternate ALF model elements
Derived property	Getter operation
Read-only property	Property + getter operation
Interface	Abstract class
Interface realization	Generalization

Furthermore, the transformation works incrementally, i.e., in case a UML model and a corresponding ALF model system already exist, model changes are propagated to the respective opposite model rather than creating those models from scratch again. This is an important feature for software development processes in practice which consist of several incremental iterations until the software system reaches its final state. On the one hand, user-supplied method bodies have to be retained when the UML model is transformed. On the other hand, in general UML model elements are referenced by other models such that if they were replaced, links from other models would get lost; in case of the UML tool presented here, those links exist from the diagram file to the UML model which would become invalid if underlying UML model elements were replaced.

The transformation definition comprises a sequence of bidirectional transformation rule calls each of which is applied to all appropriate model elements. By means of a boolean expression that at least contains a check for the correct type, the considered subset of model elements for a certain transformation rule and direction is filtered; for each model element at most one transformation rule exists for which the related boolean expression is satisfied. The execution order of the transformation rules ensures that if a model element is transformed, its container element (if any) has already been transformed resulting in a top-down traversation. The rules are applied to main model elements as well as branch model elements. For ALF operations, the respective `OperationNode` instance is called from which the respective branch model is accessed. The single rules are applied to the model elements in the following order:

1. The model roots are considered. Each UML model root instance corresponds to an ALF model root instance with a contained root package.
2. The rules **UmlClass2AlfClass** and **UmlInterface2AlfClass** are applied. UML interfaces are approximated by means of abstract ALF classes.
3. The transformation rules for associations, structured data types, enumerations, and enumeration literals are applied.
4. For UML properties and operations, three rules are provided: The rule **UmlProperty2AlfProperty** is applied to UML properties that are not derived – they correspond to ALF properties and (if they are read-only properties) to an accessing getter operation –, the rule **UmlProperty2AlfOperation** to derived UML properties – they correspond to ALF getter operations – and finally the rule **UmlOperation2AlfOperation** for UML operations – corresponding to ordinary ALF operations.
5. Parameters are considered. For technical reasons, two different rules are provided depending on the direction of the parameter.
6. UML comments are transformed to appropriate ALF documentation.
7. The rules **UmlGeneralization2AlfGeneralization** and **UmlInterfaceRealization 2AlfGeneralization** are applied. Due to the approximation of UML interfaces by means of abstract ALF classes, UML interface realizations lead to ALF generalizations.

Listing 2. Xtend class for the bidirectional transformation rule **UmlAssociation2AlfAssociation**.

```
class UmlAssociation2AlfAssociation extends UmlElem2AlfElem {
    // constructors omitted ...

    override sourceToTarget(String desc) { // UML2ALF
        sourceModel.eAllContents.filter(typeof(UmlAssociation)).forEach[a |
            val target = a.getOrCreateCorrModelElement(desc)
                    .getOrCreateTargetElem(ALF_ASSOCIATION) as AlfAssociation

            target.isAbstract = a.isAbstract
            target.name = a.name
            target.visibility = a.visibility.umlVisibilityToAlfVisibility;

            (a.eContainer.corrModelElem.targetElem as AlfPackage)
                    .classifiers += target
        ]
        super.sourceToTarget(desc)
    }

    override targetToSource(String desc) { // ALF2UML
        // completely symmetrical to sourceToTarget(...)
    }
}
```

The Xtend classes for the transformation rules have the same structure. They specialize the abstract super-class **UmlElem2AlfElem** and redefine the methods **sourceToTarget(...)** – transforming UML elements to corresponding ALF elements – and **targetToSource(...)** – transforming ALF elements to corresponding UML elements. The Xtend class for the transformation rule **UmlAssociation2 AlfAssociation** is depicted in Listing 2. Since both methods have the same structure, we only consider the method **sourceToTarget(...)**, i.e., the direction UML to ALF. The body starts with filtering the correct elements; in this case, all UML model elements that are associations and therefore have the correct type are considered. Each selected element **a** is transformed now: If it does not already exist a corresponding **target** element, a new object is created; otherwise, it exists a correspondence element for **a** and **target** such that the **target** object can be accessed. Next, the attribute values are transformed. Finally, the **target** element is added to its container (if it is not already contained) – the corresponding element for the container of **a** – that has already been transformed due to the execution order of the rules. After this iteration, the super-method is called that performs general clean-up operations as deleting model elements that have no correspondence elements any more.

Listing 3. Xtend class for the bidirectional transformation rule **UmlOpera-tion2AlfOperation**.

```
class UmlOperation2AlfOperation extends UmlElem2AlfElem {
    // constructors omitted ...

    override sourceToTarget(String desc) { // UML2ALF
        sourceModel.eAllContents.filter(typeof(UmlOperation)).forEach[o |
            val target = a.getOrCreateCorrModelElement(desc)
                        .getOrCreateTargetElem(ALF_OPERATION_NODE)
                        as AlfOperationNode
            val opDef = target.getOrCreateOperationDefinition(o)

            opDef.isAbstract =
                        o.eContainer instanceof UmlInterface || o.isAbstract
            // some more assignments omitted  ...

            // setting container omitted ...
        ]
        super.sourceToTarget(desc)
    }

    override targetToSource(String desc) { // ALF2UML
        targetModel.eAllContents.filter(typeof(AlfOperationNode)).forEach[o |
            val opDef = o.operation.implementation

            if (opDef.isGetter) {
                val source = o.getOrCreateCorrModelElement(desc)
                            .getOrCreateTargetElem(UML_OPERATION)
                            as UmlOperation

                source.isAbstract = opDef.isAbstract
                // some more assignments omitted  ...

                // setting container omitted ...
            }
        ]
        super.targetToSource(desc)
    }
}
```

Since the ALF model system consists of a collection of models each of which represents a certain portion of the context, executing transformation rules may come along with creating and deleting models. If a UML operation is transformed and a corresponding ALF `OperationNode` instance does not exist yet, the rule does not only have to create a new `OperationNode` object but also the branch model for this operation. Analogously, if a UML operation is removed, the respective branch model has to be deleted. Listing 3 shows the Xtend class for the transformation rule **UmlOperation2AlfOperation**. During the iteration over the `UmlOperation` within the method `sourceToTarget(...)`, for each object o not only the corresponding `AlfOperationNode` object but also its `AlfOperationDefinition` object is considered. This is performed by calling the operation `getOrCreateOperationDefinition(...)` returning the linked `AlfOperationDefinition` instance; if the branch model does not exist yet, it is created and the links are set correctly. The assignments – apart from setting the container – use the `AlfOperationDefinition` object directly. Within the method `targetToSource(...)` the branch model is directly accessed; since an `OperationNode` instance requires a transitively contained `OperationDefinition` child object, it is ensured that it exists.

4.5   The Integrated User Interface

One significant goal for the integrated modeling tool was that the integration is not reduced to a technical combination of both languages UML and ALF but also comprises the user interface constituting a visual integration of different editors such that an easy and fluent usage is feasible. Although a pretty wide range of models are involved in the background processes, the user should get the feeling of editing one model instead of a collection of models where each of them represents a certain portion of the context. This section describes the foundations of the implementation with respect to the user interface.

In order to facilitate an integrated user interface, an Eclipse view was created that provides the textual modifications of the ALF operations. While the class diagram is visible within the graphical editor which constitutes the main editor where the user edits the structure, the behavior is modified textually within the additional view.

Xtext provides tool support to embed generated editors within SWT composites which is used for our tool to embed the text editor within the Eclipse view. The view contents depend on the user's actions in the main editor. If the user clicks an operation or a derived property within the class diagram, the view is notified about the respective edit part and shows the embedded editor with the textual representation of the corresponding ALF operation. The complete ALF operation is now visible and can be edited as in case of a usual text editor; apart from behavioral modeling concerning the operation body, also the structural model elements related to the operation – i.e., the name, the visibility, the parameter list, and documentation – can be modified textually. The view provides a button for finishing and persisting the current modification of the respective ALF operation; when the button is clicked, the respective text file is saved, the parsing process of the ALF model is performed and eventually the ALF-to-UML transformation is induced such that the structural changes of the respective operation get visible within the class diagram. Thus, the integrated tool provides round-trip engineering with respect to structural elements of operations; all other structural model elements are edited within the diagram editor while behavior can only be edited textually.

5   Discussion

In this section, the approach presented in this paper is discussed. First, the resulting benefits are given:

Fully Executable Models. This approach overcomes the code generation dilemma that occurs when model and hand-written code evolve independently. Specifying both structure and behavior leads to a generation of fully executable source code that can be used by further programs and does not require any user interaction or code modifications afterwards; any information contained in the model is mapped adequately to the resulting source code automatically.

Convenient Notation. Our approach combines modeling structure and behavior using two different modeling languages and two different paradigms of editing models. On the one hand, the projectional diagram editor provides convenient graphical notation for modeling structural elements. On the other hand, behavior is added textually by means of the parser-based editor instead of using another graphical editor; while graphical notation for behavioral model elements can result in very large and confusing diagrams, using textual syntax results in concise model representations that are easy to read and understand.

Visual Integration. Modeling structure using UML diagrams and behavior using ALF text is not only combined technically but also visually: The different editors are combined in the modeling environment by means of appropriate Eclipse concepts. The user gets the feeling of editing one model instead of dealing with a collection of models that are involved in the background.

Interlinked Model System. Another conceivable approach to overcome the code generation dilemma could provide for modeling the structure and adding the behavior by means of code snippets in terms of plain text comments in the UML model. By contrast, our approach contains all the information of the modeled system in several models within an interlinked system; hence, all the artifacts used for the code generation – in particular the ALF operations – are persisted in terms of models within the ALF model system. In contrast to plain code snippets, cross links can be exploited to find model elements and text editor mechanisms as a content assist can be used.

Flexible Workflow. The kernel transformation converting UML models to ALF model systems and vice versa is bidirectional and incremental. Thus, a very flexible workflow is supported that allows for development processes consisting of several iterations of editing structural and behavioral model elements.

These aspects emphasize in particular the benefits of using ALF as the underlying language for expressing behavioral elements. However, using ALF comes along with a significant drawback with respect to expressiveness: Although by means of ALF a quite large range of model elements can be expressed, only a proper subset of UML is supported; thus, some elements – e.g., interfaces – cannot be expressed exactly. Nevertheless, the semantics of non-fUML elements often can be approximated pretty well using alternate components – e.g., abstract classes instead of interfaces – such that in practice, the limited expressiveness resulting from using ALF does not restrict the modeling process too hard.

6   Related Work

In the past, several tools relying on textual or graphical syntax, or even a combination thereof have been published aiming for addressing model-driven development with special emphasis on modeling behavior. While some of them are equipped with code generation capabilities, others only allow for creating models and thus only serve as a visualization tool.

Fujaba [23] is a graphical modeling language based on graph transformations which allows to express both the structural and the behavioral part of a software system on the modeling level. Furthermore, Fujaba provides a code generation engine that is able to transform the Fujaba specifications into executable Java code. Behavior is specified using *story diagrams*. A story diagram resembles UML activity diagrams where the activities are described using *story patterns*. A story pattern specifies a graph transformation rule where both the left hand side and the right hand side of the rule are displayed in a single graphical notation. While story patterns provide a declarative way to describe manipulations of the run time object graph on a high level of abstraction, the control flow of a method is on a rather basic level as the control flow in activity diagrams is on the same level as control flow diagrams. As a case study [8] revealed, software systems only contain a low number of problems which require complex story patterns. The resulting story diagrams nevertheless are big and look complex because of the limited capabilities to express the control flow.

Another textual modeling language, designed for *model-oriented programming*, is provided by **Umple**[5]. The language has been developed independently from the EMF context and may be used as an Eclipse plug-in or via an online service. In its current state, Umple allows for structural modeling with UML class diagrams and describing behavior using state machines. A code generation engine allows to translate Umple specifications into Java, Ruby, or PHP code. Umple scripts may also be visualized using a graphical notation. Unfortunately, the Eclipse-based editor only offers basic functions like syntax highlighting and a simple validation of the parsed Umple model. Umple offers an interesting approach which aims at assisting developers in rasing the level of abstraction ("umplification") in their programs [12]. Using this approach, a Java program may be stepwise translated into an Umple script. The level of abstraction is raised by using Umple syntax for associations.

Xcore[6] recently gained more and more attention in the modeling community. It provides a textual concrete syntax for Ecore models allowing to express the structure as well as the behavior of the system. In contrast to ALF, the textual concrete syntax is not based on an official standard. Xcore relies on Xbase – a statically typed expression language built on Java – to model behavior. Executable Java code may be generated from Xcore models. Just as the realization of ALF presented in this paper, Xcore blurs the gap between Ecore modeling and Java programming. In contrast to ALF, the behavioral modeling part of Xcore has a strongly procedural character. As a consequence an object-oriented way of modeling is only possible to a limited extent. For instance, there is no way to define object constructors to describe the instantiation of objects of a class. Since Xcore reuses the EMF code generation mechanism [22], the factory pattern is used for object creation. Furthermore, ALF provides more expressive power since it is based on fUML while Xcore only addresses Ecore.

The graphical UML modeling tool **Papyrus** [10] allows for creating UML, SysML, and MARTE models using various diagram editors. Additionally, Papyrus offers dedicated support for UML profiles which includes customizing the Papyrus UI to get a DSL-like look and feel. Papyrus is equipped with a

---

[5] http://cruise.site.uottawa.ca/umple.

[6] http://wiki.eclipse.org/Xcore.

code generation engine allowing for producing source code from class diagrams (currently Java and C++ is supported). Future versions of Papyrus will also come with an ALF editor. A preliminary version of the editor is available and allows a glimpse on its provided features [11]. The textual ALF editor is integrated as a property view and may be used to textually describe elements of package or class diagrams. Furthermore, it allows to describe the behavior of activities. The primary goal of the Papyrus ALF integration is using graphical and textual syntax as alternative representations of the same view on the model and not executing behavioral specifications by generating source code. While Papyrus strictly focuses on a forward engineering process (from UML to ALF), the approach presented in this paper explicitly addresses round-trip engineering.

The commercial tool **MagicDraw UML**[7] recently also provides a plug-in allowing behavioral modeling with ALF [21]. Modelers may express bodies of activities using ALF statements which are then executed either sequentially or with considerable concurrency (depending on the underlying computation platform). The plug-in integrates the **ALF Reference Implementation**[8] into the commercial tool MagicDraw UML. In order to execute UML activity, state machine, and interaction models in MagicDraw, the **Cameo Simulation Toolkit**[9] is required. The ALF plug-in allows to define executable behavior in this context. The ALF implementation for MagicDraw compiles ALF text into activity models in the background and integrates the resulting activity models within the wider UML modeling context. Furthermore, these models may be executed as parts of full system simulation scenarios.

Compared with our own solution presented in [2], the approach discussed in this paper provides a much tighter integration of UML and ALF modeling by means of a single integrated user interface. The motivation behind our approach presented in this paper is the combination of graphical and textual modeling in an integrated tool in a way such that the most appropriate formalism is used depending on the considered model elements; while structure is represented pretty intuitively using graphical elements, behavioral model elements can be expressed very precisely by a textual language. For this purpose, only ALF operations are persisted, presented, and edited textually, i.e., all other aspects of the ALF model are hidden. The modeler may focus on the current task which results in a lower cognitive complexity exposed to the user. Furthermore, instead of providing two different editors which are not connected to each other, the ALF editor is now integrated visually in the graphical editing process. When the user clicks an operation within the UML model, a specific view shows the corresponding ALF operation containing the method body; UML model and ALF text are displayed at the same time. Additionally, some actions of the tool chain are bundled such that the user does not have to take care about the technical details running in the background.

---

[7] https://www.nomagic.com/products/magicdraw.

[8] http://alf.modeldriven.org.

[9] https://www.nomagic.com/product-addons/magicdraw-addons/cameo-simulation-toolkit.

7   Conclusion

In this paper, we presented an approach which allows for modeling structure as well as behavior of a software system using an integrated tool combining two OMG standards: UML and ALF. While UML package diagrams and class diagrams are used for modeling the structure, method bodies – i.e., the behavior of a method – are specified using ALF. Fully executable Java source code may be generated from the resulting model system which can be integrated seamlessly in existing software ecosystems. The integrated user interface abstracts from the underlying set of models and provides a unified look and feel for the end user allowing for graphical as well as textual modeling. The feasibility of the approach has been demonstrated using an example workflow which may occur in real-life iterative software development processes.

References

1. Buchmann, T.: Valkyrie: a UML-based model-driven environment for model-driven software engineering. In: Proceedings of the 7th International Conference on Software Paradigm Trends, ICSOFT 2012, pp. 147–157. SciTePress, Rome (2012)
2. Buchmann, T.: Prodeling with the action language for foundational UML. In: Damiani, E., Spanoudakis, G., Maciaszek, L.A. (eds.) ENASE 2017 - Proceedings of the 12th International Conference on Evaluation of Novel Approaches to Software Engineering, Porto, Portugal, 28–29 April 2017, pp. 263–270. SciTePress (2017). https://doi.org/10.5220/0006353602630270
3. Buchmann, T.: BXtend - a framework for (bidirectional) incremental model transformations. In: Hammoudi, S., Pires, L.F., Selic, B. (eds.) Proceedings of the 6th International Conference on Model-Driven Engineering and Software Development, MODELSWARD 2018, Funchal, Madeira - Portugal, 22–24 January 2018, pp. 336–345. SciTePress (2018). https://doi.org/10.5220/0006563503360345
4. Buchmann, T., Dotor, A., Westfechtel, B.: Model-driven software engineering: concepts and tools for modeling-in-the-large with package diagrams. Comput. Sci. - Res. Dev. 1–21. https://doi.org/10.1007/s00450-011-0201-1
5. Buchmann, T., Greiner, S.: Handcrafting a triple graph transformation system to realize round-trip engineering between UML class models and Java source code. In: Maciaszek, L.A., Cardoso, J.S., Ludwig, A., van Sinderen, M., Cabello, E. (eds.) Proceedings of the 11th International Joint Conference on Software Technologies, ICSOFT 2016 - Volume 2: ICSOFT-PT, Lisbon, Portugal, 24–26 July 2016, pp. 27–38. SciTePress (2016). https://doi.org/10.5220/0005957100270038
6. Buchmann, T., Schwägerl, F.: On a-posteriori integration of Ecore models and hand-written Java code. In: Lorenz, P., Van Sinderen, M., Cardoso, J. (eds.) Proceedings of the 10th International Conference on Software Paradigm Trends, pp. 95–102. SciTePress, July 2015. https://doi.org/10.5220/0005552200950102
7. Buchmann, T., Westfechtel, B.: Using Triple Graph Grammars to Realize Incremental Round-Trip Engineering. IET Software (July 2016). https://doi.org/10.1049/iet-sen.2015.0125
8. Buchmann, T., Westfechtel, B., Winetzhammer, S.: The added value of programmed graph transformations – a case study from software configuration management. In: Schürr, A., Varró, D., Varró, G. (eds.) AGTIVE 2011. LNCS, vol. 7233, pp. 198–209. Springer, Heidelberg (2012). https://doi.org/10.1007/978-3-642-34176-2_17

9. Greiner, S., Buchmann, T., Westfechtel, B.: Bidirectional transformations with QVT-R: a case study in round-trip engineering UML class models and Java source code. In: MODELSWARD 2016 - Proceedings of the 4rd International Conference on Model-Driven Engineering and Software Development, Rome, Italy, 19–21 February, 2016, pp. 15–27 (2016). https://doi.org/10.5220/0005644700150027

10. Guermazi, S., Tatibouet, J., Cuccuru, A., Seidewitz, E., Dhouib, S., Gérard, S.: Executable modeling with fUML and Alf in Papyrus: tooling and experiments. In: Mayerhofer et al. [13], pp. 3–8

11. Guermazi, S., Tatibouet, J., Cuccuru, A., Seidewitz, E., Dhouib, S., Gérard, S.: Executable modeling with fUML and Alf in papyrus: Tooling and experiments. In: Mayerhofer et al. [13], pp. 3–8. http://ceur-ws.org/Vol-1560/paper1.pdf

12. Lethbridge, T.C., Forward, A., Badreddin, O.: Umplification: refactoring to incrementally add abstraction to a program. In: 2010 17th Working Conference on Reverse Engineering (WCRE), pp. 220–224. IEEE (2010)

13. Mayerhofer, T., Langer, P., Seidewitz, E., Gray, J. (eds.): Proceedings of the 1st International Workshop on Executable Modeling co-located with ACM/IEEE 18th International Conference on Model Driven Engineering Languages and Systems, MODELS 2015, Ottawa, Canada, 27 September 2015, CEUR Workshop Proceedings, vol. 1560. CEUR-WS.org (2016)

14. OMG: MOF Model to Text Transformation Language, v1.0. OMG, Needham, MA, formal/2008-01-16 edn., January 2008

15. OMG: Action Language for Foundational UML (ALF). Object Management Group, Needham, MA, formal/2013-09-01 edn., September 2013

16. OMG: Semantics of a Foundational Subset for Executable UML Models (fUML). Object Management Group, Needham, MA, formal/2013-08-06 edn., August 2013

17. OMG: Object Constraint Language. OMG, Needham, MA, formal/2014-02-03 edn., February 2014

18. OMG: Meta Object Facility (MOF) Version 2.5. OMG, Needham, MA, formal/2015-06-05 edn. (2015)

19. OMG: Unified Modeling Language (UML). Object Management Group, Needham, MA, formal/15-03-01 edn., March 2015

20. Schröpfer, J., Buchmann, T.: Unifying Modeling and Programming with Valkyrie. In: Hammoudi, S., Pires, L.F., Selic, B. (eds.) Proceedings of the 7th International Conference on Model-Driven Engineering and Software Development, MODELSWARD 2019, Prague, Czech Republic, 20–22 February, pp. 27–38. SciTePress (2019). https://doi.org/10.5220/0007259600270038

21. Seidewitz, E.: A development environment for the Alf language within the MagicDraw UML tool (tool demo). In: Combemale, B., Mernik, M., Rumpe, B. (eds.) Proceedings of the 10th ACM SIGPLAN International Conference on Software Language Engineering, SLE 2017, Vancouver, BC, Canada, 23–24 October 2017, pp. 217–220. ACM (2017). https://doi.org/10.1145/3136014.3136028

22. Steinberg, D., Budinsky, F., Paternostro, M., Merks, E.: EMF Eclipse Modeling Framework. The Eclipse Series, 2nd edn. Addison-Wesley, Boston (2009)

23. The Fujaba Developer Teams from Paderborn, Kassel, Darmstadt, Siegen and Bayreuth: The Fujaba Tool Suite 2005: An Overview About the Development Efforts in Paderborn, Kassel, Darmstadt, Siegen and Bayreuth. In: Giese, H., Zündorf, A. (eds.) Proceedings of the 3rd international Fujaba Days, pp. 1–13, September 2005

24. Völter, M., Stahl, T., Bettin, J., Haase, A., Helsen, S.: Model-Driven Software Development: Technology, Engineering, Management. Wiley, Hoboken (2006)

A Model-Based Combination Language
for Scheduling Verification

Hui Zhao[1(✉)], Ludovic Apvrille[3], and Frédéric Mallet[1,2]

[1] Université Côte d'Azur, I3S, INRIA, Nice, France
`vincent.zhaohui@gmail.com`
[2] I3S Laboratory, UMR 7271 CNRS, Sophia Antipolis, France
[3] LTCI, Télecom Paris, Institut Polytechnique de Paris, Paris, France

Abstract. Cyber-Physical Systems (CPSs) are built upon discrete software and hardware components, as well as continuous physical components. Such heterogeneous systems involve numerous domains with competencies and expertise that go far beyond traditional software engineering: systems engineering. In this paper, we explore a model-based approach for systems engineering that advocates the composition of several heterogeneous artifacts (called views) into a sound and consistent system model. A model combination Language is proposed for this purpose. Thus, rather than trying to build the universal language able to capture all possible aspects of systems, the proposed language proposes to relate small subsets of languages in order to offer specific analysis capabilities while keeping a global consistency between all joined models. We demonstrate the interest of our approach through an industrial process based on Capella, which provides (among others) a large support for functional analysis from requirements to components deployment. Even though Capella is already quite expressive, it lacks support for schedulability analysis. AADL is also a language dedicated to system analysis. If it is backed with advanced schedulability tools, it lacks support for functional analysis. Thus, instead of proposing ways to add missing aspects in either Capella or AADL, we rather extract a relevant subset of both languages to build a view adequate for conducting schedulability analysis of Capella functional models. Finally, our combination language is generic enough to extract pertinent subsets of languages and combine them to build views for different experts. It also helps maintaining a global consistency between different modeling views.

Keywords: CPS · MDE · Combination modeling language · SysML · AADL · Multi-view design

1 Introduction

CPSs (Cyber-Physical Systems) consists of various components and their interconnections [15]. Thus, the design of the CPSs span over numerous domains of the system. Handling requirements of different domains with different characteristics pushes model-based approaches to their limits.

This work was financially Supported by the CLARITY project and by a UCN@Sophia Labex scholarship.

S. Hammoudi et al. (Eds.): MODELSWARD 2019, CCIS 1161, pp. 27–49, 2020.
https://doi.org/10.1007/978-3-030-37873-8_2

Model-Driven Engineering (MDE) is considered as a well-established software development approach that uses abstraction to bridge the gap between the problem space and the software implementation [7,23]. MDE uses models to describe complex systems at multiple levels of abstraction. In this paradigm, models are first-class elements that represent abstractions of a real system, capturing some of its essential properties. Models are instances of modeling languages which define their abstract syntax (e.g., using a metamodel expressed in a class diagram), concrete syntax (e.g., graphical or textual), and semantics (e.g., operational or denotational by means of a model transformation) [12]. As an important issue of MDE, multi-view modeling integrates different models using various DSMLs (domain-specific modeling languages) and abstract various aspects of systems and sub-systems, such as scheduling, behaviors and functionalities. Therefore, it is critical to understand the relationship among (meta) models. The modeling languages, such as Systems Modeling Language (SysML) [10] and Architecture Analysis and Design Language (AADL) [8], have been enhanced to better handle the CPS design, but, to the best of our knowledge, none of them cover all the necessary domains to handle all the characteristics of CPSs effectively. The increasing complexity of CPSs brings a critical challenge for developers to deal with different domains. Developers have to rely on domain-specific languages to handle different domains, which results in a proliferation of languages and increasing design complexity of CPS [9,15]. Furthermore, the gaps between languages and platforms bring several problems, for example, the specification of the CPS that has problems with inconsistency and incoherency. All of those problems are exposed at integration and simulation stages, they also augment the complexity of CPS and make it skyrocketing.

To tackle these problems, a new approach is required to efficiently take advantage of each existing language and combine them together. To this end, the existing approaches can be classified into two types. The first type is to continuously integrate the necessary languages into an existing development platform, and then progressively build a comprehensive development platform. However, this type of approach could encounter a never-ending process and result in a gigantic framework, thus difficult to use, maintain, etc. The second type is to keep each language (or tool) isolated, and relate some of the elements from each language with (sub) meta-model, so as to allow different kinds of analysis offered by each method (e.g., scheduling analysis, safety analysis). Furthermore, each domain expert can work independently with the second type of approach. However, since each language has its own characteristic, such as syntax and semantics, the gaps between different languages have to be eliminated in order to handle the consistency issues.

Our previous work [27] introduced a formal approach to combine two modeling languages by defining how to link two (sub-)metamodels. More precisely, thanks to our approach, consider two models m_1 and m_2 of two different modeling languages: m_2 can automatically be augmented with some information of m_1 so as to perform verification on the enriched model (e.g., scheduling, timing, safety), and then verification results can be backtraced to m_1.

In order to validate our contribution, SysML and AADL are selected as two target languages, and their support environments (tools) Capella/Arcadia and OSATE2[1] are used to show the design of example system.

The paper is organized as follows. In Sect. 2, we first identify the workflow of the proposed approach. Then, we explicitly present the reinforced language and the operators in Sect. 3. In Sect. 4, we apply these operators on functional and physical views. To evaluate the proposed formal approach, train traction control systems are used to demonstrate the architecture and analyze scheduling in Sect. 5. Section 6 illustrate the related work. Finally, Sect. 7 concludes the paper and presents our future work. It should be noted that, in Sects. 2, 3, 4 and 5, all elements on the left of transformation rules belong to metamodels of Arcadia, and all elements on the right are from the AADL metamodels. These metamodels have been imported by default, and their prefix (e.g., *MM.Arcadia*.function) are omitted for conciseness.

2 Our Approach

In this section, we describe the workflow we propose using an example based on Arcadia and AADL, as shown in Fig. 1 [27]. Arcadia is well adapted to describe how to allocate functions, while AADL focuses on the concrete execution behaviors of components. In this paper, we use transformation to enhance Arcadia with the scheduling analysis features of AADL. The transformation is performed by proposing a set of rules and operators to specify the relationships at the M2 level. Those relations are used for model transformation purpose and a set of all relationships is called Transformation Rule Library (TRL). More specifically, these rules are used to establish a relationship between Arcadia and AADL metamodels in a Transformation Rule Library. We assume that Arcadia and AADL define concepts that can be put in relation thanks to the proposed rules.

As shown with the green part in the Fig. 1, an Arcadia function allocated to a processor can be related to a "thread" in AADL. Additional attributes in Arcadia must be added (e.g., period and execution time) when one feature has no equivalence, as shown with a red part in Fig. 1). Then, the elements of metamodels are chosen manually depending on the requirements of the project. Finally, the workflow has four steps. In step one, we can get a temporary combinational metamodel (TCM) at run time by using TRL once the equivalence relations between the two metamodels have been settled. In step two, the TCM can be used to combine an AADL model with elements of an Arcadia model, then the new AADL model can be exported into OSATE for further editing. In step three, the Cheddar analysis tool [22] is used to conduct scheduling simulation. This tool can be used to detect designing flaws, time and resources conflicts. In step four, it traces back the results to the Arcadia model in order to help the designer enhancing the performance of his/her model.

---

[1] http://osate.org/index.html.

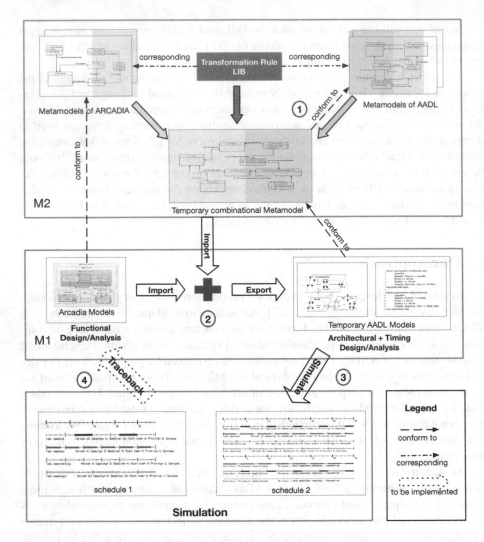

Fig. 1. Overview of workflow.

3   Model Combination Language

The proposed Language is a dedicated (meta) language to extend and enrich one DSML's capability by combining the other DSMLs. With this language, an integration engineer can explicitly capture combination scenarios at the language level. Combination pattern is used to specify different combination relationships. Specific operators are provided to build up Transformation Rule Expression (TRE), a set of TRE defines a TRL (Transformation Rule Library) which specifies how to combine different (meta) models' elements. Once the TRL is completed, it can be parsed by an automatic tool. Afterwards, the tool can perform the transformation automatically. The concept of combination language is illustrated in Fig. 2.

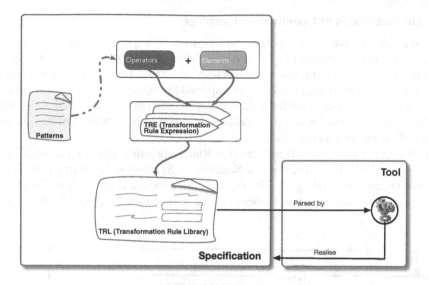

Fig. 2. Concept of combination language.

3.1 Specification

A specification consists of combination patterns and corresponding TRL. It defines what and how elements from different models are combined. Once it is specified, integration experts can share this specification thus allowing the reuse and tuning of TRL. As a specification can explicitly describe combination relationship, it also can be used to decompose models by bi-directional techniques for some decomposition needs.

3.2 Combination Patterns

Currently, We predefine a number of essential combination patterns, which provide all the declarations used in all the following examples. However, thanks to our language, designers can build other combination patterns depending on their problems and requirements. Certainly, they have to define some new combination patterns in the form of TRL.

1. *Association*: The association pattern is the most common phenomenon and easier to understand. It is used to indicates one element associate to another element and their related sub-elements (for example, its embedded element or associated attributes).
2. *Removal*: The removal pattern indicates the situation, where some element does not be needed for new models according to requirements.
3. *Correspondence*: The Correspondence pattern indicates building an equivalence relationship among a set of elements.
4. *Notation*: The notation pattern aims to hint people to add some extra information which is not existing in model. For example, the dependency relationship among the model's elements, and the nature of the elements.

3.3   Abstract Syntax of Combination Language

We give an abstract syntax of Combination Language by using a metamodel expressed
in a class diagram (shown in Fig. 3). The major element of Combination Language is
a specification that contains Patterns, Operators and TRL. The specification requires
importing at least two (meta) models. The imported (meta) models serve as a source of
a set of candidate elements for following operations. An operator selects the elements
and their attributes from imported (meta) models, and it also specifies how to combine
selected elements with a clear relationship.

Each operator contains a Transformation Rule Expression which relies on a strict
definition by EBNF (Extended Backus–Naur Form). Symbols are used to construct the
TRE. For instance, for adding security properties to a logical component of Capella, it
has to specify the corresponding element and their related attributes in TTool by using
TRE.

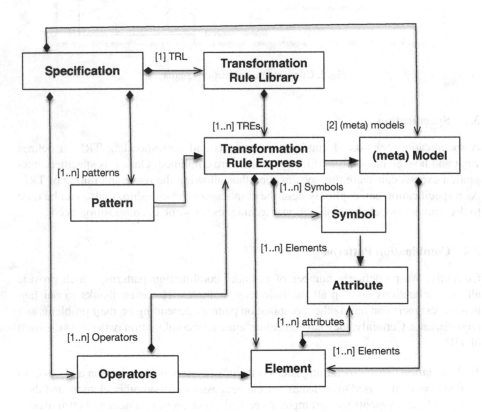

Fig. 3. A simplified view of abstract syntax of combination language.

3.4   Meta Symbol and Notations Rule Expression

In this subsection, we firstly introduce some notations and meta symbols which are fundamental elements for constructing the well-defined Transformation Rule Expressions

(see Table 1). For the propose to obtain strict definition and non-ambiguous Transformation Rule Expression pattern, we use EBNF to define TRE. EBNF is a notation technique for context-free grammars[2], often used to describe the syntax of languages [17].

Table 1. Symbols of transformation rule expression.

Symbol	Meaning
Γ	Transformation rule
;	End of rule
:	Separate elements
$\rightsquigarrow$	Transfer
<>	Parent node
{ }	Attribute
[ ]	Optional value
|	Alternative
+	Object to be created
¬	Ignorer
@	Notation

The detail literal meaning of symbols are as below:

1. A Transformation Rule Expression begins with "Γ" and ends with ";".
2. The symbol "$\rightsquigarrow$" indicates a transfer action.
3. A transfer action contains the source elements which in the left side of "$\rightsquigarrow$" and the target elements in the right side. A simple example is as bellow:

$$\Gamma <parent> \; source \; \rightsquigarrow target;$$

4. Symbol ":" separates each part of TRE.
5. An angle brackets "<>" encloses the parent node if the element has one or more parent nodes.
6. A parentheses "{ }" enclose attributes
7. A square braces "[ ]" delimit optional elements.
8. The alternative value is separated by a pipe "|". For example, The *port* has a directional attribute called *Direction* which could be *in* or *out* shown as:

$$P_{ort} : \{Direction[in|out]\}$$

9. Symbol "@" indicates the notations which are used to add some extra informations such as dependency and nature. The extra informations are handled as the same as operational value: enclosed in [ ]; separated by ";". For example, $P_{ort}@[ModelA, Security]$ means element Port belongs to ModelA and is used for

---

[2] https://en.wikipedia.org/wiki/Backus--Naur_form.

Security purpose (view). In such situation, it makes tools automatically display or hide the element P_{ort} which is in modelA and for security view in the following process.

With those symbols, we can build up plentiful TREs. Some more detailed examples of Transformation Rule Expressions are shown in the Listing 1.1.

3.5 Abstract Syntax of Rule Expression in EBNF

As we mentioned in the previous subsection, the TRE consists of one or more sequences of symbols. We list here the context-free syntax in EBNF in this subsection.

$\langle expression \rangle ::= \Gamma \langle term \rangle \leadsto \langle term \rangle; | \langle expression \rangle : \langle term \rangle; | \langle operator \rangle \langle term \rangle;$

$\langle term \rangle ::= \langle element \rangle | \langle operator \rangle \langle element \rangle | \langle operator \rangle \langle element \rangle \langle operator \rangle$

$\langle operator \rangle ::= '@' | '+' | '\neg' | '\leadsto'$

$\langle element \rangle ::= \langle element \rangle | \langle attribute \rangle | \langle optional\ value \rangle$

3.6 Operators and Semantics

The context-sensitive syntax and the operational rules could also be considered to be semantics instead of syntax. For example, the context-sensitive syntax is called static semantics in the UML specification documents from OMG [18]. In our case, it specifies how an instance of a construct can be meaningfully connected to other instances.

In order to make the TRE more clearly and precisely, we firstly present a set of relationships definitions formally. That is used to help users understand the semantics of the operator and to avoid ambiguity and misunderstanding. Secondly, we propose a set of operators to build up Transformation Rule Expression, which represents operations between (meta) models (e.g., transforming, creating, ignoring) in a systematic way. They may also help users to understand the following TRE examples.

We define a relation in the sense of set theory. Let A and B be a set of elements respectively, with a, b, c and x, y, z: model element, write $a, b, c \supset A$ and $x, y, z \supset B$.

- **Relationship:** If the ordered pair (a, x) in our relation, we write $\mathcal{R}(a, x)$ or $a\mathcal{R}x$ for simplicity. It is also a boolean function. $\mathcal{R}(a, x)$ is true means existing a relation between a and x.
- **Equivalence:** $\mathcal{E}(a, x)$ is a boolean function that is true if and only if a semantically equals to x. By function $\mathcal{E}(a, x)$ holds $\mathcal{R}(a, x) \wedge \mathcal{E}(a, x)$.
- **NotIn:** $\neg a$ is a boolean function. If it is true, that means there are any corresponding elements in set of B (x, y, z) which either have a relationship with a, nor semantically equal to a. Formally,

$$\neg \mathcal{R}(a, \{x, y, z\}) \vee \neg \mathcal{E}(a, \{x, y, z\})$$

Operators:

(a) **_Transferring Operator:_** We use $\leadsto$ indicates transferring operator, for example, $a \leadsto x$ it means that transfer from a to x, if and only if $\mathcal{E}(a, x)$ is true, in other words, a and x is _Equivalence_ relationship.

(b) **_Creating Operator:_** In the case of creating a new attribute, put the name of an attribute in the parentheses with plus "{ }+", that is used to present the option which is to be created. For example, $\Gamma a \leadsto x : \{y\}+$;, it means that transfer from a to x and add y attribute, if and only if $y \supset x$ and $\mathcal{E}(a, x) \wedge \mathcal{R}(a, y) \wedge \mathcal{R}(x, y)$ is true. An example in practice is below,

$$\Gamma Port \leadsto Port : \{Type[data|event|dataevent]\}+$$

A _port_ will be transferred to another _port_ element, and to create new attribute named _Type_ that associates to _port_ with three optional value (data, event, data and event).

(c) **_Ignoring Operator:_** This operator is used for some ignored attributes and objects. It is denoted with symbol "¬" which is in front of the object. For example, $\neg a$, it means a is **NotIn** object of set B. Formally, $\neg\mathcal{R}(a, B) \vee \neg\mathcal{E}(a, B)$.

(d) **_Notation Operator:_** This operator is used for tagging the nature of attribute of an element. There is an example: $P_{ort}@[ModelA, Security]$. It can present two attributes of element P_{ort} with two tags. One is _ModelA_, indicating that the element P_{ort} belongs to _ModelA_. In other words, It represents a dependency relationship between this element P_{ort} and element _ModelA_. Another is _Security_, represents an element P_{ort} for Security purpose. It would be used to catalog the elements for displaying or fast selecting purpose.

TRE Examples with Semantics. Transformation Rule Express (TRE) represents the transforming relationships. It would be used for guiding the integration engineer or for reading by automated transformation engine. We use some more detailed examples of Transformation Rule Expressions to explicitly explain how it works. Please refer to the TRE table which is in the Listing 1.1.

In line 1 of this example, we firstly transfer an element _port_ (it has direction attribute) of A to an object element _port_ of B, and add a new attribute _Type_ with three optional value (date, event or data event). These "type value" can be recognised by model B's DSML and the supported environment. The added attribute can be used to continue further design as well. In line 2, it is similar to previous one, but the object element _Port_ has a parent node called _feature_ which is enclosed in a pair angle brackets.

Secondly, in line 3, it shows an ignored element, in which the source element may not be found a corresponding one in the object model, or the source element is not needed by the object model. Finally, in line 4, it is a _Equivalence_ relationship between the source element and the object element, in other words, it's a set of one by one transformations which transfer "Ex_{fun}" to "_connection_", "Source" to "source" and "Target" to "target", respectively.

1 ΓP_{ort}:{Direction[in|out]} ⤳ <feature>:Port:{Direction[in|out]}:{Type[data|event|data
 event]}+;
2 ΓPP ⤳ <feature>:Port:{Direction[in|out]}+:{Type[data|event|data event]}+;
3 ΓP_{ort}:¬{ordering};
4 ΓEx_{fun}:{Source}:{Target} ⤳ <connections>:connection:{source}:{target};

Listing 1.1. The example of transformation Rule Expressions.

4 Transformation Rule Library

As we described in the above section, the Transformation Rule Express play an important role in the transformation process. Hence, in this section, we will show how to construct a set of TREs called the Transformation Rule Library (TRL). We also respectively present the following views, functional view and physical view in Arcadia (SysML) and AADL. Each view contains one or more metamodels which represents as a x-tuples.

4.1 Functional View

Logical Components in Arcadia. The logical components in Arcadia contain a set of member elements, such as logical component containers, functions, ports, and functional exchanges. In the Arcadia, Functional diagrams consist of a set of SysML blocks and its interactions, named *Logical components*; The notion of Logical components enables better expression of system engineering semantics compared to SysML, and particularly, reduces the bias towards software. SysML block definition diagrams (BDDs) and internal block diagrams (IBDs) are assigned to different abstract and refined layers, respectively. The definition of a block in SysML can be further detailed by specifying its parts; ports, specifying its interaction points; and connectors, specifying the connections among its parts and ports. This information can also be visualized using logical components in Arcadia. In the Definition 1, we present a metamodel of an instance of logical components.

Definition 1. *(Logical Component)*

 A logical component (**LC**) is 5 tuples,

$$\mathcal{LC} = <C_{omp}, F_{un}, P_{ort}, Ex_{fun}, M_{cf}>$$

where,

$$C_{omp} = \sum_{i=1}^{\infty} F_{uni}$$

is a logical component container which contains a set of functional elements.

 F_{un} is a finite set of functional block include their name and id attributes. P_{ort} is a finite set of functional ports including directions and allocation attributes. $Ex_{fun} \subseteq$

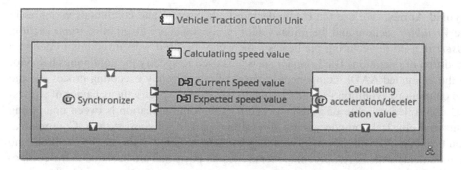

Fig. 4. An example of functional view of vehicle traction control unit in ARCADIA.

$P_{ort} \times P_{ort}$ denotes a finite set of functional exchange (connection) between two functional ports, it must be pair, one is source, another is target. $M_{cf} : \Sigma F_{un} \rightarrow C_{omp}$ allocate functions to a logical component container.

In the Fig. 4, there is a functional instance model of a part of a vehicle traction control unit in ARCADIA as an example. The blue rectangle is named logical component in Arcadia, but we consider it as a function's container, we thus call it *logical component container* C_{omp} in this paper. The green rectangle are functions F_{un} which are contained by C_{omp}. The element M_{cf} has represented this allocation relationship between logical component containers and functions $M_{cf} : \Sigma F_{un} \rightarrow C_{omp}$. The deep green square with the white triangle is the outgoing port (P_{ort}), which connects to an incoming port (P_{ort}) that is drawn as a red square with white triangle and the green line is the functional exchange between two functional ports (Ex_{fun}).

The Metamodels of Software in AADL. AADL is able to model a real-time system as a hierarchy of software components, predefined software component types in the category of the components such as thread, thread group, process, data, and subprogram are used to model the software architecture of the system.

Definition 2. *(Software Composition)*

A **SC** is a 4-tuples:

$$SC = <Type, Port, Connection, Annex>$$

where $Type$ specifies the type of components (e.g, system, process, thread). $Port$ is a set of communication point of component. Port could be different types such as **data** port, **event** port and **data event** port. And, port can specify the direction such as **in** port, **out** port, **in out** port. $Connection$ is used to connect ports in the direction of data/control flow in uni- or bi-directional. $Annex$ is defined for the refinement of component, in this paper, we used hybrid annex to explicitly describe the both discrete and continuous behavior of train traction control system.

Hybrid Annex. We use the HA to declare both discrete and continuous variables in the *Variables* section, and the initial values of constants are given in *constant* section. *Assert* is used to declaring predicates which may be used with invariants to define a condition of operation. The *behavior* section is used to specify the continuous behavior of the annotated AADL component in terms of concurrently executing processes, and use continuous evolution — a differential expression to specify the behavior of a physical controlled variable of a hybrid system. The communication between computing units and physical components are an essential part of a hybrid system, Communication between physical processes uses the channels declared in the *channel* section, and communicate with an AADL component relies on ports that are declared in the component's type. Continuous process evolution may be terminated after a specific time or on a communication event. There are invoked through timed and communication interrupt, respectively. A timed interrupt preempts continuous evolution after a given amount of time. A communication interrupt preempts continuous evolution whenever communication takes places along any one of the named ports or channels. The Definition 3 gives a metamodel of Hybrid Annex which does not exist in SysML-based environment.

Definition 3. *(Hybrid Annex)*

A *Hybrid Annex* is a 8-tuples:

$$\mathcal{HA} = <Ass, Ivar, Var_{hd}, Cons_{hd}, P_{roc}, ChP, Itr, B_{itr}>$$

where Ass is a finite set of assert for declaring predicates applicable to the intended continuous behavior of the annotated AADL component. $Ivar$ is associated with assert to define a condition of operation that must be true during the lifetime. Var_{hd} is a finite set of discrete and continuous variables. $Cons_{hd}$ is a finite set of constants which must be initiated at declaration. P_{roc} is a finite set of processes that are used to specify continuous behaviors of AADL components. ChP is a finite set of channels and ports for synchronizing processes. Itr is a finite set of time or communication interrupts. $B_{itr} : Itr \rightarrow P_{roc}$ binds interrupts to related processes.

Functional Elements Transformation Rules. The Table 2 shows the correspondence between AADL and Arcade elements. The Additional attributes column are the attributes to be created during the transformation. According to this table, we can easily write the transformation rules to transforming Arcadia to AADL on functional parts, denoted $\mathcal{LC} \rightsquigarrow \mathcal{SC} + \mathcal{HA}$. An example as below (Listing 1.2 [27]):

```
1 ΓC_omp ⤳ Type[ system|process]:{Runtime_Protection[true|false]}+;
2 ΓF_un ⤳ Type[abstract|thread]:{Dispatch_Protocol[Periodic|Aperiodic|Sporadic|
     Background|Timed|Hybrid]}+;
3 ...
```

Listing 1.2. Functional elements transformation rules example.

Table 2. Functional and Physical elements correspondence table.

Arcadia	AADL	Additional attributes	Notation
Logical component container (C_{omp})	System,Process	{Runtine_Protection[true|false]}+	@[function|AADL|scheduling]
Function (F_{un})	Abstract, Thread	{Dispatch_Protocol[Periodic|Aperiodic|Sporadic|Background|Timed|Hybrid]}+	@[function|AADL|scheduling]
Port (P_{ort})	Port	{Type[data|event|data event]}+	@[function|AADL|scheduling]
Functional Exchange (Ex_{fun})	Connection	∅	
∅	Annex	{Type[abstract| thread]}:{annex}+	@[function|AADL|scheduling]
Physical Node (N_{ode})	Device,Memory,Processor,Bus	{Dispatch_Protocol}+:{Period}:{Deadline}+:{priority}+	@[physic|AADL|scheduling]
Physical Port (PP)	∅	~PP	@[physic|AADL|scheduling]
Physical Link (PL)	Bus/BusAccess	{Allowed_Connection_Type}+:{Allowed_Message_Size}+:{Allowed_Physical_Access}+:{Transmission_Time}+	@[physic|AADL|scheduling]

4.2 Physical View

Execution Platform in AADL. Processor, memory, device, and bus components are the execution platform components for modeling the hardware part of the system. Ports and port connections are provided to model the exchange of data and event among components. Functional and non-functional properties like scheduling protocol and execution time of the thread can be specified in components and their interactions.

Definition 4. *(Execution Platform)*

A **EP** component is defined as a 3-tuples:

$$\mathcal{EP} = <EC, BA, C_{onn}>$$

where, EC defines the execution component such as processor, memory, bus and device. BA defines the BusAccess which is interactive approach between **bus** component and other execution platform components. $C_{onn} \subseteq EC \times EC$ denotes a finite set of connection between two components via bus device.

Physical Components in Arcadia. The physical component in Arcadia consists of physical Node, Port and Link. The Physical Port and Link correspond to port and bus connection in AADL. There are some choices when the physical Node is translated to AADL such as device, memory, and processor, hence the designer has to point out what type of target component during transformation by using transformation rule express.

Definition 5. *(Physical Components)*

A Physical components is 3-tuples,

$$\mathcal{PC} = <N_{ode}, PP, PL>$$

where, N_{ode} is a execution platform, named *node* in Arcadia, it could be different type of physical component (e.g, processor, board). PP is the physical component port. PL is physical link, it could be assigned a concrete type such as *bus*.

Figure 5 is shown as a part of physical instance model of vehicle traction control unit in ARCADIA. We can see the yellow parts are the physical node (N_{ode}) and the red line is the physical link (PL) named bus in this case which connects to two physical ports (PP), the small square in dark yellow.

Physical Elements Transformation Rules. According to the Table 2, we can easily write the transformation rules for physical elements. Listing 1.3 [27] shown as a part of the code to transform the physical component from Arcadia to AADL.

```
1 ΓN_ode ↝ [Device|Process|Memory|Bus]:{Dispatch_Protocol}+:{Period}:{Deadline
      }+:{priority}+;
2 ΓPP ↝ ¬PP;
3 ΓPL ↝ Bus/BusAccess:[{Allowed_Connnection_Type}+:{Allowed_Message_Size}+|{
      Allowed_Physical_Access}+:{Transmission_Time}+];
```

Listing 1.3. Physcial elements transformation rules example.

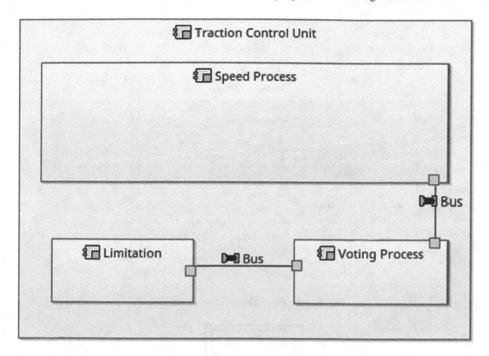

Fig. 5. An example of physical view of vehicle traction control unit in ARCADIA. (Color figure online)

What we have to especially explain is the physical link part (see line 3). The Bus device could be a logical resource or hardware component. Hence, the bus device has different properties depending on the role. When the bus is considered as a logical resource, it contains the properties *Allowed_connection_type* and *Allowed_Message_Size*. When the bus is hardware, it contains *Allowed_Physical_Access* and *Transmission_Time*. Therefore, we write the rules that either

$$\{Allowed\_Connnection\_Type\}+ : \{Allowed\_Message\_Size\}+$$

or

$$\{Allowed\_Physical\_Access\}+ : \{Transmission\_Time\}+$$

5   Case Study

To show the efficacy of our approach in transforming and using produced AADL models to analyze the properties, this section presents the experimental results of analyzing the traction controlling unit of railway signaling system. By using our proposed approach, we transfer and extend Arcadia metamodel, and design AADL using OSATE2 with the generated metamodel. once the concrete models have been created, the scheduling property is chosen to show analysis ability through Cheddar tool [22].

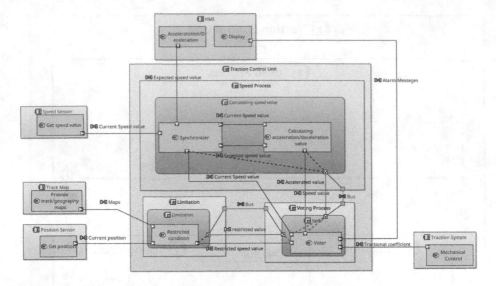

Fig. 6. Arcadia model of TCU system.

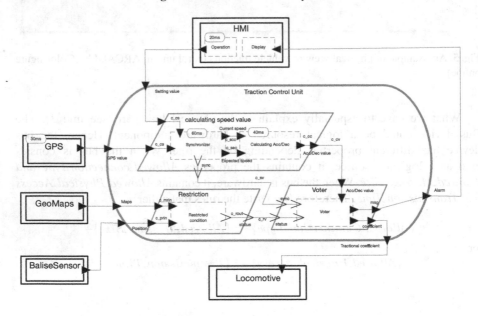

Fig. 7. AADL model of TCU system.

5.1 Train Traction Control System

Train movement is the calculation of the speed and distance profiles when a train is traveling from one point to another according to the limitations imposed by the signaling system and traction equipment characteristics. As the train has to follow the track, the movement is also under the constraints of track geometry, and speed restrictions and the calculation becomes position-dependent. The subsystem of calculating the traction effective and speed restrictions is therefore critical to achieving train safe running. Nowadays, Communication Based Train Control (CBTC) system is the main method of rail transit (both urban and high-speed train) which adopts wireless local area networks as the bidirectional train-ground communication [28]. To increase the capacity of rail transit lines, many information-based and digital components have been applied for networking, automation and system inter-connection, including general communication technologies, sensor networks, and safety-critical embedded control system. A large number of subsystems consisting of modern signaling systems of railways, therefore, system integration is one of the key technologies of signaling systems; it plays a significant role in maintaining the safety of the signaling system [26].

This paper uses a subsystem which called Traction Control Unit system (TCU) from signaling system of high-speed railway. We use this TCU system to illustrate the model transformation from engineering level to detailed architectural level and verified the instance models. The functional modules such as calculation and synchronization will be transformed using our approach, and then non-functional properties such as timing correctness and resource correctness will be verified by schedule analysis tool Cheddar [22].

First, we start with component functional views and physical view analysis by designing system models in Arcadia (shown in figure of TCU Fig. 6 [27]). The functions of the traction control system are to collect the external data by sensors such as a speed sensor. The data from Balise sensors is used to determinate the track block, and then it is going to seek the speed restriction conditions by matching accurate positioning (if the track blocks are divided fine enough) and digital geometric maps data. Meanwhile, calculating speed unit received the speed data from GPS and speed control commands from HMI (Human-Machine Interface) periodically. GPS data provides speed value periodically (we set a period of 30 seconds in this case), and HMI data sustainedly send the operation command with the period of 20 seconds till the value changed (e.g., expected speed value), then the calculating unit has to output an acceleration value and export to the locomotive mechanical system. Although they are periodic, the external data do not always arrive on time due to transmission delay or jitter. Therefore, we should use a synchronizer to make sure they are synchronized. Otherwise, the result would be wrong with asynchronous data. Similarly, to ensure the correctness of the command of acceleration (or deceleration), we applied a voting mechanism which can ensure the result is correct as much as possible. The voter must have the synchronized signal and restriction condition to dedicate to output the acceleration coefficient request to the locomotive system. The AADL diagram is shown in Fig. 7 [27].

5.2 Model Transformation

Using the Arcadia2AADL tool, the metamodel of the TCU system in Capella is translated into the corresponding AADL metamodel with the rules and approach which describes in Sect. 4. For instance, on the one hand, the function class is translated into the thread in AADL. To analyze the timing properties, several attributes also have been added such as protocol type, deadline, execution time, period.

On the other hand, the physical part element Node translates to the processor in this case. Differ from simple physical Node in Arcadia; the processor element attaches rich properties such as scheduling protocol (scheduler type), process execution time. The allocation relationships on both physical and functional parts are translated into AADL as well.

5.3 Schedule Verification

The external data and internal process work sequentially is an essential safety requirement of the system, and each task should be scheduled properly. However, in real-world, the risk of communication quality and rationality of scheduling must be taken into account. Therefore, the schedule verification is a way to evaluate system timing property. An Ada framework called Cheddar which provides tools to check if a real-time application meets its temporal constraints. The framework is based on the real-time scheduling theory and is mostly written for educational purposes [16].

```
1 thread implementation synchronizer.impl
2     properties
3     Dispatch_Protocol  => perodic;
4     Period => 100 ms;
5     Deadline => 100 ms;
6     Compute_Execution_Time => 50..60ms;
7 end synchronizer.impl;
8
9 thread implementation calalculating.impl
10     properties
11     Dispatch_Protocol  => perodic;
12     Period => 100 ms;
13     Deadline => 100 ms;
14     Compute_Execution_Time => 30ms..40ms;
15 end calalculating.impl;
16
17 thread implementation gps.position
18     properties
19     Dispatch_Protocol  => perodic;
20     Period => 40 ms;
21     Deadline => 40 ms;
22     Compute_Execution_Time => 30ms..40ms;
23 end gps.position;
24
25 thread implementation HMI.setting
26     properties
27     Dispatch_Protocol  => perodic;
28     Period => 30 ms;
29     Deadline => 30 ms;
30     Compute_Execution_Time => 20ms..30ms;
31 end HMI.setting;
```

Listing 1.4. Setting of scheduling properties.

Listing 1.4 shows a set of 4 periodic tasks (cal, pos, sync and setting) of TCU respectively, defined by the periods 100, 100, 40 and 30, the capacities 60, 40, 30 and 20, and the deadlines 100, 100, 40 and 30. These tasks are scheduled with a preemptive Rate Monotonic scheduler (the task with the lowest period is the task with the highest priority).

For a given task set, if a scheduling simulation displayed XML results in the Cheddar. One can find the concurrency cases or idle periods (see left of Fig. 8, comprise the software part and physical device part). People change the parameters directly and reload simulation; a feasible solution can be applied instead. After tuning, finally, the appropriate setting has displayed as in right of Fig. 8. According to this simulation result, people can correct the properties value in AADL, thereby ensure the correctness of system behavior timing properties.

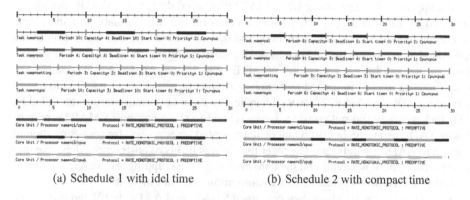

(a) Schedule 1 with idel time   (b) Schedule 2 with compact time

Fig. 8. Simulation results of tasks schedule.

6   Related Work

We have presented our approach to extending SysML-based engineering framework Capella to AADL and analyzed the relationships among Arcadia and AADL models in different view at the metamodel level. Likewise, a considerable number of studies have been proposed on "language extension, modeling languages integration and composable language components". This section provides a brief introduction to these works.

The complexity of the development of CPS has been the significant problems which puzzle the developers. It is not only from the nature of problems but also from the develop languages. Elaasar et al. has discussed [6] about the limit of UML which exacerbate the complexity of development, and proposed an approach to reduce the complexity of UML tools by implementing and adapting the ISO 42010 standard on architecture description.

Efficient integration of different heterogeneous modeling languages is essential. Modeling language integration is onerous and requires in-depth conceptual and technical knowledge and effort. Traditional modeling language integration approaches require language engineers to compose monolithic language aggregates for a specific task or project. Adapting these aggregates to different contexts requires vast effort and makes these hardly reusable. Arne Haber et al. [11] presented a method for the engineering of grammar-based language components that can be independently developed, are syntactically composable, and ultimately reusable.

In despite of existing a lot of studies on the combining SysML and AADL [4] or on the extending SysML with AADL [2]. Differ from the above studies, our approach dedicates to smoothly combine engineering platform Capella/Arcadia, AADL and its annex, and our approach can be easily applied to other languages through fine-tuning. In practice, one could design global system at a high level and then seamlessly refine the models within AADL and its annex for further analysis such as scheduling. In other words, our approach can properly extend Arcadia's design and analysis capabilities to AADL, while essentially keeping its independence.

An approach for translating UML/MARTE detailed design into AADL design has proposed by Brun et al. [3]. Their work focuses on the transformation of the thread execution and communication semantics and does not cover the transformation of the embedded system component, such as device parts. Similarly, in [25], Turki et al. proposed a methodology for mapping MARTE model elements to AADL component. They focus on the issues related to modeling architecture, and the syntactic differences between AADL and MARTE are well handled by the transformation rules provided by ATL tool, yet they did not consider issues related to the mapping of MARTE properties to AADL property. In [19], Ouni et al. presented an approach for transformation of Capella to AADL models target to cover the various levels of abstraction, they take into account the system behavior and the hardware/software mapping. However, the formal definition and rigorous syntactic of transformation rules are missed.

Behjati et al. describe how they combined SysML and AADL in [2] and provided a standard modeling language (in the form of the ExSAM profile) for specifying embedded systems at different abstraction levels. De Saqui-Sannes et al. [4] presented an MBE with TTool and AADL at the software level and demonstrated with the flight management system. Both of their works do not provide the description in a formal way.

In industrial domain applications, Suri et al. [24] proposed a model-based approach for complex systems development by separating the behavior model and execution logic of the system. Moreover, they used UML based languages to model system behavior and connected the behavior models to external physical API of CPS. It focuses on providing a solution for the modularity and interoperability issues related to Industry 4.0 from a systems integration viewpoint.

Apel et al. [1] also studied on different model driven methods for heterogenic systems for Electric vehicle. They have tried to evaluate how model-driven engineering (MDE) combined with generative frameworks can support the transfer from platform independent models to deployable solutions within the logistical domain.

The work of Kurtev [14] is used in the x-ray machine, it provided a family of domain-specific languages that integrate existing techniques from formal behavioral and time modeling. Scippacercola [21] have explored the application of model-driven engineering on the interlocking system (a subsystem of signaling system of the railway).

They discussed how to reduce efforts and costs for development, verification, and validation in a critical system.

The modeling language scientists have proposed some specific methods to weave the models as well as metamodels formally such as [13], Degueule has proposed Melange, a language dedicated to merging languages [5], and similar works like [20]. However, the structural properties are not supported.

Compared with current studies, the approach proposed in this paper has the following features:

1. A proper subset of AADL has been chosen as the transformation target including functional software composition, execution platform. We use it to describe continuous behaviors of Cyber-Physical System.
2. All of the transformations is considered at metamodel level, and then a synthesized metamodel can be used to create concrete AADL models for further analysis.
3. Transformation rules are formally defined, and then it is readable by human and easier to verify the correctness of transformation.

7 Conclusions and Future Work

In this paper, we proposed a language-based design approach for combining different modeling design artifact (called views). At the beginning of this paper, we explicitly introduce the workflow of the proposed approach. Then we give the definition of syntax and semantics of our language. We selected system engineering methodology Arcadia (based on SysML) and architectural design language AADL as a vehicle for demonstrating the effectiveness of our approach and of model combination language for scheduling verification. We did so for two reasons. Firstly, the integrating of heterogeneous components and elaborate model integrity concept in system design are challenging problems while using numerous model language to describe different views of one system (or subsystem). Since our proposed language is generic enough to extract pertinent subsets of languages, if it works well for combining Arcadia and AADL, it should also work for the others, less demanding major modifications and extra cost of learning. Secondly, Enriching the functional design with scheduling ability can discover the conflicts in the early stage and improve the performance of CPSs in practice in a better way. Hence, Our language is competent for combining the composition of several heterogeneous artifacts (views) into a sound and consistent system model.

Especially, we give a formal description of the key modeling elements of Arcadia and AADL, respectively. Then we give some example of transformation rules which guide transforming from these Arcadia metamodels to AADL formally. Finally, a case study of train traction controlling system is used to demonstrate the transformation from engineering concerned design into an architectural refinement design which can be further analyzed by scheduling properties to find flaws of functional design.

Although our proposed language-based approach is effective and has been proven by many instances in practice, there are some drawbacks to use our approach: (i) people have to spend times to learn the syntax of rules, and the writing of rule is error-prone. (ii) the traceback function is not yet implemented automatically.

In our future work, we will try to build a graphic interface to write rules, and the writing errors of the rule can be detected. We also have to implement the traceback of simulation results, which is sketched in our workflow with the arrow in dotted line. The results must be used automatically by upstream modeling framework. To this end, we have to extract the critical information from cheddar outputting file and transform to an appended file of modeling tool which can be recognized by the tool and hint user in somehow. Secondly, we will study the transformation rules for more elements of Arcadia and also for comprehensive SysML elements, even for other UML-like profiles such as MARTE. At the same time, we will continue to explore the AADL and its annex to support more analysis and formal verification of system design. Besides, the safety-critical systems have become a trend in industrial files. We will study the extension of AADL with verification of safety properties with transformation methodology.

References

1. Apel, S., Mauch, M., Schau, V.: Model-driven engineering tool comparison for architectures within heterogenic systems for electric vehicle. In: 2016 4th International Conference on Model-Driven Engineering and Software Development (MODELSWARD), pp. 671–676, February 2016
2. Behjati, R., Yue, T., Nejati, S., Briand, L., Selic, B.: Extending SysML with AADL concepts for comprehensive system architecture modeling. In: France, R.B., Kuester, J.M., Bordbar, B., Paige, R.F. (eds.) ECMFA 2011. LNCS, vol. 6698, pp. 236–252. Springer, Heidelberg (2011). https://doi.org/10.1007/978-3-642-21470-7_17
3. Brun, M., Vergnaud, T., Faugere, M., Delatour, J.: From UML to AADL: an explicit execution semantics modelling with MARTE. In: ERTS 2008 (2008)
4. De Saqui-Sannes, P., Hugues, J.: Combining SysML and AADL for the design, validation and implementation of critical systems. In: ERTS2 2012 (2012)
5. Degueule, T., Combemale, B., Blouin, A., Barais, O., Jezequel, J.M.: Melange: a meta-language for modular and reusable development of DSLs. In: Conference on Software Language Engineering, pp. 25–36. ACM (2015)
6. Elaasar, M., Noyrit, F., Badreddin, O., Gérard, S.: Reducing UML modeling tool complexity with architectural contexts and viewpoints. In: MODELSWARD, pp. 129–138 (2018)
7. Ergin, H., Syriani, E., Gray, J.: Design pattern oriented development of model transformations. Comput. Lang. Syst. Struct. **46**, 106–139 (2016)
8. Feiler, P.H., Gluch, D.P.: Model-Based Engineering with AADL: An Introduction to the SAE Architecture Analysis & Design Language. Addison-Wesley, Boston (2012)
9. Garlan, D.: Modeling challenges for CPS systems. In: 2015 IEEE/ACM 1st International Workshop on Software Engineering for Smart Cyber-Physical Systems, p. 1, May 2015. https://doi.org/10.1109/SEsCPS.2015.8
10. Group, O.M.: OMG Systems Modeling Language, May 2017
11. Haber, A., et al.: Integration of heterogeneous modeling languages via extensible and composable language components. In: 2015 3rd International Conference on Model-Driven Engineering and Software Development (MODELSWARD), pp. 19–31, February 2015
12. Harel, D., Rumpe, B.: Modeling Languages: Syntax, Semantics and All That Stuff, Part I: The Basic Stuff (2000)
13. Jezequel, J.M.: Model driven design and aspect weaving. Softw. Syst. Model. **7**(2), 209–218 (2008)
14. Kurtev, I., Schuts, M., Hooman, J., Swagerman, D.J.: Integrating interface modeling and analysis in an industrial setting. In: MODELSWARD, pp. 345–352 (2017)

15. Lee, E.A.: Cyber physical systems: design challenges. In: 2008 11th IEEE International Symposium on Object and Component-Oriented Real-Time Distributed Computing, pp. 363–369. IEEE (2008)
16. Marcé, L., Singhoff, F., Legrand, J., Nana, L.: Scheduling and memory requirements analysis with AADL. In: SIGAda, pp. 1–10. ACM (2005)
17. McCracken, D.D., Reilly, E.D.: Backus-Naur Form (BNF) (2003)
18. OMG: OMG Unified Modeling Language, April 2015
19. Ouni, B., Gaufillet, P., Jenn, E., Hugues, J.: Model Driven Engineering with Capella and AADL (2016)
20. Ramos, R., Barais, O., Jézéquel, J.-M.: Matching model-snippets. In: Engels, G., Opdyke, B., Schmidt, D.C., Weil, F. (eds.) MODELS 2007. LNCS, vol. 4735, pp. 121–135. Springer, Heidelberg (2007). https://doi.org/10.1007/978-3-540-75209-7_9
21. Scippacercola, F., Pietrantuono, R., Russo, S., Zentai, A.: Model-driven engineering of a railway interlocking system. In: 2015 3rd International Conference on Model-Driven Engineering and Software Development (MODELSWARD), pp. 509–519, February 2015
22. Singhoff, F., Legrand, J., Nana, L., Marcé, L.: Cheddar - a flexible real time scheduling framework. In: SIGAda, pp. 1–8 (2004)
23. Stahl, T., Voelter, M., Czarnecki, K.: Model-Driven Software Development: Technology, Engineering, Management. Wiley, Hoboken (2006)
24. Suri, K., Cuccuru, A., Cadavid, J., Gérard, S., Gaaloul, W., Tata, S.: Model-based development of modular complex systems for accomplishing system integration for industry 4.0. In: MODELSWARD, pp. 487–495 (2017)
25. Turki, S., Senn, E., Blouin, D.: Mapping the MARTE UML profile to AADL. In: ACES-MB, pp. 11–20 (2010)
26. Wang, J., Wang, J.: A new early warning method of train tracking interval based on CTC. IEEE Trans. Intell. Transp. Syst. 1–7
27. Zhao, H., Apvrille, L., Mallet, F.: Meta-models combination for reusing verification techniques. In: 7th International Conference on Model-Driven Engineering and Software Development, pp. 39–50. SCITEPRESS-Science and Technology Publications (2019)
28. Zhu, L., Zhang, Y., Ning, B., Jiang, H.: Train-ground communication in CBTC based on 802.11 b: design and performance research. In: CMC 2009, pp. 368–372. IEEE (2009)

The Understandability of Models
for Behaviour

Vladimir Estivill-Castro$^{(\boxtimes)}$ and René Hexel

School of ICT, Griffith University, Nathan 4111, Australia
{v.estivill-castro,r.hexel}@griffith.edu.au

Abstract. Models are used mainly to communicate among humans the most relevant aspects of the item being modelled. Moreover, for achieving impact in modern complex applications, modelling languages and tools must support some level of composition. Furthermore, executable models are the foundations of model-driven development; therefore, it is crucial that we study the understandability of executable behaviour models, especially from the perspective of modular composition. We examine the match between the delicate semantics of executable models for applications such as reactive- and real-time systems and developers' usually simple conception. Performing a series of experiments with UML statecharts and logic-labelled finite-state machines (LLFSMs), we explore understandability of event-driven vs. logic-labelled state machines as well as the architectural options for modular composition. We find that expertise in model manipulation is essential, and that clarification of the semantics of LLFSMs is necessary for them to remain formally verifiable and suitable for robotic and embedded systems.

Keywords: Model understandability · State diagram · Logic-labelled finite-state machines

1 Introduction

"Models are often, although not always, designed to be viewed by humans. In such cases, the models must be clear and easy to understand. One way to ensure this is to use a modular approach in constructing the model" [47]. The use of models to conceptualise, construct, deploy, maintain, and improve software systems would be useless if such models were not understandable by humans, or at least expert software engineers. Model-Driven Software Development (MDSD) suggests models realise a higher level of description and abstraction, as well as a more human-like approach when specifying the behaviour of software systems. Higher abstraction, away from assembly language, has been the progression of programming languages [6], and it excels with the use of models.

Modelling is essential to communicate the representation of a system, module, or function from a particular perspective, with the precise intention of enabling

Supported by Griffith University and Universiat Pompeu Fabra.

S. Hammoudi et al. (Eds.): MODELSWARD 2019, CCIS 1161, pp. 50–75, 2020.
https://doi.org/10.1007/978-3-030-37873-8_3

more comprehensive and productive analysis. But this is only true if models are understandable. Models abstract information; that is, models represent the same information as written specifications but in a more compact and compressed way. Once again, readers of such models would benefit if indeed there was no loss in translation. If the models are indeed understood, they enable focussing on relevant aspects and facilitate productive analysis, design, and deployment.

Modelling formalises requirements: *"So-called 'natural language' is wonderful for the purposes it was created for, such as to be rude in, to tell jokes in, to cheat, or to make love in (and Theorists of Literary Criticism can even be content-free in it), but it is hopelessly inadequate when we have to deal unambiguously with situations of great intricacy, situations which unavoidably arise in such activities as legislation, arbitration, mathematics, or programming."* [11].

In this paper, we review the mechanisms most commonly used to represent and model behaviour; namely, UML's statecharts [41]. We expand on a series of experiments [16], and re-iterate a series of experiments to evaluate the apparent symmetry of the **entry** and **exit** actions of state notations. In contrast to earlier work [16], we cross international, cultural, and language boundaries, contrasting results across Australia and Spain. We confirm that humans familiar with UML notation generalise rapidly and overlook intricacies of construct differences. Because MDSD uses well-established notations such as the UML, we believe it is essential to understand the profound implications of UML semantics for representing behaviour. The understandability of UML diagrams is crucial for correctness, validation, and formal verification of executable models. Software developers have highly ranked the understandability of representations among their criteria for the adoption of UML [38]. These practitioners argue against unnecessary model complexity and lack of formal semantics [38].

Our first quote highlights modularity in formal verification and model checking. Languages and modelling tools must offer a mechanism to compose simpler behaviours into more sophisticated ones in order to describe the complex interactions and responses expected of today's modern software systems. Complex systems would not be achievable if it was not for composition [48]. Therefore, in this paper, we explore the implications that nesting diagrams has as the mechanism to compose models of complex behaviours from those of simpler behaviours. Not surprisingly, this approach also runs into issues of understandability and, perhaps more seriously, scalability. Specially if one is to combine this with the mechanism of the subsumption architecture [5], such as the ability of one behaviour to suspend, and then restart or resume another behaviour.

Our observations are complementary to observations regarding the readability of formal notations: *"the familiarity with notation and structure that comes natural to [champions of formal notations] takes time, training and practice to acquire"* [20]. However, we explore further the implications for statecharts and behaviour modelling. For this, we take advantage of the theoretical and experimental validation of metrics on UML statecharts [23]. In particular, we measure NEntryA (number of entry actions), NExitA (number of exit actions), and NCS (number of composite states). Although previous experiments [23] suggest these metrics are not to be correlated with the understandability of UML diagrams, our results indicate that NEntryA (number of entry actions) and NExitA (number of exit actions) are indeed relevant for understandability of a state diagram.

Those earlier experiments suggested an inconclusive correlation between the understandability of UML state diagrams and NA (number of activities), NSS (number of simple states), NT (number of transitions), and NG (number of guards) [23]. Follow-up experimentation [7,8] reached the same conclusions.

We are of the opinion that there are other issues, besides the relevance of those metrics to the understandability of UML state diagrams, importantly the *asymmetry* of entry and exit actions. We add to the list the event-driven nature of UML. In fact if we look at logic expressions (vs events) to label transitions, earlier research, using such logic expressions represented in tabular form, found that subjects handled the task with very high accuracy [51]. The other issue, as we already alluded to, is that, although abstraction and understandability had been heralded for nesting states, this was not so evident when used in experimental settings [7,8,51]. We claim here that the issues of nesting, and the asymmetry of exit versus entry are subtle, but crucial to understandability and have, thus far, not received sufficient detailed analysis.

We argue that symmetric rules for the sequencing of entry and exit actions, while at first glance simple and straightforward, represent a series of fallacies. Our results show that these rules are hard to comprehend and to apply by software developers, especially when timing issues and composition are involved. Also, defining a semantics that results in executable models for, e.g., reactive and real-time systems is very delicate, especially if suspend/resume/restart signals cannot be ruled out between behaviours. Third, the apparently simple semantics actually results in a combinatorial explosion of states that hinders verification. We reach these conclusions from reviewing the results of a series of experiments with software developers and dissect how issues of understandability of state diagrams relate to nesting as well as being event-driven vs logic-labelled. We contrast this with the deterministic execution of logic-labelled finite-state machines (LLFSMs), which achieve model composition through a subsumption architecture using suspend/restart/resume. As a result, we propose a specific alternative semantics for LLFSMs that is suitable for robotic and embedded systems.

2   Background

While the ultimate authority on the UML is its reference documentation [37], we postulate here that it would not be uncommon for software developers to use textbooks or sources such as Wikipedia, whose English version receives more than 20 billion queries each month, for reviewing the intended meaning of the exit and entry actions of UML's states in statecharts. *"Every state in a UML statechart can have optional entry actions, which are executed upon entry to a state, as well as optional exit actions, which are executed upon exit from a state. Entry and exit actions are associated with states, not transitions. Regardless of how a state is entered or exited, all its entry and exit actions will be executed"* [46]. The most natural assumption to make is that these actions are symmetric. However, it is not hard to discover that this is not the case, e.g. when applying model-to-model transformations [32] to reduce UML statecharts with `entry` and `exit` actions into those that do not have such actions. This model-to-model transformation is justified by the indication that `entry` and `exit` are abbreviations for what otherwise would be the inefficient use of multiple states. These actions are presented symmetrically as set-up and tear-down phases: *"The value of entry and exit actions is that they provide means for guaranteed initialisation and cleanup, very much like class constructors and destructors in Object-oriented programming"* [46]. However, the transformation makes the asymmetry of `entry` explicit with respect to `exit`. In the latter, we need to remember the target state of the transition in an intermediate state.

Unfortunately, there is not much of an improvement with the *Foundational UML* (`fUML`), an executable subset of standard UML offering precise execution semantics. However, `fUML` uses Clause 15 of the UML Superstructure to define the execution semantics for statecharts. `fUML` for a state's `entry` and `exit` actions is completely symmetric as it describes Alf [36, Page 328].

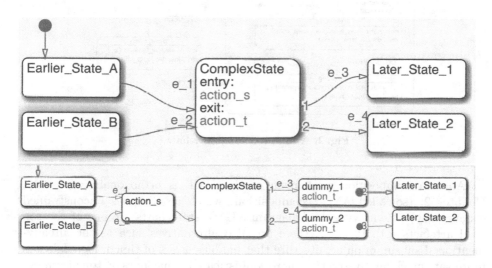

Fig. 1. Schema reflecting the model-to-model transformation that synchronises the `entry` and `exit` actions and illustrates their semantics.

The fundamental tool to handle complexity is to divide the global solution into coherent modules and compose it back from their functionality. The dominant mechanism to model complex behaviour and provide logical modularisation are hierarchies, represented by *nesting* [51] in state-based specifications, in particular, nesting sub-states (so-called OR-decomposition) [45, Chapter 2]. Some consider nested states a *"great diagrammatic simplifications when a set of events applies to several sub-states"* [12]. Others [45, Page 69] regard *hierarchically nested states* [25], as the most important invention. However, Mellor [31] highlighted several difficulties and complex semantic issues. Nested states are a mechanism to produce common facilities and simplification to event-handling policies (similarly to the *Ultimate Hook Pattern*). A notation that implies inheritance is a very powerful abstraction for sharing common features (including behaviour) and perhaps substantive of object-oriented models and the UML in particular. This abstraction capacity mostly follows Liskov's Substitution Principle [30] and implies that a sub-state of a composite state has behavioural inheritance. However, in the case of states, the *is a* relationship of inheritance is replaced by *is in (is-in-a-state)* relationship [45, Page 72]. For example, the model in Fig. 2[1] shows that when the system is in the **baking** state, it is *is-in* the **heating** state. The semantics of hierarchically nesting of states in UML is commonly specified with an interlingua approach, which again is a model-to-model transformation that flattens the model. For hierarchically nesting, *"the Cartesian product machine is used as the interlingua semantics of statecharts"* [13, Page 63].

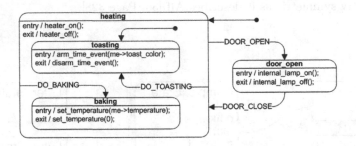

Fig. 2. A sample UML statechart.

Another composition mechanism of the UML is orthogonal regions [45, Chapter 2] (so-called AND-decomposition, which also implies unconstrained concurrency). Along with class diagrams, UML statecharts are one of the top used artefacts [41]. However, there are also alternatives such as the already-mentioned subsumption architecture that enables layers of timed, logic-labelled finite-sate machines to structure more sophisticated behaviours on top of simpler behaviours [5].

3   State-Based Diagrams

The UML is predominantly graphical. In experimental evaluations of different statechart presentations, graphical notations have been found to be preferred [51] for obtaining a high-level understanding of the system. Subjects agree that hierarchical models are easier to read than flat models and are absolutely necessary

---

[1] Figure 2 [45, Figure 2.7] appears in Wikipedia's page on UML state machines and is distributed as commons material; we also used it on our experiments.

for modelling complex systems [51]. However, subjects make the most errors when working with hierarchical models [51] and errors they would not make if the flat model was used [51]. UML statecharts are now heavily used for embedded systems, even as executable models, synthesising VHDL [49], nevertheless, remain the subject of strong criticism [4, 24, 40, 44]. While such criticism is accurate regarding the ambiguous semantics, conversely, UML is best used at the conceptual level. Therefore, we explored the issue of understandability, when the apparent syntactic sugar[2] is preserving meaning but somehow those producing the statecharts or those reading it fail to understand such shorthand notation. Despite issues of visual syntax, visual and textual standard notations enable communicating software designs to stake holders [34]. In particular, the UML can be cost-effective [14], especially when used with a degree of formality that reflects the executable code. Necessary conditions for UML to be effective were identified monitoring 20 senior developers (10 with UML experience) on five realistic maintenance tasks [14]. Despite the fact that the subjects were experienced developers, in order to level their background, a one-day UML refresher was delivered [14]. However, that research only considered class diagrams and sequence diagrams. The conclusion matches earlier observations [51] and shows that expertise with UML and usability of associated tools are strong influencing factors in the cost-effectiveness of using UML [14].

Class diagrams (structural descriptions), sequence diagrams, and stereotypes have been the focus of UML understandability [35]. The understandability of UML's use-case templates [35] was studied because of their relevance as the main communication vehicle between all stake holders, including developers. Once again, the understandability is linked to simplicity; UML artefacts must be intuitive to understand to be successful [35]. UML diagram understandability is related to cognitive load; and thus, inexperienced users struggle with diagrams that require heavy, intrinsic cognitive load correlating with diagram details [35]. *"The use case model is understandable if it allows users to recognise problem domain information and extend their understanding in problem solving."* [35]. This definition of understandable has been used with the strong recommendation [35] that for evaluating understandability, besides question accuracy, experimenters shall evaluate the time required to complete tasks: "understanding *is a cognitive process, [and] it is difficult to directly observe it, and tests to measure participants' performance were conducted to assess the level of understanding cognitively developed by each participant"* [35].

Previous work [7, 8, 16, 51] on the understandability of UML's statecharts seems restricted. The first study focused on the form of expressing transitions [51]. This study was followed by theoretical and experimental studies of the features that raise interpretation difficulty [23]. Later, the focus was that composite states add comprehensibility when users have prior familiarity with these features [8]. The counterintuitive outcome was that the experiments could not establish a direct link between composite state complexity and UML statechart

---

[2] Again, we use the model-to-model transformation of Fig. 1 to emphasise that `entry` and `exit` actions are a syntactically convenient notation.

understandability. The seemingly intuitive hypothesis would be that the use of composite states provides simplification, and thus enhances understandability; but this hypothesis is not true for inexperienced users [8].

We hypothesise that developers find UML statecharts hard to understand because their nesting usually implies uncontrolled concurrency and thus hides unexpected complexity that is intrinsically hard to reason about. That is, nesting of states, although simply described (see earlier Wikipedia quote), implies complex rules to resolve the sequence of execution. As such, we believe that logic-labelled finite-state machines (LLFSMs) are more understandable. The base of our proposal is that LLFSMs execute under a deterministic schedule. Previous research on formal verification and model checking with LLFSMs [18] demonstrates that LLFSMs avoid the exponential explosion of associated Kripke structures used by model checkers. By contrast, UML statecharts are event-driven, requiring a complex event handling process of at least five sub-steps.

Event Generation and Channeling: All generated events must be propagated to those states in all statecharts that have transitions waiting for the event.

Event Conveyance in Zero Time: Events are transported to current objects and states, theoretically with no delay and without changing the event while perfectly preserving the order of events, even in a dense-time environment.

Event Reception: Events are placed on queues (one per statechart [45]).

Event Dispatch: De-queue the event activating all responders (the listeners to the event) concurrently with *Run-Until-Completion* semantics [45].

Event Consumption: Indicates that the event has been handled; in some cases, removal from the queue is just part of this step [45].

This mechanism implies the existence of call-backs associated with the corresponding events. The Hollywood principle is often viewed favourably and used in many software patterns to seemingly minimise coupling. However, as a consequence, the call-back order of execution becomes unpredictable, requiring a model checker to evaluate all paths of execution. Formal verification must consider all possible orders in which events may be queued and de-queued. This is a fundamental source of combinatorial explosion for model checkers and cognitive load for developers. To this cognitive load we further need to add the semantics of hierarchically nesting of states in UML (or combinatorial explosion because of the Cartesian product [13, Page 63]). Moreover, UML users' cognitive load rises because they must keep in mind all aspects of the event-driven *Run-Until-Completion* semantics since *"an event can trigger a transition in all active threads, in some action threads, or in none"* [13, Page 63].

By comparison, LLFSMs offer three fundamental approaches for composition.

Control/Status Message Passing: Orthogonal behaviours with different responsibilities can synchronise through a shared memory reader/writer architecture that avoids race conditions.

Using Mechanisms to suspend/resume/restart: Enabling all sorts of rich machine hierarchies; in particular, allowing subsumption architectures.

Use of a Subsumption Switch: Wrap the actuators/effectors of a robotic/ embedded system with a module that filters commands in accordance with priorities of behavioural layers.

4 Experimental Context

We invited students from two universities (Griffith University in Australia (GU), and Universitat Pompeu Frabra in Spain, UPF) to participate in several, replicated, controlled experiments. The GU participants had completed at least one third-year, or master's software engineering (SE) course. The UPF participants had completed a second-year SE course and an elective robotics course that uses LLFSMs to create behaviours (some of the students in Spain were in their fourth year while some were in their third year). The experiments consist of either

Same Treatment of All Subjects: Everyone solves the same problem. Here, two or more aspects of a participant's performance are measured. Participant's attributes may correlate with high/low performance. For example, all subjects are required to describe everything that is communicated in a UML statechart and we measure the accuracy of describing entry versus exit behaviour per unit of time.

Different Treatment of Subjects: All subjects answer the same questions, but about a different, randomly assigned diagram, whereupon we perform an ANOVA (or $t = $ test, if two classes). We randomly divide the participants into two or three groups for tasks on equivalent, but different diagrams. We assign the groups randomly to an equivalent task; but each group proceeds with diagrams with a specific feature with the control from a diagram without the feature (for example state nesting versus a diagram with no nesting).

The method we follow starts by formulating a hypothesis, for instance *"use of composite states improves understandability of UML"*. The second step defines a measure that accounts for how quickly subjects solve a task and how accurately they solve the task. Typically we use the same measure of *"understandability efficiency"* [8] as the accuracy (the number of correct answers) divided by the time taken. Then, we define a hypothesis testing scenario; for example:

H_0: the use of composite state diagrams does *not* improve the understandability efficiency.

H_1: the use of composite state diagrams does improve the understandability efficiency.

The experiments in Australia took place during July/August 2018 while those in Spain between May/June 2019. Our experimental framework has the following aspects in common with other UML understandability studies [8,10,23].

Participant Population: The Australian students were from two different campuses in four different degree programs (one master and three undergraduate programs). The students at Universitat Pompeu Fabra were from a single campus and a single degree program (a 4-year undergraduate program).

Motivation and Persuasion: Subjects were motivated to voluntarily participate using similar incentives such as explaining that the tasks would be
illustrative of the final exam [8,10,23].

Anonymity and Voluntary Participation: Participation is voluntary and
responses were anonymous; thus, students were not evaluated on their individual performance.

Simplicity: The tasks in the experiment did not require a high level of industrial
experience. We selected relative easy to comprehend data models [10]. We
emphasised the premise that a simple data model was preferred over a more
complex one (as the focus was not the application domain nor the accuracy
with which the model reflects complex situations).

Concealed Information and Performance: We did not reveal our scoring
approaches or metrics of interest. Participants were allowed plenty of time to
complete the task.

Expertise: Students were in their final year, completing a course in software
engineering, or they were masters students who had already completed a prior
IT degree.

Long-term Preparation: Subjects received significant instruction on the main
constructs of the UML. Model-Driven development was illustrated and exer-
cised in laboratories using ARGO-UML [43] (students developed UML class
diagrams and generated code in C++, Java and SQL, analysing multiple
aspects of the mappings). Moreover, statecharts were used in laboratories
using MDSD and executable models through the QM^{TM} tool. Students were
required to review "A Crash Course in UML State Machines" [1] with overlapping content [45, Chapter 2] and distributed by Quantum®L^{e}aPs.

Pre-task Preparation: Prior to attempting the tasks, subjects were given the
opportunity to review material on UML statecharts, e.g. the earlier cited
Wikipedia page [46], plus two others [2,19].

Researchers from experimental software engineering expect only minor differences between professionals and students when participants perform relatively
small tasks [3,26]. Therefore, to support the same assumption that students as
subjects are appropriate [8,10,23] all tasks consisted of the interpretation of
UML diagrams. We argue our tasks are simple because the level of nesting was
capped at 2: at most one machine and one sub-machine. To minimise the impact
of particular visual notations [34], we used materials from others that clearly
use the same visual notation or we used a graph-layout software with the same
layout parameters (in particular, we represented statechart models as conforming to a meta-model and used an ATL transformation [27] from the meta-model
to dot [22]). The focus of our research is the semantics of the notation and its
representation on diagrams [10] (and we insist, not across visual notations [34]).

For behaviour models that produce short output, subjects were asked to
anticipate the output generated. For behaviours that generated continuous output, subjects were required to identify the main traits of the behaviour, or alternatively subjects we asked whether a particular sequence of output statements
occurred in that precise order. For example, with reference to Fig. 2, a question

asked if `internal_lamp_on()` always happened before `internal_lamp_off()`. We also emphasise that for understanding tasks (and the understandability of UML artefacts) it is common to request subjects to provide as much information as possible and to define the expected response prior to issuing the task.

5 Experimental Tasks and Results

5.1 Calibration

Our first task was an experiment with different treatment of subjects. We reproduced verbatim Cruz *et al.*'s original Figs. 5 (F5) and 6 (F6) [8] and questionnaire [8, Appendix A]. Subjects answer the same questionnaire but are randomly partitioned between the two figures. Each figure is supposed to have an equivalent UML diagram that models the same behaviour of a phone call: F5 uses nesting states while F6 has no nested states. However, F6 is a simplified version of F5 (recall the interlingua semantics of nested states). That is, F6 draws much fewer transitions than those implied by F5. This difference demonstrates that indeed, nesting suppresses many transitions that, if drawn, would (perhaps unnecessarily) clutter the diagram. Although F5 and F6 are not semantically equivalent, the questions in the questionnaire [8, Appendix A] did not explore their semantic differences. This task could be considered particularly simple, and unfortunately [8, Figure 5] or [8, Figure 6] may be translations from Spanish to English (the figures have a spelling error).

Calibration Results. Reapplying the questionnaire [8, Appendix A] shows no significant difference between nested and plain diagrams. Our experimental results are equivalent to earlier outcomes [8]. In Australia we collected responses from two campuses: 18 and 20 subjects respectively, each equally divided into the two groups (nested versus flat). In Spain, we collected responses from 21 subjects, with 11 nested and 10 flat. We measured *understandability efficiency*. While in the GU results there seems to be no significant improvement (or difference) in understandability/efficiency by using nested states, the UPF results seem to suggest even a slightly worse performance with the nested version. We offer here a new explanation derived from our earlier observations and still congruent with the original conclusions [8]. Nesting states incur in *construct redundancy* [34]. They also imply identifying a transition that is not directly leaving the source state; thus, nested states are an advanced concept. Visual notations are formal notations and "uniquely human-oriented representations" [34]. *"One should not underestimate the difficulty of reading a formal specification written in mathematical notation"* [21]. In the most Piagetian constructivist style, nested statecharts require as pre-requisite knowledge flat statecharts in a concept-map. One needs to understand the notion of state before one can capture *sub-states* (let alone the notion of *chain state* [42]). The discovery of *sub-states* revises the conceptual framework of statechart. It can only be operated efficiently if one masters the potential combinations implied by nested states. Thus, users reach command of nested statecharts when experience and regular usage assimilates the implicit semantics that the interlingua semantics implies.

5.2   Simple, Nested Model

Our second experimental task is an experiment with same treatment of all subjects. Participants must predict the output of a simple model, in particular, to comprehensively describe the information provided by the UML statechart in Fig. 2. The anticipated answer was to obtain paragraphs equivalent to those in Fig. 3. Also a questionnaire (refer to Fig. 4) that has 8 questions testing subjects on whether they could correctly identify behaviour (sequencing) on exit actions, entry action, entry and exit actions, Run-Until-Completion, State Nesting, ordering of events, ordering of nesting (priority on exiting a hierarchy of nested states), and re-entering a hierarchy of nested states.

(2 points: statechart and composite states/sub-states) This diagram models the behaviour of some device that has, fundamentally, two states: heating and door_open. The heating state has sub-states toasting and baking. Because of the solid-dot pseudo-states, this device starts in the heating state, and in the toasting sub-state. Separate states are exclusive, so the system is either in the heating state or the door_open state. Similarly, the system is either toasting or baking. However, sub-states occur within their parent state; for example baking happens always while heating.

(1 point: transitions labelled by events) An event CLOSE_DOOR will transition the system from the state door_open to heating.

(1 point: when On-Entry and On-Exit happens) An event DOOR_OPEN will cause the system to move from heating to door_open no matter what sub-state in heating. When we leave heating in this case, the action heater_off will be performed as an *exit* activity of the state heating followed by the action internal_lamp_on which is the *entry* activity of the state door_open. Here we see two actions where one happens before the other.

(1 point: nesting is described) The transitions between heating and door_open are both external transitions, but the transition of the events DO_BAKING and DO_TOASTING are internal transitions. So when DO_BAKING, no matter the sub-state in heating, we will come to the sub-state baking, but we will not execute the *exit* of heating, we will execute the *exit* of toasting (if we were in toasting, that is the action disarm_time_event is performed but heater_off is not. However, the action set_temperature of baking is performed after as the *entry* to baking. Every time the system goes out of toasting the disarm_time_event is executed. Similarly, departing form baking always executed the action set_temperature.

Fig. 3. Grading scale to assess the translation to English when interpreting the model of Fig. 2 (based on [16, Figure 3]).

Simple, Nested Model Results. Our first remarkable result is the score difference observed for subjects answering questions regarding exit actions vs entry actions on the same diagram. Our questionnaires had 8 questions: a correct answer provided one point, an incorrect one subtracted a point. For each subject, we subtracted their score for the exit answer from the score for the entry answers. The null hypothesis was that the mean of these differences is 0. For our first campus experiment, with $N = 51$ respondents, the mean of the difference scores was 3.00 with a standard deviation of 3.85. The standard error of the mean was 0.54. A t-test with 50 degrees of freedom rejects the null hypothesis (p-value less than 0.00001). The replication at the second campus had only $N = 26$ respondents; nevertheless, the mean of the score differences was 2.11, with a standard deviation of 3.97. This results in an estimate of the standard error for the mean of 0.41 and the t-test with 25 degrees of freedom also rejects the null hypothesis (p-value less than 0.00001). In Spain we only had $N = 10$ participants; nevertheless, the mean of the difference scores was 2.4 with a standard deviation of 3.33 (the standard error of the mean was 0.76). The corresponding t-test has 9 degrees of freedom and also rejects the null hypothesis at 95% significance level with p-value less than 0.049. Thus, our experimentation reveals that subjects have different capacity to answer symmetrical questions regarding `entry` sections of statecharts as opposed to `exit` sections. The mean accuracy is higher for the `entry` questions than the `exit` questions.

The diagram models the behaviour of a toaster oven. Assume that no events have been issued prior to each of the questions below, and that the two behaviours were launched concurrently in the order `Outer` followed by `Inner`. Answer only in terms of the actions: `heater_on()`, `heater_off()`, `arm_time_event(me->toast_color)`, `disarm_time_event()`, `set_temperature(me->Temperature)`, `set_temperature(0)`, `internal_lamp_on()`, and `internal_lamp_off()`.

1. If the event to DO_BAKING is received, what is/are a/the sequence of actions produced by all behaviours involved?
2. If the event to DO_BAKING is received; and later, after a few seconds, the event to DOOR_OPEN happens, what is/are a/the sequence of actions produced by all behaviours involved?
3. If the event to DO_BAKING is received, and while the action `disarm_time_event()` is being performed, the DOOR_OPEN happens, what is/are a/the sequence of actions produced by all behaviours involved?
4. If the event to DO_BAKING is received, and while the action `set_temperature(me->Temperature)` is running the DOOR_OPEN happens, what is/are a/the sequence of actions produced by all behaviours involved?
5. If the event to DO_BAKING is received, and after a few seconds the event to DOOR_OPEN happens, and while the action `set_temperature(0)` is being performed, the DOOR_CLOSE happens, what is/are a/the sequence of actions produced by all behaviours involved?
6. If the event to DO_BAKING is received, and after a few seconds the event to DOOR_OPEN happens, and while the action `heater_off()` is executing, the DOOR_CLOSE happens, what is/are a/the sequence of actions produced by all behaviours involved?
7. Write down the minimum sequence of events and conditions needed, to go from the state **toasting** to the state **baking**, and back to **toasting**, but this going back is not caused by an event to DO_TOASTING:
8. Write down the minimum sequence of events and conditions needed, to go from the state **toasting** to the state **baking**, and back to **toasting**.

Fig. 4. Questionnaire (in the style of earlier questionnaire [8, Appendix A]) to evaluate understandability of Fig. 2 and equivalent diagrams with LLFSMs (based on [16, Figure 6]).

5.3 Non-nested LLFSM

Our third experimental task is an experiment with same treatment of all subjects. Subjects were required to predict the output of the logic-labelled finite-state machine in Fig. 5a. We used the downloadable version of the `clfsm` scheduler [17] for logic-label finite-state machines and the `MiEdit` editor [15]. We used current versions of ROS under Ubuntu for the experiments (the then-current ROS-Kinetic under Ubuntu 16.04 LTS in Australia, and the updated

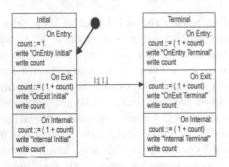 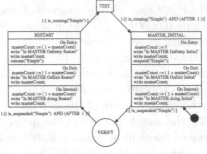

(a) A simple logic-labelled finite-state machine.

(b) A master logic-labelled finite-state machine.

Fig. 5. An arrangement of LLFSMs where the master suspends and resumes the simple LLFSM.

Ubuntu 18.04 LTS and ROS-Melodic in Spain). Subjects were provided practice in executing LLFSMs with the clfsm scheduler. Communication between LLFSMs was using the mechanisms of the ROS' middleware.

This apparently simple model has implications for understanding the notion of guards, when in a ringlet is a transition evaluated, and whether the exit is executed in a terminal state.

Non-nested LLFSM Results. The notion of logic-labelled finite-state machines (LLFSMs) could be seen as UML models with no events and only guards: LLFSMs with no events are also called *procedural state machines* [13], in that case, the model is not at the mercy of the arrival of events: *"because [the automaton] can access the input symbols at any time, it can visit states as fast as we wish"* [13, Page 15].

The discussion of the notion of *guard* is typically linked with the illustration that UML statecharts are extended state machines [45, Chapter 2]. Since there are no events in LLFSMs, their precise semantics specifies exactly when the Boolean condition is evaluated (a snapshot of all external variables is taken before commencing of a ringlet, and all guards of all transitions are evaluated in this context). But this issue is somewhat ambiguous for the UML, the expressions are meant to be evaluated upon the arrival of the event. However, events are queued in executable models and guards are evaluated during the dispatch of the event [45, Chapter 2] (recall the sub-steps to handle an event in Sect. 3).

Therefore, understandability of LLFSMs (although completely sequential), seems also to require a certain level of maturity and familiarity with UML (as we mentioned in earlier sections, most experimental evaluations of artefacts and cost-effectiveness of the UML suggest expertise and significant familiarity are required). Our results are consistent with this. We evaluated the understandability/efficiency of the subjects as the accuracy of questions about the LLFSM terminating (or running in a continuous loop), whether the execution leaves the state named **INITIAL** without executing the do (Internal) section, and whether the exit of the **TERMINAL** state is executed because no transition fires. Therefore, a fourth element is that, when in state **TERMINAL** the do does run. We had 21 respondents on our first campus, 10 graduate students and 11 undergraduate students. The accuracy divided by the time taken is used as understandability/efficiency and the values satisfy a normal distribution assumption with a Q-Q plot (for each group). The graduate students' mean understandability/efficiency is superior to that of the undergraduate students (statistically significant at a $\gamma = 95\%$ confidence level). Upon replication on the other campus, we had 6 undergraduate volunteers and 12 graduate volunteers. Despite the lower numbers, we also saw a significant result (at $\gamma = 95\%$), showing a superior understandability/efficiency for graduate students over the mean for undergraduate students. In Spain we only had 4 respondents, and all were third year students. Despite their earlier practice with LLFSMs they all made the same mistake of including the do action in the **INITIAL** although the transition fires immediately and they all include the exit action of the **TERMINAL** state despite no transition fires. All took more than 5 min to complete the task. We believe this result confirms that even the simplest UML artefacts hide very delicate issues.

5.4   Nested LLFSMs

Our the fourth task also used an executable arrangement of LLFSMs. We tested understanding of the clfsm scheduler again under the same ROS middleware. In preparation for this task, the clfsm scheduler capabilities to suspend/resume/restart one LLFSM from another LLFSM had been practiced in laboratories in the students' courses (in both Australia and Spain). Although the executable model produces continuous output, the task consisted of formulating a qualitative prediction of the execution of the arrangement in Fig. 5. This is the concurrent execution of the LLFSMs in Fig. 5a and b.

Nested LLFSM Results. We recorded the participants' accuracy relative to the time used to measure the understandability efficiency. The accuracy was regarding the correct prediction of the behaviour of the concurrent execution of two LLFSMs. The precise execution varies slightly when clfsm is invoked with the LLFSMs in Fig. 5a and b in different order. This swapping of the arrangement order slightly modifies the output. Moreover, in this case, the execution continues endlessly. Our results indicate a similar pattern as previously. The first campus had 14 undergraduate and 10 graduate students, the second campus had 10 undergraduate and 11 graduate respondents. Performance was significantly superior for graduate students at $\gamma = 95\%$. The undergraduate students seem to follow each LLFSM separately. But these subjects could not master the notion of ringlet (and of round-robin schedule of the concurrent execution of the two LLFSMs) with the same understandability/efficiency of the graduate students. In Spain we only had 6 volunteers from fourth year. Their performance was superior to the undergraduate students from Australia at a significance level of $\gamma = 95\%$, but we cannot place them above or below the Australian graduate students. This is consistent with the level of expertise. The Australian undergraduate students were in 3-year programs, while our more highly experienced participants were fourth year (Spain) or Master's students (Australia).

5.5 Subsumption and Delegation Results

This task required significant preparation. In corresponding laboratories participants had been working with examples of message passing using the ROS publisher/subscriber (`rostopics`) and client/server (`rosservices`) software patterns. They had been shown that the sequential execution of LLFSMs implies an LLFSM cannot take the role of a ROS-subscriber (LLFSMs cannot not use callbacks). The examples illustrated that the *wrapper* software pattern is applicable here. A wrapper ROS-Node that plays both the role of a subscriber and a service is placed between the publisher of a signal and the LLFSMs interested in the topic. Wrapping of `rostopic` signals (events) into a `rosservice` enables the LLFSM to act as a ROS client and query the status. One of the examples practised ahead of time by all our students was the third of the downloadable ROS LLFSMs examples [15]. Here, the elementary turtle icon of ROS is driven to walk about its environment staying away from the boundary.

The actual task comprised implementing the model presented in Fig. 2 using LLFSMs. We provided the executable code (as a ROS-package) for a service wrappers for the signals DO_BAKE and DO_TOASTING; and the signals to DOOR_OPEN and DOOR_CLOSE. The instructions of the tasks requested to emulate the nesting hierarchy of Fig. 2. The **Inner** behaviour responds to DO_BAKE and DO_TOASTING and as a result of that switches from the state **toasting** to **baking**. The second behaviour corresponds to the **Outer** behaviour that responds to DOOR_OPEN and DOOR_CLOSE. Subsequently, the behaviours are integrated. Subjects were required to commit to one of the two strategies by which LLFSMs represent state nesting: that is, subjects were asked to chose between **suspend/resume/restart** or to use a delegation (forwarding) of messages.

Subsumption and Delegation Results. A remarkable aspect of these tasks is that all groups of student volunteers, including the participants from Spain, selected the incorrect implementation pattern. None of the subjects obtained a correct implementation with LLFSMs of the model in Fig. 2.

5.6 Randomised Diagrams (Australia)

For the sixth experiment, subjects were randomly partitioned into three groups and provided the same earlier Questionnaire (Fig. 4). However, each group was provided with a different diagram. The first group was provided the diagram in Fig. 2, the second group was provided a model solution to its implementation using **suspend/ resume/restart** with LLFSMs, and the third group was provided a model solution using delegation/forwarding with LLFSMs.

Randomised Diagrams (Australia) Results. Here we first used a 3-factor ANOVA (between subjects/one-way) analysis, as we identify the three types of diagrams. If we measure the accuracy on the 8 questions in Fig. 4 divided by time, we find no evidence that the means are different. The box-plot in Fig. 6a (generated with R's `ggplot` [39]) shows not much difference, except for one outlier where one subject did extremely well for the LLFSM diagram using the delegation pattern. However, if we break the questionnaire into the four middle questions (3, 4, 5, and 6, which deal with Run-Until-Completion semantics), we can see that the results are significantly better for understandability/efficiency for diagrams with suspend/resume (refer to Fig. 6b). Conversely, on Questions 1, 2, 7, and 8, the UML diagram performs much better. Again, the 3-factor ANOVA results show no statistically significant difference. However an unpaired (two sample) t-test of the understandability/efficiency on the UML diagram versus the suspend/resume diagram does indicate the rejection of the null hypothesis at 95%. That suggests UML diagrams are understandable as long as we set up scenarios with well-spaced events, where users can follow all the consequences of one event before the arrival of another. LLFSMs seems to be the other way around. While, at a first glance, the run-until-completion semantics appears obvious and straightforward, in our experimental task denoted in Figs. 2 and 4, almost all subjects had substantial trouble with Questions 4 to 8.

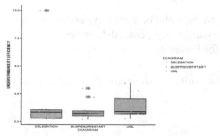
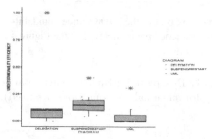

(a) Box plot of the 3-ways understandability/efficiency per model type of the Figure 4 questions.

(b) Box plot of the 3-ways understandability/efficiency per model type on Q's 3 to 6 for Figure 4.

Fig. 6. Box plots for Australian participants (the units on the right plot are half to the left plot since half the questions are used).

5.7   Randomised Diagrams (Spain)

This experiment is similar to the Randomised Diagrams experiment performed in Australia we just described (see Subsect. 5.6). However, we had only $N = 15$ participants, so we randomly divided them into only two groups, those working with the UML from Fig. 2 versus those working with a suspend/resume solution of LLFSMs. Again, the questions are those of Questionnaire (Fig. 4). Our partition results in 6 students working with the UML diagram from Fig. 2 with the other (9 participants) working with the LLFSM diagram.

Randomised Diagrams (Spain) Results. The plots in Fig. 7 show that the participants were (statistically significant) more proficient with the LLFSM diagram than with the UML diagram. Figure 7a is the total score for the questionnaire, while Fig. 7b. In this experiment, participants performed particularly poorly with those question that deal with the *Run-Until-Completion* semantics of the UML. Recall that the *Run-Until-Completion* semantics requires that the UML users keeps in mind the queue of events while resolving the current event. Most users seem to *interrupt* the handling of the current event and perform the actions of new arriving event. Note that the y-axis in the two figures in Fig. 7 is not the same scale, nevertheless, the gap between those with the UML diagram and the others widens, highlighting how challenging is to grasp the *Run-Until-Completion* semantics of the UML.

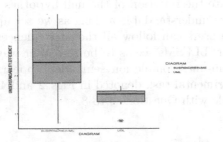 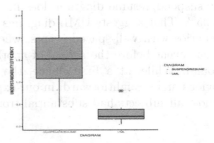

(a) Box plot of the 2-ways understandability/efficiency per model type of the Figure 4 questions.

(b) Box plot of the 2-ways understandability/efficiency per model type on Q's 3 to 6 for Figure 4.

Fig. 7. Box plots for Spanish participants (the units on the right plot are half to the left plot since half the questions are used).

6   Analysis

6.1   Lesson Learned

LLFSMs are apparently simpler because, as we mentioned, they could be considered UML statecharts without events. But LLFSMs offer a precise and unambiguous semantics that provides complete detail for execution and verification. Our results suggest that LLFSMs require significantly more maturity from participants. However, when issues of timing and order of execution become more critical, or when interpreting and understanding the effect of event showers, or the handling of events while another event is still being processed, LLFSMs are much clearer and more transparent. This is particularly supported in the Spanish replication of the experiments.

It may not be unexpected that our experiments demonstrate that enduring experience with UML is required for high understandability/efficiency. We nevertheless found some remarkable surprises. For example, we discovered that among subjects there is a strong belief that UML statecharts imply strong restrictions on the ordering of events. In particular, 32% of the first-campus group (52 respondents) indicated in one particular question that the diagram in Fig. 2 implies that DOOR_OPEN must always be followed by DOOR_CLOSED (the group on the second campus had 26 respondents, but a percentage as high as 38% also expected such an ordering of events). These responses occurred despite earlier lab demonstrations to students (prior to the questionnaire) that showed an implementation of Fig. 2 with QM^{TM}. In those demonstrations, we explicitly showed that all sequences of events of the form (DOOR_CLOSED|DOOR_OPEN)* were valid for the Outer behaviour. Our participants were a subset of the students instructed in the laboratories who experienced the execution of the implementation which displayed a behaviour that would toggle between the state **door_open** and **heating** at the right time. That is, duplication of the event DOOR_OPEN once in the state **door_open** is possible and has no effect. Moreover, 68% of these participants could not commit either way about whether the diagram implied something regarding the order of events. Only 10% could confirm that the UML diagram in Fig. 2 is at the mercy of the sequence of events coming from the environment, and its implementation (or executable model) behaves correctly only when it makes no assumptions about a benevolent environment.

6.2   Threats to Validity

Clearly, students are not professionals in the field of practice, and although, like others [28], we justified their participation, those with experience in several projects may be a different group subjects [14]. Especially since our results suggest that expertise developed with experience is a contributing factor to understandability. Since the tasks are simple or at least not very sophisticated (for example, Figs. 2 and 4), it is possible that the results could be different in other settings. For example, industrial scenarios usually involve complex behaviours of many inter-dependent statecharts [38]. Also, understandability interacts with other factors (for instance, different development tools) in more complex ways than in our controlled experiment. In particular, to remove other factors, we conducted the experiments separately, allowing at least one week in between two of them to minimise the effect of fatigue. The groups were small so we could eliminate plagiarism because we could ensure no individual received any coaching, advice, or communication with others.

Nevertheless, for evaluating understandability, the students' lack of experience signifies the difficulty in grasping the models [35]. If models were highly understandable, novice users would not exhibit the difficulties we observe. Moreover, using simple tasks for UML diagrams is a suitable approach when dealing with subjects that are students, as long as we keep in mind that the experience of users could have a more profound effect on more complex tasks [28,35].

The UML refresher material may be another issue to consider for external validity. We found the results from Spanish students somewhat surprising, regarding their inability to handle the *Run-Till-Completion* semantics of the UML, but their high performance with LLFSMs. It is possible that more practice is required with a tool such as the already mentioned QM^{TM} that implements the *Run-Till-Completion* semantics. Results may vary if participants are exposed and have more exposure to a specific model of semantics. One issue could be that Australian students effectively had little prior exposure to the notion of state machines. Neither of five programs feeding into the pool of Australian subjects had a course on automata and formal languages, while the Spanish students do have exposure to automata theory and some had exposure to a course in compilers with some content on lexical analysis. We should point out that if we compare the performance of Spanish students against Australian students under the same diagram, the Spanish students' understandability/efficiency is superior, with statistical significance, to the Australians. We can see that in Fig. 7a the mean understandability/efficiency for Spanish participants is way above 1 for all diagrams, which is where Australian participants are almost for all diagrams (refer to Fig. 6a). The same is true when we focus on the *Run-Till-Completion* semantics. The understandability/efficiency for Spanish participants is above 0.25 for all diagrams (Fig. 7b) which is above the understandability/efficiency for Australian participants in the corresponding figure (Fig. 6b). Similarly, results may vary if subjects had exposure to state diagrams from other areas.

We face the same challenges as all other studies with respect to construct validity (the suitability of the instrument to measure understandability). *Understanding* is a cognitive process, we can only measure elements that we believe reflect the level of understanding, using the common hypothesis that failure to achieve a task (such as translation into another language or into the output behaviour sequence) is linked to a lack of understanding. However, UML notations may be simply hard to learn (which may be associated with understandability). We also may not have been able to record the understanding failures accurately.

Challenges could be derived from violations to the assumptions that enable a particular analysis (that is, statistical validly), such as low effect size or statistical power. When comparing two groups, we used the t-test. Where we employ ANOVA, we assume homogeneity of variance as there does not seem to be any other factor that would invalidate this assumption. We used a Q-Q-plot to validate the assumption of normally distributed random variables. When partitioning, each value was sampled independently from any other variable to ascertain between-subject factors. However, we acknowledge that our sample sizes were smaller than those in other, similar studies. Nevertheless, we discussed results only where we could report statistical significance. Since participation was voluntary, the class sizes (where lectures and laboratories were delivered to participants) were larger than the samples reported. This self-selection of the subjects implies a potential bias. It is possible that diligent students seek more practice.

7 Asymmetric Semantics

Similar to others [9], our results suggest that hierarchical nesting of UML state-charts does not scale well. The suggestion that nesting level inversely correlates with understandability could be justified, as, when taken as executable models, UML statechart hierarchies have high McCabe Cyclomatic Complexity (the number of linearly independent paths through the execution is high as nested statecharts are an abbreviation of a single, large statechart containing the Cartesian product of states in the hierarchy). We recall that Cyclomatic Complexity is the number of linearly independent execution paths through the model.

However, the issue becomes complicated when discussing `entry` and `exit` actions. The following quote reflects a brief explanation for the roles of sections in UML statecharts. *"Regardless of how a state is entered or exited, all its entry and exit actions will be executed"* [45, Page 76]), proposing a symmetry between `entry` and `exit` actions. However, building on our earlier arguments, to illustrate further inherent asymmetry present in LLFSMs, we consider the suspension of a member of the arrangement. Suspension is a meta-action (from the perspective of the machine being suspended) that is performed by the scheduler (when triggered, e.g., by a higher-level machine in the subsumption architecture). In particular, it is quite inappropriate if a machine had been suspended (thus no longer operating) but were to execute any actions. Suspended machines must not execute any code, not even their exit actions (or, as per philosophy of the subsumption architecture, any actions are blocked from causing any effect). Figure 2 illustrates that humans interpreting the model would expect the oven would be immediately turned off when sensors report the door is open. The results of our study show a significant difference in the number of participants that preferred to treat the implementation in Fig. 2 by the `suspend`/`restart` mechanism when the `DOOR_OPEN`/`DOOR_CLOSED` (respectively) signals are detected.

Suggesting that `exit` actions are not performed in a suspended state-machine may seem to contradict the event-driven nature of UML with its associated *Run-Till-Completion* semantics—where all `exit` actions are *always* performed. Considering what happens when a machine is suspended raises the cognitive load on designers and developers when constructing or interpreting a set of statecharts. In particular, designers must consider that the suspender machine needs to account for further activity still performed by anyone who is suspended. This possibility that a suspended actor may perform any actions violates the principle of the least surprise. Moreover, the delicacies of this issue can have severe consequences in safety-critical systems (such as the radiation magnetron of a microwave), where two opposing concerns (regular operation and immediate shutdown) suddenly have to be catered for in the same (`exit`) action. We now address the critical issue of defining the semantics of a machine that receives a `suspend` with respect to the `exit` section of its current state.

We observe that the inherent asymmetry between execution context and sphere of control [29] (subsystem vs meta-action) results in an asymmetry of the `entry` and `exit` actions. Composition of larger models of LLFSMs is achieved by including further behaviours in the pre-scheduled sequential execution of an arrangement and explicitly invoking their execution (or suspension). The semantics of an arrangement of LLFSMs is that all machines in the arrangement are executing concurrently, but only one at a time is effectively running. When the holder of the execution token runs the actions associated with its current state, it executes one ringlet in the current state; then, the scheduler passes the token of execution to the next machine. The semantics for running a ringlet is defined as follows.

1. The entry action is executed if (and only if) the previous state was different to the current one.
2. The predefined sequence of transitions is evaluated; if none of them is true, the do section is executed and the ringlet finishes.
3. Alternatively, exit is executed (when a transition T fires) and the target state of T becomes the current state. This also completes the ringlet.

Thus, when arriving from another state, the entry section of a state is executed once and only once, without exception (this interpretation of transitions with identical source and target state caused some issues in SCXML [50]).

Note that, at the time a machine is suspended the suspender (another higher-level, controller machine) holds the token of execution. That is, the suspend happens outside the sphere of control [29] of the machine being suspended. Therefore, for robotic and embedded systems, which often implement the subsumption architecture [5] and suspend/resume/restart signal, a suspended machine should not run any actions after the suspension signal. For example, consider a robot design where the exit of a motion state S triggers a control signal when a transition labelled with some condition (such as an object becoming visible) fires. Suppose that a super-imposing behaviour ensures some safety constraints on the motion, for instance, that the posture is safe for the motion. If the robot were to change to an unsafe posture (a fall), the super-machine would issue a suspend but the controlled behaviour would execute the exit and drive the robot to perform a motion in an unsafe posture. In fact, if designers follow the semantics suggested here, the trigger of a motion shall not be when leaving a state, but on arrival to a state (the design is vastly improved by breaking the preparation and launching of the motion into two states, and the launching being in the entry).

As another illustration, we review the higher-level machine switching behaviour between **toasting** and **door_open** in Fig. 2. The submachine that switches between **toasting** or **baking** is the inner behaviour, and it would only receive the token of execution after being suspended, i.e. after the higher-level machine has performed the suspend. By the time the inner machine receives back the token of execution, it already is in its suspended state. Thus, it would be quite surprising if it were to resume its prior state to catch up and run some associated exit action.

To consider entry and exit actions as symmetric actions has some potential mnemonic elegance. However, the argument here is that this symmetry only applies within the sphere of control [29] of a single machine. The earlier examples serve to stress our argument. Actions in the exit are executed when one transition fires (the Boolean expression labelling it evaluates to true). Running the actions of this section while suspended results in the actions of exit being executed in a completely unpredictable context. This context is unpredictable because it is subject to all the actions of all other behaviours in the composition;

that is in the arrangement. Such a context can clearly be radically different and inconsistent with the conditions that are stated in the Boolean expressions that label the transitions leading away from the state in question. This is terribly unsafe (and thus, our argument why the example above are a poor design and the semantics favour a redesign).

Let us now focus on a further point of asymmetry pertaining the entry section. Namely, entry is executed when the operation of a machine is resumed. This is completely analogous, consistent and corresponds to having no exception when a machine is first started and the entry of its initial state is executed. Thus, the corresponding entry is executed when a LLFSM that was previously suspended is resumed or restarted. The rationale is simple, the corresponding machine is in control and able to perform its specified actions.

The earlier suggested re-design of our example robot preparing and signalling a motion corresponds to classical software engineering principles. Executing the actions of an entry section precisely, and only when one of the transitions has its guard evaluated to true, acts as a precondition (in the sense of programming by contract [33]). Thus, this semantics enforces stronger, first-principles based software development with statechart models. Among these principles are code re-use, separation of concerns, decoupling, and locality of effects, since in a layered architecture, lower layers shall be completely unaware of higher layers.

These semantics do not prevent the implementation with LLFSMs of a design using UML's composability with nested states. For example, in Fig. 2, the DOOR_OPEN signal acts as a trigger to several exit actions (in the outer and in the inner machines). Because this is a UML design, the exit actions are aimed at reversing the corresponding entry actions. For instance, suspending the inner machine and not executing its exit would leave the toaster on. The problem is that the UML design hides that the super-machine requires cooperation from its sub-machine. This assistance ought to be made explicit through notification (to the sub-machine) of a condition. This is clearly a delegation pattern (and forwarding of a corresponding signal). When the system is in the state baking, it is also in the state toasting and thus it shall listen to DOOR_OPEN as well. Moreover, the order in which all the nested states execute their corresponding exit actions becomes explicit by using delegation. Note, however, that the original description of nested-state semantics by Harel prioritised first the super-state over the sub-state, but UML has revised this interpretation and now an inverse prioritisation is used. This, once more, highlights the significance of clear, accessible semantics to the designer. Thus, our discussion here emphasises the importance of characterising the scenarios where the subsumption architectural pattern of independent components is applicable, versus those situations where other patterns, such as delegation and communication, are applicable. Making these explicit to software engineers may alleviate the confusion that exists, as our experiments have revealed.

8   Conclusions

Our experiments have shown that the simplistic model of symmetry between entry and exit actions does not even hold true when tested against simple, nested models. Perhaps unsurprisingly, more experienced participants (masters students) showed a superior capability in their levels of understanding compared to less experienced participants (undergraduate students).

The wide-spread use of state diagrams for model behaviour for the ever growing number of embedded devices (just consider the Internet of Things) makes it imperative that executable models, such as LLFSMs, delineate the precise semantics derived from the entry and exit asymmetry. We have argued for a semantics where exit is executed upon leaving the state in the sphere of control of the current machine. The experiments show that the interaction of nesting states with UML's *Run-Till-Completion* semantics is particularly hard to grasp.

Overall, our study shows that, while complex, nested models are hard to interpret for humans, a precise semantics (as is necessary for verifiable, executable models) needs to be intuitive for human understandability. Importantly, compared to the literature, where seemingly simple, symmetric semantics have led to often counter-intuitive or difficult-to-comprehend system behaviours, we have demonstrated an asymmetry in participants' understanding of entry vs exit behaviour that supports our hypothesis of an intrinsically asymmetric execution semantics leading to a more intuitive system behaviour.

References

1. A crash course in UML state machines (2015). https://www.state-machine.com/ doc/AN_Crash_Course_in_UML_State_Machines.pdf. Accessed 20 June 2019
2. State machine diagram tutorial (2018). https://www.lucidchart.com/pages/uml-state-machine-diagram. Accessed 20 June 2019
3. Basili, V.R., Shull, F., Lanubile, F.: Building knowledge through families of experiments. IEEE Trans. Softw. Eng. **25**(4), 456–473 (1999)
4. Börger, E., Cavarra, A., Riccobene, E.: Modeling the dynamics of UML state machines. In: Gurevich, Y., Kutter, P.W., Odersky, M., Thiele, L. (eds.) ASM 2000. LNCS, vol. 1912, pp. 223–241. Springer, Heidelberg (2000). https://doi.org/10.1007/3-540-44518-8_13
5. Brooks, R.: A robust layered control system for a mobile robot. IEEE J. Robot. Autom. **2**(1), 14–23 (1986)
6. Colburn, T., Shute, G.: Abstraction in computer science. Minds Mach. **17**(2), 169–184 (2007)
7. Cruz-Lemus, J.A., Genero, M., Manso, M.E., Morasca, S., Piattini, M.: Assessing the understandability of UML statechart diagrams with composite states–a family of empirical studies. Empir. Softw. Eng. **14**(6), 685–719 (2009)
8. Cruz-Lemus, J.A., Genero, M., Manso, M.E., Piattini, M.: Evaluating the effect of composite states on the understandability of UML statechart diagrams. In: Briand, L., Williams, C. (eds.) MODELS 2005. LNCS, vol. 3713, pp. 113–125. Springer, Heidelberg (2005). https://doi.org/10.1007/11557432_9

9. Cruz-Lemus, J.A., Maes, A., Genero, M., Poels, G., Piattini, M.: The impact of structural complexity on the understandability of UML statechart diagrams. Inf. Sci. **180**(11), 2209–2220 (2010)
10. De Lucia, A., Gravino, C., Oliveto, R., Tortora, G.: An experimental comparison of ER and UML class diagrams for data modelling. Empir. Softw. Eng. **15**(5), 455–492 (2010)
11. Dijkstra, E.W.: Foreword. In: Hinchey, M.G., Dean, N.C. (eds.) Teaching and Learning Formal Methods, pp. vii–viii. Elsevier, Amsterdam (1996)
12. Douglass, B.P.: Doing Hard Time: Developing Real-Time Systems with UML, Objects, Frameworks, and Patterns. Addison-Wesley, Boston (1999)
13. Drusinsky, D.: Modeling and Verification Using UML Statecharts: A Working Guide to Reactive System Design, Runtime Monitoring and Execution-based Model Checking. Newnes, Oxford (2006)
14. Dzidek, W.J., Arisholm, E., Briand, L.C.: A realistic empirical evaluation of the costs and benefits of UML in software maintenance. IEEE Trans. Softw. Eng. **34**(3), 407–432 (2008)
15. Estivill-Castro, V., Hexel, R.: Downloads (2016). http://mipal.net.au/downloads. php. Accessed 20 June 2019
16. Estivill-Castro, V., Hexel, R.: Resolving the asymmetry of on-exit versus on-entry in executable models of behaviour. In: 7th International Conference on Model-Driven Engineering and Software Development, MODELSWARD, pp. 51–63 (2019)
17. Estivill-Castro, V., Hexel, R., Lusty, C.: High performance relaying of C++11 objects across processes and logic-labeled finite-state machines. In: Brugali, D., Broenink, J.F., Kroeger, T., MacDonald, B.A. (eds.) SIMPAR 2014. LNCS (LNAI), vol. 8810, pp. 182–194. Springer, Cham (2014). https://doi.org/10.1007/978-3-319-11900-7_16
18. Estivill-Castro, V., Hexel, R., Rosenblueth, D.A.: Efficient model checking and FMEA analysis with deterministic scheduling of transition-labeled finite-state machines. In: 3rd World Congress on Software Engineering, WCSE 2012, pp. 65–72. IEEE Computer Society (CPS), Wuhan (2012)
19. Fakhroutdinov, K.: State Machine Diagrams (2009). https://www.uml-diagrams. org/state-machine-diagrams.html. Accessed 20 June 2019
20. Finney, K.: Mathematical notation in formal specification: too difficult for the masses? IEEE Trans. Softw. Eng. **22**(2), 158–159 (1996)
21. Finney, K., Fedorec, A.M.: An empirical study of specification readability. In: Hinchey, M.G., Dean, N.C. (eds.) Teaching and Learning Formal Methods, pp. 117–129. Elsevier, Amsterdam (1996)
22. Gansner, E.R., Koutsofios, E., North, S.: Drawing graphs with dot (2015). https:// www.graphviz.org/pdf/dotguide.pdf. Accessed 20 June 2019
23. Genero, M., Miranda, D., Piattini, M.: Defining metrics for UML statechart diagrams in a methodological way. In: Jeusfeld, M.A., Pastor, Ó. (eds.) ER 2003. LNCS, vol. 2814, pp. 118–128. Springer, Heidelberg (2003). https://doi.org/10. 1007/978-3-540-39597-3_12
24. Glinz, M.: Problems and deficiencies of UML as a requirements specification language. In: 10th International Workshop on Software Specification and Design, p. 11. IEEE Computer Society (2000)
25. Harel, D., Politi, M.: Modeling Reactive Systems with Statecharts: The STATE-MATE Approach. McGraw-Hill, New York (1998)
26. Höst, M., Regnell, B., Wohlin, C.: Using students as subjects–a comparative study of students and professionals in lead-time impact assessment. Empir. Softw. Eng. **5**(3), 201–214 (2000)

27. Jouault, F., Allilaire, F., Bézivin, J., Kurtev, I.: ATL: a model transformation tool. Sci. Comput. Program. **72**(1), 31–39 (2008). https://doi.org/10.1016/j.scico.2007. 08.002. Special Issue on Second issue of experimental software and toolkits (EST)
28. Kitchenham, B.A., et al.: Preliminary guidelines for empirical research in software engineering. IEEE Trans. Softw. Eng. **28**(8), 721–734 (2002)
29. Kopetz, H.: Real-Time Systems - Design Principles for Distributed Embedded Applications. RTSS, 2nd edn. Springer, Boston (2011). https://doi.org/10.1007/ 978-1-4419-8237-7
30. Liskov, B.H., Wing, J.M.: A behavioral notion of subtyping. ACM Trans. Program. Lang. Syst. **16**(6), 1811–1841 (1994)
31. Mellor, S.J.: UML point/counterpoint: modeling complex behavior simply. Embedded Syst. Program. **13**, 38–42 (2000)
32. Mens, T., Van Gorp, P.: A taxonomy of model transformation. Electron. Not. Theor. Comput. Sci. **152**, 125–142 (2006)
33. Mitchell, R., McKim, J., Meyer, B.: Design by Contract, by Example. Addison-Wesley, Reading (2002)
34. Moody, D.: The "physics" of notations: toward a scientific basis for constructing visual notations in software engineering. IEEE Trans. Softw. Eng. **35**(6), 756–779 (2009). https://doi.org/10.1109/TSE.2009.67
35. Mustafa, B.A.: An experimental comparison of use case models understanding by novice and high knowledge users. In: New Trends in Software Methodologies, Tools and Techniques - 9th SoMeT 2010. Frontiers in Artificial Intelligence and Applications, vol. 217, pp. 182–199. IOS Press (2010)
36. Object Management Group: Action language for foundational UML (Alf) – concrete syntax for a UML action language. Version 1.1. Technical report formal/2017-07-04, An OMG Action Language for Foundational UML Publication (2017). Normative reference: http://www.omg.org/spec/ALF/1.1
37. Object Management Group: OMG unified modeling language version 2.5.1. Technical report formal/2017-12-05, OMG Object Management Group Publication (2017). Normative reference: http://www.omg.org/spec/UML
38. Petre, M.: UML in practice. In: International Conference on Software Engineering, ICSE 2013, pp. 722–731. IEEE Press, Piscataway (2013)
39. R Core Team: R: A Language and Environment for Statistical Computing. R Foundation for Statistical Computing, Vienna, Austria (2016). https://www.R-project. org/
40. Reggio, G., Astesiano, E., Choppy, C., Hussmann, H.: Analysing UML active classes and associated state machines - a lightweight formal approach. In: Maibaum, T. (ed.) FASE 2000. LNCS, vol. 1783, pp. 127–146. Springer, Heidelberg (2000). https://doi.org/10.1007/3-540-46428-X_10
41. Reggio, G., Leotta, M., Ricca, F., Clerissi, D.: What are the used UML diagrams? A preliminary survey. In: 3rd International Workshop on Experiences and Empirical Studies in Software Modeling (EESSMod 2013 Co-Located with MODELS 2013), vol. 1078, pp. 3–12. CEUR (2013)
42. Richardson, M.: Guideline: Statechart Diagram. https://tinyurl.com/ RichardsonStatechart (2015). Accessed 09 Oct 2019
43. Robbins, J.E.: Cognitive support features for software development tools. Ph.D. thesis, Department of Information and Computer Science, University of California, Irvine (1999). Advisor: Prof. D. F. Redmiles
44. Rumpe, R.: Executable modeling with UML - a vision or a nightmare? In: Issues and Trends of Information Technology Management in Contemporary Associations Volume 1, pp. 697–701. Idea Group Publishing (2002)

45. Samek, M.: Practical UML Statecharts in C/C++, Second Edition: Event-Driven Programming for Embedded Systems. Newnes, Newton (2008)
46. Samek, M.: UML State Machine (2009). https://en.wikipedia.org/wiki/UML_state_machine. Accessed 20 June 2019
47. Seshia, S.A., Sharygina, N., Tripakis, S.: Modeling for verification. Handbook of Model Checking, pp. 75–105. Springer, Cham (2018). https://doi.org/10.1007/978-3-319-10575-8_3
48. Shaw, M.: Toward higher-level abstractions for software systems. Data Knowl. Eng. **5**(2), 119–128 (1990)
49. Wood, S.K., Akehurst, D.H., Uzenkov, O., Howells, W.G.J., McDonald-Maier, K.D.: A model-driven development approach to mapping UML state diagrams to synthesizable VHDL. IEEE Trans. Comput. **57**(10), 1357–1371 (2008)
50. World Wide Web Consortium: State chart XML (SCXML): State machine notation for control abstraction, 1 September 2005
51. Zimmerman, M.K., Lundqvist, K., Leveson, N.: Investigating the readability of state-based formal requirements specification languages. In: 24th International Conference on Software Engineering, ICSE, pp. 33–43 (2002)

A Role Modeling Based Approach
for Cyber Threat Analysis

Bastien Drouot$^{(\boxtimes)}$, Fahad R. Golra, and Joël Champeau

Lab STICC UMR6285, ENSTA Bretagne, Brest, France
bastien.drouot@ensta-bretagne.org,
{fahad.golra,joel.champeau}@ensta-bretagne.fr

Abstract. Using DSMLs, the domain experts can express their models in a language that is relevant to the problem area. However, it also adds the complexity of interoperability between these languages, specially for application areas that encompass multiple domains. One such application area, Cyber Threat Analysis (CTA), is at the intersection of various domains that can evolve independently: system modeling, attacker modeling and threat description. In this paper, we present an approach to address CTA interoperability issues based on role modeling. The proposed language provides a mechanism to define shared semantics between DSMLs relative to the CTA. The concept of a role is central to our approach, presented as Role4All framework. These roles allow us to federate different DSMLs to generate an attacker's viewpoint. Our approach is illustrated using a case study on the development of an attacker's viewpoint based on the federation of multiple domain models. Interoperability between the domain models is crucial to apply dedicated algorithms and interpretations on the attacker's viewpoint. We used this attacker viewpoint to simulate attacks on a system for security analysis.

Keywords: Model federation · Role modeling · DSML
interoperability · Cyber threat analysis · Simulation

1 Introduction

Model driven engineering (MDE) is being used in different phases of system development life cycle for various systems like embedded systems, safety critical systems, *etc.* [14]. MDE is also used for different objectives like knowledge management, systems analysis (both structural and behavioral) and performance evaluation (worst case analysis, scheduling) [22]. In this paper, we present a modeling approach and framework applied to the cybersecurity domain. Cybersecurity is one of the active research domains where models are being used, especially to support the integration of digital subsystems [1].

Our work focuses on cyber threat analysis based on system modeling and dynamic attacker knowledge to anticipate an attacker's behavior. Due to the large scope of cyber threat analysis, the modeling space uses multiple Domain

© Springer Nature Switzerland AG 2020
S. Hammoudi et al. (Eds.): MODELSWARD 2019, CCIS 1161, pp. 76–100, 2020.
https://doi.org/10.1007/978-3-030-37873-8_4

Specific Modeling Languages (DSMLs); each dedicated to provide abstractions for a specific sub-domain like system representation, vulnerability definition, attacker competencies hypothesis, *etc.* In this cybersecurity context, we face two main issues (1) creation of an attacker viewpoint from the set of heterogeneous DSMLs (2) dynamicity of the attacker viewpoint according to the evolution of the attacker knowledge.

The attacker viewpoint aggregates several concepts from various domains to characterize the behavior and the competencies of an attacker relative to the considered system. To define this viewpoint in conjunction with the system model, we face a problem of interoperability between several DSMLs that model a system from different concerns or domains [3]. So one of the underlying issues to create the attacker viewpoint is to tackle the problem of DSMLs interoperability.

On the modeled viewpoint, we must be able to interpret and execute an attack scenario to simulate the attacker behavior. The attack scenario interpretation should be able to interpret the stepwise evolution of an attack to update the attacker view. To support such dynamically evolving view, the framework should be able to support the changes in DSML entities, which at times even changes the semantics of interpretation. This dynamic semantics change in the context of modeling approaches *e.g.* object (re) classification, remains an open issue.

To solve the interoperability issue between heterogeneous DSMLs, in our previous work, we proposed a model federation solution based on role modeling in the context of cyber threat analysis [6]. Our previous work relies on the concept of roles to interpret the model elements of a base model (DSML). In this article, we have focused on the dynamicity for the modeled elements. The main contribution of our work can be categorized as: (1) a role modeling based approach for the interoperability of heterogeneous DSMLs that allows the modification of interpreted concepts at runtime, (2) A dynamic attacker viewpoint that updates the attacker view according to the advances of an attack by taking into account new knowledge obtained from each attack step and (3) the lessons learned from developing this solution, through the implementation of an interpreter, for simulating attack scenarios.

The rest of the paper is organized as follows. In Sect. 2, we present cyber threat analysis as the context for the application of role modeling based federation approach. Then in Sect. 3, we discuss the modeling context by describing the state of the art on DSML interoperability and the concept of views. We describe the proposed framework, Role4All in Sect. 4. Then, in Sect. 5 we present our role modeling based methodology on the cybersecurity case study. Then, we demonstrate the interpretation and simulation of cyber threat analysis case study in Sect. 6. In Sect. 7 we share the lessons learned from the development and application of our framework and conclude in Sect. 8.

2 Cyber Security Context

In section we explain the background of this research work. Remaining within the context of cybersecurity, we expand on the concepts of Cyber Threat Analysis and Cyber Threat Modeling.

2.1 Cyber Threat Analysis

Contrary to other reactive security approaches like intrusion detection, cyber threat analysis (CTA) is a proactive approach to anticipate a cyber security crisis. CTA aims to look for vulnerabilities pertinent to a particular system or organization by taking into account the current vulnerability knowledge and analyzing it against anticipated attacker's behavior. Assumptions about the attacker's system knowledge and the goals for a probable attack are used to anticipate the attacker's behavior. Cyber threat analysis can be performed using a combination of some of the following methods [4,7,13].

- *Modeling*: System elements are conceptualized to produce an abstraction of the system under study. The objective is to gather information so as to create a representation of the current knowledge of the system.
- *System discovery*: The knowledge of a system depends on the current view of the real system. System discovery uses observations and actions that can be performed on a system to extend some specific knowledge about it.
- *Vulnerability exploitation*: A vulnerability is "*a weakness of an asset or control that could potentially be exploited by one or more threats.*" [17]. These vulnerabilities can be exploited by the attacker to achieve certain goals. Vulnerability exploitation is performed to play the attack scenario based on attacker ability, system access and system configuration.

System discovery can be simulated through models and models can also be used to emulate vulnerability exploitation by playing attack scenarios. As modeling can be used to realize all of these three methods, we prefer cyber threat modeling to perform cyber threat analysis.

2.2 Cyber Threat Modeling

Threat modeling is about using models to analyze security issues for the concerned systems. These models are used for developing abstractions of the system, threats, attackers and some other details like system element configurations [27]. Different threat modeling approaches have different takes on how and what needs to be brought into focus when modeling threats [20,23]. Our study of different definitions and use of common themes to identify relevant models and associated DSMLs, highlights the modeling part of threat modeling and allows a clear distinction between the system, threats and attackers.

- *System modeling* characterizes the system by describing the system's behavior, its features, its boundaries, etc. In this context, we are interested in two sub-categories of system modeling *i.e.* the system topology and the system configuration. System topology models an arrangement of the system elements and the network between them. In this paper, we use PimCa[1] [12] as

---

[1] PimCa specification is confidential. However we will present some details about PimCa DSML and its metamodel in Sect. 5.1.

the DSML to describe the system topology. This language is defined by a cyber security entity of the French Ministry of Armed Forces to represent and analyze a system at several levels of abstraction *i.e.* from conceptual to physical levels. The system configuration is based on structured data defining hardware and software components of the system elements.

- *Attacker modeling* characterizes the attacker and his behavior *i.e.* the attacker's goal, the attacker's competencies and attack scenarios. The attacker's competencies are based on the description of an attack in the common vulnerability scoring system (CVSS) [19]. His current knowledge of the system is represented by a specific view on the system that keeps updating step-by-step throughout the execution of the attack.

- *Threat description* explains the possible vulnerabilities of the system. Every system has vulnerabilities; most of them referenced in a library. We chose to limit our vulnerabilities to a single library *i.e.* the National Vulnerability Database (NVD) [30].

In order to cover all these models, the set of DSMLs used in this study are PimCa, structured data of configuration, National Vulnerability Database (NVD) and the structured data of attacker competencies. Moreover, for the generation and stepwise animation of the attacker viewpoint, we interpret model elements with a guarded command interpreter [5,15], which executes the attack scenario.

3   Modeling Context

This section presents the issues related to DSML interoperability and view dynamicity in general and specifically focuses on it from the perspective of role modeling.

3.1   Model Interoperability

Interoperability between different formalisms and paradigms is a recurrent issue in a development process, specifically when Model Driven Engineering (MDE) approaches are brought into the picture. This interoperability challenge makes it hard to conceive a system that is composed of multiple heterogeneous DSMLs. Traditionally, the issue of interoperability is handled through integration, unification or federation approaches [16].

Integration approach is based on the definition of a common modeling language that is built around the union of all the concepts of the different formalisms/languages [8]. This approach is applied if each formalism contains only a few concepts. It is also important that the number of formalisms remain fixed because any new DSML integration requires the redefinition of the entire integrated language which is a major drawback of this approach.

The unification mechanism is based on the identification of common concepts between the formalisms and the definition of the correspondence between these core concepts and the concepts of the modeling languages [11]. This approach is usually named as the pivot/reference language approach. It is the most used approach to conceptualize and implement interoperability between several formalisms. In the case of a limited number of concepts, pivot language is a powerful solution if any concept of the languages finds its correspondence in the pivot definition. However, accurate and precise definition of the pivot language remains a difficult task. If the definition is too abstract, important language concepts (or properties) can be lost. On the other hand, defining a rich pivot language produces an overly broad pivot language that faces the same problems as of integration approaches.

Instead of defining a common language definition, model federation approach focuses on modeling the semantics of the links between the concepts of heterogeneous languages [9, 21]. These links or relationships define the correspondence between the concepts without a concrete pivot language definition. The main goal of the federation is to specify the interoperability by concentrating on the semantic definitions without modifying the language concepts. A common advantage of all federation approaches is the clear separation between the DSML elements and the semantic modeling relative to the federation context (the federation elements). A DSML element can have several semantic interpretations within the same federation and at the same time several DSML elements can share the same semantic interpretation.

Bi-directional transformations are a good option to handle interoperability between different DSMLs [29]. However, when the DSMLs are evolving or when dynamic interpretation of the model elements is needed (*i.e.* the interpretation of an element can change over time), bi-directional transformations do not provide enough support to handle such situations. Another limitation of bi-directional transformations is that they are usually limited to using MetaObject Facility Specification (MOF) metamodels at both ends of a transformation. This limits the heterogeneity of DSMLs within the universe of MOF.

We chose to apply the federation approach to ensure the DSML interoperability for the cyber threat analysis. CTA is still in its infancy and lacks mature frameworks and languages. Thus, the DSMLs used in this domain are constantly evolving. Evolution is a major concern when choosing an approach to tackle DSML interoperability issues. The chosen model federation approach should be able to integrate new languages and it also needs to cater the evolution of DSML definitions. In this context, the approach for handling interoperability issues should be dynamic. The dynamic interoperability ensured by role modeling is one of the main topics that we will expand upon in the next section.

3.2   Role Modeling

Role modeling has its roots in some earlier works in data modeling during the seventies. As a natural extension, roles were used in object-oriented design and implementation, and modeling and metamodeling. Steimann presents a short survey on role modeling which emphasizes the ontological definition of roles [28]. Roles are used to add dynamicity to the classic type-based approaches [18] and to define dynamic interfaces which can be adapted over time [10]. Furthermore, these roles can be used on multiple abstraction levels *i.e.* metamodeling, modeling, and implementation.

In our context, the natural type is provided by a metaclass of the DSML definition, and roles provide the semantic interpretation of these elements according to the current role being played by the type. Roles are successfully used to interconnect heterogeneous design tools in order to create tool chains for system design. Seifert et al. [26] connect various models produced by different modeling tools using the concept of roles. Moreover, for the model exchange process between multiple tools, roles have also been used to preserve the semantics of model entities [2].

To handle the interoperability between different DSMLs in the context of cybersecurity, we chose role modeling using Role4All framework [24]. We propose a federation approach using role modeling and present a simulator based on roles.

4   Framework for Interoperability

In this section, we present Role4All, our proposed framework for model federation using the concept of role to define dedicated viewpoints and to map these viewpoints to several DSMLs. It is based on the earlier works by Schneider et al. [24]. We will present this framework in the already described context of cyber threat analysis (Sect. 4.1) and then we focus on:

- Modeling dynamic views *i.e.* attacker view (Sect. 4.2).
  Federation of cyber security DSMLs (Sect. 4.3).
- Execution of attack scenario according to the attacker viewpoint (Sect. 4.4).

4.1   Role4All Framework

Role modeling has its roots in some earlier works in data modeling during the seventies. As a natural extension, roles were used in object-oriented design and implementation, and modeling and metamodeling. Steimann presents a survey on role modeling which emphasizes the ontological definition of roles [28]. Roles are successfully used to interconnect heterogeneous design tools in order to create tool chains for system design. For example, Seifert et al. [26] connect various models produced by different modeling tools using the concept of roles. Moreover, for the model exchange process between multiple tools, roles have also been used to preserve the semantics of model entities [2]. Furthermore, roles can be used on multiple abstraction levels *i.e.* metamodeling, modeling, and implementation.

A significant effort has been made to provide an exhaustive formalized feature list to characterize and define the concept of role in the context of modeling. Kuhn et al. [18] present a list of 26 classifying features of roles from the state of the art that describe different aspects of a role modeling language. The first 15 features in this list were originally presented by Steimann [28]. In view of these works, each role language definition carries a subset of these 26 features. As

proposed in these works, we selected and established the relevant list of features
to ensure our needs for the proposed framework, Role4All. Table 1 presents a list
of role features, categorized in three groups to better demonstrate how they are
implemented in the proposed framework.

- (V) Viewpoint features: These features are supported to design an attacker
  viewpoint (Sect. 4.2).
- (F) Federation features: These features are supported to federate data from
  the cyber security DSMLs (Sect. 4.3).
- (S) Simulation features: They are supported to play attack scenarios through
  the attacker viewpoint (Sect. 4.4).

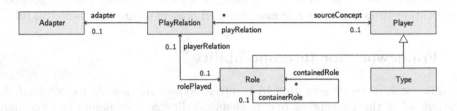

Fig. 1. Role4All metamodel.

Role4All metamodel substructure, presented in Fig. 1, is based on five main
classes named: Role, Player, Type, Adapter and PlayRelation. A role is an interpretation of a base type in a specific context. The base type is provided by a
metaclass of the DSML definition, and roles provide the semantic interpretation
of these elements according to the current role being played by the type. Hence
a base type, developed in its own context of a specific intent, can be used in
another context by giving it a different role. We discuss a role at three abstraction levels *i.e. roleClass*, *role* and *roleInstance*. *RoleClass* is the "Role" entity
presented in the Role4All metamodel, a *role* is a modeling element that conforms to the *roleClass* and a *roleInstance* is conformed to a *role*. Similar naming
convention is used throughout the paper for other entities of the metamodel *e.g.
player*, *type playRelation* and *adapter*.

A *player* is an abstract modeling element that is interpreted through a *role* in
the new context. We like to explain this interpretation as, *"a player plays the role
of* something". *Player* is specialized as a *type* that refers to a modeling element
of the base model *i.e.* a cyber security DSML in our context. This is shown in the
Role4All metamodel by a *typeClass* as a specialization of a *playerClass*. Hence
we can say that "a *type* as a *player* can play a *role.*"

An *adapter* is responsible for transforming *player* properties into *role* properties. Seen from the perspective of traditional MDE approaches, we place the
transformation relevant code in the definition of the *adapter*. A *playRelation*
links a *player* to a *role* through an *adapter*. This pattern allows us to dynamically change the semantics of a relationship (interpretation) between a *role* and

a *player*. This interpretation is carried by the adapter, which can be replaced without modifying a *role* or a *player*. For example, a person p is considered as a student from the perspective of a university and at the same time as an employee from the perspective of a company. In our metamodel, p is a *playerInstance* which can play two *roles*: student or employee. If p play the *role* of the student, we associate p with a *roleIntance* rs through a *playRelationInstance* p_{rs} and an *adapterInstance* a_{ps}. In this example, rs is an instance of the *role* student and a_{ps} is an instance of the *adapter* responsible for transforming person properties into student properties.

Table 1. Classification of role features by Steimann and Kuhn et al.

Feature	Category
1. Roles have properties and behaviors	V
2. Roles depend on relationships	
3. Objects may play different roles simultaneously	V
4. Objects may play the same role several times	V
5. Objects may acquire and abandon roles dynamically	S,F
6. Sequence of role acquisition and removal may be restricted	
7. Unrelated objects can play the same role	V
8. Roles can play roles	S, F
9. Roles can be transferred between objects	F
10. The state of an object can be role-specific	
11. Features of an object can be role-specific	
12. Roles restrict access	
13. Different roles may share structure and behavior	F
14. An object and its roles share identity	
15. An object and its roles have different identities	V
16. Relationships between roles can be constrained	
17. There may be constraints between relationships	
18. Roles can be grouped and constrained together	F
19. Roles depend on compartments	
20. Compartments have properties and behaviors	
21. A role can be part of several compartments	
22. Compartments may play roles like objects	
23. Compartments may play roles which are part of themselves	
24. Compartments can contain other compartments	
25. Different compartments may share structure and behavior	
26. Compartments have their own identity	

Categories: (V)iewpoints, (F)ederation and (S)imulation

4.2   Viewpoint Definition

In this subsection we first present Role4All metamodel and then describe the features that define a role and how these features are supported by Role4All. Moreover we present how the Role4All metamodel gathers these features together.

Role4All metamodel substructure (presented Fig. 1) is based on four main classes named: PlayRelation, Role, Player and Adapter. We discuss a role at three abstraction levels *i.e. roleClass, role* and *roleInstance. RoleClass* is the "Role" entity presented in the Role4All metamodel, a *role* is a modeling element that conforms to the *roleClass* and a *roleInstance* is an instance of a *role*. Similar naming convention is used throughout the paper for other entities of the metamodel like *Player, PlayRelation* and *Adapter*. A *player* is a modeling element that is interpreted as a *role* in the federation according to the new context. We like to explain this interpretation as, *"a player plays the role of something in a federation"*. As modeled in the Role4All metamodel, a *typeClass* is a specialization of a *playerClass i.e.* a type as a player can play a role. A *typeClass* in the metamodel refers to a modeling element of the source DSMLs for a federation. For example, a doctorate student remains a student when seen from the perspective of research, and the same doctorate student can play the role of a teacher from the perspective of teaching.

A federation allows one to develop a viewpoint from existing models. A viewpoint in Role4All is defined through a role model. In some situations a *role* can also play another *role*, which allows among other things to create a viewpoint on a viewpoint. In order to realize this, the *roleClass* in the metamodel is a specialization of a *playerClass*. In Role4All, an *adapter* is responsible for transforming *player* properties into *role* properties. In comparison to traditional MDE approaches we place the code relevant to the transformation in the definition of the *adapter*. In Role4All, a *playRelation* links a *player* to a *role* through an *adapter*. This pattern allows us to dynamically change the semantics of a relationship (Interpretation) between a *role* and a *player*. This interpretation is carried by the adapter, which can be replaced without modifying a *role* or a *player*.

Like in other role modeling approaches, Role4All *roles* define a viewpoint of one or several model elements. The *roleClass* satisfies a subset of the 26 features presented in Table 1. As previously explained, we need to create a single viewpoint to define a common semantics for several DSMLs. In order to attain this objective, our language implements the concept of role in a fashion that satisfies features 1, 3, 4, 7 and 15. Each of these features are satisfied by a different capability of the *roles*:

- *Feature 1* demands roles to have properties and behaviors. In Role4All, a *role* conforms to the *roleClass* with behaviors and properties. So the operational semantics of a role is defined by the properties and the methods encapsulating behaviors.
- *Features 3 and 4* deal with different simultaneous interpretations and the same interpretation over multiple times. In Role4All a *role* may be linked

with many *players* through several *playRelations*. This is handled in Role4All metamodel by the *many (*)* cardinality between "Player" and "PlayRelation". In addition a *player* may be linked to the same *role* several times through a different *adapter*.

- *Feature 7* defines a viewpoint related to different elements of different languages. The pattern using *roleClass*, *playerClass* and *adapterClass*, allows various *players* to be linked with the same *role*, with a specific *adapter*.
- *Feature 15* requires a separation between the model elements by keeping their different native identities. As explained previously, a *role* and a *player* conform of different classes in Role4All metamodel.

4.3   Federation with Role4All

The main goal of the federation approach is to define relationships between different formalisms. A federation reifies the cross cutting concerns of these formalisms. The resulting federation model has two main properties: first, it concretizes the dynamics of the relationships between different formalisms and second, it ensures consistency between the model elements of these different formalisms. The main features to support the federation are:

- *Feature 5* describes the capacity to attach and de-attach roles dynamically. The *playerClass* has a method `play` that allows a *playerInstance* to play a role. This method generates a *playRelationInstance* and an *adapterInstance* and then links the *playerInstance* to the *roleInstance* using them. Moreover, the removal of a *playRelationInstance* entitles a *playerInstance* to dynamically leave a role.
- *Feature 8* deals with the adaptation of viewpoint definition such that roles themselves can play a role. The *roleClass* is a subclass of *playerClass*, so a role has the inherited behavior (especially the method `play`). Therefore, a *roleInstance* can also play a *role*.
- *Feature 9* allows transferring a role to/from another model element. A *roleInstance* can be transferred to a *playerInstance* via the creation of a new *playRelationInstance* or a mutation of the older relation.
- *Feature 13:* describes the sharing of structure and behavior between federated *roles*. A *role* conforms to the *roleClass*. Inheritance mechanism is used to define *roles* that share behavior and structure with another *role*.
- *Feature 18* groups *roles* so that a federation model can be developed. The *roleClass* with the bidirectional relation *containerRole/containedRoles* allows a *roleInstance* to contain other *roleInstances* or to be contained by another *roleInstance*. This allows the language to define role sets through this association. The behavior of the container includes constraints applicable to all the contained *roleInstances*.

Feature 5, 8 and 9 are inherent properties of our role modeling language to ensure that *roles* are dynamic and that they can serve for interoperability between different formalisms. Indeed, if new concepts (or properties) are required in the federation definition, we add *roles* to adapt this definition. Furthermore, if concepts (or properties) are no longer necessary in the federation definition, we can detach the corresponding *roles* and also remove the associated *playRelation-Instance* and *adapterInstance*. These *role* capacities ensure a dynamic definition of the federation approach.

Feature 13 and 18 ensure consistency between *roles* and model elements. In the Role4All metamodel (Fig. 1), this feature is supported by the reflexive containment reference on the *roleClass*. If each of the *containedRoles* is connected with a model element, this containment allows to gather a logical assembly of *roleInstances*, in order to define a set of federated *roleInstances*. This also maintains the overall behavior of this set based on local *role* behaviors and supports broadcasting notifications which come from the local behavior.

4.4 Interpretation Viewpoint in Role4All

Role4All framework allows the generation of dedicated viewpoints such as an interpretation or a simulation viewpoint. The CTA context deals with the attacker, so we focus on the direct interpretation of the attacker viewpoint. As illustrated in Fig. 2 the attacker viewpoint is applied on several DSMLs and the interpretation is applied on the attacker viewpoint.

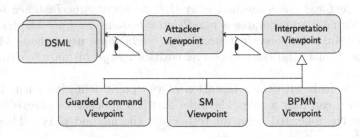

Fig. 2. Interpretation viewpoint pattern.

Some role features already described in the previous sections are also relevant to the definitions of an interpreter viewpoint, they are identified by an 'S' in Table 1 and are described hereafter:

- *Feature 5* allows the simulated elements to dynamically acquire or abandon roles. The simulation language of the framework allows this feature. For example, a model element with an attached role of "clean element" can switch to the role "corrupt element", if it is compromised.
- *Feature 8* allows a role to play another role. This feature is also supported by the framework. One can define a simulation viewpoint (role model) that is itself based on another viewpoint (role model) of the system.

The *interpretation viewpoint* is refined according to the type of viewpoint being interpreted and the objective of interpretation. Figure 2 presents three different interpreters/simulators: a guarded command interpreter, a state machine interpreter (SM) and a process interpreter BPMN. For example, the guarded command viewpoint used for the interpretation described in Sect. 5 is defined by a role model containing two *roles*: *BlockRole* and *BlocksListRole*. A *Block-Role* has a guard and a command and a *BlocksListRole* has variables and several *BlockRoles*. These two *roles* are used to adapt the information from the attacker viewpoint in a way that it can be interpreted by the interpreter.

Both guards and commands are the attributes of a *BlockRole* element of the interpretation viewpoint. For the guarded command viewpoint, a guard is:

- an evaluation of properties defined in a *roleInstance*
- evaluated in an interpreter (*e.g.* the guarded command interpreter).

A command in the guarded command viewpoint is:

- a trigger for the methods defined in a *roleInstance*
- executed by the guarded command interpreter.

In the context of cybersecurity, we use the interpreter to simulate the attacker behavior on the system. The selected interpreter allows a stepwise simulation of an attack through the attacker viewpoint of a system. The simulation of role models uses the execution semantics defined within the *roles*. We expand on the use of simulation mechanism for cyber threat analysis in the next section.

5   Role Modeling for Cyber Threat Analysis

In this section, we simulate an attack on a system based on a role interpretation offered by Role4All. In this approach, the attacker viewpoint of the system is modeled using roles. The attacker viewpoint uses role modeling to create a semantic viewpoint based on the federation of several DSMLs used in cyber threat analysis.

We demonstrate the use of role modeling for CTA using a case study of an attack simulation. The discussed scenario of this case study is enacted on a network system composed of two parts: an attacker having access to the Internet and a target local network which embodies most enterprise architectures with a web server and a local network. In this architecture (as shown in Fig. 3a), Kali machine symbolizes the attacker's computer and the Internet is abstracted by a switch connecting this machine to the local network. The target local network consists of three subnets, all protected by the same Firewall. The cyber threat analysis includes a risk analysis which emphasizes that the ActiveDirectory is a critical resource as it contains the authentication data (logins and passwords) for the users. In our example the ActiveDirectory is the target of the attack scenario.

Unlike penetration testing on a real system [13], the expected benefit of a modeling approach is to promote experimentation and analyze several system

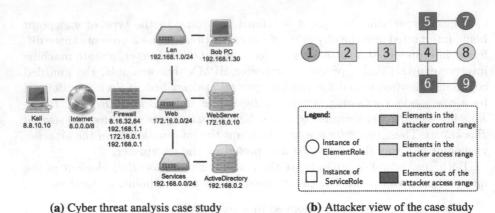

(a) Cyber threat analysis case study   (b) Attacker view of the case study

Fig. 3. Different views of CTA case study.

configurations and scenarios according to different attacker competencies. In the next sections, we present the details of our approach by describing the modeling space, federation for viewpoint development and the interpreter for simulating the attacks.

5.1 Modeling Space

In Sect. 2.2 we introduced following DSMLs used in the context of cyber threat analysis.

1. PimCa [12], a DSML defined by a cyber security entity of the French Ministry of Armed Forces, describing the system topology.
2. A vulnerability DSML, based on a subset of the NVD data structure [30], describing vulnerabilities of system elements.
3. A configuration DSML, based on structured data, describing the configurations of system elements.
4. An attacker competencies DSML, based on CVSS [19], describing the attacker's competencies to attack the system elements.

We illustrate an abstraction of the configuration DSML metamodel in Fig. 4a, as one of the metamodels used for the development of the attacker viewpoint. In this metamodel, a *Configuration* is composed of *Elements* which can be an *Environment*, a *Service* or an *Application*. In this case study, each node in the system topology has a configuration model *e.g.* the configuration of WebServer is presented in Fig. 5a. This textual model represents the configuration of the WebServer as: a server running Windows 2000 V5.2 (*Environment*) providing a Network Service used by two *Applications i.e.* WordPress V3.6.1 and Symposium V14.11. With this configuration we describe a web server using WordPress and Symposium plugins.

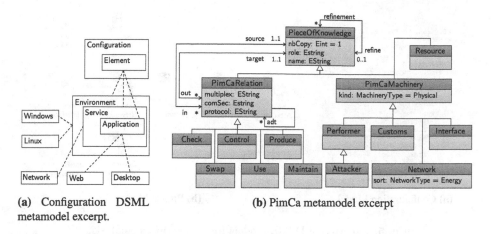

(a) Configuration DSML metamodel excerpt.

(b) PimCa metamodel excerpt

Fig. 4. Excerpts of DSML metamodels in cyber threat analysis.

These versions of the applications used on this server contain certain vulnerabilities[2]. The `WebServer` is part of a network and is connected with others network elements.

In our case study we model the connections between network elements using PimCa. An excerpt of concepts of PimCa metamodel is presented in Fig. 4b. This metamodel allow us to model several element types such as an *Attacker*, a *Network* or an *Interface*. Each of these elements is a *PimCaMachinery*. In PimCa metamodel, *PimCaMachineries* are interconnected through *PimCaRelations*. *Check*, *Swap*, *Control*, *Use*, *Produce* or *Maintain* are the different types of *PimCaRelations* that can be used to interconnect *PimCaMachineries*. Figure 5b presents the PimCa model used in the case study. In this model, each network element is defined as one of the types of a *PimCaMachinery*. For example, `Kali` is a user of the `WebServer` that wants to control the `ActiveDirectory`, hence he is modeled as an *Attacker* and the `WebServer` is modeled as an *Interface*. The attacker *uses* the `WebServer` through several *Network* elements. `BobPC` *controls* the `WebServer` and the `ActiveDirectory`. The network connection between the system elements is model by *Swap* relations *e.g.* `BobPC` is connected with `WebServer` through four *Swap* relations.

Finally, like the `WebServer`, each element of the system has configurations described in a the configuration DSML and relations described in another PimCa DSML. Moreover, `WebServer` and the others system elements have vulnerabilities (described in NVD DSML) and attacker competencies (described in the attacker competencies DSML). The attacker viewpoint federates several information sources about the system *e.g.* the attacker view on the `WebServer` federates, among others information, the configuration (Fig. 5a) and the PimCa model (Fig. 5b). To federate these models, we group information from several sources

---

[2] We will explain the link between these applications and vulnerabilities in the next section.

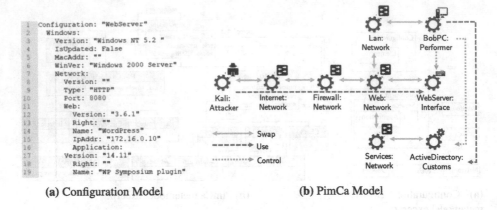

```
1  Configuration: "WebServer"
2    Windows:
3      Version: "Windows NT 5.2 "
4      IsUpdated: False
5      MacAddr: ""
6      WinVer: "Windows 2000 Server"
7      Network:
8        Version: ""
9        Type: "HTTP"
10       Port: 8080
11       Web:
12         Version: "3.6.1"
13         Right: ""
14         Name: "WordPress"
15         IpAddr: "172.16.0.10"
16         Application:
17       Version: "14.11"
18         Right: ""
19         Name: "WP Symposium plugin"
```

(a) Configuration Model

(b) PimCa Model

Fig. 5. Excerpts of DSML models for cyber threat analysis.

and synchronize them. Lets take an example of such grouping and synchronization from our case study. The federation of the two models *i.e.* configuration and the PimCa models (shown in Fig. 5) would include the following activities.

– We federate the name and the version of the *Applications* running on the WebServer with relations (*Swaps* and *Controls*) coming to the WebServer *PimCaMachinery*. So, the attacker view on the WebServer federates the WordPress V3.6.1 *Application*, the Wp Symposium plugin V14.11 *Application*, the *Control* relation between BobPC and WebServer, the *Swap* relation between Web and WebServer and the *Use* relation between Kali and WebServer.
– We synchronize the *name* of the WebServer *PimCaMachinery* from PimCa model with the "Configuration" attribute of the Configuration model which has the value "WebServer" (first line of the configuration model in Fig. 5a). Indeed, these two synchronized elements describe the same information *i.e.* the name of WebServer.

The federation mechanism using to federate and synchronize information from different DSMLs is detailed in the next section.

5.2 Role Models for the Generation of Federated Viewpoint

In this section we create a viewpoint federating information from various DSMLs using role modeling. This is a viewpoint (Fig. 3b) on the network system from the perspective of an attacker. In Role4All, a viewpoint is defined by a role model containing multiple *roles*. The attacker viewpoint is defined using five *roles*, two describing system elements (*ElementRole* and *ServiceRole*) and three describing the related concepts (*ConfigurationRole*, *CompetenciesRole* and *Vulnerability-Role*). Each of these *roles* is modeled in Fig. 6 and presented below:

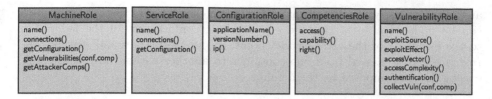

Fig. 6. Attacker role model.

- *ElementRole*: This *role* models the elements that contain relevant information regarding the attacker goals *i.e.* the attacker must control or corrupt these elements. An *ElementRole* has a name, references to the system topology connections, a configuration, some vulnerabilities and a list of attacker competencies. The instances of *ElementRole* are depicted as circles in Fig. 3b.
- *ServiceRole*: This *role* provides a view on the system elements by modeling elements that render a service to the system (the attacker must use or bypass these elements for a successful attack). A *ServiceRole* has a name, some references to the system topology connections and a configuration. The instances of *ServiceRole* are shown as boxes in Fig. 3b.
- *ConfigurationRole*: It models an interpretation of the configuration of system element from the point of view of the attacker. A *ConfigurationRole* consists of an application name associated with a version number, and an ip address.
- *CompetenciesRole*: It specifies the attacker's competencies with regard to a system topology element *i.e.* the attacker's access to system elements (physical, adjacent network, network), the attacker's access rights (none, user, administrator) and the attacker's skill level (Low, Medium, High).
- *VulnerabilityRole*: It describes the vulnerabilities of a system element from the point of view of an attacker. A *VulnerabilityRole* has a name, a reference to the exploit description in the vulnerability database, effect description with respect to the exploit, some access requirements and a complexity level. A *VulnerabilityRole* is generated by applying a filter (composed of *ConfigurationRoles* and *CompetenciesRoles*) on a vulnerability database. Typically the NVD database is too rich and detailed, therefore we model only the relevant vulnerabilities to reach the target scenario.

In order to understand the dynamicity of our approach, it is important to understand the instantiation mechanism of the *roles*. The reflexive containment association of the *roleClass* in Role4All metamodel (shown in Fig. 1) allows the definition of *containerRoles* and *containedRoles*. A *roleInstance* referencing other *roleInstances* using this association is a *containerRole* and the referenced *roleInstances* are the *containedRoles*. The metamodel of Role4All does not explicitly define any other relationship between *roles*, as a result the language does not allow any other relationship between two roles. This is the reason why we do not see any association between the *roles* in Fig. 6. The reason behind this design choice is that the role model does not link the *roles* at design-time, it is the instantiation scheme that ensures the relationships between the *role instances* at the runtime. Two main advantages of this choice are: (1) these relationships can be updated even at runtime *e.g.* dynamic conformance of the federation to the evolution of the attacker viewpoint, in our case study and (2) any *role instance* can be moved from one container to another without any constraint, except the ones imposed by the domain.

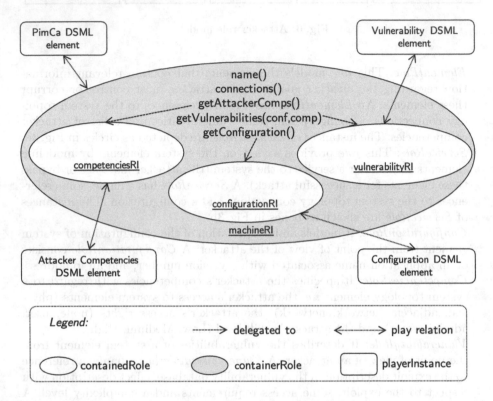

Fig. 7. A view of the cyber threat analysis federation.

Views being the instances of viewpoints; we generate them by federating several DSML elements at runtime. Figure 7 presents a view based on the viewpoint defined by the role model shown in Fig. 6. This view represents two kind of relationships *i.e.* between *roleInstances* themselves and between *roleIntances* and *playerInstances*. *ElementRI*, in this view, is a *containerRole* instance of *ElementRole*. This *containerRole* contains three *containedRoles i.e. compInstance* (instance of *CompetenciesRole*), *vulnInstance* (instance of *VulnerabilityRole*) and *confInstance* (instance of *ConfigurationRole*). A *containerRole* can have several methods to access information from different *playerInstances* belonging to different DSMLs. However, by design of the Role4All metamodel, a *roleInstance* is connected to only one *playerInstance*. In order to realize such an implementation where one *roleInstance* needs to be connected to multiple *playerInstances*, the *containerRole* delegates the responsibility of accessing information to individual *containedRoles*, each connected to a different *playerInstance*. The *containedRoles* can themselves act as *containerRoles*, when a complex hierarchy is required. The containment relationship between the roles allows the *containerRole* to delegate method calls to the *containedRoles*. In the view presented in Fig. 7, the *name()* and *relation()* methods of the *elementRI* reference information of the external DSML elements directly (named *PimCaWebServer*). However the rest of the methods are delegated to the *containedRoles* for accessing information in respective DSMLs.

The relationship between the *elementRI* and a PimCa DSML element (as shown in Fig. 7) is a relationship between a *roleInstance* and a *playerInstance*. Such relationships depicted in this Figure are simplified to facilitate comprehension. In fact, a *roleInstance* is connected to a *playerIntance* through a *playRelationInstance*, as illustrated in Fig. 8. This *playRelationInstance* realizes the connection between them by using an *adapterIntance*. For example the play relation between *elementRI* and a *PimCaMachinery* is realized through a *playRelationInstance*. This relation is adapted by an instance of the *adapter* named *ElementRoleToPimCaMachinery*. This *adapter* contains the code relevant to the transformation between *PimCaMachinery* and the *elementRole*. A detailed example of the definition and use of an *adapter* is given in [25].

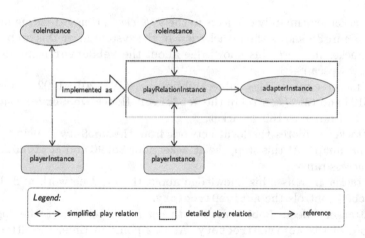

Fig. 8. Implementation of the play relation.

6 Simulation for Cyber Threat Analysis

6.1 Interpretation Using Roles

Role4All enables interpreting a role model to perform a simulation using a dedicated viewpoint and an interpreter (as presented in Sect. 4.4). This interpreter is based on stepwise evolution of guarded commands language, formalized by Dijk-stra [5]. At each step all the guards are evaluated and the commands with guard evaluated to true are selected. The interpreter allows an interactive execution, i.e. at each step the user selects a command to execute among the triggerable commands. Moreover, the interpreter also allows a random execution, i.e. at each step a randomly selected command is executed among the triggerable ones. The guards and commands used by the interpreter are the ones created by the inter-preter viewpoint. As explained in Sect. 4.4, commands trigger *role* methods and guards are the evaluations of the *role* properties (*roles* conform to the attacker role model in our example). For CTA, we defined two kinds of commands *i.e.* attacker commands are the ones executable by the attacker and system com-mands are the ones related to the normal execution of the system. To test our interpreter, we interactively execute an attack scenario through the attacker view of the case study (Fig. 3b).

During this interpretation, the attacker view of the system evolves in two ways: the attacker can extend his control range by taking control of new system elements, or he can discover his access range (after taking control of a new element) by communicating to the newly accessible elements. The access and control ranges are shown in Fig. 3b. The selected attack scenario consists of 7 steps listed below:

1. The attacker legitimately connects to the *webServer*, thus extending his access range. Figure 3b shows the attack view of the system after this step.
2. The attacker increases his knowledge about the `webServer` using dedicated tools *e.g.* wpscan[3].
3. The attacker exploits the vulnerabilities *e.g.* CVE-2014-10021[4] and CVE-2016-5195 and takes control of the `webServer`. Hence, `webServer` is added to the control range to this attacker.
4. The attacker explores the local network from the `webServer` using dedicate tools *e.g.* nmap[5]. At this step, the attacker adds `BobPC` and `ActiveDirectory` to his access range.
5. The attacker increases his knowledge about the local network and discovers that `BobPC` controls the `ActiveDirectory`.
6. The attacker infects `BobPC` with a *trojan horse* to collect the login and password of the `ActiveDirectory`. At this point in time, the attacker has extended his control range from `Kali` to `WebServer` and `BobPC` and gains access to `ActiveDirectory`.
7. The attacker connects to `ActiveDirectory` using the authentication details collected in the previous step. At this step, the attacker achieves his goal by taking control of `ActiveDirectory`.

To execute this attack scenario we created 18 system commands and 6 attacker commands. Each of these commands are in fact calling the behavior

---

[3]   https://wpscan.org/.

[4]   The identification number corresponds to the US National Vulnerability Database.

[5]   https://nmap.org/.

definitions (methods) of *roles* from the attacker role model. The system commands allowed us to carry out simple tasks on the system, such as switching on/off a system element (*i.e.* a node/machine of the network). The attacker commands were of two kinds: *"get information about a node"* and *"take control of a node by exploiting a vulnerability"*. In these commands a node is a system element like `WebServer`, `BobPC` or `ActiveDirectory` and a vulnerability is an instance of *VulnerabilityRole*.

As described earlier, a guard is an evaluation of properties defined in a *roleInstance* whereas a command is a trigger of methods defined in a *roleInstance*. For executing a command, its guard should be true *e.g.* the command:*"get information about the* `WebServer`*"* needs the guard:*"*`WebServer` *is in access range"* to be true for its execution. Once executed, this command extends the attacker access range. In fact, this command triggers the `getConfiguration`, `getVulnerabilities` and `getAttackerCompetens` methods of *elementRoleInstance*. Once the attacker's access or control range is extended, the associated PimCa model is updated with the corresponding *PimCaRelation i.e.* a *use* relation is added for every addition to the access range and a *control* relation is added for every new addition to the control range, as shown in Fig. 5b.

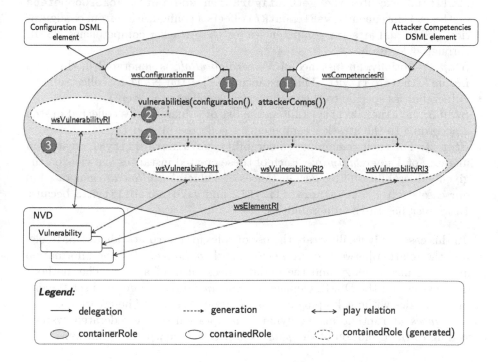

Fig. 9. Cyber threat analysis using federation at runtime.

6.2   Dynamic Update of the Federated Models

During step 2 of the attack scenario presented in the previous section, the command *"get information about the WebServer"* triggers `getConfiguration`, `getVulnerabilities` and `getAttackerCompetens` methods. These methods belong to `wsElementRI`, an instance of *ElementRole* that describes a view of the `webServer`. `WsElementRI` is a *containerRole* containing two *containedRoles i.e.* `wsConfigurationRI` and `wsCompetenciesRI`. `WsConfigurationRI`, an instance of *ConfigurationRole*, is part of the view on `webServer` that concerns the configuration. `WsCompetenciesRI`, an instance of *CompetenciesRole*, is part of the view on `webServer` that concerns attacker's competencies. The `getConfiguration` method of `wsElementRI` delegates the responsibility of accessing the configuration to `wsCompetenciesRI`. Similarly, the `getAttackerCompetens` method of `wsElementRI` delegates the responsibility of accessing the competencies to `wsCompetenciesRI`. The `getVulnerabilities` method has a more complex behavior. Figure 9 illustrates the federation mechanism triggered by this method in three steps:

- *Step 1:* To collected information from external sources, `getVulner abilities` executes the `getConfiguration` and `getAttackerCompetens` methods. Consequently, `wsElementRI` collects a configuration from configuration DSML and attacker competencies for the Attacker competencies DSML through delegation.
- *Step 2:* Initially, an instance of *VulnerabilityRole* is generated in this step *i.e.* `wsVulnerabilityRI`. This instance queries the NVD to collect all the vulnerabilities specific to the configurations collected in step 1.
- *Step 3:* `wsVulnerabilityRI` filters the list of vulnerabilities collected in step 2 according to the attacker competencies collected in step 1.
- *Step 4:* For each remaining vulnerability, `wsVulnerabilityRI` creates an instance of *VulnerabilityRole*. Each of these created instances is a view on the given vulnerability. Three new instances of *VulnerabilityRole* are generated in our case study *i.e.* `wsVulnerabilityRI2` and `wsVulnerabilityRI3` because *webServer* has three vulnerabilities.

In this case study we illustrate the use of roles for interpretation of DSML elements, the relation between *containerRole* and *containedRoles*, the information propagation methodology and the update mechanism of a view. The methods of the roles act on the DSML elements (*playerInstances*) to get and set the element properties without keeping a copy of these elements. The creation of new *roleInstances* at runtime allows dynamic adaptation of the federated system, according to the evolution of the *players* and to the viewpoint definitions.

7   Lessons Learned

This research project was carried out for the french ministry of armed forces, where the problem at hand was to simulate multiple attack scenarios. Due to the non disclosure agreement, we are not able to disclose any sensitive information regarding the analysis. However, we would like to share the lessons learned from this project on cybersecurity that used model driven engineering to solve the issues at hand.

- *The Ability to Update Views at Runtime.* View based approaches usually define viewpoints on a meta level. During the runtime, these viewpoints are instantiated to get actual views on the models. During runtime, these views interpret the base model entities as defined by the semantics chosen as the meta level. However, most of these approaches do not support the modification of such interpretations at runtime. During this project we came across a problem, where the interpretation, relying on a base model element, had to replace the based model element during the execution. In terms of traditional MDE, it would mean to change the transformation definition during the execution of a transformation. The use of role instances allow switching the role being played by a player on the fly. Using the pattern with adapter and playrelation helped us resolve this problem on an implementation level. However, further work is needed to tackle the co-evolution of dynamic views and the base models.

- *Dynamicity is Necessary for an Attacker View.* Most of the current cybersecurity approaches following a *persona non grata* approach, present a mechanism to view the system from an attacker's perspective. These approaches tend to present the attacker view as a predefined static view that does not take into account the evolution of the attacker's perspective during the attack. Such systems are good for analyzing and proposing attack preventive measures, however they fall short on how to respond when an actual attack in undergoing. We solved this problem by taking into account the advances of the attacker with each attack step. However, we find that other kinds of dynamicity would further strengthen the attacker point of view. For example, the attacker view should also take into account, the state of the system. A industrial robot in the context of Industry 4.0 might be more vulnerable in one state than another.

- *Generating Attack Models Facilitates Security Analysis.* Attack models are generally used in the domain of cybersecurity for classification of security threats. These attack models then serve as input for various cyber threat analysis approaches. They are normally developed through brainstorming sessions arranged by the security experts. Generating of attack models can facilitate security analysis. While exhaustive analysis of attack scenarios via formal methods seems idealistic for the moment, generating multiple attack paths from a given configuration seems clearly possible. Combined with the dynamic aspect of the attacker view, it could enable multiple scenarios exploration. Such tools would greatly facilitate complex and multi-step attack design and thus produce increasingly precise analysis. For example, attack trees and attack graphs generation could be partially automated via these scenarios. In particular, it could bridge the gap between pentesting and attack trees/graphs.

8   Conclusion

Handling interoperability between different DSMLs remains tedious and is generally handled by traditional model driven engineering methodologies *e.g.* model transformations. When dynamicity comes into play, where models are continuously evolving, it becomes hard to use the traditional mechanisms. We claim that the model federation approach provides a viable solution to handle DSML interoperability. In this paper, we demonstrated that role modeling provides the capacity to define a shared semantics between different DSMLs. The goal of role modeling is to act as a semantics viewpoint on the model elements. These model elements remain independent of the federated model and no transformations are applied. A role model uses behavioral functions to access and update model elements without creating intermediate model elements. We have formalized the concept of role in our language through Role4All metamodel. The framework offers an extension mechanism so that multiple connectors for classic data formats like XML, JSON, *etc.* can be added to it. In this paper, we apply role modeling based methodology to perform cyber threat analysis. This analysis needs to use data and meta-data from different tools in different formalisms and then correlate and process it as federated data. We presented an interpreter for the framework that is capable of simulating the roles. We used this interpreter to simulate an attack on a system. Our future perspectives on this research work are to propose mechanisms for formal verification of the federated models. This would allow us to use formal verification to generate all possible attack scenarios based on different topologies, system configurations, vulnerability knowledge and attacker competency levels.

References

1. Basin, D., Doser, J., Lodderstedt, T.: Model driven security: from UML models to access control infrastructures. ACM Trans. Softw. Eng. Methodol. (TOSEM) **15**(1), 39–91 (2006)
2. Champeau, J., Leilde, V., Diallo, P.I.: Model federation in toolchains. In: MODELS Companion Proceedings (2013)
3. Combemale, B., Deantoni, J., Baudry, B., France, R.B., Jézéquel, J.-M., Gray, J.: Globalizing modeling languages. Computer **47**(6), 68–71 (2014)
4. Conti, M., Dargahi, T., Dehghantanha, A.: Cyber threat intelligence: challenges and opportunities. In: Dehghantanha, A., Conti, M., Dargahi, T. (eds.) Cyber Threat Intelligence. AIS, vol. 70, pp. 1–6. Springer, Cham (2018). https://doi.org/10.1007/978-3-319-73951-9_1
5. Dijkstra, E.W.: Guarded commands, nondeterminacy, and formal derivation of programs. In: Gries, D. (ed.) Programming Methodology. MCS, pp. 166–175. Springer, New York (1978). https://doi.org/10.1007/978-1-4612-6315-9_14
6. Drouot, B., Champeau, J.: Model federation based on role modeling. In: Proceedings of the 7th International Conference on Model-Driven Engineering and Software Development, MODELSWARD 2019, Prague, Czech Republic, 20–22 February 2019, pp. 72–83 (2019)

7. Elahi, G., Yu, E., Zannone, N.: A vulnerability-centric requirements engineering framework: analyzing security attacks, countermeasures, and requirements based on vulnerabilities. Requir. Eng. **15**(1), 41–62 (2010)
8. Emerson, M., Sztipanovits, J.: Techniques for metamodel composition. In: OOPSLA-6th Workshop on Domain Specific Modeling, pp. 123–139 (2006)
9. Golra, F.R., Beugnard, A., Dagnat, F., Guerin, S., Guychard, C.: Addressing modularity for heterogeneous multi-model systems using model federation. In: Companion Proceedings 15th International Conference on Modularity, pp. 206–211. ACM (2016)
10. Gottlob, G., Schrefl, M., Röck, B.: Extending object-oriented systems with roles. ACM Trans. Inf. Syst. (TOIS) **14**(3), 268–296 (1996)
11. Hardebolle, C., Boulanger, F.: ModHel'X: a component-oriented approach to multi-formalism modeling. In: Giese, H. (ed.) MODELS 2007. LNCS, vol. 5002, pp. 247–258. Springer, Heidelberg (2008). https://doi.org/10.1007/978-3-540-69073-3_26
12. Hemery, D.: PimCa: Définition du langage. Technical report, DGA Maitrise de l'Information, January 2015
13. Holik, F., Horalek, J., Marik, O., Neradova, S., Zitta, S.: Effective penetration testing with Metasploit framework and methodologies. In: 2014 IEEE 15th International Symposium on Computational Intelligence and Informatics (CINTI), pp. 237–242. IEEE, November 2014. https://doi.org/10.1109/CINTI.2014.7028682
14. Hutchinson, J., Whittle, J., Rouncefield, M., Kristoffersen, S.: Empirical assessment of MDE in industry. In: Proceedings of the 33rd International Conference on Software Engineering, pp. 471–480. ACM (2011)
15. Ishida, T.: Q: a scenario description language for interactive agents. Computer **35**(11), 42–47 (2002)
16. ISO 14258:1998 - Industrial automation systems - Concepts and rules for enterprise models. Standard, International Organization for Standardization, Geneva, CH, August 1998
17. ISO/IEC 27000:2016 - Information technology - Security techniques - Information security management system - Overview and vocabulary. Standard, International Organization for Standardization, August 2016
18. Kühn, T., Leuthäuser, M., Götz, S., Seidl, C., Aßmann, U.: A metamodel family for role-based modeling and programming languages. In: Combemale, B., Pearce, D.J., Barais, O., Vinju, J.J. (eds.) SLE 2014. LNCS, vol. 8706, pp. 141–160. Springer, Cham (2014). https://doi.org/10.1007/978-3-319-11245-9_8
19. Mell, P., Scarfone, K., Romanosky, S.: Common vulnerability scoring system. IEEE Secur. Priv. **4**(6), 85–89 (2006)
20. Myagmar, S., Lee, A.J., Yurcik, W.: Threat modeling as a basis for security requirements. In: Symposium on Requirements Engineering for Information Security (SREIS), vol. 2005, pp. 1–8. Citeseer (2005)
21. Niemoller, J., Mokrushin, L., Vandikas, K., Avesand, S., Angelin, L.: Model federation and probabilistic analysis for advanced OSS and BSS. In: 2013 Seventh International Conference on Next Generation Mobile Apps, Services and Technologies (NGMAST), pp. 122–129. IEEE (2013)
22. Osis, J.: Model-Driven Domain Analysis and Software Development: Architectures and functions. IGI Global, Hershey (2010)
23. Pauli, J., Xu, D.: Threat-driven architectural design of secure information systems. In: Proceeding of First International Workshop on Protection by Adaptation, PBA 2005, Miami (2005)

24. Schneider, J.P., Champeau, J., Lagadec, L., Senn, E.: Role framework to support collaborative virtual prototyping of system of systems. In: 24th International Conference on Enabling Technologies: Infrastructure for Collaborative Enterprises (WETICE), pp. 144–149. IEEE (2015)
25. Schneider, J.P., Champeau, J., Teodorov, C., Senn, E., Lagadec, L.: A role language to interpret multi-formalism system of systems models. In: 9th Annual IEEE International Systems Conference (SysCon), pp. 200–205. IEEE (2015)
26. Seifert, M., Wende, C., Aßmann, U.: Anticipating unanticipated tool interoperability using role models. In: Proceedings of the First International Workshop on Model-Driven Interoperability, pp. 52–60. ACM (2010)
27. Shostack, A.: Threat Modeling: Designing for Security. Wiley, Hoboken (2014)
28. Steimann, F.: On the representation of roles in object-oriented and conceptual modelling. Data Knowl. Eng. **35**(1), 83–106 (2000)
29. Stevens, P.: A landscape of bidirectional model transformations. In: Lämmel, R., Visser, J., Saraiva, J. (eds.) GTTSE 2007. LNCS, vol. 5235, pp. 408–424. Springer, Heidelberg (2008). https://doi.org/10.1007/978-3-540-88643-3_10
30. Zhang, S., Caragea, D., Ou, X.: An empirical study on using the national vulnerability database to predict software vulnerabilities. In: Hameurlain, A., Liddle, S.W., Schewe, K.-D., Zhou, X. (eds.) DEXA 2011. LNCS, vol. 6860, pp. 217–231. Springer, Heidelberg (2011). https://doi.org/10.1007/978-3-642-23088-2_15

Static Data-Flow Analysis
of UML/SysML Functional Views
for Signal and Image Processing
Applications

Andrea Enrici[1]([✉]), Ludovic Apvrille[2], Renaud Pacalet[2], and Minh Hiep Pham[2]

[1] Nokia Bell Labs, 91620 Nozay, France
andrea.enrici@nokia-bell-labs.com
[2] LTCI, Télécom Paris, Institut Polytechnique de Paris, 75013 Paris, France
{ludovic.apvrille,renaud.pacalet,minh.pham}@telecom-paris.fr

Abstract. The complexity of heterogeneous Multi-Processor Systems-on-Chip stretches the limits of software development solutions based on sequential languages such as C/C++. While these are still the most widely used languages in practice, model-based solutions appear to be an efficient alternative. However, the optimized compilation of models for multi-processor systems still presents many open research problems. Among others, static data-flow analyses for models require the adaptation of traditional algorithms used in program analysis (iterative and worklist algorithms). These algorithms operate on Control-Flow Graphs with a unique start node (i.e., a node without predecessors) and assume that every basic block is reachable from this start node.

In this paper, we present a novel combination of the well-known iterative and worklist algorithms that examines a Control-Flow Graph where basic blocks can be reached by paths that originate from different start states. We apply this solution to functional views of signal and image processing models denoted with UML Activity and SysML Block diagrams. We demonstrate its effectiveness on interval analysis and show that significant reductions in the number of visits of the models' control-flow graphs can be achieved.

Keywords: Static data-flow analysis · Optimizing model compilation UML/SysML · Multi-Processor System-on-Chip

1 Introduction

Thanks to the continuous evolution of semiconductor process technologies, tens or hundreds of processors can nowadays be integrated into single chips. These Multi-Processor Systems-on-Chip (MPSoCs) have emerged in the last two decades as an important class of systems that are widely used in networking, communications, signal processing and multimedia among other applications.

© Springer Nature Switzerland AG 2020
S. Hammoudi et al. (Eds.): MODELSWARD 2019, CCIS 1161, pp. 101–126, 2020.
https://doi.org/10.1007/978-3-030-37873-8_5

Two branches of MPSoC platforms currently exist: homogeneous and hetero-geneous. Homogeneous multi-processors are largely used for High-Performance Computing (HPC) applications. They are composed of multiple instances of identical processors (e.g., Intel x86 CPUs) that provide general-purpose capa-bilities. Heterogeneous multi-processors are typically used in application-specific domains (e.g., signal and image processing, embedded systems) and are com-posed of processing elements (e.g., Digital Signal Processors - DSPs - Field Pro-grammable Gate Arrays - FPGAs) with specific functionalities and performance characteristics (e.g., throughput, latency, power consumption).

Because of their heterogeneity, the development of application control code for heterogeneous MPSoCs is considered more difficult than in the case of homo-geneous systems. By application control code, we refer to the code that runs in the user space of an Operating System (or an equivalent software stack - hence the adjective *application*) and governs the execution of an application (hence the adjective *control*). Software developers are not only faced with issues that are typical of parallel programming (e.g., synchronization, deadlocks, choice of task granularity). They must also consider how to efficiently parallelize applications, how to map and schedule parallel functions onto execution units as well as how to interface hardwired accelerators (e.g., FPGAs, Graphics Processing Units - GPUs).

Model-Based Software Engineering (MBSE) [38, 39] is a software development paradigm that can alleviate the programming of heterogeneous MPSoCs. MBSE combines domain-specific modeling languages to abstract the structure, behavior and requirements of a system under design, with transformation engines and generators. The latter analyze models and produce artifacts such as source code, simulation, verification inputs or alternative model representations.

Modeling languages like UML and SysML offer graphical constructs that have a higher abstraction level (i.e., task-level[1]) than the constructs natively available in C/C++[2]. Constructs in UML and SysML have a rich semantics (e.g., block-ing, non-blocking read/write operations) that enables the expression of complex control-flow interactions (e.g., hierarchical composition, dispatch/reception of signals). Unfortunately, some of these constructs cannot be efficiently examined by standard techniques for static data-flow analysis that were developed for single-processor programs in sequential languages.

In this paper, we present an algorithm that processes a Control-Flow Graph (CFG) derived from the specification of parallel functions. Unlike standard CFGs

---

[1] By the term task, we denote the most coarse-grain unit of work that the programming model of an execution unit in a target MPSoC platform offers to the programmer. In the literature, the term task can be ambiguous and alternatives include process, light-weight process, thread (for execution), step, request, or query (for work). For instance, given a general-purpose CPU equipped with an Operating System (OS), a task is equivalent to an OS process. Given a Digital Signal Processor and its software stack, operations such as Fast-Fourier Transforms, signal modulations can run as tasks.

[2] In the context of our work, C/C++ are the reference programming languages with which signal and image processing applications for MPSoCs are developed [20].

from single-processor programs, this CFG has multi start nodes (i.e., nodes without predecessors) and basic blocks are reachable on paths that can originate from multiple start nodes. Our solution reduces the number of visits that are necessary to analyze the Control-Flow Graphs (CFGs) of UML/SysML models, with respect to a simple combination of standard techniques used in *program* analysis. We demonstrate the efficiency of our algorithm for the interval analysis of functional views expressed with UML Activity diagrams, SysML Block Definition and SysML Internal Block diagrams. The design of these diagrams is supported by TTool/DIPLODOCUS [42], a UML/SysML toolkit for the hardware/software co-design of data-flow systems.

The rest of this paper is organized as follows. Section 2 positions our approach for optimizing model compilation with respect to existing solutions. Section 3 positions our static analysis algorithm with respect to related work. Section 4 illustrates our contribution. Section 5 describes the analysis of UML/SysML functional views for a testbench of signal and image processing applications. Section 6 concludes this paper.

2   Optimizing Compilation of UML/SysML Models

In [35], existing approaches for the design of Digital Signal Processing applications for MPSoCs are classified as compiler-based, language-extension, model-based and platform-based, according to where the application's parallelism is treated.

Compiler-based approaches take as input standard sequential languages (e.g., C) and produce software by means of a parallelizing compiler. The latter automatically inspects the input specifications to find parallelizable regions of code (e.g., time consuming loops), partitions each such a region into a set of concurrent tasks and maps them onto the available processors. A prominent example of such an approach is the MPSoC Application Programming Studio (MAPS) [32].

Because of the current limitations in the automatic extraction of parallel regions [35], language-extension approaches require the programmer to explicitly define these regions by enriching the source code with annotations and/or calls to Application Programming Interfaces (APIs). A prominent example of C language extended with annotations is OpenMP [5]. Well-known examples of languages extended with APIs are OpenCL [1], the Compute Unified Device Architecture (CUDA) [4], the Message Passing Interface (MPI) [3] and the MATLAB toolboxes MATLABMPI [28] and MPITB [10].

Model-based approaches use Models of Computations (MoCs) with a formally well-defined semantics (e.g., Synchronous Data Flow [31] - SDF - Kahn Process Networks [27] - KPN - MATLAB/Simulink [2]) to explicitly reveal the parallelism in an input application. The latter is described as a set of concurrent modules interconnected by data-dependencies in the form of buffers. As an application's intrinsic parallelism is explicitly revealed by the input language, parallelization consists in mapping the modules to processors.

Platform-based approaches, such as the Common Intermediate Code (CIC) [30], can be seen as a new type of compiler for parallel processing. CIC provides to the user an intermediate parallel programming model that is independent of a target platform. A CIC translator automatically maps an input specification to constructs of the CIC intermediate parallel programming model and into target-specific code.

With respect to the above taxonomy, our approach can be classified as model-based. The main difference with existing model-based approaches is that we use UML/SysML diagrams as input specifications rather than a formal MoC such as SDF or KPN. The reason for this choice being that the execution semantics of these MoCs is focused on the communication between concurrent modules. These MoCs ignore the modules' internal behavior that describes the production and consumption of information. This prevents a model compiler from implementing aggressive optimizations that are based on a module's internal behavior. An example of this limitation can be seen from the work in [17]. Here, the authors propose a memory optimization technique that is based on scripts that describe the internal memory use of SDF actors in an input application. We advocate that the richer execution semantics of (some) UML/SysML diagrams facilitates the MPSoC programming with respect to MoC-based approaches. Indeed, it avoids the user and the compiler to optimize an input application based on specifications in different languages. Thanks to static analysis techniques such as the one described in this paper, an optimizing compiler can automatically detect optimization opportunities without forcing the user to specify code regions where optimizations can take place.

An approach that also attempts to optimize models before code generation is described in [14,15]. Their approach is based on GUML, a GCC front-end for UML that allows to generate binary executables from UML State Machines. GUML translates input UML diagrams into GIMPLE, which is one of GCC's many intermediate representation formats used by GCC for optimization purposes. The authors propose two levels of optimizations that aim at reducing the binary code size, with respect to the binary that is obtained by compiling C++ code that is automatically generated from UML by means of standard design patterns (e.g., State Pattern, State Table Transition, Nested Switch Case Statements). At first, GUML eliminates the dead code that can be present in C++ code due to the presence of unreachable states. Secondly, GUML removes redundant expressions in state machines by analyzing the CFG that is generated directly from UML rather than from the C++ code that is generated from UML diagrams. From the viewpoint of the compilation approach, the main difference with our work is that we propose a meta-compiler that clearly separates the optimized model compilation from the compilation of C code. Our approach generates software binaries in two compilation steps. However, besides pure software implementations, it also allows to target pure hardware and hardware/software implementations via High-Level Synthesis.

The approach that we follow to generate optimized software from executable UML/SysML models is shown in Fig. 1. In the context of our research, we develop control software that executes as an application in the user-space of an Operating System (or equivalent software stack in a target platform). This software governs

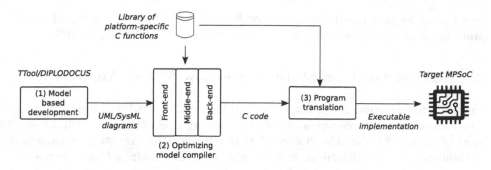

Fig. 1. MPSoC software development from UML/SysML models - revised from [22].

the execution of data processing and transfer operations that can be implemented as both hardware and/or software components (e.g., Intellectual Property blocks in a FPGA, software tasks). For this reason, we model a system with a combination of UML/SysML diagrams, rather than UML only. In Fig. 1, UML/SysML diagrams are created in TTool/DIPLODOCUS [42], step (1). These diagrams denote: (i) the functionality of an application, (ii) the architecture and communication protocols of the target MPSoC platform and (iii) their mapping. In this phase, models are used as the primary artifact for software development. They are created, edited and debugged (e.g., formal verification, simulation, profiling) until legal specifications are obtained that respect some desired constraints (e.g., throughput, latency, power consumption). This is similar to the way code is created, edited and debugged in Integrated Development Environments (IDE) such as Eclipse CDT [19].

Model-based specifications are compiled into C code, step (2) in Fig. 1, by an optimizing compiler. This compiler's structure is the same as those of traditional programming languages [40]: it includes a front-end for parsing and analysis, a middle-end for optimization and a back-end for code generation. The output code of the model compiler in Fig. 1 can be further developed as in traditional software engineering. In the case of our methodology, the output control software does not include the algorithmic part of computation and communication operations. The corresponding code is provided by an external library (e.g., I/O specific code, platform-specific code for OS or middleware) that is specific to the target MPSoC platform.

The output C code (control, data processings and transfers) can be further used to produce pure hardware (e.g., a hardware IP-based design), pure software (e.g., an application running on top of an Operating System) or mixed hardware/software implementations (e.g., some functionalities are executed by a general-purpose control processor and some are accelerated in hardware) as indicated by step (3) in Fig. 1. Different *translators* must be used accordingly: Computer Aided Design (CAD) toolsuites (e.g., Xilinx Vivado High Level Synthesis) or traditional programming-language compilers (e.g., GNU/gcc/g++, Clang). In the latter case, our optimizing model compiler can be seen as a *meta-compiler* that coordinates the overall compilation process, on top of multiple single-processor compilers for each execution unit of the target MPSoC.

3   Related Work on Static Data-Flow Model Analysis

Similarly to techniques for program analysis [34], static data-flow *model* analysis provides solutions to reasoning about the value and relations (e.g., definitions, use) of data (e.g., Variables, Objects) that influence the execution of models, without actually running them. Static analysis provides useful solutions in many domains, most notably in optimizing compilers to efficiently produce code, in software testing to detect anomalies and in security to detect malicious behaviors. To the best of our knowledge, we appear to be the first to propose the use of static data-flow analysis on a combination of UML Activity, SysML Internal Block and Block Definition diagrams. Similarly, we found no related work that applies this type of analysis to optimizing model compilers.

Generally speaking, data-flow-based analyses for models is not possible without adapting traditional algorithms from program analysis (Sect. 4). The reason for this is that edges in control-flow graphs that are derived from models are instances of associations or references defined in a given meta-model. These edges denote relationships between objects which may have an arbitrary semantics that depends on the meta-model's domain. Two elements in a model may be connected by means of multiple paths that originate from different start nodes (i.e., nodes without predecessors).

Relevant work that perform static data-flow analysis on UML models can be found in [13,23,29,37,43,44]. In [37], the authors propose an approach for static analysis based on attribute grammars and data-flow analysis. As a solution, they propose a modified version of the iterative algorithm that dynamically discovers dependencies between data-flow equations while analyzing a model.

In [23], the authors present an extended Activity diagram metamodel, called Concurrent Control Flow Graph (CCFG), to support control-flow analysis of UML 2.0 Sequence diagrams. The authors define a mapping based on the Object Constraint Language that is formal and verifiable. This mapping is defined in the form of consistency rules between a Sequence diagram and a CCFG.

Specifically, the work in [13,29,43] are dedicated to the analysis of Statecharts for software testing. The authors in [29] discuss the generation of test cases from UML State Machines, for a set of criteria to be tested. Here, data-flow analysis is used to identify the points in the input models where variables are defined and used. This work examines control-flow graphs that are derived by transforming UML State Machines into Extended Finite State Machines, where hierarchical and concurrent states are flattened. With respect to our work, communications between Classes are not considered and broadcast communications are eliminated when in the transformation to Extended Finite State Machines.

The main contribution in [13] is a technique that guides the coverage of UML Statecharts for test data selection in the context of fault detection. Based on definition-use pairs of variables, this technique selects the best transition tree that is used as a data for the coverage of UML Statecharts. In our work, a control-flow graph is entirely derived from the input UML/SysML diagrams. Conversely, in [13] the authors use a special Event Action Flow Graph that only represents events and actions, where operation contracts and guard conditions are expressed in the Object Constraint Language (OCL).

The IF toolset [43] is an environment for the modeling and validation of heterogeneous real-time systems. The toolset includes a translator for input UML Statecharts and Class diagrams and a static analyzer. These tools make use of an intermediate representation formalism, called IF, and support live-variable analysis, dead-code elimination and variable abstraction. In the IF toolset, the input diagrams represent systems implemented in software. Conversely, our UML/SysML diagrams can also capture mixed hardware/software or purely hardware implementations.

The work in [44] is an approach that builds a data structure from all the associations between definitions and use (DU) of variables in UML State Machines. Statecharts are specified with the abstract syntax of the UML Action Specification Language [33]. An input Statechart is parsed, its control-flow graph is extracted and stored in an adjacency matrix that is traversed to identify all the DU pairs. To enhance the scalability of their approach, the authors also present a set of mapping rules that allow to port their solution to virtually any concrete syntax of the UML Action Specification Language. However, no effective application of this approach is detailed.

In the domain of network applications and distributed software, the Go language [7,18] is a relative newcomer that has gained considerable attention in recent years. The language supports concurrency by means of two constructs: channels and light-weight threads called *goroutines*. Concurrent goroutines exchange data via channels in a similar way to Communicating Sequential Processes [24] and Occam [26]. In principle, Go channels are similar to the UML/SysML operators that we use to exchange information between Activities. Go channels cannot be associated to arbitrarily complex communication protocols as with ProtocolStateMachines. However, they have certain characteristics that make our analysis framework not reusable in the case of the Go language. The static analysis of channel-based communication [12] is similar to pointer analysis: channels are referenced shared data where pointers to channels can be communicated over channels or stored and passed to sequential procedures together with other references.

4 Static Data-Flow Model Analysis

In this section, we propose an algorithm for the static data-flow analysis of parallel applications at task-level of abstraction. We denote an application's functional view with UML Activity (AD) and SysML Block diagrams (i.e., SysML Block Definition and Internal Block diagrams - shortened to BDs). UML ADs are used to capture the internal behavior of tasks, whereas SysML BDs are used to capture the structure of the data and control dependencies between tasks.

Our static analysis serves the purpose of detecting optimization opportunities both within a single task (intra-task) and between parallel tasks (inter-task).

With respect to specifications in the C programming language, our UML/SysML-based specifications are positioned at a higher level of abstraction. Still, a UML AD's can be seen as equivalent to an entire C program. Dedicated UML constructs, called InvocationActions, can be used to reference UML ADs similarly to procedure calls in the C language. Thus, existing techniques for program interprocedural analysis [25,36] can be reused to examine both synchronous and asynchronous invocations of UML Activities.

Instead, novel techniques are needed to efficiently account for Control-Flow Graphs with multiple start nodes and edges that originate from the modeling constructs that denote the communication protocols for the exchange of information among parallel functions (e.g., SendObjectActions, ReceiveObjectActions).

The algorithm that we present here is implemented in the optimizing model compiler's frontend of Fig. 1.

4.1   The Control-Flow Graph for a Functional View

Because in data-flow analysis the order of statement matters, it is more convenient to view a specification (be it code or a model) as a Control Flow Graph (CFG). Generally speaking, a CFG is a directed graph, where nodes correspond to statements and edges represent possible flows of control. In this paper, we do not describe the process that transforms our UML/SysML diagrams into a CFG. UML/SysML have a graphical formalism that explicitly separates between flows of data and control with different Tokens and Edges. Therefore, a CFG is obtained by visiting the control dependencies in diagrams. Sequences of constructs with no branches in, except for the entry, and no branches out, except for the exit, are grouped into CFG nodes (basic blocks).

Processings. The CFG that results from the composition of UML ADs and SysML BDs is a directed graph $G^* = <N^*, E^*>$. G^* can be also seen as a supergraph formed by the composition of a set of control flowgraphs $N^* = \{G_1, G_2, \ldots, G_n\}$. Each such a control-flow graph $G_i = <N_i, E_i>$ represents a UML Activity: nodes N_i are the Activity's modeling constructs and edges E_i are the Activity's ControlFlowEdges. One of these flowgraphs, G_{source}, represents the source Activity that is the application's entry point (this is similar to the CFG for the main() procedure in the C programming language). At least one of the control-flow graphs in N^* is a sink node in G^* that we denote G_{sink}. It is the application's exit point. E^* is the set of (super)edges in G^* that represent information dependencies between Activities. As said before, an application's structural view is specifically expressed in our contribution with SysML BDs. Thus, edges in E^* correspond to the Relationships among SysML Blocks.

Each Activity's CFG G_i has a unique start node (i.e., UML InitialNode) and can have multiple exit nodes (i.e., UML ActivityFinalNode and FlowFinalNodes). Remaining nodes represent the modeling statements (e.g., Actions, ControlNodes). Thus, an expanded view of G^* presents multiple start nodes, one for each task. For each such a start node, not all the basic blocks in the expanded view of G^* can be reached.

Communications. In UML/SysML, communication protocols can be specified in many ways: UML Actions with a profile-specific semantics (e.g., blocking, non-blocking), ProtocolStateMachines, Sequence diagrams, Activity diagrams or a combination thereof [21]. Our UML/SysML formalism uses Actions with read and write communication primitives to describe point-to-point communications. More complex protocols (e.g., DMA transfers, broadcast transfers) can be described with a combination of Activity and Sequence diagrams [21]. In this paper, we focus on the static analysis of point-to-point communications and we postpone the study of more complex protocols to future work. We focus on analyzing Actions which read/write semantics can be blocking or non-blocking. For this reason, in addition to the ordinary *intra*-graph edges that connect nodes within a single G_i, we create *inter*-graph (super)edges for each pair SendObjectAction-ReceiveObjectAction from a sender G_i to a receiver G_j.

Generally speaking, we advocate that for both simple and complex protocols, the protocols' control-flow graphs must be included in the global functional view's CFG and analyzed together with the CFGs of processings. When complex communication protocols are present, synchronous/asynchronous call and return nodes and edges must be added to the functional view's CFG G^*. This allows to reuse techniques from interprocedural program analysis.

4.2   The Control-Flow Graph Analysis

Static analysis propagates information related to the flow of data along edges in a CFG. This is done according to the edges' transformation functions that account for the semantics of nodes. Common visitation algorithms stem from two approaches: the iterative search and the worklist algorithm.

In the iterative search (Algorithm 1), given a node n, the current state of the information associated to the node is saved (line 5 in Algorithm 1). At each CFG visitation, a node is examined once (line 6 in Algorithm 1). If the state of the output information changes after processing the node (lines 7–9 in Algorithm 1), then a flag is activated to trigger successive visitations.

The worklist algorithm (Algorithm 2) is based on examining the CFG's edges. These are stored in a list (line 1 in Algorithm 2). Edges are iteratively popped out of the worklist (line 3 in Algorithm 2) and information is propagated from the edge's source to its destination node (lines 4–5 in Algorithm 2). If any changes occur then successor edges[3] are pushed into the worklist. The analysis repeats until it reaches a fixed-point that corresponds to the worklist being empty (line 2 in Algorithm 2).

During a CFG visitation (i.e., the examination of all CFG nodes), the worklist algorithm immediately propagates changes to neighboring nodes. Edges are stored back into the worklist and examined in the next iteration. Therefore, a

---

[3] We always imply forward analysis. Predecessor edges must be considered in the case of backward analysis.

complete visitation of all nodes may require multiple examinations of the same node. Conversely, the iterative search always examines nodes once per visitation, but it waits until the next visitation of the entire CFG to propagate a change.

Algorithm 1. The iterative search algorithm.

```
 1  changed = true;
 2  while changed do
 3  |   changed = false;
 4  |   for ∀node n do
 5  |   |   old = out[n];
 6  |   |   process(n);
 7  |   |   if old ≠ out[n] then
 8  |   |   |   changed = true;
 9  |   |   end
10  |   end
11  end
```

In the context of our research, analyzing an expanded view of G^* purely on the basis of the iterative or worklist algorithm would not work. These algorithms were designed for Control-Flow Graphs that are derived from single-processor programs. These CFGs have a single start node from which paths originate that reach all basic blocks. Instead, a hierarchical combination of these algorithms is necessary, where the top-most algorithm is used to visit the tasks that compose G^* and the lower-most algorithms visits the basic blocks that compose each of the tasks $\{G_1, G_2..., G_n\} \in G^*$.

We combined Algorithms 1 and 2 as proposed in [9]. The iterative search has a more global nature in because, at each iteration, it computes data flows for all CFG's nodes. This makes it a suitable candidate to examine inter-Activity dependencies and thus direct visitations of the entire supergraph G^*. The worklist algorithm, instead, has a more local nature as it propagates data flows locally to a node's successors only (predecessors in case of backward analysis). This makes it an ideal candidate to examine intra-Activity dependencies.

Nonetheless, this simple combination may still result in unnecessary visitations. The iterative algorithm must not propagate local changes from a previous iteration to all nodes in G^*. Similarly, at each visitation, the worklist algorithm should explore a node's successors/predecessors only when information from *all* its incoming edges is available (i.e., information that is propagated on both inter- and intra-Activity edges).

We call our combination of Algorithms 1 and 2 the Combined Iterative Blocking Worklist (CIBW) and present it in Algorithms 3 and 4. Specifically for this paper, Algorithms 3 and 4 are a further improvement of the version described in [22]. More in details, lines 1–10 in Algorithm 3 in [22] and line 16 in Algorithm 4 in [22] were specific to the case of *acyclic* super-graphs. Here, we removed this constraint and present a CIBW algorithm that also handles cyclic super-graphs.

Algorithm 2. The worklist algorithm.

```
1  worklist ← {start edge};
2  while worklist ≠ ∅ do
3  |   worklist ← worklist \ e;
4  |   old = out[e];
5  |   process(e);
6  |   if old ≠ out[e] then
7  |   |   for p ∈ succ[e] do
8  |   |   |   worklist ← worklist ∪ p;
9  |   |   end
10 |   end
11 end
```

In Algorithm 3, Activities' CFGs are iteratively visited until no changes occur when data-flow information is propagated. The algorithm iteratively searches the (super)nodes of G^* at the level of abstraction of the whole supergraph. Each node in G^* is processed only if the data-flow information of any of its successors (predecessors in the case of backward analysis) has changed as indicated by a set of pending graphs P (lines 7–17). To retain the fairness of the original iterative approach, each node is visited exactly once on each iteration (line 6). Thus, the same Activity's CFG cannot be explored in consecutive iterations.

An Activity's CFG is visited by a blocking version of the worklist search, in Algorithm 4. This algorithm operates on a worklist of edges that is composed of the set of intra-Activity edges. At lines 4–11, exploration proceeds like in the classical worklist search (Algorithm 2). Exploration can be suspended and an Activity can be marked as pending (lines 13–15) if the edge under analysis originates from a task that has not yet been visited. Hence the name *blocking worklist*. The condition at line 13 guarantees the absence of deadlocks when blocking the analysis. Deadlocks may arise when an edge connects two tasks that belong to the same cycle in G^*. Upon completing the analysis, the current Activity is removed from the pending list P, line 23.

4.3   The Performance Gain of the CIBW Algorithm

We evaluate the gain of the CIBW algorithm, with respect to a non-blocking combination of the iterative and worklist algorithms. This is given in Eq. 1 by the ratio between number of *propagations* $\mathcal{N}$ of data-flow facts between CFG's nodes N^*.

$$g = 1 - \frac{\mathcal{N}^{blocking\ worklist}}{\mathcal{N}^{non-blocking\ worklist}} = 1 - \frac{\mathcal{N}^{bw}}{\mathcal{N}^{nbw}} \tag{1}$$

This gain can be expressed analytically only for graphs with a simple topology (see Sect. 5). In this case, we can express the gain, Eq. 2, in terms of the number of unnecessary propagations $\mathcal{N}^u$ that are performed by the non-blocking worklist for each node $n \in N_i$ that receives an inter-Activity edge.

Algorithm 3. The Combined Iterative Blocking Worklist algorithm.

```
   /* G* =< N*, E* > the control-flow super-graph                              */
   /* analysis[] the state of the analysis; each entry corresponds to a basic block in
      G*                                                                       */
   /* p_start ... p_end: the set of basic blocks of task p                     */
   /* P the set of pending tasks to analyze                                    */
   /* In forward analysis P is initialized with G_source                       */
   /* In backward analysis P is initialized with G_sink                        */
   /* In forward analysis Next(x) is the set of successor tasks of task x in G* */
   /* In backward analysis Next(x) is the set of successor tasks of task x in G* */
 1 changed = true;
 2 while changed do
 3  |  changed = false;
 4  |  foreach p ∈ P do
 5  |  |   P ← P \ p;
 6  |  |   old := analysis[ p_start, ..., p_end ];
 7  |  |   < blocked, analysis[] >= blocking_worklist( p, analysis );
 8  |  |   if blocked then
 9  |  |   |   changed = true;
10  |  |   end
11  |  |   else
12  |  |   |   if old ≠ analysis[ p_start, ..., p_end ] then
13  |  |   |   |   changed = true;
14  |  |   |   |   foreach s ∈ Next( p ) do
15  |  |   |   |   |   P ← P ∪ s;
16  |  |   |   |   end
17  |  |   |   end
18  |  |   end
19  |  end
20 end
```

$$g = \frac{\mathcal{N}^u}{\mathcal{N}^{bw} + \mathcal{N}^u} \qquad (2)$$
$$where\ \mathcal{N}^{nbw} = \mathcal{N}^u + \mathcal{N}^{bw}$$

Unnecessary propagations are those that propagate partial information without collecting, for nodes connected by inter-Activity edges, information from all incident edges, both inter-task and intra-task. $\mathcal{N}^u$ is zero in two cases. First, in case n has no successors. Second, in case no path exists from an Activity's InitialNode to n, where all nodes in the path operate on the same set of data D_n (Variables and/or Objects) as n. In all other cases, $\mathcal{N}^u$ is different from zero and depends on two factors: (i) the number of n's successors that operate on D_n and (ii) the type of paths (acyclic or cyclic) that these successors belong to.

Given a path where at least one node operate on D_n or a superset of D_n, the value of $\mathcal{N}^u$ is given by Eq. 3, for $n's$ successors. These successors are visited either once, if they belong to a linear path, or k_p times, one per each iteration, if they belong to a cyclic path. The coefficient k_p is defined by the number of iterations that are necessary to reach the analysis' fixed point.

$$\mathcal{N}^u = \sum_{\forall\ path\ p\ \in\ CFG,\ i\ \in\ p} v_i^p$$

$$v_i^p = \begin{cases} 1 & D_n \subseteq D_i,\ i \notin cycle \\ k_p & D_n \subseteq D_i,\ i \in cycle \end{cases} \qquad (3)$$

Algorithm 4. The blocking worklist algorithm.

```
1  Function blocking_worklist( G_a = < N, E >, analysis[] ):
       /* G_a = < N, E > the UML Activity's CFG for task a          */
       /* worklist the list of CFG edges E                          */
       /* e_{x→y} the directed edge from nodes x to y               */
       /* analysis[ x ] stores the abstract state of the analysis for basic block x  */
       /* f_{x→y}(analysis[ x ]) is the transfer function of edge e_{x→y} applied to the
          abstract state of the analysis for basic block x. It does not modify the state
          stored in analysis[ x ]. It returns the relevant data-flow facts that the edge
          transfers to y.                                           */
       /* In forward analysis Next(x) is the set of successor of basic block x in N  */
       /* In backward analysis Next(x) is the set of successor of basic block x in N  */
2      worklist ← E;
3      while !empty( worklist ) do
4          e_{n→m} ← worklist.pop();
5          temp ← analysis[ m ] ⊓ f_{n→m}( analysis[ n ] );
6          if temp ⋢ analysis[ m ] then
7              analysis[ m ] ← temp;
8              foreach p ∈ N, p ∈ Next( m ) do
9                  |  worklist.push( e_{m→p} );
10             end
11         end
12         else
13             if n ∈ G_b, m ∈ G_a, a ≠ b, {G_a, G_b} ∉ cycle in G*, G_b ∈ P then
14                 |  P ← P ∪ G_a;
15                 |  return < true, analysis[] >;
16             end
17         end
18     end
19     P ← P \ G_a;
20     return < false, analysis[] >;
21 End function
```

In Eq. 3, i indexes the successors of n, D_i denotes the data set on which the i-th node operates and D_n the data set onto which n operates. A path p is defined as a succession of nodes that starts either at the Activity's InitialNode or at node n. A path p can terminate at an ActivityFinalNode or at a FlowFinalNode or at n itself or at any other node m that receives a different inter-Activity edge.

From these definitions and from Eq. 3, we can define a lower and an upper bound for the number of unnecessary propagations on a path p, $\mathcal{N}_p^u$, as in Eq. 4.

$$L_p \leq \mathcal{N}_p^u \leq (k_p \times L_p) \tag{4}$$

In Eq. 4, $\mathcal{N}_p^u$ is comprised between L_p, in case p is a linear path, and $k_p \times L_p$, in case p is cyclic. By L_p, we denote the number of nodes in p that operate on D_n.

4.4 Discussion

The CIBW algorithm can be used for the analysis of compositions of UML ADs, regardless of the presence of a SysML BD. In practice, the presence of SysML BDs is necessary only if ProtocolStateMachines are to be used. We developed this algorithm to analyze the CFG of models created in TTool/DIPLODOCUS [41]. The DIPLODOCUS profile does not provide global variables and diagram references (to support the modeling of hardware implementations); information among tasks is passed-by-value and cannot be shared between more than two tasks (a producer and a consumer).

Our CIBW algorithm can serve as a starting point for UML/SysML profiles where global variables and diagram references are supported. In profiles where the synchronous invocations of tasks is allowed, valid paths in G^* that result from matching invocation-return sites can be analyzed by including standard *meet over all valid paths* (MVP) techniques from program analysis. Instead, in cases where asynchronous invocations of tasks are permitted, an engineer wishing to reuse the CIBW algorithm must provide a dedicated mechanism to handle the unbounded set of pending asynchronous calls. Techniques such as the one in [25] can be leveraged to this purpose.

Similarly to optimizing compilers that operate on source code, our approach also trades off precision for efficiency, e.g., when join operations are applied in order to reduce two abstract states to one. Model-checking techniques could be leveraged to improve the precision of our analysis, if the set of reachable abstract states is seen as the reachability tree that denotes the possible executions of an input application [11]. Because all reachable abstract states are stored separately in the set of reachable states (i.e., absence of join operations between states), model-checking techniques can automatically add path-sensitivity to the analysis.

5   Case Study

In this section, we demonstrate the effectiveness of the CIBW algorithm on reducing the number of unnecessary propagations of data-flow facts in CFGs, with respect to the non-blocking case. We apply the CIBW algorithm to perform interval analysis of UML/SysML functional views of different domains, namely signal and image processing applications. We first demonstrate the reduction in CFGs' visits on single Activity diagrams. In this case, we examine UML ADs for two different functional views of a 5G channel decoder (receiver side, uplink SC-FDMA, single antenna case, Physical Uplink Shared channel - xPUSCH). Subsequently, we show the reduction in data-flow facts' propagations for the entire super control-flow graphs (composition of multiple Activities) of a set of testbench applications.

We create and edit functional views with TTool/DIPLODOCUS [42], a framework for the hardware/software co-design of data-dominated systems from UML/SysML diagrams. More precisely, TTool [41] is the name of the toolkit that allows to create, edit and validate UML/SysML diagrams. DIPLODOCUS [8] is the name of the profile dedicated to the hardware/software co-design of data-flow systems. In DIPLODOCUS, concurrent Activities communicate by means of blocking or non-blocking read/write Actions. The latter operate on *logical* First-In First-Out (FIFO) buffers that can be of finite or infinite size. A read primitive blocks on empty buffers until enough items are written to the FIFO. A write operation suspends on a full buffer until enough items are consumed.

As previously said, from the viewpoint of the compiler optimizations, interval analysis allows to automatically quantify the amount of samples that are produced and consumed by tasks in a signal/image processing applications. It also allows to quantify a task's internal memory consumption. These values can be used by the compiler for memory management, e.g., to determine the size of memory regions that can be shared among tasks.

Value analysis can also be used for other purposes. In [22], we motivated our work with the need for early check of model-based designs of Cloud-Radio Access Network architectures [16]. In this context, our analysis algorithm can be applied to single models (both platform independent and dependent) for checking properties against a desired set of requirements, constraints and performance characteristics, among other criteria. Furthermore, it can be applied to automatically inspect different design alternatives and assist Design Space Exploration frameworks in determining the best spatial partitioning (mapping) and temporal partitioning (scheduling) for a target platform. For instance, given a target platform with limited memory, the CIBW analysis could determine which, among multiple designs, is the best candidate that consumes the less memory.

5.1 The Application of the CIBW Algorithm to Individual Activities

The block diagram of the signal-processing operations for the 5G decoder that we consider first is shown in Fig. 2. We consider functional views that are representative of two possible MPSoC implementations of the decoder. In both cases, the execution of the signal-processing operations in Fig. 2 is governed by a Controller that we modeled with a dedicated source Activity.

In the first implementation, that we call *sparsely controlled* each of the processing operations in Fig. 2 is denoted with two Activities, which structure is represented by the SysML Blocks in Fig. 2. Figure 3b shows the Activity that captures the pure processing of data (transformation of input samples). Figure 3a shows the Activity that captures the control related to a pure processing Activity. In this implementation, the exchange of control information is distributed between operations but accompanies the data dependencies between tasks (Task_EvtIn and Task_EvtOut in Fig. 3a). This implementation targets

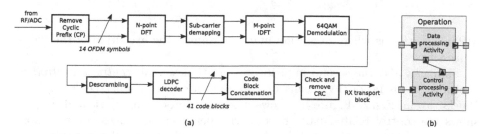

Fig. 2. The block diagram of the 5G channel decoder (a). Operations are modeled with the SysML Blocks in (b), with data dependencies (blue Ports) and control dependencies (brown and purple Ports) - revised from [22].

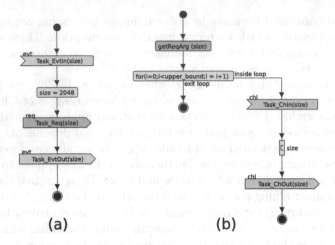

Fig. 3. The UML Activities for the *sparsely* controlled MPSoC implementation: the control part (a) and the data-processing part (b).

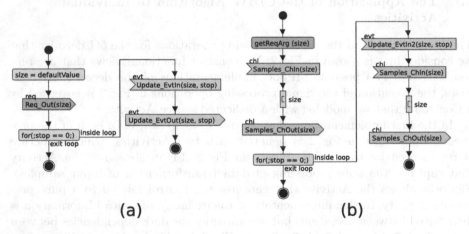

Fig. 4. The UML Activities for the *centrally* controlled MPSoC implementation: the control part (a) and the data-processing part (b) - revised from [22].

MPSoC platforms where execution units coordinate the execution of the data-processings.

Similarly, also the second implementation, that we call *centrally controlled*, captures an operation by means of two Activities interconnected by SysML Blocks as in Fig. 2. Figure 4b shows the pure processing part and Fig. 4a shows the control related part. Here, each operation exchanges control information (e.g., number of samples to process) with the Controller Activity only (`Update_EvtIn` and `Update_EvtIn2` in Fig. 3a). This implementation targets MPSoC platforms where control is centralized to a general-purpose processor.

We precise to the reader that, in [22], we erroneously inverted the figures and table entries for sparsely and centrally controlled implementations. This has been corrected in the current section.

In these implementations, we denoted each decoder's view with a SysML BD containing 11 SysML Composite Block Components: 1 for each operation in Fig. 2 as well as one Source and one Sink that respectively emit and collect samples. For each operation, we created separate Activities for managing the control information to/from the Controller and for the processing of input/output samples. This modeling strategy allows to target MPSoC platforms where the two Activities can be mapped to different processors. Thus, each Composite Block Component contains 2 SysML Primitive Block Components each containing a UML AD such as the diagrams in Figs. 3 and 4.

Evaluation. Table 1 lists statistics for the number of CFGs' visits for single Activities in both implementations. The numbers in Table 1 are expressed as a function of n_v that indicates the number of different values for the control variables that are dispatched by the Controller to ADs. The parameter n_v in Table 1 corresponds to k_p in Eq. 3.

In the centrally controlled implementation, applying Eq. 1 to the entries in Table 1 results in no gain for the blocking worklist. For a control Activity (Fig. 4), both CIBW and CINBW result in no unnecessary propagations because all variables are uninitialized and no information is propagated to the successors of the first ReceiveObjectAction. In data-processing Activities (Fig. 4), data-flow facts are propagated an equal number of times by both CIBW and CINBW as no inter-Activity dependency that modifies the value of control Variables in present.

In the sparsely controlled implementation, the Controller dispatches two different values for Variables `size` and `stop`, thus $n_v = 2$. The number of propagations of the CIBW algorithm for the Activities in Fig. 3 is the sum of the propagations for the nodes (excluding nodes for control statements) outside the loop and those inside the loop: $4 + 4n_v$ and $2 + 2n_v$, respectively. The number of unnecessary propagations for the CINBW algorithm is equal to 3 as node `Update_EvtIn2(size, stop)` can propagate the value of `size` to three successors, for a processing Activity (Fig. 3). It is equal to 1 for a control Activity as updates on the value of `size` can only be propagated to `Update_EvtOut(size, stop)` (Fig. 3). For both types of Activities, the number of unnecessary propagations does not depend on n_v because of the absence of further ReceiveObjectActions in the diagrams' loops, other than `Update_EvtIn()`, `Update_EvtIn2()`.

For individual control Activities, applying Eq. 1 for the case of the CIBW algorithm yields a gain equal to 14.3%. For individual data-processing Activities, the gain amounts to 20%.

Refined Expression of the CIBW Gain. Based on our experience, the structure of the diagrams in Figs. 3 and 4 is generic to other signal-processing applications. This allows us to fix a CFG topology and to further refine Eq. 1 in order to analytically express a generic gain, as in Eq. 5.

Table 1. Statistics for interval analysis on the two views of the 5G decoder - revised from [22].

Type of Activity diagram	Nb. of CFG nodes	Nb. of propagations CIBW $\mathcal{N}^{bw}$	Nb. of propagations CINBW $\mathcal{N}^{nbw}$
Sparsely controlled implementation			
Data processing	5	$5n_v$	$13n_v$
Control processing	3	$3n_v$	$3n_v$
Centrally controlled implementation			
Data processing	9	$4 + 4n_v$	$4 + 4n_v + 3$
Control processing	5	$2 + 2n_v$	$2 + 2n_v + 1$

$$g = 1 - \frac{n^{pred} + n^{loop} \times n^{it}}{n^{pred} + n^{loop} \times n^{it} + n^{succ}} \tag{5}$$

Here, n^{pred} is the number of predecessors of the ReceiveObjectAction, n^{succ} the number of its successors, n^{loop} denotes the number of nodes in the loop. The values for these parameters are fixed by the CFG's topology. The only parameter that can vary is n^{it}, the number of iterations. The latter is related to the number of times that novel information must be propagated to the nodes in the loop. The gain g as a function of n^{it} can be studied by means of the limits in Eqs. 6 and 7.

$$\lim_{n^{it} \to 0} 1 - \frac{n^{pred} + n^{loop} \times n^{it}{}^{0}}{n^{pred} + n^{loop} \times n^{it}{}^{0} + n^{succ}} = \frac{n^{succ}}{n^{pred} + n^{succ}} \tag{6}$$

$$\lim_{n^{it} \to +\infty} 1 - \frac{n^{pred}{}^{0} + n^{loop} \times n^{it}}{n^{pred}{}^{0} + n^{loop} \times n^{it} + n^{succ}{}^{0}} = 0 \tag{7}$$

In Eq. 6, the gain is dominated by the number of successor nodes n^{succ} that operate on the same data sets as those received by the ReceiveObjectAction. Because a single ReceiveObjectAction is present in the loop body, in Eqs. 5–7, the parameters n^{pred}, n^{succ} account for the number of propagations at the first iteration of the CIBW algorithm. Whereas, $n^{loop} \times n^{it}$ denotes the number of propagations at successive iterations. Therefore, in this case, the CIBW reduces the number of propagations during the first visitation only. For successive visitations, the blocking mechanism is no longer more beneficial.

Instead, Eq. 7 tells us that when nodes in the loop are frequently visited, the performance of the CIBW degenerate to that of the CINBW. This occurs when the Controller dispatches to ReceiveObjectActions a large number of different values for the control variables.

However, if we consider models with multiple ReceiveObjectActions in the loop body, the blocking worklist effectively reduces the number of propagations at all visitations. Here, the gain is expressed by Eq. 8, where $n^{succ}(r)$ is the number of successors of a ReceiveObjectAction r that operate on the same data set, D_r. $\sum_r n^{succ}(r)$ is the sum of a given ReceiveObjectAction r's successors, over all ReceiveObjectActions. r_1 is the first ReceiveObjectAction, $n^{pred}_{r_1}$ is the number of r_1's predecessors and $n^{succ}_{r_1}$ is the number of r_1's successors.

$$g = 1 - \frac{n^{pred}_{r_1} + n^{it} \times n^{loop}}{n^{pred}_{r_1} + n^{succ}_{r_1} + n^{it} \times (\ n^{loop} + \sum_r n^{succ}(r)\ )} \tag{8}$$

In this case, for a large number of visitations, g does not degenerate to zero, Eq. 9, as opposed to Eq. 7.

$$\lim_{n^{it} \to +\infty} g() = 1 - \frac{n^{loop}}{n^{loop} + \sum_r n^{succ}(r)} = \frac{\sum_r n^{succ}}{n^{loop} + \sum_r n^{succ}} \tag{9}$$

In Eq. 9, the term $\sum_r n^{succ}(r)$ is defined by the relative position of ReceiveObjectActions. It is always greater or equal than 1. This is the case of a a diagram where the loop's body has only 2 ReceiveObjectActions.

5.2   The Application of the CIBW Algorithm to Complete Applications

Given an application's supergraph G^*, the total gain is computed as the ratio of the number of propagations for all Activities (Eq. 1). This gain depends on the combination between the supergraph's topology and the topology of each task's CFG (see previous sub-section). We applied the CIBW and CINBW to a benchmark composed of 4 signal processing applications (including the 5G decoder described above) and 3 image-processing applications:

- The Welch Periodogram Detector (WPD), Fig. 6, is an energy detection algorithm used for sensing the spectrum and detecting when a given frequency band can be opportunistically used. Our model refers to the implementation described in [6].

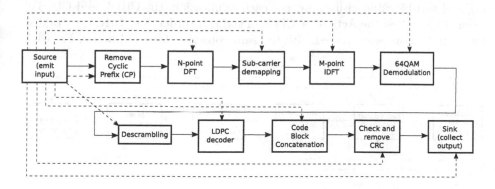

Fig. 5. The control-flow graph of application 5G decoder at task level of abstraction.

- The High Order Cumulants (HOC), Fig. 7, as implemented in [6], that is used in cognitive radio by a transmitter to sense the spectrum and detect if another user is currently transmitting in the same frequency range. The HOC algorithm operates on segments of an input stream that are processed to extract a score. The occupancy of a specific frequency range is determined by accumulating scores over a given classification period and by comparing the accumulated scores with a pre-computed threshold.
- RASTA-PLP (RelAtive SpecTrA - Perceptual Linear Prediction), Fig. 10 is an approach used in speech processing. It is applied to Perceptual Linear Prediction techniques to reduce the influences of a communication channel's frequency response.
- The Sobel filter, Fig. 9, is used in edge detection algorithms. It creates an approximation of the image's gradient by using intensity values in a region around each image's point in order to approximate the corresponding image's gradient.
- SUSAN (Smallest Univalue Segment Assimilating Nucleus), Fig. 8, is a noise-filtering algorithm that preserves an image's structure by smoothing over those neighbors which are part of a region centered around a given pixel. It works by taking an average over all of the pixels in the locality which lie in a region denoted as USAN (Univalue Segment Assimilating Nucleus).
- A JPEG encoder, Fig. 11, encodes an image in the JPEG (Joint Photographic Experts Group) format. JPEG is commonly used for lossy compression of digital images.

In Figs. 5, 6, 7, 8, 9, 10 and 11, control dependencies among tasks are represented by continuous edges for the sparsely-controlled implementation and by dotted edges for the centrally-controlled implementation. In sparsely-controlled implementations, control dependencies connect the same tasks as data-dependencies.

Table 2 reports on the results for interval analysis on our benchmark applications. Here, the number of propagations correspond to the number of times that new data-flow facts are propagated in the CFG. We counted these propagations by tracking how many times line 7 in Algorithm 4 is executed in both blocking and non-blocking visitations. For each application, the CIBW and CINBW algorithms visited the Activities' CFGs in the same order. Similarly, the worklist for each Activity was created with the same ordering for CFG nodes. For each

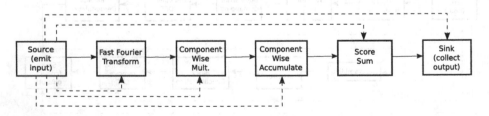

Fig. 6. The control-flow graph of application WPD at task level of abstraction.

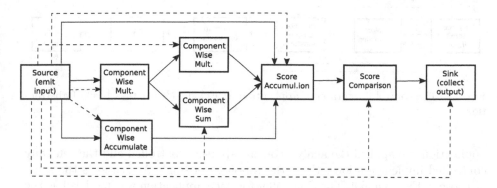

Fig. 7. The control-flow graph of application HOC at task level of abstraction.

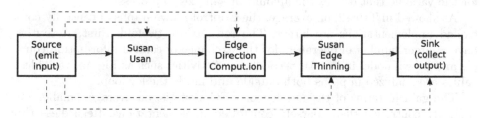

Fig. 8. The control-flow graph of application SUSAN at task level of abstraction.

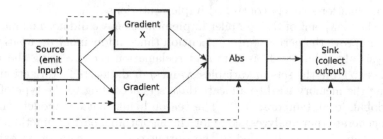

Fig. 9. The control-flow graph of application Sobel at task level of abstraction.

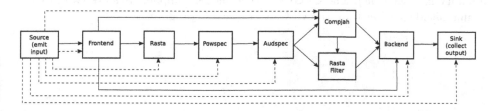

Fig. 10. The control-flow graph of application RASTA-PLP at task level of abstraction.

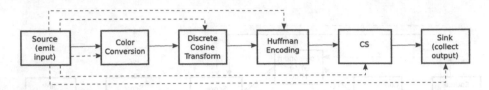

Fig. 11. The control-flow graph of application JPEG encoder at task level of abstraction.

application, we applied the analysis on the sparsely controlled and the centrally controlled implementations. Here, the topology of single Activities is the same as those in Figs. 3 and 4. The Controller for each application was modeled as the source Activity that emits the samples to process. For the sake of simplicity, we reported results for a scenario where the Controller communicates a single value for the variable that defines the amount of samples to process.

As showed in Table 2, on average, the Control-Flow Graphs of centrally controlled implementations are larger. The reasons are twofold. First, Activities have a larger number of operators for the exchange of control information (purple and brown nodes in Fig. 4). Secondly, in Activities such as Fig. 4b, variables' values are analyzed in paths both outside and inside the for-loop.

The gain in terms of the number of CFG visits is, on average, smaller for centrally controlled than sparsely controlled implementations. Regardless the type of implementation, as expected, the number of visits with the CINBW algorithm is larger. Due to the higher number of exchanges of control information in centrally controlled implementations' models, the CIBW algorithm needs more visitations than for sparsely controlled implementations.

From the viewpoint of the compiler implementation, we did not include techniques to improve the performance (execution time and memory occupation) of the analysis algorithm, such as data-sets reclamation (i.e., re-using the memory needed to store the sets of variables' values) or data-sets factorization (i.e., factorizing the memory used to allocate data sets according to the type of variables - global, local, temporary) [9]. The reason being that our model compiler does not generate (nor analyzes) code for the algorithmic part of functionalities. This algorithmic part is included in the output code by means of an external library of C functions (Fig. 1). The model compiler is, instead, involved in analysis and optimizing the control part of an input application (scheduling and memory management). The CFGs that the model compiler uses are two orders of magnitude smaller than the CFGs of typical C programs.

Table 2. Statistics for interval analysis on the CFGs of a set of benchmark applications.

Application	Nb. of CFG nodes in G^*	Nb. of propagations CIBW $\mathcal{N}^{bw}$	Nb. of propagations CINBW $\mathcal{N}^{nbw}$	Gain $1 - \mathcal{N}^{bw}/\mathcal{N}^{nbw}$
Sparsely controlled implementations				
5G Decoder	62	131	596	78%
WPD	38	71	185	62%
HOC	44	90	202	55%
JPEG encoder	48	99	464	78%
RASTA-PLP	58	146	846	83%
Sobel	40	79	315	75%
SUSAN	42	86	524	84%
Centrally controlled implementations				
5G Decoder	84	200	632	68%
WPD	42	105	204	49%
HOC	54	132	240	45%
JPEG encoder	56	140	475	71%
RASTA-PLP	67	203	616	67%
Sobel	40	101	382	74%
SUSAN	48	117	400	71%

6 Conclusions and Future Work

In this paper we presented a framework to perform static data-flow model analysis on functional views of signal-processing applications denoted by UML Activity and SysML Block diagrams. Our approach considers the functionality of both the computations and the communication protocols that can be expressed in ProtocolStateMachines associated to the Ports of SysML Blocks. We also proposed a visiting algorithm that combines well-known iterative and worklist searches with a blocking mechanism that considers the semantics of blocking communication primitives. We demonstrated that this mechanism can significantly reduce the number of unnecessary visits that would result from ignoring the blocking primitives.

We believe that many opportunities are present for future work, e.g., the analysis of communication protocols with more complex primitives than blocking/non-blocking read/write operations, the introduction of model-checking techniques to improve precision, as discussed in Sect. 4.4. In the next paragraph, we detail the opportunity that we consider to be the most relevant for the complete development of our optimizing model compiler.

As described in Sect. 2, among the existing solutions for the programming of MPSoC platforms, our approach is positioned in the category of model-based solutions. Currently, all these solutions use formal Models of Computation

(MoCs). We claimed that the richer execution semantics of UML/SysML is advantageous because it allows a compiler to perform more aggressive optimizations based on the specifications for the internal behavior of tasks. These behaviors are absent in MoC-based formalism where tasks are seen as blackboxes. While more limited in expressiveness, MoC-based formalism have proven to be suited to capture system-level characteristics such as scheduling or memory consumption of an application as a whole. For this reason, we believe that SDF and KPN could be used more effectively as compiler's intermediate representations rather than input formalisms for the front-end. In this scenario, where UML/SysML are the input languages and SDF/KPN are the intermediate representations, semantics analysis is also necessary. It would ensure that a programmer correctly describes, with UML/SysML diagrams, an application that also matches the semantics of the intermediate representations that are internally used by the compiler to make system-level optimizations.

References

1. Khronos OpenCL: the open standard for parallel programming of heterogeneous systems. https://www.khronos.org/opencl
2. MathWorks Simulink. https://www.mathworks.com/products/simulink
3. Message Passing Interface (MPI). https://www.mpi-forum.org/
4. nVidia CUDA: General-purpose parallel computing architecture. https://www.nvidia.com/cuda
5. OpenMP: API specification for parallel programming. https://www.openmp.org/
6. Spectrum and Energy efficiency through multi-band Cognitive Radio: D6.3. Report on the implementation of selected algorithms. https://cordis.europa.eu/project/rcn/93076/reporting/fr
7. The Go programming language. https://golang.org/
8. Apvrille, L., Muhammad, W., Ameur-Boulifa, R., Coudert, S., Pacalet, R.: A UML-based environment for system design space exploration. In: ICECS, pp. 1272–1275 (2006)
9. Atkinson, D.C., Griswold, W.G.: Implementation techniques for efficient data-flow analysis of large programs. In: ICSM, pp. 52–61 (2001)
10. Baldomero, J.: Message passing under MATLAB. In: HPC, pp. 73–82 (2001)
11. Beyer, D., Gulwani, S., Schmidt, D.A.: Combining model checking and data-flow analysis. In: Clarke, E., Henzinger, T., Veith, H., Bloem, R. (eds.) Handbook of Model Checking, pp. 493–540. Springer, Cham (2018). https://doi.org/10.1007/978-3-319-10575-8_16
12. Bodden, E., Pun, V.K.I., Steffen, M., Stolz, V., Wickert, A.: Information flow analysis for go. In: ISOLA, pp. 431–445 (2016)
13. Briand, L.C., Labiche, Y., Lin, Q.: Improving statechart testing criteria using data flow information. In: ISSRE, pp. 104–114 (2005)
14. Charfi, A., Mraidha, C., Boulet, P.: An optimized compilation of UML state machines. In: ISORC, pp. 172–179 (2012)
15. Charfi, A., Mraidha, C., Gérard, S., Terrier, F., Boulet, P.: Toward optimized code generation through model-based optimization. In: DATE, pp. 1313–1316 (2010)
16. Checko, A., et al.: Cloud RAN for mobile networks - a technology overview. IEEE Commun. Surv. Tutor. **17**(1), 405–426 (2015)

17. Desnos, K., Pelcat, M., Nezan, J.F., Aridhi, S.: Distributed memory allocation technique for synchronous dataflow graphs. In: SiPS 2016 (2016)
18. Donovan, A., Kernighan, B.: The Go Programming Language. Addison-Wesley, Boston (2015)
19. Eclipse CDT. http://www.eclipse.org/cdt/
20. EE Times: Embedded Software Stuck at C. Technical report, November 2007
21. Enrici, A., Apvrille, L., Pacalet, R.: A UML model-driven approach to efficiently allocate complex communication schemes. In: Dingel, J., Schulte, W., Ramos, I., Abrahão, S., Insfran, E. (eds.) MODELS 2014. LNCS, vol. 8767, pp. 370–385. Springer, Cham (2014). https://doi.org/10.1007/978-3-319-11653-2_23
22. Enrici, A., Apvrille, L., Pacalet, R.: Efficient data-flow analysis of UML/SysML diagrams for optimized model compilation of hardware-software systems. In: MODELSWARD, pp. 86–97 (2019)
23. Garousi, V., Briand, L.C., Labiche, Y.: Control flow analysis of UML 2.0 sequence diagrams. In: Hartman, A., Kreische, D. (eds.) ECMDA-FA 2005. LNCS, vol. 3748, pp. 160–174. Springer, Heidelberg (2005). https://doi.org/10.1007/11581741_13
24. Hoare, C.: Communicating sequential processes. Communun. ACM **21**(8), 666–677 (1978)
25. Jhala, R., Majumdar, R.: Interprocedural analysis of asynchronous programs. In: POPL, pp. 339–350 (2007)
26. Jones, G., Goldsmith, M.: Programming in Occam2. Prentice-Hall International, Upper Saddle River (1988)
27. Kahn, G.: The semantics of a simple language for parallel programming. In: IFIP Congress, pp. 471–475 (1974)
28. Kepner, J.: MatlabMPI. J. Parallel Distrib. Comput. **64**(8), 997–1005 (2004)
29. Kim, Y.G., Hong, H.S., Bae, D.H., Cha, S.D.: Test cases generation from UML state diagrams. IEE Proc.-Softw. **146**(4), 187–192 (1999)
30. Kwon, S., Kim, Y., Jeun, W., Ha, S., Paek, Y.: A retargetable parallel programming framework for MPSoC. TODAES **13**(39), 39:1–39:18 (2008)
31. Lee, E.A., Parks, T.M.: Dataflow process network. Proc. IEEE **83**(5), 1235–1245 (1995)
32. Leupers, R., Aguilar, M.A., Eusse, J.F., Castrillon, J., Sheng, W.: MAPS: a software development environment for embedded multicore applications. In: Ha, S., Teich, J. (eds.) Handbook of Hardware/Software Codesign, pp. 917–949. Springer, Dordrecht (2017). https://doi.org/10.1007/978-94-017-7267-9_2
33. Mellor, S.J., Balcer, M.: Executable UML: A Foundation for Model-Driven Architectures. Addison-Wesley Longman Publishing Co., Inc., Boston (2002)
34. Nielson, F., Nielson, H.R., Hankin, C.: Principles of Program Analysis. Springer, Heidelberg (2010)
35. Park, H., Oh, H., Ha, S.: Multiprocessor SoC design methods and tools. IEEE Sig. Process. Mag. **26**(6), 72–79 (2009)
36. Reps, T., Horwitz, S., Sagiv, M.: Precise interprocedural dataflow analysis via graph reachability. In: POPL, pp. 49–61 (1995)
37. Saad, C., Bauer, B.: Data-flow based model analysis and its applications. In: Moreira, A., Schätz, B., Gray, J., Vallecillo, A., Clarke, P. (eds.) MODELS 2013. LNCS, vol. 8107, pp. 707–723. Springer, Heidelberg (2013). https://doi.org/10.1007/978-3-642-41533-3_43
38. Schmidt, D.C.: Model-driven engineering. IEEE Comput. **39**(2), 25–31 (2006)
39. Selic, B.: The pragmatics of model-driven development. IEEE Softw. **20**(5), 19–25 (2003)

40. Torczon, L., Cooper, K.: Engineering a Compiler, 2nd edn. Morgan Kaufmann Publishers Inc., San Francisco (2007)
41. TTool (2006). http://ttool.telecom-paristech.fr
42. TTool/DIPLODOCUS (2006). http://ttool.telecom-paristech.fr/diplodocus.html
43. VERIMAG: IF: Intermediate Format and Verification Tool set (2018). http://www-verimag.imag.fr/article58.html?lang=en
44. Waheed, T., Iqbal, M.Z.Z., Malik, Z.I.: Data flow analysis of UML action semantics for executable models. In: Schieferdecker, I., Hartman, A. (eds.) ECMDA-FA 2008. LNCS, vol. 5095, pp. 79–93. Springer, Heidelberg (2008). https://doi.org/10.1007/978-3-540-69100-6_6

Umple-TL: A Model-Oriented, Dependency-Free Text Emission Tool

Mahmoud Husseini Orabi[(⊠)] [iD], Ahmed Husseini Orabi[(⊠)] [iD],
and Timothy C. Lethbridge[(⊠)] [iD]

School of Electrical Engineering and Computer Science,
University of Ottawa, 800 King Edward Avenue, Ottawa, Canada
{mhuss092, ahuss045, timothy.lethbridge}@uottawa.ca

Abstract. We describe the text-emission templating capabilities of Umple (Umple-TL) and compare this Umple feature to other technologies for text generation. Umple, which is written in itself, combines modeling synergistically with programming in languages like Java and C++. Umple-TL further builds on these synergies. With the use of Umple-TL, we eliminated dependencies on third-party libraries for text emission. We demonstrate how Umple-TL attains benefits such as smaller and faster executables, target-language independence and IDE independence. We compare Umple-TL and other text emission tools in order to show how Umple-TL can overcome many of the challenges a tool can face. The word 'template' in this paper refers to patterns for the generation of output, and not to generic types, another common use of the term.

Keywords: Umple · Umple-TL · Templates · Text emission

1 Introduction

Umple is a textual model-oriented programming language that supports code generation for different target languages such as Java, C++, PHP, and Ruby [1]. The master code is written in Umple syntax, which insulates the developer from ever having to see generated code. Users can also inject additional target-language code directly into the textual model.

A key objective of Umple is to make software development simpler by adding modelling and other constructs to base languages. This also includes the core features of UML such as state machines, composite structure, and associations [1, 2].

In this paper, we show how we extended Umple with a text-generation-templating sub-language we call Umple-TL. The word 'template' here refers to patterns of text to output, not to generic types, which is another use of the term 'template' in programming languages. In this paper, we explain Umple-TL in detail and compare it to other text-generation technologies.

Languages such as PHP were designed with generation of textual output as their motivating use case. But languages such as Java do not come with built-in template mechanisms and rely on verbose method calls to generate text.

There are a wide variety of contexts where generating formatted textual content is an essential requirement: These include generation of data formats such as XML and

© Springer Nature Switzerland AG 2020
S. Hammoudi et al. (Eds.): MODELSWARD 2019, CCIS 1161, pp. 127–155, 2020.
https://doi.org/10.1007/978-3-030-37873-8_6

html, generation of modelling and programming language code (in metaprogramming and code generation), generation of messages for inter-process communication, and generation of user interfaces.

Templates are just one of many abstractions that have been added to Umple as a necessary step to achieve Umple's overall goals. Our intent is to obtain synergies by combining templates with modelling in an easy-to-use language.

A distinguishing feature of Umple-TL is that it supports template development for *multiple target languages*, allowing reuse of templates across such languages.

In Sects. 4 and 5, we explain how Umple as a template language (Umple-TL) is used. The examples shown in this paper can be instantly run in the UmpleOnline online editor (try.umple.org), the Umple Eclipse plugin or the Umple command line compiler.

This paper is a significant extension of the our previous MODELSWARD conference paper [3] providing much greater detail, additional case studies, and more evaluation. Specifically, in Sect. 3, we discuss common challenges that the developers of text emission tool can face. In Sects. 4 through 6 we show more examples of using Umple-TL. In Sect. 8, we discuss how Umple overcomes the challenges presented in Sect. 3, and we also show a comparison between Umple-TL and other common text emission tools.

2 Other Text Emission Tools

There are many text emission tools available to developers. These include Java Emitter Templates (JET), Apache Velocity, Acceleo, Epsilon Generation Language (EGL), Xpand, and Xtend. Later in the paper we compare Umple-TL to these tools. Here we provide an overview of the capabilities of the tools.

JET, now deprecated, was one of the most commonly-used Eclipse-based textual generation tools due to its ease of use and straightforwardness. A developer needed to create a Java project containing the JET nature. JET has a JSP-like syntax, in which a skeleton template was used to customize text emission. JET did not provide a direct way to define rules that relate different JET files. It reduced the complexity of text emission by using a single parameter-less emitter method. However, this forced additional configuration, Eclipse dependencies, and code development restrictions.

Velocity template engine (VTL) is an Apache Velocity project [4] that aims to provide generation units based on a model-view-controller (MVC) pattern. It depends on third-party runtime libraries to generate the outputs of the VM files. As a result, a Velocity configuration as well as the VM files must be a part of the product release.

Acceleo (or MTL) is an Eclipse project that enables UML modelling with code generation support. It follows the Object Management Group (OMG) specifications for the model to text language (MTL) standard. Acceleo requires additional Eclipse libraries such as EMF and Ecore, and it requires experience with these to use it. A model can have a hierarchical representation in order to define and associate the generation units, as well as the parameters and items required to generate the content of template files; i.e. Model Template (MT).

Similarly, Xtend is an Eclipse-based project. It was initially released as a part of the Xtext project [5] but then became a standalone Eclipse project. Xtend is intended to replace Xpand. Xtend tries to improve the Java programming language by introducing additional capabilities and major features such as functional programming, text emission, operator overloading, and dynamic typing. Such features are influenced by many languages and projects such as Scala and Xpand. Similarly to Velocity, Xtend is restricted to Java applications only and requires a runtime library.

Epsilon generation language (EGL) is an Eclipse project that provides several code generation options such as text emission. A model is used to manage the content of a generation process similarly to Acceleo. However, Epsilon has an advantage over Acceleo in that it does not have specific restrictions on certain model types. The Epsilon model connectivity (EMC) layer is used to enforce a model-driven paradigm by associating metamodels of several types such as EMF or XML. Epsilon script provides features such as expression statements, polymorphism and annotations. However, such capabilities are dependent on a runtime library, similarly to Velocity and Xtend.

3 Challenges

Designing a text emission tool gives rise to various challenges. Some of the most important are listed in this section, based on what we faced during the development of Umple-TL. These can be seen as requirements for an ideal text emission tool.

3.1 Challenges Relating to the Source Language

The first group of challenges is requirements for the source language that the developer uses to describe the sort of output to be emitted (Box 1 in Fig. 1).

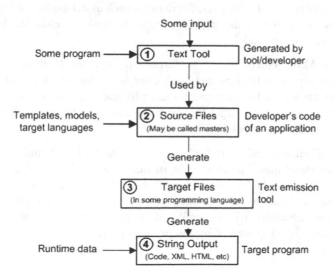

Fig. 1. The process of text emission [3].

Constraints and Emission Flow. A text emission tool must provide a way to help a developer specify constraints and other forms of execution control in their source files; these will determine how or when target strings will be generated. For example, in C++, the keyword "friend" is reserved; a tool should give a way for developers to set constraints to prevent having this keyword appear improperly in the generated target C++ files. Later in the chapter when discussing this requirement, we will show that Umple-TL has an ability to specify arbitrary control constructs that can serve as constraints; Umple also has a built-in OCL-like constraint mechanism that injects preconditions and postconditions into any method. Together these can be used to ensure detect issues that may result in malformed target files or runtime string output'.

Transformation Rules. A tool should ideally support rule-based transformation across different schemas. Based on rules specified in the source language, it should be possible to alter the string outputs without the need for a lot of rework to the source. For example, it should be easy in the source to direct the target to switch between generating XML and Json output.

3.2   Challenges Relating to Both Source and Target

The second group of challenges relate to both the source and target language.

Representation Consistency. The source and generated target files must have a consistent hierarchical representation.

Target Code Efficiency. A generated target file is expected to be efficient, i.e. it must avoid issues such as unnecessary loops or redundant string manipulations.

Target Code Readability. The generated target code must be properly represented using appropriate spacing, indentation, variable naming and so on. Altering the generated output is something that must be avoided for the same reasons programmers do not modify compiler output. However, for reasons such as debugging and certification, it may be necessary to read the target code, so it must be readable. Also, not all generated output will be 'code'.

File Structure Management. At both source and target levels, there may be many files of different types; the file structure used, even in the same tool, can differ between the source and target files. For example, a source file can have an extension tailored for a text emission tool, while the target file can have another extension such as Java class or even two extensions as would be the case in C++.

Reusability. When required, a source or generated target file should be reusable by other source or target files. The challenges in that case are mostly related to how the generated target files can be linked together. For example, while a user is developing a source file and they want to reuse another source file, they should not need to think about how this reusability will be enforced at the level of the target files. Such enforcement must be taken care of by the text emission tool.

Pattern Support. There is a gap between the source and target files. The main challenge is related to how to enforce the same level of abstraction or transfer patterns between the levels. For example, a user while developing source files can follow patterns such as facade or builder; the target files must follow the same pattern.

Comment Support. A tool must provide a way to add comments to the source file, and have them transferred to the target file. In particular, the tool might need to generate comments in the target file to allow traceability back to the source file. Comments in the source files are valuable for maintainability, reusability and all other well-known reasons for commenting source. Comments in the target files are helpful for debugging or investigation purposes.

Debugging Support. Debugging ought to be facilitated at the level of source files. When issues occur in generation of target files or runtime generation, the developer ought to be provided with information pointing back to the relevant points in the source. The best approach is to allow full debugging or tracing at the source level, so the developer never has to see the target files. But if this is not fully supported, then when running a debugger on the target files, the developer should be easily pointed back to the source files.

Additional Flexibility Aspects. Sophisticated tools provide several options that help users to handle the content to be emitted; examples include allowing multiple text emission methods and unlimited size of target code and runtime strings. Reusability, which we referred to above, is one aspect of flexibility. Flexibility can also be increased if a tool can incorporate target language expressions; this will be explained later in this section. Some tools may put many restrictions on how text content is emitted. Other tools may have limited solutions, such as the number of emitting methods; this causes the development time to be increased in order to cope with such limitations.

3.3 Challenges Relating to Text Generation

The third group of challenges relates to the string output generated by the target code (i.e. the text generated by the generated generator).

Consistency of Text Formatting. Generation output must be consistent. In this context, we are referring to consistent output regardless of the inputs or applied constraints used. For example, whitespace such as for indentation at the start of lines ought to appear consistently across all output (something not available in many tools). A text emission tool hence ought to provide a way for a user to define whitespace formatting.

Content Protection. This refers to preventing end users of the generated systems (Box 4 in Fig. 1), from accessing the content of text to be emitted. Failing to protect emitable text content can pose major security or privacy issues.

3.4   Modelling Support in Text Generation Technology

The fourth group of challenges relates to modelling support.

Modelling Support. Use of abstract models to represent the source and target languages as well as data in the runtime system can facilitate text emission. Basing emission on models is one of the code generation approaches on which we focus.

Input Model Restrictions. A model-based tool usually enforces certain types of models, metamodels, or schemas. This will require tool users to work with the model types that this tool supports. For example, several tools require the use of the Eclipse Modelling Framework (EMF). In addition, obviously, any limitations that may exist in the supported models will also appear in the text emission tool. Some tools such as Epsilon Generation Language (EGL), can overcome such issues by allowing users to select different types of models [6].

3.5   Additional Challenges

Additional challenges can appear based on the tool used; this is what the fifth group focuses on.

Workflow Complexity. Many tools give a large number of options to the developers to handle code generation but unfortunately, this may cause workflow complexity to be increased. For instance, a user may be required to use different editors and wizards, switch back and forth among different types of files, and propagate updates across different places.

IDE Dependencies. This is a part of the workflow complexity mentioned above. Some tools require developers to use a specific IDE. This poses problems in several contexts: the user may happen to have selected a different IDE, or needs to run the tool outside an IDE (e.g. in a scripting language), Or the user may want to use the tool in a very simple manner, but would be forced to set up the tool in the IDE to get any work done. Many tools only run in Eclipse; an ideal tool should easily run both inside and outside Eclipse.

Third-Party Library Independence. This means that a tool only requires integration in the development environment. The tool should not have to be integrated into a released product (Box 4 in Fig. 1). For example when using Velocity [4] the Velocity Engine has to be incorporated into the built final product, which can result in problems as Velocity changes over time, and also results in increased system size.

Target Language Restrictions. A tool may require developers to be familiar with specific languages such as Java. This can be considered a part of workflow complexity, since users will need to learn how to use the language imposed by a tool. An ideal tool would be able to work with several different programming languages.

Structural Complexity. This is also a part of workflow complexity. The structural complexity of some sophisticated tools can be high due to requiring users to deal with several types of files; this can be the case even for very simple text output. For instance, a developer may be required first to write a metamodel file. Second, the developer may need to write a model. Third, they might need to write a template file that uses the model in order to specify text content to be emitted. Finally, the developer may need to write configuration and launch files in order to produce results.

Syntax Complexity. Typically, a tool has its own script or language. The syntax complexity of a script or language of a tool obviously causes the complexity of a tool to be increased in general. Syntax complexity may increase as well when users are asked to be familiar with specific metamodels or schemas.

Target Language Expressions. The script or language of tool is not necessarily expected to be as sophisticated as commonly used target programming languages such as Java and C++; otherwise, this will appear as reinventing the wheel. At least the basic features of a target language must be supported such as variable declaration. While using a tool to emit text content, a user may need to use target language expressions in order to handle the content dynamically. However, relying on a tool's language or script to handle expressions may have limitations. For instance, a tool may support "for" loops but not "while" loops. As a solution, it could be a good idea if a tool allows users to write expressions using target language sntax. For instance, if a target language is Java, then a user should be able to write expressions in Java. However, users will still need to use the language provided by the tool.

4 Main Concepts of Umple-TL

Umple-TL provides synergies because it blends UML constructs and templates constructs (Fig. 2). Umple-TL's text emission API is language independent and supports multi-target blocks, i.e. blocks that can contain C++ and Java simultaneously.

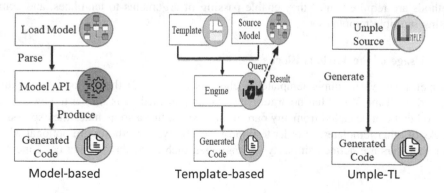

Fig. 2. Types of text emission.

The core elements of Umple-TL are as below:

Umple Source Text: This is the master code of the system under development. It includes templates, model constructs, and methods written in the syntax of the selected target language; i.e. C++, Java, and so on. Umple-TL is used to generate text from templates, which are defined as a part of the source model (text). The Umple compiler processes the source text to produce the entities below.

Compiled (Generated) Code: This is generated by the Umple compiler in a target language. It is intended to be ignored by the programmer and should be treated like bytecode or object code from a compiler. This is executed to produce the following.

Runtime Output Text: This is emitted when the compiled code is executed. It could be any type of text, including error messages, html, and so on. If the Umple source text describes a compiler, then the runtime output would be code itself. This is the case with Umple, which compiles *itself*. A key motivation for Umple-TL to make it easier for Umple to develop its own code generators [7].

The two key elements in Umple-TL source text are *templates* themselves and *emitter methods*.

- Templates: These describe the runtime output text to be generated. A template is a specialized Umple attribute with a unique label and a body defined within a block delimited by ≪! and !≫. Table 1 describes the blocks that can be nested inside the outer delimiters.
- Emitter methods: These are invoked to create outputs based on one or more templates. The keyword 'emit' is used to indicate these (Snippet 1 – Line 3).

An Umple-TL template is an attribute meaning that it follows the same restrictions an attribute has. For instance, a name cannot start with a number, nor have the same name as any other attribute or template.

In a similar manner, an emitter method is a specialized Umple method, meaning that it must follow the naming conventions imposed on normal Umple methods. Arguments to the emitter method are referred to in expression and code blocks.

A template class must at least have one emitter method or template. Emitter methods are required since they enable passing of arguments to templates, and composing multiple templates

4.1   Usage of the Various Blocks

Snippet 1 shows a simple template labelled as t1 (Line 2) that is used by emitter method, e1 (Line 3) that has no arguments. An emitter method is similar to any regular method that can be called from any part of the system; this also includes the expression blocks of other templates. In order to improve usability, parentheses are optional when no parameters are defined similarly to languages such as Scala (Snippet 6 – Line 4).

```
1   class TemplateTest1{                                          Umple
2        t1 <<! My Template !>>
3        emit e1()(t1);
4   }
```

Snippet 1. A simple Umple-TL example.

(Line 2 - Snippet 2) demonstrates the use of a code block delineated by ≪# and #≫. The code in the block can be in any target language that Umple supports; i.e. Java and C++. We use Java in the examples in this paper use Java. An Umple developer must write valid code according to the target language's syntax.

```
1   class TemplateTest2{                                          Umple
2        t2a <<!<<#if(b)#>>This will be output if b is true !>>
3        t2b <<! ... and this will always be output !>>
4        emit e2(Boolean b)(t2a, t2b);
5   }
```

Snippet 2. Umple-TL example illustrating a code block and multiple templates.

Table 1. A summary of the syntax for the blocks used to write templates in Umple-TL.

Block type	Description
≪! {b} !≫	**Top Level:** Defines the start and end of a template body. The {b} represents arbitrary text to output, with any of the following nested within
≪={e} ≫	**Expression:** Computes strings to be inserted into the text. The {e} represents any expression in the target language that returns a string, such as a variable or method invocation
≪# {c} #≫	**Code:** Code in the target language to define logical conditions (e.g. to make output of parts of the template optional) and loops. The content of code blocks is not appended to the runtime output text, but instead appears in the compiled code
≪/* */≫	**Comment:** Material not added to the runtime output, but which does appear in the compiled code. Comments could also be placed in code blocks, but using comment blocks requires less nesting
≪$ ≫	**Exact space:** Specifies whitespace that will appear at the beginning of every line in the runtime output text

(Lines 4 - Snippet 2) also shows an emitter method e2() that has an argument, b, referred to in template t2a (Line 2). The emitter method also demonstrates emission of two templates.

There are two variables string1 (Line 2) and string2 (Line 3) in Snippet 3. Umple creates a getter method for any public attribute; i.e. getString1() and getString2 (Lines 5 and 6). Snippet 2 has two expression blocks. The first uses the getString1(), and the second directly appends the value of string2.

```
1   class TemplateTest3{                                              Umple
2       String string1;
3       String string2;
4
5       t3<<! String1=<<=getString1()>>; String2=    <<=string2>>!>>
6       emit generate1()(t3);
7   }
```

Snippet 3. Using assign statements in Umple-TL.

A developer can use a combination of expression and code blocks. Snippet 4 has an expression block where a for loop is used to emit parts of the content of the template block. The number of times is indicated by the argument *iterations*. Snippet 4 also has a comment block (Line 3).

```
1   class TemplateTest4{                                              Umple
2       t4 <<!
3       <</* Use iterations to control output*/>>
4       <<# for(int index=0;
5           index<iterations; index++){#>>
6           Iteration <<=index>>;<<#
7           }#>>!>>
8       emit generate1(int iterations)(t4);
9   }
```

Snippet 4. An Umple-TL example using expression and code blocks.

By default, whitespace in a template is preserved in the runtime output. However, a user may need to generate different indentation, such whitespace at the start of lines, in different contexts. It can also be used to make the emitted code readable.

To control the indentation in runtime output, the developer can write an exact space block. This will fix the indentation of its contents no matter how that output is generated (e.g. from an expression, variable, or plain text).

Snippet 5 has two templates, internalTemplate and t5. t5 internally invokes generated emitter method internalGenerate() using exact space markers (Line 2). There are four whitespaces after the ≪$, which means that they will appear in all lines of the runtime output. Alternatively, a developer can pass he number of indentations when calling the method generate().

```
1   class TemplateTest5{                                              Umple
2      t5 <<!<<$   internalGenerate()>>,!>>
3      internalTemplate<<!Some content!>>
4
5      emit generate()(t5);
6      private emit internalGenerate()(internalTemplate);
7   }
```

Snippet 5. An example of exact space handling.

4.2 Emitter Methods

An emitter method's name can be followed by two sets of parentheses. In such a case, the first is used to list the arguments, and the second is used to list the templates to emit.

A developer needs to list the templates to be used for text emission in an emitter method (Snippet 6). A generated emitter method will output the content of all of the referenced templates according to their defined order.

If there is just one set of parentheses, then it refers to the list of templates with the assumption that the method has no arguments.

The visibility of an emitter method is public by default (Snippet 6 – Line 4). Thus, adding the public keyword to an emitter method will not make a difference in visibility (Line 3).

```
1   class TemplateTest{                                               Umple
2      t6 <<! My Template !>>
3      public static emit generate1()(t6);
4      emit generate2(t6);
5   }
```

Snippet 6. Emitter method examples.

Snippet 7 shows an example of an emitter method that outputs three templates.

(Snippet 8 - Line 9) shows a private emitter method internalGenerate(), which means that it can only be called internally (Line 3).

```
1   class TemplateTest{                                               Umple
2      t7a <<!Content1!>>
3      t7b <<!Content2!>>
4      t7d <<!Content3!>>
5
6      emit generate1()(t7a, t7b, t7c);
7   }
```

Snippet 7. Multiple references to templates in an emitter method

```
1   class TemplateTest{                                              Umple
2     internalTemplate<<! Some content !>>
3     t8<<!<<=internalGenerate()>>!>>
4
5     emit generate()(t8);
6     private emit internalGenerate()(internalTemplate);
7   }
```

Snippet 8. An internal invocation of an emitter method

The basic distinction between an emitter method and template, is that an emitter method is used to utilize a template or a group of templates, and to define other features such as formatting. In order to improve usability in the future, we need to generate a default emitter method for each template, so users can directly define templates without needing to define emitter methods if there is no special logic behind using these templates.

5   UML Constructs and Generation Templates

Umple-TL can use the UML modelling, separation-of-concerns and template features of Umple in a synergistic way. Umple UML modelling constructs include associations, state machine, and composite structure. Separation of concerns features include mixins, traits and aspects [8]. This synergy is one of the key contributions of our work. In this section, we will focus on using templates with state machines.

Snippet 9 shows an Umple model that displays course information based on the number of the registered students. Each student has a name and id, while a course has a name and description. There is an association between a course and students (Line 4), so that a course can have zero or more students and a student may or may not be in a course.

A course has four statuses, Opened (Line 25), Registered (Line 38), Withdrawn (Line 45), and Closed (Line 46). The template information changes based on the status. If a course status is Opened, all information including fees will be displayed; otherwise, it will not. The description and number of students are displayed regardless of the course status. If a course is in the Registered status, information such as last day to withdraw is shown.

Figure 3 shows the state machine defined in Snippet 9. The logic of the state machine is given textually in Lines 24–48.

```
1    class Course {                                                          Umple
2       String name;
3       String description;
4       0..1 -- * Student student;
5       cr <<!
6       !>>
7       courseInfo <<!
8       Course: <<=getName()>>
9       Description: <<=getDescription()>>
10      Number of registered students: <<=numberOfStudent()>>
11      <<# switch(getStatus()) {#>><<# case Opened:#>>
12      <<# switch(getStatusOpened()) {#>><<# case
13   WithoutLateRegistrationFees:#>>
14      Last day to register without late fees <<=d1>>
15      <<# case WithLateRegistrationFees :#>>
16      Last day to register with late fees <<=d2>>
17      <<# } #>>
18      <<# case Registered:#>>
19      Last day to withdraw from a course <<=d2>>
20      <<# } #>>
21      !>>
22
23      status{
24         Opened {
25            register -> Registered;
26            close -> Closed;
27            WithoutLateRegistrationFees {
28               register -> Registered;
29              deadLinePassed -> WithLateRegistrationFees;
30            }
31            WithLateRegistrationFees {
32               register -> Registered;
33               deadLinePassed -> Closed;
34            }
35         }
36
37         Registered {
38            requestToWithdrow -> Withdrawn;
39            LastDayToWithdraw {
40               requestToWithdrow -> Withdrawn;
41               deadLinePassed -> Closed;
42            }
43         }
44         Withdrawn { }
45         Closed {
46            open -> Opened;
47         }
48      }
49
50      emit printCourseInfo(String d1, String d2,
51         String, d3 )(courseInfo, cr);
52   }
53
54   class Student{
55      String name;
56      Integer id;
57   }
```

Snippet 9. An example of using UML constructs to develop templates.

```java
1    Student student1 = new Student("Name1", 1234);
2    Student student2 = new Student("Name2", 432);
3    String d1="JA 1"; String d2="FE 1"; String d3="AP 1";
4
5    Course course = new Course("Course1", "This is a course");
6    course.addStudent(student1);
7    course.addStudent(student2);
8
9    System.out.println(course.printCourseInfo(d1,d2,d3));
10   //Course: Course1
11   //Description: This is a course
12   //Number of registered students: 2
13   //Last day to register without late registration fees JA 1
14   //Last day to register with late registration fees FE 1
15   //Last day to withdraw from a course AP 1
16
17   course.close();
18   System.out.println(course.printCourseInfo(d1,d2,d3));
19   //Course: Course1
20   //Description: This is a course
21   //Number of registered students: 2
22
23   course.open();
24   System.out.println(course.printCourseInfo(d1,d2,d3));
25   //Course: Course1
26   //Description: This is a course
27   //Number of registered students: 2
28   //Last day to register without late registration fees JA 1
29   //Last day to register with late registration fees FE 1
30   //Last day to withdraw from a course AP 1
31
32   course.register();
33   System.out.println(course.printCourseInfo(d1,d2,d3));
34   //Course: Course1
35   //Description: This is a course
36   //Number of registered students: 2
37   //Last day to withdraw from a course AP 1
```

Snippet 10. An invocation example of Snippet 9.

Snippet 10 shows output of the generated code of Snippet 9 in green as lines of comments. In Snippet 10, there are two students; both are added to a course. A course status is Opened by default. The first information printed is full course information, given that the course status is Opened. The output is shown in Lines 10–15.

In Line 17, the status of the course switches to Closed. The output in that case (Lines 19–21) only shows the basic information about the course, as well as its registered students.

The status switches back to Opened (Snippet 10 - Line 23). The output is in Lines 25–30, which is identical to the Lines 10–14.

Finally, the status changes to Registered (In Line 31), which is similar to the Closed state, but additionally shows the last day to withdraw (Lines 34–37).

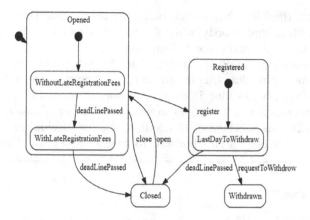

Fig. 3. The state machine diagram of Snippet 9—generated automatically by Umple [3].

5.1 Declarative Examples

In this section, we show three Umple-TL examples for HTML page generation. The first example (Snippet 11) is more specific, and hence requires a few lines to execute (Snippet 12). The second example (Snippet 13) is more generic, so it can support dynamic table generation, but will require more lines of code to define custom tables (Snippet 14). The last example (Snippet 15) shows the user of traits and aspect-orientation in Umple.

```
1    class HtmlTemplate {                                              Umple
2      htmlTemplate <<!
3        <html>
4          <body>
5            <table>
6              <<# for  (String name: names) {#>>
7                <tr>
8                  <td>
9                    <<=name>>
10                 </td>
11               </tr>
12             <<#}#>>
13           </table>
14         </body>
15       </html>
16     !>>
17
18     emit printHTML(List<String> names)(htmlTemplate);
19   }
```

Snippet 11. HTML template generation (1).

```
1    System.out.println(new HtmlTemplate().printHTML(Arrays.asList(new      Java
2    String[]{"Row1", "Row2", "Row3"})));
3
```

Snippet 12. An invocation example of Snippet 11.

In Snippet 13, HtmlNode has two attributes, tag and content. The tag attribute is a valid html tag such as html or body, while the content is optional with an empty value by default; it refers to the text content of an html node.

There is an association attribute, children (Line 5). Associations are one of the key features that Umple provides. Umple provides all different types and variations of associations. In (Snippet 13 - Line 5), the type of association used is optional unbound self-reflexive; this means that it refers to an unlimited number of children of the same class, HtmlNode (or its subclasses). In addition, this list of children can be empty, which means that it is fine for an HtmlNode to have an empty list of children.

```
1    class HtmlNode{                                                      Umple
2        String tag;
3        String content= "";
4
5        0..1--* HtmlNode children;
6
7        nested <<!<<#for(HtmlNode node: children) {
8            #>><<=node.generate()>><<#
9        }#>>!>>
10
11       print <<!<<<=tag>>>
12       <<=content>><<<=nestedPrint()>>
13       </<<=tag>>>!>>
14
15       emit generate()(print);
16       private emit nestedPrint()(nested);
17   }
```

Snippet 13. HTML template generation (2).

There are two emitter methods for two templates, print and nested. The print template is the main template that is used to print out the content of an HtmlNode instance. The content of an HtmlNode instance includes the nested content of its children in nested ways. The *nested* template loops the child list of an HtmlNode instance. A child node itself can have a list of children. This continues recursively until a node does not have any children.

Snippet 14 shows how the model written in Snippet 13 can be used to print out similar content to Snippet 11.

5.2   Traits and Aspect Orientation

Some tools such as JET [9] can help developers easily write template skeletons, which will contain sharable text content across all generated files; a typical use might be to inject a copyright statement in each file. However, the generated files do not necessarily require sharing all text content. In such a case, developers will need to write additional skeletons causing development to be more complicated than necessary. Other commonly-known text emission tools such as Epsilon Generation Language (EGL) [10] and Xtend [5] may require developers to bureaucratically add copyright statements to all template files.

```java
1   HtmlNode html = new HtmlNode("html");
2   HtmlNode body = new HtmlNode("body");
3   html.addChild(body);
4
5   HtmlNode table = new HtmlNode("table");
6   body.addChild(table);
7
8   for (String label : Arrays.asList(new String[] {
9       "Row1", "Row2", "Row3" })) {
10      HtmlNode row = new HtmlNode("tr");
11      table.addChild(row);
12
13      HtmlNode tableData = new HtmlNode("td");
14      tableData.setContent(label);
15      row.addChild(tableData);
16  }
17
18  System.out.println(html.generate());
```

Snippet 14. An invocation example of Snippet 13.

This dilemma mentioned above can be overcome by using the aspect-oriented features Umple provides. Aspect-orientation can be used in conjunction with the trait feature of Umple [11]. Traits allow developers to create external partial definitions that can be used by other classes. In other words, a trait contains attribute and method definition similarly to classes; when a class uses a trait type, the attributes and methods of this trait are mixed into that class.

```umple
1   class Helper {
2       copyright <<//Some copyright>>;
3       static emit copytightEmit()(copyright);
4   }
5
6   trait Extension {
7       before generate* {
8           Helper._copyrightEmit(0, sb);
9       }
10  }
11
12  class Template {
13      isA Extension;
14
15      myContent1 <<! Some content1 !>>
16      myContent2 <<! Some content2 !>>
17
18      emit generate1()(myContent1);
19      emit generate2()(myContent2);
20  }
```

Snippet 15. An example encompassing the features of aspect-orientation, traits, and templates.

Snippet 15 shows an example that defines two classes named Helper and Template in addition to a trait named Extension. Helper has an emitter method used statically to add a copyright statement. The template has two emitter methods, generate1, and generate2; both emitter methods add different template content. As well, Template is a type of the Extension trait. When the Extension trait is used as a part of a class, its definitions will be mixed into that class.

According to Line 7 in Snippet 15, Extension looks for all methods starting with the word "generate", using the wildcard symbol "*". This means that for the case of Template, there will be two matches for generate1 and generate2. According to Line 8, for each match, a call to the static helper method, copyrightEmit will be made. This call will be put at the very beginning of the method body of each emitter method in Extension.

Snippet 16 shows a portion of the code added at the beginning of each generated emitter method of Template. This means that a copyright statement will be added before each emitter method.

```java
1   public StringBuilder _generate1(Integer numSpaces,
2       StringBuilder sb) {
3       Helper._copyRightEmit(0, sb);
        ....
4   }
5
6   public StringBuilder _generate2(Integer numSpaces,
7       StringBuilder sb) {
8       Helper._copyRightEmit(0, sb);
        ....
9   }
```

Snippet 16. An example of a generated Java code using aspect-orientation, trait, and template features.

From the example above, we can see the benefits of using the Umple features of aspect-orientation and traits to alter the behavior of templates in an easy way. These Umple features maintain the Umple straightforwardness of having a single artifact model, while applying additional behavior.

6   Demonstration of Practical Value

We use three approaches to evaluate our work. First, we demonstrate the value of our work in practice in this section. Second, we demonstrate the use of concrete metrics. Third, we show a comparison between Umple and other text emission tools based on the key challenges we listed in Sect. 3.

A practical demonstration of using Umple-TL is that the Umple compiler is written in Umple, with all artifact generation (diagram DSLs, Java, C++, Ruby, PHP, XML interchange data, etc.) using Umple-TL.

Before UmpleTL, the Umple compiler had used JET [9] to emit the text of generated artifacts [12]. However, JET was deprecated, and we faced limits on its capacity (maximum size of strings). For JET replacement, we considered a variety of solutions, including Eclipse tools such as Acceleo [13]. However, that would have tied Umple to both Eclipse and Acceleo; it would also have added a lot of complexity for developers. We wanted a very simple solution, hence we developed Umple-TL to fit synergistically with other Umple features while at the same time making template generation available for all Umple-developed applications.

After Umple-TL, a tool was developed to automatically transform all templates written in JET into Umple-TL [12]. This tool was applied to the Umple compiler and various other projects, with translation being accomplished in just a few minutes! The Umple compiler has hence become an extremely large test-case for Umple-TL, and also has proved that it works effectively.

Table 2. Evaluation. Marginally better values in italics; values that are more than 4% better in red bold.

Generators	JET			Umple		
	MasterSource LOC	Generated Java LOC	Generation time (ms)	MasterSource LOC	Generated Java LOC	Generation time (ms)
Java	*11594*	21283	5988	11877	**20287**	**4741**
PHP	*4760*	7544	3938	4909	*7444*	**3031**
C++				5409	10549	7908

The real-time C++ code generator in the Umple compiler was directly written in Umple-TL from the beginning, which demonstrate that manual coding of Umple-TL is usable. It uses the Umple-TL features and capabilities more extensively than the generators automatically converted from JET, since it offers a comprehensive set of features as compared to JET. For instance, the LOC of the master source in C++ is less than half the LOC of the master source in Java, although C++ is more verbose than Java.

7 Performance Measures

Performance of a templating tool can be measured based on the templating code, generated code, and generation time. Both templating and generation code should have smaller size, which helps improve the generation time.

In the following we compare the performance of the Umple compiler when it used Jet, as of release 1.23.1, on March 22, 2016 [14], and its performance in release 1.24.0 the same day, after it was converted to use Umple-TL [15]. Note that Umple has been enhanced since the day of that conversion so the metrics as of the latest Umple release [16] will be different.

The metrics are presented in Table 2 and further illustrated in Figs. 4 and 5. In Table 2 we compare the templating code written in JET (left), with the code written in Umple-TL (right).

Code size is measured in Lines of code (LOC) and translation time for a set of test cases is measured in milliseconds. The generators shown in our comparison are Java [17], and PHP [18] as transcoded from Jet. Data for C++ templates manually written in Umple-TL [19] is shown for comparison in Table 2. The master source code refers to code written either in Umple-TL or JET, while the generated code refers to the code of the Umple compiler generated (by Jet of Umple-TL) in Java.

In Java and PHP, we can see that the master LOC is almost the same as the Umple-TL. However, Umple-TL is a bit larger, because it must be enclosed in a class (Snippet 1). The PhP generation template code LOC count is smaller (for both Jet and Java templates) than the Java generation template code because Umple supports fewer features when generating Php.

The C++ generator, which supports the same features as the Java generator, requires many fewer lines of template code, as it better employs Umple-TL features, resulting in 45% LOC reduction.

The emission time of Umple-TL was faster than Jet in both Java and PHP generators (Fig. 5).

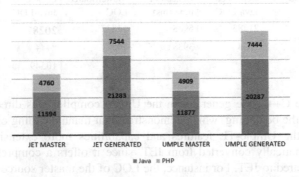

Fig. 4. LOC comparison between Jet (left) and Umple (right). Master is the source in Jet or Umple.

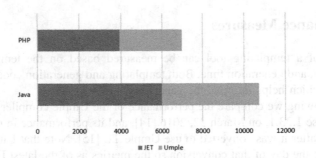

Fig. 5. Generation time comparison.

8   A Comparison of Templating Tools for Text Generation

In this section, we compare Umple-TL against other tools commonly used for text emission (Table 3). The tools include Java Emitter Templates (JET), Apache Velocity [4], Acceleo [13], Epsilon generation language (EGL) [6, 10], Xpand [20], and Xtend [5]. Our selection depends on whether a tool satisfies most of the challenges and requirements listed in the previous section. Not all of the challenges and requirements are shown in Table 3. For instance, we did not include pattern support, and instead focused on generation dynamicity and modelling support. When a tool supports modelling with high generation dynamicity, this may imply that the generation gap patterns will be decreased. JET is in our list of comparison as Umple's compiler formerly used JET before the introduction of Umple-TL (Sect. 6).

Reusability is an open-ended criterion that may not be simple to specify for a tool. Instead, we focus on other criteria such as generation dynamicity, transformation rules, input model restrictions, syntax complexity, structural complexity, and target language expressions. Meeting these criteria mean that the reusability of a tool will be increased.

Comments support is present in all tools; hence, we did not add it to our comparison.

For *file structure management*, we found that this not directly related to a tool itself, but mostly related to the type of text a developer intends to emit. For instance, generating C++ code will require generation of both header and body files. In such a context, our focus will be on that a tool should have lower workflow and structural complexity.

For *target code readability*, we found that other criteria such as formatting complexity and debugging support are enough for our comparison. We did not include *target code efficiency* in or comparison; assessing this aspect can be a completely different topic of discussion.

In terms of *representation consistency*, other aspects such as less structural complexity, high generation dynamicity, and the presence of modelling support could help users to have a consistent representation.

The criterion of the *ability to specify constraints,* is not included as constraints can directly be defined using the tool or target language expressions. In addition, rule-based transformation gives more options to handle constraints.

Consistency of text formatting is maintained when formatting complexity is decreased. Thus, we found that it will be enough to refer to formatting complexity in our comparison.

In Table 3, for the criteria, workflow complexity, structural complexity, syntax complexity, and formatting complexity, the rating can be low, medium, or high. A tool is assumed better if it has a low complexity. The same rating scale is used for generation dynamicity. A tool is presumably better if it has high generation dynamicity.

For debugging support, this can be applied at the level of source files, runtime, generation, or a combination of them, as explained in the previous section. A tool can support many of those types of debugging, while other tools may not provide any type of debugging.

For other criteria, they are all yes/no answers to determine whether a feature is supported or whether it follows certain restrictions. The desirable features of a tool are set in bold in Table 3.

Commonly used programming languages such as PHP and Go can be directly used for text emission. PHP is included in our comparison, since it is a good example on how text emission can be directly handled using a programming language. Technically, when using a tool such as JET, we can say that we use Java for text emission; however, when we refer to PHP in our comparison, we mean that PHP can be used directly for text emission without additional tools or extensions. Any programming language can still be directly used for text emission without additional extensions; however, this will require additional development effort and unfortunately mostly it will be unnecessary or replicate the effort done by other text emission tools.

Table 3. A comparison of template development tools; bold font means better.

	JET	Velocity	Acceleo	Xpand	Xtend	Epsilon	PHP	Umple-TL
Workflow complexity	**Low**	**Low**	Medium	High	**Low**	Medium	Medium	**Low**
IDE dependencies	Eclipse	**None**	Eclipse	Eclipse	Eclipse	Eclipse	**None**	**None**
Third-party library dependencies	Yes	**No**	Yes	Yes	Yes	Yes	**None**	**No**
Target language expressions	**Yes**	No	No	No	No	No	No	**Yes**
Input model restrictions	**No**	**No**	Yes	Yes	**No**	**No**	**No**	**No**
Modelling support	No	No	**Yes**	**Yes**	No	**Yes**	No	**Yes**
Transformation rules	No	No	**Yes**	**Yes**	**Yes**	**Yes**	No	**Yes**
Structural complexity	Medium	**Low**	Medium	High	**Low**	Medium	**Low**	**Low**
Generation dynamicity	Low	Medium	Medium	Medium	**High**	**High**	**High**	**High**
Syntax complexity	**Low**	**Low**	Medium	High	**Low**	Medium	**Low**	**Low**
Debugging support	Runtime	None	**All**	Runtime	Runtime	**All**	Runtime	Runtime
Content protection	**Yes**	No	**Yes**	**Yes**	**Yes**	**Yes**	No	**Yes**
Formatting complexity	Medium	Medium	Medium	Medium	Medium	**Low**	Medium	**Low**
Generator language restrictions	Yes	Yes	Yes	Yes	Yes	**No**	**No**	**No**

8.1 Tool Discussion

In this section, we discuss the results of each table entry except for Umple-TL. The discussion of Umple-TL will come in the next section.

In terms of *workflow complexity*, JET, Velocity, and Xtend are easy to use. Xpand has the highest complexity due to the effort spent to configure its workflow. The workflow of Acceleo and Epsilon is less complex than Xpand. We marked the workflow complexity of Epsilon as medium not as low, since a user is required to be familiar with model-to-text transformation and the Epsilon Model Connectivity (EMC) layer in order to use their metamodels. In addition, Epsilon requires implementing configuration or launch files in order to get an Epsilon file running.

We marked the workflow complexity of PHP as medium not as low, since PHP requires developers to be familiar with additional paradigms such as the client/server architecture. It is important to mention that assessing the workflow complexity of text emission of a programming language is not straightforward. For instance, in C++, developers are not required to be familiar with the client/server architecture; however, C++ requires a lot of effort for compilation and configuration.

All of the entries mentioned have *IDE dependencies* except for Velocity and PHP. However, no tool has *third-party library dependencies* except for Velocity. It is well-known that in PHP, there are no restrictions to specific IDEs or libraries; developers have the liberty to choose development environment they find convenient. This is the case for all the most widely-used programming languages.

JET is the only tool that controls emission using *target language expressions* (Java in the case of Jet) as opposed to a custom language. As mentioned, relying on custom expressions in a tool can cause limitations as a tool will not necessary be able to handle as comprehensive a set of expressions as compared to a sophisticated language such as Java. The PHP entry is marked as "no", since the concept of target languages does not exist at all when using a programming language directly for text emission.

In terms of *input model restrictions*, only Acceleo and Xpand enforce restrictions to use Ecore to develop models. However, in terms of *modelling support*, they are the tools that directly provide modelling support. Other tools such as Xtend can use additional libraries such Xtext to support modelling. Epsilon overcomes this tradeoff, since a user has the liberty to decide the type of models to be used using the Epsilon Model Connectivity (EMC) layer. In Umple, we managed to overcome this tradeoff as well, since Umple can be used as an object-oriented programming language as well as being a modelling language.

We did not mark for PHP that it supports modelling, since modelling features are not a part of its built-in features or constructs. Although, in fact, PHP or any sophisticated programming language can support some aspects of modelling such as classes and inheritance, we do not consider their level of abstraction to be sufficient to be called modelling languages.

Only model-based tools such as Acceleo, Xpand, and Epsilon can provide a support for *transformation rules*. It is important to mention that Xtend can be used with Xtext in order to support model-related features. Transformation rules can be supported in PHP but this will require additional effort in a similar manner to modelling support. Thus, we marked the transformation rules in PHP as "no".

In JET, a template file must use a skeleton file; this adds additional complexity to its text emission structure, and thus, we marked JET's *structural complexity* as medium. On the other hand, in Xpand, we mentioned that a template file depends on the developed metamodels and models; both add more complexity to its text emission structure and thus we decided to mark their complexity as high.

In an Acceleo template, a developer needs to follow the structure specified in their model; this causes the complexity to be increased and become medium. We marked the structural complexity of Epsilon as medium, since users work with different types of files such as Epsilon files, metamodels, launch files, and Epsilon transformations.

Epsilon provides a complete solution for code generation and contains several features represented in different types and syntax. Similarly to any language, a user will need a fair amount of time in order to get used to most features of a language such as Epsilon [10]. However, we did not mark the structure complexity of Epsilon as high as a user does not necessarily need to learn about all Epsilon features in order to get their text emission working.

Xtend and Velocity directly use a single template file; thus, we marked their structural complexity as low. We also marked the structural complexity of PHP as low, since the main artifact the developers work with is "*.php" files. PHP developers still work with other artifacts such as HTML, CSS, and JavaScript files. The structural complexity varies among different programming languages if they are going to be used for text emission directly. For instance, in C and C++, developers must work with two artifact types; headers and bodies, while Java developers only need to write Java files. Typically, in any development process, additional configuration and launch files are required; this is a part of the IDE selected for the development, which we referred to earlier in this section.

In terms of *generation dynamicity*, we found that of the tools that existed prior to this research, Xtend and Epsilon provide the most dynamic solutions. A developer is able to write as many emitter methods as they want with a variable number of parameters; there are no restrictions on how they should implement their text emission content. Velocity, Epsilon, Acceleo, and Xpand provide enough solutions to handle dynamicity but in not in as flexible a way as Xtend and Epsilon; this is why we marked them as medium. On the other hand, we marked JET is low as it does not provide a direct way to have dynamic parameters. We marked the generation dynamicity of PHP as high; this is the case for any sophisticated programming language if it were to be included in our comparison.

The syntax complexity of all pre-existing tools is low except for Xpand and Acceleo. In Xpand, a developer will need to move among different parts of the template file in order to understand what this template does; thus, we marked the syntax complexity of Xpand as high. On the other hand, Acceleo is not as complex as Xpand in terms of syntax complexity; however, it assumes that a developer is familiar with Ecore constructs and methods; this is why we marked its complexity as medium.

We marked the syntax complexity of Epsilon as medium instead of low, since a user needs to use the Epsilon Model Connectivity (EMC) layer to control the meta-model type used.

We marked the syntax complexity of PHP as low, since PHP is a commonly used programming language. This statement may be challenged by others when comparing with different programming languages; this depends on what programming language a developer prefers,

We found that only Acceleo and Epsilon support all types of *debugging*. For example, Epsilon provides a traceability feature to debug or audit a transformation process [10].

On the other hand, in JET, debugging is limited but there is at least a workaround to debug the generated classes at runtime; debugging the generated classes at runtime can be sufficient. If there is any syntax in a JET file, there will be direct compiler errors in its generated file.

The same workaround can be applied for Xpand; additionally, in Xpand, the tool support has several features for validation and error highlighting such as the Check language. In Xtend, the debugging is at the runtime level, since the Xtend files are automatically generated. On the other hand, Velocity does not have any type of debugging support even at runtime since the generated files are not produced. Alternatively, a developer can use log statements.

Debugging in PHP depends on the IDE used and the user-written code. Any sophisticated programming language is usually supported by many tools or IDEs, which usually offer debugging as one of its features. Thus, we marked PHP that it supports runtime debugging.

All entries provide support for *content protection* except for Velocity and PHP. In Velocity, template files are required to be a part of the release build in order to have in-memory generation of its template. Such an issue can cause security concerns. Content protection in PHP is one of the major discussion points that always arise when developing an application or library. When developing a PHP library, it may not be straightforward to protect template content; thus, we did not mark that PHP has content protection. This is not necessarily the case for other programming languages. For instance, in C++ and Java, developers have a lot of options to hide or compile their solutions as binary files.

For *formatting complexity*, we refer to aspects such as spacing and indentation. When a tool enables developers to write their code directly without being wrapped in a method, the spacing and indentation will not be a problem; in other words, what a developer sees in their source files will be what they get in the generation. Those tools include Velocity, Acceleo, and Xpand. Such tools still do not provide APIs to enable a user to shift or control the spacing or indentation of their text content directly. It is important to mention that users can still find a way to handle format. For example, in Xpand, a user can define a method to add some spaces or tabs; however, this does not come as a part of the language semantics, which is why we marked its formatting complexity as medium not low.

We marked the formatting complexity of Epsilon as low, since Epsilon provides a way to set a formatter object. Using a formatter object, a user can make a sequence of calls to format a generated text as they require [10]. However, this formatting feature takes place after the text is already generated, which reduces the developer's control.

On the other hand, in both JET and Xtend, the output descriptors are written in an emitter function; a developer will always need to shift their text content and make them aligned with their methods. This will be annoying to the developer as they will need to do that for all methods. As well, like the abovementioned tools, there is no way to control the number of spaces used; thus, a developer will need to do this manually at all places in code. We marked the formatting complexity of PHP as medium, since it is the developers' responsibility to handle text format.

8.2 Umple Discussion

In terms of *workflow complexity*, a developer will only need to work with a single artifact, an Umple model. An Umple model can encompass the required emission information such as metamodels and models. The model could be in a single file, or several, at the discretion of the developer.

There are no *IDE dependencies* required whatsoever when using Umple-TL. A developer has the liberty to use their IDE of interest; they can even directly use UmpleOnline (try.umple.org) editor and then download the generated files. There are no *third-party library dependencies* for both development and release builds; in fact, Umple is written in itself as an Umple model to be generated without additional tools involved. For the tools that we studied, even those that provide third-party independent solutions, they do not provide independence at the development level.

In terms of *target language expressions*, Umple enables users to write their expressions in the syntax of the target language. A user even has the freedom to switch among different target languages such as C++ and Java; other tools that we listed restrict a developer to use a specific target language.

There are no *input model restrictions* in Umple. A developer can directly write their Umple model and use the appropriate target language that fits their needs; they will not find themselves in a situation where they have to use a specific target language or model schema.

Obviously, there is *modelling support* in Umple, since it is a model-oriented language. Umple incorporates UML constructs into template development. In other words, in Umple, a model-oriented approach is applied on the models being implemented, not at the tool level only. We noticed that sometimes, enforcing a model-oriented paradigm can be turned into a burden of complexity as we showed in Xpand and Acceleo.

Being a model-oriented language means that *transformation rules* can be applied on the written Umple models. In Umple, there are many transformation options such as Java, C++, PHP, Ecore, and XMI. Although a developer has to choose a target language for certain expressions, basic for-loops, while-loops and if-then expressions can be specified the same in Java and C++, allowing a set of templates to be used across target languages.

Umple has low *structural complexity*, since it provides a configuration-free solution. As previously mentioned, a model can encompass all information including the configuration information. The process is simple as a user writes a model and then generates output.

Umple-TL provides many solutions to handle generation dynamicity. Developers are not tied to a specific emitter method or number of emitter methods; they are able to define their emitter methods, as they require. The number of parameters to be specified in an emitter method is dynamic; the developer is able to control and define the parameters. Making changes to the parameter signature of an emitter method is straightforward, since all information is represented in a single model artifact. A user is able to invoke and use other template classes within another template class. As well, a template class can be designed to serve as helpers or static classes.

Umple follows the C-family syntax conventions, which is desirable for many developers, since commonly-used languages such C, C++, and Java follow this style. As a result, Umple has a low *syntax complexity*. A developer will not need to worry about learning a new script representation in order to start using Umple-TL.

In terms of *debugging support*, Umple still does *not* provide tool support for debugging at the model level. Alternatively, a user is able to debug the generated files. Line numbers from the source Umple are injected as comments into the generated code, allowing ease of traceability. As well, there is a tracing support in Umple, which enables the developers to write trace statements in their Umple models as a way to debug generated files at runtime.

Content protection is provided by Umple, since developers will only need to use the generated files for their product releases.

In terms of *formatting complexity*, we showed how Umple-TL provides APIs to handle space and string manipulation. The solutions provided help optimize performance; we indicated for example that the string buffer instance is shared across different nested template calls.

Umple-TL follows a similar approach as JET and Xpand in terms of having inline definitions for templates. For example, a user can define a template that will apply tabs or carriage returns. In addition, a feature such as aspect orientation offers flexible options when writing redundant content such as tabs and copyrights.

All existing tools have *generator language restrictions* to Java for all of them except PHP. Being inspired by UML, in Umple-TL, we rely on the multi-language feature of Umple to enable developers to write their models in their target language of interest such as Java, C++, and PHP. We showed template examples in two different target languages, C++ and Java.

9 Conclusions

Text-emission is a common capability required in many types of programs: It is needed to create user interfaces, such as by generating html, or to communicate among programs, such as through XML or JSON. It is also needed for metaprogramming, i.e. generating programs in other languages.

In this paper we show how the text-emission capability of Umple, called Umple-TL, has several advantages as compared to other text-generation technologies, while taking advantage of and integrating with Umple's textual model-driven engineering capabilities. Umple provides a unified approach to develop executable models that can be written in both textual and visual notations. Umple does not depend on third-party libraries nor specific IDEs. It keeps models language-agnostic and supports multiple target languages including C++, Java, and PHP.

With the introduction of Umple-TL, developers are able to develop templates as a part of the Umple syntax itself. Hence, all template development can be in Umple without asking developers to switch among different development contexts, compilers, file types or IDEs.

Some other distinguishing feature of Umple-TL are the following:

- Templates can be reused to produce systems with different target execution languages.
- Templates can be generated from UML modeling constructs such as associations and state machines. For example, different output can be generated in different states.
- Templates can produce highly readable output through the management of indentation whitespace.
- Several separation-of-concerns mechanisms can be synergistically combined when generating templates. These include emitter methods, mixins, traits and aspects.

We provided a detailed comparison between Umple-TL and other common text emission tools such as Xpand, Xtend, Epsilon, and Acceleo. We also illustrated how Umple-TL can help reduce both the emission time and generated code size, while not impacting source size.

We presented the challenges in development of a text-emission tool, and showed by example how Umple-TL overcomes such challenges. We illustrated many of Umple-TL's capabilities through a series of examples. Of particular note is that Umple (and hence UmpleTL) is written in itself.

Acknowledgments. This research was supported by OGS, NSERC, and ORF.

References

1. Orabi, M.H., Orabi, A.H., Lethbridge, T.: Umple as a component-based language for the development of real-time and embedded applications. In: Proceedings of the 4th International Conference on Model-Driven Engineering and Software Development, pp. 282–291 (2016)
2. Husseini Orabi, M., Husseini Orabi, A., Lethbridge, T.C.: Component-based modeling in umple. In: Proceedings of the 6th International Conference on Model-Driven Engineering and Software Development, pp. 247–255 (2018)
3. Orabi, M., Orabi, A., Lethbridge, T.: Umple as a Template Language (Umple-TL). In: Proceedings of the 7th International Conference on Model-Driven Engineering and Software Development, Prague, Czech Republic, pp. 98–106 (2019)
4. Carnell, J., Harrop, R., Mittal, K.: Velocity template engine. In: Mittal, K. (ed.) Pro Apache Struts with Ajax, pp. 317–357. Apress, Berkely (2006). https://doi.org/10.1007/978-1-4302-0252-3_10
5. Xtend: Xtend (2017). http://eclipse.org/xtend/. Accessed 01 Jan 2015
6. Rose, L.M., Paige, R.F., Kolovos, D.S., Polack, F.A.C.: The epsilon generation language. In: Schieferdecker, I., Hartman, A. (eds.) ECMDA-FA 2008. LNCS, vol. 5095, pp. 1–16. Springer, Heidelberg (2008). https://doi.org/10.1007/978-3-540-69100-6_1
7. Orabi, M.H.: Facilitating the representation of composite structure, active objects, code generation, and software component descriptions for AUTOSAR in the umple model-oriented programming language. Ph.D. thesis, University of Ottawa (2017)
8. Badreddin, O., Lethbridge, T.C., Forward, A.: A test-driven approach for developing software languages. In: MODELSWARD 2014, International Conference on Model-Driven Engineering and Software Development, pp. 225–234 (2014)
9. Eclipse: JET Tutorial (Introduction to JET) (2003). https://eclipse.org/articles/Article-JET/jet_tutorial1.html. Accessed 01 Oct 2017
10. Kolovos, D., Rose, L., García-Domínguez, A., Paige, R.: The Epsilon Book. Eclipse Public License (2015)
11. Abdelzad, V., Lethbridge, T.C.: Promoting traits into model-driven development. Softw. Syst. Model. **16**, 997–1017 (2015)
12. Umple: JETToUmpleTL (2018). https://github.com/umple/JETToUmpleTL. Accessed 01 July 2017
13. Acceleo: Acceleo eclipse page (2017). http://www.eclipse.org/acceleo/. Accessed 01 Oct 2017
14. Umple: Github Umple (2016). https://github.com/umple/umple/releases/tag/v.1.23.1. Accessed 01 July 2017
15. Umple: Github Umple (2016). https://github.com/umple/umple/releases/tag/v.1.24.0. Accessed 01 July 2017
16. Github Umple: Github Umple (2018). https://github.com/umple/umple/releases/latest. Accessed 01 July 2017

17. Github Umple: Github Umple (2018). https://github.com/umple/umple/tree/master/UmpleToJava/UmpleTLTemplates. Accessed 01 July 2017
18. Github Umple: Github Umple (2018). https://github.com/umple/umple/tree/master/UmpleToPhp/UmpleTLTemplates. Accessed 01 July 2017
19. Github Umple: Github Umple (2018). https://github.com/umple/umple/tree/master/UmpleToRTCpp/UmpleTLTemplates. Accessed 01 July 2017
20. Eclipse Modeling Framework (EMF). http://www.eclipse.org/modeling/emf. Accessed 01 July 2017

Dataset Management Using Metadata

David Milward(✉)

Oxford University, Oxford, UK
david.milward@cs.ox.ac.uk
http://www.cs.ox.ac.uk

Abstract. Correct data analysis depends on good quality data, and that means having data in a form that can be consistently queried, profiled and managed, easily and repeatedly. The healthcare sector, in particular the growing field of personalised medicine, has some of the most complex and diverse datasets. However, they are mostly heterogeneous datasets, and not always easy to merge into a form that is useful for the data scientists and researchers that are attempting to carry out data analysis. This paper describes key factors needed to automate the process of integrating such datasets, it is based upon experience working with standards-compliant metadata registries in precision medicine.

1 Introduction

This paper extends the work in Model Driven Engineering in Healthcare [23], which describes experimentation carried out in the healthcare domain aimed at automating dataset curation. This paper provides a clear motivational example of how the improvements to the ISO11179-based metadata registry, described in the previous work, have resulted in a significant reduction in time and effort spent in data preparation tasks. Additional detail has been provided on the improvements made to the *meta-model* and domain specific language (DSL) developed as part of this project.

One of the fundamental problems in data science is how to derive high quality data from multiple heterogeneous sources, and for the most part the process of "data wrangling", getting data from multiple sources into a form which can be analysed, is a highly tedious process involving a high degree of expert guidance in the curation process. This paper describes how the principles of model driven engineering can be applied to reduce this involvement, it provides details on a meta-model and domain specific language developed specifically to address this problem, as well detailing experiments carried out in mapping of ontologies, vocabularies and data models.

There is little doubt that the current landscape of the internet and the availability of large amounts of computing power provide a surplus of valuable data, especially in the healthcare domain, from which new knowledge can be obtained. Data is being collected not just in hospitals, but on devices used and worn by patients, and this data if correctly matched up can provide valuable feedback

© Springer Nature Switzerland AG 2020
S. Hammoudi et al. (Eds.): MODELSWARD 2019, CCIS 1161, pp. 156–181, 2020.
https://doi.org/10.1007/978-3-030-37873-8_7

on the efficacy of treatment regimes and new drugs. However, the capability of the hardware has run far ahead of the ability of software to integrate that data, always assuming there is willingness to do so.

In the next section we review the objectives of the research effort, in the section following on Data Standards, we look at the kind of data being handled, and the standards which are being used in the healthcare sector at present. After this is a section on Methodology, which describes the approach to tackling the research, following on is a section detailing the results. These are discussed in the next section, this is followed with a look at other related work going on in the field and that is followed by conclusions.

2 Objectives

The objectives in carrying out this research were to examine ways of automating the process of curating data elements for the construction of research datasets. In particular to explore ways to ensure the preservation of semantics in the datasets being curated. The data pipeline may involve several individual transformations of datasets, with anonymization techniques being applied before the data is stored in its final data warehouse, and it is essential that the data semantics be preserved if the information is to be of any use to researchers. Our aim was to find formal ways of automating dataset curation and management. By formal, we mean based in mathematical or logic theory, enabling a repeatable set of rules to be derived for this process. We approached this problem by breaking the problem into components by asking the following questions:

- What data is needed for the research area, and how should it be specified?
- How does a researcher find the data they need?
- How can a catalogue of datasets be assembled and managed effectively?
- What are the time consuming areas in this process?
- Can datasets be mapped automatically through the explicit specification of their semantics?
- Can these time-consuming processes be automated? If so, how?

We then applied the methodology described later on to experiment with different technologies to achieve solutions to these questions.

3 Background

This section provides a quick overview of the way in which data is structured, stored and organised in the healthcare sector, we have included brief overviews of the key data standards encountered in the course of this research.

3.1 Data

Data exists in many forms, primarily we are concerned in this study with health-care data, which for the most part is derived from clinical systems and applications, however in this discussion, we also consider data from mobile devices, Internet of Things (IOT) and social media. Data can be stored in many forms, the following section gives a brief overview of current data storage practise in the healthcare sector.

Spreadsheet and Delimited Date. This is data extracted from databases or spreadsheets, and it is normally stored in a tabular format, with column headings or field names defining the data types of columns, and with one column containing identifiers to link the data to a patient record. In many cases these data tables are anonymized, to hide the identity of the patient.

Laboratory Reports. These may also be provided as tabular data, but they normally provided as pdf files, based on a template, with attached media files, containing some sort of laboratory specific data, such as X-Ray images attached. In some cases these will be simple text or numerical data files, in a specific laboratory specific format. Often these will be linked using a unique identifier to other patient record information.

XML and JSON. Some data is being provided using JSON and XML, most of this is fairly similar to the tabular data provided from spreadsheets and databases, although potentially the structure can be more complex.

Textual Data. This is data provided in textual reports, normally word or PDF files, and it is referred to as unstructured data. There is some degree of structure in the language which is re-inforced with medical terminology, but it is not based on a defined or formal model.

Big Data. This is not yet common in our experience in the healthcare sector, but it is likely to become so in the near future. The standard storage for Hadoop and big data engines is a storage file, of which there are three in common usage: ORC, Parquet and AVRO. The first two are column-based, whilst the last is row-based, the latter also has the ability to store the complete data schema, i.e. the metadata, in the file.

Relational Database. For the most part the output from relational databases is in text delimited or XML forms, as discussed earlier, there is the possibility to output in a SQL format, but unless the whole database is going to be replicated this is not a flexible way to transfer or move data.

3.2   Data Standards

Data Standards are used in healthcare, and are seen as a key component "for unleashing the potential of clinical data for diverse scenarios of (re-) use" according to a book recently published called "Fundamentals of Clinical Data Science" [28]. In practise data standards are used lin an ad-hoc fashion, and are often not built into software applications, but applied to reporting packages as an afterthought. An outline of some of the different data standards is given in Table 1.

Table 1. A sample of data standards in healthcare.

Name	Description	Origin
SNOMED CT	Clinical Terminology	International Health Terminology Standards Development Organisation (IHTSDO)
HL7 v2/v3	Messaging Standard	Health Level Seven International
OpenEHR	Open Electronic Health Record, object model and terminology	openEHR Foundation
Fast Healthcare Interoperability Resources (FHIR)	Describes data formats, elements and an API for exchanging electronic health records	Health Level Seven International
NHS Data Dictionary	Variety of standards for data elements, classifications and value sets	NHS Digital
OMOP Common Data Model	A standardised common data model	OHDSI
Clinical Document Architecture (CDA)	XML-based markup standard for clinical documents	Health Level Seven International
Digital Imaging and Communications in Medicine (DICOM)	File format and networking protocol for file exchange	National Electrical Manufacturers Association (NEMA)
Continuity of Care Record (CCR)	The CCR standard is a patient health summary standard	ASTM International (and others)
Dataset.XML	Protocol for communication of study results	Clinical Data Interchange Standards Consortium (CDISC)
Laboratory Data Model (LAB)	XML format for exchange of laboratory data	Clinical Data Interchange Standards Consortium (CDISC)
Operational Data Model (ODM)	XML schema for modeling electronic Case Report Forms (CRFs)	Clinical Data Interchange Standards Consortium (CDISC)
Health informatics - Electronic Health Record Communication (EN 13606/ISO13606)	European Standard for an information architecture to communicate Electronic Health Records (EHR)	International Organization for Standardization
MEDCIN	standardized medical terminology	Medicomp Systems, Inc
Medical Dictionary for Regulatory Activities (MedDRA)	Clinically validated international medical terminology, dictionary and thesaurus	International Federation of Pharmaceutical Manufacturers and Associations (IFPMA)
RxNorm	Vocabulary for clinical drugs	U.S. National Library of Medicines

During the course of this work the first six of these data standards were frequently referenced, the others less so or possibly not at all. A brief summary of the different standards follows.

3.3 SNOMED CT

SNOMED CT is a clinical terminology, consisting of medical terms, codes, definitions and relationships, Originally called the systemised nomenclature of medicine (SNOMED) in 1975, it has been combined with a number of other terminologies since then to become SNOMED CT, and it is now it is probably the most widely used clinical terminology in the world. It is now defined using description logic, which allows a number of features, probably the most notable is the existence of both pre- and post-coordinated terms. Post-coordinated terms allow new terms to be composed from combinations of exisiting terms using an expression language, however, this can result in particular complex terms being expressed using both a pre-coordinated and a post-coordinated term. This complexity is not popular with many organizations tasked with implementing SNOMED CT. SNOMED CT has over 300,000 terms defined, and more than 1.3 million relationships.

3.4 Fast Healthcare Interoprability Resources (FHIR)

Fast Healthcare Interoperability Resources (FHIR) is the latest set of standards from the *Health Level 7* standards body, who previously developed a number of other standards including HL7 Version 2.x Messaging Standard, HL7 Version 3.x Messaging Standard, Continuity of Care Document (CCD) and Clinical Document Architecture (CDA). They have been widely adopted by both the American National Standards Institute (ANSI) and the International Standards Organization (ISO). The standard defines a messaging REST(API) which can exchange resources, these are built using XML or JSON using a pre-defined set of models, describing most instances of data exchange in the healthcare domain.

3.5 International Classification of Diseases (ICD)

The World Health Organisation (WHO) manages a set of clinical diagnostic codes collectively known as the International Classification of Diseases(ICD). ICD-11 is the current version of the standards, however ICD-10/9/8 are in common usage in the UK. It has evolved from proposals in 1860 to classify hospital data, in particular causes of death. The standard started with a simply system for classifying death called the Bertillon Classification of Causes of Death, introduced in 1890, since then the classification has progressed in a coding system called the International Statistical Classification of Diseases, Injuries, and Causes of Death into the International Classification of Diseases. As well as descriptions of diseases it includes signs, symptoms, abnormal findings, complaints, social circumstances, and external causes of injury or disease.

ICD-11 provided full ontological and terminological support for the whole systems, using the web ontology language as its formal basis. It also has mappings into SNOMED CT which uses the same formal specification basis.

3.6   OpenEHR - ISO EN 13606

This is an open source standard developed from the ground up by clinicians, guided by the ISO13606 [12] standard. The standard itself specifies a means for communicating part or all of the electronic health record (EHR) of one or more identified subjects of care between EHR systems, or between EHR systems and a centralised EHR data repository. The openEHR websites states that "the openEHR mission is the construction of an open, vendor neutral platform for electronic health records and interoperable clinical and research data. The openEHR Foundation was established in 2003 in pursuit of this ambition. Its work has been framed and informed by three guiding principles: technical rigour, clinical engagement and trust."

3.7   OMOP CDM

The research organisation called the Observational Health Data Sciences and Informatics (OHDSI) took over a program, from the FDA and the Pharmaceutical Industry to develop a common data model. The motivation stems from side effects that were not spotted quickly enough in drugs-trial programs, due to the diverse way in which data was stored and analysed. The idea behind a common data model is that if data is transformed and stored in a uniform pre-defined format, then the same queries can be run continuously over the data, and any new anomalies, such as negative interactions between different treatment regimes, can be spotted quickly. The common data model is used widely in the US and Europe and has been used successfully to carry out large-scale statistical analysis across patients taking prescribed medication. There are other common data models in use, OMOP CDM has been selected for use by Genomics England, and recently emerged as the best common data model for a community EHR-registry [9].

3.8   LOINC

The Logical Observation Identifiers Names and Codes (LOINC), was started in 1994 and first released in 1997. It is a standard for identifying health measurements, observations, and documents connected with medical laboratory reports. It encompasses a rich catalog of codified measurements, laboratory tests, and clinical measures as well as templates for reports, documents and forms. It is centred on pathology, and is more granular and detailed in this area than either SNOMED CT or the ICD-11, and can be used in conjunction with FHIR to encode laboratory information into FHIR messaging services.

3.9   NHS Data Dictionary

Version 3 of the NHS Data Dictionary is a standard for clinical models, forms and data elements used within the NHS. It is based on a core UML data model, which is transformed and made available through HTML browsers on the NHS

Data Dictionary website, and through a variety of packaged datasets available through the NHS's Terminology Reference Data update (TRUD) service website, alongside NHS-conformant versions of SNOMED CT, ICD-10, and Read codes.

3.10   ISO11179

ISO11179 is a standard for metadata registries, and a fairly detailed description of the standard was included in [23]. We repeat some key details about ISO11179 in this section. Its purposes are listed in the standard as being the following:

> ISO/IEC 11179 addresses the semantics of data, the representation of data and the registration of the descriptions of that data. It is through these descriptions that an accurate understanding of the semantics and a useful depiction of the data are found.

Furthermore the standard states that it's purpose is to promote:

- standard description of data
- common understanding of data across organizational elements and between organizations
- re-use and standardization of data over time, space, and applications
- harmonization and standardization of data within an organization and across organizations
- management of the components of descriptions of data
- re-use of the components of descriptions of data

ISO11179 Structure. The standard is all about using metadata to improve interoperability and we repeat the following which taken from the standard:

> ISO/IEC 11179 addresses the semantics of data, the representation of data and the registration of the descriptions of that data. It is through these descriptions that an accurate understanding of the semantics and a useful depiction of the data are found.

The purpose of ISO/IEC 11179 is to promote the following:

- standard description of data
- common understanding of data across organizational elements and between organizations
- re-use and standardization of data over time, space, and applications
- harmonization and standardization of data within an organization and across organizations
- management of the components of descriptions of data
- re-use of the components of descriptions of data

Part 3 of the standard provides a registry meta-model, specified using UML diagrams, and it was thus chosen as the starting point for building this implementation. There is a warning at the beginning of Part 3, stating that this part *prescribes a conceptual model, not a physical implementation* This part of ISO/IEC 11179 also prescribes a list of basic attributes (see clause 12) for situations where a full conceptual model is not required or not appropriate. The other 5 parts were used to inform the core metadata registry metamodel as specified in ISO11179: Part 3.

Semantic Interoperability. One of the key ideas behind ISO11179 is that of semantic interoperability, and although semantic interoperability is not directly referenced in the standard, there are many references to the *semantics* of a data element, and how this can be assigned to data element by application of the standard. For instance part One states that "Metadata registries (MDR), addresses the semantics of data, the representation of data, and the registration of the descriptions of that data. It is through these descriptions that an accurate understanding of the *semantics* and a useful depiction of the data are found.". The text continues with "An MDR manages the *semantics* of data.".

Users of ISO11179 metadata registries assert that if a data element has the same object class and property, then this is sufficient to capture the semantics and context of a data element. Users of ISO11179 conformant metadata registries also claim that semantic equivalence can be achieved through careful classification and naming of data elements, Part 1 A.5.2 states that: "All this means care must be applied when using the MDR, both from the metadata management perspective and the perspective of the user of data described by it. Two different organizations might register descriptions of equivalent data in the form of data elements, yet those data elements might look substantially different. Looked at in a different way, just because two data element descriptions differ does not mean they cannot be describing similar if not equivalent data."

Thus the standard strives to include semantics into the canonical metadata registry design, however, it does not put forward a way of coding the semantics to make them machine readable.

4   Methodology

What was clear from looking at the problems facing researchers was that an accessible, set of standard descriptions for datasets and data elements, one which can be searched and accessed remotely, and which is machine readable is needed. As this is one of key items that ISO11179 seeks to promote (see Sect. 3.10), it became our starting point for developing the framework.

Having defined our objective as being to explore the ways in which dataset management could be made more efficient, the next stage of the research looked at the following key areas:

- (a) Experimentation to see if an ISO11179 compliant metadata registry could replace the use of excel files to specify datasets.

- (b) In addition to test the ISO11179 implementation to see if it would improve semantic interoperability between heterogeneous datasets.
- (c) If there are other techniques, such as model driven engineering that could be applied to this problem of automating dataset curation

Initially we developed a standards-compliant metadata registry, and started, with the help of clinicians to populate it. This proved very difficult on account of the training needed to understand the model being used. In effect datasets and ontologies familiar to the researchers had to be mapped to the ISO11179 meta-model. We modified the meta-model, but still found it very difficult. We then started from scratch, and build a new meta-model, informed by the principles identified in ISO11179. This journey is documented in [23]. The final meta-model and language is described in the result's section.

4.1 Motivational Example

Consider a very simplified example of the problems associated with collecting and analysing large quantities of heterogeneous data. Let's take as an example the idea that a data scientist needs a monthly update from 4 hospital trusts to make a particular analysis, and for this she needs 3 key data items: gender, clinical finding, outcome, in addition to the patient details, and date of outcome/finding, to carry out this analysis. Let's suppose this data is being updated on a monthly basis, so in the course of a year we have 12 datasets being input, from each of 4 hospital trusts, making a total of 48 datasets. Let's also suppose that this analysis is carried out over a 4-year period. In total we are seeking to examine 48 monthly datasets for each Trust, since there are 4 trusts and 3 key data points, this makes a total of 576 data points, although date and id will also be needed to position the data, so that gives 6 data items in each dataset, giving 1152 data items.

It may be that each trust is sending the data directly from the system of origin, however, it is more likely it has already been curated against some internal or possibly external data standard. For our purposes here we can assume that one Trust is sending the data on an ad-hoc bases, and the other 3 are referencing the data to national standards, let's assume 2 Trusts use the NHS Data Dictionary for some items and LOINC for other items and that 1 Trust uses SNOMED CT as a data standard.

If no data standards are being used then each data item from each trust needs to be examined and compared to the destination data item specification, it is possible that the data item specification may be the same, but it is more likely that some kind of transformation will be required. If data standards are being used, then it is necessary to determine how they are being used. For instance it may be that instead of using full codes shortened enumerations are being used instead, so these need to be mapped to the target code in the standard.

Figure 1 shows the way the data might look when input to our research data aggregation system, let's call this the input state. The data from each trust consists of 4 records covering 6 data items, however the headers are not

Trust A

case_id	gender	clinical finding	date of finding	outcome	date of outcome
14d9e460-63cb-43e4-b323-fee2bb408eab	female	Alcohol excess	04 November 2010	Complete Remission/Response	10 February 2015
208b87e8-f96f-419c-a659-c94a1b4c12b7	male	Hepatitis B virus infection	04 November 2010	Stable Disease	18 May 2018
2cb6ca17-edc8-4b84-896b-dc8a3aca5e25	male	Alcohol excess	18 May 2012	Progressive Disease	10 February 2015
e80deff0-6d18-4093-8d6d-ee481e4d06ac	male	Hepatitis B virus infection	18 May 2012	[Not Available]	18 May 2018

Trust B

case_id	sex	finding		outcome	
349e01b0-0c88-4321-839e-0a84edf11a73	1	A	4/11/10	3	10/2/17
31798d61-fb34-49dc-a20e-091c1a20eb6a	2	A	2/12/10	4	18/5/17
4631400b-1c96-4074-b779-7cbc77a49d99	2	B	18/4/12	2	10/2/17
4631400b-1c96-4074-b779-7cbc77a49d99	2	C	12/5/12	1	18/5/18

Trust C

case_id	gender	clinical finding		result	
e7d1b042-5b1c-4c29-b501-a5ef4810ecd2	1	1	04/11/2010	A2	10/02/2015
6013a4fd-89cf-48a7-a465-c7b644afb4a5	1	4	04/11/2010	A3	18/05/2018
7abb4883-60b7-4882-b946-1a4665889257	4	3	18/05/2012	B2	10/02/2015
7abb4883-60b7-4882-b946-1a4665889257	2	7	18/05/2012	E4	18/05/2018

Trust D

case_id	sex	finding		status	
14d9e460-63cb-43e4-b323-fee2bb408eab	1	3	14/11/2010	A2	10/02/2015
208b87e8-f96f-419c-a659-c94a1b4c12b7	2	4	05/11/2010	A3	18/05/2018
2cb6ca17-edc8-4b84-896b-dc8a3aca5e25	6	3	15/05/2012	B2	10/02/2015
e80deff0-6d18-4093-8d6d-ee481e4d06ac	7	4	15/05/2012	E4	18/05/2018

Fig. 1. Illustrative sample of heterogeneous data.

Trust	case_id	gender	clinical finding	date of finding	outcome	date of outcome
A	14d9e460-63cb-43e4-b323-fee2bb408eab	8532	4052460	04/11/2010	4014046	10/02/2015
A	208b87e8-f96f-419c-a659-c94a1b4c12b7	8507	45615497	04/11/2010	36309215	18/05/2018
A	2cb6ca17-edc8-4b84-896b-dc8a3aca5e25	8507	4052460	18/05/2012	2618003	10/02/2015
A	e80deff0-6d18-4093-8d6d-ee481e4d06ac	8507	45615497	18/05/2012	0	18/05/2018
B	349e01b0-0c88-4321-839e-0a84edf11a73	8532	45615497	04/11/2010	0	18/05/2018
B	31798d61-fb34-49dc-a20e-091c1a20eb6a	8507	45615407	02/12/2010	36309215	10/03/2017
B	4631400b-1c96-4074-b779-7cbc77a49d99	8507	40319607	18/04/2012	4014046	18/05/2017
B	4631400b-1c96-4074-b779-7cbc77a49d99	8507	4148231	12/05/2012	2618003	10/02/2017
C	e7d1b042-5b1c-4c29-b501-a5ef4810ecd2	8532	40319607	04/11/2010	36309215	18/05/2018
C	6013a4fd-89cf-48a7-a465-c7b644afb4a5	8532	45615497	04/11/2010	4014046	10/02/2015
C	7abb4883-60b7-4882-b946-1a4665889257	0	4148231	18/05/2012	2618003	18/05/2018
C	7abb4883-60b7-4882-b946-1a4665889257	8507	4052460	18/05/2012	36309215	10/02/2015
D	14d9e460-63cb-43e4-b323-fee2bb408eab	8532	45615497	14/11/2010	4014046	18/05/2018
D	208b87e8-f96f-419c-a659-c94a1b4c12b7	8507	40319607	05/11/2010	2618003	10/02/2015
D	2cb6ca17-edc8-4b84-896b-dc8a3aca5e25	0	4052460	15/05/2012	4014046	18/05/2018
D	e80deff0-6d18-4093-8d6d-ee481e4d06ac	0	40319607	15/05/2012	36309215	

Fig. 2. Illustrative sample of homogeneous research quality data.

necessarily the same, and neither is the data formatting. Our researcher needs consistent data in the form shown in Fig. 2, let's call this the research state where the data is conforming to the target data model, in this case the OMOP Common Data Model.

What effort is required to transform the dataset in Fig. 1 to the dataset shown in Fig. 2? How can we describe and specify the process so that it can be automated? What techniques can be used to carry out this automation process? The amount of data in this simple example is relatively small for illustrative purposes, but to be useful, we need to be able to apply the techniques evaluated to datasets of much larger sizes, at least 1000 times as large.

We assume here that if a dataset is coded to a known data standard, then all the relevant checks can be carried out by machine, apart from the initial linking of the source dataset to the target dataset.

Consider data input from Trust A going into the research data system. It is an ad-hoc dataset, arguably it has a kind of data dictionary in that the header descriptions provide metadata which applies to the whole column of data. A lookup has to be performed from this header or data description to the OMOP code, and then each text item needs to be translated. Since there is no definition for the ad-hoc data we need to perform 4 manual transformation (MT) checks, one for each data item, and we need to do this for each input data report which arrives, unless we are prepared to make assumptions with regard to the data input. In practise this would probably involve our researcher writing a script to transform the data input, and then needing to check the output, at least for errors, manually each time it is run. It is likely over this 4-year period that data formats will change at least twice. For the period of the study we will therefore need to carry out 192 MT's, just for Trust A, which is sending out data on an ad-hoc basis. If this was the case for all the trusts then we would be looking at figure of 764 MT's.

For the other 3 Trusts two data standards are in play, so we need to build a transformation from each data input(source) item to each research(target) data item. A manual transformation check will be needed to verify a particular link from the data input format to the research data format. Since there are only 2 data standards in play we need only identify 8 links to make the transformation for the 12 items originating from the 3 Trusts. This may change of course if any of the standards are updated, which is quite likely in a 4 year period. So let us assume the standards change twice in this period, it means that over the 48 month period we will need to update these 8 links twice, so in terms of manual transformation checks we can assign a value of 24 for the period.

Overall, we can see that having standards in play reduces the amount of manual checking from a factor of 764 to 216 MT's, an approximate 80% reduction in manual intervention. If we now add into our model the notion that the data being sent over more than just 2 nodes. Very often data will originate in one patient record system in a Hospital Trust, but it will then be transferred to another Trust in the same group, or to a staging area, such a Genomic Medicine Centre, which is responsible for aggregating that data. This means that it will go through another layer of transformation. In other words, the journey from source to the researcher will involve twice as many transformation potentially.

Our researcher is looking at 3 key data items, and to do this the data pipeline will require 216 MT's. If we extend the data set to one containing say 600 data items, and assume that it passes 2 sets of transformations then we get a figure of 86,400 MT's over the period. This may not seem that excessive, but the problem is that each manual transformation check requires human computation and a repetitious attention to detail, and this is not something everybody is good at. If one check takes 30 s then it will take about 4.5 months to ensure the datasets are conformant. This is a significant amount of time over a 4-year working period, time much better spent on data analysis.

If these checks can be carried out automatically then we are likely to improve the data quality as well as reducing the time taken to obtain high quality research data. If we manage to get all 4 Trusts to stick to 2 data standards, then we can reduce the manual checks to 24 for 3 data items, which translates to 480 MT's, and at 30 s each we arrive at about 4 h of tedious checking over the 4-year period. The rest of the transformation and checking work can be carried out by machine. This motivational example shows how the amount of time taken to ensure transformational correctness and data quality can be reduced by significant factors by using a standards based approach. We still need to show the most efficient way of implementing that approach.

Examples of Coding for the Example Datasets. For person phenotypic sex in the NHS Data Dictionary we use:

- 1 Male
- 2 Female
- 9 Indeterminate (unable to be classified as either male or female)

But for Person stated gender we use:

- 0 Not Known
- 1 Male
- 2 Female
- 9 Not Specified

So these codes will need to be linked to the target gender codes as used in OMOP:

- FEMALE (concept_id=8532)
- MALE (concept_id=8507)
- UNKNOWN INFORMATION (concept_id=0)

A researcher will need to check that the transformations are correct, and may assume from the data that the source is from a dataset using the *phenotypic sex* codes, getting a series of digits: 1, 2, 9 which are relatively easy to map to the target dataset values of 8507, 8532 and 0 respectively. However if the source has changed to another application using *Person Stated Gender* we may start getting a 0 appearing in the dataset. It maybe that the researcher is informed of the change, or it may be that this may be flagged as a data error. Either way the researcher will need to check the transformation, and then decide whether to map the new data element value in the source file of 0 to a value of 0 in the target file in addition to the existing 9 to 0 mapping, or whether to ignore it altogether. If the researcher has been told of the change, or perhaps there is some metadata indicating this change in the source dataset, then this is a relatively easy change to implement. However, if there is suddenly a significant number of *0 values* in the dataset, the researcher will need to check back to confirm what change has happened, has the value enumeration changed, or is the dataset suddenly suffered a deprecation in data quality. In this case it's highly likely that will be mapped, however, a dataset which has all its entries mapped to male or female is telling a different story to one which has perhaps 5% mapped to *unknown*. These differences may affect the final analysis being carried out, in this example the dataset is fairly trivial, however it illustrated the potential for changes in the dataset, and it also shows why checking transformations manually can be a very time-consuming process.

Once we get into the clinical detail, even for these 3 data elements, we start to see much more complicated sets of values for data elements representing more complex medical concepts, for Loinc we have:

- 1 Identifies as male http://snomed.info/sct ©: 446151000124109 Identifies as male gender (finding) LA22878-5
- 2 Identifies as female http://snomed.info/sct ©: 446141000124107 Identifies as female gender (finding) LA22879-3
- 3 Female-to-male transsexual http://snomed.info/sct ©: 407377005 Female-to-male transsexual (finding) LA22880-1
- 4 Male-to-female transsexual http://snomed.info/sct ©: 407376001 Male-to-female transsexual (finding) LA22881-9
- 5 Identifies as non-conforming http://snomed.info/sct ©: 446131000124102 Identifies as non-conforming gender (finding) LA22882-7
- 6 Other LA46-8
- 7 Asked but unknown

and for SNOMED CT we have:

- 1. Feminine gender (finding SCTID: 703118005)
- 2. Gender unknown (finding: SCTID: 394743007)
- 3. Gender unspecified (finding:SCTID: 394744001)
- 4. Masculine gender (finding SCTID: 703117000)
- 5. Non-binary gender (finding SCTID: 1066981000000107)
- 6. Surgically transgendered transsexual (finding SCTID: 407375002)
- 7. Surgically transgendered transsexual, female-to-male (SCTID: 407379008)
- 8. Surgically transgendered transsexual, male-to-female (SCTID: 407378000)
- 9. Transgender identity (finding:SCTID: 12271241000119109)

The 7 LOINC values can be mapped directly to the 9-value SNOMED CT listing, however, in some cases mis-matches can occur and more metadata is required to make the mapping. For instance, in transforming a data item linked to SCTID: 407375002 to a LOINC based dataset it is not known in detail whether the Surgically transgendered transsexual is male-to-female or female-to-male and therefore the mapping would probably be to item 5 or 6. A further transformation back to SNOMED CT would lose the information which was previously present in the dataset.

In the NHS Data Dictionary National Codes, for the Cancer Outcomes and Services Data Set, LIVER CIRRHOSIS CAUSE TYPE is recorded during a Liver Cancer Care Spell, and this data element has 6 different enumerations: 1: Alcohol excess, 2: Hepatitis B virus infection, 3: Hepatitis C virus infection, 4: Non alcohol related fatty liver disease, 5: Hereditary haemochromatosis, 6: Other (not listed).

This motivational example shows how the manual checking time for transforming data items firstly is time-consuming, tedious and requires a high level of expertise. It also shows how the time factor can be reduced by applying machine readable data standards to dataset management. By a simple example we have

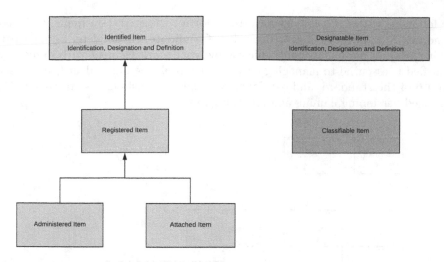

Fig. 3. Types of items in a metadata registry (Reproduced from ISO111179 Part 6 4.2).

shown how employing a machine readable standard the time taken to manage these datasets can be reduced from 4.4 months to 4 h. We will show later that this time can be reduced to minutes by using metadata registries efficiently to store the data standard profile in a machine readable manner.

4.2   Key Issues Highlighted by ISO11179

Following the initial tests on an ISO11179 compliant metadata registry, documented in [23], the standard was consulted to examine which parts were useful to the study and which were not. Implementing an ISO11179 compliant metadata registry did not allow us to achieve our object of formally defining a way to automate and curate datasets. However, there were a number of lessons learnt during this exercise which enabled us to take issues identified in the standard and apply them to the problem.

Managing Versions. Naming is dealt with in depth in Part 5, and administration of data items is dealt with in Part 6. The practice of naming administrative models as detailed in the standard was too complex for us, for instance in the standard data items are divided into registered items, administered items, designatable items, identifiable items, classifiable items and attached items, as per Fig. 3, which has been reproduced from the standard. This we found could be simplified, since every item in the registry needs to be registered and administrated so we made no distinction, and had all data elements being derived from *registeredItems*. The standard also mandates that all items are given unique identities, and that a status be registered for all items. The standard gives the following list of possible *lifecycle*states for a registered data item: Preferred Standard, Standard, Qualified, Recorded, Candidate, Incomplete, Superseded. Having a clear naming system which allow each data element to be uniquely identified is essential to managing datasets, we took the ideas identified in Part 5 and 6 of the standard, and developed a simpler publishing system which also embraced versioning,naming and identification.

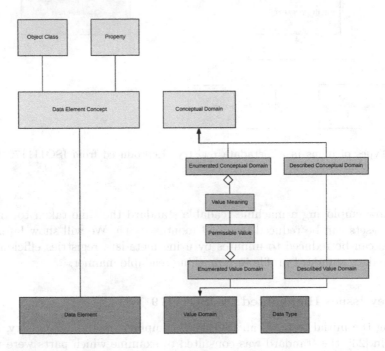

Fig. 4. ISO11179-meta-model (Reproduced from ISO111179 Part 3 section 11, tables 9, 11, and 13).

Semantics. Part 1 of the standard states that:

> There are semantic, syntactic, and lexical rules used to form a naming convention. Names are a simple means to provide some semantics about data constructs, however the semantics are not complete

The topic of forming a naming system is further tackled in part 5, however, no particular set of rules is prescribed, so whilst it is acknowledged that rules are needed to define a naming convention which can provide semantics, no indication of how to build such a system is given. Furthermore, the use of names to provide some kind of semantic equivalence is ruled out in Part 5 section 1:

> It is out of scope of the naming rules to establish semantic equivalence of names among different languages. Naming must be supplemented by other

methods such as ontologies or controlled vocabularies in establishing semantic equivalence.

If we go back to the start of the standard we see that semantics are core to the concept of a metadata registry:

The contextual semantics are described by the data element concept (DEC). The DEC describes the kinds of objects for which data are collected and the particular characteristic of those objects being measured. The symbolic semantics are described by the conceptual domain (CD). A CD is a set of categories, not necessarily finite, where the categories represent the meaning of the permissible values in a value domain - the allowed values for a data element. The names, definitions, datatype, and related objects that are associated with a particular object in an MDR give that object meaning. The depth of this meaning is limited, because names and definitions convey limited information about an object. The relationships that object has with semantically related objects in a registry provides additional information, but the additional information is dependent on how many semantically related objects there are.

In the next section we examine the meta-model provided by the standard.

The Meta-model. Initially an ISO11179 based meta-model was used in the basic architecture of the metadata registry, used to register and curate datasets as described earlier on. However during the study 8 problems were identified, which were listed in [23]. Some of these were problems with the way in which the standard was expressed, and some were problems with the meta-model itself. The key problems relating to the meta-model were;

- ISO11179 introduces representational items, such as *Conceptual Domain, Data Element, Data Element Concept, etc*, indicating that they are part of the *standard or ideal metadata registry meta-model* with no indication of how the ISO11179-compliant models so defined are generated, used or related, nor how data can be transformed into this particular model or what the actual advantage is over any other meta-model/model.
- Basic types used in the *meta-model* include types which in most computer science contexts would be viewed as derived types, this makes implementation needlessly difficult and confusing.
- The introduction asserts that metadata registry is specified in the form of a conceptual data model, however, despite references to other standards, and a brief explanation in ISO/IEC 11179-3 Third Edition 15-02-2015 Annex, E no formal definition of what is meant by *conceptual data model* is provided.
- Value domains are specified with the same definition that is used to describe data types.

In addition, the representational items Object Class, Property and Conceptual domain were thought to serve no useful purpose, and could be replaced by a set of relationships and relationship types which would allow contextual and semantic issues to be expressed through linking to other data elements, in particular to elements from managed terminologies and ontologies. The ISO-meta-model from Part3–10 is illustrated in Fig. 4. To address these problems and others documented in [23], a new meta-model and meta-modelling language was proposed, which is described in the next section.

5   Results

The core of this research involved software development using an iterative, agile methodology. Much of the success therefore depended on how effectively the systems developed can be used by practitioners in the field. The key results of this research were to build a data pipeline for Genonics England. They have used this platform over the past 3 years and continue to do so, the benefits can be listed as follows:

- Specifying exact data models for research (rather than using a preset data standard built for another purpose)
- Providing the data description in a machine readable format, that can be used by automatic software generation applications to develop, for example, online research questionaires.
- Reduction in time and effort, as illustrated in the motivational example
- The ability to validate data automatically using a variety of rules and constraints stored in the MDR, thus raising the quality of data accepted into the research pipeline
- The ability to access and search for similar data elements from different datasets and models.
- The capability to generate XML and XSL schemas automatically based on curated dataset descriptions.
- The capability to map between different data elements in different data models, due to unambiguous identification.

5.1   MDML - Metadata Modelling Language

The key requirements which were identified during the initial phase of work were as follows:

- A well understood set of representational items or entities in the core model
- A consistent meta-model formally specified.
- A clear specification allowing deferent features to be easily identified and evaluated
- A consistent type system
- The ability to link together different kinds of terminologies, ontologies, data models, and programming models.

– A method of linking together elements in different models, and importing data elements from one model into another model, so that well-defined data elements can be shared across a number of models.
– A clear cut identification systems for data elements.

The overall result is a meta-model, part of which is illustrated in Fig. 5

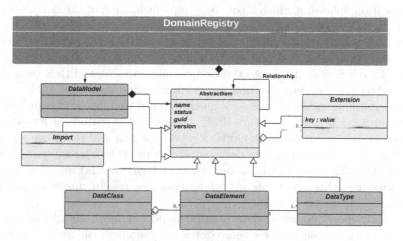

Fig. 5. MDML meta-model.

The key change to the meta-model concerned the adoption of a more common grouping or containment paradigm, so that data elements can be grouped using the notion of a class, rather than a classifier or object class as in the standard. This provides a more flexible and intuitive means of grouping data elements, however data elements can be contained in many different classes, unlike class attributes in UML they are not specific to a particular class.

Another change is that every data item in the registry is in effect a data item, or registered item, they all have a unique identifier which is related to the publishing system. Every data item can be related to every other data item, and every data item can have metadata attached, using the extension mechanism. A data element has a data type, the notion of value domains has been dropped, mostly because it was difficult to explain the difference between a *value domain* and a *data-type* to data professionals working on the project.

MDML Specification. The MetaData Modelling Language (MDML), originally named the Metadata Management Language, is designed to address the specific healthcare interoperability problems discussed earlier, although the specification is of a general nature and the language can be applied to datasets outside the healthcare domain. We specified the language formally, using the Z notation, because we wanted to examine potential semantic possibilities, however this exercise was not successful so we then then implemented it as a Domain Specific Language (DSL) using the ECore-based XText Language toolkit. The 8 problems discussed in the last section point to a need to capture data structures, relationships, and rules. Ideally, this language should have the core features of an entity-relationship or object modelling notation, as well as the ability to express logical constraints on values and value sets. The Unified Modeling Language (UML) is a widely-used notation which meets this basic requirement, and was initially considered as a candidate, but rejected in favour of the DSL approach.

The abstract language syntax and constraint semantics are specified using the Z notation, following which a concrete implementation of the language using the XText [7] toolkit of the ECore/EMF modelling framework [6]. ECore may be seen as a widely-used implementation of the UML MOF standard—for the purposes of data language definition, there are no significant differences between the two. ECore is embedded into the Eclipse environment and thus comes with a range of widely-used visualisation, programming and modelling tools.

The publishing model arrived at is much reduced from the ISO standard, and only 4 states are defined, these are draft, finalised, deprecated (or superseded), and deleted. While developing a model it's composition and structure are going to be *mutable*, however once a model is agreed, it needs to become *immutable* or *finalised*. A finalised model will have a fixed, externally-valid name: a globally-unique identifier, this will enable any references to be used in automatic processes in a reliable and robust fashion.

Currently most published data standards do not have any globally-unique identifier which can be used by heterogeneous systems in different locations to refer to during any shared operation or communication.

The new meta-model has the notion of hierarchical classes, as does UML, this allows most groupings of data elements to be included using a containment relationship. A dataclass therefore has a set of members, each a named data item. It has also a name, a textual definition, and a constraint. There are two notions of factorisation in class declarations, both of which should be familiar from object modelling: a class may 'contain' other classes, corresponding to an extension of scope or control in implementation; a class may also 'extend' other classes, in the sense of extending or re-using an existing class declaration. These other classes are declared at the same level, and thus the connections to them are represented using identifiers.

A data class is represented by the following schema:

$$
\begin{array}{|l}
\hline
\_DataClass_____ \\
DataItem \\
contains, extends : \mathbb{P}\ Path \\
members : Name \nrightarrow DataItem \\
\hline
\forall\, n : \mathrm{dom}\ members \bullet (members\ n).name = n \\
\hline
\end{array}
$$

Names are unique within a model. A model has a name, a textual definition, and an identifier. It may import the contents of other models. It contains a set of classes, enumerations, and primitive types: every class, enumeration, or primitive that we will consider is declared in exactly one model. It has a status, indicating whether or not it has been finalised: this is a key distinction, as only finalised or immutable models may be used as a basis for determining interoperability. As mentioned before, finalised models will be allocated a globally-unique identifier.

$$Status ::= draft \mid final \mid deprecated \mid deleted$$

A data model is represented by the following schema:

$$
\begin{array}{l}
\rule{0pt}{0pt} \\
\hline
\textit{Model} \\
\hline
\textit{DataItem} \\
imports : \mathbb{P}\,Name \\
classes : Name \nrightarrow DataClass \\
enumerations : Name \nrightarrow Enumeration \\
primitives : Name \nrightarrow Primitive \\
status : Status \\
\hline
\forall\, n : \operatorname{dom} classes \bullet (classes\ n).name = n \\
\forall\, n : \operatorname{dom} enumerations \bullet (enumerations\ n).name = n \\
\forall\, n : \operatorname{dom} primitives \bullet (primitives\ n).name = n \\
\hline
\end{array}
$$

Names of classes, enumerations, and primitives must be unique within a model. A metadata registry is an administered collection of data models, subject to specific constraints upon the way in which models are created, edited, and published. For the purposes of this chapter, a registry or catalogue may be represented as an instance of (a subtype of) the following schema:

$$
\begin{array}{l}
\hline
\textit{Collection} \\
\hline
models : Name \nrightarrow Model \\
\hline
\end{array}
$$

This is only an illustrative sample of the specification, which informed the Xtext grammar which is described in the next section.

MDML Language. XText is a language toolkit, which works initially by defining a set of rules to form a grammar, this is similar to an EBNF grammar, but has a slightly different syntax. However it is a formal set of rules which can be related directly to the specification, which in turn is related back to the requirements derived from the original experimentation. Due to space restrictions we are only reproducing a part of the language here to illustrate the process used to develop the language.

```
DomainRegistry :
(registeredItems += DataModel)*
;
```

This definition is simply defining the item of a DomainRegistry as being something which can contain zero to many registered items, each of which must be a DataModel. We then move on to define a DataModel:

```
DataModel:
'DataModel' name = QualifiedName
'status:' status = Status 'domainid:'
guid = GUID  '@' '(' Version ')'  '{'
(elements += DataItem)*
(relations += Relationship)*
(constraint += Constraint)*
(predicate += Predicate)*
'}'
;
```

A DataModel is defined by a qualified name and a 'modelid' composed of a unique id and a version. The QualifiedName needs to be an identifier, the id needs to be an integer and the version is a semantic versioning [24] identifier (e.g. 0.1.2 or X.Y.Z). Semantic versioning uses the convention that the first digit indicates a new version, the use of which will break previous codebases, the second digit indicates new functionality added in a backward compatible manner, and the third digit indicates a backward compatible update to the model.

5.2   User Traction

Initially an ISO11179 compliant metadata registry was built using the Grails(java) platform, and a number of data standards were uploaded and transformed into the ISO meta-model. As is discussed in [23] this was not successful, the meta-model was not understood, and relationship between "headers" on a spreadsheet and *data elements, data element concepts, value domains, concept domains, object classes and properties* was simply not intuitive. As a result, the model was changes and simplified, this was still not enough and the new meta-model was developed. Initially, it was felt that using the new language in the Eclipse platform would be simpler and easier than specifying data models using excel spreadsheet, however this turned out not to be the case. As a result, the meta-model was re-built on the *grails* platform, and this rapidly became the framework of choice, since the web-based user interface was definitely preferred over the excel spreadsheet alternative.

This framework was adopted by Genomics England to promote a standard description of data elements across all the Genomic Medicine Centres providing data to Genomics England. It was and still is being used to promote a common understanding of data across NHS Trusts involved in the project, allowing re-use of datasets and descriptions of data, and allowing relationships to map data flowing between applications using different standards. The time savings have not been quantitatively measured for practical reasons, but have been estimated using the motivational example introduced earlier on.

6 Discussion

For small scale datasets it is clear that automatic curation and metadata-based tooling is a big overhead, and it is only now that large amounts of data are being integrated and collected into large data-warehouses that problems are appearing, as identified in [26]. By taking a model-driven approach we are able to record all aspects of a data element using a variety of different tools, and apply these to different scenarios.

Formal description logic based ontologies are extremely good artefacts for specifying complex research subjects, and they are now an established way to manage and share knowledge, especially in the biological sciences domain. Classes, concepts, elements/properties, constraints and relationships can be easily recorded, for both data descriptions (upper ontologies) and for instance data. While they allow some degree of semantic interoperability, the problem of evolution is still actively being researched [20], and there is no established way of automatically monitoring versioning. We present a means of doing so, metadata registries built using the MDML meta-model have versioning and identification built in, so a REST call on the metadata registry will by default return the current version of a particular model or ontology.

Most of the key aspects of ontologies can be stored in such a registry and can be addressed using the same REST/JSON api as for relational or XML based data models. In fact, although we have implemented the framework using a java/grails/RDBMS based framework there is no reason why a graph database, or triple store could not be used to store the data. It may indeed be an interesting avenue for further research, especially for solving complex matching problems, since many of the techniques already tried an tested in the field of *Ontology Matching* could be applied.

The use of a metadata registry based on MDML provides the ability to cross reference concepts from ontologies with data elements which are defined in data models, this has enabled rules to be added, mostly as regular expressions derived from ontological constraints, and stored on data-type items. In the Genomics England, case a shared library of data elements and types has been developed that has been used across another 20 or so data models, simplifying the curation, validation and data-landing processes.

7 Related Work

As previously identified, the big data world uses ETL processes to extract data from disparate sources, and yet it appears that data scientist's time is largely spent (50–80%) with data wrangling [19]. This is also logged as a problem in the Big Data world [16], since extract-load-transform (ETL) processes can be carried out in most big data toolkits, but they are very intensive manual tasks, take up a lot of time, and slow down the analysis pipeline. The study on "Data context informed Data Wrangling" [14] proposes a datalog system with a number of algorithms to apply rules from a number of sources, and identifies metadata as a key component in informing those processes.

The paper on data wrangling by Terrizano et al. [11] identifies the licensing and copyright aspects of managing data, which we haven't mentioned at all in this study, but which are partially answered in the MDML metadata registry, and this is an area which is calling for more research as there is little doubt that much data is being collected with scant regard to its provenance, ownership and legal status. Developments in automatic transformations such as reported in [2] will also contribute to study of automated data wrangling where preformated models are not defined.

The work described in this paper has been informed by work carried out by colleagues at the University of Oxford on the CancerGrid project [3], where an ISO/IEC 11179-compliant metadata registry was developed as detailed in [4]. Initially the test software for these studies was developed using the eXist XML database, but it was found to have problems scaling once the number of data elements increased over about 10,000, and so new work was carried out to build a more scalable metadata registry using java-based web frameworks.

The CaBIG initiative by the National Cancer Institute in the USA was one of the first applications of ISO11179 [15,17]. Sinaci and Erturkmen [30] describe a semantic metadata registry framework where Common Data Elements (CDEs) are exposed as Linked Open Data resources. Ulrich et al. [32] report on building a hybrid architecture consisting of an ISO 11179-3 conformant MDR server application for mediating and translating data elements into Fast Health Interoperability Resources (FHIR) [10] for the North German Tumor Bank of Colorectal Cancer.

Tao et al. [31] present case studies in representing HL7 Detailed Clinical Models (DCMs) and the ISO11179 model in the Web Ontology Language (OWL); a combination of UML diagrams and Excel spreadsheets were used to extract the meta-models for fourteen HL7 DCM constructs. A critical limitation of this approach is that the transformation from meta-models to their ontological representation in OWL is based on a manual encoding. Leroux et al. [18] use existing ontologies to enrich OpenClinica forms.

Schlieter et al. [27], Atanasovski [1] apply model driven engineering techniques to healthcare problems, Marcos et al. [21] describes the implementation of an OpenEHR system. The problems with integrating data encoded using different datasets and terminologies are clearly identified by Jian [13], and solutions using OpenEHR technology are put forward in [22].

In the Model Driven Health Tools (MDHT) [25] project, the HL7 Clinical Document Architecture (CDA) standard [5] for managing patient records is implemented using Eclipse UML tools [8]. MDHT supports only the CDA standard, whereas the Model Catalogue can interoperate with any metadata standard. The CDA standards are large and complex: Scott and Worden [29] advocate a model-driven approach to simplify the HL7 CDA.

8 Conclusion

MDML is a domain specific language which has been used effectively to reduce expert involvement in tedious data wrangling tasks. We have not been able to measure the full effect of this during the study as it has been an iterative evolutionary process. Also the amount of data being examined now is well in excess of the amount that a human expert could be expected to validate, so it is safe to say that by using manual techniques, data validation would not have been carried out on the core dataset. Instead it would have been carried out by researchers on their local copy while carrying out specific analysis tasks on an ad-hoc basis. This would have meant that each researcher would have been carrying out the same validation in parallel, on their local subset of data. Such a situation would be much less efficient than maintaining a high quality data repository that can be accessed without having to carry out data wrangling tasks locally.

Using a model driven engineering paradigm in data-wrangling has provided an effective implementation of the main goals identified in ISO11179, using an updated meta-model and applying a simplified version and identification protocol for data-sets. This gives the ability to identify complex data patterns as models and identify them with a globally unique identifier. In turn, this enables rules associated with data elements, or with relationships between data elements, to be applied to data-sets using automated techniques, for validation, transformation and linking. In doing this the degree of complexity is reduced, the data becomes easier to manage, and the human intervention in the process is significantly reduced.

This research effort, carried out with Genomics England, resulted in the use of a model-driven metadata registry that has significantly reduced tedious 'data-wrangling' work. In addition the generation of simple *low code* software applications has been simplified. Applications such as web-based questionaires, excel, word and xml reports have been automatically generated due to the application of model driven engineering techniques.

In summary the application of model-driven engineering techniques to the principles identified in the ISO11179 standard has led to a significant increase in the amount of automation possible in the data wrangling, data validation and data management process.

Acknowledgements. I would like to acknowledge the help of Adam Milward, Kathy Farndon, Amanda O'Neill and Samuel Hubble at Genomics England, and Jim Davies, Charles Crichton, Steve Harris and James Welch at the University of Oxford.

References

1. Atanasovski, B., et al.: On defining a model driven architecture for an enterprise e-health system. Enterp. Inf. Syst. **12**(8–9), 915–941 (2018). https://doi.org/10.1080/17517575.2018.1521996
2. Bogatu, A., Paton, N.W., Fernandes, A.A.A.: Towards automatic data format transformations: data wrangling at scale. In: Calì, A., Wood, P., Martin, N., Poulovassilis, A. (eds.) BICOD 2017. LNCS, vol. 10365, pp. 36–48. Springer, Cham (2017). https://doi.org/10.1007/978-3-319-60795-5_4

3. Davies, J., Gibbons, J., Harris, S., Crichton, C.: The CancerGrid experience: metadata-based model-driven engineering for clinical trials. Sci. Comput. Program. **89**, 126–143 (2014)
4. Davies, J., et al.: Domain-specific modelling for clinical research. In: SPLASH Workshop on Domain-Specific Modelling, October 2015. http://www.dsmforum.org/events/dsm15/Papers/Davies.pdf
5. Dolin, R.H., et al.: HL7 clinical document architecture, release 2. J. Am. Med. Inform. Assoc. **13**(1), 30–39 (2006)
6. Eclipse: Ecore tools (2008). http://eclipse.org/ecoretools/
7. Eclipse: Xtext: Eclipse project (2008). https://eclipse.org/Xtext/
8. Eclipse-Foundation: Eclipse MDT UML2 tools (2018). https://eclipse.org/modeling/mdt?project=uml2
9. Garza, M., Fiol, G.D., Tenenbaum, J., Walden, A., Zozus, M.N.: Evaluating common data models for use with a longitudinal community registry. J. Biomed. Inform. **64**, 333–341 (2016). https://doi.org/10.1016/j.jbi.2016.10.016
10. The HL7-FHIR-Foundation: Fast health interoperability resources (2017). https://www.hl7.org/fhir/
11. Terrizzano, I.G., Schwarz, P.M., Roth, M., Colino, J.E.: Data wrangling: the challenging journey from the wild to the lake. pdfs.semanticscholar.org (2015). https://pdfs.semanticscholar.org/2a24/f587b68a1ef6539b4ed8725dfe76f0ed40e2.pdf
12. ISOTC215: Health informatics - electronic health record (EHR) standard (2008). http://www.en13606.org/
13. Jian, W.S., et al.: Building a portable data and information interoperability infrastructure framework for a standard Taiwan electronic medical record template. Comput. Methods Programs Biomed. **88**(2), 102–111 (2007). https://doi.org/10.1016/j.cmpb.2007.07.014. http://www.sciencedirect.com/science/article/pii/S0169260707001848
14. Koehler, M., et al.: Data context informed data wrangling. In: 2017 IEEE International Conference on Big Data (Big Data), pp. 956–963, December 2017. https://doi.org/10.1109/BigData.2017.8258015
15. Komatsoulis, G.A., et al.: caCORE version 3: implementation of a model driven, service-oriented architecture for semantic interoperability. J. Biomed. Inform. **41**(1), 106–123 (2008)
16. Konstantinou, N., et al.: Thevada architecture for cost-effective data wrangling. In: Proceedings of the 2017 ACM International Conference on Management of Data, pp. 1599–1602 (2017)
17. Kunz, I., Lin, M.C., Frey, L.: Metadata mapping and reuse in caBIG. BMC Bioinform. **10**(Suppl 2), S4 (2009)
18. Leroux, H., McBride, S., Lefort, L., Kemp, M., Gibson, S.: A method for the semantic enrichment of clinical trial data. In: Health Informatics: Building a Healthcare Future Through Trusted Information; Selected Papers from the 20th Australian National Health Informatics Conference (HIC 2012), vol. 178, p. 111. IOS Press (2012)
19. Lohr, S.: For big-data scientists, 'janitor work' is key hurdle to insights. New York Times (2014). https://www.nytimes.com/2014/08/18/technology/for-big-data-scientists-hurdle-to-insights-is-janitor-work.html
20. Mahajan, A., Kaur, P.: A review on evolution and versioning of ontology based information systems. IOSR J. Comput. Eng. (IOSR-JCE) **17**(42), 35–43 (2015)

21. Marcos, M., Maldonado, J.A., Martínez-Salvador, B., Boscá, D., Robles, M.: Interoperability of clinical decision-support systems and electronic health records using archetypes: a case study in clinical trial eligibility. J. Biomed. Inform. **46**(4), 676–689 (2013). https://doi.org/10.1016/j.jbi.2013.05.004
22. Martínez-Costa, C., Menárguez-Tortosa, M., Fernández-Breis, J.T.: An approach for the semantic interoperability of ISO EN 13606 and OpenEHR archetypes. J. Biomed. Inform. **43**(5), 736–746 (2010). https://doi.org/10.1016/j.jbi.2010.05.013. http://www.sciencedirect.com/science/article/pii/S1532046410000821
23. Milward, D.: Model driven data management in healthcare. In: Proceedings of the 7th International Conference on Model-Driven Engineering and Software Development, MODELSWARD, vol. 1, pp. 107–118. INSTICC, SciTePress (2019). https://doi.org/10.5220/0007391101070118
24. OMG: Semantic versioning (2003). https://semver.org/
25. Open-Health-Tools: model driven health tools (2008). https://projects.eclipse.org/proposals/model-driven-health-tools
26. Press, G.: Cleaning big data: most-time-consuming, least enjoyable data sciencetask. Forbes (2016). https://www.forbes.com/sites/gilpress/2016/03/23/data-preparation-most-time-consuming-least-enjoyable-data-science-task-survey-says/
27. Schlieter, H., Burwitz, M., Schönherr, O., Benedict, M.: Towards model driven architecture in health care information system development. In: 12th International Conference on Wirtschaftsinformatik (WI 2015), March 2015
28. Schulz, S., Stegwee, R., Chronaki, C.: Standards in healthcare data. In: Kubben, P., Dumontier, M., Dekker, A. (eds.) Fundamentals of Clinical Data Science, pp. 19–36. Springer, Cham (2019). https://doi.org/10.1007/978-3-319-99713-1_3
29. Scott, P., Worden, R.: Semantic mapping to simplify deployment of HL7 v3 clinical document architecture. J. Biomed. Inform. **45**(4), 697–702 (2012)
30. Sinaci, A.A., Erturkmen, G.B.L.: A federated semantic metadata registry framework for enabling interoperability across clinical research and care domains. J. Biomed. Inform. **46**(5), 784–794 (2013). https://doi.org/10.1016/j.jbi.2013.05.009. http://www.sciencedirect.com/science/article/pii/S1532046413000750
31. Tao, C., Jiang, G., Wei, W., Solbrig, H.R., Chute, C.G.: Towards semantic-web based representation and harmonization of standard meta-data models for clinical studies. AMIA Summits Transl. Sci. Proc. **2011**, 59–63 (2011)
32. Ulrich, H., Kock, A.K., Duhm-Harbeck, P., Habermann, J.K., Ingenerf, J.: Metadata repository for improved data sharing and reuse based on HL7 FHIR. Stud. Health Technol. Inform. **228**, 162–166 (2016)

The Art of Bootstrapping

Andreas Prinz[1](✉) ⓘ and Gergely Mezei[2] ⓘ

[1] Department of ICT, University of Agder, Grimstad, Norway
andreas.prinz@uia.no
[2] Department of Automation and Applied Informatics,
Budapest University of Technology and Economics, Budapest, Hungary
gmezei@aut.bme.hu

Abstract. Language workbenches are used to define languages using appropriate meta-languages. Meta-languages are also just languages and can, therefore, be defined using themselves. The process is called bootstrapping and is often difficult to achieve.

This paper compares four different bootstrapping solutions. The EMF environment and the Meta-Programming System (MPS) use a compiled bootstrapping for their own definition. The platforms LanguageLab and DMLA are using interpreted bootstrapping. This paper compares these kinds of bootstrapping and relates them to the definition of instantiation. Besides the structural aspects of the bootstraps, the dynamism is also elaborated. It is shown how the bootstrap is related to the execution environment. Finally, the level of changeability is also discussed. It is shown that all approaches are quite similar and provide very flexible environments.

Keywords: Language workbench · Bootstrapping · Metamodelling

1 Introduction

Metamodelling [12] is an approach to define languages using metalanguages. In turn, these languages can be used to define specifications (programs) of new languages. Typically, one would use a metamodelling environment, also called language workbench[1] [7,9,25,28], to define languages and metalanguages. The metalanguages are also languages and thus they can be defined using the same or different metalanguages. This process is called bootstrapping, and it is mainly an advantage for the workbench developers. In general, the term 'bootstrapping' is used in several contexts, e. g. to refer to the process to load the initial constructs of an engine to start it. In this paper, bootstrapping refers to a self-descriptive process that acts as the base point of modelling. Bootstrapping is typically not visible to the users. This paper discusses the similarities

---

[1] There are also grammar-based language workbenches in addition to the metamodelling environments.

© Springer Nature Switzerland AG 2020
S. Hammoudi et al. (Eds.): MODELSWARD 2019, CCIS 1161, pp. 182–200, 2020.
https://doi.org/10.1007/978-3-030-37873-8_8

and the differences between four language workbenches, namely Eclipse Modeling Framework (EMF) [24], JetBrains Meta Programming System (MPS) [3,22], LanguageLab [11] and Dynamic Multi-Layer Algebra (DMLA) [5].

EMF is tightly connected to the Eclipse [4] infrastructure. In particular, it is used for the structure definitions of many Eclipse projects. EMF provides high-level descriptions of classes and their relationships similar to MOF [17]. EMF descriptions are simple class diagrams that are translated into Java classes that integrate with the Eclipse infrastructure. Another output from the EMF specifications is an exchange storage format XMI [18] the production of which is auto-generated.

The open-source industrial-strength *Meta-Programming System (MPS)* is provided by the company Jetbrains. MPS has several meta-languages covering a wide range of language-design elements in order to support comprehensive language design. All the meta-languages within MPS are defined using MPS itself making the platform bootstrapped. MPS features a language called Base Language resembling Java, which is then available for language extension and development inside MPS. For example, it is possible to define new constructs for Java (Base Language) within MPS. In the project mbeddr [26], MPS provides an almost complete definition of C++, allowing C++ to be used and extended within MPS. This is exactly what mbeddr does: extending C++ in MPS with state machines and units for use in embedded device programming.

LanguageLab is an academic project at the university of Agder, Norway. It is not concerned with an industrial strength environment, but rather with the concepts that are needed to make metamodelling user-friendly and feasible. The main goal of LanguageLab is to show the essential concepts of metamodelling in a clear and understandable tool, such that it can be used in university teaching [10]. In the same way as MPS, also LanguageLab is bootstrapped such that the few meta-languages of LanguageLab are defined within LanguageLab.

Dynamic Multi-Layer Algebra (DMLA) is also an academic project. It is developed at the Budapest University of Technology and Economics, Hungary. DMLA provides an environment, where stepwise refinement of concepts is possible from the highly abstract initial ideas to the fully concretized final specifications. The approach ensures rigorous validation along the whole process based on constraints specified during the refinement. The goals of the approach are achieved by a multi-layer modelling structure with a built-in, fully modelled operation language. The initial modelling structure, i.e. the bootstrap of DMLA is self-describing and self-validating.

These four language workbenches have different focus. EMF is mostly related to defining structure. The general idea of MPS is to provide the user with as much as possible help in defining languages and using known notation when possible. LanguageLab is focused on a clean environment, and in this context, it tries to avoid exposing the underlying language of the platform to the user. DMLA has focus on validated multi-layer modelling and refinement.

All four platforms are implemented in Java, and this is very visible in EMF and MPS, but not much visible in LanguageLab and DMLA. All four platforms are used to define themselves, and this paper compares these four self-definitions.

The paper starts with an introduction of the essential terms and concepts of metamodelling in Sect. 2. In Sect. 3, more details of the four platforms are provided, before we describe their bootstrap in Sect. 4. Runtime aspects are discussed in Sect. 5. Finally, we conclude in Sect. 6.

2   Terminology

This section introduces the concepts and terms used in metamodelling in general, and in EMF, MPS, LanguageLab and DMLA in particular. We use basically the terms of MPS in this paper, and indicate the different terms used in EMF, LanguageLab, and DMLA.

Metamodelling is an application of model-driven development [1] to language engineering and compiler construction. Instead of implementing language tools and compilers by hand for each domain-specific language, a model of the language is created. From the model, tools are automatically generated [16]. This way, languages can be designed quickly for the programming tasks at hand [29].

A *language description* has several different aspects, which together give a complete description of all important properties of the language. There are the aspect groups e.g. of structure or semantics, as well as a group of tool-related aspects. In this paper, we focus mainly on the most relevant aspects for bootstrapping, namely structure, constraints, and semantics. Concrete syntax is not important in this context, since we can always use a predefined concrete syntax based on the abstract syntax.

The structure (abstract syntax, metamodel) aspect defines the *concepts* that are used in the language and their relationships with each other. In EMF a 'concept' is represented by a 'class'. LanguageLab uses the term 'type', while DMLA uses the term 'entity' instead.

Concepts can own *properties* (of basic types) and *children* (enclosed concepts). Properties are called 'attributes' in LanguageLab and EMF. Children are referred to as 'aggregates' in LanguageLab, while in EMF, they are represented by containment associations. In DMLA, the term 'slot' is used for both of the terms mentioned above. A slot is a placeholder that can have constraints on its type, or cardinality and can have a value. The value can be a primitive or complex value (child).

In modelling, relations between concepts are essential. Typical examples are inheritance, containment, aggregation and UML-like association relations. The containment relation is already discussed in the previous paragraph. Inheritance is referred to as *parent*, while associations are called *references* in EMF, MPS and LanguageLab. In DMLA, containment and association are not distinguished, thus, the term 'slot' is also used for references, while inheritance is currently not supported natively.

The abstract syntax introduces a large range of possible specifications. However, not all of them are meaningful, and thus, constraints are often used to define additional conditions for valid specifications. For example, there can be size constraints (not more than one parent), or type constraints (the actual parameter type must match the formal parameter type), or reference constraints (attribute types have to be defined in the enclosing scope). Constraints are boolean conditions that all have to be true for a specification to be valid.

The meaning of programs in a language is defined by its semantics. There are two main ways to achieve this: transformations (compiler) and executions (interpreter). In the first case, the model is mapped to another model or to source code, and then this other representation is executed. A typical example is a code generator that produces Java code from the model. In the second case, we have a virtual machine that can directly interpret the language models. This is discussed in more detail in Sect. 5.

3   Language Workbenches

In this section, we present the four language workbenches EMF, MPS, Language-Lab, and DMLA. They are selected because they provide very different views onto languages and bootstrapping, and they have different focus.

3.1   EMF

The Eclipse Modeling Framework (EMF) [24] is possibly the most complete and without doubt the most well-known modelling platform nowadays. EMF and Ecore (the underlying modelling foundation) are often referred to as the defactor standard of modelling. There exist many tools and applications using and extending the Eclipse-based framework of EMF in many fields, including visual modelling, metamodeling and model processing. Models are specified in XML Metadata Interchange (XMI) from which EMF provides tools and runtime support to produce a set of Java classes for the model, and also a set of adapter classes that enable viewing and editing of the model. EMF has runtime support for manipulating the models including change notification, persistence support and a reflective API for manipulating modelled objects generically. The platform focuses not only on models themselves but also on editing the models. EMF provides a basic editor and several ways to extend the editor in a textual or visual way.

From the modelling point of view, EMF is based on Ecore which itself is a reference implementation of the EMOF standard [19]. Although MOF has four modelling layers, in practice, EMF is restricted to two modelling layers (metamodel and model) from the users point of view, while the core metamodel of Ecore is self-defining.

Although the potential extension points of an EMF domain are countless, the usual modelling scenario is often code-based, not modelled. Typically, the user creates the structural definition of her domain model based on the Ecore metamodel. Then the definition is refined by additional constraints (OCL constraints or custom, Java validation methods) if required. If execution semantics is needed, the user may implement the corresponding methods in Java and execute them from the modelling environment, or use approaches such as Kermeta3 [13] to overcome the limitations of Ecore. To sum up, in case of EMF, only the structural aspect of the model definitions is modelled by its bootstrap.

3.2 MPS

JetBrains MPS is a metaprogramming system which is being developed by JetBrains. MPS is a tool to design domain-specific languages (DSL). It uses projectional editing which allows users to overcome the limits of language parsers, and build DSL editors using text, tables and diagrams. It implements language-oriented programming [29]. MPS is an environment for language definition, a language workbench, and an integrated development environment (IDE) for such languages.

Developers from different domains can benefit from domain specific language extensions in general purpose programming languages. For example, Java developers working with financial applications might benefit from built-in support for monetary values. Unfortunately, traditional text based languages are subject to text ambiguity problems which makes such extensions problematic.

MPS supports composable language definitions. This means that languages can be extended, and embedded, and these extensions can be used, and will work, in the same program in MPS. For example, if Java is extended with a better syntax for collections and then again extended with a better syntax for dates, these extensions will work well together.

MPS solves grammar ambiguity issues by working with the abstract syntax tree directly. In order to edit such a tree, a text-like projectional editor is used.

MPS provides a reusable language infrastructure which is configured with language definition languages. MPS also provides many IDE services automatically: editor, code completion, find usages, etc.

The boostrap of MPS includes a definition of almost complete Java called Base Language. It also provides languages for collections, dates, closures and regular expressions. All meta-languages (language definition languages) of MPS are defined in MPS, with languages for structure, editor, constraints, type system, and generator.

For better applicability of MPS, there is also a connection to C and C++ given by the project mbeddr [26]. Its main purpose is to provide support for the development of embedded system using MPS. It has languages tailored to embedded development and formal methods: core C language, components, physical units, and state machines.

3.3 LanguageLab

In metamodel-based language design, a major challenge is to be able to operate on an adequate level of abstraction when designing a complete computer language. There are several different technologies, meta-languages and tools in use for defining different aspects of a language, that may or may not satisfy the needs of a DSL developer when it comes to abstraction level. Before starting the design and development of the LanguageLab workbench, we set out to examine what concepts are needed for defining the different aspects of a computer language, and discuss how to apply them on a suitable level of abstraction. If the abstraction level is too high, the definition of behaviour may be a challenge, while if the abstraction level is too low, the language developer will spend too much time on unnecessary details.

The LanguageLab platform facilitates operation on a suitable abstraction level. It provides user-friendliness and a low threshold to getting started, in order to make it useful for teaching of metamodelling. The platform is open for third party language modules and it is intended to facilitate reuse of language modules, modular language development and experiments with multiple concrete syntaxes. Another goal is to supply some basic guidelines for developing LanguageLab modules that can further add to the features and capabilities of the LanguageLab platform.

Based on experiences from teaching, the core LanguageLab is a very simple metamodel-based language definition platform, attempting to remove some of the complexity of the more popular existing tools. This simplicity allows students to grasp the basic principles of metamodelling by working on small language examples on a suitable level of abstraction for each relevant language aspect.

In LanguageLab, a language definition consists of one or more modules with structured elements that can be run as an IDE for that language. Program (code) specifications work in the same way. Specifications can also be run as programs and create the intended execution as described by the language used.

LanguageLab exists as a simple prototype based on Eclipse/EMF. There is also a more advanced version built in MPS. LanguageLab is simplistic by design.

3.4 DMLA

The Dynamic Multi-Layer Algebra (DMLA) [5] is a multi-layer modelling framework based on Abstract State Machines (ASM) [2]. DMLA consists of two parts: (i) the Core containing the formal definition of modelling structures and their management functions; and (ii) the Bootstrap having a set of essential reusable entities for all modelled domains in DMLA. We have intentionally separated the two parts to be able to use the same structure with different bootstraps, like a computer, which can be used with different operating systems.

According to the Core, each concept is defined by a 4-tuple (unique ID, meta-reference, attributes and concrete values). Besides these tuples, the Core also defines basic functions to manipulate the model graph, for example, to create new model entities or query existing ones. This solution makes it possible to create a virtual machine handling the concepts and simulating the ASM functions and thus act as an implementation-independent interpreter for the models.

Although the tuple-based structure is defined by the Core, it is useless without a proper bootstrap. The role of the Bootstrap is to define the basic, essential built-in building blocks for practical modelling. For example, concepts such as

'Entity', 'Slot' and 'Constraint' are introduced here. Based on the complete setup of these initial concepts, the definition of domain models is possible. Instantiation in DMLA means gradual constraining and thus has several peculiarities. Whenever a model concept claims another concept as its meta-concept, the framework automatically validates if there is indeed a valid instantiation between the two concepts. Similarly to concepts, slots are also automatically validated against their meta-slots (each slot has a reference to its meta-slot). The rules of valid instantiation are not encoded in an external programming language (e.g. Java), but modelled by the bootstrap. The operations needed for encoding the concrete validation logic of instantiation are modelled by their abstract syntax tree (AST) representation as 4-tuples within the bootstrap.

In DMLA, multi-level behaviour is supported by 'fluid metamodeling', that is, instead of following a rigid hierarchy between the modelling levels, each concept can refer to any other concept along the complete meta-hierarchy, unless the reference is found to be contradictory to the validation rules. This way, instantiation in DMLA acts as a refinement relation, where the concepts to be refined can be referenced anywhere within the modelling space. DMLA also supports horizontal refinement, when previously existing slots are cloned, not concretized, but new slots may be added and thus the original concept may be extended. Note that this behaviour is very similar to inheritance, therefore we use it to simulate inheritance relationships.

From the practical applications point of view, there are two major versions of DMLA workbenches. The old version has an XText-based editing environment, where users can edit their models using our scripting language, DMLAScript [27]. DMLAScipt is only syntactic sugar to hide the tuple-based structure from users. The models defined by the scripts are translated to tuples and the tuples to Java. The generated code acts as a set of instructions for the underlying abstract state machine developed in Java. The main limitation of this approach is that the model is validated as a whole and dynamic modification is not supported. In other words, one can define a hierarchy of refinements and validate it, but cannot apply operations on the models interactively. In order to solve this, we are working on a new workbench based on GraalVM [20] and Truffle [21]. In this new environment, we provide a complete virtual machine for the users, which can be used interactively, e.g. run operations altering the modelling concepts. In this paper, we will refer to only this new version of DMLA.

4   Bootstrap

Bootstrapping is connected to a circularity in definition. In the context of language workbenches, this means that one language is defined using itself or a set of languages is defined using that same set. It is a good idea to distinguish between the bootstrap situation and the bootstrap process.

Bootstrap Situation. The bootstrap situation is a static situation describing how languages and concepts depend on each other. For normal use in a language workbench, new languages are defined using existing meta-languages. Here, the new languages depend on the meta-languages, as they are defined using them. The meta-languages are just used and have no dependency on the new languages.

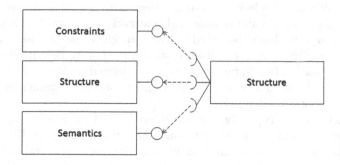

Fig. 1. Circularity between languages.

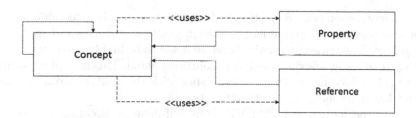

Fig. 2. Circularity between concepts.

Looking at the meta-languages themselves, they are typically also defined using the same meta-languages, thereby establishing a circular definition-use dependency. For example, the structure meta-language is defined using three meta-languages: the structure meta-language, the constraint meta-language and the semantics meta-language (Fig. 1).

Just by looking at the language level, it is hard to open up the challenge of circularity. Instead, it is valuable to look at the dependencies on the concept level. In Fig. 2, we show the details of the circularity displayed in Fig. 1 from the concept level's point of view. The three concepts 'Concept', 'Property', and 'Reference' are defined in the structure language, but all of them are in fact instances of the concept 'Concept'. They are concepts and therefore they may have properties (like a name), children (like methods) and references (like a type), which are instances of Property, Child and Reference, respectively. The dependency relationship that leads to the circularity is the instantiation relation.

Language workbenches may offer different solutions, but at the very core, they have to answer the same question: how are the concepts defined using each other?

Bootstrap Process. The bootstrap process is the technical process that leads from a situation without circularity to the situation with circularity. Often, this is a technically challenging step and is difficult to understand, see [14,23].

In the process of bootstrap, the definition of Concept needs reference to properties, children and references, but in order to achieve this, we need to have the concept of property, containment and reference, respectively. However, the definition of property should be based on the concept 'Concept' that we are just trying to create. Often, it is possible to start with empty definitions that can be filled later, leading to several concepts to be defined at once and referencing each other. This leads to a tightly coupled set of concepts together forming the essence of the bootstrap definition.

The tricky part is typically the self-reference, which would imply that a concept is defined before it is defined, which is impossible. Often, this situation has to be established using means from outside the language workbench. In this paper, we focus more on the bootstrap situation as the process is only needed once, and then the bootstrap situation can be used again and again.

4.1 The Bootstrap of EMF

The main motivation behind creating EMF was to have a universal modelling and model processing platform that can be used in practical scenarios and application development. The infrastructure is therefore made to be highly customizable and easy to extend using a flexible modelling solution behind. This modelling solution is Ecore [24], which has a strong resemblance with the EMOF variant of MOF [17], but has more focus on practical functionality.

Ecore is the metamodel for EMF. It is self-defining because it is used to explain its own classes. The elements and the structure of Ecore are translated into native Java classes, which again are used to represent the metamodel of Ecore. This way, Ecore concepts act more as interface specifications rather than implementation classes, since their logic is not modelled. For example, the root concept EObject has a method eContainer() that returns its container concept (or null, if it does not have one), but it is not specified in Ecore how the container is retrieved. More precisely the specification is available but only as an informal textual description written in English.

The reason for this is that EMF is only a structural tool with focus on navigating and manipulating the concepts and their properties. ECore does not take into account aspects of constraints or semantics. The structural parts described by Ecore can be extended by constraints as EAnnotations. From the practical points of view, several methods exist to handle the constraints e.g. adding annotated Java methods, or using projects such as Eclipse OCL [6]. However, from the theoretical points of view, unfortunately, this also means that Ecore itself does not support adding and validating constraints.

There is no support for modelling the operation logic (i.e. dynamic semantics) in Ecore either. Similar to constraints, we can easily attach methods to the model written in Java, or use Eclipse-based projects to model the operations, but Ecore is capable only to describe the interface of operations.

Ecore, as an interface specification, is not only able to describe itself, also the complete infrastructure of EMF is built upon the current version of Ecore. So changes to the Ecore, although possible, might invalidate many Eclipse projects being build using EMF, since the Java implementation relies on existing concepts and relations between the concepts.

4.2   The Bootstrap of MPS

MPS uses all its meta-languages for the bootstrap, i.e. structure, editor, constraints, behaviour, typesystem, intentions, accessories, generator, runtime, actions, dataflow, refactorings, textgen and version control. Based on the focus of this paper, we only consider the aspects structure, constraints, and typesystem as well as generator (semantics). All the other aspects are mainly used to improve the user experience, and the bootstrap works also without them.

This leads to the language dependencies shown in Fig. 3, which are explained in more detail in the next subsection. At the concept level, the name of the self-referential concept is *ConceptDeclaration*, not *Concept*. Properties and references are instances of *ConceptDeclaration*, and they are attached to the concept declarations as already shown in Fig. 2. This way they are not involved in the direct circularity. A similar argument applies to *EditorDeclaration* and *ConstraintDeclaration*, which are instances of *ConceptDeclaration*. They are attached to concept declarations using references.

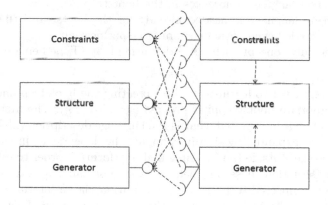

Fig. 3. Bootstrap in MPS and LanguageLab.

The bootstrapping process in MPS is enabled by the generated Java code. In a first attempt, the code is created semi-automatically, and then the loop is established and the new code generation will recreate the correct code. After the loop is existing, also changes to the bootstrap situation are possible.

4.3 The Bootstrap of LanguageLab

The bootstrap of LanguageLab is shown in Fig. 3. This figure depicts three languages in their meta-language role on the left, and in their language role on the right. Still, the languages are the same as indicated by the same name.

There are two kinds of dependencies in Fig. 3: use dependencies and references. A use dependency is a connection between a meta-language and a language, i.e. an arrow from the right to the left. Essentially it means that a description is dependent on the language it is written in. A reference is given between languages on the same meta-level. In our case, both the constraints language and the generator language depend on the structure language, as the constraint and the generator descriptions always refer to their concept description.

At the concept level, the situation is very similar as before. Here, the name of the self-referential concept is 'Type', not 'Concept'. Property and Reference are instances of Type, and they are attached to Types. In the same way, Constraint and Semantics are instances of Type and they are attached to Types using references, see again Fig. 2.

This leads to the the structure language being central to the bootstrap, as indicated in Fig. 3. There are the following reasons for the structure language being special, all of them being related to the Type concept.

– The structure language has five incoming dependencies, three with instantiation to structure, constraints, and semantics, and two as references from constraints and semantics to Type. In fact, these two references are the only incoming cross-language references in the bootstrap.
– The structure language is needed already for the bootstrap situation. This means it is needed even without running a specification.
– Type is the only concept with a self-definition loop (Type being defined by a Type).

LanguageLab has two features to allow creating the bootstrapping situation using an appropriate bootstrapping process (see also [23]). The first feature is that LanguageLab is interpreted, that is the language description (file) is used as it is. This can be exploited by simply changing the dependency in the language description file (i.e. outside the LanguageLab platform) in order to establish the bootstrapping situation. A second helpful feature of LanguageLab is that each language use is connected to its language definition via an interface, where the actual language can be exchanged when the instance is loaded. This means that there is no direct connection between language use and language definition. With these interfaces, bootstrapping is even possible within the platform itself.

4.4 The Bootstrap of DMLA

In this paper we give a brief summary of the bootstrap elements to illustrate the mechanisms. For more details, please refer to [5].

The bootstrap of DMLA is not structured using meta-languages: the definition of constraints and operations are merged with the structural parts. They are not separated, because the structure, the validation (constraints) and the dynamic behaviour (operations) are all essential when creating model definitions, none of them would work without the other two. The main reason behind is that even the definition of type and cardinality checking are modelled. For example, by changing the implementation of the built-in TypeConstraint entity, one can alter what type conformance means. Note that the term 'implementation' refers here to an operation fully modelled by tuples of DMLA, not to a method written in code. This is why DMLA is said to be self-validating, as the validation methods are essential parts of the bootstrap model. Although in DMLA the bootstrap is not structured into separate languages, we have the same challenges to solve: the definition of the basics of structure, constraints and execution.

The topmost concept is referred to as 'Base', all other concepts are direct or indirect instances of it. Base grants three features for its instances: (i) the ability to have slots (properties, children and references), (ii) the ability to have constraints and (iii) it also defines the basic validation formulae.

The first feature grants composability. Note that even the definition of 'slot' is modelled (by the concept SlotDef), not hard coded.

The second feature (constraint containment) is used to fine-tune instantiation rules. Constraints (originated from the concept 'Constraint') are re-usable validation logic definitions and they are intensively used to specify type-, and cardinality restrictions as mentioned earlier, since no a priori instantiation rules are implemented. The same mechanism can also be used to add custom, user-defined constraints to further restrict instantiation.

The third feature of 'Base' (validation formulae) is responsible to define how to collect attached constraints of the given concept and evaluate them. The formulae are defined as operations and they are stored in slots. Instances may refine these formulae, but each concept is validated against all formulae of its meta-concepts (along the whole hierarchy). This means that the formulae may be extended making them more rigorous, but they cannot be relaxed.

All other concepts defined in the bootstrap inherit the behaviour described above since they are originated from Base. It is worth mentioning that besides the structural, and constraint-related concepts, the elements of the operation language (the expressions and statements composing an operation) are also modelled. In order to achieve this, every language element has a corresponding entity and when an operation is defined, its abstract syntax tree is built from the instances of these entities. For example, all conditional statements refer to the concept 'If' as their meta-concept.

Note that unlike in the case of the other three approaches, in DMLA, the bootstrap definition is not available as a pre-compiled binary code, when domain languages and models are built. Instead, the bootstrap is interpreted every time it is used. This way, the bootstrap situation is not handled differently than the usual models. The same rules, the same validation logic applies to the concepts of the bootstrap as for modelling concepts of other domains. Handling all concepts uniformly simplifies the underlying framework and helps in eliminating errors.

5   Dynamic Semantics

The discussion so far was related to the structure and the static aspects. Even though this is the central aspect of a language, the semantics is needed to make the language work. The structure allows us to talk about descriptions (specifications), i.e. drawings and texts. In contrast, the semantics talks about running systems and executions of the descriptions. Moreover, the semantics is the place to solve the bootstrapping circularity, as the circularity is between the description of a language and its later use, i.e. an execution.

5.1   Executing Specifications

The description provided by the model elements is passive in nature. It does not allow any activities and it will not change by itself. It has to be placed in a proper environment to be activated. We will refer to this environment as the *execution machine*. The execution machine is always bound to a language, which is the language of the descriptions it can run. The execution machine can be concrete, like a concrete computer for machine code, or abstract like the Java virtual machine for Java.

An execution machine is in some sense physical, as it can be used and executed. It has an innate ability to create executions for a description that is placed into it. In order to describe these machines, we will consider an abstract view of executions as sequences of runtime states. These runtime states are structured, and their structure is coming from the specification under execution and from additional structures used by the execution machine. As an example, if we specify a class Person in Java, then the structure of Person objects will be available as a template in Java runtime states. Figure 4 shows several examples how specification elements (descriptions) can appear at runtime (as instances).

description	instance
class	object
attribute	slot
reference	slot
method	activation record
variable	reference to a value
if	branching activity
while	looping activity
assignment	changing a reference to a value

Fig. 4. Different possible execution instantiations.

In addition to structures described by the models, the runtime state may also include elements like a program counter and exception storage. These additional structure parts are not derived from the specification but created by the execution machine mainly to help in managing the execution of the model. The structure of these additional parts is universal in the sense that it is not affected by the current specification but only by the execution machine. This also means that if we run the same specification more than once in an executuion machine, then the runtime states may differ. Often, the possible runtime states are called the runtime environment (RTE). Note that by observing the run of a program using a debugger, the current runtime state is observed.

It is the task of the execution machine to provide a way to embody the current runtime state and also to define the rules of when and how to advance the state based on the specification and the language semantics. This way, it is an execution engine which turns descriptions into living things, see also the left side of Fig. 5. Here, the specification is written in the Spec language. The execution machine for the specification (EM 4 Spec) is bound to the specification language. The running specification is placed inside the execution machine. It will have runtime states as given by the language semantics.

Introducing the execution machine breaks the self-reference loop, as the machine is working based on the laws of nature (it is physical), and the loop is embedded in the working of the execution machine.

From the abstraction levels point of view, the use of an execution machine is a vertical process in the sense that the specification – a high-level description (text) – is turned into low-level runtime states and state changes of the running specification, see again Fig. 4. For the sake of clarity, we refer to this vertical process as *execution instantiation*. It is depicted as the arrow between the running specification and the specification itself in Fig. 5. Execution instantiation relates to structural constructs like classes and methods, but also to dynamic constructs like expressions and statements.

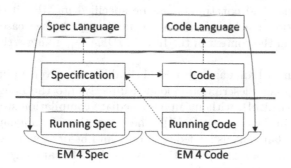

Fig. 5. Semantic approaches.

5.2 Compiling Specifications

Execution can also be achieved by translating the specification into another specification in a different language that has already an execution semantics, i.e. an execution machine. We will refer to this translation as compilation. In contrast to the aforementioned execution instantiation, compilation is a horizontal process, as the result is not an execution, but still a description. We can consider several compilation steps, but in the end, there has to be a final step to execute the description.

Figure 5 shows the same execution situation for the code (to the right) as the situation for the specification (to the left). The code is run in its own execution machine. For our discussion, we consider the connection between the original description and the final execution as a similar runtime connection, see the arrow from the running code to the specification in Fig. 5. It is irrelevant how many compilation steps are between the description and the execution - it is still one vertical step.

5.3   Semantics in the Case Languages

In EMF, there are three stages of language definitions: (i) the language description is created as the instance of the meta-languages which are later saved in the form of an XMI file; (ii) from the description Java source code is generated (compilation step); (iii) the Java source files are compiled to bytecode (compilation step), which is then loaded and thereby activated in EMF runtime (execution step). EMF runtime is basically the same as Eclipse runtime. EMF is not a complete language definition framework - the constraints and semantics parts are missing. Typically, they are specified using Java, so stage (ii) is not needed for the semantics part. From stage (iii), the JVM execution machine enriched with Eclipse functionality takes over and handles the compiled specification, thus allowing to close the bootstrapping cycle.

In MPS, the process is very similar, but MPS has its own file format and does not use XMI. In addition, MPS has meta-languages for all aspects, such that the semantics and constraints can be specified in MPS itself. Otherwise, the JVM execution machine is again the final stop. In the case of MPS, the JVM is running in the context of the IntelliJ IDEA [8], giving a richer execution machine.

The situation in LanguageLab is slightly different, given by its interpretive nature. The language description is loaded directly into the LanguageLab execution machine (LLEM), without an intermediate compilation step. The LLEM itself is defined in Java (using EMF). The semantics of LanguageLab ensures that the defining language is loaded read-only and before its instances. Changes to this language are not done until the next load of the language. This way it is possible to close the bootstrap loop.

DMLA is also interpretive and does not need a compiler step. At runtime, all specifications are given as tuples translated from DMLAScript. This way, the Core component of DMLA can be considered the execution machine for DMLA, implemented based on GraalVM and Truffle. DMLA allows changes of languages and specifications at any time at any level (even in the bootstrap). The effect of changing a concept is immediately reflected by the runtime state of the execution machine.

Both LanguageLab and DMLA are interpretive language environments allowing a complete definition of a language including semantics. The semantics is given by the underlying execution machine. Both environments can specify languages and specifications in the same framework in their languages. We can refer to these connections as in-level instantiation, which is a different instantiation than the execution instantiation introduced earlier. Execution instantiation crosses the machine boundary, while in-level instantiation is on the same level, i.e. instances are still descriptions.

LanguageLab uses its languages to extend its (generic) execution machine with the language-specific parts of the language loaded, thereby creating a specialized execution machine for the language loaded. In this situation, the language and the execution machine cannot be changed. In contrast, DMLA uses its generic execution machine for both the language and the specification. This way, the level of specification is left only at the very end of the process by the execution machine, when the machine evaluates the final form of models by interpreting them. This solution allows a very flexible change handling as explained in the next section.

5.4   Changeability

Many modelling environments are not modelled, but hard-coded and available only as a binary. In contrast to these approaches, having a self-defining, modelled bootstrap allows to modify, fine-tune or refactor the basic modelling principles and thus the modelling mechanisms much easier. Changing the bootstrap means to change all its aspects, namely structure, constraints, and semantics.

Here it is essential to remember that changes to a meta-language might make all its own definitions invalid, such that the whole platform does not work any longer. It is important to make sure that the changes maintain validity. This is discussed in more detail in [15].

Therefore, we consider the gradual change of the bootstrap situation rather than a complete replacement of it. This way, the previous self-references stay intact and the result of the bootstrap is comparable with the situation before. We assume that the changes to the bootstrap still fit with the underlying execution machine. In some sense, this sound like there is not much difference between hard-coded and bootstrapped environments. However, a bootstrap has only a few (typically far less than ten) self-referential concepts that are not allowed to change, in contrast to the hard-coded situation, where we have dozens (sometimes hundreds) of such concepts.

Changing the bootstrap of EMF is not easy. The platform, the modelling environment and the extensions (thus the whole Eclipse modelling ecosystem) rely heavily on the binaries generated from the EMF bootstrap, thus any modification to the bootstrap may cause problems. The meta-languages for EMF are Java and EMF. The bootstrap modification would work in two steps: first the new language is defined, and then it is compiled and used. As long as the generated code still adheres to the Eclipse platform requirements, such changes are possible and have been done before.

MPS is open to changes as long as the generated code fits into its execution machine (a variant of the IntelliJ [8] platform). This implies that the structure, constraint, and generator languages can be partly or completely replaced, but the core of the bootstrap, the Concept being an instance of itself, cannot be changed. The modification of the bootstrap is a two-step process similarly to EMF: first, the new languages are defined, and then the languages are compiled in order to be available for use. It is used frequently to create new versions of the meta-languages of MPS.

The situation in LanguageLab is similar, although the platform is interpreted. All meta-languages can be changed or replaced, as long as they still fit into the LanguageLab execution machine.

In the case of DMLA, the bootstrap can be easily modified. There are only a few core concepts (Base, Slot, Constraint) and basic operational statements (e.g. conditional statement), whose structure and semantics must not be modified, but otherwise, all other elements of the bootstrap and even the validation logic can be easily modified without needing to change anything in the execution machine. This is also true for operations including their inner implementation. They are executable not only directly by the execution machine, but also callable from operations. Since operation definitions are composed of model elements, they can also be changed by operations, thus it is possible to create self-changing, self-refactoring models. It is even possible to create an operation that changes its own definition.

6   Conclusion

Self-defining language workbenches tend to be more flexible and more consistent than environments defined by an external language. The methods of bootstrapping of a compiler have been discussed and used for decades in the field of the classical programming languages, but nowadays, similar solutions are needed in the field of model-based language workbenches as well. Having a precise, adaptable, self-describing bootstrap definition is not an easy task to achieve and even then, we are only at halfway, since the challenge of evaluating the definition is also to be solved.

In this paper, we have compared the bootstrapping strategies and mechanisms of four modelling platforms: EMF, MPS, LanguageLab, and DMLA. Although both the main goals and the modelling paradigms are different in the approaches, it is clearly visible that the basic constructs involved in the bootstrap situation are very similar for them.

On the language level, bootstrapping gives a very tight connection between all the involved meta-languages, which might seem to make bootstrapping impossible. However, the situation becomes solvable if we look at the concept level, where there is normally just a few concepts that are self-referential or mutually referencing each other. All four platforms have similar solutions to define the very core concepts of the bootstraps, although there are differences: EMF focuses merely on the structural aspects, MPS and LanguageLab have different languages to handle structure, constraints and semantics, while DMLA has only one language that covers all of these features.

The actual bootstrapping is given by the execution of the languages in an execution machine, which can be accessed directly (interpretive) or via transformations (compiled). In the compiled case (as in EMF and MPS), the language description is translated to another language, which is then run in its own execution machine (an extended Java VM). In the case of an interpretive approach, there are two options: (i) the execution machine can be specialized to each language and be able to handle specifications of this language as in LanguageLab; or (ii) the execution machine can be generic and both language descriptions and specifications are evaluated by the execution machine directly as in DMLA.

As the paper shows, bootstrapping is not an easy task to solve. The art of bootstrapping is multicoloured. Existing approaches are very similar in some sense, but at the same time, they are also very different. The main goal of having a self-describing bootstrap can be achieved in different ways depending on the main requirements of the users. Practical approaches, such as EMF and MPS, focus on usability and expressivity, while academic approaches, such as LanguageLab and DMLA, focus on creating a theoretically pure solution. By elaborating the main challenges of creating a bootstrap, we believe that this paper can act as a guideline to choose the right approach for the specified needs and to create new solutions having their own bootstrap.

References

1. Atkinson, C., Kühne, T.: Model-driven development: a metamodeling foundation. IEEE Softw. **20**(5), 36 41 (2003). https://doi.org/10.1109/MS.2003.1231149
2. Boerger, E., Stark, R.: Abstract State Machines: A Method for High-Level System Design. Springer, Heidelberg (2003). https://doi.org/10.1007/978-3-642-18216-7
3. Campagne, F.: The MPS Language Workbench, Vol. I. Fabien Campagne (2014)
4. D'Anjou, J., Fairbrother, S., Kehn, D., Kellerman, J., McCarthy, P.: The Java Developer's Guide to Eclipse. Addison-Wesley, Boston (2005)
5. DMLA Developers: Dynamic multi-layer algebra (DMLA) official webpage. https://www.aut.bme.hu/Pages/Research/VMTS/DMLA. Accessed 12 June 2019
6. Eclipse OCL. http://projects.eclipse.org/projects/modeling.mdt.ocl. Accessed 12 June 2019
7. Erdweg, S., et al.: The state of the art in language workbenches. In: Erwig, M., Paige, R.F., Van Wyk, E. (eds.) SLE 2013. LNCS, vol. 8225, pp. 197–217. Springer, Cham (2013). https://doi.org/10.1007/978-3-319-02654-1_11
8. Fields, D., Saunders, S.: IntelliJ Idea In Action. Dreamtech Press, New Delhi (2006)
9. Fowler, M.: Language workbenches: The killer-app for domain specific languages? http://www.martinfowler.com/articles/languageWorkbench.html (2005)
10. Gjøsæter, T., Prinz, A.: Teaching computer language handling - from compiler theory to meta-modelling. In: Fernandes, J.M., Lämmel, R., Visser, J., Saraiva, J. (eds.) GTTSE 2009. LNCS, vol. 6491, pp. 446–460. Springer, Heidelberg (2011). https://doi.org/10.1007/978-3-642-18023-1_14
11. Gjøsæter, T., Prinz, A.: Languagelab 1.1 user manual. Technical report, University of Agder (2013), http://brage.bibsys.no/xmlui/handle/11250/134943

12. Gonzalez-Perez, C., Henderson-Sellers, B.: Metamodelling for Software Engineering. Wiley Publishing, Hoboken (2008)
13. Kermeta3 developers: Kermeta3 homepage: K3 - breathe life into you metamodel. http://diverse-project.github.io/k3/index.html. Accessed 12 June 2019
14. Konat, G., Erdweg, S., Visser, E.: Bootstrapping domain-specific meta-languages in language workbenches. In: SIGPLAN Not, vol. 52, no. 3, pp. 47–58 (2016). https://doi.org/10.1145/3093335.2993242
15. Meijler, T.D., Nytun, J.P., Prinz, A., Wortmann, H.: Supporting fine-grained generative model-driven evolution. Softw. Syst. Model. 9(3), 403–424 (2010). https://doi.org/10.1007/s10270-009-0144-1
16. Nytun, J.P., Prinz, A., Tveit, M.S.: Automatic generation of modelling tools. In: Rensink, A., Warmer, J. (eds.) ECMDA-FA 2006. LNCS, vol. 4066, pp. 268–283. Springer, Heidelberg (2006). https://doi.org/10.1007/11787044_21
17. Object Management Group: Meta Object Facility (MOF) Core Specification. Object Management Group (2006). http://www.omg.org/cgi-bin/doc?formal/2006-01-01.pdf
18. Object Management Group: XML Metadata Interchange. Object Management Group (2015). https://www.omg.org/spec/XMI/About-XMI/
19. OMG: MOF 2.5.1. specification. https://www.omg.org/spec/MOF/2.5.1/. Accessed 12 June 2019
20. Oracle: Graalvm. https://www.graalvm.org/. Accessed 12 June 2019
21. Oracle: Truffle GitHub. http://github.com/oracle/graal/tree/master/truffle. Accessed 12 June 2019
22. Pech, V., Shatalin, A., Völter, M.: JetBrains MPS as a tool for extending java. In: Proceedings of the 2013 International Conference on Principles and Practices of Programming on the Java Platform: Virtual Machines, Languages, and Tools, PPPJ 2013, pp. 165–168. ACM (2013). https://doi.org/10.1145/2500828.2500846
23. Prinz, A., Shatalin, A.: How to bootstrap a language workbench. In: Proceedings of the 7th International Conference on Model-Driven Engineering and Software Development, MODELSWARD 2019, Prague, Czech Republic, 20–22 February 2019, pp. 345–352 (2019). https://doi.org/10.5220/0007398203450352
24. Steinberg, D., Budinsky, F., Paternostro, M., Merks, E.: EMF: Eclipse Modeling Framework 2.0, 2nd edn. Addison-Wesley, Boston (2009). Professional
25. Stoffel, R.: Comparing language workbenches. In: MSE-seminar: Program Analysis and Transformation, pp. 18–24 (2010). http://wiki.ifs.hsr.ch/SemProgAnTr/files/ComparingLanguageWorkbenches-Roman-Stoffel-2010-12-23.pdf
26. Szabó, T., Voelter, M., Kolb, B., Ratiu, D., Schaetz, B.: Mbeddr: extensible languages for embedded software development. In: Proceedings of the 2014 ACM SIGAda Annual Conference on High Integrity Language Technology, HILT 2014, pp. 13–16. ACM, New York (2014). https://doi.org/10.1145/2663171.2663186
27. Urbán, D., Theisz, Z., Mezei, G.: Self-describing operations for multi-level metamodeling. In: Proceedings of the 6th International Conference on Model-Driven Engineering and Software Development, MODELSWARD 2018, Funchal, Madeira - Portugal, 22–24 January 2018, pp. 519–527 (2018). https://doi.org/10.5220/0006656105190527
28. Völter, M.: Generic tools, specific languages. Ph.D. thesis, TU Delft, Delft University of Technology (2014). http://resolver.tudelft.nl/uuid:53c8e1e0-7a4c-43ed-9426-934c0a5a6522
29. Ward, M.P.: Language oriented programming. In: Software-Concepts and Tools, vol. 15, no. 4, pp. 147–161 (1994) http://www.tech.dmu.ac.uk/~mward/martin/papers/middle-out-t.pdf

A Framework for Multi-level Modeling of Analog/Mixed Signal Embedded Systems

Daniela Genius[1](✉), Rodrigo Cortés Porto[1,3], Ludovic Apvrille[2],
and François Pêcheux[1]

[1] Sorbonne Université, LIP6, CNRS UMR 7606, Paris, France
daniela.genius@lip6.fr
[2] LTCI, Télécom Paris, Institut Polytechnique de Paris, Sophia Antipolis, France
[3] Technische Universität Kaiserslautern, Kaiserslautern, Germany

Abstract. Embedded systems are commonly built upon heterogeneous digital and analog integrated circuits, including sensors and actuators. Model-driven approaches for designing software and hardware are generally limited to the digital parts of systems. In the present paper, we adopt a global view on the extensions made to an integrated modeling and simulation tool, TTool. In this tool, the verification and virtual prototyping of embedded systems is described at different abstraction levels and extended in order to handle analog/mixed-signal systems. An extensive case study spans these levels and illustrates the usefulness of our approach.

1 Introduction

Many model-driven techniques have been proposed for designing both digital software and hardware. High level models are employed to specify the functionality of the system, and subsequent model transformations are applied until a virtual prototype containing software and hardware can be generated. However, embedded systems—e.g. robotics, automotive and medical systems—are frequently built upon heterogeneous hardware components such as processors, FPGAs, DSPs, hardware accelerators, digital and analog analog/mixed signal (AMS) and radio frequency (RF) circuits. In early design phases, a high-level representation that includes both digital and analog descriptions is necessary in order to quickly explore the design space, taking into account both digital and AMS/RF components. Obviously, at such a high level of abstraction, speed of design space exploration prevents us from using precise models.

The paper gives an overview of our recent contribution [27] and completes several aspects that have not yet been treated beforehand. Our model-driven approach offers operators and views in order to capture digital and analog domains at several abstraction levels. This approach is supported by the free software TTool [6]. TTool can capture digital/analog aspects and generate a virtual prototype combining SystemC and SystemC-AMS in order to evaluate

© Springer Nature Switzerland AG 2020
S. Hammoudi et al. (Eds.): MODELSWARD 2019, CCIS 1161, pp. 201–224, 2020.
https://doi.org/10.1007/978-3-030-37873-8_9

the system under design. The paper focuses both on modeling capabilities and simulation aspects e.g. ways to combine AMS simulation with event-based (SystemC) simulation. An important aspect regarding simulation which is addressed in the paper is the problem of synchronization between time domains. The overall approach is explained with toy examples before being demonstrated with an automotive braking application.

In the next section, we give an overview of existing approaches targeting the modeling and/or co-simulation of cyber-physical systems. Section 3 presents the basic concepts behind the simulation of analog components. Section 4 explains how digital and analog components can be modeled and evaluated altogether. Section 5 illustrates the usefulness of the approach with a realistic system. Finally, Sect. 6 concludes the paper and gives a perspective on future work.

2   Related Work

Several well established tools in analog/mixed signal design, like *Ptolemy II* [35] [42], are based upon a data-flow model. They target heterogeneous system design by defining several sub domains [21] using hierarchical models. Instantiation of elements controlling the time synchronization between domains is left to the responsibility of designers. Recently, a co-simulation framework for timing verification of cyber-physical systems [29] from Ptolemy models, named *Metronomy*, has been developed.

Metropolis [7] is also based on high level models and facilitates the separation of concerns between computation and communication aspects. Heterogeneous systems are taken into consideration, yet heterogeneity can only be represented using processes, mediums, quantities and constraints. Hierarchical models are not allowed. Metro II [18] introduces hierarchy and allows so-called *Adaptors* for data synchronization, which serve as a bridge between the semantics of components belonging to different Models of Computation (MoCs). The model designer still has to implement time synchronization by means of constraints, assertions, annotators and schedulers. As a common simulation kernel handles the entire process execution (digital and analog), MoCs are not well separated.

From the Micro Electro Mechanical Systems (MEMS) community [10] stems an approach which can transform structural SysML diagrams into VHDL-AMS code. It is thus closely related to our work, but limited to its domain and generates VHDL specifiations, which are less flexible than most other approaches for expressing different Models of Computation, VHDL being essentially a hardware description language on register transfer level.

Discrete Event System Specification (DEVS [14]) is a modular and hierarchical formalism for modeling and analyzing general systems. DEVS supports discrete events and continuous systems. Continuous functions can be described by differential equations, or hybrid systems. A dozen of platform implementations based on DEVS exist, ranging from Petri Net over object oriented to Python based [12,41,50].

Modelica [22] is an object-oriented modeling language for component-oriented systems containing e.g. mechanical, electrical, electronic and hydraulic components. Classes contain a set of equations that can be translated into objects running on a simulation engine. Yet, since time synchronization is not predefined, the simulation engine must manipulate objects in a symbolic way in order to determine an execution order between components of different MoCs.

UML/SysML based modeling techniques such as MARTE and Gaspard2 [23, 48] are extremely popular for capturing the behavior of embedded systems, but less widely used for heterogeneous system design [44]. Furthermore, with very few exceptions such as [39, 46], they do not support refinement until cycle/bit accurate level virtual prototypes nor provide OS support for full-system simulation. Co-simulation between different Models of Computation is usually out of scope, too.

The B method [1] and more recently Event-B [2] model systems at different abstraction levels and makes it possible to mathematically prove consistency between refinement levels. Based on set theory and the B language, the B method is well established in large-scale public/private projects (urban transports etc.). To our knowledge, no extensions to cyber-physical systems have been proposed.

Several frameworks based on SystemC [32], a library of C++ classes, makes it possible to model (digital) hardware. For instanfe, HetSC [31], HetMoC [51] and ForSyDe [40] all have the disadvantage that instantiation of elements and controlling the synchronization have to be managed by the designer.

The following works stem from the analog/mixed signal hardware design domain, where SystemC-AMS extensions [3] is about to become a standard, describing an extension of SystemC with AMS and RF features [47]. The usual approach for linking the digital part of a heterogeneous system with SystemC-AMS is to rely on the *Discrete Event* (DE) parts of SystemC AMS extensions. For instance, *Timed data Flow* (TDF) adds support for signals where data values are sampled with a constant time step.

In the scope of the BeyondDreams project [9], a mixed analog-digital systems proof-of-concept simulator has been developed, based on the SystemC AMS extension standard. Another simulator is proposed in the H-Inception project [30]. All of these approaches rely on SystemC AMS code i.e. they do not provide a high-level interface for specifying the application.

3 Basic Concepts

First, let us briefly introduce two fundamental concepts and two associated tools. On the one hand, *Timed data Flow* as implemented in [19], on the other hand, multi-level modeling and virtual prototyping as implemented in TTool [6].

3.1 Timed Data Flow

SystemC AMS predefines several Models of Computation, e.g. the Timed Data Flow (TDF) Model of Computation, which is based on the timeless Synchronous

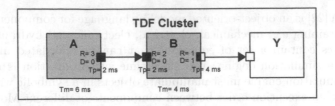

Fig. 1. TDF cluster [27].

Data Flow (SDF) semantics [36]. At each time step, a TDF module reads a fixed number of samples from each of its input ports, then executes the processing function, and finally writes a fixed number of samples to each of its output ports. TDF modules can interact with the discrete world (such as digital MPSoC platforms) using converter ports.

Figure 1 shows a graphical representation TDF cluster. Discrete DE modules are represented as white blocks, TDF modules as gray blocks, TDF ports as black squares, TDF converter ports as black and white squares, and finally TDF signals as arrows. So-called **converter ports**, shown as black-and white squares, serve as interface between the TDF and DE MoC. For the SysML-like notation supported by TTool, we will adhere to this representation.

TDF modules have the following attributes:

- Module Timestep (**Tm**) denotes the period during which a module is activated. One module is activated only if there are enough samples available at its input ports.
- Rate (**R**). A module reads or writes a fixed number of data samples each time it is activated. This number is annotated to the ports and it is known as the *Port Rate*.

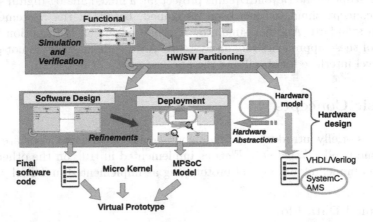

Fig. 2. Hardware/Software partitioning and Code generation for MPSoC platforms [27]. (Color figure online)

- Port Timestep (**Tp**) is the period during which each port of a module is activated. It also denotes the time interval between two samples that are being read or written.
- Delay (**D**). A Delay D can be assigned to a port to make it store a given number of samples each time it is activated, and read or write them in the next activation.

SystemC-AMS extensions, already mentioned in Sect. 2, define models of computations e.g. for TDF modules. We rely on a reference implementation [19] for generating the simulation code of the analog parts.

3.2 Modeling Tool

TTool [6] is a SysML based, free and open-source software initially designed for model-based engineering of (digital) embedded systems at different abstraction levels: functional, partitioning, software design, and deployment. To each of these levels, as shown in Fig. 2 taken from [27], is associated separate *panels*, which allow designers to model systems using a SysML-like notation. The method underlying these levels explains how to take hardware/software partitioning decisions at a high level of abstraction and to regularly validate them during software development [39].

Software and hardware tasks to be partitioned are first captured within the functional abstraction level. Software tasks used in deployments are captured in the software design abstraction level. In both partitioning and deployment, the computation part of tasks is deployed to processors or hardware accelerators, and the communication and storage parts are deployed to communication and storage elements e.g. buses and memories.

TTool allows verification and fast (and high-level) simulation of digital parts. It also supports cycle/bit accurate virtual prototyping on a Multi-Processor System-on-Chip (MPSoC) based on the *SoCLib* [45] public domain library written in SystemC. As SystemC-AMS is an extension to SystemC, relying on TTool for integrating analog/mixed signal components was natural. The next section discusses this integration.

4 Integration of Analog Components

In the following, we show how TDF concepts can be integrated into SysML-like models and in TTool, while keeping in mind our objective to generate correct-by-construction simulation code i.e. handling potential synchronization problems between domains before simulation starts. The philosophy of TTool also requires that all parts of the model are check against syntax (and against a few semantic aspects as well) **before** any code is generated.

Figure 2 uses orange circles to explain how the methodology described before have been adapted in order to support AMS components in TTool. Hardware parts, shown on the lower right, can be simulated with a cycle-accurate precision.

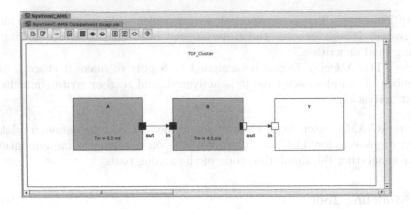

Fig. 3. SystemC-AMS diagram of Fig. 1 in TTool SystemC-AMS panel.

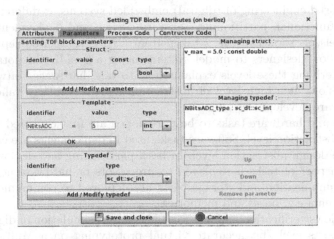

Fig. 4. TDF module parameters [27].

Analog/Mixed Signal components are not represented on the partitioning level since the decision to have them implemented in hardware or software is not in the hands of the designer of the embedded platforms. AMS components are thus captured in deployment diagrams, from which the hardware top cells and the descriptions of the mapping of software objects to processors, memories and communication elements are generated for simulation purpose.

Our contribution is twofold: we represent SystemC-AMS components in Deployment Diagrams and are able to generate the communication between digital and analog parts in the simulation/prototyping code.

4.1 Representing Analog Components

In our extension to TTool, analog and digital parts of a system are first designed in different **panels**. As a consequence, we have enhanced the graphical interface

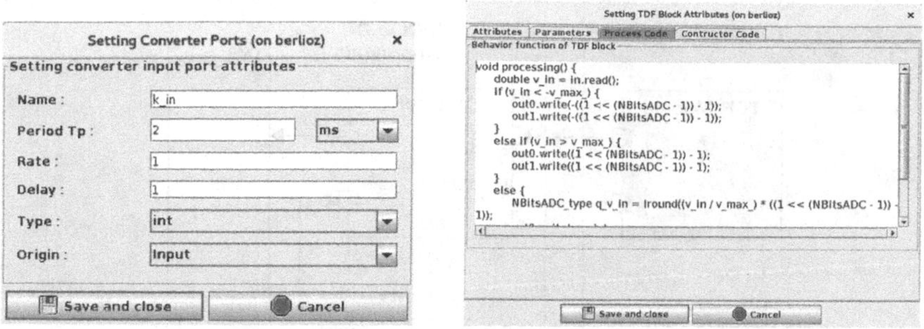

Setting Converter Ports (on berlioz) ✕

Setting converter input port attributes

Name :   k_in

Period Tp :   2   ms

Rate :   1

Delay :   1

Type :   int

Origin :   Input

💾 Save and close   ⊗ Cancel

Setting TDF Block Attributes (on berlioz) ✕

Attributes | Parameters | Process Code | Contructor Code

Behavior function of TDF block

```
void processing() {
    double v_in = in.read();
    if (v_in < -v_max ) {
        out0.write(-((1 << (NBitsADC - 1)) - 1));
        out1.write(-((1 << (NBitsADC - 1)) - 1));
    }
    else if (v_in > v_max ) {
        out0.write((1 << (NBitsADC - 1)) - 1);
        out1.write((1 << (NBitsADC - 1)) - 1);
    }
    else {
        NBitsADC_type q_v_in = lround((v_in / v_max ) * ((1 << (NBitsADC - 1)) -
1));
```

💾 Save and close   ⊗ Cancel

Fig. 5. TDF port parameters (left) and processing function (right) [27].

of TTool with an abstract way to capture SystemC-AMS blocks with DE components, TDF modules and converter ports. Each TDF cluster must designed in its own panel because SystemC-AMS must calculate a separate schedule [3] for each of them.

As mentioned before, TDF modules can be connected together or with DE modules relying on TDF, DE and ports, respectively. The panel provides graphical representations of these elements. The graphical interface also offers a toolbar to select the different components (modules, ports) and connectors between ports.

Figure 3 shows a TTool AMS panel for the design of the introductory example, which contains two TDF modules (gray blocks) and a DE module (white block) interconnected through their respective ports and signals.

Module Parameters. The name and Timestep of a module can be set and its time resolution selected (s, μs, ns). The parameters of a TDF module such as its internal variables or template parameters can also be set up, as shown in Fig. 4.

A TDF block has as its attributes name and Timestep. As attributes, variables and constants can be declared.

Port Parameters. Port parameters can be captured as shown in Fig. 5. For readability, the port Timestep and Delay do not appear in the TDF block visible on the panel but can be obtained and specified by clicking on the port (Fig. 5).

Converter ports have the same attributes, while attributes of DE ports are slightly different (no need to specify Rate and Delay, but indicating the sensitivity to a clock signal is required). TDF and converter ports have a name, a Timestep, a Rate and a Delay. Furthermore, it has to be specified whether it is an input or an output port (called *origin* in the window), and which is the type of data to be transmitted.

Processing Function. Representing analog components in an abstract way is quite difficult since most components are more or less unique. Thus, we decided

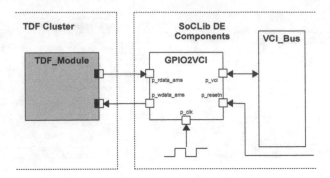

Fig. 6. GPIO2VCI component.

that it would be best if users could directly enter a code to describe functions' behavior. For instance, Fig. 5 shows on the right the processing function for a n-bit analog-digital converter as described by [5].

Valid Schedule. TTool takes as input a SysML system representation to compute a valid *schedule* for each cluster. This determines the correct execution order of TDF modules within the cluster, such that data flow characteristics (sampling rate, sampling period, etc.) are consistent. To compute this schedule, TTool relies on the classical sequential scheduling algorithm of [37] known as *list scheduling*. This algorithm uses an ordered list of the nodes to generate the schedule. Nodes are the TDF blocks and arcs are the signals. TTool builds this list based on the order in which the TDF blocks are created on the panel. Note that there can be several valid schedules. In the example of Fig. 1, a valid schedule would be ABABB.

4.2   Connecting AMS Components to the MPSoC

If the deployment model contains only SystemC-AMS clusters, TTool generates stand-alone SystemC AMS TDF code of the components as well as the SystemC-AMS top cells from the mixed graphical/textual descriptions, and supplies a Makefile. In case software code is also deployed, processors, buses and memories must also be generated. In order to run application software, we thus combine TDF clusters with a MPSoC suitable for full-system simulation.

For this purpose, the SoCLib library provides hardware models, written in SystemC. In particular, it allows the use of a micro kernel [8], able to load and execute cross-compiled software for several processor cores (MIPS, ARM, ...). SoCLib is based on the shared memory paradigm. Components are interconnected based on the *Virtual Component Interconnect* (VCI) [49] protocol. These components can be initiators i.e. they issue requests (e.g. CPUs) or targets that respond to these requests (e.g. RAM memory), sometimes both (DMA, coprocessor wrapper).

The main idea for the integration of SystemC-AMS and SoCLib components into TTool is that the analog components will act as **targets** for the SoCLib initiator digital components (CPUs, hardwareaccelerators, DMA, ...). The generated top cell is thus composed of SoCLib modules and interfaces to the SystemC-AMS clusters. It is also important to mention that a TDF cluster may contain custom DE modules which are not part of the SoCLib library.

In order to connect both worlds, we have introduced a generic *adapter* module that can be used as an interface between SystemC-AMS modules and SoCLib interconnect components [16]. This component is modeled as a **general-purpose input/output** (GPIO) adapter to VCI, called **GPIO2VCI** in the following.

Figure 6 shows the model of the GPIO2VCI component which plays the role an interface between the SystemC-AMS modules (*TDF_Module* belonging to a TDF Cluster) and the SoCLib VCI interconnect component (*VCI_Bus*). Data are exchanged via ports *p_rdata_ams* and *p_wdata_ams*, respectively, *p_vci* communicates with the SoCLib/VCI world. There is also a clock and a reset port. The component is manually inserted in the graphical interface of the panel, then its instantiation and connection, in particular the required lines in the top cell, are automatically generated.

The GPIO2VCI fulfills the rules for writing cycle-bit precise SystemC simulation models of SoCLib. These writing rules, listed in [28], specify that cycle-bit accurate components are built by one or several **Finite State Machines** (FSM) and have clearly defined internal registers. The FSM can be described by three types of functions. The `transition` function, which is triggered once per cycle on the rising edge of the clock, computes the next values of the registers, depending on their current values and the values of the input signals. The `genMoore` function, which is triggered once per cycle on the falling edge of the clock, computes the values of output signals that depend on the internal registers. Finally, the `genMealy` function, which is triggered once per cycle on the falling edge of the clock, computes the values of output signals that depend on the internal registers and the values of the input signals.

4.3 Solving Causality Problems

Due to their different Model of Computation, AMS components require to execute their simulated behavior apart from the rest of the system: yet, they regularly have to synchronize with the digital platform. The SystemC kernel is thus **controlling** the AMS kernel which runs continuously until it is interrupted by an access to a converter port by a TDF cluster.

When a TDF module accesses its input converter port, the DE simulation time advances until it is equal to the TDF simulation time of the input converter port. Later, if an access to an output converter port occurs with a TDF simulation time that is less than the new DE simulation time, a time synchronization issue occurs. To avoid this situation, the TDF simulation time of the output converter ports always needs to be greater or equal than the DE simulation time.

This problem was exposed in [4] and resolved with the help of colored timed Petri Nets [33] derived from the SystemC AMS code.

According to [17], when a SystemC-AMS simulation is being executed, the execution of the SystemC DE simulation kernel is blocked while the SystemC-AMS simulation kernel continues running. As a consequence, during this period the DE simulation time (t_{DE}) does not advance at all, while the TDF simulation time (t_{TDF}) runs according to the Timesteps of the TDF modules and ports. On access to a TDF converter port, the SystemC-AMS simulation kernel is interrupted and yields to the SystemC DE simulation kernel. This way, t_{DE} advances until it is equal to t_{TDF}. In general, t_{TDF} runs ahead of t_{DE}, but in some scenarios, $t_{TDF} \geq t_{DE}$ i.e. t_{DE} may be greater than t_{TDF}: this is a causality problem.

In [4], synchronization at converter ports is modeled with the help of Colored Timed Petri Nets derived from the SystemC-AMS code. Causality issues between TDF and DE MoC are then automatically checked. However, this is done on SystemC-AMS code, whereas [15] proposes a way to detect causality issues from SysML models and also shows that only accesses to TDF *input* converter ports affect synchronization.

The following algorithm presented in [16], of which a detailed version is shown in [15], solves causality issues by iterating over additional Delays and recomputing schedules until all causality issues are solved.

```
 1: procedure DETECTTIMESYNCISSUES
 2:     for each Module in Static Schedule do
 3:         for each Converter Port do
 4:             if Input Converter Port then
 5:                 advance t_DE
 6:                 compute max_t_DE
 7:             else if Output Converter Port then
 8:                 compute t_TDF of port
 9:                 if !(t_TDF ≥ max_t_DE) then
10:                     Time synchronization issue detected
11:                     Suggest port Delay to fix it
12:                 end if
13:             end if
14:         end for
15:     end for
16: end procedure
```

Based on the static schedule for one complete TDF cluster period, each time a TDF module is executed, for each accessed input converter port, the DE simulation time (t_{DE}) advance as shown in line 5, and the maximum t_{DE} is stored as shown in line 6. Then, for each accessed output converter port, the TDF simulation time (t_{TDF}) is computed (see line 8). The t_{TDF} of each port should be greater than or equal to the maximum stored DE simulation time, as shown in line 9. If this condition fails, there is a causality problem and a Delay in the output converter port where the issue was detected is suggested.

4.4   MPSoC Virtual Prototype

GPIO2VCI components are visible in the AMS diagram, as shown in Fig. 7, where our initial cluster is connected to a mono processor platform. Yet, only the connection is represented on the AMS panel by the GPIO2VCI. Also, there can be more than one such connections, one for each TDF cluster. Clicking on one of the GPIO2VCI components opens the corresponding TDF cluster.

Conversely, TDF clusters are displayed in the Deployment Diagram, see Fig. 8. Here, we map a monolithic toy software (a hello world message followed by the printout of *values* generated by a sine wave generator in the AMS cluster), represented by a block named *software* on a mono processor named *CPU0*.

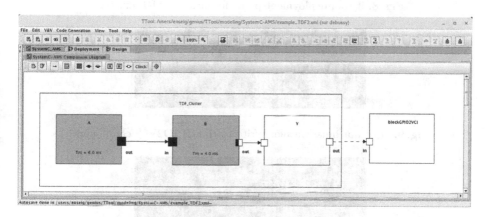

Fig. 7. Adding a GPIO2VCI component.

4.5   Simulation of the Virtual Prototype

Since model-driven approaches expect to ideally provide model validation **before** code generation (and thus simulation), we propose a way to statically identify synchronization problems [15]. Basically, based on the static schedule for one complete TDF cluster period, each time a TDF module is executed, for each accessed input converter port, the DE simulation time (t_{DE}) advances, and the maximum t_{DE} is stored. Then, for each accessed output converter port, the TDF simulation time (t_{TDF}) of each port should be greater or equal than the maximum stored t_{DE}. If this condition fails, it means there is a causality problem with the time synchronization and a delay in the output converter port where the issue was detected will be suggested to the designer in order to resolve the problem. The schedulability of the analog part is validated using the schedulability check of SystemC-AMS [37], thus before code is generated.

Figures 9 and 10 show the simulation of the integration of SystemC-AMS and SoCLib SoC components: a write operation to the GPIO2VCI thus to the analog part, followed by a read from the GPIO2VCI.

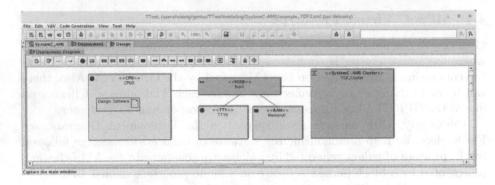

Fig. 8. TTool deployment panel featuring a TDF cluster.

```
sink0 @ 1021 ns: 0
sink0 @ 1022 ns: 0
@1022 ns: Writing to address 0xC1200000 value = 25
sink0 @ 1023 ns: 16.5328
sink0 @ 1024 ns: 17.1137
sink0 @ 1025 ns: 17.6777
sink0 @ 1026 ns: 18.2242
sink0 @ 1027 ns: 18.7528
sink0 @ 1028 ns: 19.2628
```

Fig. 9. Host machine console: Write to the GPIO2VCI component.

```
sink0 @ 1916 ns: -12.0438
sink0 @ 1917 ns: -12.726
@1917 ns: Reading from address 0xC1200004 value =-12
sink0 @ 1918 ns: -13.3957
sink0 @ 1919 ns: -14.0521
sink0 @ 1920 ns: -14.6946
sink0 @ 1921 ns: -15.3227
sink0 @ 1922 ns: -15.9356
sink0 @ 1923 ns: -16.5328
```

Fig. 10. Host machine console: Read from the GPIO2VCI component.

4.6   Trace Generation

While it possible to generate cycle accurate *vcd* traces of the digital signals in
the original version of TTool, the integration of SystemC-AMS necessitates the
tracing of the analog, thus continuous, signals. Thus, our tool contains additional
mechanisms for trace generation of the analog part of the simulation.

SystemC-AMS tracing using the `sca_trace` primitives is invoked for each
analog cluster. This function, if activated from the TTool graphical interface,
allows to create one trace file per cluster. Code lines are generated and inserted
in the SystemC-AMS code of the cluster.

Listing 1.1 shows how tracing is handled for the top cell under consideration A tabular trace file is created with a given name. signals connecting the
GPIO2VCI component to the TDF cluster are added to the trace, then the tracing functions that have been created in the cluster's SystemC-AMS code are
invoked. Traces can then be displayed with a tool adapted to analog traces, like

GAW - Gtk Analog Wave viewer [43]. As usual, traces of the SystemC digital part can displayed with e.g. gtkwave [11].

```
sca_util::sca_trace_file *tfp = sca_util::sca_create_tabular_trace_file("analog_trace");
sca_util::sca_trace(tfp,signal_to_ams0,"signal_to_ams0");
sca_util::sca_trace(tfp,signal_from_ams0,"signal_from_ams0");
Cluster0_0.trace_Cluster0(tfp);
...
sca_util::sca_close_tabular_trace_file(tfp);
```

Listing 1.1. Tracing for the AMS components invoked in the top cell.

5   Case Study

Our contribution to tackle digital and analog systems is illustrated by an automotive embedded system designed in the scope of the EVITA European project [20] and for which code generation was presented in [38]. Recent on-board Intelligent Transport (IT) architectures comprise a very heterogeneous landscape of communication network technologies (e.g., LIN, CAN, MOST, and FlexRay) that interconnect in-car Electronic Control Units (ECUs).

We apply in the following, step by step, the general methodology developed in [25] concerning the digital part along with the new techniques introduced in [27].

Among the use cases addressed by EVITA, we selected the automatic braking function [34]. Basically, this function works as follows: an obstacle is detected by another automotive system which broadcasts that information to neighboring cars. A car receiving such information has to decide whether it is concerned with this obstacle. This decision includes a plausibility check function that takes into account various parameters, such as the direction and speed of the car, and also information previously received from neighboring cars. Once the decision to brake has been taken, the braking order is forwarded to relevant ECUs. Last but not least, the presence of this obstacle is forwarded to other neighboring cars in case they have not yet received this information.

5.1   Partitioning

The *functional view* in Fig. 11 describes of a set of abstract communicating tasks; green boxes representing TLM modules). Functional abstraction allows us to avoid capturing the exact data processing algorithms, but rather to consider only abstract computation complexity. Each individual task describes its abstract functional behavior using communication operators, computation elements, and control elements. Thanks to data abstraction, we consider only the size of the data sent or received, and ignore details such as type, values, or names.

Then, mapping intends to partition functions between software and hardware implementations. Figure 12 shows the deployment diagram. The architecture is modeled as a graph built upon execution (light blue), communication (orange), and storage (light turquoise) nodes. Execution nodes are for example CPUs and hardware accelerators. Our extension allows a representation of analog/mixed

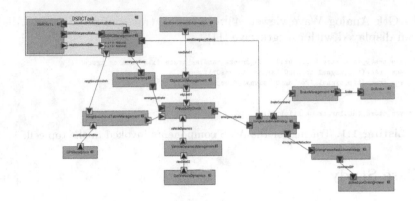

Fig. 11. Functional view. (Color figure online)

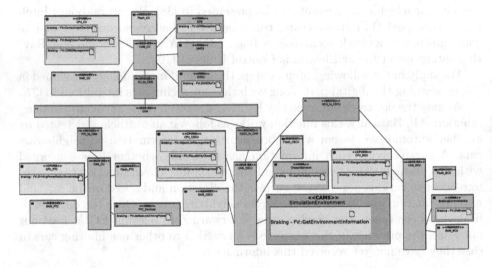

Fig. 12. Partitioning level mapping view. (Color figure online)

signal modules, which are execution nodes too. Communication nodes include bridges and buses, storage nodes are memories.

A function mapped onto a processor will be implemented in software, and a function mapped onto a hardware accelerator (darker turquoise) is implemented in hardware. Functions to be implemented in hardware are either digital or analog functions. In our example, all sensors obtaining information from the environment are modeled as analog blocks.

An evolution with regards to [27] is that analog blocks can now be made explicit on the partitioning level as a particular kind of hardware accelerators, named *CAMS* (abbreviating SystemC-AMS) as shown on the bottom center of Fig. 12: the simulation environment is subsumed in the light purple block named *SimulationEnvironment*, which is slightly enlarged for better readability.

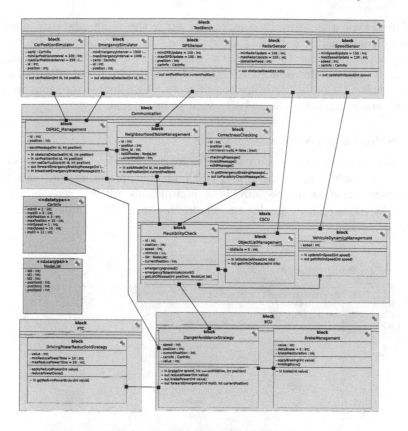

Fig. 13. Block diagram from [38].

5.2 Software Design

Once the partitioning is done, software can be designed and verified with TTool. Figure 13 shows the former software block diagram taken from [38], with the five sensors at the top: there, sensors are captured as software components. Now, they can be removed from the software design diagram since the partitioning decision has already been taken for the analog blocks: they do not need to be considered any more during software design.

Other software components are grouped according to their destination ECU:

- **Communication ECU** manages communication with neighboring vehicles.
- **Chassis Safety Controller ECU (CSCU)** processes emergency messages and sends orders to brake to ECUs.
- **Braking Controller ECU (BCU)** contains two blocks: *DangerAvoidanceStrategy* determines how to efficiently and safely reduce the vehicle speed, or brake if necessary.
- **Power Train Controller ECU (PTC)** enforces the engine torque modification request.

To prototype the software components with the other platform elements (hardware components, operating system), we must map the software components to a model of the target system. Mapping can be performed using the deployment features introduced in [24]: such a **deployment diagram** is a SysML representation of hardware components, their interconnection, software tasks and communication channels between software tasks.

5.3   Modeling Sensors

Before, since sensors were captured as software tasks, code generation from software design resulted in having a C/POSIX code representing the behavior of these sensors, leading to too unrealistic simulations All five sensors are now replaced by more realistic analog models in the form of five independent TDF clusters.

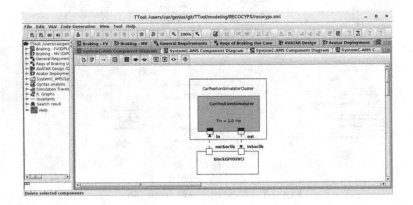

Fig. 14. TTool panel with model of the *CarPositionSimulator* sensor.

Figure 14 shows the AMS panel of the textitCarPositionSimulator sensor that gives information on surrounding cars *id* (e.g., car position).

From TDF information (Rate, Delay, ...), TTool infers, if possible, missing parameters, and then computes a coherent schedule, and finally generates SystemC-AMS code, comprising ports, Delays and interfaces [15]. Cluster output is read by the *DSRSC_Management* block (see Fig. 13). Often, complex data structures of more than one parameter are transmitted in channels (here, *id* and *position*). Currently, they have to be transmitted one by one, basic type by basic type. Thus, *id* and *position* require two sequential write operations to the out port in the processing code and two corresponding read operations in the entry code.

We can easily model the randomized choice of an integer between 1 and 5 (*id*) and between 3 and 10 (*position*) stemming from the data type of Fig. 13. The code of this simple processing function is shown on the right of the figure in a separate window. The *write* primitive sends one integer value to the *out* converter port.

5.4   Interaction of Analog Blocks with the Software Design Level

In contrast to the purely digital model of the same application, the functional blocks pertaining to the sensors are no longer represented in the software design level block diagram, since they are represented by analog blocks captured in five separate SystemC-AMS panels. In Fig. 13, thus, the upper row of tasks named *TestBench* disappears.

A library named *libsyscams* has been provided to contain read and write primitives on the side of the MPSoC, the *read_gpio2vci* and *write_gpio2vci* functions. As shown above, *CarPositionSimulator* issues two random values from its output port, *EmergencySimulator* does the same. By executing these software functions, the CPU of the digital platform is able to exchange (i.e. read or write) values with the analog components.

On the side of the MPSoC platform, according to TTool's semantics, the *DSRSC_Management* block nondeterministically reads from either block, or read a *broadcastEmergencyBrakingMessage* from a third, the *DangerAvoidanceStrategy* block. In the current version, the first two blocks being replaced by sensors modeled in SystemC-AMS, this semantics should be preserved.

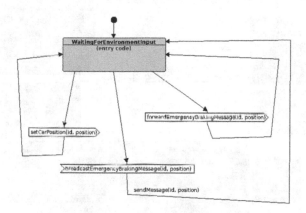

Fig. 15. *DSRSC_Management* block state machine containing link to the entry code.

Let us now consider the state machine of the *DSRSC_Management* block (Fig. 15). In [27], we show how to use **entry code** that can be contained in a state to call *libsyscams*. This is the case of the *WaitForEnvironmentInput* state. We read nondeterministically either the input from *CarPositionSimulator* or *EmergencySimulator*, whenever values are available on either. This nondeterminism, which was in the past expressed by the semantics of TTool's channels between software blocks, must now be reflected in the entry code of the software block's state machine as well. Figure 16 shows the successive operations: we call the *read_gpio2vci* primitive and check whether data was successfully read and in that case, go on to the next operation. If there are several parameters (here *id* and *position*), they must be read sequentially.

Fig. 16. *WaitingForEnvironmentInput* state entry code.

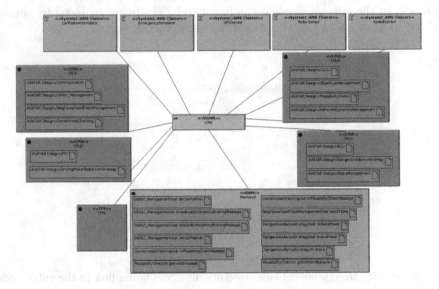

Fig. 17. Deployment diagram of the active braking application.

5.5 Deployment

Figure 17 shows the extended *deployment diagram* giving an overview of the mapping of software tasks and channels. Where the software tasks are mapped onto the CPU, the channels between the tasks on the memory. TDF clusters are displayed as gray boxes along with digital components, interconnected to the central (digital) interconnect through GPIO2VCI components as detailed below. For a better overview, the diagram contains sensors as gray boxes, each one corresponding to a SystemC-AMS cluster connected via a GPIO2VCI. Clicking

Fig. 18. Validation and code generation window.

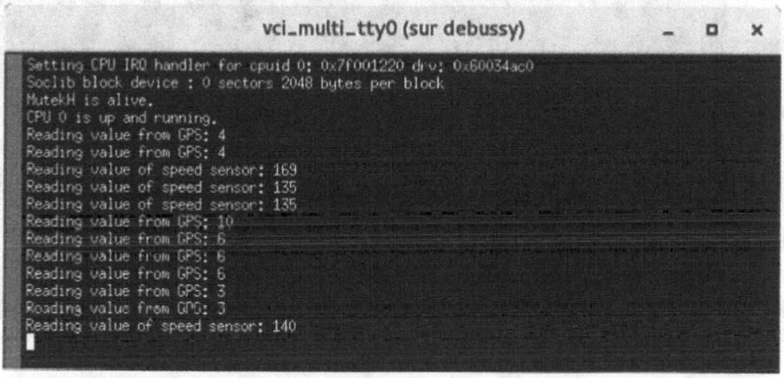

Fig. 19. TTY of the SoCLib simulation showing system boot and first input from the sensors.

on the box opens the corresponding SystemC-AMS panel. A fifth CPU which used to simulate the sensor execution is no longer in use.

The generated MPSoC platform consists of a digital SoC based on SoCLib components connected to the analog hardware components, modeled using SystemC-AMS code. On the SoCLib side, a MIPS32 CPU, a 1 MB RAM memory and a TTY terminal are modeled in SystemC. This virtual prototype is capable of running **software** (limited to communicating some values and command in the case study) and a lightweight **operating system** [8].

5.6   Running the Application

TTool first checks the coherency of the block and port parameters before computing a valid TDF schedule for each TDF cluster, taking into account synchronization issues between the TDF and DE world [27]. This is done in a so-called

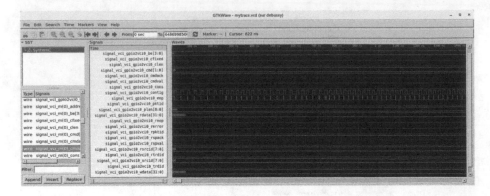

Fig. 20. Digital trace generated from TTool's simulation.

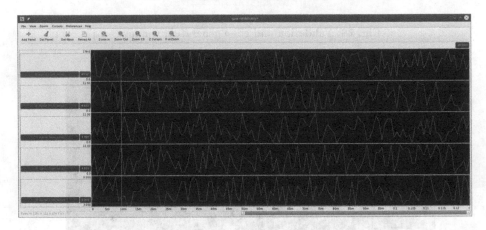

Fig. 21. Analog trace generated from TTool's simulation.

validation window (Fig. 18). Once the cluster schedule is validated, code generation can be started from another dialog window.

Figure 19 shows the start up of the software application and first incoming measurements of the sensors (randomized values in plausible ranges were used for simulation). Figure 20 shows part of the simulation vcd trace of the AMS version, containing the digital signals; we focus on the signals on one of the *gpio2vci* interfaces. In Fig. 21, the five incoming signals from the five sensors are traced with GAW.

In the light of former work, we examine latencies [26]. The most important latency is the one between the detection of an emergency situation and the moment when the braking really occurs.

As can be seen in Fig. 22, the message is issued by *ForwardEmergency-BrakingMessage*, left hand side of the figure) and received by reading from channel *brake* (right hand side). In the simulated situation, the latency is of $1918 - 1681 = 237\,\mu\text{sec}$. Figure 23 finally shows the sequence diagram obtained

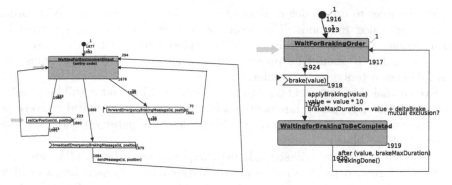

Fig. 22. Latency checkpoints between emergency detection (write to channel *ForwardEmergencyBrakingMessage*) and braking (reading from channel *brake*). Automates arc annotated with values obtained by running the interactive simulation.

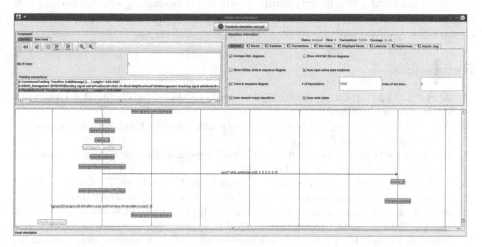

Fig. 23. Emergency situation in a sequence diagram.

at software design level, indicating that there is an emergency message, but that particular message can be ignored.

6 Conclusion and Perspectives

The paper shows the integration of SystemC-AMS (TDF) components into a multi-level modeling tool for complex embedded systems. Starting from a SysML-like representation and progressively refining, we obtain, by model transformation, a cycle-accurate virtual prototype.

Virtual prototyping can be obtained from the last refinement stage, taking into account both analog and digital parts of the system. To this end, a library was created to provide read and write functions between digital and analog components.

Yet, in order to use analog components, C code needs to be inserted in order to capture analog functions. The resulting code is thus no longer correct by construction. In the future, this should be replaced by specific read and write operators. Also, it should be possible to transmit structured data types and multiple parameters more conveniently.

Even if analog components tend to be unique, we think that it will be possible to select a set of typical components such as filters, analog/digital converters, sine sources, and sinks. We plan to provide a library of parametrizable versions of such building blocks.

Yet, TDF models are still strongly oversimplified as in the EVITA industrial case study, further detail was not available. We are currently modeling a medical appliance with a strong proportion of analog blocks, stemming from an Open Source project [13], for which we have access to full implementation details.

Latency measurements are currently limited to the digital part. The feedback of simulation results is still only semi-automatic. Automating and extending this mechanism to the entire system should enable us to propose a full design space exploration environment for Analog/Mixed Signal systems.

References

1. Abrial, J.R.: The B-Book: Assigning Programs to Meanings. Cambridge University Press, Cambridge (2005)
2. Abrial, J.R.: Modeling in Event-B: System and Software Engineering. Cambridge University Press, Cambridge (2010)
3. Accellera Systems Initiative: SystemC AMS extensions Users Guide, Version 1.0. Accellera Systems Initiative, March 2010
4. Andrade, L., Maehne, T., Vachoux, A., Ben Aoun, C., Pêcheux, F., Louërat, M.M.: Pre-simulation formal analysis of synchronization issues between discrete event and timed data flow models of computation. In: Design, Automation and Test in Europe, DATE Conference, March 2015
5. Andrade Porras, L.: Principles and implementation of a generic synchronization interface between SystemC AMS models of computation for the virtual prototyping of multi-disciplinary systems. Ph.D. thesis, Université Pierre et Marie Curie (2016)
6. Apvrille, L.: Webpage of TTool (2011)
7. Balarin, F., Watanabe, Y., Hsieh, H., Lavagno, L., Passerone, C., Sangiovanni-Vincentelli, A.L.: Metropolis: an integrated electronic system design environment. IEEE Comput. **36**(4), 45–52 (2003)
8. Becoulet, A.: Mutekh. http://www.mutekh.org
9. Beyond Dreams Consortium: Beyond Dreams (Design Refinement of Embedded Analogue and Mixed-Signal Systems) (2008–2011). http://projects.eas.iis.fraunhofer.de/beyonddreams
10. Bouquet, F., Gauthier, J.M., Hammad, A., Peureux, F.: Transformation of SysML structure diagrams to VHDL-AMS. In: 2012 Second Workshop on Design, Control and Software Implementation for Distributed MEMS, pp. 74–81. IEEE (2012)
11. Bybell, T.: GTKWave Viewer (2019). http://gtkwave.sourceforge.net
12. Capocchi, L., Santucci, J.F., Poggi, B., Nicolai, C.: DEVSimPY: a collaborative python software for modeling and simulation of DEVS systems. In: 2011 IEEE 20th International Workshops on Enabling Technologies: Infrastructure for Collaborative Enterprises, pp. 170–175. IEEE (2011)

13. echOpen Community: Designing an open-source and low-cost echo-stethoscope (2017). http://www.echopen.org/
14. Concepcion, A.I., Zeigler, B.P.: DEVS formalism: a framework for hierarchical model development. IEEE Trans. Softw. Eng. **14**(2), 228–241 (1988)
15. Porto, R.C.: Integration of SystemC-AMS simulation platforms into TTool. Master's thesis, Technische Universität Kaiserslautern (2018)
16. Porto, R.C., Genius, D., Apvrille, L.: Modeling and virtual prototyping for embedded systems on mixed-signal multicores. In: RAPIDO (2019)
17. Damm, M., Grimm, C., Haas, J., Herrholz, A., Nebel, W.: Connecting SystemC-AMS models with OSCI TLM 2.0 models using temporal decoupling. In: FDL, pp. 25–30 (2008)
18. Davare, A.: A next-generation design framework for platform-based design. In: DVCon, vol. 152 (2007)
19. Einwich, K.: SystemC AMS PoC2.1 Library, COSEDA, Dresden (2016)
20. EVITA: E-safety vehicle intrusion protected applications. http://www.evita-project.org/
21. Fong, C.: Discrete-time dataflow models for visual simulation in ptolemy II. Master's report, Memorandum UCB/ERL M 1 (2001)
22. Fritzson, P., Engelson, V.: Modelica—a unified object-oriented language for system modeling and simulation. In: Jul, E. (ed.) ECOOP 1998. LNCS, vol. 1445, pp. 67–90. Springer, Heidelberg (1998). https://doi.org/10.1007/BFb0054087
23. Gamatié, A., et al.: A model-driven design framework for massively parallel embedded systems. ACM Trans. Embed. Comput. Syst. **10**(4), 39 (2011)
24. Genius, D., Apvrille, L.: Virtual yet precise prototyping: an automotive case study. In: ERTSS 2016, Toulouse, January 2016
25. Genius, D., Li, L.W., Apvrille, L.: Model-driven performance evaluation and formal verification for multi-level embedded system design. In: 5th International Conference on Model-Driven Engineering and Software Development (MODELSWARD 2017), Porto, Portugal (2017)
26. Genius, D., Li, L.W., Apvrille, L.: Multi-level latency evaluation with an MDE approach. In: 6th International Conference on Model-Driven Engineering and Software Development (MODELSWARD 2018), Funchal, Portugal (2018)
27. Genius, D., Cortés Porto, R., Apvrille, L., Pêcheux, F.: A tool for high-level modeling of analog/mixed signal embedded systems. In: 7th International Conference on Model-Driven Engineering and Software Development (MODELSWARD 2019), Prague, Czech Republic (2019)
28. Greiner, A.: Writing efficient cycle-accurate, bit-accurate SystemC simulation models for SoCLib, September 2017. http://www.soclib.fr/trac/dev/wiki/WritingRules/Caba. http://www.soclib.fr/trac/dev/wiki/WritingRules/Caba. As of: 16 October 2018
29. Guo, L., Zhu, Q., Nuzzo, P., Passerone, R., Sangiovanni-Vincentelli, A., Lee, E.A.: Metronomy: a function-architecture co-simulation framework for timing verification of cyber-physical systems. In: Proceedings of the 2014 International Conference on Hardware/Software Codesign and System Synthesis, p. 24. ACM (2014)
30. H-Inception Consortium: Heterogeneous Inception Project (2012–2015). https://www-soc.lip6.fr/trac/hinception
31. Herrera, F., Villar, E.: A framework for heterogeneous specification and design of electronic embedded systems in SystemC. ACM Trans. Des. Autom. Electron. Syst. (TODAES) **12**(3), 22 (2007)
32. IEEE: SystemC. IEEE Standard 1666-2011 (2011)

33. Jensen, K., Kristensen, L.M.: Coloured Petri Nets. Modelling and Validation of Concurrent Systems. Springer, Heidelberg (2009). https://doi.org/10.1007/b95112
34. Kelling, E., et al.: Specification and evaluation of e-security relevant use cases. Technical report, Deliverable D2.1, EVITA Project (2009)
35. Lee, E.A.: Disciplined heterogeneous modeling. In: Petriu, D.C., Rouquette, N., Haugen, Ø. (eds.) MODELS 2010. LNCS, vol. 6395, pp. 273–287. Springer, Heidelberg (2010). https://doi.org/10.1007/978-3-642-16129-2_20
36. Lee, E.A., Messerschmitt, D.G.: Synchronous data flow. Proc. IEEE **75**(9), 1235–1245 (1987)
37. Lee, E.A., Messerschmitt, D.G.: Static scheduling of synchronous data flow programs for digital signal processing. IEEE Trans. Comput. **C–36**(1), 24–35 (1987). https://doi.org/10.1109/TC.1987.5009446
38. Li, L., Apvrille, L., Genius, D.: Virtual prototyping of automotive systems: towards multi-level design space exploration. In: DASIP (2016)
39. Li, L.W., Genius, D., Apvrille, L.: Formal and virtual multi-level design space exploration. In: Pires, L.F., Hammoudi, S., Selic, B. (eds.) MODELSWARD 2017. CCIS, vol. 880, pp. 47–71. Springer, Cham (2018). https://doi.org/10.1007/978-3-319-94764-8_3
40. Niaki, S.H.A., Jakobsen, M.K., Sulonen, T., Sander, I.: Formal heterogeneous system modeling with SystemC. In: 2012 Forum on Specification and Design Languages (FDL), pp. 160–167. IEEE (2012)
41. Ninios, P., Vlahos, K., Bunn, D.W.: OO/DEVS: a platform for industry simulation and strategic modelling. Decis. Support Syst. **15**(3), 229–245 (1995)
42. Ptolemy.org (ed.): System Design, Modeling, and Simulation using Ptolemy II (2014)
43. Quillevere, H.: Gtk Analog Wave Viewer (2019). http://www.rvq.fr/linux/gaw.php
44. Selic, B., Gérard, S.: Modeling and Analysis of Real-Time and Embedded Systems with UML and MARTE: Developing Cyber-Physical Systems. Elsevier, Amsterdam (2013)
45. SocLib Consortium: The SoCLib project: an integrated system-on-chip modelling and simulation platform. Technical report, CNRS (2003). www.soclib.fr
46. Taha, S., Radermacher, A., Gérard, S.: An entirely model-based framework for hardware design and simulation. In: Hinchey, M., et al. (eds.) BICC/DIPES -2010. IAICT, vol. 329, pp. 31–42. Springer, Heidelberg (2010). https://doi.org/10.1007/978-3-642-15234-4_5
47. Vachoux, A., Grimm, C., Einwich, K.: Analog and mixed signal modelling with SystemC-AMS. In: ISCAS (3), pp. 914–917. IEEE (2003). http://ieeexplore.ieee.org/xpl/mostRecentIssue.jsp?punumber=8570
48. Vidal, J., de Lamotte, F., Gogniat, G., Soulard, P., Diguet, J.P.: A co-design approach for embedded system modeling and code generation with UML and MARTE. In: DATE, pp. 226–231. IEEE (2009)
49. VSI Alliance: Virtual Component Interface Standard (OCB 2 2.0), August 2000
50. Zeigler, B.P., Kim, D.: Distributed supply chain simulation in a DEVS/CORBA execution environment. In: WSC 1999, 1999 Winter Simulation Conference Proceedings. Simulation-A Bridge to the Future (Cat. No. 99CH37038), vol. 2, pp. 1333–1340. IEEE (1999)
51. Zhu, J., Sander, I., Jantsch, A.: HetMoC: heterogeneous modelling in SystemC. In: 2010 Forum on Specification & Design Languages (FDL 2010), pp. 1–6. IET (2010)

Towards Multi-editor Support
for Domain-Specific Languages Utilizing
the Language Server Protocol

Hendrik Bünder[1](✉) and Herbert Kuchen[2](✉)

[1] itemis AG, Bonn, Germany
buender@itemis.de
[2] ERCIS, University of Münster, Münster, Germany
kuchen@uni-muenster.de

Abstract. In model-driven software development (MDSD) projects, frequently domain experts and developers work together on the same model. However, they have quite different preferences concerning tools for working with a model. While developers require a powerful integrated development environment (IDE), domain experts are overwhelmed by the amount of functionality of an IDE and its confusing user interface. They prefer a simple editor, often provided as a web application, which does not require a local installation. Currently, both stakeholders typically agree on a common tool, which is frustrating for at least one of them. The Language Server Protocol (LSP) is a standard that aims to include language smarts into simple editors without turning them into IDEs. Originally, it has been designed for programming languages. In the present paper, we will give evidence based on a case study and a corresponding SWOT analysis that it is even more beneficial for a textual domain-specific language (DSL) as it is often used in MDSD. We will focus on the language workbench Xtext which supports the LSP. In particular, we will investigate how the LSP can be used to integrate a DSL into different development tools (editors and IDEs). Supplementing the SWOT analysis, we have also evaluated the practical relevance of the LSP.

Keywords: Textual domain-specific languages · Model-driven development language server protocol · Case study

1 Introduction

Domain-specific languages (DSLs) enable the efficient creation of complex software systems by allowing to describe the concepts of a particular domain in a typically declarative and semantically rich way. Due to their high level of abstraction, the documents written in a DSL are typically called *models* rather than programs. Such models are captured in an either textual or graphical notation. In model-driven software development, the models are automatically transformed into documents on a lower level of abstraction. Frequently, they are directly

© Springer Nature Switzerland AG 2020
S. Hammoudi et al. (Eds.): MODELSWARD 2019, CCIS 1161, pp. 225–245, 2020.
https://doi.org/10.1007/978-3-030-37873-8_10

transformed into the source code of the selected programming language. One key factor to success for a domain-specific language is a mature editor support that includes language smarts such as syntax highlighting, validations, and code completion.

Focusing on textual DSLs, there is a variety of potential editors. On one side of the scale, simple text editors such as VI [16] or Microsoft Notepad can be used. While these editors focus on simple and fast text changes, they do not support any language-specific smarts. On the other side of the scale, sophisticated integrated development environments (IDE) come with a feature rich, language specific editor. Additionally, they provide an ecosystem for analyzing, running, testing, and debugging source code.

For creating mature editor support for DSLs, language workbenches such as MPS [5], Spoofax [13], and MontiCore [15] offer many features. Based on the integration into IDEs such as Eclipse [33] or IntelliJ [12], language editors can be created quickly by semi-automated processes. Although this integration enables the fast creation of language specific editors, it also couples the editor to the host IDE.

Since DSLs are often edited by both, technical and non-technical users, conflicting requirements arise. The technical users prefer the DSL editor to be deeply integrated into the IDE that is best for their use case. For example, a developer implementing an application in JavaScript [23] might prefer Visual Studio Code [18]. Alternatively, a developer implementing an application in Java [1] or C++ [29] might prefer the Eclipse IDE. Since a DSL might describe different parts of an application or provide multiple generators, it should be easily integrated into different IDEs. On the other hand, DSLs have to provide an editor that is optimized for non-technical users. In contrast to developers, non-technical users are distracted by the overloaded user interfaces of IDEs and prefer simple editors. Yet, they should be supported by all the language smarts that are key factor to success for a DSL. In addition, non-technical users favor web-based editors where no additional installation is required.

The stated requirements cause a lot of effort for toolsmiths, since they have to provide editors for different IDEs, text editors, and browsers. Consequently all language smarts such as code completion or syntax highlighting have to be implemented in the programming language used by the IDE or tool in which the editor should be integrated. Since this is not an economically reasonable strategy, toolsmiths tend to support only a single IDE. Thereby, developer productivity decreases due to the fact that the supported IDE for the DSL might not be the ideal IDE for enhancing, testing, running, and debugging the source code generated from the DSL. Additionally, non-technical are forced to used IDE to collaborate instead of a more concise web browser based editor.

The Language Server Protocol (LSP) [22] introduced by Microsoft, RedHat and Codenvy decouples the language smarts from the actual editor integration. While intended to provide editor support for general purpose programming languages, it can equally well be used for DSLs. The LSP is supported by the Xtext language workbench. DSLs built upon the Xtext language workbench support all LSP features including multi-IDE, multi-Editor and browser integration. In order to exemplify the steps required to integrate an arbitrary DSL into multiple editors, we have conducted a case study. In addition, we have performed an analysis of strengths, weaknesses, opportunities and threats (SWOT) of leveraging the Xtext LSP integration. The present paper is an extended version of a preceding conference paper [4]. In order to supplement the SWOT analysis, we have now also analyzed the utilization of the LSP. The analysis focuses on open source github projects that have been implemented utilizing Xtext and the LSP. In order to also get an idea of the usage of the Xtext and LSP integration in proprietary closed source projects, the Eclipse textual modeling framework (TMF) forum was analyzed in order to evaluate, how extensively the topic is being discussed.

The present paper is structured as follows. First, Sect. 2 gives an overview of the LSP. In Sect. 3, the Entity-DSL implemented in the context of the case study is described. Further, we outline the results of the conducted SWOT analysis identifying the potential of the LSP in combination with the Xtext language workbench. Section 4 presents our observations from analyzing open source projects utilizing the Xtext and LSP integration. It also presents our results from examining the Eclipse TMF (Xtext) forum. Section 5 summarizes and discusses our results, before we describe related work in Sect. 6. Finally, we conclude in Sect. 7.

2   Overview of the Language Server Protocol

This section describes the language server protocol [22]. Readers who are familiar with it, can skip this section. A more detailed presentation can be found in [4].

In order to enable the comfortable editing of the overwhelming variety of existing programming languages, editor- and IDE-vendors face the challenge to support corresponding sophisticated *language smarts* for them. Well-known examples of language smarts are *goto definition*, *hovers* and *code completion*. At the same time, the number of editors and IDEs is growing steadily. Therefore, providing editor support for all languages in all available integrated development environments and editors creates an $O(n \times m)$ complexity.

Through separation of language smarts and editor integration, the LSP strives for mitigating this issue. By providing a server process in charge of language smarts and a client process integrating the results into the specific editor, both parts become independent. The implementation of language server and development-tool extension is supported by mature Software Development Toolkits (SDK) that encapsulate low-level communication leading to the efficient creation of client and server processes. By communicating through the standardized LSP, development tool and language server can be implemented separately even in different programming languages. The separation of concerns in combination with the feature rich protocol decreases the complexity to $O(n + m)$ [28].

Since the introduction of the LSP in 2016, more than 50 language servers have been implemented covering languages such as Python, Ruby, and Java.

Additionally, development-tool extensions are available for more than 10 IDEs and editors such as VSCode or Eclipse [28]. The advantages of the LSP are not only useful for programming languages but also for textual domain-specific languages, since they require the same language smarts. Currently, only the Xtext language workbench for developing DSLs supports the LSP. Thus, we use this workbench in the sequel.

The LSP architecture specifies a client and a server process that communicate through the standardized LSP. The protocol specifies capabilities that represent possible messages exchanged between client and server process [22]. In order to provide the right features for the right editor, development tool and language server exchange supported `Capabilities` during the initial communication. In order to enable the extension of the LSP for a specific language, the LSP offers `ExperimentalCapabilities`. Instantiations of these `Capabilities` are not part of the protocol. Thus, development tool and server have to be extended manually to support these custom features.

The language server will ignore missing `Capabilities` and expect these language smarts not to be supported by the development tool. For the requested `Capabilities`, the language server answers with the `Capabilities` it supports [20].

While the number of features supported by the LSP is increasing steadily, there are six key features [28], namely *code completion* (supported by 90% of the language-server implementations), the *hover* feature (see Fig. 1; 88% support), *goto definition* (83% support), *workspace symbol* (causing a search for the given symbol in the whole workspace; supported by just 60% of the servers), *find references* (63% support), and *diagnostic* (causing a notification back to the development tool; 78% support). The Xtext language workbench supports all these six key features.

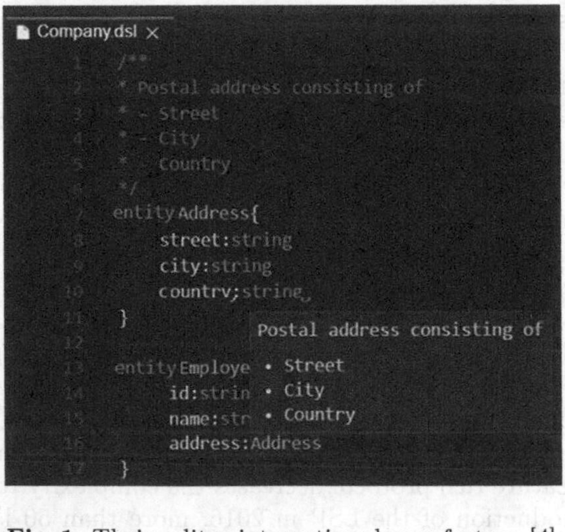

Fig. 1. Theia editor integration: hover feature [4].

The LSP has its limitations. For instance, it solely focuses on integrating language smarts. Well-known IDE features such as building, testing, running and debugging source code remain IDE-specific. Other protocols care about such features [3,14]. Comparing the development-tool extension capabilities to features provided by native IDE integration reveals additional shortcomings. For example leveraging the native Eclipse integration of Xtext DSLs provides mature UI features such as outline view, project-creation wizards, or type hierarchies [32]. The trade-off for integrating language smarts into multiple editors is the loss of such advanced user-interface features.

Language servers and the corresponding development-tool extensions can either be used by cloning the respective github repository or by installing an extension through a market place of the respective IDE or editor.

3 Case Study: Language Server Protocol with Xtext DSLs

A case study was conducted to quantify the efforts required to provide a language server and two development-tool extensions for a simple example DSL. The language server is supposed to provide the six key features as explained in Sect. 2. The IDE integration is exemplified by providing a development-tool extension for Theia as well as for Eclipse.

Figures 2 and 3 show the expected integration into Theia and Eclipse, respectively. The grammar of the example DSL will be explained in the next subsection. As shown by the two figures, both editors provide content sensitive proposals determined by the language server. However, the keyword highlighting is not supported by the LSP. Thus, it had to be implemented for each IDE separately.

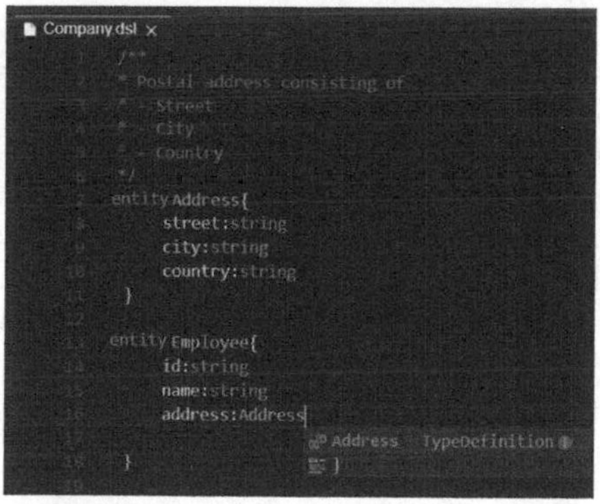

Fig. 2. Theia Editor Integration [4]. 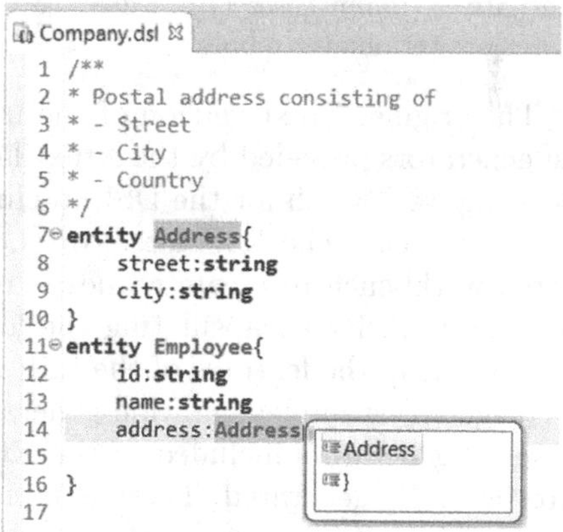   **Fig. 3.** Eclipse Editor Integration [4].

A detailed description on how the language server and the development tools have been implemented will be explained in the next subsections.

3.1   Language Server Implementation of an Entity-DSL

Our simple example DSL allows to describe entities with operations and properties. Its simplified grammar in EBNF format is shown in Listing 1.1. Readers, who are familar with Xtext, can find the original syntax description in Xtext format in the Appendix.

A model consists of a sequence of entities. An entity has an identifier as its name and it may inherit from another entity (keyword extends). Moreover, it may have an arbitrary amount of features, i.e. properties and operations. An operation has an identifier as its name, an optional list of parameters and a return type. A property has an identifier as its name and a type. A type can reference an entity by its name or it can be a primitive type, i.e. string, number, or boolean.

```
Model:
   Entity*;
Entity:
   'entity' ID ('extends' ID)? '{' Feature* '}';
Feature:
   Property | Operation;
Property:
   ID ':' Type;
Operation:
   'op' ID '(' (Parameter (',' Parameter)*)? ')'   (':' Type)?;
Parameter:
   ID Type;
Type :
   Primitive |   EntityReference;
EntityReference :
   ID;
Primitive :
   'number' | 'string' | 'boolean';
```

Listing 1.1. EBNF rules for the Entity-DSL. A * suffix indicates an arbitrary number of repetitions; a ? suffix indicates an optional element. Vertical bars separate alternatives. Parentheses () are used to limit the sope of a * or ? suffix. Symbols in quotes are terminal symbols.

The original Xtext version of the mentioned DSL syntax serves as input for the generators provided by the Xtext language workbench that create the corresponding workbench for the DSL, including abstract syntax tree, parser, linker, formatting, etc. The LSP for Java (LSP4J) framework is utilized by the generated workbench to create requests, responses and notifications in accordance with the LSP. By encapsulating the low-level JSON communication through a Java API [24], the features of the LSP are available to the generated Java-based language-server implementation generated from the Xtext grammar. Due to the powerful generators included in the Xtext language workbench, all six key features are fully generated. There is no manual implementation required.

3.2   Building a Development-Tool Extension for the Theia IDE

As desktop and cloud IDE, Theia integrates different languages based on the LSP. In addition, Theia separates backend processes and the graphical user interface. Thereby, the frontend can either be a browser or a desktop application, while at the same time the backend process is executed locally or remotely on a cloud-based infrastructure [30].

Language servers in Theia are provided through a backend extension, that is capable of configuring the language server. Theia uses dependency injection mechanisms [8] to provide extensions. Listing 1.2 shows the code required to inject the Entity-DSLs backend extension. Here and in the following listings, we do not expect the reader to understand every detail. The listings rather serve to demonstrate that the implementation requires very limited effort.

The `BaseLanguageServerContribution` class from the LSP-specific Theia framework is extended by the `EntityDslContribution`. As shown in Listing 1.2, there are two working modes for the language server. First it can run as local sub-process on the same machine. Alternatively, it can be executed remotely using web-socket communication [7]. The client-specific libraries encapsulate the details for establishing the connection.

```
@injectable()
class EntityDslContribution extends BaseLanguageServerContribution {

  start(clientConnection: IConnection): void {
    let socketPort = getPort();
    if (socketPort) {
      this.connectToRemoteServer(clientConnection,socketPort)
    } else {
      this.connectToLocalServer(clientConnection)
    }
  }
}
```

Listing 1.2. Registering a Language-Server Extension in Theia.

After the backend extension has been registered, language smarts can be provided through the Theia editor. However, the keyword highlighting as shown in Fig. 2 has to be specified by a frontend extension. Within this extension, the keywords are specified and it is determined, how they should be highlighted. Moreover, the frontend extension contains information about the file extensions handled by the given language server. Listing 1.3 exemplifies how the "globPatterns" method of the `EntityDslClientContribution` must be overwritten to bind the language server to the file extension.

```
@injectable()
export class EntityDslClientContribution extends
    BaseLanguageClientContribution
{
  protected get globPatterns() {
    return ['**/*.dsl'];
  }
}
```

Listing 1.3. Binding the ".dsl" file extension to the language server.

By providing a backend and frontend extension as shown above the Theia IDE can provide language smarts for the Entity-DSL as shown in Fig. 2.

3.3   Building a Development-Tool Extension for the Eclipse IDE

Xtext as language workbench and also the language tooling created by the workbench are heavily integrated into Eclipse through its plugin mechanism. Thereby, Xtext DSL editors within Eclipse have a lot of default features included, such as outline views or type hierarchies. Yet, for the purpose of the case study, the Entity-DSL should provide an editor for the Eclipse IDE based on the LSP. Fortunately, the language server for the Eclipse (LSP4E) framework [6] encapsulates low-level communication through a Java-API.

The basic mechanism for providing extensions to the Eclipse ecosystem is by utilizing its plugin architecture [33]. The LSP-based editor support for the Eclipse IDE will also be provided by a specific plugin that extends the LSP4E plugins extension point [10]. The DSL-agnostic extension point "org.eclipse.lsp4e.languageServer" provided by the LSP4E plugin is extended as shown in Listing 1.4. It delegates the implementation to the `EntityDslLanguageServerClass`. This class handles all DSL-specific features for the Entity-DSL.

```
<extension point="org.eclipse.lsp4e.languageServer">
  <server id="org.eclipse.lsp4e.languages.dsl"
    class="org.eclipse.lsp4e.languages.dsl.EntityDslLanguageServer"
    label="Entity-DSL Language Server">
  </server>
</extension>
```

Listing 1.4. Registering a Language Server Extension in Eclipse.

The implementation of the `EntityDslLanguageServer` that extends the LSP4E framework class `ProcessStreamConnectionProvider` is shown in Listing 1.5. The language server is started as soon as a file with the file extension ".dsl" is opened. The `createLauncherCommand` method returns the command required to start a sub-process running the language server. Next, the `ProcessStreamConnectionProvider` computes the working directory for the language server.

```
public class EntityDslLanguageServer extends ProcessStreamConnectionProvider
  {
  public MyDslLanguageServer() {
    setCommands(createLauncherCommand());
    setWorkingDirectory(workingDirectory());
  }
}
```

Listing 1.5. Entity-DSL Extension.

If the language server is running on a remote host, the `ProcessOverSocketStreamConnectionProvider` class from the LSP4E plugin can be extended. Thereby, the communication to an already running language server on a remote host can be realized via a web-socket infrastructure.

```
public class EntityPresentationReconciler extends PresentationReconciler {
  private Set<String> keywords = new HashSet<>(Arrays.asList(new String[] {
    "entity", "extends", "op", "string", "number", "boolean"}));
}
```

Listing 1.6. Keyword Definition for Syntax Highlighting.

As for the Theia extension, the correct highlighting within the editor needs to be specified by providing an additional class. For the Eclipse IDE the `PresentationReconciler` is extended by the `EntityPresentationReconciler` that defines syntax highlighting for comments and keyword in the Entity-DSL as shown in Listing 1.6.

While integrating LSP-based editors into Eclipse and Theia is comparable on a conceptual level, both require tool-specific implementations. Defining syntax highlighting and the start-up of the language server are the main concerns of both development-tool specific extensions. Nevertheless, regarding programming language, architecture, and API both development tools are significantly different.

3.4   Experimental Results of Implementing the Entity-DSL

To quantify the effort of integrating a DSL editor into two different IDEs leveraging the LSP, the time required to implement a language server and the respective development-tool extensions was measured. The first part of the case study was the language-server implementation based on the EBNF-like grammar of the Xtext language workbench. Due to the fact that parser, linker and all required classes for the six key features of the language server as specified in Sect. 2 have been generated completely, the language server implementation could be finished in about two hours (Table 1).

Table 1. Effort for implementing the Entity-DSL [4].

Task	Time (in minutes)
Language Server Implementation	127
Theia Editor Integration	414
Eclipse Editor Integration	317

The implementation of the Theia integration required more manual effort, since a backend and frontend extension had to be provided. Since both required manual implementation, configuration and testing the overall effort was about 7 h. Due to some conceptual similarities between the Theia and Eclipse extension, implementing the Eclipse integration took only a little bit more than 5 h. In general, the fast implementation of all three parts was mainly enabled by the sophisticated SDKs that encapsulate the low-level communication.

In addition to the case study, the efforts spent on providing three extensions in context of the Yakindu Solidity Tools project were analyzed. The project provides an integrated development environment for Ethereum/Solidity based smart contracts [37].

As shown by Table 2, the Yakindu Solidity Tools project provides three language server based editor integrations, namely for Theia, Visual Studio Code,

Table 2. Effort for implementing Multi Editor Support for the Solidity IDE.

Task	Time (in minutes)
Language Server Implementation	350
Theia Editor Integration	835
VSCode Editor Integration	725
Atom Editor Integration	680

and Atom. The creation of the language-server implementation took around 350 min in total. All three editor extensions required a little bit more than a day of work with 835, 725 and 680 min of effort, respectively. Since the Yakindu Solidity IDE supports more keywords and DSL-specific functionality the implementation took more effort for all four compared to the Entity DSL.

It is clear that the observations from two projects cannot achieve statistical significance. In order to achieve that we would need to investigate hundreds of projects, which is not realistic taken into account the duration and costs of such projects. However, observations from the considered projects nevertheless give a rough idea of the effort required to provide multi-editor support for a DSL. They indicate that providing support for multiple editors can be provided with moderate effort using the Language Server Protocol and that this approach is substantially easier and faster compared to a native integration.

3.5   Analysis of the Potential of the Language Server Protocol

Based on the case study, a SWOT analysis [11] has been conducted in order to get a comprehensive view on the potential of the LSP for multi-editor support of DSLs. By analyzing strengths and weaknesses as well as opportunities and threats, the potential of the LSP is examined internally and with respect to the external environment. By investigating the strengths of the LSP, advantages increasing the market penetration will be identified. In addition, weaknesses and threats will be determined that must be eliminated or mitigated to ensure the success of the LSP.

The analysis starts with evaluating the internal strengths of the LSP. By specifying a standardized protocol for development tool and language server to communicate, language smarts can be implemented once and integrated multiple times. The LSP consequently establishes a solid foundation for multi-editor integration not only for general-purpose programming languages but also for domain-specific languages. Reducing the overall integration complexity to $m + n$ rather than $m \times n$, multiple editors can be integrated efficiently.

The lightweight JavaScript Object Notation (JSON) format used for exchanging messages in combination with the JSON-RPC protocol ensures compact payloads. By reducing the amount of data sent back and forth between language server and development tool, efficient communication over a network is possible.

Although both processes are currently running on a single machine, the JSON-RPC protocol enables a good user experience when editing text files.

Being able to support multiple editors is especially advantageous for domain-specific languages. Domain models might be specified collaboratively by technical and non-technical team members. While technical users might prefer a certain IDE, such as Eclipse or VSCode, in which the editor needs to be integrated seamlessly, non-technical users typically prefer a browser-based interface to a simple editor such that no additional tool needs to be installed. This reduces the distribution and maintenance costs. Moreover, browser-based editors can be designed to be more concise and clearly structured compared to IDEs that are confusingly overloaded with buttons and menus from a non-technical user's perspective.

The LSP provides a flexible approach to extend the protocol using custom capabilities. Thereby, toolsmiths can provide language- or editor-specific language smarts. In contrast to the LSP capabilities, the editor integration has to be built manually. Consequently, these smarts might not be supported by all editors. In the long run, the LSP might adopt custom extensions that provide value for the majority of programming languages.

In contrast to the strengths of the LSP, the following weaknesses can be identified. Since the LSP is founded on the assumption that one language server serves one development tool, the number of parallel language servers quickly rises in multi-language scenarios. Editing three or more languages in parallel is a valid scenario. In such a situation, the programming language to implement the language server has to be chosen with respect to its memory footprint. Three language servers implemented in Java will all run in their own Java Virtual Machine (JVM) on a single machine allocating approximately 3 GB of memory. Taking into account the size and complexity of the different languages, a poor user experience might result. Yet, there are more memory efficient SDKs, e.g. utilizing JavaScript, to implement the language server.

Since every development-tool extension requires its own implementation in the programming language suitable for the development tool, the toolsmiths have to decide which editors to support. Therefore, DSL-editor providers require knowledge about providing extensions for Theia, VSCode, or Eclipse. In addition, every extension has to be tested separately to ensure matching user experience in terms of keyword highlighting or validations.

By separating language-server implementations on a conceptual level, they become independent and scalable. Yet, there is no communication between different language servers, leading to continuous re-implementations of basic features. In contrast to native IDE integration, language servers now have to implement functionality, e.g. to resolve classes from a classpath, that otherwise could have been reused.

The language server was built in order to provide sophisticated editor support in multiple editors for textual programming languages. Since the Xtext language workbench supports the LSP, it can also used for DSLs. The combination of Xtext and LSP works seamlessly, because Xtext is also based on text files. However, DSLs can also be implemented using projectional editors such as IntelliJ's Meta Programming System (MPS) [9]. Further, there is a variety of graphical DSLs to specify domain models. Since the language server does not support any of the two approaches, powerful alternatives or extensions to textual domain-specific languages are ignored.

In addition to internal strengths and weaknesses, the SWOT analysis also analyzes external factors in form of opportunities and threats. The first opportunity lies in the spread of domain-specific languages which are by now widely adopted in research and practice. While language workbenches, such as Xtext or MPS, support the fast implementation of sophisticated DSLs, the editor funtionality is often bound to a single IDE. Yet, developers demand different IDEs for different languages or projects. Moreover, non-technical users refuse to interact with IDEs after all. A holistic DSL that enables collaboration of technical and non-technical users needs multi-editor support in order to enable the efficient creation and maintenance of domain models. In an industry where the number of programming and domain-specific languages as well editors and IDEs is rising steadily, the LSP provides a solution to efficiently provide multi-editor support.

One important requirement for multi-editor support is to enable non-technical users to engage in the creation of domain models. Since DSLs are describing abstract technology agnostics constructs, such as insurance contracts or banking products [34], non-technical users need to be able to engage in the creation. While DSLs integrated into heavyweight IDEs are confusing due to the amount of menus, buttons and toolbars, web-based editors are perceived as more concise and clearly structured. Moreover, web-based approaches eliminate additional tool installations. In addition to an IDE integration, the LSP enables the parallel use of web-based editors such as Monaco [21], that can be easily integrated into web-browsers. Providing a browser-based editor lowers the barrier for non-technical users and fosters collaboration on domain models.

Our SWOT analysis closes with examining threats regarding the LSP. Since the LSP is the first standardized approach to provide multi-editor support, there are no technological alternatives. On the one hand, this makes it unlikely that the LSP will be replaced by a competing approach. On the other hand, the investments in development tools and language servers depend on the LSP. These investments would be lost, if the LSP was discontinued.

Providing high-level DSLs quickly generates the demand for multi-notation support including tables, formulas, or charts. Projectional language workbenches such as MPS offer such functionality, but are currently limited to supporting only a single editor. In order to gain more market share, the LSP needs to be enhanced to handle DSLs based on projectional editors.

Browser-based multi-notation language workbenches provide web editors for DSLs typically on a high-level of abstraction. WebGME [17] is a famous example from this category that provides a browser-based editor to specify browser-based DSL editors. In general, multi-notational editors provide an alternative to parser-based languages utilizing the LSP. Yet, approaches like WebGME lack support for native IDE or multi-editor integration.

4   Utilization of the Language Server Protocol

As mentioned above, a relevant threat when relying on the LSP is that the LSP could be abandoned, when it is not used widely enough. Thus, as a supplement to our SWOT analysis, we will now investigate the utilization of the LSP in practice. First, open-source projects built upon the LSP and Xtext were analyzed. Second, the Eclipse TMF (Xtext) forum and its LSP-related threads were examined. While the first indicates the actual market penetration of LSP-based Xtext editors in the open-source community, the second demonstrates how intensive the topic is discussed in the Xtext community, including closed-source projects.

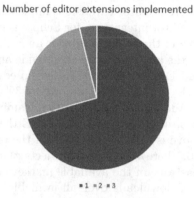

Fig. 4. Number of editor extensions implemented.

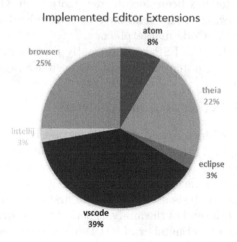

Fig. 5. Kind of editor integration.

4.1   LSP-Based Xtext Solutions in Practice

The first part of the analysis started with crawling all the 98 found open-source github repositories utilizing the LSP for academic or commercial purposes. Projects using Xtext and LSP integration solely for demonstration or testing purposes have been excluded. A manual inspection revealed that out of the 98 search results only 51 had an actual implementation of the language server and only 27 of those had at least one development-tool extension implemented.

As shown in Fig. 4, about 70% of all projects only provide one editor extension. Out of the 27 projects, only 7 implement two development-tool extensions which is equal to 25%. Only the Solidity-IDE project [37] provides three editor extensions namely for Atom, Theia and Visual Studio Code.

Figure 5 shows the different editor extensions implemented using the LSP for the 27 projects. Since the editor integration for Eclipse is more effective using the native integration, only 3% of the projects provide an Eclipse extension using the LSP. Further, only 3% of the analyzed projects provide an extension for IntelliJ. In contrast to IntelliJ and Eclipse, Atom is rather an editor than an IDE. It is only supported by 8% of the projects. The majority of 39% provides an extension for Visual Studio Code. Additionally, 29% of the examined projects provide a browser extension based on the LSP. The Theia IDE that was also used in the case study mentioned above is enhanced by 22% of the projects.

As depicted in Fig. 6, there are only 6 projects that provide their editor extensions through at least one of the available marketplaces. The y-axis shows the cumulative number of downloads over all available stores or marketplaces for the given projects. The *JHipster* IDE is the clear outlier with more than 20,000 downloads; most of them through the VSCode marketplace. The projects *yang*, *plexus-interop*, and *ex.xtext.lsp* have been downloaded between 5,000 and 1,700 times. While for the first two, the downloads stem from the VSCode marketplace only, the latter has been downloaded more than 3,000 times from the IntelliJ marketplace. *ck2xtext* and *scila* have been downloaded 707 and 98 times, respectively, from the VSCode marketplace.

We can conclude that the LSP is significantly used in practical open-source projects, although its full potential has not yet been leveraged.

4.2   Eclipse TMF (Xtext) Forum Analysis

In order to analyze to which extent the LSP feature is discussed by the Xtext community, the Eclipse TMF (Xtext) forum was examined. The forum is the main point of discussions about features and best practices regarding Xtext. Since the LSP support is part of Xtext since version 2.11.0 that was released February 1, 2017, the analysis starts from the first quarter of 2017. The first quarter of 2019 marks the end of the analysis period that is divided quarterly. For the given time period a total number of 981 threads were discussed in the Xtext forum. The analysis was done based on the subject and creation date of each thread. In order to count all topics regarding the LSP, all subjects mentioning the words *Language Server Protocol*, *language server*, or *LSP* were counted. In

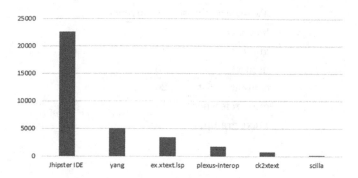

Fig. 6. Cumulative Downloads of Editor Extensions.

addition, subjects using the words *vscode*, *Visual Studio Code*, or *Theia* were counted as LSP related. The analysis focuses on the subjects of the threads rather than on the entire discussion. Thus, we only take those questions into account that specifically focus on the topic.

In order to compare the search results for LSP-related topics to other important topics in the forum, the subject headlines were analyzed to find the two-word phrases, which occurred most frequently. Table 3 shows the six two-word phrases most frequently occurring in the subjects of the threads in descending order of occurrences. While the first three show no direct relation to a specific Xtext topic, the last three are all related to specific features of the Xtext workbench.

Based on the results of the text analysis, the subjects of the threads were analyzed for the questions regarding content assist, cross reference and xtext grammar. Since the topic content assist is synonymously named proposal provider or code assist, these terms were included in the search query. For the other two topics, no additional terms were required. Yet, for questions regarding Xtext grammar subjects only mentioning the word grammar without Xtext were also counted. All four analyses were done in a case-insensitive way.

Figure 7 shows the results for the four topics. The first questions regarding the LSP Xtext integration were asked in the second quarter and third quarter of 2017. While there are two questions on average per quarter regarding LSP, there are also quarters such as the fourth quarter of 2017, where no questions were asked. Although being only the third most often occurring topic based on Table 3, "Xtext grammar" is questioned most often with an average of more than 7 questions per quarter. "Content assist" is questioned regularly in the Xtext forum and with an average of four question per quarter more often than the LSP topic. The fourth topic related to cross-references is discussed in less than two question per quarter on average.

Although, the absolute number of LSP-related topics in the considered form is not impressive, these topics are nevertheless among the most active topics

Table 3. Two-word phrases in thread subjects.

Two-word Phrase	Occurrences
how to	76
xtext 2	40
in xtext	35
content assist	26
cross reference	18
xtext grammar	14

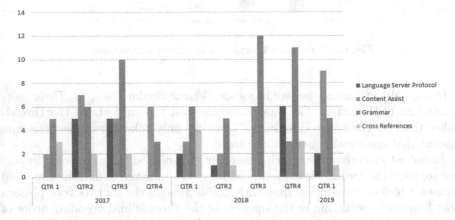

Fig. 7. Questions asked per topic and quarter in the Xtext TMF (Xtext) forum.

in that forum. Thus, the topic is relevant, although its importance has still a potential to rise.

5   Discussion

The LSP offers a standardized mechanism that enables an easy integration of language smarts into different editors and IDEs. As the case study has shown, the Xtext language workbench integrates this feature to provide arbitrary DSLs for different development tools. While the integration is slightly specific for each tool, the language server parts for the key features are generated completely. Thereby, LSP-based DSL editors can be created quickly as Subsect. 3.4 has shown. Although the results from the case study are supported by the findings from the real world open source project Yakindu Solidity Tools, additional projects should be analyzed to further support our claims. The SWOT analysis conducted as second part of the case study shows that the LSP addresses the right requirements, since the number of DSLs and development tools is steadily increasing. Yet, the Xtext and LSP integration is limited to textual DSLs, hence ignoring sophisticated alternatives such as MPS-based projectional DSLs.

However, our analysis of the utilization of LSP-based DSLs in real world projects has revealed that the full potential of the LSP has not yet been leveraged. There are currently 27 open source projects utilizing Xtext and LSP. Only six of them are listed on an official marketplace. Projects such as JHipster that are utilizing Xtext and LSP and the corresponding market places to distribute the development-tool extension can be seen as early adopters. In addition, we know of several large DSLs that are implemented as company-specific closed source solutions. In order to get an idea, of the overall importance of the LSP, including closed-source projects, we have analyzed the amount of questions asked about the language server and Xtext integration. As shown in Fig. 7 there are between four and six questions asked per quarter about the LSP. Comparing it to the other topics that are available in the Xtext forum, the number of LSP-related questions is not impressive but steady.

According to our experience, especially large companies using Xtext have a deeply integrated Eclipse-based tool chain. However up to now, their main focus remains on Eclipse as primary IDE. Therefore, they prefer the powerful native Eclipse integration, which has turned out to be frustrating for non-technical users such as domain experts.

On the road to multi-editor support for arbitrary DSLs, the Xtext language workbench integrating the LSP marks an important milestone. Separating language smarts and editor functionality enables an efficient distribution of editor integrations for a broad variety of editors and IDEs. In addition, the standardized protocol establishes the minimal features for sophisticated editor support as listed by the community-driven LSP-site [28]. Moreover, the Xtext-LSP integration can increase the efficiency of model-driven software development with DSLs by integrating the language smarts into the IDE or editor that is most appropriate for running, testing, and debugging the generated code.

Since the LSP-based DSLs also support web-editors, they can be a valid alternative to other approaches. By integrating LSP-based Xtext DSLs into web-browsers, also non-technical users can interact with the domain model. The results from Sect. 4 substantiate this. They show that 25% of the LSP-based DSLs provide a browser integration. By providing a web-based editor, technical and non-technical team members can contribute to the domain models using their favorite editor.

6   Related Work

Textual Domain-Specific Languages can be divided into two categories, namely internal and external. While internal DSLs are embedded into a host language [34], external DSLs have their own tool support [31]. The creation of domain-specific editors is supported by language workbenches that provide frameworks to specify abstract syntax, parser, editor, and generators [9]. While MontiCore and MPS provide generators to create DSL editors that could be integrated into Eclipse or IntelliJ, Xtext and Spoofax focus on Eclipse-based extensions. In addition, Spoofax provides experimental support for an IntelliJ integration [13].

Likewise, Xtext has a strong focus on Eclipse-based extensions and lacks contributions for constantly supporting an IntelliJ integration [36].

In addition to approaches integrating language editors into classical IDEs, there is a variety of web-based language workbenches. These web-based language workbenches are divided into client-server and cloud-based Modeling as a Service (MaaS) approaches by Popoola et al. [25]. Modeling platforms from the latter category such as WebGME, CLOOCA, GenMyModel, MORSE, and MDEForge provide their services without requiring on-premise hardware. In contrast, client-server based approaches such as ModelBus, AToMPM, and DSLForge must be installed on a local server. In addition to relying on proprietary protocols [26], none of the language workbenches provides integration into editors or IDEs, such as Atom [2] or Eclipse, respectively.

While there exists a lot of research around language workbenches for textual external DSLs and web-based language workbenches, little attention has been paid to providing a multi-editor support for combining editor, IDE and browser-based integration. By introducing the LSP, Microsoft, RedHat, and Codenvy laid the foundation for providing language smarts in different development tools through a standardized protocol [22]. With Xtext being the first language workbench fully implementing the LSP [19] an additional milestone on the way towards multi-editor support was reached in 2017 [35]. While Rodriguez-Echeverria et al. [27] have already proposed an LSP infrastructure for graphical modeling, little attention has been paid to multi-editor integration of textual domain-specific languages.

7   Conclusions

We have reported the results of a case study conducted to quantify the effort required to integrate an Xtext DSL into different editors or IDEs utilizing the LSP. While the language server part can be generated completely based on an Xtext grammar, each development-tool extension has to be implemented specifically. However, the total integration costs are significantly below providing individual IDE-specific extensions. In addition, the SWOT analysis has revealed great potential of the LSP for standardizing and distributing language smarts for different editors and IDEs. However, exclusively targeting textual editors ignores alternative approaches such as projectional or graphical DSLs.

The LSP represents a major step towards multi-editor support for domain-specific languages. By separating language smarts and development-tool extensions by a standardized protocol, the integration costs for supporting multiple editors significantly decrease. However, the analysis of real world projects shows that there are only a few projects leveraging the Xtext-LSP integration and the ecosystem around it, e.g. marketplaces for development-tool extensions, to its full extent. Further research is required to analyze, whether these projects are early adopters or whether the Xtext-LSP integration is targeting only a niche market.

Large companies that build their tool-chains on top of the Eclipse ecosystem appreciate the seamless integration of different plugins that enables the efficient creation of workbenches. The LSP is built on the assumption that every language server is independent and does not interact with other languages servers. While this approach increases the scalability, it also introduces disadvantages, since every language server has to re-implement certain functionality. The assumption that this separation of language servers and the consequent reimplementation of basic features hinders large companies to adopt the LSP, has to be substantiated by further research.

The contributions of this paper are the following. First, we have conducted a case study to quantify the efforts for implementing a DSL and integrating its editor into two different IDEs. Our case study has shown that this can be done with moderate effort. In addition, we have reported on the findings from a SWOT analysis performed to identify the potential impact of the LSP for textual domain-specific languages. Moreover, we have supplemented the findings of the SWOT analysis by investigating open-source github projects and the Eclipse TMF (Xtext) forum in order to examine the practical relevance of the LSP. The combination of the case study and the analysis of real world projects shows that the Xtext-LSP integration offers great potential that currently is not leveraged to its full extent.

Appendix: Syntax of Entity DSL in Xtext Format

```
Model:
    entities+=Entity*;
Entity:
    'entity' name=ID ('extends' superType=Entity)?
    '{' features+=Feature* '}';
Feature:
    Property | Operation;
Property:
    name=ID ':' type=Type;
Operation:
    'op' name=ID '(' (params+=parameter(',' params+=parameter)*)?')'
    '(' ':' returntype=Type)?;
Parameter:
    name=ID type=[Type];
Type :
    {Primitive} name=Primitive |  EntityReference;
EntityReference :
    {EntityReference} entityDefinition=[Entity];
Primitive :
    'number' | 'string' | 'boolean';
```

Listing 1.7. Grammar Rules for the Entity-DSL in Xtext format.

References

1. Arnold, K., Gosling, J., Holmes, D.: The Java Programming Language. Addison Wesley Professional, Boston (2005)
2. Atom: A hackable text editor for the 21st century (2019). https://atom.io/
3. BSP: Build server protocol (2019). https://github.com/scalacenter/bsp

4. Bünder, H.: Decoupling language and editor – the impact of the language server protocol on textual domain-specific languages. In: Hammoudi, S., Ferreira, P.L., Selić, B. (eds.) Proceedings of the 7th International Conference on Model-Driven Engineering and Software Development (MODELSWARD 2019), pp. 131–142. Prag (2019). https://doi.org/10.5220/0007556301310142, publication status: Published

5. Campagne, F.: The MPS Language Workbench: Meta Programming System, 3rd edn. Campagnelab, New York (2016). version 1.5.1 edn

6. Eclipse: Eclipse LSP4E (2018). https://projects.eclipse.org/projects/technology.lsp4e

7. Fette, I., Melnikov, A.: The websocket protocol. Technical report (2011)

8. Fowler, M.: Inversion of control containers and the dependency injection pattern (2004)

9. Fowler, M.: Language workbenches: The killer-app for domain specific languages (2005). https://www.martinfowler.com/articles/languageWorkbench.html

10. Gamma, E., Beck, K.: Contributing to Eclipse: Principles, Patterns, and Plug-ins. Addison-Wesley Professional, Boston (2004)

11. Helms, M.M., Nixon, J.: Exploring SWOT analysis - where are we now?: a review of academic research from the last decade. J. Strategy Manag. **3**(3), 215–251 (2010). https://doi.org/10.1108/17554251011064837

12. JetBrains: IntelliJ IDEA (2018). https://www.jetbrains.com/idea/

13. Kats, L.C., Visser, E.: The spoofax language workbench: rules for declarative specification of languages and IDEs. In: Proceedings of the ACM International Conference on Object Oriented Programming Systems Languages and Applications, OOPSLA 2010, pp. 444–463. ACM, New York (2010). https://doi.org/10.1145/1869459.1869497

14. Kichwas Coders: Debugging protocol vs. language server protocol (2018). https://kichwacoders.com/2017/11/08/debug-protocol-vs-language-server-protocol/

15. Krahn, H., Rumpe, B., Völkel, S.: Efficient editor generation for compositional DSLs in eclipse. arXiv preprint arXiv:1409.6625 (2014)

16. Lamb, L., Robbins, A.: Learning the vi Editor, 6th edn. O'Reilly & Associates, Sebastopol (1998)

17. Maróti, M., et al.: Next generation (meta) modeling: web-and cloud-based collaborative tool infrastructure. In: MPM@ MoDELS, vol. 1237, pp. 41–60 (2014)

18. Microsoft: Code editing. Redefined (2018). https://code.visualstudio.com/

19. Microsoft: Implementations - language servers (2018). https://microsoft.github.io/language-server-protocol/implementors/servers/

20. Microsoft: Language server protocol specification - initialize (2018). https://microsoft.github.io/language-server-protocol/specification#initialize

21. Microsoft: Monaco editor - about (2018). https://microsoft.github.io/monaco-editor/

22. Microsoft: Overview - what is the language server protocol (2018). https://microsoft.github.io/language-server-protocol/overview

23. Mikkonen, T., Taivalsaari, A.: Using JavaScript as a real programming language (2007)

24. Spönemann, M.: The language server protocol in Java (2018). https://typefox.io/the-language-server-protocol-in-java

25. Popoola, S., Carver, J., Gray, J.: Modeling as a service: a survey of existing tools. In: MODELS (Satellite Events), pp. 360–367 (2017)

26. Rodriguez-Echeverria, R., Izquierdo, J.L.C., Wimmer, M., Cabot, J.: An LSP infrastructure to build EMF language servers for web-deployable model editors. In: Proceedings of the Second Workshop on Model-Driven Engineering Tools (MDETools 2018), pp. 1–10. CEUR (2018)
27. Rodriguez-Echeverria, R., Izquierdo, J.L.C., Wimmer, M., Cabot, J.: Towards a language server protocol infrastructure for graphical modeling. In: Proceedings of the 21th ACM/IEEE International Conference on Model Driven Engineering Languages and Systems, pp. 370–380. MODELS 2018. ACM, New York (2018). https://doi.org/10.1145/3239372.3239383
28. Sourcegraph: Languageserver.org (2018). https://langserver.org/
29. Stroustrup, B.: The C++ Programming Language. Pearson Education India, Bengaluru (2000)
30. Theia.org: Theia - cloud and desktop IDE (2018). https://www.theia-ide.org
31. Tomassetti, F.: The complete guide to (external) domain-specific languages (2017). https://tomassetti.me/domain-specific-languages
32. Vogel, L., Milinkovich, M.: Eclipse Rich Client Platform. Vogella series, Lars Vogel (2015). https://books.google.de/books?id=AC4_CQAAQBAJ
33. Vogel, L., Beaton, W.: Eclipse IDE: Java Programming, Debugging, Unit Testing, Task Management and Git Version Conrol with Eclipse, 3rd edn. Vogella Series, Vogella, Lexington (2013)
34. Völter, M.: DSL Engineering: Designing, Implementing and Using Domain-Specific Languages. CreateSpace Independent Publishing Platform, Lexington (2013)
35. Xtext: Xtext 2.11.0 release notes (2017). https://www.eclipse.org/Xtext/releasenotes.html#/releasenotes/2017/02/01/version-2-11-0
36. Xtext: Idea support (2018). https://www.eclipse.org/Xtext/releasenotes.html
37. Yakindu: Yakindu solidity tools (2019). https://yakindu.github.io/solidity-ide/

Executing Scenario-Based Specification with Dynamic Generation of Rich Events

David Harel[1], Guy Katz[2(✉)], Assaf Marron[1], Aviran Sadon[3], and Gera Weiss[3]

[1] Weizmann Institute of Science, Rehovot, Israel
{David.Harel,assaf.marron}@weizmann.ac.il
[2] The Hebrew University of Jerusalem, Jerusalem, Israel
guykatz@cs.huji.ac.il
[3] Ben-Gurion University of the Negev, Be'er Sheva, Israel
sadonav@post.bgu.ac.il, geraw@cs.bgu.ac.il

Abstract. Scenario-Based Programming (SBP) is an approach to modeling and running complex, event-based, system behavior by composing narrower views of overall behavior. In this paper we introduce significant extensions to the strict interfaces by which scenarios in existing SBP frameworks specify what the system must, may, or must not do, and to the mechanisms that execute these scenarios: (i) we allow events with a multitude of variables and parameters; each event can become an entire model, and each event selection can be the selection of a major section of the new state of the system and the environment; (ii) we extend the basic *request/block* SBP interfaces with a rich set of composable constraints and functions, which can describe desired and undesired variable assignments, where each constraint may relate to all variables or to just a subset thereof; (iii) we introduce a central, application-agnostic mechanism for adding *optimization* to standard event selection; and (iv) we relate our method to Null-Space Behavior (NSB)—a successful compositional approach in control theory. We demonstrate these language-independent concepts through several use cases that are implemented in a variety of languages and solvers.

Keywords: Scenario-Based Programming · Behavioral programming · Constraint solvers · SMT solvers · NSB · Mathematica · MATLAB-Simulink Z3 · Python

1 Introduction

One of the key goals in Model Driven Engineering (MDE) is creating executable models, which, on one hand, represent how engineers and other stakeholder conceive a problem and a system, and, on the other hand, can be used directly

---

This paper substantially extends the paper titled "On-the-Fly Construction of Composite Events in Scenario-Based Modeling Using Constraint Solvers", published in Modelsward 2019 [48].

© Springer Nature Switzerland AG 2020
S. Hammoudi et al. (Eds.): MODELSWARD 2019, CCIS 1161, pp. 246–274, 2020.
https://doi.org/10.1007/978-3-030-37873-8_11

for automatic generation of system and environment behavior: for simulation, for formal analysis, and for final production deployment. *Scenario-Based Programming (SBP)* [16,40,45] tackles this challenge by offering dynamic, run-time, composition of *scenarios*, each of which specifies a narrow facet of the system's behavior, as might be described in a requirements document, resulting in cohesive integrated system behavior. Individual scenarios describe both desired behaviors, which should be manifested in the system as a whole, and undesired (or even forbidden) behaviors, which the system should avoid. The SBP principles are general, i.e., language agnostic. They have been implemented in dedicated frameworks, such as the Play-Engine and PlayGo for the visual language of Live Sequence Charts (LSC) [39,40] and ScenarioTools [22] for the textual Scenario Modeling Language (SML). Furthermore, SBP has been implemented as libraries in programming languages like Java [41], C++ [30], and JavsScript [4], and has been amalgamated with the Statecharts visual formalism [53]. SBP has been successfully used in modeling complex systems, including industrial manufacturing, biological modeling, web-servers [30], cache coherence protocols [32], robotic controllers [25], and in new approaches for intelligent software-development assistant tools [32–34,52].

In this work, we expand SBP capabilities by allowing more expressive specification of each scenario's view of the composite behavior, and richer techniques for composing these views.

The principles of execution mechanisms used in current behavioral programming tools are as follows. System and environment behavior is modeled as a sequence of discrete events, each perhaps with one or two parameters (e.g., traffic light turns green, vehicle starts moving, vehicle makes a 45° right turn); all scenarios are run in parallel and are synchronized at predetermined points; at every synchronization point each scenario declares a discrete set of events it would like to see triggered, termed *requested events*, and a set of events it forbids from being triggered, termed *blocked events*; the underlying SBP infrastructure then selects for triggering *a single* event that is requested by at least one scenario and is not blocked by any scenarios; the selected event is then broadcast to all scenarios; scenarios can react to that event and change their declarations; and the execution continues until the next synchronization point is reached. An example appears in Fig. 1.

Some of the benefits of SBP stem from these intuitive [19] and succinct [31] expression and composition semantics, reducing the cognitive load that might be imposed by a single composite automaton, or depicting visually the actual conditions of which events are allowed in which composite states. The approach also renders scenario-based models more amenable to automatic analysis using formal compositional techniques [21,28,29,32,37], and even makes it easier to automatically distribute, repair and synthesize such models [23,24,26,35,57,58].

Here is how we would like to extend the current capabilities of SBP:

1. We wish to allow for rich events that may have multiple numeric and discrete parameters. This need is clear in the context of modern systems, such as autonomous driving, advanced robotics, and more. We believe that in this area there is a gap in most, if not all, software engineering approaches.

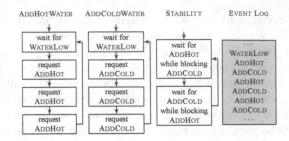

Fig. 1. (From [36]) A scenario-based system for controlling the water level in a tank with hot and cold water taps. Scenarios are depicted as parallel-running transition systems that synchronize at every state. The scenario object ADDHOTWATER repeatedly waits for WATERLOW events and requests the event ADDHOT three times; the scenario object ADDCOLDWATER performs a symmetrical operation with cold water. In a model that includes only the objects ADDHOTWATER and ADDCOLDWATER, the three ADDHOT events and three ADDCOLD events may be triggered in any order during execution. In order to maintain the stability of the water temperature in the tank, the scenario object STABILITY enforces the interleaving of ADDHOT and ADDCOLD events, by using event blocking. The execution trace of the resulting model appears in the event log.

In particular, it may well be that the recent trend to employ machine learning (ML) techniques directly to a large variety of complex problems is fueled not only by the great success of computational learning techniques in solving certain kinds of problems. It is quite accepted that for complex systems even if all rules and specifications needed for a procedural solution were available, e.g., from domain experts, or by extraction from statistical and ML tools, there are no practical engineering techniques for using these rules in building the system so that it is robust, efficient, predictable, analyzable and maintainable.

2. We would like to be able to view events as entire instances of object models of the system and the environment, enabling new assignments to any and all variables in a single synchronization point. As will be seen later, this concept of finding object model instance aligns well with the terminology of constraint solvers, which aim to find a *model* that satisfies the given constraints. These instantaneous models are not to be confused with the model of the system, which describes the objects in the system and their behaviors.

3. We want to extend the basic *request/block* SBP interfaces with a richer set of composable constraints which may relate to all variables or to just a subset thereof; further, these constraints may be organized in hierarchies or priorities of various kinds, and interfere with (or override) each other in more ways than the request/block protocol allows.

4. We would like to add intelligence and insight to the event (or model) selection, such that when multiple solutions satisfy the constraints, optimization techniques may be introduced, to select a preferred solution.

These extensions can be thought of as enhancing SBP's concept of *event selection* to a form of *event construction*. We accomplish them by allowing the scenarios to present rich constraints in languages accepted by a variety of constraint solvers, and then having the SBP infrastructure invoke a solver and/or optimizer at every synchronization point to solve a composite formula, which is assembled from the declarations of all scenarios.

The work described in this paper extends our previous work [48] in several ways. First, we introduce here an extension to SBP that performs constraint resolution with optimization. Additionally, we study the concept of variable targeting in constraint specifications. We also demonstrate the applicability of our approach using additional use-cases, discuss its applicability to real-time settings, and compare the solutions it yields to related solutions proposed in the literature, particularly Null-Space behavior (NSB). Our extensions demonstrate that through the proposed enhancements to SBP, the concept of rich events can be expanded so that the entire state of the system and its environment, with its numerous variables and parameters, can be determined by behavioral decisions at every step. We propose the concept of variable targeting with proper labeling and meta processing, and implement it in Python/Z3. Finally, we introduce an implementation of the extended SBP principles, using Wolfram Mathematica.

The paper is organized as follows. In Sect. 2 we provide some necessary background on SBP and on constraint solvers. In Sect. 3 we provide the formal definitions of how SBP is to be extended to allow for the new capabilities, and in Sect. 4 we describe certain technical aspects of the implementation of SBP with various solvers. In Sect. 5 we review the main capabilities of the new approach and illustrate them with specific example applications. In Sect. 6 we review related work, and we conclude in Sect. 7.

2   Background

2.1   Scenario-Based Modeling

Formally, a scenario-based specification/model/program consists of modules termed *scenarios*. All scenarios run in parallel. Each scenario repeatedly declares sets of events which, from its own perspective, should, may, or must not occur at that particular point in time during the execution. The simultaneously-running scenarios are repeatedly synchronized, and a central mechanism selects events that constitute the integrated system behavior. Ideally, the scenarios do not interact with each other directly— all interactions are carried out through the common event selection and broadcasting mechanism.

Following the definitions in [41, 49], we define a scenario object O over event set E as a tuple $O = \langle Q, \delta, q_0, R, B \rangle$, where the components are interpreted as follows:

- Q is a set of states, each representing one of the predetermined synchronization points;
- q_0 is the initial state;

- $R : Q \to 2^E$ and $B : Q \to 2^E$ map states to the sets of events requested and blocked at these states, respectively; and
- $\delta : Q \times E \to 2^Q$ is a transition function indicating how the object reacts when an event is triggered.

Scenario objects can be composed, in the following manner. For objects $O^1 = \langle Q^1, \delta^1, q_0^1, R^1, B^1 \rangle$ and $O^2 = \langle Q^2, \delta^2, q_0^2, R^2, B^2 \rangle$ over a common event set E, the composite scenario object $O^1 \parallel O^2$ is defined by $O^1 \parallel O^2 = \langle Q^1 \times Q^2, \delta, \langle q_0^1, q_0^2 \rangle, R^1 \cup R^2, B^1 \cup B^2 \rangle$ where:

- $\langle \tilde{q}^1, \tilde{q}^2 \rangle \in \delta(\langle q^1, q^2 \rangle, e)$ if and only if $\tilde{q}^1 \in \delta^1(q^1, e)$ and $\tilde{q}^2 \in \delta^2(q^2, e)$; and
- The union of the labeling functions is defined in the natural way; i.e., $e \in (R^1 \cup R^2)(\langle q^1, q^2 \rangle)$ if and only if $e \in R^1(q^1) \cup R^2(q^2)$, and $e \in (B^1 \cup B^2)(\langle q^1, q^2 \rangle)$ if and only if $e \in B^1(q^1) \cup B^2(q^2)$.

A *behavioral model* M is simply a collection of scenario objects $O^1, O^2, \ldots, O^n$, and the executions of M are the executions of the composite object $O = O^1 \parallel O^2 \parallel \ldots \parallel O^n$. Each such execution starts from the initial state of O, and in each state q along the run an enabled event is chosen for triggering, if one exists (i.e., an event $e \in R(q) - B(q)$). Then, the execution moves to state $\tilde{q} \in \delta(q, e)$, and so on.

2.2   Constraint Solvers

Broadly speaking, constraint solvers are tools that take as input a set of constraints given as a formula φ over a set of variables V, and either (i) return a variable assignment that satisfies φ, or (ii) state that no such variable assignment exists. As mentioned above, a satisfying assignment is usually called a *model*, but we will try to refrain from using that term, so as to not confuse it with the model of the system under development. Different solvers differ in the kinds of constraints they allow as part of their input, and many popular solvers operate on constraints given in restricted forms of first order logic. The performance of these solvers (and the complexity of the problems they solve) also closely depends on the kinds of inputs they allow. Automated solvers have become widespread and highly successful in the last decades, particularly in tasks related to program analysis and verification [5,14].

The types of candidate solvers relevant to our work are as follows:

Boolean Satisfiability (SAT) Solvers. These are solvers that operate on a set V of Boolean variables, and limit the constraint input φ to be a quantifier-free propositional formula over the variables of V. The solver then attempts to find a Boolean assignment that satisfies φ. For example, for $V = \{p, q\}$, the formula $\varphi_1 = (p \lor q) \land (p \lor \neg q)$ is satisfiable, and one satisfying assignment is $p, \neg q$, whereas the formula $\varphi_2 = (\neg p \lor \neg q) \land p \land q$ is unsatisfiable. Although the Boolean satisfiability problem is NP-complete, there exist many mature tools that can solve instances that appear in practice, and which contain hundreds of thousands of variables [54]. A particular kind of SAT solver, called *MaxSAT*, attempts to find a Boolean assignment that satisfies as many of the input constraints as possible (and not necessarily all of them).

Linear Programming (LP) Solvers. LP solvers operate on a set V of rational variables, and the constraint formula φ is a conjunction of linear constraints, often referred to as a *linear program*. For example, for the variables $V = \{x, y, z\}$, the constraint $\varphi_3 = (x \leq 5) \wedge (x + y \leq z)$ is satisfiable, whereas the constraint $\varphi_4 = (x \leq 5) \wedge (y \leq 2) \wedge (x + y \geq 20)$ is unsatisfiable. The general linear programming problem is known to be solvable in polynomial time, although many solvers use worst-case exponential algorithms that turn out to be more efficient in practice [13].

Satisfiability Modulo Theories (SMT) Solvers. These solvers can be regarded as generalized SAT solvers, capable of handling formulas in rich fragments of first order logic. The satisfiability of the formulas is checked subject to (i.e., *modulo*) *background theories*, which intuitively restrict the search only to satisfying assignments that "make sense" according to these certain theories. For example, considering the theory of arrays of integer elements with variable set $V = \{a, b\}$, the formula $\varphi_5 = (a[3] \geq b[5]) \wedge (a[4] \leq b[0])$ is satisfiable, whereas the formula $\varphi_6 = (a = b) \wedge (a[4] \neq b[4])$ is unsatisfiable. Modern SMT solvers support many theories of interest, including various arithmetic theories, the theory of uninterpreted functions, and theories of arrays, of sets, of strings, and others [6]. Furthermore, these background theories can be combined: for example, one can define formulas that include arrays of integers or sets of strings, etc. The SMT problem is, in general, undecidable, although certain background theories afford efficient decision procedures.

Numeric Optimization Solvers. For some optimization problems, it is beneficial to apply solvers that are guaranteed to terminate after a finite number of steps. Some tools, such as MATLAB and Mathematica, implement iterative algorithms that after a finite number of steps terminate, either converging to an optimal solution or providing an approximation thereof if one has not yet been discovered. Such solvers are useful, for example, when implementing a controller for generating real-time feedback in the context of a physical system, such as an autonomous car, a drone, a robot, etc.

The above kinds of solvers are used for many tasks in academia and industry, and all are highly successful. Many mature tools supporting them exist, and a great deal of research is being put into improving them further.

3 New Extension Mechanisms

3.1 Formal Definitions of the New Event Generation Mechanism

The mechanism underlying our extensions of SBP is as follows. At each synchronization point, instead of declaring sets of requested and blocked events, each scenario object O_i can instead declare a set of constraint formulas $\Phi = \{\varphi_i^1, \ldots, \varphi_i^l\}$ that are intended as guiding rules for a solver-based mechanism that assembles the events. Further, these constraint formulas are *labeled* by a labeling function L_i, which maps each formula φ_i^k into a subset of a finite set of predefined labels (or tags) $\mathcal{L}$. The labels then provide additional meta information/semantics that can guide the SBP infrastructure in assembling and composing the various formulas, such as distinguishing *must* constraints from *may* constraints, assigning different priorities to some constraints, etc.

At each synchronization point, the execution mechanism collects from all scenarios the sets of constraint formulas $\Phi_1, \ldots, \Phi_n$, and assembles them into a global constraint formula φ. This formula is then passed as input to a constraint solver. If the formula is found to be satisfiable, the result (i.e., the satisfying assignment returned by the solver) is broadcast to all scenarios, which can then change their states and declarations. When no satisfying assignment is found, the system takes no action, and waits for an external event, as described in [42]. Alternatively, when the set of scenarios also includes scenarios that play the role of (i.e., simulate) the environment, no additional external events can be expected, and the system can then stop or terminate for further debugging.

Formally, we modify the definitions of SBP to support the new capabilities, via integration with constraint solvers, as follows. Let V denote a set of variables. (Note: the goal of the SBP infrastructure is to assign a value to each of these variables, at each synchronization point.) Let $\mathcal{L}$ denote a finite set of labels. We define a scenario object O over V and $\mathcal{L}$ as a tuple $O = \langle Q, \delta, q_0, C, L \rangle$, where Q is a set of states and q_0 is the initial state, as before. The function C (which replaces the labeling functions R and B in the original definition of SBP) maps each state $q \in Q$ to a set of constraint formulas $\Phi = \{\varphi^1, \ldots, \varphi^l\}$ over the variables of V. The function L maps each state to a labeling of these constraint formulas; i.e., $L : Q \times \xi \to 2^{\mathcal{L}}$, where ξ represents the set of all possible formulas. By convention, we require that $L(q, \varphi) = \emptyset$ for every φ such that $\varphi \notin C(q)$. The transition function δ is now defined as $\delta : Q \times A(V) \to 2^Q$, where $A(V)$ is the set of all possible assignments to the variables of V. Intuitively, given a specific state q and a variable assignment $\alpha \in A(V)$ (as may be chosen by the solver-assisted execution infrastructure), invoking $\delta(q, \alpha)$ returns the set of states into which the object may transition.

In order to account for the new constraint formulas, we modify the composition operator for scenario objects, as follows: for scenario objects $O^1 = \langle Q^1, \delta^1, q_0^1, C^1, L^1 \rangle$ and $O^2 = \langle Q^2, \delta^2, q_0^2, C^2, L^2 \rangle$ over a common variable set V and a common label set $\mathcal{L}$, the composite scenario object $O^1 \parallel O^2$ is defined by $O^1 \parallel O^2 = \langle Q^1 \times Q^2, \delta, \langle q_0^1, q_0^2 \rangle, C, L \rangle$, where $\langle \tilde{q}^1, \tilde{q}^2 \rangle \in \delta(\langle q^1, q^2 \rangle, \alpha)$ if and only if $\tilde{q}^1 \in \delta^1(q^1, \alpha)$ and $\tilde{q}^2 \in \delta^2(q^2, \alpha)$. The constraint-generating function C is defined as $C(\langle q^1, q^2 \rangle) = C^1(q^1) \cup C^2(q^2)$; i.e., the constraints defined by the individual objects are combined and become the constraints defined by the composite object. We define $L(\langle q^1, q^2 \rangle, \varphi) = L^1(q^1, \varphi) \cup L^2(q^2, \varphi)$, using again the convention that $L^i(q^i, \varphi) = \emptyset$ if $\varphi \notin C^i(q^i)$.

The key difference between our extended semantics and the original is only in the event selection mechanism. As before, a *behavioral model* M is a collection of scenario objects $O^1, O^2, \ldots, O^n$, and the executions of M are the executions of the composite object $O = O^1 \parallel O^2 \parallel \ldots \parallel O^n$. Each such execution starts from the initial state of O, and after each state q along the run a variable assignment α is assembled, by invoking a constraint solver on a formula φ constructed from $C(q)$ according to the constraint labeling L. Specifically, we assume that the modeler also provides a *constraint composition rule* ψ. Given the constraint-generating function C and the labeling function L, ψ *interprets* the labels in L and thus dictates how to construct for every state q the constraint formula φ that should be passed along to the solver, and/or how, in general, to treat the various constraints (e.g., applying conjunctions, disjunctions and negations, applying priorities among scenarios, or applying various optimization goals when multiple solutions exist). The execution then moves to state $\tilde{q} \in \delta(q, \alpha)$, and so on.

3.2   Extension of the Request/Block Semantics of SBP

The original semantics of SBP, as defined in [41,49], can be obtained from the new one as follows. We allow only two labels $\mathcal{L} = \{\text{"Request"}, \text{"Block"}\}$ representing request constraints and block constraints respectively. In addition, we define the variable set V to contain precisely one variable e, representing the triggered event. Next, we syntactically restrict the constraint formulas φ_i to be of the form $e = c$ for some constant c; and finally, for any state q we define the constraint composition rule to be:

$$\psi(q, C, L) = (\bigvee_{\varphi \in C(q) \mid \text{"Request"} \in L(q,\varphi)} \varphi) \wedge (\bigwedge_{\varphi \in C(q) \mid \text{"Block"} \in L(q,\varphi)} \neg\varphi) \qquad (1)$$

Intuitively, at each state, each scenario object can declare events it requests (expressed as constraints tagged with the label "*Request*"), and those it wants to block (expressed as constraints tagged with the label "*Block*"). The constraint composition rule then translates these individual constraints into a global formula representing the fact that the triggered event needs to be requested and not blocked; i.e., it should satisfy the conjunction of being requested with the negation of being blocked.

When using these particular restrictions, the straightforward solver of choice is a SAT solver: since the formula φ only contains propositional connectives and the variable e can only take on a finite number of values, we can encode these possible values using a finite set of Boolean variables (this process is often called *bit-blasting*). A modern SAT solver can then be used for selecting the triggered event very quickly, in a way that is likely to enable an execution that is sufficiently fast for many application domains.

Beyond just SAT solvers, we propose in this paper to use SMT solvers. This allows for richer constraint languages that employ theories such as the theory of real numbers. Further, we do not restrict V to contain only a single variable. This enables the constraint resolutions to yield not only the choice of a value or event from a set of candidates, but an assignment of values to an entire system configuration.

As explained in more detail in Sect. 5.6, to make sure that all variables are properly assigned, and to comply with the scenario's intentions of which variable should constrain the values of each other variable, we enrich the "Request" tagging and labeling with a subset S of the set V of variable names, i.e., we use the labels $\mathcal{L} = \{ "Request(S)" | S \subseteq V \} \cup \{ "Block" \}$. The following formula extends formula (1), in stating that for each variable in V there must be at least one constraint satisfied in the constraint resolution, which stated that it wishes that this variable be set.

$$\psi(q, C, L) = \tag{2}$$

$$\left(\bigwedge_{v \in V} \left(\bigvee_{\varphi \in C(q) \ | \ "Request(S)" \in L(q,\varphi), v \in S} \varphi \right) \right) \wedge \left(\bigwedge_{\varphi \in C(q) \ | \ "Block" \in L(q,\varphi)} \neg\varphi \right)$$

4 Implementation Infrastructure

To demonstrate and evaluate our approach, we developed proof-of-concept applications on multiple platforms.

The first implementation uses MATLAB/Simulink. Scenario objects generate their constraints as strings containing textual descriptions of the constraints. These strings are then passed into MATLAB's equation and system solver, which is called `solve`. The solution yielded by the solver is then translated into variable values that flow along the classical Simulink connectors as input to other blocks, driving standard Simulink behavior. The results of this behavior (i.e., the effect on the environment) are also fed back into the scenarios, which can then change the constraints they present. See Sect. 5.7 for more details on this case study.

In a second, experimental implementation, described in Sect. 5.8, we used solvers and optimizers of Wolfram's *Mathematica* to create composite behavior from SBP-like specifications.

A third implementation, used in the code examples in this paper, is based on the Python language and the Z3 SMT solver [17]. We use Python and Z3 to implement the event selection formula (2). To simplify the specifications, we also added the label `Wait-For` that allows a scenario to maintain its declaration as long as the condition tagged by this label is not met. The default for this tag, if not present, is `True`, i.e., if a scenario does not specify an explicit "Wait-For" condition, its request and block statements are valid for the next event only. Note that since formulas that are labeled only with "Wait-For" do dot appear in Eq. (2) they do not affect event construction, only the progress of the scenarios.

In our implementation, each scenario object is coded as a Python *generator*. A generator is a function that can pause itself and pass control back to its caller at any point, using the `yield` idiom. It can then be subsequently resumed when it is re-invoked with the language's `next` idiom. The infrastructure mimics the parallel execution, as follows (the core of the execution mechanism code for a similar system appears in [48]). It calls each generator sequentially, waiting for it to yield control, and then calls the next one. When all scenarios reach their respective synchronization points, the infrastructure collects the constraints passed by the scenarios (in the form of a Python *dictionary* containing Z3 constraints labeled by keys from the set {Request (S), Block, and Wait-For}). It then invokes the solver to obtain an assignment for all variables of V that satisfies Eq. (2). We also support the label Request (without the set S) that is automatically translated to the label Request (S), where S is the set of all the variables that appear in the labeled formula.

5   Modeling with the New Composition Principles

What can be achieved by using this new composition mechanism? How does it help system engineers and modelers? We review these capabilities via several illustrative examples:

1. An extension of the water-tank example with hot and cold water taps.
2. A UAV/drone that is capable of maneuvers in three dimensional space.
3. A software installation management system and/or software product line management system, where dependencies and conflicts among software libraries/features/packages determine which component is to be installed or included in a particular delivery.
4. Solving the *Towers of Hanoi* puzzle. In this application the scenarios describe the (a) essence of the puzzle, i.e., the initial state (all disks on one peg), the goal (all disks are on some other peg), and rules (e.g., disks on a peg must be ordered by decreasing diameter); and (b) behavioral scenarios for executing an iterative solution.
5. Navigating a flock/swarm of robots, in two-dimensional space, towards a destination, while bypassing obstacles. The goal is to move all robots towards a configuration where the set's centroid ("center of gravity") is at a pre-specified destination, while the individual robots avoid colliding with the obstacles, whose boundaries were also pre-specified.

Listings of actual scenarios for these applications/models are available as part of the supplementary material [15].

5.1   Constructing Rich Multi-variable Events

We now illustrate the richness of the events that can be modeled our extension.

In the drone example, the UAV is capable of simultaneous vertical and horizontal maneuvers. We can define V to include two variables, $V = \{v, h\}$, where v represents the vertical angular velocity and h the horizontal angular velocity. One scenario can set upper and lower bounds on the vertical angular velocity, say due to the drone's mechanical limitations, and another can limit the horizontal angular velocity (see Fig. 2). Here we require no labeling of the constraints, i.e. $\mathcal{L} = \emptyset$, and the constraint composition rule ψ is a simply a conjunction of all the individual constraints.

true   true

Fig. 2. Two scenario objects, represented as transition systems (state machines) that, respectively, put hard limits on the vertical and horizontal angular velocities of the drone. Each scenario has a single synchronization point, as indicated by its single state, in which it contributes a constraint (e.g., $\varphi_1 = -5 \leq v \leq 5$) to the global constraint set. The only transition, a self loop that does not depend on the variable assignment returned by the solver, indicates that the scenario continues to contribute this constraint, regardless of the satisfying assignment discovered by the solver.

Without any additional limitations, i.e., if only these two scenarios existed in the system, the constraint formula at any synchronization point would be

$$\varphi = \varphi_1 \wedge \varphi_2 = (-5 \leq v \leq 5) \wedge (-10 \leq h \leq 10)$$

Because the constraints are arithmetical, linear constraints, we can use an LP solver to dispatch them; and indeed, in this case an LP solver will return an assignment such as $v = 3, h = 0$. Other scenario objects in the system, referred to as actuator scenarios, may then receive and process these values, and through appropriate APIs adjust the drone's engines accordingly.

Let us now extend the example with a particular flight situation, where another scenario navigates the drone to its destination, and that scenario is requesting a right turn at an angular velocity of at least 6 degrees per second:

$$\varphi_3 = h \geq 6$$

We also add an obstacle-detection scenario that detected the presence of a cellular-communication antenna tower up ahead, and which, in order to circumvent the obstacle, is requesting that the elevation be increased or that a left turn be initiated:

$$\varphi_4 = h \leq -3 \vee v \geq 2$$

When the solver is given the global constraint formula $\varphi = \wedge_{i=1}^{4}\varphi_i$, it can *construct* the composite event by yielding the solution $h = 8, v = 3$, which satisfies all constraints by both turning right and increasing the drone's altitude.

In the Towers of Hanoi example (see detailed scenarios in Sect. 5.5 and in the supplementary material), we observe how the scenarios form a complete configuration; i.e., they specify which disc should reside on which peg, and which pegs would be designated as source and destination respectively. Thus, in each step, the SBP execution mechanism implicitly constructs the entire three-peg configuration. The instructions for the actual moving of a disk from one peg to another, is (purposely for this example) only implicit, in contrast to more standard programming where this step would be at the core of the program.

5.2   Rich Constraint Specifications

While the events and the environment configurations are greatly enriched by supporting the assignment of many variables in every step, one should note that feeding the solvers with arbitrary expressions allows scenarios to introduce constraints that in themselves are rich. For example, a scenario can introduce an irregularly-shaped obstacle by describing the curve of its boundary in a single expression. Or, the effect of gradually changing speeds and friction coefficients as a car slows down or swerves on an uneven road, can be introduced as a single rich function of time and location.

5.3   Enhanced Incrementality

Figure 3 lists the Python code for the water tank system, depicted as a set of transition systems in Fig. 1. During execution, the satisfying assignments obtained by the solver alternate between assigning hot to true and cold to false, and vice versa.

```
hot = Bool('hot')
cold = Bool('cold')

def mutual_exclusion():
    yield {Block: And(cold,hot), WaitFor: false}

def three_hot():
    for i in range(3):
        yield {Request([cold,hot]): hot, WaitFor: hot}

def three_cold():
    for j in range(3):
        yield {Request([cold,hot]): cold, WaitFor: cold}

def no_two_same_in_a_row():
    m=yield {}
    while True:
        if is_true(m[cold]):
            m=yield {Block: cold}
        if is_true(m[hot]):
            m=yield {Block: hot}
```

Fig. 3. A solver-based SBP specification for the water-tank application. The hot (resp., cold) variables/flags indicate that a dose of hot (resp., cold) water is to be added to the tank. The rules/requirements are: (1) do not add hot and cold doses at the same time; (2) add three doses of hot water; (3) add three doses of cold water; (4) never add two doses of the same type consecutively.

```
temp = Real('temp')

def hot_temp():
    while True:
        yield {Block: And(hot, temp <= 50),
               WaitFor: false}

def cold_temp():
    while True:
        yield {Block: And(cold, temp >= 50),
               WaitFor: false}

def after_hot_temp():
    while True:
        m=yield {WaitFor: hot}
        while is_true(m[hot]):
            m=yield {Block: temp <= 20}

def after_cold_temp():
    while True:
        m=yield {WaitFor: cold}
        while is_true(m[cold]):
            m=yield {Block:  temp >= 80}
```

Fig. 4. New requirements for the water tap model: (1) the temperature of a hot event must be above 50; (2) the temperature of a cold event must be below 50; (3) the temperature of an event that follows a hot event must be above 20; (4) the temperature of an event that follows a cold event must be below 80.

Consider now a customer-driven requirements change. E.g., the requirement prohibiting two consecutive doses of the same type is removed, and the customer decides to add requirements about water temperature, as presented in Fig. 4 and its caption. In an SBP model, one can simply add and remove the respective lines of scenario code. These additional requirements introduce a new solver variable temp. The new scenarios can control this new variable, and the solver can handle it, in addition to preexisting variables, without changing other scenarios. Note that the remaining scenarios are unaware of the new variable.

5.4   Rich Constraint-Composition Semantics

So far, we have seen two examples for constraint composition rules (annotated as ψ above): *request-and-block* and *conjunction*. We now demonstrate another composition rule.

In a system for managing software package dependencies, package A may *require* package B and/or it may be *incompatible* with package C, and thus cannot be installed alongside C. The *state* of the entire system is the set of currently installed software packages. Finally, the system is given a user-supplied goal, such as `install Package A`, and is then required to install A and any prerequisite packages, while removing the smallest number of packages currently installed with which A and its dependencies are incompatible.

To model this, we can utilize a *MaxSAT* solver, whose input formula consists of subformulas labeled either *hard* or *soft*. The solver finds an assignment that satisfies the hard constraints and as many of the soft constraints as possible. For each package dependency, we will specify a scenario that adds a hard constraint representing this dependency, and we will model the currently-installed packages as soft constraints that are introduced by designated scenarios. The MaxSAT solver will thus return an assignment such that the goal package and its prerequisites are installed while the number of previously installed packages that are removed is minimized [2,51].

More specifically, the variable set V consists of a Boolean variable for each software package, e.g. $\{x_A, x_B, x_C, \ldots\}$, which are true if and only if the package is installed. Actuator scenarios respond to changes in variable values by installing or removing a package. Our label set is $\{h, s\}$, indicating whether a constraint is hard or soft, respectively. Each dependency is represented by a dedicated object; for example, the requirement "A requires B" is encoded by the top scenario object in Fig. 5. Other objects are used for encoding the soft constraints representing the currently installed packages; an example appears in the bottom scenario object in Fig. 5.

The composition rule ψ constructs the formula φ (to be passed to the MaxSAT solver) as the conjunction of the individual scenario objects' constraints, and marks these constraints as hard or soft according to their labels.

Fig. 5. Software-package Management Example: (Left) A scenario object that specifies that installing A requires B and labels the constraint as *hard* for the MaxSAT solver. (Right) A scenario that adds x_B as a soft constraint if package B is currently installed (left state), and contributes no constraints if it is not installed (right state). Switching between the states is performed according to the assignment discovered by the solver; specifically, it depends on whether x_B is assigned to true or not. We assume the package is initially installed.

5.5   Combining "Stories" with Constraints

An important feature of SBP is the ability of each scenario object to describe an aspect of system behavior as a "story"; i.e., a *scenario* of events in time. This description does not mandate, as in standard programming, a complete step-by-step prescription of all process steps.

We illustrate this concept via the Towers of Hanoi example. Our SBP model for solving the puzzle is based on the following iterative (rather than recursive) algorithm:

Repeat the following two steps: (1) move the smallest disk to the "next" peg to the right (cyclically, or modulo three); and then (2) move "any" disk that is not the smallest (there is only one option for this).

Using the Python/Z3 implementation of SBP, the (rich) events, or system states can be modeled using the following state variables:

```
peg1 = Const('peg1', SetSort(IntSort()))
peg2 = Const('peg2', SetSort(IntSort()))
peg3 = Const('peg3', SetSort(IntSort()))

source, dest = Ints("source_dest")
```

The variables source and dest are used to model the next action to be taken.

Note that the variables peg1, peg2, and peg3, which represent the disks on the three pegs, are sets. Recomputing them at every step further illustrates the richness of events and event selection, as discussed in Sect. 5.1. Furthermore, observe that in this particular model we use sets rather than ordered entities such as arrays or lists. We can do so for two independent reasons: (a) the particular system is for executing a solution, and not for solving the puzzle, and as in other models, not *all* assumptions must be explicitly coded; (b) in the representation of the problem in the SMT solver the "identity" of a disk is also its size and its location in the linear order (much as a collection of two-dimensional vectors $\langle x, y \rangle$ can imply relative locations for multiple pairs of points in a 2D space without explicitly stating this fact).

The main scenario that provides the core steps of the algorithm states that the variables source and dest should be chosen so that, repeatedly, (1) disk zero is moved one peg to the right (cyclically), and (2) disk zero is not moved:

```
def cycle():
  while True:
    yield {Request([source, dest]):
            And(min(peg(source)) == 0,
                dest == nxtMod3(source))}

    yield {Request([source, dest]):
            min(peg(source)) != 0}
```

This ability to use SBP to extract and highlight the core steps of an algorithm into separate scenarios, distinguishing them from technicalities like initialization, termination, data management and other mandatory bookkeeping, is discussed in greater detail in the proposal for *Scenario-Based Algorithmics* [44].

We model the rest of the behavior of the solution with the following scenarios:
- The values of variables source and dest must always be different from each other and in the range 1,2,3 (notice the use of the blocking idiom):

```
def ranges():
  yield {Block: Or(source < 1, source > 3,
                   dest < 1, dest > 3,
                   source == dest),
         WaitFor: false}
```

This scenario is coded to never resume and change states; its constraints always hold, though the same behavior could be exhibited with a specification that contains a loop that resumes after any event (WaitFor: True) and then returns to the same state.
- The initial state of the pegs is $\langle\{0,\ldots,n\},\emptyset,\emptyset\rangle$:

```
def init():
  yield {Request: And(peg1 == FullSet(),
                      peg2 == EmptySet(),
                      peg3 == EmptySet())}
```

- The smallest disk on the source peg must be smaller than the smallest disk on the destination peg:

```
def size():
  yield {Block: min(peg(dest)) < min(peg(source)),
         WaitFor: false}
```

- The source peg must not be empty:

```
def nonempty():
  yield {Block: IsEmpty(peg(source),
         WaitFor: false}
```

- The smallest disk from the src peg should move to dest peg:

```
def actuator():
 m = yield {}

 while True:
     src = pegs[m.eval(source).as_long()-1]
     dst = pegs[m.eval(dest).as_long()-1]
     thrd = (set(pegs) - {src, dst}).pop()

     d = m.eval(min(src)).as_long()

     m=yield {Request([peg1, peg2, peg3]):
                 And(eqSet(dst, m.eval(SetAdd(dst, d))),
                     eqSet(thrd, m.eval(thrd)),
                     eqSet(src, m.eval(SetDel(src, d))))}
```

5.6   Specifying Targeted Constraints

Using the constraint solvers allows each scenario to relate to some variables, while ignoring others. This is another source of expressive power. However, since the solver must, at every step, assign values to each of the variables, it is the modeler's responsibility to specify for each variable at least one scenario that requests a value for it. While this is normally not a significant burden, there are some fine points that must be handled, and for which we offer a particular interface.

Consider the situation in Fig. 6, where two scenarios deal with separate variables, x_1 and x_2, respectively. The first scenario requests that x_1 be greater than 50, and the second requests that x_2 be greater than 50. In traditional SBP, if each of these two scenarios were to request, say, the coordinates for a robot's destination, exactly (and only) one of the two requests would be satisfied, but both scenarios would be able to react to the choice (e.g., abandon requests that were not chosen, or maintain the request until it is satisfied, perhaps after visiting the destination that was chosen first). However, the current case is different. Since the first scenario is not aware of the second one, the designer implicitly assumes that the only may constraint for x_1 is that it be greater than 50, hence it does not expect the solver to allow an assignment to x_1 that is smaller than 50. According to our semantics, however, the composition rules produces the constraint $\psi = x_1 > 50 \lor x_2 > 50$, which is satisfied, e.g., by the assignment $\{x_1 = 0, x_2 = 51\}$. A way to avoid this unintended behavior is to label each proposition with the variable that it is aware of and to solve for each set of variables separately. Another way to avoid the problem is to look for assignments that maximize the number of satisfied may constraints, e.g., by using solvers that optimize the number of satisfied clauses.

```
def scenario1():
  yield {Request: x₁ > 50}

def scenario2():
  yield {Request: x₂ > 50}
```

Fig. 6. Unintended behavior with the Request semantics when using Equation (1). Solving $(x_1<50) \lor (x_2>50)$, the assignment $\{x_1 = 0, x_2 = 51\}$ is valid, despite the fact that no scenario specified that x_1 may be smaller than 50.

In another case that must be handled, recall that, when specifying a constraint like $x = y$, a modeler may have different intents: whether the values for both x and y are to be chosen, or the value for x should be chosen such that it is equal to the value of y that was determined by other means, or the value for y should be implied by that of the predetermined value of x. The need to distinguish between these intents is particularly important in our setting, where the constraint solver may be asked to set (almost) all variables of the system and its environment, and may thus yield surprising results, such as having a vehicle avoid an obstacle by moving the obstacle. Using existing idioms to specify environment assumptions, like "the coordinates of this obstacle cannot change" is not enough, because the intent to change or not change a particular variable may vary from one scenario to another, or from one scenario state to another, even within the same scenario.

In our implementation, we address this by using the labeling system. E.g., specifying `Request[source,dest]` in the algorithm "story" scenario, and `Request[peg1,peg2,peg3]` in the disk-moving actuator scenario, we indicate that the first request is to assign values only to `source` and to `dest` and the second request is to assign values only to `peg1`, `peg2`, and `peg3`.

The event selection mechanism is then changed to not only satisfy one request while obeying all blocking statements, but to satisfy at least one request for changing each of the variables for which there exists a request.

Thus, removing the `[source,dest]` and the `[peg1,peg2,peg3]` from the above labels would allow for assignments that are consistent with one of the two requests but are not consistent with the other one (since in SBP not all requests must be satisfied).

The labeling of which variables can be set by a particular constraint is optional. When absent, the default is that the request applies to all, and only, the variables mentioned in the request.

This feature can be seen to provide additional expressive power, as follows. The formal definition and the implementation allow the additional tagging of the requests to include labels that are not necessarily variable names, or are variable names but ones that are not mentioned in the particular mathematical formulation of the constraint at hand. Thus, a scenario can specify that its requested constraints may be ignored altogether if other constraints labeled in the same way are satisfied.

5.7 Real-Time Reactivity

Even though solvers are designed to apply complex mathematical and logical operations and extensive searches, they can be also be used in real-time reactive systems that need to provide fine-grained discretization of near-continuous behavior.

To illustrate this, consider a model for a controlled follower rover that needs to track a leader rover while keeping a safe distance from it. The follower must accommodate nearly-arbitrary leader behavior, constrained only by basic, reasonable bounds on the leader's speed and turn angles. This served as a challenge problem in the MDETOOLS'18 workshop, where the organizers supplied a simulator for driving the participants' demonstrations. (See mdetools.github.io/mdetools18/challengeproblem.html.)

The simulator periodically emits the locations of the rovers, the distance between them, and the heading angle of the follower. The follower advancement and turning is controlled by setting the power for the left and right wheels.

The scenarios' code is shown in Fig. 7: (i) bounds: the bounds for the pR and pL variables, indicating the power to the right and left wheels; (ii) forward.backward: forward and backward motion in reaction to relative distance; i.e., when the rovers are too far apart or too close the follower accelerates, decelerates or even reverses its direction; (iii) spin: steering towards the leader by turning the wheels when the relative angle (based on the latest simulator input) exceeds a specified value (3°), the follower turns left or right towards the leader; (iv) turnpowers: calculating the needed wheel power(s) for an already-triggered turn.

This example demonstrates the ability to construct complex behavior at run time, using distinct, modular, behavioral aspects.

The resulting system behavior is indeed very similar to the one presented in [20], which resulted from using SBP without a constraint solver, employing direct request-and-block logic, and which could request only finite sets of events. The use of constraint-solvers enabled, e.g., the spin() scenario, to specify infinitely many options and allows, as demonstrated by the turnpowers() scenario, to further decompose the specification and to better align with the requirements.

The real-time capabilities of this solver-based composition is further demonstrated in the Patrol Vehicle example (described here only briefly, in order to fit space constraints), this time in a MATLAB/Simulink framework, using MATLAB solvers. This is a simulation of an autonomous vehicle that moves repeatedly in a fixed route in the shape of the figure eight, and is subject to strict speed demands and constraints, as reflected by the following scenarios: (1) always attempt to accelerate to a maximum pre-specified speed; (2) when arriving at a sharp curve, reduce speed below a specified value until exiting the curve; and (3) after driving at a speed that is higher than a certain value for longer than a certain time limit, reduce the allowed speed and acceleration to be below some other limits, for a certain amount of time (e.g., to avoid overheating or wearing out of the motor).

In addition to the real-time perspective, this example also illustrates the ability to model "stories" (see Sect. 5.5) that progress from one state to another and present different constraints at different times and states. Thus, for example, specifying the speed constraints that hold only *after* detecting the arrival at (or departure from) a sharp curve, or *after* the passage of a certain amount of time, appears quite intuitive and well aligned with the stated requirements. This can be contrasted with the less intuitive use of ever-present constraints, each constantly requiring a conjunction of conditions, e.g., current-speed-and-current-road-curvature, or, current-speed-and-time-since-certain-past-event.

5.8 Event Construction with Optimization

In this section, we show how the computational tools (namely, solvers) can also be applied to enrich the event construction with optimization of event-selection and variable assignment choices. This optimization capability is a step towards being able to manage multiple concurrent prioritized goals. This part of the work is inspired by the *Null Space Behaviour* (NSB) technique [1] in control theory, where composition and optimization of controllers is based on linear matrix operations,

```
def bounds():
  yield {Block: Or(pL < −MAX, pL > MAX, pR < −MAX, pR > MAX),
         WaitFor: false}

def forward_backward():
  while True:
    if dist > CLOSE:
      if dist < FAR:
        yield {Request([pL,pR]): pL = pR = MAX·(dist−CLOSE)/(FAR−CLOSE)}
      else:
        yield {Request([pL,pR]): pL = pR = MAX}

    else:
      if dist > VERY_CLOSE:
        yield {Request([pL,pR]): pL = pR = MAX·(dist−CLOSE)/(CLOSE−VERY_CLOSE)}
      else:
        yield {Request([pL,pR]):  pL = pR = −MAX}

def spin():
  while True:
    if abs(dir_error) > 3:
      if dir_error > 0:
        yield {Request([pL,pR]): pL > pR, Block: Not(pL > pR)}
      else:
        yield {Request([pL,pR]): pL < pR, Block: Not(pL < pR)}
    else:
      yield {}

def turnpowers():
  yield {Block: And(pL ≠ pR , Or(pL ≠ 0, pR ≠ 40), Or(pL ≠ 40, pR ≠ 0)),
         WaitFor: false}
```

Fig. 7. Main scenarios of the leader-follower rover model (see explanation in the text).

and where computing solutions for lower priority goals is done within the *null space* of the matrices used for the achieving higher priority goals.

This richer example also further illustrates other key properties discussed earlier. These include the ability to construct decisions with a multitude of variables; the ability to compose scenarios, each of which has a partial view of the system behavior; and, more importantly, the ability to specify what can or cannot be changed in the system and its environment.

The system in this example coordinates and guides the motion of a flock of robots (a.k.a. a multi-robot) in a two-dimensional space, as proposed in [1]. Both our approach and NSB are based on first designing simple controllers for achieving individual aspects of the required behaviour, and then composing them into a combined controller, whose emergent behaviour addresses all the requirements together.

The requirements for the flock's motion are: (i) the centroid ("center of gravity") of the flock should move in the direction of a specified point; (ii) a robot may not travel faster than 10 meters per second; (iii) initially, the robots are placed at equal distances on (the perimeter/curve of) a given circle; (iv) while moving, the robots should strive to maintain the circle formation; (v) the robots should stay within a specified rectangular region; (vi) the robots should not path through a specified elliptical obstacle; (vii) the centroid should also not pass through the given elliptical obstacle; (viii) the robots should maintain a minimal specified distance between any two.

In this implementation, the solver we used is the "FindMinimum" procedure from Wolfram's Mathematica.

We formalized each requirement as an objective function or a blocking constraint to be presented to the solver. Specifically, we created a separate module/formula for each requirement. This modeling approach helps engineers and other stakeholders examine how the behaviour of a system might change when individual requirements are added, removed, or changed.

The solver was used to steer the multi-robot iteratively, in a greedy approach. Conceptually, at each step, all possible movements of the flock were considered and an optimal one was chosen. The resulting motions of each step were used to move the robots' coordinates, and this information then served as the input for forming the equations for the next step. In future enhancements additional parameters can be considered in subsequent steps, such as past speeds and directions, in the interest of creating smoother motion or detecting situations where a robot is stuck in a tight corner.

The simulation ran successfully at about 20 steps per second (i.e., at intervals of 50 ms), thus supporting the claim that solvers can be used for real-time control systems. Clearly, faster processors now enable the running of new and complex computational tools for applications that previously demanded solutions to focus on leanness and efficiency (as in the case of NSB).

The use of the Mathematica solver enables composing the controllers in a way that manages goals hierarchically. One approach is to nest the calls for finding optimal solutions, and pass the results of each invocation as a constraint on the search for the next-lower goal in the hierarchy ladder. This can be done as follows:

$$\arg\max\{f_2(x,v) \colon v \in \arg\max\{f_1(x,v) \colon v \in \mathbb{R}^{2n}\}\}$$

Here, n is the number of robots, $x \in \mathbb{R}^{2n}$ is a vector representing the positions of the robots in the plane, $v \in \mathbb{R}^{2n}$ is a vector representing the horizontal and vertical velocities that the controller needs to assign to the robots, and f_1 and f_2 represent the higher-priority and lower-priority goal functions, such as reaching the target destination, avoiding an obstacle, or preserving a formation.

The idea in this formulation is to only create sets of commands that are optimal with respect to the high-priority function, while using the low-priority function as a secondary consideration within the first solution space (similarly to sorting database records by a primary and secondary sort keys).

Other composition rules can support more refined controller combinations; e.g., composing the constraints in parallel to achieve a joint objective function, and controlling goal priorities via weights as opposed to solving for one goal and only then for the other.

The general characteristics of the solution's emergent behaviour is similar to the behaviours shown in the NSB paper [1]. In particular, casual observation makes it clear that in both cases global solutions are handled with narrower local views; i.e., the scenario-weaving mechanism returns the control commands only for a specific time instance. A detailed comparison of the two approaches according to criteria like solution quality (e.g., successful termination, path length and smoothness of trajectory and speed), computational cost/efficiency, the ability to provide formal correctness proofs, and ease of development, is beyond the scope of the current paper.

The demonstration of SBP with Mathematica is still in early stages. We have not built interfaces between a procedural/scripting language like Java or Python to Mathematica. Hence, the present example does not (yet) demonstrate the SBP capabilities of scenarios that follow a "story", changing states and declaration following the occurrence of relevant events. Given that SBP principles are language agnostic, and our experience with developing such interfaces in multiple languages and environments, we regard this issue is a technicality.

Other interesting challenges we encountered include the following. First, there were several technical issues to be addressed. For example, the solver was not able to cope with rectangular and other non-elliptical obstacles. Clearly, this should not be attributed to the use of SBP, and we expect that engineers will be able to specify constraints and objective functions that indeed test the limits of each solver's capabilities.

A second issue is that, as stated earlier, the solver is applied locally, in very short time intervals, and without look-ahead or backward planning. This can cause some robots to get stuck in tight corners, not recognizing that they have to reverse some distance in order to get back on track. Finding a composition technique that allows for global solutions, e.g., for adding a requirement that the path be the shortest possible, or that it meet some other overall conditions, remains as future research. Note that global solutions do not mandate look-ahead that is provided by the execution infrastructure. As in NSB, the individual scenarios can contain the needed logic. For example, the flock may apply the "right hand rule" a localized approach to finding paths in certain mazes; or pilot/scout robots can explore the perimeter of the obstacle, reporting to others, who then plan a trajectory with straightforward geometry. Specialized sensors (simulating ordinary long-distance vision, or the availability of maps) can detect obstacles from a distance, triggering bypass trajectories that are less likely to get stuck in narrow crevasses. Alternatively, recovery scenarios can exercise "simulated annealing", detecting when robots are stuck and driving them to return and explore new directions.

Another important issue is verification, and especially, compositional verification. The basic-style SBP lent itself very well to compositional verification, which helps tackle the state explosion that often hinders application of formal methods to complex reactive systems [29]. How does one specify the assumptions and guarantees of scenarios when their declarations include complex assertions that are understood only by rich solvers? A first step could be to use yet another kind of solver for composing behaviors, one that is geared especially for such a verification purpose [18].

6   Related Work

In this paper, we propose a particular approach to run-time composition of behavior, namely, extending the composition rules of existing SBP-style frameworks with specification and solving of constraints. We now briefly compare SBP to other mechanisms for execution-time composition of events, with a special focus on the present context of constraint specifications (an earlier, related analysis appears in [45]).

An important feature of SBP is its intuitiveness and succinctness. These properties are a consequence of the ability to specify forbidden behavior directly and explicitly, rather than doing so using control-flow conditions, designed to prevent certain pieces of code or specification from actually doing the undesired action. In SBP, this feature was originally embodied in the use of concrete lists of requested events and filter-based blocking. Using this paper's extensions, this is done with constraint solvers. For example, one can now build and test the specification that a vehicle is not allowed to enter a road intersection when the traffic light is red, even before having coded how vehicles behave. Other approaches, such as business-workflow engines, simulation engines, and tools for test-driven development, often support intuitive specification of executable use cases and scenarios, but their support for generic composition of multiple allowed scenarios and forbidden scenarios is limited. Conventional object oriented and procedural programming, logic programming and functional programming languages provide for composition of behaviors, but the requirements' use cases and scenarios are not directly visible in the code. Instead, they are typically reflected only in emergent properties of the actual execution.

The principles of SBP have been implemented in several languages, in both centralized and distributed environments. These implementations have positioned SBP as a design pattern for using constructs like messaging, semaphores and threads, and concepts such as agent-orientation for achieving incrementality and alignment of code with a set of requirements.

Publish-subscribe is a related framework for parallel composition, which does not provide language support for forbidden behavior. Aspect oriented programming [50] supports specifying and executing cross-cutting program instructions on top of a base application, but, unlike SBP, it does not allow for specifying forbidden behavior, state management within an aspect, or symmetry between aspects and base code.

Other behavior-based models, such as Brooks's subsumption architecture [12], Branicky's behavioral programming [11], and LEGO Mindstorms leJOS (see [3]), call for constructing systems from behaviors. The SBP formalism is language-independent, has multiple implementations, and extends in a variety of ways each of the coordination and arbitration mechanisms used by those architectures.

The execution semantics employed by SBP is similar to the event-based scheduling of SystemC [46], which uses cyclical co-routine scheduling by synchronization, evaluation, update and notification. SBP is different from SystemC in that it offers support for specifying scenarios and forbidden scenarios that directly correspond with the original requirements, while SystemC provides a particular framework for composing parallel components in certain designs and architectures. In SBP, synchronization is an inherent technique for continuously complying with the constraints posed by the requirements, whereas in SystemC synchronization is used for the coordination of an otherwise parallel component execution. This also implies differences in the semantic details of synchronization, queuing, event selection, and state management within each parallel component.

The BIP language (behavior, interaction, priority) [8] utilizes the concept of glue for assembling components. It pursues goals similar to SBP's, with a focus on correct-by-construction systems. SBP is more geared towards the execution of intuitively specified behaviors and constraints, and the run-time resolution of these constraints.

As mentioned earlier, SBP has recently been implemented using the visual formalism of Statecharts. The Yakindu Statecharts tool now offers an extension of Statecharts' original support for concurrent, orthogonal and hierarchical state machines [27] with the optional specification of requested and blocked events in any state, accompanied by an enhanced event selection semantics [53]. These enhancements provide the formal definitions of SBP principles, which are based on transition systems and state machines (see, e.g., [41]), with a direct, concrete executable implementation that is readily understood by humans. This allows to directly cast inter-object behaviour, which typically modelled with Statecharts and other state-based languages, in the same formalism and language as intra-object behaviour.

In SBP, the direct execution and/or simulation of a model is termed *play-out*. Play-out is achieved by considering all constraints of the various scenarios before each event selection. Thus, the computational burden required for each runtime decision depends mainly on the number of scenarios, and does not depend on the number of states in each scenario or on the nondeterministic branching in future system and environment behavior. In contrast, many general program synthesis approaches for reactive systems (see, e.g., [9]) apply planning, model-checking, and other techniques to resolve environment assumptions and specification constraints a-priori. This gives rise to a strategy (e.g., a deterministic finite automaton) for successfully handling all possible environment behaviors that may be encountered in all reachable program states. Synthesis has been applied to SBP specifications with the request-and-block idioms in, e.g., [43].

General synthesis techniques typically have to deal with very large state graphs. Often, this is done via run-time planning (also termed online/on-the-fly synthesis) (see, e.g., [10]). In this approach, an execution mechanism considers a single starting state of the system and its environment, thus limiting the number of system and/or environment actions considered in the search. Such a technique was implemented in SBP in, e.g., *smart play-out* [38]. An intriguing future research avenue is to perform run-time look-ahead, or complete program synthesis during development, for SBP specifications with rich constraint specifications like the ones discussed in this paper. Such research could include identifying categories of constraint specifications that are richer than the filters and lists used in traditional SBP, but which are still more amenable to synthesis than arbitrary constraints.

Our proposed use of constraint solvers to directly control the execution of SBP specifications differs from other uses of these tools in the verification and analysis of systems, including *symbolic execution* [55], *bounded model-checking* [7], *concolic testing* [56], and others. SMT solvers have previously been applied in performing such analysis tasks also in the context of SBP; e.g., by extending SMT solvers to deal more efficiently with transition systems [47] and by using the solvers to efficiently prove compositional properties for collections of SBP scenarios [29].

7 Conclusion

We have described a substantial extension of the Scenario-Based programming design and modeling approach for complex systems. By enabling the invocation of general, rich, and well-proven solvers and optimizers at every decision that the system makes, we enable modelers to perform sophisticated, yet trusted, composition of modular requirement specifications. At the same time, each narrow requirement can itself be as deep and rich as the domain professional that presented it wishes it to be. The enhancements allow scenario objects to interact with each other in far more subtle and intricate ways than is possible with only the original request-and-block idioms. All these capabilities enable engineers to use SBP in order to more directly create faithful models of complex systems. The theoretical principles of this extension are demonstrated through numerous applications that explore the capabilities, and limits, of the approach.

Future research directions include making intelligent run-time decisions using look-ahead (with model checking facilities), development-time and run-time program synthesis, and applying machine learning techniques for improving program decisions over time. These tools exist already in basic forms for traditional SBP, and have been shown to be useful. However, extending them to the present formulation will entail accounting for the more flexible event selection process.

References

1. Antonelli, G., Arrichiello, F., Chiaverini, S.: The NSB control: a behavior-based approach for multi-robot systems. Paladyn, J. Behav. Robot. **1**(1), 48–56 (2010)

2. Argelich, J., Lynce, I.: CNF instances from the software package installation problem. In: Proceedings of 15th RCRA Workshop on Experimental Evaluation of Algorithms for Solving Problems with Combinatorial Explosion (2008)
3. Arkin, R.C.: Behavior-Based Robotics. MIT Press, Cambridge (1998)
4. Bar-Sinai, M., Weiss, G., Shmuel, R.: BPjs: an extensible, open infrastructure for behavioral programming research. In: Proceedings of 21st ACM/IEEE International Conference on Model Driven Engineering Languages and Systems (MODELS), pp. 59–60 (2018)
5. Barrett, C., Kroening, D., Melham, T.: Problem Solving for the 21st Century: Efficient Solvers for Satisfiability Modulo Theories. London Mathematical Society and Smith Institute for Industrial Mathematics and System Engineering (2014)
6. Barrett, C., Tinelli, C.: Satisfiability modulo theories. In: Clarke, E., Henzinger, T., Veith, H., Bloem, R. (eds.) Handbook of Model Checking, pp. 305–343. Springer, Cham (2018). https://doi.org/10.1007/978-3-319-10575-8_11
7. Biere, A., Cimatti, A., Clarke, E., Zhu, Y.: Symbolic model checking without BDDs. In: Cleaveland, W.R. (ed.) TACAS 1999. LNCS, vol. 1579, pp. 193–207. Springer, Heidelberg (1999). https://doi.org/10.1007/3-540-49059-0_14
8. Bliudze, S., Sifakis, J.: A notion of glue expressiveness for component-based systems. In: van Breugel, F., Chechik, M. (eds.) CONCUR 2008. LNCS, vol. 5201, pp. 508–522. Springer, Heidelberg (2008). https://doi.org/10.1007/978-3-540-85361-9_39
9. Bloem, R., Jobstmann, B., Piterman, N., Pnueli, A., Saar, Y.: Synthesis of reactive(1) designs. J. Comput. Syst. Sci. **78**(3), 911–938 (2012)
10. Blum, A.L., Furst, M.L.: Fast planning through planning graph analysis. Artif. Intell. **90**(1–2), 281–300 (1997)
11. Branicky, M.: Behavioral Programming. In: Working Notes AAAI Spring Symposium on Hybrid Systems and AI (1999)
12. Brooks, R.: A robust layered control system for a mobile robot. Robot. Autom **2**(1), 14–23 (1986)
13. Chvátal, V.: Linear Programming. Freeman W.H., New York (1983)
14. Clarke, E., Henzinger, T., Veith, H., Bloem, R.: Handbook of Model Checking. Springer, Heidelberg (2018). https://doi.org/10.1007/978-3-319-10575-8
15. Harel, D., Katz, G., Marron, A., Sadon, A., Weiss, G.: Supplementary Material for Scenario-based Programming with Rich Event Construction (2019). http://www.b-prog.org/ccismw19
16. Damm, W., Harel, D.: LSCs: breathing life into message sequence charts. J. Formal Methods Syst. Des. (FMSD) **19**(1), 45–80 (2001)
17. de Moura, L., Bjørner, N.: Z3: an efficient SMT solver. In: Ramakrishnan, C.R., Rehof, J. (eds.) TACAS 2008. LNCS, vol. 4963, pp. 337–340. Springer, Heidelberg (2008). https://doi.org/10.1007/978-3-540-78800-3_24
18. Frehse, G., et al.: SpaceEx: scalable verification of hybrid systems. In: Gopalakrishnan, G., Qadeer, S. (eds.) CAV 2011. LNCS, vol. 6806, pp. 379–395. Springer, Heidelberg (2011). https://doi.org/10.1007/978-3-642-22110-1_30
19. Gordon, M., Marron, A., Meerbaum-Salant, O.: Spaghetti for the main course?: observations on the naturalness of scenario-based programming. In: Innovation and Technology in Computer Science Education, ITiCSE 2012. ACM (2012). https://doi.org/10.1145/2325296.2325346
20. Greenyer, J., Bar-Sinai, M., Weiss, G., Sadon, A., Marron, A.: Modeling and programming a leader-follower challenge problem with scenario-based tools. In: Proceedings of 21st ACM/IEEE International Conference on Model Driven Engineering Languages and Systems (MODELS), pp. 376–385 (2018)

21. Greenyer, J., Gritzner, D.: Generating correct, compact, and efficient PLC Code from scenario-based GR(1) specifications. In: System-Integrated Intelligence: Challenges for Product and Production Engineering (SYSINT) (2018)

22. Greenyer, J., et al.: ScenarioTools—a tool suite for the scenario-based modeling and analysis of reactive systems. J. Sci. Comput. Program. **149**, 15–27 (2017)

23. Greenyer, J., Gritzner, D., Katz, G., Marron, A.: Scenario-based modeling and synthesis for reactive systems with dynamic system structure in scenariotools. In: Proceedings of 19th ACM/IEEE International Conference on Model Driven Engineering Languages and Systems (MODELS), pp. 16–23 (2016)

24. Greenyer, J., et al.: Distributed execution of scenario-based specifications of structurally dynamic cyber-physical systems. In: International Conference on System-Integrated Intelligence: Challenges for Product and Production Engineering (SYSINT), pp. 552–559 (2016)

25. Gritzner, D., Greenyer, J.: Synthesizing executable PLC code for robots from scenario-based GR(1) specifications. In: Seidl, M., Zschaler, S. (eds.) STAF 2017. LNCS, vol. 10748, pp. 247–262. Springer, Cham (2018). https://doi.org/10.1007/978-3-319-74730-9_23

26. Harel, D. Kantor, A., Katz, G., Marron, A., Weiss, G., Wiener, G.: Towards behavioral programming in distributed architectures. J. Sci. Comput. Program. (J. SCP) **98**, 233–267 (2015)

27. Harel, D.: Statecharts: a visual formalism for complex systems. J. Sci. Comput. Program. (J. SCP) **8**(3), 231–274 (1987)

28. Harel, D., Kantor, A., Katz, G.: Relaxing synchronization constraints in behavioral programs. In: McMillan, K., Middeldorp, A., Voronkov, A. (eds.) LPAR 2013. LNCS, vol. 8312, pp. 355–372. Springer, Heidelberg (2013). https://doi.org/10.1007/978-3-642-45221-5_25

29. Harel, D., Kantor, A., Katz, G., Marron, A., Mizrahi, L., Weiss, G.: On composing and proving the correctness of reactive behavior. In: Proceedings of 13th International Conference on Embedded Software (EMSOFT), pp. 1–10 (2013)

30. Harel, D., Katz, G.: Scaling-up behavioral programming: steps from basic principles to application architectures. In: International Workshop on Programming Based on Actors, Agents, and Decentralized Control (AGERE!), pp. 95–108 (2014)

31. Harel, D., Katz, G., Lampert, R., Marron, A., Weiss, G.: On the succinctness of idioms for concurrent programming. In: Proceedings of 26th International Conference on Concurrency Theory (CONCUR), pp. 85–99 (2015)

32. Harel, D., Katz, G., Marelly, R., Marron, A.: An initial wise development environment for behavioral models. In: Proceedings of 4th International Conference on Model-Driven Engineering and Software Development (MODELSWARD), pp. 600–612 (2016)

33. Harel, D., Katz, G., Marelly, R., Marron, A.: First steps towards a wise development environment for behavioral models. Int. J. Inf. Syst. Model. Des. (IJISMD) **7**(3), 1–22 (2016)

34. Harel, D., Katz, G., Marelly, R., Marron, A.: Wise computing: toward endowing system development with proactive wisdom. IEEE Comput. **51**(2), 14–26 (2018)

35. Harel, D., Katz, G., Marron, A., Weiss, G.: Non-intrusive repair of reactive programs. In: Proceedings of 17th IEEE International Conference on Engineering of Complex Computer Systems (ICECCS), pp. 3–12 (2012)

36. Harel, D., Katz, G., Marron, A., Weiss, G.: Non-intrusive repair of safety and liveness violations in reactive programs. Trans. Comput. Collect. Intell. (TCCI) **16**, 1–33 (2014)

37. Harel, D., Katz, G., Marron, A., Weiss, G.: The effect of concurrent programming idioms on verification: a position paper. In: Proceedings of 3rd International Conference on Model-Driven Engineering and Software Development (MODELSWARD), pp. 363–369 (2015)

38. Harel, D., Kugler, H., Marelly, R., Pnueli, A.: Smart play-out of behavioral requirements. In: Aagaard, M.D., O'Leary, J.W. (eds.) FMCAD 2002. LNCS, vol. 2517, pp. 378–398. Springer, Heidelberg (2002). https://doi.org/10.1007/3-540-36126-X_23

39. Harel, D., Maoz, S., Szekely, S., Barkan, D.: PlayGo: towards a comprehensive tool for scenario based programming. In: Proceedings of 10th International Conference on Automated Software Engineering (ASE), pp. 359–360 (2010)

40. Harel, D., Marelly, R.: Come, Let's Play: Scenario-Based Programming Using LSCs and the Play-Engine. Springer, Heidelberg (2003). https://doi.org/10.1007/978-3-642-19029-2

41. Harel, D., Marron, A., Weiss, G.: Programming coordinated behavior in Java. In: D'Hondt, T. (ed.) ECOOP 2010. LNCS, vol. 6183, pp. 250–274. Springer, Heidelberg (2010). https://doi.org/10.1007/978-3-642-14107-2_12

42. Harel, D., Marron, A., Weiss, G., Wiener, G.: Behavioral programming, decentralized control, and multiple time scales. In: Proceedings of 1st SPLASH Workshop on Programming Systems, Languages, and Applications Based on Agents, Actors, and Decentralized Control (AGERE!), pp. 171–182 (2011)

43. Harel, D., Segall, I.: Synthesis from live sequence chart specifications. Comput. Syst. Sci. **78**(3), 970–980 (2012)

44. Harel, D., Marron, A.: Toward scenario-based algorithmics. In: Böckenhauer, H.-J., Komm, D., Unger, W. (eds.) Adventures Between Lower Bounds and Higher Altitudes. LNCS, vol. 11011, pp. 549–567. Springer, Cham (2018). https://doi.org/10.1007/978-3-319-98355-4_32

45. Harel, D., Marron, A., Weiss, G.: Behavioral programming. Commun. ACM **55**(7), 90–100 (2012)

46. IEEE: Standard SystemC Lang. Ref. Manual. IEEE (2006)

47. Katz, G., Barrett, C., Harel, D.: Theory-aided model checking of concurrent transition systems. In: Proceedings of 15th International Conference on Formal Methods in Computer-Aided Design (FMCAD), pp. 81–88 (2015)

48. Katz, G., Marron, A., Sadon, A., Weiss, G.: On-the-fly construction of composite events in scenario-based modeling using constraint solvers. In: Model-Driven Engineering and Software Development, MODELSWARD 2019, pp. 141–154 (2019). https://doi.org/10.5220/0007573801410154

49. Katz, G.: On module-based abstraction and repair of behavioral programs. In: Proceedings of 19th International Conference on Logic for Programming, Artificial Intelligence and Reasoning (LPAR), pp. 518–535 (2013)

50. Kiczales, G., et al.: Aspect-oriented programming. In: Aksit, M., Matsuoka, S. (eds.) ECOOP 1997. LNCS, vol. 1241, pp. 220–242. Springer, Heidelberg (1997). https://doi.org/10.1007/BFb0053381

51. Mancinelli, F., Boender, J., Di Cosmo, R., Vouillon, J., Durak, B., Leroy, R.: Treinen: managing the complexity of large free and open source package based software distributions. In: Proceedings of 21st IEEE/ACM International Conference on Automated Software Engineering (ASE), pp. 199–208 (2006)

52. Marron, A., et al.: Six (im)possible things before breakfast: building-blocks and design-principles for wise computing. In: Proceedings of 19th ACM/IEEE International Conference on Model Driven Engineering Languages and Systems (MODELS), pp. 94–100 (2016)

53. Marron, A., Hacohen, Y., Harel, D., Mülder, A., Terfloth, A.: Embedding scenario-based modeling in statecharts. In: Proceedings of 5th International Workshop on Model-Driven Robot Software Engineering (MORSE) (2018)
54. Nadel, A.: Understanding and improving a modern SAT solver, Ph.D. thesis, Tel Aviv University (2009)
55. Păsăreanu, C., Visser, W.: A survey of new trends in symbolic execution for software testing and analysis. Int. J. Softw. Tools Technol. Transf. **11**(4), 339–353 (2009)
56. Sen, K.: Concolic testing. In: Proceedings of 22nd IEEE/ACM International Conference on Automated Software Engineering (ASE), pp. 571–572 (2007)
57. Steinberg, S., Greenyer, J., Gritzner, D., Harel, D., Katz, G., Marron, A.: Distributing scenario-based models: a replicate-and-project approach. In: Proceedings of 5th International Conference on Model-Driven Engineering and Software Development (MODELSWARD), pp. 182–195 (2015)
58. Steinberg, S., Greenyer, J., Gritzner, D., Harel, D., Katz, G., Marron, A.: Efficient distributed execution of multi-component scenario-based models. Commun. Comput. Inf. Sci. (CCIS) **880**, 449–483 (2018)

Evaluating the Multi-variant Model Transformation of UML Class Diagrams to Java Models

Sandra Greiner$^{(\boxtimes)}$ and Bernhard Westfechtel

Applied Computer Science I, University of Bayreuth, 95440 Bayreuth, Germany
{sandra.greiner,bernhard.westfechtel}@uni-bayreuth.de

Abstract. When the two disciplines, *software product line engineering* (SPLE) and *model-driven software engineering* (MDSE), come together *multi-variant model transformations* (MVMTs) are almost indispensable tool support.

Variability annotations are boolean expressions used in annotative SPL engineering (SPLE) for expressing in which products model elements are visible. Developing the SPL in a model-driven way requires various model representations, e.g., Java models for generating the source code. Although model transformations are the key essence of MDSE and can be used to generate these representations from already existing (model) artifacts, they suffer from not being able to handle the variability annotations automatically. Thus, the developer is forced to annotate target models manually contradicting the goal of both disciplines, MDSE and SPLE, to increase productivity. Recently, approaches have been proposed to solve the problem using, e.g., traces, to propagate annotations without changing the transformation itself. In this paper we utilize a generic framework allowing to evaluate whether the target model of arbitrary (reuse-based) MVMTs was annotated correctly. In particular, for two different product lines we illuminate the transformation of UML class diagrams to Java models from which we finally can generate source code. On the one hand, we examine the quality of different post-processing annotation propagation strategies, on the other hand, the scalability of the framework itself.

Keywords: Model-driven software engineering · Software product line engineering · Multi-variant model transformations · Annotative approach

1 Introduction

When the two disciplines, *software product line engineering* (SPLE) and *model-driven software engineering* (MDSE), come together in *model-driven product line engineering* (MDPLE), *multi-variant model transformations* (MVMTs) are almost indispensable tool support.

© Springer Nature Switzerland AG 2020
S. Hammoudi et al. (Eds.): MODELSWARD 2019, CCIS 1161, pp. 275–297, 2020.
https://doi.org/10.1007/978-3-030-37873-8_12

SPLE applies the paradigms of *organized reuse* and *variability* for increasing productivity when developing a set of closely related products. In the phase of *domain engineering* the superimposition of the products is developed in the *platform*. Thereafter, in the phase of *application engineering* products are derived from the platform and prepared for delivery [29]. Feature models [21] capture the common and varying parts of the products as *features*. In annotative approaches [2] the artifacts at the domain engineering level are associated with variability annotations resulting in a superimposed (150%) model. In the ongoing we denote a boolean expression over features from the feature model as *annotation*. By providing a selection of the features in a *feature configuration* a model filter derives configured models from the platform by removing elements.

Quite alike, MDSE [34] aims to increase the level of productivity by raising the level of abstraction when developing software. Metamodels define the syntax for concrete models from which eventually running source code should be generated. The EMF framework [35] establishes the de-facto standard in the academic world for model-driven development.

In MDPLE [9,10,16] models are the main development artifacts in the phase of domain engineering. Applying an annotative approach in model-driven SPLE means that model elements are associated with annotations. Typically, not only one single model but various types of models establish a model-driven product line. For instance, a UML class diagram [28] may capture the structure of the platform and an database may be necessary to store the objects which eventually requires an object-relational mapping. In addition, from the models source code needs to be created. *Model transformations* are the key essence in MDSE for creating target representations in an automated way. They allow for transforming source (input) models to target (output) representations in different modes, e.g., *model-to-model* (M2M) or *model-to-text* (M2T) transformations, creating either a model or text, e.g., source code.

Despite the fact that model transformations are well established in MDSE, a priori they do not regard annotations attached to the model elements in MDPLE. Consequently, state-of-the-art model transformations create a superimposed target model but neglect the annotations. Since annotating the target model manually is a tedious task, contradicting the general purpose of MDSE and SPLE to increase productivity, there is the need for the SPLE engineer to automatically propagate annotations from the source to the target representation. Solutions supporting this task are referred to as *multi-variant model transformations* (MVMT) [32]. A variety of approaches has been proposed, like lifting [30], extending the execution with aspects [13], a higher order transformation [41] or applying an a-posteriori propagation [12,14,42].

In [15] we have presented a framework for executing MVMTs and for evaluating their outcome generically. This paper extends the conference paper and contributes

- an extended motivating example in Sect. 2.1, detailing the case study used in Sect. 5.
- an evaluation of the performance of different post-processing strategies and the home automation system as a large case study.
- revised discussion regarding the bottleneck of evaluating the commutativity criterion and of applying post-processing propagation strategies.

The following section motivates the necessity of multi-variant model transformations. Thereafter, we provide an overview on existing approaches and motivate why a framework for their evaluation is necessary. In Sect. 4 the architecture of the evaluation framework is sketched and one realization is presented in the following example. Finally, related work is shortly discussed and a conclusion is drawn.

2   Motivation

This section motivates why multi-variant model transformations are essential to MDPLE and derives basic requirements such transformation should adhere to.

2.1   Graph Product Line

In [26] the authors introduce a product line for graphs. We take up this example and use it to illustrate the need for MVMTs. As depicted in Fig. 1, the feature model (on the right hand side) consists of the mandatory features Nodes and Edges. Edges are refined by the optional features Directed and Weighted and nodes may be colored. Optionally, a graph may include a search mechanism which is either depth first search DFS or breadth first search BFS (XOR feature

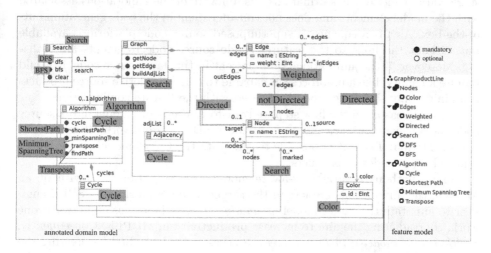

Fig. 1. Feature model and annotated domain model for the Graphs product line.

group). Further `Algorithms` may be present for analyzing the graph structure, like computing a `Minimum Spanning Tree`.

As a starting point for developing the product line in a model-driven way, its *structure* can be defined in an Ecore class diagram [35]. The model consists of a class `Graph` containing `nodes` and `edges`. The optional colored nodes are realized by a unidirectional reference to the respective class and `Weighted` edges by a corresponding attribute. In the case of undirected graphs, nodes and edges are linked with a one bidirectional reference whereas in the case of directed graphs two bidirectional references are designed to distinguish the source from the target node of an edge. The algorithms are implemented in respective operations.

In order to keep track in which products a (domain) model element should be present, the elements are associated with annotations, i.e., boolean expressions over the features of the feature model. For instance, the class `Color` is only present in colored graphs. Based on a feature configuration providing each feature of the feature model with a selection state, custom-oriented models are derived.

When generating source code from the models, the programs are not deliverable, yet, because still *behavior*, in form of method bodies, is missing. For delivery, for instance the search algorithms, have to be implemented if they are selected in the product. Assuming the MDPLE engineer implements the algorithm, e.g., for the DFS algorithm, for the first product, it is at least necessary to copy the method body to each further product shipped with the DFS feature. However, this contradicts the aim of organized reuse in SPLE. Thus, the algorithms should not be implemented in the phase of application engineering but in the phase of domain engineering.

For that reason, source code should be created for the complete Graph product line (instead of for each configured product) allowing to implement the method bodies only once. While it is possible to prevent the method bodies from being overwritten upon regeneration, the Ecore code generator – like all single-variant model transformations – is unaware of the annotations associated with the model elements and does not consider them in the code generation out-of-the-box. As a consequence, a superimposed source code platform is available but without the links to the features single source code fragments are realizing. Moreover, if the annotations were present in the Java source code, it would require a facility, like a preprocessor, capable to correctly derive source products containing only the source code associated with the feature configuration.

For that reason, in the first step we transform the Ecore model into a source code model, like the Java model from the MoDisco framework [4] in a M2M transformation. Then, it is possible to annotate the target model and to apply a model filter to derive products.

Again, without a variability-aware model transformation, i.e., without an MVMT, the annotations are lost in the target model requiring the SPLE engineer to annotate the target model *manually*, which is laborious and error-prone work, contradicting the aim to increase productivity in MDPLE. Consequently, *multi-variant model transformations* are necessary, which, besides creating the target model, propagate the annotations from the source to the target model automatically. Then, it is possible to include the method body once in the respective methods of the Java model. Since the annotations are attached to the Java model, the product delivery becomes a simple derivation steps without requiring additional handwork.

2.2   Requirements

From above example we can postulate the following requirements that need to be fulfilled by a multi-variant model transformation.

First of all, multi-variant model transformations are used in *MDPLE environments*, which offer integrated tool support for model-driven product line engineering. As a consequence, two groups are confronted with such framework: on the one hand, the requirements of the *user*, on the other hand, the requirements of the *builder* of the MDPLE tool need to be satisfied.

The *user* requires *automated* and *correct* tool support:

- **Automation:** The multi-variant model transformation should propagate annotations from the source to the target model *automatically*.
  As stated in the previous section, the laborious and error-prone task of manually annotating the target model contradicts the aim of increasing efficiency and productivity in software engineering.
- **Correctness:** The multi-variant model transformation should propagate annotations *correctly*, i.e., for each feature configuration applied to the source and target model the filtered products should be consistent.
  Consistency is defined on product level and, thus, by the single-variant transformation as stated in Sect. 3.1.

On top of that, the *tool builder* of an MDPLE environment, further may postulate the subsequent requirements:

- **Reuse:** Multi-variant model transformations should *reuse* (already existing) single-variant model transformations.
  An MVMT extends a single-variant model transformation inasmuch as it executes the SVMT and propagates variability annotations, in addition. Therefore, a tool builder would like to reuse already existing single-variant model transformation technology and specifications.
- **Genericity:** In a *generic* way single-variant model transformations should be extended to multi-variant transformations, minimizing the effort of the tool builder.

The requirements of the end user, stated in the first place, are hardly debatable and should be supported in any MDPLE environment. Contrastingly, the tool builder's requirements may depend on the respective MDPLE environment:

On the one hand, there are *closed environments* with a small set of built-in model transformations, all written in the same language. In this case, it may be sufficient to extend each of the single-variant transformation definitions manually, by editing the respective transformation definition.

On the other hand, there are *open environments* in which neither the type of models nor the model transformations are fixed. For instance, MDPLE environments such as Feature Mapper [16] and Famile [8,9] support arbitrary EMF-based domain models [35] and make no assumptions on the tools operating on these models (including model transformation tools and their underlying transformation languages). In such environments, a generic approach to realizing multi-variant model transformations is indispensable.

3   Overview

This section defines the correctness requirement for MVMTs at first, followed by a categorization and overview on already existing approaches to MVMTs.

3.1   Correctness

The most important requirement for this contribution is the criterion of correctness. For evaluating the validity of the target models of the MVMT, a commutativity criterion has been postulated in [30]. We use the criterion for assessing the quality of the annotations propagated to the target model. As sketched in Fig. 2, the criterion requires to filter both, the annotated source model m_s and the annotated target model m_t, by a feature configuration fc. The resulting products m'_t and m''_t can be compared after transforming the filtered source product m'_s. If the target products are the same for each valid feature configuration the MVMT is said to *commute*. In different words, path one (1), i.e.m filtering and applying the t_{sv}, must result in the same target models as path two (2) which first transforms (t_{mv}) once and filters afterwards.

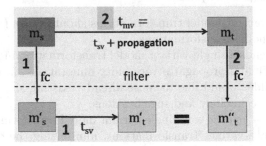

Fig. 2. Commutativity criterion: filtering the superimposed models m_s and m_t by all valid feature configurations fc should result in consistent products where the source product is transformed with the reused SVMT for the comparison of m'_t and m''_t. [Adapted from [15].]

To this end, the validity of the filtered target models is ensured in the following way: It is assumed the source model m_s is valid and correctly annotated such that each derived product m_s' is valid as well. Furthermore, with a valid model m_s' as input t_{sv} creates a valid target model m_t'. Since m_t'' should equal m_t', it is ensured that m_t'' is valid, too. If all filtered products m_t'' are valid, the superimposed target model m_t is semantically correct, too.

3.2   Error Measurement

For measuring the quality of the annotations propagated to the target model m_t, we introduce two errors, an absolute error and a severity error. The absolute error counts each feature configuration resulting in at least one mismatch on product level as erroneous whereas the severity error takes the number of the affected model elements into account. Thus, the absolute error is measured by counting the number of feature configurations in which commutativity is violated and by comparing it with the number of all valid feature configurations:

Definition 1 (Absolute error). *Let n be the number of all valid feature configurations and let v be the number of feature configurations in which a strategy violates commutativity with $v \leq n$. Then, the absolute error err_{abs} can be computed in the following way:*

$$err_{abs} = \frac{v}{n}$$

This error rate is rather rigorous since it counts a feature configuration as wrong as soon as there is one difference between the models m_t' and m_t''. For that reason, the error could be relaxed by considering the number of differences between m_t' and m_t'' and comparing it with the number of elements in the multi-variant target model m_t. Summing these error rates up and dividing them by the number of valid feature configurations gives a hint on the overall error in terms of the affected elements (severity of the error).

Definition 2. *Let n be the number of all valid feature configurations. Let $|m_t|$ be the cardinality of m_t, i.e., the number of annotated elements in the target model. Let further $diff$ be the number of differences between m_t' and m_t''. Then, the severity error err_{sev} is calculated as follows:*

$$err_{sev} = \frac{\sum_{i=1}^{n}\left(\frac{\#diff_i}{|m_t|}\right)}{n}$$

Both error rates allow to draw conclusions on the quality of the MVMT with respect to fulfilling commutativity.

3.3   Existing Approaches

Different approaches for automating the annotation of model elements exist, which can be roughly categorized in *black-box* and *white-box* solutions depending on the fact whether *no* or *all* internals (i.e., the contents of the transformation) are exploited, respectively. All of them, however, have in common that existing transformations or the existing tool environments are reused to some extent.

Lifting [30] and higher order transformations as presented in [33] can be classified as white-box solutions. Lifting changes the semantics of the execution engine and is defined for in-place graph transformations but was also applied in out-place transformations with a graph-like DSL [11]. The solution based on higher order transformations in ATL transformations [33] is specific to the language ATL [19] and not generally applicable. While both approaches are based on *reusing* existing technology, both require to change this technology.

In contrast, pure black-box approaches do not intervene in the functionality of the reused transformation engine. Instead, they exploit the existing technology and the created artifacts during the transformation for propagating the annotations from the source to the target model *orthogonally* to the transformation.

Firstly, in [7] this behavior is supported by using the provided DSL *MySync* allowing to specify corresponding elements in the source and target models. The SVMT is executed as it stands. Thereafter, the annotations are propagated to the corresponding elements as stated in the mappings. So far, this approach works only for metamodels conforming to the Ecore meta-metamodel. Moreover, it requires the user to manually specify the corresponding elements for each new kind of input or output metamodel.

Another approach to achieve the desired behavior is trace-based propagation as proposed in [42]. A generic trace model serves as interface for different kinds of traces. Annotations of source elements are applied to their corresponding target elements as recorded in the trace. It is a generic approach since it is independent of the applied transformation language and the input and output metamodel. The approach only requires a trace to be persisted. Therefore, it may support various transformation tools, like the ATL/EMFTVM [41], medini QVT [17] or QVT-d [43], Bxtend [5] and eMoflon [25].

Please note: Traces vary with respect to the granularity of the persisted information. As stated in [42] at least three categories can be distinguished: *incomplete*, *generation-complete* and *complete* traces. The first category only stores one source and one target element in so called *correspondence graphs*, being the key element in triple graph grammars (TGGs) [31]. In these realizations further dependent elements are determined from the basic mappings. In contrast, generation-complete traces persist all source and all target elements of a rule application whereas complete traces distinguish the elements of the target model with respect to the fact whether they have already been present before applying a rule (context elements) or they have been created due to applying a rule. Depending on the granularity of the trace, the propagation of annotations may have to be adapted. The authors provide a computation model for transformations based on complete traces which is proved to fulfill commutativity.

Quite differently, if the transformation language supports aspect-oriented programming [22], a generic aspect could be provided to transfer the annotations [13]. The aspect should attach the annotation of the element triggering its execution to the created target element. In the cited approach this behavior is implemented for the Xpand language [23] supporting M2T transformations only. Thus, annotations are integrated as preprocessor directives and products filtered by using a preprocessor. While the approach is specific to the language Xpand (language-dependent), it can be categorized as black-box approach since transformation rules are not analyzed.

4 Evaluation Framework

In order to keep this article self-contained, this section highlights key elements of the evaluation framework and illustrates how it can be extended to measure the performance regarding the runtime.

4.1 Architectural Overview

As depicted in Fig. 3, the evaluation framework needs to execute all the steps of the commutativity criterion presented in Sect. 3.1. The necessary inputs to the system are the annotated source and target model, m_s and m_t, respectively, as well as the feature model (fm) and the single-variant transformation (t_{sv}) which has been reused to create m_t. The output of the evaluation is the answer, whether the commutativity criterion is satisfied. Moreover, when commutativity is violated, the differences should be made available. In the figure, all yellow boxes represent interfaces which have to be replaced by realizations specific to the respective MDPLE tool. All of them are part of the abstract Evaluator which offers the single steps solely in single methods or bundled altogether in one evaluate() method. Furthermore, the results of the evaluation should be persisted and made available to the product line engineer. Please note: although only one instance of the feature configuration (fc) and the products (m'_s, m'_t and m''_t), respectively, is shown in Fig. 2, the evaluation takes all valid feature configurations into account.

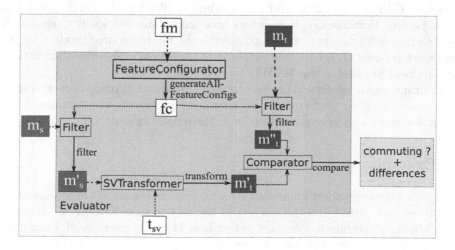

Fig. 3. Overview on the architecture of the MVMT evaluation framework (Color figure online).

The evaluation takes place in the following steps: At first, a FeatureConfigurator is supposed to generate all valid feature configurations. For sufficing the
evaluation of commutativity, it is obligatory to generate all valid configurations,
even if the number of them might increase exponentially with respect to the
number of optional features in the feature model. One alternative is to *sample*
the configurations, which is discussed in Sect. 6. Given the set of feature configurations, the source and the target model are both filtered by each configuration.
We employ two Filters because the representation of the target model may differ
from the source model's one in as much as a second filter for the target may
be required. For instance, if source code is generated in a M2T transformation,
instead of a model filter a preprocessor will remove deselected parts from the
superimposed source code.

Before comparing the products, the filtered source products m'_s have to be
transformed by the SVTransformer which is the instance that should have been
reused to create the target model m_t. Thereafter, each pair of the filtered (m''_t)
and the transformed (m'_t) target product is compared by the Comparator. Therefore, the comparator must correspond with the representation of the target models, e.g., for models a comparison based on the EMFCompare framework [3] can
take place or a pure textual String compare when source code or model files
should be compared literally.

4.2 Runtime Measurement

The components necessary for executing the transformation and evaluating it
have been explained in [15] extensively. Here, we like to provide some extensions. Firstly, the evaluator is extended to provide runtime measurements. In
a fine granular way, the evaluator provides runtime measurements of the single evaluation steps. The evaluator measures the runtime of filtering the source
model by each configuration and the runtime of filtering the target model in
the same way. Furthermore, it measures how much time was spent to create all
valid feature configurations and to transform the filtered source product m'_s to
the target product. Likewise, the executor of the MVMT provides the runtime
measurement of running the MVMT.

Runtime measurements allow for comparing different propagation strategies
with respect to their performance. Furthermore, measuring the runtime of the
evaluation steps may reveal bottlenecks in the evaluation method.

5   Example

The goal of the evaluation framework is to verify whether an MVMT commutes.
In [12] we have introduced the real-world use case of transforming instances of
the UML class diagram to instances of the Java MoDisco metamodel. Primarily,
this example demonstrated how the evaluation framework works and what kind
of output is generated. Here we like to take up this example and extend it by
measuring its performance with respect to the runtime of the evaluation steps.

In addition, we examine different strategies to determine missing annotations in partially annotated models. Moreover, the section present a second product line for home automation systems (HAS) which is picked to demonstrate the strengths and limitations of the evaluation method.

5.1 Setup

In the following examples we focus on the evaluation of trace-based propagation [42] in real-world scenarios transforming UML into Java. The source models are built with the MDPLE tool *FAMILE* [9], i.e., they consist of a UML domain model and an associated mapping model. The mapping model contains a mapping element for each domain model element. The mapping element associates the domain model element with an annotation. A feature model defines the features that are allowed to be used for annotations.

At first, the FeatureConfigurator iterates the feature model and generates all valid configurations, taking into account AND, OR and XOR feature groups and *requires* and *excludes* relationships between features. The model filter, integrated in FAMILE, removes – based on a feature propagation strategy – deselected elements. It is a hierarchical filter which ensures the validity of the derived products by including or excluding elements which initially would have been removed or kept, respectively. For instance, if a child element is included but its parent is not selected, the children will be deselected as well. Elements without an annotation are assumed to be globally visible, i.e. present in each feature configuration. Finally, the models have to be compared. Since EMFCompare provides a mature framework for comparing models conforming to the same metamodel, we utilize its mechanism to conduct a pure structural comparison of two models.

Transformation. The reused SVMT is the Bxtend transformation presented in [6]. It is a bidirectional transformation based on a correspondence model, i.e., on 1:1 traces. As discussed in [14] and [12], 1:1 traces typically leave parts of the target model without an annotation since in reality 1:1 mappings only occur rarely. Thus, post-processing strategies have been proposed to annotate the elements still missing an annotation after an initial propagation. We apply each strategy in our use case and compare the measurements regarding the error values and the runtime.

To keep this article self-contained, we summarize here the post-processing strategies for incomplete traces in a nutshell. The algorithms assume each model is structured as a spanning containment tree. Each node represents a model element where the contained nodes are the children of the node and the container is the parent node. Then, each element missing an annotation is added to a list of open elements in a preorder traversal of the tree. In the case the root of the domain model misses an annotation, the root feature of the feature model is taken as annotation.

Thereafter, the list of open elements is iterated with one of the following strategies to compute the missing annotations:

1. **TRUE.** Iterates the list from the beginning and assigns the annotation `true`. This strategy is comparable with our hierarchical filter, which a priori assumes that a element is globally visible in the case it does not carry an annotation.
2. **Container.** Iterates the list from the beginning and assigns the annotation of the parent node to an element without annotation.
3. **Contained.** Iterates the list from the end and assigns the disjunction of the annotation of the element's children nodes. In the case leafs of the tree miss an annotation, the annotation *true* is assigned.
4. **Combined.** Combines strategy two and three: Firstly, it iterates the list from the beginning and assigns the annotation of the container. Secondly, it iterates the list from the end and combines the container annotation of each element in a conjunction with the disjunction of the children annotation.

To this end, the single-variant transformation creating a Java model for a given UML class diagram is a BXtend transformation as described in [6]. For each UML association the transformation specification creates a class declaration in the Java model capturing the two association ends as field declarations. For each UML class a Java class declaration is created and a compilation unit which is necessary to represent the corresponding Java file that is generated by the MoDisco source code generation. This situation for the class Color of the Graph product line is sketched in Fig. 4. The figure also drafts the rule for transforming UML classifiers on the right hand side: Besides the compilation unit, a parameterized type is created for each UML classifier in order to represent complex types with multiplicities greater than one. The Bxtend trace, however, records only main correspondences, i. e., for example a UML class and the created Java class declaration. Both, the compilation unit and the parameterized type are left from the incomplete trace as written with BXtend but would be present in a complete trace. Please note: The Java Model element, shown in the figure, is the root of the Java MoDisco model and, thus, annotated with the root feature in our propagation mechanism.

Technical Details. The system, on which we conducted the performance measurements, was an Intel i7-5600U 2.60 GHz × 4 processor with 16 GB of memory (Ubuntu 18.04.2). In the case it was possible each measurement was run 5 times. We removed the first runtime which was an outlier most probably resulting from missing compiler optimization. The arithmetic mean was taken from the four remaining measurements. Detailed numbers can be found online[1].

5.2   Graph Product Line

In the first scenario we consider the Graph product line presented in Sect. 2 on instance level. However, it is modeled as a UML class diagram instead of an

---

[1] http://btn1x4.inf.uni-bayreuth.de/mvmt/uml2java.

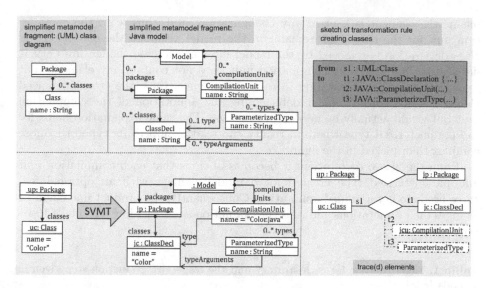

Fig. 4. Simplified example of Java MoDisco metamodel and the snippet of the transformed models. On the right, one transformation rule and the trace corresponding to the snippet is sketched.

Ecore model. In total, the source model comprises 140 elements from which 325 target elements are created.

The components necessary for executing and evaluating the transformation have been explained in [15] extensively. In addition to the error values, we measure the runtime in this contribution. Furthermore, we compare the applied strategies with respect to their correctness and their runtime performance.

Error Values. At first, we compare the error values computed in each strategy. The results reveal that the error is always of the same size. In each strategy the absolute error is 100% and the severity error is 48.26%. Furthermore, looking at the number of mismatches in each strategy, reveals that the differences are the same in corresponding feature configurations.

From the above observation, we can conclude that applying any of the strategies makes no difference with respect to the mismatches between the products in this use case. This is due to the capabilities of the hierarchical filter and mostly depends on the structure of the metamodel as sketched in Fig. 4. In detail, we see from the difference files, that compilation units and parameterized types are not present in the transformed target model m'_t whereas they remain in the filtered model m''_t. Both kinds of elements are contained in the overall container of the Java model, the Model which is annotated with the root feature GraphProductLine. As a consequence, for instance the annotation of a compilation unit is either true (strategy: true), GraphProductLine (strategy:container), true (strategy: contained) or GraphProductLine and true (strategy:combined), respectively. To this end, this means the element is kept in any configuration, and, thus, e.g., the compilation unit for the class Color remains in the model although the corresponding class declaration is removed by the model filter in the case the feature Color is deselected. Moreover, the compilation unit does not contain any elements but references the class declaration in a cross reference, thus, the cross-referenced element is not considered for determining the annotation of the compilation unit but would actually be needed in this case. The same explanation holds for the parameterized type where in reality the relationship to its type(s) is more complex than picked in the figure.

From the above description, it becomes obvious that each compilation unit and parameterized type created for a model element with an optional features needs to get a refined annotation. Consequently, the product line engineer changes their annotations and runs the evaluation again yielding a result of 100% **correctness**.

Table 1. Mean runtime for each strategy and the respective evaluation step given in seconds [sec].

Strategy	generateFeatConfig	source filter	target filter	t_{sv}	t_{mv}	path 1	path 2
true	0.467	2.262	1.570	27.85	0.050	30.11	1.620
container	0.502	1.427	2.488	27.80	0.067	29.23	2.556
contained	0.498	1.362	1.777	26.71	0.098	28.07	1.875
combined	0.465	1.564	2.758	26.20	0.056	27.76	2.814
mean	0.483	1.654	–	27.14	–	–	–

Runtime. The mean runtime measurements are enumerated in Table 1. It can be seen that the time consumptions of each strategy are almost of the same size. Generating 180 feature configurations for the feature model with nine optional features takes about 0.5 s which is still feasible. The source filter for filtering a domain model with 150 elements is slightly faster than the target filter, filtering 325 elements. Most of the time is spent for running the single-variant model transformation 180 times which takes about half a minute (27.14 s). Please note: it is possible to compute the mean for the methods generating all feature configurations, filtering the source model and transforming the resulting product since all of them act on the same input and produce the same output. Solely, the multi-variant transformation and the target filter behave either differently or work on different input, respectively.

In contrast, the multi-variant transformations (t_{mv}) run all in the same amount of size (0.05–0.1 s). Furthermore, it becomes obvious that the combined strategy does not consume significantly more runtime for iterating the list of open elements twice but is of the same size. The comparably high value for the contained strategy may be caused by the fact that for each element missing an annotation its list of children elements is iterated which is requires more time than only looking up the annotation of one element, like the parent in the strategy using the container.

More importantly, in the last two columns of Table 1 the two paths of the commutativity diagram have been compared as described in Sect. 3.1. We do not add the time for generating all feature configurations, which is performed on both paths but summarize in the first path the time spent for filtering the source model and transforming the resulting products which is almost 30 times slower than using the MVMT and filtering thereafter (path 2). This clearly demonstrates a further benefit of applying MVMT which is time reduction.

5.3 Home Automation System (HAS)

The second product line we utilize for the evaluation is one for home automation systems (HAS) adapted from the descriptions in [29]. In general, it includes mostly technical design decision where we focused on modeling the structure.

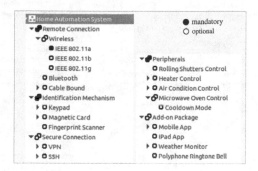

Fig. 5. Feature model for the home automation system.

The feature model is depicted in Fig. 5. It comprises the mandatory mechanisms Remote Connection, Identification Mechanism and Peripherals. The remote control contains an OR group of wireless, bluetooth and cable support. If a wireless connection is chosen at least the feature IEEE 802.11a must be selected which is obligatorily required by the other two IEEE standards. Furthermore, one or two of the identification mechanisms can be selected and any of the peripherals (OR) can be integrated. The mircowave oven may include an optional cooldown mode. As secure connection either SSH or VPN can optionally be added to the HAS. Finally, there is a number of optional add-ons. In total, with respect to the dependencies between the features and the minimum and maximum of allowed selected features, the feature configurator finds 16560 valid feature configurations.

Figure 6 sketches the structure of the UML class diagram by placing the included classes in their corresponding packages. In total, it is 221 elements being part of the domain model and the created target model comprises 509 elements. Out of the 221 source model elements we have annotated all packages and classifiers including associations in the mapping model. Most of the annotations are quite straight-forward and can be deferred from the names of the model elements. Please note, the package wifi is included whenever Wireless or Bluetooth is selected. The Cooldown Mode for microwave ovens is implemented in a state chart, which we have omitted for the sake of simplicity in this contribution.

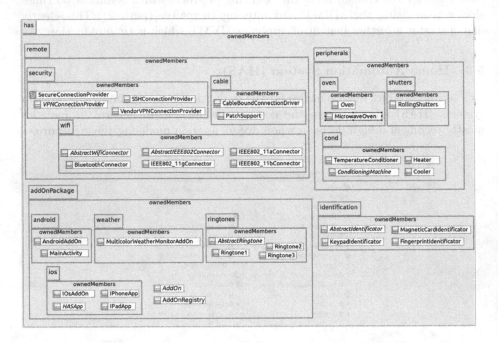

Fig. 6. UML Package diagram for the home automation system.

Executing the MVMT creating 509 elements does not significantly influence the runtime of the transformation which takes now about 0.2 s, i.e., about 0.39 ms to create one element which is comparable with the Graph scenario where it takes about 75 ms/325 = 0.23 ms to create one element (which still depends in detail on the respective strategy). Table 2 enumerates the arithmetic mean of the runtime measurements in each strategy. In contrast to the measurements of the Graph product line, in this scenario the strategy utilizing the contained elements is even faster than the one using containers. However, as in the first scenario there is no significant difference between each strategy regarding the runtime since each one takes about 0.2 s.

However, this scenario is introduced mainly to exemplify the limitations of the commutativity evaluation. In terms of the number of valid feature configurations it is still possible to generate the 16560 configurations in a feasible amount of time which takes 3.234 min in the mean (running it 5 times). However, consecutively filtering and transforming is hard to accomplish. Moreover,

Table 2. Mean runtime of multi-variant model transformation in each strategy in the HAS use case, measured in seconds.

	true	container	contained	combined
t_{mv} [sec]	0.197	0.210	0.186	0.216

storing the feature configurations and difference files becomes expensive as well. Due to the high number of feature configurations it was not possible to run the complete evaluation more often than once. It is possible to filter the source and target model once and to store all the products which took 5.76 and 6.49 min, respectively. However, running the transformation afterwards, is not possible out-of-the-box because the default Java heap is too small to keep the source models and target models all in memory to finally compare them. Otherwise, not keeping the models in memory would increase the runtime for loading and unloading the respective model pairs. Moreover, if the models are not kept in memory and running the transformation directly, it still takes more than one day to execute all transformations.

As a consequence, this example demonstrates that a brute force approach of evaluating commutativity by using all valid feature configurations is only feasible up to a limited amount of configurations. For large product lines alternatives have to be applied which can also be integrated in our framework.

5.4 Threats to Validity

Some threats to validity have to be mentioned. At first, although we have picked a real-world use case with relevant models from a practical point of view, the domain models are still small but w.r.t. the number of elements. Moreover, definitely not all kind of relationships between source and target model elements are present in the UMl to Java use case. There are more mapping relationships possible, e.g., having to deal with information loss. For instance, the Family to Person use case [1] may also reveal differences for the single post-processing strategies regarding the error values.

Furthermore, the measurements were conducted at maximum 5 times. This number was picked in order to have a number which still allows to store all feature configurations and models in smaller use cases without exploiting too much memory. In addition, we were able to run parts of the evaluation in the HAS case study in a feasible amount of time. For better accuracy, however outliers in terms of the longest and shortest runtime should also be removed from the measurements which in turn requires more measurement executions. We only removed the first measurement which took always the most time for setting up the system and not being optimized by the compiler.

6   Discussion

First of all, as illustrated in the first scenario the evaluation framework allows for evaluating consistency of MVMTs. By that, it is possible to detect strengths and weaknesses of propagation approaches. The scenario shows that with above approach complete and correct automation of propagating annotations may become impossible in real-world applications. Nonetheless, the example also reveals that errors can be detected and may be fixed with a very small amount of effort.

In this section two points stand out to be discussed. On the one hand, the post-processing strategies can be evaluated based on the results in the UML2Java use case. On the other hand, the scalability of the commutativity evaluation as presented in this contribution needs to be considered.

To both product lines we have applied four the post-processing strategies introduced in Sect. 5.1. We measured their performance on both product lines and their quality with respect to the error values in the Graph product line. Looking at the runtime of the different strategies reveals that there are no significant differences. Although the more complex one (strategy combined), which iterates the list of elements, awaiting an annotation, twice, takes a little longer in the case there are more elements to be annotated (HAS use case) but still remains in the same amount of time. Regarding the quality of the strategies the computed error values in the Graph product line are the same in each strategy. However, this is mostly caused by the properties of the transformation and the corresponding metamodels. In the case of the Java MoDisco model a better accuracy would be achieved, if the annotations of cross references were taken into account. However, generalizing this approach means to collect all annotations of cross referenced elements in addition to the containment relationships but would also require to consider realization relationships, like inheritance. Thus, its complexity rises significantly and elements which may be irrelevant or already included anyway would be taken into account additionally. As a consequence, from the results it is recommendable to use the combined strategy which is more accurate but still not expensive.

In the second place, evaluating commutativity completely does not scale very well. It is feasible for a small number of configurations (up to ca. 400 configuration), for larger numbers the evaluation runs out of memory and takes too long. For only generating 16560 configurations and filtering both models by each configuration the framework already spends more than 15 min taken together. The consecutive single-variant model transformation on all products exceeds the default Java heap size and running it standalone requires about one day for only transforming all models. For that reason, we propose to integrate sampling strategies picking only a representative number of configurations and running the evaluation on these samples only. For instance, there is various forms of coverage-based sampling [18, 27] which apply t-wise strategies or distance-based sampling [20] which promises to covert the configuration space more uniformly in an efficient way. Instead of our feature configurator which creates all valid feature configurations one of aforementioned mechanisms could be integrated to create only a representative set of valid feature configurations to evaluate commutativity.

7   Related Work

Transforming product lines has gained popularity in the last few years. Thereby, the term "multi-variant model transformation" may be interpreted differently: *transformation* of *multi-variant models*, the focus of our contributions, and *multi-variant transformation* of *models*, as addressed in [37,38]. In addition, *transformations of product lines* [39], covering both feature and domain models, goes beyond the scope of our work in which we evaluate the transformation of artifacts in a single software product line. Moreover, the tool presented in [24] allows for summarizing families of (slightly varying) transformations into a product line which is not the focus of our work.

Various strategies to transform a multi-variant source model into a multi-variant target model are discussed in Sect. 3.3. To the best of our knowledge, so far there is no common means to evaluate the quality of the resulting target models with a generic framework. In addition, solutions which are formally proven [36,40,42] ensure the transformation behaves correctly, if the underlying computational model is satisfied. However, if the computational model is violated, our framework helps to find out where the transformation fails and why it fails. This allows for improving the MVMT solution for supporting more (general) use cases.

Sampling mechanisms as mentioned to circumvent the bottleneck of generating all valid feature configurations are not always specific to SPLE but often aimed to support arbitrary configurable system.

8   Conclusion

Summing it up, this paper presents an evaluation framework for multi-variant model transformations. In a real-world use case of model transformations where UML class diagrams are transformed in a Java source code model, two scenarios are illuminated. The two well-known product lines show the strengths and weaknesses of the framework.

In the future we like to use the strength of the framework to further evaluate different MVMT approaches and to give recommendations but also like to work on the weakness of handling exploding numbers of feature configurations, e.g., by including sampling mechanisms.

References

1. Anjorin, A., Buchmann, T., Westfechtel, B.: The families to persons case. In: Proceedings of the 10th Transformation Tool Contest (TTC 2017), Co-located with the 2017 Software Technologies: Applications and Foundations (STAF 2017), Marburg, Germany, 21 July 2017, pp. 27–34 (2017). http://ceur-ws.org/Vol-2026/paper2.pdf
2. Apel, S., Janda, F., Trujillo, S., Kästner, C.: Model superimposition in software product lines. In: Paige, R.F. (ed.) ICMT 2009. LNCS, vol. 5563, pp. 4–19. Springer, Heidelberg (2009). https://doi.org/10.1007/978-3-642-02408-5_2

3. Brun, C., Pierantonio, A.: Model differences in the eclipse modelling framework. UPGRADE **IX**(2), 29–34 (2008)
4. Bruneliere, H., Cabot, J., Jouault, F., Madiot, F.: MoDisco: a generic and extensible framework for model driven reverse engineering. In: Proceedings of the IEEE/ACM International Conference on Automated Software Engineering, ASE 2010, pp. 173–174. ACM, New York (2010). https://doi.org/10.1145/1858996.1859032
5. Buchmann, T.: BXtend - a framework for (Bidirectional) incremental model transformations. In: Proceedings of the 6th International Conference on Model-Driven Engineering and Software Development, MODELSWARD 2018, Funchal, Madeira - Portugal, 22–24 January 2018, pp. 336–345 (2018). https://doi.org/10.5220/0006563503360345
6. Buchmann, T., Greiner, S.: Bidirectional model transformations using a handcrafted triple graph transformation system. In: Software Technologies, 11th International Joint Conference, ICSOFT 2016, Lisbon, Portugal, 24–26 July 2016, Revised Selected Papers, pp. 201–220 (2016). https://doi.org/10.1007/978-3-319-62569-0_10
7. Buchmann, T., Greiner, S.: Managing variability in models and derived artefacts in model-driven software product lines. In: Proceedings of the 6th International Conference on Model-Driven Engineering and Software Development, MODELSWARD 2018, Funchal, Madeira - Portugal, 22–24 January 2018, pp. 326–335 (2018). https://doi.org/10.5220/0006563403260335
8. Buchmann, T., Schwägerl, F.: Ensuring well-formedness of configured domain models in model-driven product lines based on negative variability. In: 4th International Workshop on Feature-Oriented Software Development, FOSD 2012, Dresden, Germany, 24–25 September 2012, pp. 37–44 (2012). https://doi.org/10.1145/2377816.2377822
9. Buchmann, T., Schwägerl, F.: FAMILE: tool support for evolving model-driven product lines. In: Joint Proceedings of Co-located Events at 8th ECMFA, CEUR WS, Lyngby, Denmark, pp. 59–62, July 2012. http://btn1x4.inf.uni-bayreuth.de/publications/ECMFA-Buchmann2012.pdf
10. Czarnecki, K., Antkiewicz, M., Kim, C.H.P., Lau, S., Pietroszek, K.: Model-driven software product lines. In: Companion to the 20th Annual ACM SIGPLAN Conference on Object-Oriented Programming, Systems, Languages, and Applications, OOPSLA 2005, San Diego, CA, USA, 16–20 October 2005, pp. 126–127 (2005). https://doi.org/10.1145/1094855.1094896
11. Famelis, M., et al.: Migrating automotive product lines: a case study. In: Theory and Practice of Model Transformations - 8th International Conference, ICMT 2015, Held as Part of STAF 2015, Proceedings, L'Aquila, Italy, 20–21 July 2015, pp. 82–97 (2015). https://doi.org/10.1007/978-3-319-21155-8_7
12. Greiner, S., Westfechtel, B.: On determining variability annotations in partially annotated models. In: Proceedings of the 13th International Workshop on Variability Modelling of Software-Intensive Systems, VAMOS 2019, Leuven, Belgium, 6–8 February 2019. https://doi.org/10.1145/3302333.3302341
13. Greiner, S., Westfechtel, B.: Generating multi-variant java source code using generic aspects. In: Proceedings of the 6th International Conference on Model-Driven Engineering and Software Development, MODELSWARD 2018, Funchal, Madeira - Portugal, 22–24 January 2018, pp. 36–47 (2018). https://doi.org/10.5220/0006536700360047

14. Greiner, S., Westfechtel, B.: Improving trace-based propagation of feature annotations in model transformations. In: Proceedings of MODELS 2018 Workshops: ModComp, MRT, OCL, FlexMDE, EXE, COMMitMDE, MDETools, GEMOC, MORSE, MDE4IoT, MDEbug, MoDeVVa, ME, MULTI, HuFaMo, AMMoRe, PAINS Co-located with ACM/IEEE 21st International Conference on Model Driven Engineering Languages and Systems (MODELS 2018), Copenhagen, Denmark, 14 October 2018, pp. 584–593 (2018). http://ceur-ws.org/Vol-2245/me_paper_2.pdf

15. Greiner, S., Westfechtel, B.: Generic framework for evaluating commutativity of multi-variant model transformations. In: Proceedings of the 7th International Conference on Model-Driven Engineering and Software Development, MODELSWARD 2019, Prague, Czech Republic, 20–22 February 2019, pp. 155–166 (2019). https://doi.org/10.5220/0007585701550166

16. Heidenreich, F., Kopcsek, J., Wende, C.: FeatureMapper: Mapping features to models. In: Companion Proceedings of 30th ICSE, pp. 943–944. ACM, Leipzi, May 2008. https://doi.org/10.1145/1370175.1370199

17. ikv++ technologies: medini QVT. ikv++ technologies (2018). http://projects.ikv.de/qvt

18. Johansen, M.F., Haugen, Ø., Fleurey, F.: An algorithm for generating t-wise covering arrays from large feature models. In: 16th International Software Product Line Conference, SPLC 2012, Salvador, Brazil , 2–7 September 2012, vol. 1, pp. 46–55 (2012). https://doi.org/10.1145/2362536.2362547

19. Jouault, F., Allilaire, F., Bézivin, J., Kurtev, I.: ATL: a model transformation tool. Sci. Comput. Program. **72**(1–2), 31–39 (2008). https://doi.org/10.1016/j.scico.2007.08.002

20. Kaltenecker, C., Grebhahn, A., Siegmund, N., Guo, J., Apel, S.: Distance-based sampling of software configuration spaces. In: Proceedings of the 41st International Conference on Software Engineering, pp. 1084–1094. ICSE 2019. IEEE Press, Piscataway (2019). https://doi.org/10.1109/ICSE.2019.00112

21. Kang, K.C., Cohen, S.G., Hess, J.A., Novak, W.E., Peterson, A.S.: Feature-oriented domain analysis (FODA) feasibility study. Technical Report CMU/SEI-90-TR-21, Carnegie-Mellon University, Software Engineering Institute, November 1990

22. Kiczales, G.: Aspect-oriented programming. In: Proceedings of the 27th International Conference on Software Engineering, ICSE 2005, St. Louis, MO, USA, p. 730. ACM, New York (2005). ISBN: 1-58113-963-2. https://doi.org/10.1145/1062455.1062640

23. Klatt, B.: Xpand: a closer look at the model2text transformation language. Language **10**(16), 2008 (2007)

24. de Lara, J., Guerra, E., Chechik, M., Salay, R.: Model transformation product lines. In: Proceedings of the 21th ACM/IEEE International Conference on Model Driven Engineering Languages and Systems, MODELS 2018, Copenhagen, Denmark, 14–19 October 2018, pp. 67–77 (2018). https://doi.org/10.1145/3239372.3239377

25. Leblebici, E., Anjorin, A., Schürr, A.: Developing emoflon with emoflon. In: Theory and Practice of Model Transformations - 7th International Conference, ICMT 2014, Held as Part of STAF 2014, . Proceedings, York, UK, 21–22 July 2014, pp. 138–145 (2014). https://doi.org/10.1007/978-3-319-08789-4_10

26. Lopez-Herrejon, R.E., Batory, D.: A standard problem for evaluating product-line methodologies. In: Bosch, J. (ed.) GCSE 2001. LNCS, vol. 2186, pp. 10–24. Springer, Heidelberg (2001). https://doi.org/10.1007/3-540-44800-4_2

27. Marijan, D., Gotlieb, A., Sen, S., Hervieu, A.: Practical pairwise testing for software product lines. In: 17th International Software Product Line Conference, SPLC 2013, Tokyo, Japan, 26–30 August 2013, pp. 227–235 (2013). https://doi.org/10.1145/2491627.2491646

28. Object Management Group, Needham, MA: Unified Modeling Language (UML), formal/17-12-05 edn. March 2017

29. Pohl, K., Böckle, G., van der Linden, F.: Software Product Line Engineering: Foundations Principles and Techniques. Springer, Berlin (2005). https://link.springer.com/book/10.1007%2F3-540-28901-1

30. Salay, R., Famelis, M., Rubin, J., Sandro, A.D., Chechik, M.: Lifting model transformations to product lines. In: 36th International Conference on Software Engineering, ICSE 2014, Hyderabad, India, 31 May–07 June 2014, pp. 117–128 (2014). https://doi.org/10.1145/2568225.2568267

31. Schürr, A.: Specification of graph translators with triple graph grammars. In: Mayr, E.W., Schmidt, G., Tinhofer, G. (eds.) WG 1994. LNCS, vol. 903, pp. 151–163. Springer, Heidelberg (1995). https://doi.org/10.1007/3-540-59071-4_45

32. Schwägerl, F., Buchmann, T., Westfechtel, B.: Multi-variant model transformations - a problem statement. In: ENASE 2016 - Proceedings of the 11th International Conference on Evaluation of Novel Approaches to Software Engineering, Rome, Italy 27–28, April 2016, pp. 203–209 (2016). https://doi.org/10.5220/0005878702030209

33. Sijtema, M.: Introducing variability rules in atl for managing variability in mde-based product lines. In: Proceedings of MtATL, vol. 10, pp. 39–49 (2010)

34. Stahl, T., Völter, M., Bettin, J., Haase, A., Helsen, S.: Model-Driven Software Development - Technology, Engineering, Management. Pitman, London (2006). http://eu.wiley.com/WileyCDA/WileyTitle/productCd-0470025700.html

35. Steinberg, D., Budinsky, F., Paternostro, M., Merks, E.: EMF Eclipse Modeling Framework. The Eclipse Series, 2nd edn. Addison-Wesley, Boston (2009)

36. Strüber, D., Rubin, J., Arendt, T., Chechik, M., Taentzer, G., Plöger, J.: Variability-based model transformation: formal foundation and application. Formal Aspects Comput. **30**(1), 133–162 (2018). https://doi.org/10.1007/s00165-017-0441-3

37. Strüber, D., Peldzsus, S., Jürjens, J.: Taming multi-variability of software product line transformations. In: Russo, A., Schürr, A. (eds.) FASE 2018. LNCS, vol. 10802, pp. 337–355. Springer, Cham (2018). https://doi.org/10.1007/978-3-319-89363-1_19

38. Strüber, D., Schulz, S.: A tool environment for managing families of model transformation rules. In: Echahed, R., Minas, M. (eds.) ICGT 2016. LNCS, vol. 9761, pp. 89–101. Springer, Cham (2016). https://doi.org/10.1007/978-3-319-40530-8_6

39. Taentzer, G., Salay, R., Strüber, D., Chechik, M.: Transformations of software product lines: A generalizing framework based on category theory. In: 20th ACM/IEEE International Conference on Model Driven Engineering Languages and Systems, MODELS 2017, Austin, TX, USA, 17–22 September 2017, pp. 101–111 (2017). https://doi.org/10.1109/MODELS.2017.22

40. Taentzer, G., Salay, R., Strüber, D., Chechik, M.: Transformation of software product lines. In: Tichy, M., Bodden, E., Kuhrmann, M., Wagner, S., Steghöfer, J.P. (eds.) Software Engineering und Software Management 2018, pp. 51–52. Gesellschaft für Informatik, Bonn (2018)

41. Wagelaar, D., Iovino, L., Ruscio, D.D., Pierantonio, A.: Translational semantics of a co-evolution specific language with the EMF transformation virtual machine.

In: Theory and Practice of Model Transformations - 5th International Conference, ICMT 2012, Proceedings, Prague, Czech Republic, 28–29 May 2012, pp. 192–207 (2012). https://doi.org/10.1007/978-3-642-30476-7_13

42. Westfechtel, B., Greiner, S.: From single- to multi-variant model transformations: trace-based propagation of variability annotations. In: Proceedings of the 21th ACM/IEEE International Conference on Model Driven Engineering Languages and Systems, MODELS 2018, Copenhagen, Denmark, 14–19 October 2018, pp. 46–56 (2018). https://doi.org/10.1145/3239372.3239414

43. Willink, E.D.: The micromapping model of computation; the foundation for optimized execution of eclipse qvtc/qvtr/umlx. In: Theory and Practice of Model Transformation - 10th International Conference, ICMT 2017, Held as Part of STAF 2017, Proceedings, Marburg, Germany, 17–18 July 2017, pp. 51–65 (2017). https://doi.org/10.1007/978-3-319-61473-1_4

Modeling and Analysis of Partitions on Functional Architectures Using EAST-ADL

Christoph Etzel[✉] and Bernhard Bauer

Institute of Computer Science, University of Augsburg, Augsburg, Germany
{christoph.etzel,bauer}@informatik.uni-augsburg.de

Abstract. The complexity in automotive systems engineering is increasing over the last decade. Autonomous driving and new comfort functions are some reasons for this growing complexity. With the introduction of multi-core processors in automotive system architectures, the shift from sequential to parallel thinking is more and more important in the different development phases. Based on the EAST-ADL, we present an approach to support the design process for distributed systems by using partitioning as an additional viewpoint on the architecture level. Therefore, we developed an extension to the EAST-ADL for partitioning and show automatic partitioning analysis on different architecture abstractions. These derived partitions can support system designers during the design process of functional architectures, by having a first insight how independent the functional components are structured from a data dependency viewpoint. This gives hints for the allocation of functions to hardware in later stages of the development process.

Keywords: System architecture · Model-driven systems engineering · Automotive systems engineering

1   Introduction

The trend of model-driven development to manage complexity during system development is still ongoing. Automotive systems are containing more and more hard- and software parts and forming huge distributed systems. In 2007 a BMW 7 contained 67 embedded devices providing 270 functions interacting with the user [19] and this further increased to 100 Electronic Control Units (ECUs) in premium vehicles around 2013 [14]. With the development of autonomous vehicles and its increased demand for additional sensors and data, the required computing power and the system complexity will further rise to assure a safe and comfort driving experience. Replacing single-core ECUs with multi-core systems

This work was partially funded within the project ARAMiS II by the German Federal Ministry for Education and Research with the funding ID 01IS16025. The responsibility for the content remains with the authors.

S. Hammoudi et al. (Eds.): MODELSWARD 2019, CCIS 1161, pp. 298–319, 2020.
https://doi.org/10.1007/978-3-030-37873-8_13

is a possible way to lower the system complexity in vehicles [1]. This is an intensive discussed topic and first vehicles using multi-core architectures are on the road [15]. To utilize these newly created systems including the embedded multi-core technique, a "parallel thinking" is required already from the start of the system development. Having a well-designed abstract system model during early design steps, helps deriving it further down towards the concrete system. Starting the design process at the system level includes many different models and stakeholders and there exists no golden standard of methods and frameworks [7]. In the automotive domain many projects use a bottom-up approach [15]. Such an approach has the high probability to not fully understand the big picture of the system and therefore detailed analysis of the whole system are hard to achieve.

Model-based approaches can provide customized views for the current development situation to the stakeholders. This supports achieving their engineering and optimization tasks, by focusing on the level of intention. Different abstraction levels, starting with a high level view in the early stage to a more detailed technical view in a later stage, is a common way to manage development complexity. The architecture description language EAST-ADL supports such an approach by providing on the one side a step-wise refinement and on the other side dealing with cross-cutting issues. Allover, EAST-ADL allows modelling of requirements, features, functional components, timing constraints, safety constraints and other engineering related information.

The focus of our work is to support system designers during their architectural design decisions. We support the propagated "parallel thinking" through analyzing and parallelization of the logical and component-based architectures to achieve partitions, based on data dependencies. The partitioning shall give the system designer a starting point how and how well parts of the architecture can be distributed, e.g., without stressing the bus system (communication overhead). Sets of components in a partition may be executed independently from components in other partitions. To get a better understanding of the partitions, key figures for partitions are calculated. The partitioning analysis support the system designer to choose a suitable hardware architecture for system functions. The current version of EAST-ADL supports functional composition modeling, but has no modeling notations to express partitions. We introduce an extension of the EAST-ADL to store information about partitions and present partitioning algorithms to compute such partitions from an architectural model.

This paper is an extended version of our previous published work at MODELSWARD 2019 [6]. In this version, we added an additional partitioning algorithm (KaFFPa) and used it to evaluate the Single Entry Region (SER) analysis. First, introduce EAST-ADL and the used partitioning algorithms to perform our analysis. In Sect. 3 we present our approach and tooling. This is followed (Sect. 4) by the extension of the EAST-ADL meta-model with elements to handle partitioning information on in the model. Section 5 shows how the algorithms are applied to different target abstraction levels to find partitions and which key figures can be calculated to get a better understanding of a partition. The approach is evaluated in a case study showing a brake-by-wire system example (Sect. 6). The paper completes with the conclusion and giving an outlook for further research.

2   Preliminaries

This chapter introduces existing languages, methods and algorithms used in this paper.

2.1   EAST-ADL

EAST-ADL stands for 'Electronics Architecture and Software Technology - Architecture Description Language' and is maintained by the EAST-ADL Association [5]. Its focus is on capturing engineering information for automotive electronic system development. It offers elements to capture requirements, features, functions, software & hardware components and communication in a standardized form. The system's implementation is not part of the EAST-ADL, but the established AUTomotive Open System ARchitecture (AUTOSAR) standard [2] is used. While AUTOSAR's most abstract concept is the software architecture, the EAST-ADL provides means to model the system architecture and capture essential engineering information on this stage [3].

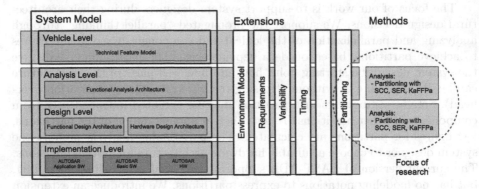

Fig. 1. EAST-ADL abstraction levels with the containing models and cross cutting extensions. On the right hand side the partitioning extension and methods provided in this research. [6] (Color figure online)

The current release of the EAST-ADL2 [4] describes four abstraction levels to model the vehicle in different levels of detail (see left hand side of Fig. 1). The **Vehicle Level** includes a Technical Feature Model of the electric and electronic system. It can be used as a software product line by using decomposition and variability to allow different feature configurations. The **Analysis Level** includes the Functional Analysis Architecture (FAA). On this level, the features of the Vehicle Level are realized by abstract functions. These functions are connected through devices (e.g., sensors or actuators) to the vehicle environment, defining the systems boundary. The **Design Level** includes the Functional Design Architecture (FDA) and the Hardware Design Architecture (HDA). The FDA realizes the abstract function of the FAA with an implementation-oriented aspect. This includes software, middleware and hardware abstraction. The HDA captures physical resources and their connections and is used to allocate functions from the FDA to hardware entities. The **Implementation Level** is the connection to the AUTOSAR system model. The EAST-ADL is aligned with AUTOSAR and elements of the Design Level can be mapped to AUTOSAR entities [20]. These alignment and mapping capabilities enable traceability through the models during the whole development process.

Beside these abstraction levels, EAST-ADL is extended by several cross-cutting concern extensions, spanning over the layers of abstraction. Figure 1 shows the abstraction levels with their models horizontal and the extensions (cross-cutting concerns) are vertically aligned over all levels. Examples for these extensions in are Environment, Requirements, Variability and Timing. In this paper, we present an additional extension called *Partitioning* and methods applicable using this extension. Our contributions are marked with a red circle in Fig. 1. Since the focus of our research is on the Functional Analysis Architecture (FAA) and the Functional Design Architecture (FDA) we provide a more detailed description of these two abstraction levels. Both architectures contain a component-based architecture model to capture the system information. The elements of the architectures are build up using a type/prototype concept similar to AUTOSAR. The basic elements are *FunctionTypes* and *FunctionPrototype*. A *FunctionType* is an abstract function component description and gets instantiated by one or more *FunctionPrototypes*. A *FunctionType* contains *FunctionPorts*, which can be connected together using *FunctionConnectors*. Hierarchical architectures are realized by the specializations of *FunctionType* on the Analysis and Design Level (*FunctionAnalysisType* and *FunctionDesignType*), which can own parts in form of *FunctionAnalysisPrototypes* respectively *FunctionDesignPrototypes*. *FunctionConnectors* linking owned prototypes are called assembly connection, while a connection between a port of the type itself and a prototype is called delegation connection.

Besides the FDA, the Design Level includes the Hardware Design Architecture (HDA) to model the hardware system. The HDA defines the connectivity, capabilities and basic safety characteristics of technical architectures, e.g., the execution units (ECUs) including their cores and the communication paths. This information can be expressed using the following elements from the EAST-ADL modeling language (again using type/prototype concept): *HardwareComponentType* is the basic element for the specializations *Node*, *Sensor*, *Actuator* and *ElectricalCompmonent*. It defines *HardwarePorts* and *HardwarePins* of the component and the embedded connections. An ECU is a *Node* element and its cores are contained *HardwareComponentPrototypes* of type *Node*. *HardwarePortConnectors* forming the bus system by connection ports and are capable to store information about the bus type and speed. *HardwarePorts* containing *HardwarePins* and these pins are connected using *HardwareConnectors*, forming the bus system.

Since every abstraction level defined by the EAST-ADL includes a complete model of the whole system, a full tracebility between the levels can be realized. This is supported by linking elements of different abstraction levels together using the *Realization* relationship. E.g., a function on the FAA is realized by a group of functions on the FDA. Using realization links, this can be documented for later development stages or analyzes.

The EAST-ADL abstraction levels can be seen as equivalents to the phases of a system developing life cycle. For example, the abstraction levels can be used/mapped to phases of the V-Modell XT [30] as follows: the Vehicle Level, including its feature models, is part of the systems requirements analysis; the Analysis and Design Level are used in the system analysis, system architecture and system design phase; the Implementation Level belongs to the software architecture phase. Another example is the ATESST2 project, which released a methodology guideline for the development with EAST-ADL2 [27]. It defines a top-down development process and we embed our partitioning analysis into it, by making suggestions at which point of the process the partitioning step should be performed.

2.2   Partitioning Algorithms

In this section, partitioning algorithms used in this paper are explained. The strongly connected components algorithm is a classical algorithm from graph theory, while the extended single entry region algorithm is a more recent publication dedicated to AUTOSAR systems. Karlsruhe Fast Flow Partitioner (KaF-PPa) algorithm is a state of the art multilevel graph partitioning algorithm.

Strongly Connected Components. Strongly connected components (SCCs) are highly interconnected nodes in a directed graph. Tarjan [26] presents definitions for strong connectivity in graphs and an algorithm for computing the strongly connected components. A (sub-)graph is called strongly connected if there exists a path between each pair of nodes. A partition is formed by the set of strongly connected components.

Feedback loops, which are a very common pattern in automotive control systems, would form such a strongly connected component. Therefore, we see potential in applying the SCC on EAST-ADL architectures of the Analysis and Design Level.

Potts et al. [18] applied the SCC algorithm on system of systems (SoS) to support architectural decision making.

Single Entry Region. The Single Entry Region (SER) analysis is a data dependency graph analysis for AUTOSAR system description models introduced by Kienberger et al. in [12] and further refined in [11,13]. It is based on work of [8,9,17,28]. The analysis tries to identify regions having a loose coupling to other parts of the system and therefore be somewhat isolated. A SER is described by the following three properties:

- The number of nodes is greater or equal to two.
- All input dependencies from nodes outside the SER are routed over a single "entry node".
- There is a path from the "entry node" to any other node inside the SER.

The SER analysis is performed on an AUTOSAR system description model, namely on the component-based architecture formed by *Runnable Entities* (AUTOSAR's atomic executable and schedulable units) and their data dependencies. From our point of view, the analysis can be used for every appropriate type of dependency in a graph. Since the components of an AUTOSAR system description model are derived from the FDA on EAST-ADL's Design Level and the FDA and FAA are component-based architectures with data dependencies, we adopt the SER analysis to EAST-ADL.

KaFFPa. KaFFPa (Karlsruhe Fast Flow Partitioner) is a multilevel graph partitioning approach [22]. In a first step, it contracts the initial graph to create smaller graphs and does a first partitioning of this contracted graph. Then the contraction is reverted at each level and a local improvement is done to optimize the partitions on the coarser levels. The algorithm partitions the graph into a predetermined number of partitions, often denoted as k. The graph may contain weighted nodes and/or edges to describe the workload of a node or the communication of an edge, for example.

The KaFFPa algorithm is embedded in the KaHIP (Karlsruhe High Quality Partitioning) framework, which is public available [24]. Since the algorithm is reported to have very promising results in partitioning [21] and is easy available by using the public framework, we chose it for our approach.

3   Our Approach

Our approach has the goal to support the system designer during his architectural design decisions in order to have an architectural model that is well suited for further fine-grained development. Partitioning, in our context, is the process of grouping the system under development (SUD) into different parts without changing its functional component-based architecture. It is not intended to provide concrete mappings of functional components to hardware elements. The approach provides additional views on the SUD, depending on which criteria the partitioning is performed. We identified the FAA on the Analysis Level and the FDA on the Design Level as targets for our partitioning.

By using the extension mechanism of the EAST-ADL, the EAST-ADL system model remains unchanged and is only extended with new elements. The new extension makes use of already available EAST-ADL modeling concepts to define its elements and use them for structuring system model elements. Figure 2 shows the extension called "Partitioning" and its meta-model elements to express partitions. Also elements to store additional information not yet available in the EAST-ADL meta model, but helpful for analyzing a SUD, are specified. Since

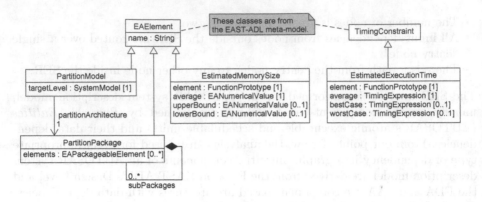

Fig. 2. The "Partitioning" meta-model extension. [6]

there are only references to elements in the system model, the FAA on the Analysis Level or the FDA on the Design Level remain unchanged.

A short example shows how this works: For example, on the Analysis Level, the SUD is described by the FAA using functional devices and analysis functions. The functional devices are the connection to the environment; using sensors to get data from the environment and actuators to interact with it. Typically, chains of *AnalysisFunctions* link sensors to actuators, by performing calculations on the sensors data and react accordingly through the actuators. The connections between the devices and functions are modeled by ports to provide and receive data, which are linked together with function connectors. This component based description of the architecture together with additional data defined in the extensions is used to determine partitions, which can be persisted with the proposed *Partitioning* extension.

Tooling

AutoAnalyze. The extension of EAST-ADL and the analyses are implemented in our tool AutoAnalyze. It is based on the Eclipse Modeling Framework[1], the Model Analysis Framework[2], EATOP[3] and Artop[4]. This allows us to load, edit and save models defined with the EAST-ADL meta-model by using the EAXML format.

KaHIP. KaHIP (Karlsruhe High Quality Partitioning) is a framework for doing graph partitioning with different algorithms [24]. It includes KaFFPa (Karlsruhe Fast Flow Partitioner), the multilevel graph partitioning algorithm we use

---

[1] Eclipse Modeling Framework (EMF) https://www.eclipse.org/modeling/emf/.

[2] Model Analysis Framework - Data-flow based model analysis (MAF) https://www.informatik.uni-augsburg.de/en/chairs/swt/ds/projects/mde/maf/.

[3] Eclipse EATOP Project https://www.eclipse.org/eatop/.

[4] AUTOSAR Tool Platform (Artop) https://www.artop.org/.

in this paper and several other algorithms. KaHIP uses the Metis file format as explained in the Metis 4.0 user guide [10,23]. AutoAnalyze is extended to export a graph in the Metis format, which then can be loaded into the KaHIP framework.

4 EAST-ADL Partitioning Extension

The focus of our approach is not limited to partition architectures on the different abstraction levels provided by EAST-ADL, but also to have a standardized way to retain and exchange the partition information. EAST-ADL structures the system model into different abstraction levels and it shall be possible to have multiple partition models per abstraction level. This is motivated by the idea that partitioning can be done with different goals to achieve different views on the model. These goals influence the selection and weight of properties going into the calculation, resulting in many possible partition views on the system. While the content of the architectures is diverse for every abstraction level, the meta-model elements shall be shared to support a common handling of partitioning in every use case. The newly introduced elements are derived from already specified elements in the EAST-ADL to be compatible with it. In the following definitions, most elements from the EAST-ADL meta-model can be identified by the prefix "EA", for example, *EAElement* and *EANumericalValue* are both from the EAST-ADL infrastructure package. The EAST-ADL meta-model contains some none prefixed elements, we will indicate if such an element is used. Besides having a good compatibility and extensibility using basic elements of the EAST-ADL, the partitioning extension fully benefits of already available concepts, e.g., connecting elements using EAST-ADL realization links to achieve a full traceability over the model.

The complete "Partitioning Extension" can be seen in Fig. 2. On the left hand side are the meta-model elements to capture partitions and on the right hand side are elements to support the analysis of partitions. The root of the new partitioning elements is *PartitionModel*, pointing to the architectural model which is partitioned. It is derived from *EAElement*, an abstract metaclass of the EAST-ADL meta-model, defining an identifiable and named element. The *EAElement* has some attributes omitted in the figure, for example, the UUID attribute, as a global unique identifier, an expressive name and a comment attribute for additional descriptions. The partition model contains two associations the *targetLevel* and *partitionArchitecture*. The *targetLevel* is used to link the partition model to the level it partitions the architecture; i.e., the *AnalysisLevel* or *DesignLevel* object which are of the EAST-ADL meta-model super type *SystemModel*. The association *partitionArchitecture* points to the root package of the partition architecture. Since the partitioning is done independently on every abstraction level, only elements that are part of the target level are allowed to be linked in the partition architecture and its nested packages.

Name. PartitionModel
Description. The *PartitionModel* is used to organize the partition architecture of an abstraction level.
Generalizations. EAElement
Attributes. No additional attributes.
Associations.
  targetLevel : SystemModel [1]
  partitionArchitecture : PartitionPackage [1]
Constraints. All (nested) referenced elements in the *partitionArchitecture* shall be part of the referenced *targetLevel*.
Semantics. *PartitionModel* is the representation of a nested set of partitions for a specific system abstraction level.

PartitionPackages are used to collect elements belonging to a partition, by using the *elements* association. The reason to define a new class *PartitionPackage* instead of using the already existing EAST-ADL meta-model element *EAPackage* is that an *EAPackage* uses a composition to aggregate the containing elements, while a *PartitionPackage* shall only provide an association to the elements in the architecture. Using the association a duplication of elements is avoided and changes to properties of elements in the architecture have not to be mirrored to the partition model. The *subPackages* association contains sub partitions and is realized using a composition. A *PartitionPackage* can contain multiple elements and packages to enable hierarchical partition architectures. To achieve a sound hierarchy, the association to elements in the target architecture shall be only once and as deep as possible in the *subPackages* structure.

Name. PartitionPackage
Description. The PartitionPackage is used to form partitions of elements.
Generalizations. EAElement
Attributes. No additional attributes.
Associations.
  elements : EAPackageableElement [0..*]
  subPackages : PartitionPackage [0..*] {comp.}
Constraints. No additional constraints
Semantics. *PartitionPackages* can be used to organize *EAPackageableElement* that form a partition. The packages can be structured hierarchically, where each level may contain variable number of *EAPackageableElements* and sub packages forming sub partitions.

The two elements *PartitionModel* and *PartitionPackage* enable a structural description of partitions. They link to elements in the architecture using associations and by this mechanism, no change of the architectures themselves is necessary.

  The EAST-ADL includes already multiple extensions for different purposes. The timing extension, for example, defines modeling elements to specify timing constraints and other timing related information to enable timing analysis.

Despite the existing extensions, there are still some elements missing from our point of view that would be helpful for analyzing partitions. To allow a more accurate partitioning of an architecture, two additional elements are defined, to store estimated values of memory footprints and execution time.

The element *EstimatedMemorySize* is used to capture the estimated memory footprint of a component. For example, this element can be used to balance partitions based on the memory size or to get an idea of the memory requirements of a partition. It has an association to an element in the system model and three values describing its estimated average memory size in bytes and optional upper/lower bound values to define a spectrum the memory size varies. The *element* and *average* associations are mandatory, otherwise no meaningful statement could be made.

Name. EstimatedMemorySize
Description. The estimated size of memory used by the function in bytes.
Generalizations. EAElement
Attributes. No additional attributes.
Associations.
> element : FunctionPrototype [1]
> average : EANumericalValue [1]
> upperBound : EANumericalValue [0..1]
> lowerBound : EANumericalValue [0..1]

Constraints. If set, the values shall comply to $lowerBound \leq average \leq upperBound$.
Semantics. The *EstimatedMemorySize* stores the estimated or measured average memory size in bytes and optional an upper/lower bound.

The EAST-ADL timing extension describes an execution time constraint specifying the upper and lower bound run-time of an event. We introduce an *EstimatedExecutionTime* element, storing estimated or measured average execution time of a function and optionally a best and worst case value. It makes use of the already defined elements *TimingConstraint* and *TimingExpression* in the EAST-ADL timing package. *TimingExpression* allows the specification of a time including a unit and a time base. The *EstimatedExecutionTime* element is derived from the element *TimingConstraint*. The average, best and worst case elements are derived from *TimingExpression*. The *element* and *average* associations are mandatory, otherwise no meaningful statement could be made. In a SUD all defined values have be in line with already defined execution time constraints.

Name. EstimatedExecutionTime
Description. The estimated execution time of the function.
Generalizations. TimingConstraint
Attributes. No additional attributes.
Associations.
> element : FunctionPrototype [1]
> average : TimingExpression [1]

bestCase : TimingExpression [0..1]
worstCase : TimingExpression [0..1]

Constraints. If set, the values shall comply to
$bestCase \leq average \leq worstCase$.

Semantics. The *EstimatedExecutionTime* stores the estimated or measured values of the average execution time and optional a best/worst case value.

5   Partitioning Analysis

In this section, we describe how the SCC, SER and KaFFPa algorithms are used to automatic search for partitions on the architectures of the Analysis and Design Level. Partitions are formed by sets of functional components and analysis is done independently on the Analysis and Design Level. Besides using an algorithm to compute sets of partitions, an engineer can manually model partitions or modify the generated partitions afterwards.

5.1   Parameters for the Analysis

The main focus on our analysis are on supporting the engineer in understanding the architecture from the data dependency viewpoint. In our use cases we identified additional kinds of relevant clustering parameters: communication between functions and resource usage of functions. The communication is closely related to the data dependencies, since the data has to be transferred between the functions. Therefore, the amount of data exchanged between functions and the coupling of those can be taken into account. On the resource side execution time, execution frequency and memory consumption are values of interest. Using the newly introduced meta-model elements and already available elements in the EAST-ADL three parameter to consider these viewpoints: Data Flow Weight, Function Computational Time Weight and Function Memory Weight.

Data Flow Weight. For the communication perspective we introduce a parameter to describe a weight for the data exchanged on a connection between two functions. The size of the transferred data can be calculated using the *EADatatype* specified for the connection and the repetition of the transfer, which can be derived of the function triggering (*FunctionTrigger*).

Function Computational Time Weight. This parameter combines our introduced *EstimatedExecutionTime* element to estimate the computing time in conjunction with function triggering to get an idea how a processor is utilized by a function.

Function Memory Weight. Using the newly specified *EstimatedMemorySize*, the memory footprint either of the binary or the resource usage during runtime including temporary memory can be calculated.

These parameters can either be used in partition search algorithms or to calculate key figures of a partition. E.g., partitions can be rated by their memory footprint summing up the Function Memory Weight of every component, or by their Function Computational Time Weight, if it is assumed that the set of functions in one partition is executed sequentially. These key figures are indicators for the system designer to judge about the architecture and possibly perform a refactoring.

5.2   EAST-ADL Analysis Level

The Analysis Level includes an abstract functional representation of the architecture captured in the FAA. This architecture is designed very early in the development process during the system analysis phase [27]. From a methodology point of view, the partitioning shall be placed in the development process after the task to specify the analysis function details. The result of partitioning analysis can then be used to further refine the architecture in an iterative way.

Before starting the analysis on the FAA, we have implemented multiple model pre-checks in our tool, such as if all directions of the ports and the binding to the function connectors are reasonable. For example, if two functions are connected via "IN" ports a warning is raised. The same applies to "OUT" ports. Additionally, it should be noted that a client-server connection in the model is interpreted as a bi-directional connection between the components.

SCC Analysis. The first analysis implements the strongly connected component search. The directed graph consists of the analysis function prototypes as the vertices and the function connectors as the directed edges between the vertices. Since the SCC algorithm analyzes paths between the vertices, only the communication between the functions is taken into account to form partitions.

The results of the strongly connected component search is transferred into a partitioning model, where a set of strongly connected functions forms a partition. For every detected set with more than one component a *PartitionPackage* is created referring to the containing functions. An example with three graphs can be seen in Fig. 3. The sets of strongly connected components enclosing more than one element are visualized with the same color. In the graph on the bottom of the figure is a single element "Prototype3" not colored (white background), since it forms a strongly connected set containing only itself and sets with just one element do not need a distinct color.

SER Analysis. Another implemented algorithm is the Single Entry Region (SER) analysis, which was developed for AUTOSAR system description models [13]. A brief general description can be found in Sect. 2.2. We adapted the algorithm to fit to the EAST-ADL Analysis Level. For this purpose, every *AnalysisFunctionPrototype* contained in the FAA represents a node. The dependencies between the nodes are formed by the function connectors between the prototypes. The dependency weights are calculated by using the introduced Data Flow Weight parameter and summing it up for every connection between a pair

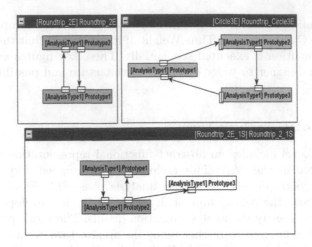

Fig. 3. Three examples of graphs with strongly connected components. [6] (Color figure online)

of nodes. The output of the algorithm are regions containing sets of *Analysis-FunctionPrototype*s. This gets transferred into the partitioning model such that every calculated region forms one partition.

KaFFPa. The KaHIP framework offers graph partitions algorithms with variable strategies. For our problem domain, we choose the KaFFPa algorithm and transfer the architectures to the METIS format, which serves as the input format. The *AnalysisFunctionPrototype*s of the FAA form the nodes of the graph. Optionally, the nodes can be weighted using the introduced parameters Function Computational Time Weight and Function Memory Weight introduced in Sect. 5.1. In contrast to the SCC and SER analyses, which use directed graphs, KaFFPa expects undirected graphs with only one edge between a pair of nodes. As a result, the direction information of the function connectors is ignored and every set of connections between two components becomes an edge. The weight of the edge is calculated by summing up the weights of all connections in this set. The weight itself is defined by the introduced Data Flow Weight (see Sect. 5.1), and therefore depends on the exchanged data type (to calculate the size of the data) and how often it is exchanged.

These information form a graph, which is complete to be partitioned using KaFFPa. To run KaFFPa, it needs a parameter k, defining the number of partitions the graph should be divided into. At present, this has to be provided by the engineer conducting the analysis.

The output of KaFFPa is a text file containing as many lines as nodes in the graph. Each of these lines represents a node and the value in the line represents the partition block ID. With the information how input graph was generated (knowing which *AnalysisFunctionPrototype* is which node), the output file is transferred into the partitioning model such that all nodes with the same block ID form one partition.

5.3   EAST-ADL Design Level

The Design Level includes an implementation-oriented functional model of the architecture captured in the FDA. Looking into the design process, the FDA is specified during the design phase in parallel with the HDA [27]. This newly introduced partitioning step shall be placed in the development process after the task to specify the design details, but before the allocation the functions to the HDA. The result of partitioning analysis can then be used to further refine the architecture in an iterative way and as an input artifact to the HDA allocation task.

Since the elements of the FDA are very similar to the ones used for the analysis of the FAA on the Analysis Level, the SCC, SER and KaFFPa analysis are analogous to the analyses explained into detail in Sect. 5.2. The graphs are formed by function prototypes and function connectors. Even the pre-checks and the handling of client-server connections are identical.

By using a partition model of our analysis an engineer can allocate functions to elements of the HDA. Elements grouped into one partition by these two algorithms are candidates to be allocated on one node, because they communicate with each other. Placing them on one node or closely connected nodes can reduce the communication overhead. The HDA can also serve as a starting point to determine the parameter k for KaFFPa. k should be at least as high as the number of cores which are available to run components of the architecture on. KaFFPa includes an option to use a mapping algorithm, which performing a mapping which is communication and topology aware [25]. In Sect. 7 we discuss shortly, why this is not reasonably applicable for our approach in the automotive domain.

6   Case Study - Brake-by-Wire System Example

To evaluate the proposed approach a case study on an example architecture is carried out, showing the results of the SER and KaFFPa in detail. Since our approach tries to help an engineer understanding his/her model, we compare the different partitioning results between algorithms not by minimum cut values or other parameters, for example, but doing an expert review. It should be noted, that the SCC analysis would not find partitions with more than one component in this particular example and is therefore not discussed further. Nevertheless, we picked this model, because it illustrates the SER analysis, the differences to KaFFPa and the partition transition during the development process very clearly.

The "Brake-by-Wire for four-wheel vehicles" model is originally from the EAST-ADL Association and published on their website[5].

---

[5] Brake-by-Wire System II (http://www.east-adl.info/Resources.html) (Accessed July 12, 2019).

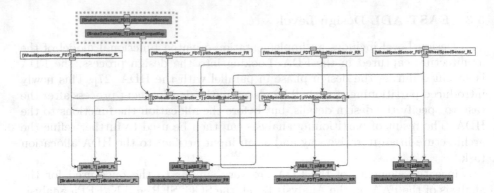

Fig. 4. Functional Analysis Architecture (FAA) of Brake-by-Wire Example. The colored elements are SER partitions. [6] (Color figure online)

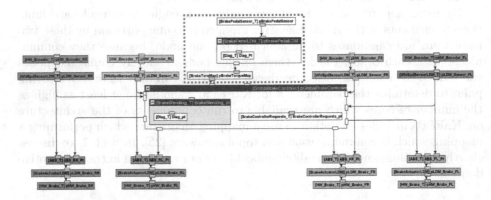

Fig. 5. Functional Design Architecture (FDA) of Brake-by-Wire Example. The colored elements are SER partitions. [6] (Color figure online)

The FAA on the Analysis Level consists of 16 components and 26 connections between these (see Fig. 4). The main function is a *pGlobalBrakeController*, which gets data from four wheel speed sensors, the vehicle speed and the requested brake force. The vehicle speed is calculated by the *pVehSpeedEstimator* getting data from the wheel speed sensors. The vehicle speed is provided to the *pGlobalBrakeController* and the four ABS controllers. The brake force is calculated by the *pBrakeTorqueMap* with data from the *pBrakePedalSensor*. The four ABS controllers are sending data to each brake actuator. The colored components in Fig. 4 are partitions computed by the SER analysis. The upper green colored partition consists of two components (*pBrakePedalSensor* and *pBrakeTorqueMap*), the lower four partitions are each formed by the ABS and the brake actuator of one wheel. All three properties that a partition created by SER analysis must fulfill are very well recognizable. The partitions have more than one element, all dependencies from outside into the partition pass through an entrance node and there is a path between every pair of nodes.

The SER analysis found five partitions and six single elements, so we set $k = 11$ for KaFFPa, since the six single elements are partitions of $size = 1$. Using this setting, we can compare the results of both algorithms. To understand the output of the analysis with KaFFPa, we give the numbering of the components as generated for the input graph: 1: *pBrakePedalSensor*, 2: *pBrakeTorqueMap*, 3: *pWheelSpeedSensor_FL*, 4: *pWheelSpeedSensor_FR*, 5: *pWheelSpeedSensor_RR*, 6: *pWheelSpeedSensor_RL*, 7: *pGlobalBrakeController*, 8: *pVehSpeedEstimator*, 9: *pABS_FL*, 10: *pBrakeActuator_FL*, 11: *pABS_FR*, 12: *pBrakeActuator_FR*, 13: *pABS_RR*, 14: *pBrakeActuator_RR*, 15: *pABS_RL*, 16: *pBrakeActuator_RL*. In Listing 1.1 the output of KaFFPa for the FAA can be seen. Each line represents a node from the input graph and contains the block ID of the node. Line 1 is the first node *pBrakePedalSensor*, associated with block/partition number 2. Line 2 *pBrakeTorqueMap*, block/partition number 3. ... It can be seen that the partitions on the bottom of Fig. 4, the components 9–16, are identical generated by KaFFPa. A difference comes up for *pWheelSpeedSensor_RL* and *pVehSpeedEstimator* (lines 6 and 8), which are packed together in one partitions (block ID 7). The SER analysis puts *pBrakePedalSensor* and *pBrakeTorqueMap* (lines 1 and 2) together, which is from viewpoint of an expert review the more natural choice. Other values for k did not lead to a better evaluation result in the expert review. In our evaluation the best results to help the engineer to get a better understanding of the FAA is the SER analysis.

The design architecture (see Fig. 5) is derived from the FAA. It contains 28 components and 27 connections (some components are for diagnoses, their connections to components outside the scope of this braking example have been omitted). For example, a wheel speed sensor from the functional analysis architecture is now more detailed by using two components. One is a hardware encoder providing the digital hardware signal and the other is a local device manager (LDM) encapsulating the hardware device specific parts. On the actuator side, a similar detailing is performed by using a LDM and a hardware function component for the realization. Two components for diagnose tasks are also embedded in the example. One is a diagnose component in the *pBrakePedalLDM* and the other one in the *pGlobalBrakeController*.

The partitions found using the SER algorithm are very similar to the ones on the analysis architecture. On the bottom, every ABS component together with a LDM and the actuator form a partition. Four new partitions are originated from the decomposition of the wheel speed sensors into hardware encoders and LDMs. A difference can be seen looking at the former partition of the *pBrakePedalSensor* and *pBrakeTorqueMap*, which is for a better recognition marked with a square of orange dots in both figures. Because a diagnose component (*Diag_Pt*), which provides data to other components not visible in this figure, is embedded in the *pBrakePedalLDM*, it is not marked as a potential partition on this level. An option to in- or excluding diagnose components in the analysis is part of our

Listing 1.1. Output partitioning FAA using KaFFPa with $k = 11$.

1	2
2	3
3	4
4	0
5	6
6	7
7	4
8	7
9	5
10	5
11	1
12	1
13	10
14	10
15	8
16	8

Listing 1.2. Output partitioning FDA using KaFFPa with $k = 10$.

1	7
2	7
3	1
4	0
5	0
6	9
7	9
8	6
9	6
10	2
11	2
12	1
13	0
14	4
15	4
16	9
17	8
18	8
19	6
20	5
21	5
22	2
23	3
24	3

Listing 1.3. Output partitioning FDA using KaFFPa with $k = 12$.

1	1
2	1
3	1
4	8
5	8
6	0
7	2
8	5
9	5
10	4
11	4
12	3
13	7
14	7
15	6
16	2
17	11
18	11
19	5
20	9
21	9
22	3
23	10
24	10

framework. Turning it off, the components *pBrakePedalSensor*, *pBrakePedal-LDM* and *pBrakeTorqueMap* get together in one partition. Since there is no flag in the EAST-ADL meta-model to identify diagnose components, we are using a naming schema (the prefix "*Diag_*") to recognize these components.

For KaFFPa we discuss two outputs with $k = 10$ (number of partitions and solo components in SER analysis excluding the diagnose components) and $k = 12$ (including diagnose components). The model was simplified for the paper and the expert review by just using *pBrakePedalLDM* and *pGlobal-BrakeController*, while not explicitly modeling the diagnose components and the *BrakeConrollerRequests_pt* for the KaFFPa input file. The lines to component mapping is as follows: 1: *pBrakePedalSensor*, 2: *pBrakePedalLDM*, 3: *pBrake-TorqueMap*, 4: *pHW_Encoder_RR*, 5: *pLDM_Sensor_RR*, 6: *pHW_Encoder_RL*, 7: *pLDM_Sensor_RL*, 8: *pHW_Encoder_FR*, 9: *pLDM_Sensor_FR*, 10: *pHW_-Encoder_FL*, 11: *pLDM_Sensor_FL*, 12: *GlobalBrakeController*, 13: *ABS_RR_Pt*, 14: *pLDM_Brake_RR*, 15: *pHW_Brake_RR*, 16: *ABS_RL_Pt*, 17: *pLDM_Brake_-RL*, 18: *pHW_Brake_RL*, 19: *ABS_FR_Pt*, 20: *pLDM_Brake_FR*, 21: *pHW_Brake_-FR*, 22: *ABS_FL_Pt*, 23: *pLDM_Brake_FL*, 24: *pHW_Brake_FL*.

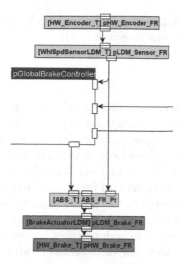

Fig. 6. Zoom into KaFFPa partitioning results ($k = 10$ and $k = 12$) of the FDA Brake-by-Wire Example.

In comparison to the SER analysis results, a noticeable difference in the KaFFPa results for $k = 10$ and $k = 12$ is that all encoder and sensor elements are in a partition together with the ABS component. Figure 6 shows an example of the partitions for the set of elements to control the front right brake. For Listing 1.2 these are the block IDs 6 and 5 and for Listing 1.3 the block IDs 5 and 9. This shows the difference to the SER characteristic, there all input edges have to be routed over a single entry node, while KaFFPa does partitioning on undirected graphs. From the expert review point of view, the SER results are more useful to get an understanding which groups of components may be executed independently whereas KaFFPa tries minimizing the cutting. An additional difference in the partitioning for $k = 10$ is that the components *pBrakePedalSensor*, *pBrakePedalLDM* and *pBrakeTorqueMap* do not form one partition. While the first two form a partition (block ID 7), the *pBrakeTorqueMap* is placed together with the *GlobalBrakeController* (block ID 1). While this may be an optimal choice from the algorithms perspective, it would not be the natural one of an engineer. We evaluated the KaFFPa output for values of k from [8,16], but did not find more useful sets for our approach.

In summary, the results of the SER are preferable for identifying independent parts from the data flow perspective, while the KaFFPa partitions optimize the data throughput. An open point is how to determine the value of k to get results, which help the engineer understanding the architecture. Since the technical architecture, which the systems is deployed on, is in most cases heterogeneous, k equals number of ECUs or cores may not be a useful selection.

Using the analysis results, an engineer can check if the transition from the analysis architecture to the design architecture is sound (e.g., having a closer look, why one partition is now missing) and link the partitioned elements to elements of the HDA. This allocation is supported by the key figures, which can be calculated for the partitions (see Sect. 5.1).

7   Related Work

Using the KaHIP framework, the KaFFPa offers an option to perform a process mapping communication and topology aware process mapping developed by [25]. It was designed to address the mapping problem on modern supercomputer systems and several assumptions have been made. The hardware topology is hierarchically organized and every hierarchy level is identical. For example, every node in the topology has the same number of processors and every processor the same number of cores. This also applies to the distance value of the communication links inside each hierarchy level, which is assumed to be identical. On the other hand, automotive technical system architectures are very heterogeneous, containing different bus systems (high/low data transfer rates, non-/deterministic, ...) and ECUs (high/low performance, different architectures, ...). In addition, there are timing and safety requirements that require certain properties of individual hardware elements and thus constrain the mapping. Considering the differences, the KaFFPa process mapping is not a useful option for our problem domain, specifically for the HDA allocation task.

Marinescu et al. [16] propose a modeling extension for EAST-ADL and model analysis with the focus on resource-usage. The analysis is applied on the FDA using a priced timed automata to predict resource usage and optimizing resource utilization. In contrast to our approach, theirs is focusing on resource usage and allocation, while ours is proposing a general extension to describe partitions and algorithms focusing on the analysis of data dependencies. A mapping of parts of our extension to theirs is possible, e.g., *EstimatedMemorySize* (ours) to *MemoryConstraint* (theirs). In the development process, their resource-usage analysis is placed after ours during the development of the Design Level elements.

Walker et al. [29] have developed a multi-objective optimization approach for EAST-ADL system architectures. Such an automation to rapidly explore architecture variants enables system designers to focus on the challenging parts. Their framework allows the connection of various analyses using an *Analysis Wrapper*. The analyses are performed independently and just provide their results to the optimization engine. This extension mechanism would make it possible to use our partitioning analysis in their framework. However, there has to be done further research how to derive and rate quantitative criteria for the optimizer from the partitioning models.

8   Conclusion and Further Research

In this paper, we presented an approach to support system designers during the development process by doing partitioning on functional architectures. Therefore, we proposed an extension to the EAST-ADL meta-model to capture partitions without the need to alter the architecture. Additionally two elements are added to the extension to extend the analysis with additional information concerning the memory consumption and executing time of functions. These elements can be used to calculate key figure values of the partitions to get a better understanding of them. We presented three algorithms (SCC, SER and KaFFPa) to perform an automated analysis for partitions on the architectures of the Analysis and Design Level (FAA and FDA). These analyses are independent of the partitioning extension, if no persistence of the partitions is needed to perform further analyses. Moreover, we applied the new approach to a small case study from the EAST-ADL consortium and specifically done an expert review to compare the SER and KaFFPa results with regard to our goals.

The results concerning our approach are very promising and in the next steps we will evaluate it with additional scenarios. The best working approach for getting a better understanding of the architecture and its potential for parallelization, seems to be the SER analysis. We will further refine the introduced analysis for partitioning of functional models on these levels of abstraction. We think the proposed approach is not limited to the EAST-ADL modeling language and can be transferred to similar concepts even outside the automotive domain. Examples for other languages are SysML[6] and AADL[7], both strongly influenced the EAST-ADL specification [3].

References

1. Arbeitskreis Multicore, BICCnet Innovationszirkel Embedded Systems: Relevanz eines Multicore-Ökosystems für künftige Embedded Systems: Positionspapier zur Bedeutung, Bestandsaufnahme und Potentialermittlung der Multicore-Technologie für den Industrie- und Forschungsstandort Deutschland (2011). https://www.bicc-net.de/workspace/uploads/subfeatures/downloads/positionspapier_multicore_oekosys-1323952449.pdf. Accessed 15 July 2019
2. AUTOSAR: AUTOSAR website (2019). https://www.autosar.org/. Accessed 15 July 2019
3. Blom, H., et al.: EAST-ADL: An architecture description language for automotive software-intensive systems in the light of recent use and research. Int. J. Syst. Dynam. Appl. (IJSDA) **5**(3), 1–20 (2016)
4. EAST-ADL Association: EAST-ADL Domain Model Specification. Version V2.1.12 (2013)
5. EAST-ADL Association: EAST-ADL website (2018). http://www.east-adl.info/. Accessed 15 July 2019
6. Etzel, C., Bauer., B.: Extending EAST-ADL for modeling and analysis of partitions on functional architectures. In: Proceedings of the 7th International Conference on Model-Driven Engineering and Software Development : MODEL-SWARD, INSTICC, vol. 1, pp. 169–178. SciTePress (2019). https://doi.org/10.5220/0007688301690178
7. Gajski, D.D., Abdi, S., Gerstlauer, A., Schirner, G.: Embedded System Design: Modeling, Synthesis and Verification. Springer, New York (2009)

---

[6] Issued by the OMG, http://www.omgsysml.org/.
[7] Issued by the SAE International, http://www.aadl.info/.

8. Gotz, M., Roser, S., Lautenbacher, F., Bauer, B.: Token analysis of graph-oriented process models. In: 13th Enterprise Distributed Object Computing Conference Workshops, pp. 15–24, September 2009. https://doi.org/10.1109/EDOCW.2009.5332020

9. Johnson, R., Pearson, D., Pingali, K.: Program structure tree: computing control regions in linear time. In: Proceedings of the ACM SIGPLAN Conference on Programming Language Design and Implementation (PLDI), pp. 171–185. ACM January 1994

10. Karypis, G., Kumar, V.: A fast and high quality multilevel scheme for partitioning irregular graphs. SIAM J. Sci. Comput. **20**(1), 359–392 (1998). https://doi.org/10.1137/S1064827595287997

11. Kienberger, J.: Systematic and Methodical Analysis, Validation and Parallelization of Embedded Automotive Software for Multiple-IEU Platforms. Ph.D. dissertation, University of Augsburg (2019)

12. Kienberger, J., Minnerup, P., Kuntz, S., Bauer, B.: Analysis and validation of AUTOSAR models. In: Proceedings of the 2nd International Conference on Model-Driven Engineering and Software Development, pp. 274–281. MODELSWARD 2014, SCITEPRESS - Science and Technology Publications, Lda, Portugal (2014). https://doi.org/10.5220/0004701002740281

13. Kienberger, J., Saad, C., Kuntz, S., Bauer, B.: Efficient parallelization of complex automotive systems. In: Balaji, P., Leung, K.C. (eds.) Proceedings of the 7th International Workshop on Programming Models and Applications for Multicores and Manycores, pp. 40–49. ACM (2016). https://doi.org/10.1145/2883404.2883421

14. Lukasiewycz, M., et al.: System architecture and software design for electric vehicles. In: IEEE (ed.) Design Automation Conference (DAC), 2013 50th ACM/EDAC/IEEE, pp. 1–6 (2013)

15. Macher, G., Höller, A., Armengaud, E., Kreiner, C.: Automotive embedded software: migration challenges to multi-core computing platforms. In: IEEE 13th International Conference on Industrial Informatics (INDIN), pp. 1386–1393, July 2015. https://doi.org/10.1109/INDIN.2015.7281937

16. Marinescu, R., Enoiu, E.P.: Extending EAST-ADL for modeling and analysis of system's resource-usage. In: IEEE 36th Annual Computer Software and Applications Conference Workshops, pp. 532–537, July 2012. https://doi.org/10.1109/COMPSACW.2012.99

17. Ottenstein, K.J., Ottenstein, L.M.: The program dependence graph in a software development environment. SIGPLAN Not. **19**(5), 177–184 (1984). https://doi.org/10.1145/390011.808263

18. Potts, M., Sartor, P., Johnson, A., Bullock, S.: Hidden structures: using graph theory to explore complex system of systems architectures. In: International Conference on Complex Systems Design & Management. CSD & M, December 2017

19. Pretschner, A., Broy, M., Kruger, I.H., Stauner, T.: Software engineering for automotive systems: a roadmap. In: Future of Software Engineering, pp. 55–71 (2007). https://doi.org/10.1109/FOSE.2007.22

20. Qureshi, T.N., Chen, D.J., Lönn, H., Törngren, M.: From EAST-ADL to AUTOSAR software architecture: a mapping scheme. In: Crnkovic, I., Gruhn, V., Book, M. (eds.) ECSA 2011. LNCS, vol. 6903, pp. 328–335. Springer, Heidelberg (2011). https://doi.org/10.1007/978-3-642-23798-0_35

21. Sanders, P., Schulz, C.: Engineering multilevel graph partitioning algorithms. CoRR abs/1012.0006 (2010), http://arxiv.org/abs/1012.0006

22. Sanders, P., Schulz, C.: High quality graph partitioning. In: Bader, D.A., Meyer-henke, H., Sanders, P., Wagner, D. (eds.) Graph Partitioning and Graph Clustering, 10th DIMACS Implementation Challenge Workshop, Georgia Institute of Technology, Proceedings, Contemporary Mathematics 2012, Atlanta, GA, USA, February 13–14, vol. 588, pp. 1–18. American Mathematical Society (2012). https://doi.org/10.1090/conm/588, http://www.ams.org/books/conm/588/11700

23. Sanders, P., Schulz, C.: Kahip v2.10 - karlsruhe high quality partitioning - user guide. CoRR abs/1311.1714 (2019), http://arxiv.org/abs/1311.1714

24. Schulz, C.: KaHIP website (2018). http://algo2.iti.kit.edu/kahip/. Accessed 15 July 2019

25. Schulz, C., Träff, J.L.: Better process mapping and sparse quadratic assignment. In: Iliopoulos, C.S., Pissis, S.P., Puglisi, S.J., Raman, R. (eds.) 16th International Symposium on Experimental Algorithms (SEA 2017). Leibniz International Proceedings in Informatics (LIPIcs), vol. 75, pp. 4:1–4:15. Schloss Dagstuhl-Leibniz-Zentrum fuer Informatik, Dagstuhl, Germany (2017). https://doi.org/10.4230/LIPIcs.SEA.2017.4, http://drops.dagstuhl.de/opus/volltexte/2017/7603

26. Tarjan, R.: Depth-first search and linear graph algorithms. SIAM J. Comput. 1(2), 146–160 (1972). https://doi.org/10.1137/0201010

27. The ATESST2 Consortium: Methodology guideline when using EAST-ADL2. Deliverable D5.1.1 V1.1 (2010)

28. Tip, F.: A survey of program slicing techniques. J. Program. Lang. 3, 121–189 (1995)

29. Walker, M., et al.: Automatic optimisation of system architectures using EAST-ADL. J. Syst. Softw. 86(10), 2467–2487 (2013). https://doi.org/10.1016/j.jss.2013.04.001

30. Weit, E.V.: V-Modell XT: Das deutsche Referenzmodell für Systementwicklungsprojekte Version 2.2 (2018)

A Framework for Flexible Program Evolution and Verification of Distributed Systems

Olaf Owe[1]([⊠]), Elahe Fazeldehkordi[1,3]([⊠]), and Jia-Chun Lin[1,2]([⊠])

[1] Department of Informatics, University of Oslo, Oslo, Norway
{olaf,elahefa,kellylin}@ifi.uio.no
[2] Department of Information Security and Communication Technology,
NTNU Gjøvik, Gjøvik, Norway
[3] Department of Technology Systems, University of Oslo, Oslo, Norway

Abstract. Program evolution may reveal bad design decisions, misunderstandings, erroneous code, or erroneous specifications, because problems made early in the design of a system may not be discovered until much later in the life-time of the system. Non-trivial changes of old code may be necessary. Flexibility in making such changes is essential, especially in a distributed setting where the system components are updated independently. In this setting re-verification is challenging. We consider flexibility with respect to what changes can be made as well as what can be efficiently reverified.

In this paper we propose a flexible framework for modeling and evolution of distributed systems. It supports unrestricted modifications in such systems, both in code and specifications, and with support of verification and re-verification. We consider on the setting of concurrent and object-oriented distributed programs, and introduce a core high-level modeling language supporting active objects. We allow *multiple inheritance* because it gives added flexibility during evolution, allowing a wider class of software changes. To avoid undesired effects of multiple inheritance, we apply a *healthy* binding strategy. We prove that the framework supports *Modification Independence* and *Hierarchy Independence*, which requires healthy binding. We demonstrate that our framework can deal with verification of software changes that are not possible in comparable frameworks.

Keywords: Program evolution · Program reasoning · Software changes · Multiple inheritance · Healthy binding · Active objects · Concurrency · Re-verification · Evolution flexibility · Modification independence · Hierarchy independence

1 Introduction

There is a need for program evolution in modern systems, because of long lifetime and changing environmental needs. System development is a complicated

© Springer Nature Switzerland AG 2020
S. Hammoudi et al. (Eds.): MODELSWARD 2019, CCIS 1161, pp. 320–349, 2020.
https://doi.org/10.1007/978-3-030-37873-8_14

process where many kinds of mistakes can be made over time, including bad design decisions, unclear specifications, misunderstandings, and erroneous code or specifications. Problems or bad design decisions made early may not be discovered until much later. Redesigning or modifying code made at an early stage in the software development may have severe implications on the overall system. Making changes may create new problems that are hard to foresee. These kinds of problems are severe in the setting of concurrent programs where the interaction of the different concurrent units is complicated, and also in the setting of object-oriented programs where inheritance, late binding, and code reuse cause dependencies between the classes. A systematic approach, in which the consequences of a software change can be formalized, would be advantageous. Formal methods could be helpful in supporting specification and analysis of program properties. However, formal methods are mainly oriented towards developing correct specifications and programs, rather than the process of redoing earlier decisions. It is therefore interesting to look at formal frameworks with support for unrestricted software changes, and such that the framework can detect possible consequences. A trivial approach to reasoning about program changes is to re-verify and reprove all results whenever a change has been made. However this is time-consuming and expensive, especially for large software systems. Ideally we would like to reprove as little as possible, without losing soundness. This is critical in the setting of distributed systems where the system components are updated independently.

We focus on the setting of distributed, concurrent, and object-oriented systems, and introduce a framework for modeling, development, and evolution of such systems – with support of verification. Our framework includes several life cycle aspects such as formal requirement specification, system design, executable modeling, analysis, and maintenance. This means that one can avoid translation between different formalisms. The framework allows unrestricted changes in code and requirements, and includes a theory for reverification of a changed system. We consider programming mechanisms for efficient, imperative style programming in a distributed setting, including non-blocking as well as blocking remote method calls, combined with suspension and scheduling control of processes inside an object. Our goal is *flexibility*, in the sense of support of unrestricted software changes and with simplicity of reverification, more specifically, that the framework makes it possible to do desired changes in software and requirements (*Modification Independence*, Theorem 1), and that the effect of changing one class is limited to that class and possibly subclasses inheriting from it (*Hierarchy Independence*, Theorem 2). We show that we can deal with software changes that are not possible to verify in comparable frameworks.

A framework that allows the simplest reverification of any given software change, has the best flexibility. Clearly incremental and modular reasoning are preferable, as well as limiting the number of modules to be affected by a given change. It is desirable to avoid reverification of the whole system when possible. Flexibility depends on the choice of programming and specification constructs, their semantics, as well as the reasoning system. In particular flexibility is affected by the choice of abstraction mechanisms. For instance, for shared variable concurrency it is hard to analyze the effect of software changes, even with an advanced reasoning framework. And synchronization by signaling is notoriously hard to reason about. In the setting of behavioral subtyping, a change in a subclass may violate superclasses requirements, thereby limiting flexibility.

Flexibility demands programming languages with a compositional semantics and compositional reasoning frameworks. Compositional reasoning of classes is supported by several approaches. Our framework is based on a programming paradigm with compositional semantics, *cooperative scheduling* to support object-local synchronization control, using *interface abstraction* to reduce dependencies between classes, and the use of *communication histories* to enable compositional specification and reasoning.

In the presence of class inheritance, modularity of each subclass is advantageous, as cross-class dependencies hinder flexibility. The strong dependencies of behavioral subtyping can be reduced with the notion of *lazy behavioral subtyping* [8,9]; however, reasoning requirements to local calls in a superclass are imposed on subclasses, which limits flexibility. A framework for evolution based on this approach is given in [11].

We observe that changing a class C in the middle of a class hierarchy may in general affect existing subclasses as well as superclasses. Clearly code inherited from C in subclasses could lead to inconsistencies, since C is changed. And requirements imposed on C from superclasses may also lead to inconsistencies, something which may in general be remediated by changes in these superclasses, thereby affecting other subclasses of these superclasses as well. This makes reasoning about changes of classes difficult. However, the effect on superclasses depends on the semantics of class inheritance. Therefore the choice of class inheritance semantics is essential, in particular when it comes to inheritance of requirements. If a class is changed, it is undesirable that its superclasses also need to be modified, as this will destroy flexibility. This is the case in approaches where requirements are pushed from superclasses to subclasses, as in the case of behavioral subtyping.

In order to avoid this inherent flexibility limitation, we build on an approach with *separation of the reuse of code from the reuse of specifications* to allow unrestricted reuse of code and specifications. In particular we build on the approach of *behavioral interface subtyping* [20] where each class is only required to satisfy its own interface specifications, and any invariant or other local specifications given in the class. This means that a method redefined in a subclass is allowed to break the requirements of the superclass. This opens up for more liberal modifications than earlier work based on lazy behavioral subtyping [8,9]. As no superclass requirements are imposed on a subclass, this allows full control of the inheritance of code and of requirements when a subclass is defined, and when it is modified. In this way we may avoid inconsistent specifications due to inheritance. In our approach we can avoid inconsistencies due to superclass requirements, simply by controlling which requirements to inherit.

The notion of multiple inheritance allows adjustments in the inheritance hierarchy in the middle without removing existing inheritance relationships, simply by adding superclasses (and superinterfaces) as needed. This gives added flexibility during evolution, while allowing backwards compatibility. However, multiple inheritance has been criticized for too much flexibility and ambiguity issues, as exemplified in the diamond problem. We therefore add syntax for resolving ambiguities statically by using class names to limit the binding, and insisting on the healthiness condition suggested in [9], which implies that a local call appearing in a class C may only bind to a class below or above C, and not to a class in a different branch than that of C. Thus program changes in other branches than C will not affect the binding of such calls. The addition of superclasses during program evolution makes it possible to adjust the inheritance hierarchy and to reuse code from added superclasses. For instance, a service-oriented system defined by a class S defining online purchases of tickets of some kind may be extended with functionality for subscription to newsletters (of the relevant kind) and such that newsletters are sent to the subscribing customers. This extension can be done by adding the subscription class as an additional subclass of S and adding the relevant subscription interface as an interfaces of S. Without support of multiple inheritance this extension would not be possible when S already has a subclass from before.

Our framework allows unrestricted changes of code and specifications (assuming type correctness). This means that one may write combinations of code and specifications that are inconsistent, for instance when a class does not satisfy the requirements of its interface(s). The framework will detect such inconsistencies so that they may be resolved, by changing code and/or specifications. In order to determine the consequences of changes in a (super)class, the framework needs to keep track of dependencies of local calls. We show that our framework can deal with software changes that are not possible to verify in comparable frameworks, and show how to reason within a hierarchy where some classes are verified and others not. We demonstrate our framework by examples.

Our approach is modular in the sense that the consistency of a class is determined by looking at the class itself, its interface(s), and reused code from superclasses. In order to analyze a software modification, one must first determine the affected code, in particular subclasses, and for each such subclass one must reverify the affected parts (after redesign of any inconsistent parts). Incremental reasoning is achieved by not letting a class impose restrictions on its subclasses. The present work extends the framework of [22] by adding multiple inheritance. As argued, multiple inheritance provides significant improvements in flexibility and simplicity during evolution since it enables added functionality just by adding superclasses and interface support in the middle of a class hierarchy, where needed. Thus multiple inheritance can be more useful in the program evolution phase than in the original program design phase.

Outline. Section 2 gives the programming setting for our framework, and Sect. 3 gives a summary of history-based specification and reasoning, including an example. Section 4 describes the proof obligations generated by our framework, simplifying [21]. In Sect. 5, we show how the framework is extended to deal with software changes. Finally, we discuss related work (Sect. 6) and give a conclusion (Sect. 7).

2 Language Setting

Our setting is distributed systems, and we focus on asynchronously communicating objects, so-called *active objects*, supporting blocking and non-blocking remote calls, without support of remote field access. In this setting, verification of a system of concurrent objects can be done compositionally, verifying each class separately, letting the specification of each class and interface refer to its local history [21]. The local history of an object reflects the time sequence of communication events such as method calls and returns, involving the object. Each class can be verified in a sequential manner, and a compositional rule states that a global invariant about the global history can be obtained by conjunction of the local invariants on local histories together with a wellformedness predicate relating the local histories to the global history.

We consider *multiple inheritance*, because this gives the freedom to extend the inheritance hierarchy during evolution, which greatly adds to the flexibility of changing programs. A class can then inherit from several superclasses while removing/adding/redefining method definitions, method specifications and invariants. As customary, we require a non-cyclic inheritance graph. And fields w may be added (an initial value r may be given, otherwise the default value of the type is used). Class parameters are concatenated, and so are fields and initialization code. In case of a diamond-shaped inheritance, where the top superclass is inherited through several superclasses, the top superclass is inherited only once. This is achieved by the binding strategy. Method names (and field and class parameter names) can be qualified by a class name so that the occurrence is unique in the given class. This provides fine-grained control of the inherited names. For local calls we may use a class name to make the name unique, and similarly for fields and class parameters. Dot-notation as in $o.n(\ldots)$ and *this* $C.n(\ldots)$ is reserved for late-bound method calls, while the colon notation $C : n(\ldots)$ is reserved for static local method calls. If a field w is ambiguous due to multiple inheritance, we use the syntax $C:w$ for a field as seen in a superclass C. We insist on *healthy binding*, which means that an internal call made by a method defined in class C must bind to a class hereditarily related to C (as defined below).

We consider a core high-level imperative modeling language, given in Fig. 1, inspired by the concurrency model of Creol [15] – extended to multiple inheritance. The language is executable with an interpreter in Rewriting logic/-Maude [5]. The language is similar to that of [22], which considered only single inheritance. A program consists of a number of interfaces and classes. A class may implement a number of interfaces and inherit a number of (super)classes. The reflexive and transitive extension of the subclass relation is denoted $\le$. If $A \le B$, we say that A *is below* B, and B *is above* A; and we say that A and B are

$$
\begin{array}{lll}
Pr & ::= [In^*\ Cl]^+ & \text{program} \\
In & ::= \textbf{interface}\ F[\textbf{extends}\ F^+]^?\{S^*\ I^*\} & \text{interface declaration} \\
Cl & ::= \textbf{class}\ C\,[([T\,cp]^+)]^?\,[\textbf{implements}\ F^+]^? & \text{class definition} \\
   & \quad [\textbf{inherits}\ [C(\bar{e})]^+]^?\,[\textbf{removing}\ m^+]^? & \text{inheritance mechanisms} \\
   & \quad \{[T\,w\,[:=r]^?]^*\ s^?\ M^*\ S^*\ I^*\} & \text{class body} \\
M & ::= T\ m([T\,x]^*)\ B\ P^* & \text{method definition} \\
S & ::= T\ m([T\,x]^*)\ P^* & \text{method signature} \\
B & ::= \{[[T\,x\,[:=r]^?]^+;]^?\,[s;]^?\ \textbf{return}\ r\} & \text{method body} \\
T & ::= F\ |\ \mathsf{Any}\ |\ \mathsf{Void}\ |\ \mathsf{Bool}\ |\ \mathsf{String}\ |\ \mathsf{Int}\ |\ \mathsf{Nat}\ |\ \ldots & \text{types} \\
v & ::= x\ |\ w & \text{variables (local or field)} \\
e & ::= \mathsf{null}\ |\ \mathsf{this}\ |\ \mathsf{caller}\ |\ v\ |\ cp\ |\ f(\bar{e})\ |\ (e) & \text{pure expressions} \\
r & ::= e\ |\ \textbf{new}\ C(\bar{e})\ |\ e.m(\bar{e})\ |\ \mathsf{this}\ C.m(\bar{e})\ |\ [C]^?:m(\bar{e}) & \text{right-hand-side/call/new} \\
s & ::= \textbf{skip}\ |\ [v:=]^?r\ |\ s;s & \text{basic statements} \\
  & \quad |\ \textbf{await}\ v:=e.m(\bar{e})\ |\ \textbf{await}\ e & \text{suspending statements} \\
  & \quad |\ \textbf{if}\ e\ \textbf{then}\ s\,[\textbf{else}\ s]^?\ \textbf{fi} & \text{if statement} \\
P & ::= [\,[\,A,A\,]\,]^+\,[\textbf{where}\ A^+]^? & \text{pre-/postcondition pairs} \\
I & ::= \textbf{inv}\ A^+\,[\textbf{where}\ A^+]^? & \text{invariant specification}
\end{array}
$$

Fig. 1. Language syntax. Specification elements are written in blue. F denotes an interface name, C a class name, m a method name, cp a formal class parameter, w a field, x a method parameter or local variable. We use [ ] as meta parentheses and superscripts $*$, $+$, and ? for repetition, non-empty repetition, and optional parts, respectively. Expressions e are side-effect free, and $\bar{e}$ denotes a (possibly empty) expression list. Assertions A are first order Boolean expressions and may refer to the local communication history $\mathbf{h}$. A **where** clause defines auxiliary functions used for specification purposes. Other statements, such as while loops, can be added. (Color figure online)

hereditarily related if either A is below B or A is above B. Class instances represent concurrent and active objects. Local data structures are defined by (build-in or user-defined) data types. An interface can extend other (super)interfaces and add declarations of methods, behavioral constraints, and invariants.

A variable referring to an object is typed by an interface, not by a class. A variable declared of interface F is called an F variable. Through type checking the language guarantees that for an F variable, the object referred to by the variable at run-time implements F. This is called the *interface substitution principle* [15, 17, 23]. We distinguish between *public methods*, those exported through an interface of the class, and *private methods*, those that are not exported through any interface of the class. Note that interface abstraction defines the publicness, rather than keywords such as private and public. Thus a public method in a class may be private in a subclass (and vice versa).

We allow remote calls of public methods with the syntax $v := o.m(\bar{e})$ where $\bar{e}$ the list of actual parameters and o is the callee. The value resulting from the call is assigned to the variable v. (The assignment part may be omitted if this value is not needed). A remote call $v := o.m(\bar{e})$ is type correct if the interface of o supports a method m such that the type of the actual parameters $\bar{e}$ is a subtype of the formal parameters of m and the output type of m is a subtype of the type of v. Since verification is done after type checking, we assume type correct programs, and assume that a class does not offer two declarations of the same method name. (If needed we could index the method name by the input and output type in order to make them distinct).

We allow both late-bound and static-bound local method calls, syntactically indicated by dot-notation and colon-notation, respectively. Local calls have the syntax $v := this.m(\bar{e})$ and $v := this\ C.m(\bar{e})$ (where C limits the binding of m) for late-bound calls, or $v := C:m(\bar{e})$ for static-bound calls, where this refers to the current object. We let this have the enclosing class as its type. Public methods are required to maintain the class invariant. Private methods may only be called locally, and may be called in states violating the invariant. A static local call $: m(...)$ binds to the method m defined in the enclosing class C, if any, and otherwise to the closest inherited m, using a depth-first, then left-first, traversal of the superclasses of C. If neither C nor its superclasses has a method m, the call is statically illegal. The static local call $B : m(...)$ (for $C \leq B$) binds to the method m defined in class B or inherited by B, as defined for a local call $: m(...)$ appearing in class B. The class qualification (B) enables the programmer to select which version of a redefined method is needed. A late-bound local call $this\ B.m(...)$ is legal if $B : m(...)$ is legal and binds to the class closest to that of the executing object, as explained in detail in Sect. 3.2. The local call $this\ C.m(...)$ when occurring in class C, may be abbreviated to $this.m(...)$. Note that all legal calls will have a binding. Type checking ensures that there exists a binding, following [17].

In order to allow non-blocking calls, the language offers a suspension mechanism, programmed by **await** statements. An object may perform at most one process at a given time, and suspended processes are placed on a process queue local to the object. When the active process is suspended or completed (by a **return** statement), an enabled process from the process queue may be resumed. We consider conditional suspension (by means of a Boolean expression) and call-related suspension, suspending while the return value from a remote call has not arrived. The call **await** $v := o.m(\bar{e})$ suspends the current process and places the remaining part of the process in the queue, and it is enabled when the result from the call has arrived to the object. In the meantime the object may execute enables processes or handle incoming calls. Note that the callee o may be this, in which case the call will be done by the object. However, we may not suspend on a local call to a private method (since the syntax **await** $v := C : m(\bar{e})$ is not part of the language) as this would complicate the class invariant reasoning, as explained below.

The behavior of methods may be specified by pre/post specifications. This is needed for reasoning about local calls, for which the invariant may be violated, and is in particular useful for private methods, and other locally called methods. Multiple pre/post specifications of each method are allowed, and a class may implement multiple interfaces. A class without an **implements** list will implement the empty interface Any, which is the superinterface of all interfaces.

When an interface **extends** another (super)interface, all declarations and specifications are inherited. When a class **inherits** another class (the superclass), all code and specifications are inherited unless redefined: A pre/post pair (P) is inherited unless another is stated, an invariant (I) is inherited unless another is stated, the initialization code (s) is inherited unless another is stated, and a method body (B) is inherited unless the method is redefined or removed. Likewise, the implementation clause of the superclass is inherited unless a new implementation clause is provided, in which case the superclass implementation clause is not inherited.

The syntax **removing** $m_1, m_2....$ expresses that the listed methods should not be inherited, thereby defining "negative" inheritance. By type checking it must be ensured that public methods are not removed and that the remaining methods in C (including inherited ones) do not (directly or indirectly) lead to a call on a removed method. The purpose of a removal is to make a semantically simpler subclass, where irrelevant or problematic code is eliminated. In particular this can be used to make verification easier, and even avoid verification problems for instance when an invariant is redefined. Removal of fields will mainly be a typing issue. For simplicity, we assume read-only access to method and class parameters.

Apart from standard statements, we have included multiple inheritance, both static and late-bound calls, as well as cooperative scheduling and suspension allowing non-blocking calls, something which is useful in a distributed concurrent setting. Recursive calls are allowed, and while statements can easily be added.

3 History-Based Specification

The abstract state of an object is captured by the time sequence of communication events that have occurred so far involving the object. In a given state this sequence is finite. Thus finite communication sequences suffice for safety reasoning, called *histories*. Interface, class, and system specifications are expressed by means of histories. *Global histories* capture all communication events in a distributed system (or subsystem), and *local histories* capture all communication events seen from a given object. The local history **h** of an object o is part of the global history H, and these are related by the equation $\mathbf{h} = H/o$ where H/o denotes the projection of the global history H to all communication events involving o as either the sender or receiver.

The invariant of an interface F may refer to the local history **h** and this, but not fields since these are not visible at the interface level. When seen from another class or interface with a larger alphabet, the F invariant must hold on the alphabet of F. The invariant of a class C may refer to fields, the local history **h**, class parameters, and this. This invariant must be maintained by each public method of the class (possibly inherited), and a class must satisfy each implemented interface using projection on the history to reflect the subset of methods visible through the interface. A method specification may in addition refer to the formal parameters (including the caller) and logical variables (primed variables), and a postcondition may talk about the result (return). When seen from another class with a larger alphabet, a C invariant must hold on the alphabet of C.

The local history **h** of a class/interface is the time sequence of communications events seen by this object, considering the following kinds of events:

- a method call made by this object, denoted this $\rightarrow o.m(\bar{e})$
- a method call received by this object, denoted $o \twoheadrightarrow$ this.$m(\bar{e})$ (for m in the class)
- a method return made by this object, denoted $o \leftarrow$ this.$m(\bar{e}; e)$ (for m in the class)
- a method return received by this object, denoted this $\twoheadleftarrow o.m(\bar{e}; e)$, as well as
- a creation event made by this object, denoted this $\rightarrow o.$ **new** $C(\bar{e})$

where o represents the other part in the communication. In practice, specifications using histories will often be concerned about method completions, i.e., $\leftarrow$ and $\twoheadleftarrow$ events, and possibly creation events, since these capture the essential input/output relations. (This is the case for our examples.) For a given method call, the $\leftarrow$ event precedes the $\twoheadleftarrow$ event, which is formalized by a wellformedness predicate (wf) below.

Sequence Notation: A sequence is either *empty* or of the form $q; x$ where q is a sequence and x an element. The notation q/s denotes the projection of q restricted to elements in the set s, $q \leq q'$ denotes that q is a prefix (head subsequence) of q', x **before** x' **in** q denotes that x appears before any occurrence of x' in q, i.e., $length(q'/x) \leq length(q'/x')$ for any prefix q' of q. For a global history H, there must be a meaningful ordering of the events, i.e., the history must be *wellformed*, defining $wf(H)$ by the conjunction of:

$$(o \rightarrow o'.m(\bar{e})) \text{ } \textbf{before} \text{ } (o \twoheadrightarrow o'.m(\bar{e})) \text{ } \textbf{in} \text{ } H$$
$$(o \rightarrow o'.m(\bar{e})) \text{ } \textbf{before} \text{ } (o \leftarrow o'.m(\bar{e}; e)) \text{ } \textbf{in} \text{ } H$$
$$(o \leftarrow o'.m(\bar{e}; e)) \text{ } \textbf{before} \text{ } (o \twoheadleftarrow o'.m(\bar{e}; e)) \text{ } \textbf{in} \text{ } H$$
$$(o' \rightarrow o.\textbf{new}\,C(\bar{e})) \, \textbf{before} \, (o \rightarrow o''.m(\bar{e}')) \, \textbf{in} \, H$$
$$(o' \rightarrow o.\textbf{new}\,C(\bar{e})) \, \textbf{before} \, (o'' \rightarrow o.m(\bar{e}')) \, \textbf{in} \, H$$

expressing that messages are sent before they are received, that method invocation must precede method return, and that a creation event of o must precede other o events. The conjunction of these properties (universally quantified) expresses the wellformedness predicate, used in the compositional rule for global reasoning. The rule for object composition essentially says that the global invariant is the conjunction of the wellformedness predicate and all object interface invariants, each referring to its own alphabet. Since the alphabets of the objects are by definition disjoint, the wellformedness predicate is needed to connect the different object invariants.

We let **h**$/F$ denote the projection of a local history **h** to the events visible through F, i.e., events of the form this $\rightarrow o.$ **new** $C(\bar{e})$, this $\rightarrow o.m(\bar{e})$, and this $\twoheadleftarrow o.m(\bar{e}; e)$, as well as events of the form $o \twoheadrightarrow$ this.$m(\bar{e})$ and $o \leftarrow$ this.$m(\bar{e}; e)$ for m offered by F. The same notation applies to classes C, projecting to this $\rightarrow$

and this $\leftarrow$ events as well as $\rightarrow$ this.m and $\leftarrow$ this.m for m defined or inherited in the class. An invariant $I(\mathbf{h})$ of an interface F is understood as $I(\mathbf{h}/F)$ in a subinterface or class. We therefore define $I_F(\mathbf{h})$ as $I(\mathbf{h}/F)$, and similarly for classes, defining $I_C(\mathbf{h}) \triangleq I(\mathbf{h}/C)$.

In general history-based invariant specification is more expressive than pre-/post conditions since a pre/post pair (P, Q) of a method m with parameters $\overline{x}$ can be formulated as the invariant (caller $\leftarrow$ this.$m(\overline{x};$ return)) $\in h \wedge P \Rightarrow Q$ where P and Q may refer to this, caller, and $\overline{x}$, and Q also to return, and $\mathbf{h}$. For instance, one may express that the return event of a method *hire* implies that the object has received the return of a method *check budget* with OK as result. However, a specification expressible as a pre/post specification can be simpler to read and write than the corresponding invariant.

3.1 A Bank Example

Figure 2 shows a minimalistic example defining a class BANK and a subclass BANKPLUS, as well as related interfaces and a possible CLIENT class. The example is taken from [22]. The code illustrates suspension, non-blocking and blocking calls, static and late-bound local calls. Interface and type names are capitalized while class names are written in upper case letters. The keyword **inv** identifies invariants and the keyword **where** identifies auxiliary function definitions. In assertions, **inv** refers to the current invariant, while C : **inv** refers to the invariant of class C.

Interface Bank states that the balance (as returned by bal) is the sum of amounts deposited (by add) or withdrawn (by sub) from the bank account, ignoring unsuccessful add and sub calls. In addition it states that add calls always succeed. Interface PerfectBank extends Bank by stating that also sub calls succeed, while interface BankPlus extends Bank by stating that the balance is always nonnegative. Interface Client (here omitted) includes methods salary (for receiving salary) and bill (for paying a bill).

The specifications of interface Bank and class CLIENT illustrate history-based specification, with inductive definitions of sum and allpaid. Functions are defined by a set of equations. The left hand sides can be seen as patterns, using underscore (_) to match any expression and letting ***others*** match any other case not covered by the other left hand sides. The auxiliary function *sum* calculates the balance from the local history. Note that only method-return events are used in the specification as other kinds of events are covered by the ***others*** equations. This is a typical situation for objects with "reactive" behavior as illustrated here.

The subclass BANKPLUS inherits the pre/post specifications of bal and add from BANK, but not the ones for upd and sub, which are redefined and therefore not inherited. In fact, the subclass violates the pre/post specifications for upd and sub in BANK. BANKPLUS does not support the BANK interface PerfectBank. Therefore the **implements** clause is redefined and not inherited. The await statement in class CLIENT allows the client to be responsive to salary reception calls and bill payment calls in case the *sub* call takes much time. However, it is

```
interface Bank {
  Bool sub(Nat x)
  Bool add(Nat x) [true, return= true]
  Int bal() [true, return= sum(h)]
  where sum(empty) = 0,
        sum(h; (_←this.add(x;true))) = sum(h)+x,
        sum(h; (_←this.sub(x;true))) = sum(h)−x,
        sum(h; others) = sum(h) }

interface PerfectBank extends Bank {
  Bool sub(Nat x) [true, return= true] }

interface BankPlus extends Bank {
  inv sum(h)>=0 }


class BANK implements PerfectBank {
  Int bal:=0; -- a field defining the balance
  Bool upd(Int x) {bal:=bal+x; return true} [true, return= true]
      [inv, bal=sum(h)+x and return=true]
  Bool add(Nat x) {return this.upd(x)} [true, return= true]
  Bool sub(Nat x) {return this.upd(−x)} [true, return= true]
  Int bal() {return bal} [true, return=bal]
  inv bal=sum(h) }

class BANKPLUS implements BankPlus inherits BANK {
  Bool upd(Int x) {Bool ok:=(bal+x>=0);
    if ok then ok:=BANK:upd(x) fi; return ok}
      [inv, bal>=0 and bal=sum(h)+if return then x else 0]
      [b'=bal, return=(b'+x>= 0)]
  Bool sub(Nat x) [b'=bal, return=(b'>= x)]
  inv BANK:inv and bal >=0 }

class CLIENT implements Client {
  Seq[String] paid; -- a field keeping track of paid bills
  Bank acc:= new BANK; -- the banc account of the client
  Bool salary(Nat x) {return acc.add(x)}
  Bool bill(String kid, Nat x, Bank y) { Bool ok:=false;
    if kid ∉ paid then await ok:=acc.sub(x);
     if ok then y.add(x); paid:=(paid;kid) fi
    fi; return ok}
  inv paid=allpaid(h) --- paid corresponds to successful bill payments
  where allpaid(empty) = empty,
        allpaid(h; _←this.bill(k,x,y;true))=(allpaid(h);k),
        allpaid(h; others)=allpaid(h) }
```

Fig. 2. A bank example with a client class [22].

then possible that two bills with the same kid are both paid. This would not be possible if the *sub* call is made as a blocking call.

In this example, the subclass does not obey the requirements imposed by behavioral subtyping, nor by lazy behavioral subtyping. The redefinition of upd in BANKPLUS does not satisfy the BANK postcondition of upd, and therefore the verification of the redefined upd will not succeed when using the framework of lazy behavioral subtyping (since the BANK postcondition of upd is needed for the local upd calls in the verification of BANK and therefore pushed to subclasses). In our framework, the BANK postcondition of upd is not imposed on the subclass, and the example can be verified without problems.

```
class BANK2 implements PerfectBank, BankPlus inherits BANKPLUS {
  Bool upd(Int x)
    {await bal+x>=0; bal:=bal+x; return true}
    [inv, bal=sum(h)+x and bal>=0 and return]
  Bool sub(Nat x) [true, return= true] }
```

Fig. 3. A possible subclass of class BANKPLUS [22].

Figure 3 shows a subclass of BANKPLUS that could be meaningful in a distributed setting. A transaction is delayed as long as the balance is insufficient. This is done by means of an await statement, which suspends the sub activation, but does not block the object. Note that sub is inherited but not its specification. Class BANK2 implements the additional interface PerfectBank, and it inherits from BANKPLUS the invariant and all pre/post specifications, except the ones for upd and sub, which are violated. Again reasoning with behavioral subtyping or lazy behavioral subtyping breaks down, because the reasoning about the (late-bound) calls to upd in BANK depends on the postcondition of upd, and therefore it is imposed on all subclasses in the case of lazy behavioral subtyping. Our framework allows flexible reuse of code and specifications, without verification problems, avoiding harmful superclass requirements.

Consider next that class BANKPLUS is changed for instance by redefining sub by

$$\text{Bool sub(Nat x) } \{\textbf{return } \text{BANK:sub(x+1)}\}$$

A fee of 1 unit is incorporated in the withdrawal. In this case, class BANKPLUS can still be reverified, but the subclass BANK2 is indirectly affected by this change, and it is no longer a PerfectBank (because of the fee). Thus to avoid this inconsistency, class BANK2 should be modified, say by removing Perfect-Bank as an interface.

If a subclass of BANK redefines add and sub without using upd, that subclass may remove method upd. And a subclass of BANK implementing an interface with add, but not sub, and with the same class invariant as class BANKPLUS, may remove method sub in order to make invariant reasoning simpler.

3.2   Reasoning About Late Binding and Static Binding

Statically bound calls are resolved at compile time, while late bound calls are bound at runtime. In either case the behavior of the call depends on the class of the object executing the method, called the *actual class*, since the behavior may (possibly indirectly) depend on late bound calls inside the method body. For $C1$ and $C2$ subclasses of C, it may be that there is a local call $this.n(\overline{x})$ in method m of C, and if n is redefined in both $C1$ and $C2$, an m call will bind n differently depending on the actual class. For instance in the Bank example, a call to sub binds to BANK:sub, but the $this.upd$ call in the body of BANK:sub binds to BANKPLUS:upd or BANK:upd depending on the class of the executing object, BANKPLUS or BANK, respectively.

To formalize the binding of late-bound and static calls, we introduce three functions, $bind(A, m)$, $bind(A, B, m)$, and $bind(A, B, C, m)$, where $A \leq B$ and $B \leq C$. We let the function $bind(A, m)$ return A if it has a definition of m, otherwise the closest class with a definition of m considering the superclasses above A, using a depth-first, left-fist traversal. This is used for binding a static call : $m(...)$ appearing in class A and also for a static call $A : m(...)$ appearing in subclass of A. We let the function $bind(C, B, m)$ return C if C has a definition of m, otherwise the closest superclass of C with a definition of m using a depth-first, left-first search of the superclass hierarchy of C, restricted to classes hereditarily related to B. Similarly, $bind(C, B, A, m)$ returns the closest superclass of C hereditarily related to both B and C, using a depth-first, left-first search of the superclass hierarchy. When C is known, $bind(C, .., m)$ can be calculated, even with an open-ended class hierarchy.

A late-bound local call $this.m(...)$ appearing in a class B binds to $bind(C, B, m)$ where C is the class of the executing object. The late-bound local call $this\ A.m(...)$ appearing in a class B binds to $bind(C, B, A, m)$ with $B \leq A$ and C and B as above. For a late-bound local call the binding can be calculated statically for a given actual class of the executing object, $this$.

In the case of verification based on behavioral interface subtyping, we reconsider each possible actual class of this. Thus for each subclass of C (defined so far), we reconsider the verification of any inherited or reused methods. For each subclass C', the binding can then be done at verification time, binding a call this.m appearing in C to $bind(C', C, m)$ and binding $C : m(..)$ to $bind(C, m)$ as explained.

A complication in reasoning about local calls is that a release point (programmed by an **await** statement) should maintain the invariant of the actual class (say D) as opposed to the enclosing class (C). Thus reasoning about a release point occurring in a method $C : m$ must consider the invariant of the actual class, which may be a subclass (D) of C. We therefore index the derivation symbol ($\vdash$) both with the class of the executing object D as well as with the class of the enclosing object C, using the notation $\vdash_{D,C}$. In the setting of behavioral interface subtyping, reasoning is done for each choice of D. For a method inherited from C, we derive properties by means of $\vdash_{D,C}$, thereby letting all relevant proof obligations from C be reconsidered for each subclass D.

In reasoning with behavioral subtyping, this is not needed since reasoning about method m of C is made (once) for all actual D. The latter approach makes reasoning simple when it succeeds, at the cost of redefinition flexibility – whereas in our system, based on behavioral interface subtyping, we may differentiate the different versions of an inherited method in the different subclasses. This gives more fine-grained reasoning (and specification) control, which is valuable in the setting of flexible code reuse and program evolution. A pre/post specification of m in C will be based on the invariant of C, which may be different from that of D. Therefore a pre/post specification of m in C cannot in general be guaranteed in a subclass D if $C\colon m$ has local calls or release points.

For example, consider two executions of a late-bound m call occurring in class A with $C1$ and $C2$ as the actual classes. These can be referred to by $C1\colon m$ and $C2\colon m$, respectively. We have that $bind(C1, A, m) = bind(C2, A, m)$ when the closest definition of m (hereditarily related to A) is in a common superclass of $C1$ and $C2$. A call to m with C as the actual class may cause a local call this.$n(y)$ (directly or indirectly). In the verification, this call will then be re-analyzed with C as the actual class, using the binding $bind(C, A, n)$ where A is the class enclosing the call, and a static call $D : n(y)$ with C as the actual class will be re-analyzed using the binding $bind(D, m)$. The analysis of these call is the same when $bind(C, A, m) = bind(D, A, m)$ and the method body has no local calls to methods redefined below D and no release points.

For partial correctness reasoning, we consider theorems of the form

$$\vdash_{C,A} [P]\ s\ [Q]$$

where C is the actual class and A is the class enclosing s, and the Hoare triple $[P]\ s\ [Q]$ states that if the statement(list) s is executed in a state satisfying the precondition P the final state will satisfy the postcondition Q provided the execution of s terminates (using square brackets rather than curly brackets since the latter are part of the programming language syntax). Figure 4 presents sample proof rules needed for the example, modifying the rules in [22] (using a double-indexed proof symbol). Note that the axiom schema for assignment is as for sequential programs without aliasing. If we had allowed remote field access, this would no longer hold. The notation Q_e^v denotes (capture-free) textual substitution replacing all free occurrences of the variable v by the expression e. Similarly, $Q_{e,e'}^{v,v'}$ denotes simultaneous replacement (v by e and v' by e'). Rules for sequential composition and if-statements are as usual. Rules for while-loops and recursive calls are also standard, but are omitted here for brevity.

For a class C we use $\vdash_{C,A}$ to prove the pre/post verification conditions for objects of that class, for code inherited from A. For code in class C this corresponds to normal class-based reasoning ($\vdash_{C,C}$). For code inherited from A, reasoning about release points and local or self calls depends on C, which reflects the actual class of this object, as well as A. Note that reasoning about late-bound self calls reduces to reasoning about static local calls: According to rule self call, the late-bound self call $v := $ this $B.m(\overline{x})$ is equivalent to the static call $v := D\colon m(\overline{x})$ where D is given by $bind(C, A, B, m)$. Thus the binding depends on the class of assign $\qquad\qquad\qquad\qquad\qquad\qquad \vdash_{C,A} [Q_e^v]\, v := e\,[Q]$

history $\qquad\qquad\qquad\qquad\qquad\qquad \vdash_{C,A} [h' = \mathbf{h}]\, s\, [h' \le \mathbf{h}]$

await guard $\qquad\qquad\qquad\qquad\qquad \vdash_{C,A} [I_C \wedge L]\ \mathbf{await}\ b\,[b \wedge I_C \wedge L]$

new $\qquad\qquad \vdash_{C,A} [\forall v'.\, fresh(v', \mathbf{h}) \Rightarrow Q_{v',\mathbf{h};(\mathsf{this} \to v'.\, \mathsf{new}\, C(\bar{e}))}^{v,\mathbf{h}}]\, v := \mathbf{new}\ C(\bar{e})\,[Q]$

simple call $\qquad\qquad\qquad\qquad \vdash_{C,A} [Q_{\mathbf{h};(\mathsf{this} \to o.m(\bar{e}))}^{\mathbf{h}}]\, o.m(\bar{e})\,[Q]$

blocking call $\qquad \vdash_{C,A} [\forall v'.\, o \ne \mathsf{this} \wedge Q_{v',\mathbf{h};(\mathsf{this} \to o.m(\bar{e}));(\mathsf{this} \leftarrow o.m(\bar{e};v'))}^{v,\mathbf{h}}]\, v := o.m(\bar{e})\,[Q]$

non-blocking call $\qquad\qquad \dfrac{\vdash_{C,A} [P]\ \mathbf{await}\ true\ [\forall v'.\, Q_{v',\mathbf{h};(\mathsf{this} \leftarrow o.m(\bar{e};v'))}^{v,\mathbf{h}}]}{\vdash_{C,A} [P_{\mathbf{h};(\mathsf{this} \to o.m(\bar{e}))}^{\mathbf{h}}]\ \mathbf{await}\ v := o.m(\bar{e})\,[Q]}$

self call $\qquad\qquad\qquad \dfrac{\vdash_{C,A} [P]\ v := bind(C, A, B, m) : m(\bar{e})\,[Q]}{\vdash_{C,A} [P]\ v := \mathsf{this}\ B.m(\bar{e})\,[Q]}$

implicit self call $\qquad\qquad \dfrac{\vdash_{C,A} [P]\ v := bind(C, A, m) : m(\bar{e})\,[Q]}{\vdash_{C,A} [o = \mathsf{this} \wedge P]\ v := o.m(\bar{e})\,[Q]}$

static call $\qquad \dfrac{\vdash_{C,A} [P]\ body_{bind(B,m):m}\ [Q_{\mathbf{h};(\mathsf{this} \leftarrow \mathsf{this}.m(\bar{e};v))}^{\mathbf{h}}]}{\vdash_{C,A} [P_{\bar{e},\mathsf{this},\mathbf{h};(\mathsf{this} \to \mathsf{this}.m(\bar{e}))}^{\bar{x},\mathsf{caller},\mathbf{h}} \wedge L]\, v := B : m(\bar{e})\,[Q_{\bar{e},\mathsf{this},v}^{\bar{x},\mathsf{caller},return} \wedge L]}$

sequence $\qquad\qquad\qquad \dfrac{\vdash_{C,A} [P]\, s\,[Q] \qquad\quad \vdash_{C,A} [Q]\, s'\,[R]}{\vdash_{C,A} [P]\, s;s'\,[R]}$

if-then-else $\qquad\qquad \dfrac{\vdash_{C,A} [P \wedge b]\, s\,[Q] \qquad \vdash_{C,A} [P \wedge \neg b]\, s'\,[Q]}{\vdash_{C,A} [P]\ \mathbf{if}\ b\ \mathbf{then}\ s\ \mathbf{else}\ s'\ \mathbf{fi}\,[Q]}$

Fig. 4. Hoare-style rules and axioms. Primed variables represent fresh logical variables, $fresh(v', \mathbf{h})$ expresses that v' does not occur in $\mathbf{h}$, and L denotes a local assertion, i.e., without occurrences of fields. In rules self call and static call, we assume that v does not occur in e (otherwise we would need a primed variable, v'). In rule static call we assume that $\bar{x}$ is the formal parameter list (which is read-only). Note that binding is calculated at verification time.

the executing object C, restricted by A and B. The binding $bind(C, A, B, m)$ can be calculated at verification time since C, A, and B are known. We have that the self call $v := \mathsf{this}.m(\bar{e})$ abbreviates $v := \mathsf{this}\ A.m(\bar{e})$ where A is the enclosing class, and similarly that the static call $v := \; : m(\bar{e})$ abbreviates $v := \; A : m(\bar{e})$. Thus rules for these special cases are omitted. For instance, reasoning about the late-bound call $v := \mathsf{this}.m(\bar{x})$ reduces to reasoning about the static $v := : m(\bar{x})$ if the class of this has a redefinition of m. Rule static call states that reasoning about $v := B : m(\bar{e})$ reduces to reasoning about $body_{bind(B,m):m}$, adding effects on the history, where $body_{C:m}$ denotes the body of the definition of method m in class C.

The *body* of a method definition $m(\overline{x})\{s; \textbf{return } e\}$ is given by

$\mathbf{h} := (\mathbf{h}; caller \twoheadrightarrow this.m(\overline{x}));$

$s; \text{return} := e;$

$\mathbf{h} := (\mathbf{h}; caller \leftarrow this.m(\overline{x}; \text{return}))$

incorporating the effects on the local history reflecting method call reception and method return. Since each class is analyzed separately, we obtain a modular and incremental verification system suitable for an open-ended class hierarchy, not unlike [7]. In the analysis of a class C we may need to consider super-classes of C, but not subclasses. We may reuse superclass verification results as follows: For code inherited from a superclass B, we may derive $\vdash_{C,B} [P] s [Q]$ from $\vdash_{B,B} [P] s [Q]$ when s has no release points and no local calls leading to calls of methods redefined below B. Otherwise $\vdash_{C,B} [P] s [Q]$ can be established by a new analysis of s and of any locally called methods in s. In particular $\vdash_{C,B} [P] v := B\!:\!m(\overline{x}) [Q]$ follows from $\vdash_{B,B} [P] v := B\!:\!m(\overline{x}) [Q]$ when $B : m$ has no release points nor local calls. In contrast to behavioral subtyping and lazy behavioral subtyping, no requirements are imposed on subclasses.

4 Proof Obligations

For each class C we must ensure that it satisfies the stated requirements, i.e., that the **implements** clause is satisfied (syntactically and semantically), that the class invariants are maintained by each method (except private ones), and that the stated pre/post specifications are satisfied by the corresponding methods of the class.

In this proof, inherited methods must be considered, while superclass implementation claims, superclass invariants, and superclass pre/post specifications, are not considered unless inherited. Each class is verified in this sense, taking inherited superclass code into consideration. Together with correct typing of object variables, this ensures that each object variable will satisfy its declared interfaces, and each object of run-time class C will satisfy the interfaces of C. This ensures that the compositional rule (Sect. 5.1) for reasoning about active object systems is sound. Furthermore, each late-bound local call with C as the run-time class of the caller/callee will satisfy the pre/post specification given in C since class C is statically verified. This is reflected in the composition rule, which considers all verified callee classes.

We formalize the proof obligations expressing the correctness of a program, a class, an interface claim, a class invariant, and a method specification. We define the following proof obligations, identifying the actual class and the enclosing class:

Definition 1 (Program and Class Correctness).
A program P is correct, denoted $\vdash P \textbf{ ok}$, if each class in the program is correct.
   A class C is correct, denoted $\vdash C \textbf{ ok}$, iff

⊢ C **sat** F *for each interface* F *specified in the* **implements** *clause of* C,

⊢ C **inv** I *for each stated (or explicitly inherited) invariant* I *of* C,

⊢$_{C,C}$ $m(\overline{x})$ **sat** $[P,Q]$ *for each method* $m(\overline{x})$ *defined in* C, *and each specification* $[P,Q]$ *stated (or inherited) in* C *for* m,

⊢$_{C,A}$ $m(\overline{x})$ **sat** $[P,Q]$ *for each method* $m(\overline{x})$ *inherited from* A, *and each specification* $[P,Q]$ *stated (or inherited) in* C *for* m,

where

⊢$_{C,A}$ $m(\overline{x})$ **sat** $[P,Q]$ *is verified by proving* ⊢$_{C,A}$ $[P]$ $body_{bind(C,A,m):m}$ $[Q]$ *(as explained above).*

⊢ C **inv** I *is verified by proving* ⊢$_{C,C}$ $m(\overline{x})$ **sat** $[I,I]$ *for each public method* $m(\overline{x})$ *in* C, *and by proving* ⊢$_{C,A}$ $m(\overline{x})$ **sat** $[I,I]$ *for each public method* $m(\overline{x})$ *inherited from* A, *and by proving that the invariant holds initially, i.e.,* I *holds when* h *is replaced by the empty history and fields by initial values.*

⊢ C **sat** F *is verified by proving that the conjunction of the invariants* $I_i(h)$ *of* C *implies the invariant of* F, I_F *(considering methods visible through* F, *as explained in Sect. 3):*

$$\wedge_i I_i(h) \Rightarrow I_F(h/F)$$

Note that type checking ensures that all methods of F are offered in C, with a signature better or equal to that of F (i.e., contravariant parameter types and covariant return types). And it ensures that removed methods are not directly or indirectly called from C, and that private methods of C are not directly or indirectly called with **await**.

For a subclass C' of C, ⊢$_{C,A}$ $m(\overline{x})$ **sat** $[P,Q]$ need not imply ⊢$_{C',A}$ $m(\overline{x})$ **sat** $[P,Q]$ even if m is not redefined, since the binding of local calls appearing in the body of m in C may bind differently in the context of C' (i.e., $bind(C,A,n)$ versus $bind(C',A,n)$, respectively). In general ⊢$_{C,A}$ $m(\overline{x})$ **sat** $[P,Q]$ depends on redefinition of m or locally called methods and possible C invariants in case of suspension (by **await** statements). A redefinition in C' of a locally called method may violate the supertype specification of that method. A suspension point performed on a C' object can only guarantee that the C' invariant is maintained, which could be weaker than the C invariant. We therefore track these dependencies, and we may conclude that ⊢$_{C,A}$ $m(\overline{x})$ **sat** $[P,Q]$ implies ⊢$_{C',A}$ $m(\overline{x})$ **sat** $[P,Q]$ if ⊢$_C$ $m(\overline{x})$ **sat** $[P,Q]$ does not depend on any redefined code and that any invariant used in the verification is respected by C'.

For a method m defined in B without local calls or suspension points, we have that the theorem ⊢$_{C,A}$ $B:m(\overline{x})$ **sat** $[P,Q]$ reduces to ⊢$_{C,C}$ $m(\overline{x})$ **sat** $[P,Q]$. This gives a practical way of reusing proofs from superclasses.

4.1   Verification of the Bank Example

Let B denote BANK and BP denote BANKPLUS. Let I_B denote the invariant of B and I_{BP} that of BP. According to our definition of class correctness, we get the following verification conditions for class BANK ($\vdash B\,\mathbf{ok}$):

$$\vdash\quad I_B \Rightarrow I_{PerfectBank}(\mathbf{h}/PerfectBank) \tag{1}$$

$$\vdash_{B,B}\ bal(x)\ \mathbf{sat}\ [true, \mathsf{return} = bal] \tag{2}$$

$$\vdash_{B,B}\ add(x)\ \mathbf{sat}\ [true, \mathsf{return} = true] \tag{3}$$

$$\vdash_{B,B}\ sub(x)\ \mathbf{sat}\ [true, \mathsf{return} = true] \tag{4}$$

$$\vdash\quad I_B\,{}^{h,bal}_{empty,0} \tag{5}$$

$$\vdash_{B,B}\ bal(x)\ \mathbf{sat}\ [I_B, I_B] \tag{6}$$

$$\vdash_{B,B}\ add(x)\ \mathbf{sat}\ [I_B, I_B] \tag{7}$$

$$\vdash_{B,B}\ sub(x)\ \mathbf{sat}\ [I_B, I_B] \tag{8}$$

$$\vdash_{B,B}\ upd(x)\ \mathbf{sat}\ [I_B, bal = sum(\mathbf{h}) + x \wedge \mathsf{return} = true] \tag{9}$$

In addition we must verify the PerfectBank pre/post conditions, which follow by the corresponding BANK pre/post conditions (2,3,4). In particular, the postcondition $\mathsf{return} = sum(\mathbf{h}/PerfectBank)$ follows by (2) and I_B. Here (1) represents the entailment of the PerfectBank invariant, which in this case is an empty obligation since PerfectBank has no invariant, (2,3,4) are requirements from BANK, (5) states that I_B holds initially, (6,7,8) state the invariance of I_B, and (9) represents the additional pre/post specifications of upd given in BANK. Verification conditions (2,5,6) and (9) are trivial, (3,4) and (7,8) follow from (9), treating the **return** e of a public method $m(\overline{x})$ as the assignment return $:= e$, followed by $\mathbf{h} := (\mathbf{h}; (\mathsf{caller} \leftarrow \mathsf{this}.m(\overline{x}; \mathsf{return})))$ according to the definition of *body*.

For class BANKPLUS we must verify $\vdash BP\,\mathbf{ok}$, which amounts to the verification conditions given in Fig. 5. These represent the entailment of the BankPlus invariant (10), the inherited pre/post specifications of BankPlus (11,12), the initial satisfaction of I_{BP} (13), the invariance of I_{BP} (14–16), and the pre/post specification of upd given in BANKPLUS (17). Here (10,13,14) are trivial and (11) reduces to (2) by observing that $\vdash_{BP,B}\ bal(x)\ \mathbf{sat}\ [P, Q]$ equals $\vdash_{B,B}\ bal(x)\ \mathbf{sat}\ [P, Q]$ (for any $[P, Q]$) since there are no local calls nor release points. Then (12,15,16) follows by using (17). For the local call in the redefined upd we observe that proofs about $B:upd(x)$ do not depend on the actual class since the body has no local calls. We may therefore reuse the specification of upd from BANK when analyzing the call $BANK:upd(x)$ in class BANKPLUS. Then verification of (17) is straightforward, and verification of (18) reduces to the trivial condition $b' = bal \Rightarrow \mathbf{if}\ bal + x \geq 0\ \mathbf{then}\ b' + x \geq 0 = true\ \mathbf{else}\ b' + x \geq 0 = false$. Moreover, the verification above can easily be mechanized.

Consider BANKPP, abbreviated $B2$, of Fig. 3. We have that I_{B2} is I_{BP}. Figure 6 gives the verification obligations for $\vdash B2\,\mathbf{ok}$. Here (19,23) reduce to (10,13) since I_{B2} is the same as I_{BP}. Since reasoning about $bal(x)$ does not depend on the actual class, (20) reduces to (2). Furthermore, (24) is trivial, and (20,22,25,26) follow by (27). For (27) we use Hoare-style reasoning and must verify that the given pre/post specification is satisfied by the body of upd, which is:

$$\vdash \ I_{BP} \Rightarrow sum(\mathbf{h}/BankPlus) \geq 0 \qquad (10)$$

$$\vdash_{BP,B} bal(x) \ \mathbf{sat} \ [true, \mathsf{return} = bal] \qquad (11)$$

$$\vdash_{BP,B} add(x) \ \mathbf{sat} \ [true, \mathsf{return} = true] \qquad (12)$$

$$\vdash \ I_{BP} {}^{\mathbf{h},bal}_{empty,0} \qquad (13)$$

$$\vdash_{BP,B} bal(x) \ \mathbf{sat} \ [I_{BP}, I_{BP}] \qquad (14)$$

$$\vdash_{BP,B} add(x) \ \mathbf{sat} \ [I_{BP}, I_{BP}] \qquad (15)$$

$$\vdash_{BP,B} sub(x) \ \mathbf{sat} \ [I_{BP}, I_{BP}] \qquad (16)$$

$$\vdash_{BP,BP} upd(x) \ \mathbf{sat} \ [I_{BP}, bal \geq 0 \wedge bal = sum(\mathbf{h}) + \mathbf{if} \ \mathsf{return} \ \mathbf{then} \ x \ \mathbf{else} \ 0] \qquad (17)$$

$$\vdash_{BP,BP} upd(x) \ \mathbf{sat} \ [b' = bal, \mathsf{return} = (b' + x \geq 0)] \qquad (18)$$

Fig. 5. Verification conditions for class BANKPLUS.

$$\vdash \ I_{B2} \Rightarrow sum(\mathbf{h}/BankPlus) \geq 0 \qquad (19)$$

$$\vdash_{B2,B} bal(x) \ \mathbf{sat} \ [true, \mathsf{return} = bal] \qquad (20)$$

$$\vdash_{B2,B} add(x) \ \mathbf{sat} \ [true, \mathsf{return} = true] \qquad (21)$$

$$\vdash_{B2,B} sub(x) \ \mathbf{sat} \ [true, \mathsf{return} = true] \qquad (22)$$

$$\vdash \ I_{B2} {}^{\mathbf{h},bal}_{empty,0} \qquad (23)$$

$$\vdash_{B2,B} bal(x) \ \mathbf{sat} \ [I_{B2}, I_{B2}] \qquad (24)$$

$$\vdash_{B2,B} add(x) \ \mathbf{sat} \ [I_{B2}, I_{B2}] \qquad (25)$$

$$\vdash_{B2,B} sub(x) \ \mathbf{sat} \ [I_{B2}, I_{B2}] \qquad (26)$$

$$\vdash_{B2,B2} upd(x) \ \mathbf{sat} \ [I_{B2}, bal = sum(\mathbf{h}) + x \wedge bal \geq 0 \wedge \mathsf{return} = true] \qquad (27)$$

Fig. 6. Verification conditions for class BANK2.

$$\mathbf{await} \ bal + x \geq 0; bal := bal + x; \mathsf{return} := true; \mathbf{h} := (\mathbf{h}; (caller \leftarrow this.upd(x; \mathsf{return})))$$

(since we may here ignore all $\rightarrow$ events) which reduces to the condition

$$I_{B2} \wedge bal + x \geq 0 \Rightarrow (bal + x = sum(\mathbf{h}; (caller \leftarrow this.upd(x; true))) + x \wedge bal + x \geq 0)$$

which is trivial since *upd* events do not affect *sum* due to the **others** equation. The example shows that: Verification of a class is done by inspecting the class and its superclasses, and does not impose any proof obligations on subclasses. Reasoning about static and late-bound local calls are handled by the actual class context. Proof obligations can often be reduced to already verified superclass obligations. The verification conditions we have seen are easily verified and thus easily automated.

5   Evolutionary Program Changes

During evolution of a system there may be a series of program changes, including changes of existing classes as well as additions of new classes and interfaces. For instance, an existing class in the middle of a class hierarchy may by augmented by adding a new class as a superclass and by adding new implementation clauses. And one may introduce a new interface to make two independent subsystems interact, adding support of the new interface in one or more existing classes.

In general, an existing class D may be changed by adding methods and fields, replacing methods, changing inheritance clauses, implementation clauses, removal clauses, and/or specifications. This can be understood by replacing the whole class definition by another definition. The updated class D may in general have a number of subclasses (at the time when D is updated) and these are implicitly modified if they inherit or reuse code from D. Thus, we need to reverify the redefined D, but in addition we need to consider the affected subclasses of D.

Definition 2 (System Change). *A system change is given as a sequence of* **introduce** *and* **update** *definitions. We use the syntax* **introduce** *In for adding an interface definition In and the syntax* **introduce** *Cl for adding a class definition Cl, with In and Cl as defined in Fig. 1. We use the following syntax for defining class updates:*

> **update class** $D \, [([T \; cp]^+)]^?$
> $[\textbf{implements also}^? \; F^+]^?$
> $[\textbf{inherits also}^? \; C(\overline{e})]^?$
> $[\textbf{removing also}^? \; m^+]^?$
> $\{[T \; w \; [:= r]^?]^* \; s^? \; M^* \; S^* \; I^*\}$

This class update modifies an existing class D by adding class parameters cp^+ (if present), changing the interface support to F^+ (if present), adding superclasses $[C(\overline{e})]^+$ (if present), removing methods m^+ (if present), adding fields w^+ (if present), adding initialization code s (if present), adding/redefining method definitions M^* (if present), changing method specifications S^* (if present), and changing the invariant to I^* (if present). For any optional item omitted, there is no change from the original class. This is somewhat similar to the semantics of inheritance, except that the modifications are made on an existing class rather than a new subclass. In order to limit duplication of old code, we use the quasi class name OLD to refer to elements of the original version of the class, thus the redefinition of a method m may contain the call $OLD : m(...)$ to reuse the old version of m. In contrast to static calls, such a call is textually expanded using the original definition (since the original definition may be removed). Similarly, $OLD : \textbf{inv}$ expands to the old invariant. We may use the keyword **also** in **implements**, **inherits**, and **removes** clauses, to define added elements. Thus **inherits also** C means that the updated class inherits C in addition to the classes inherited by the original version of the class.

An example of a class update is given in Fig. 7. Here the transaction-oriented bank version given by BANK 2 is changed so that one can check earlier transactions. This is done by letting the BANK 2 class inherit SAFETRANS in addition to the old superclass, thereby using multiple inheritance. The SAFETRANS class stores transactions in a secure manner, by giving limited read access, through checking if a given transaction has happened or not, and restricting write access to append. (For brevity the class is minimalistic.) The *upd* method of BANK 2 is then updated using the append method of SAFETRANS. The added invariant states that the transactions defined by SAFETRANS corresponds to the history as defined in Bank. Note that $sum(\mathbf{h})$ is here understood as $sum(\mathbf{h}/Bank)$. The example shows the usefulness of multiple inheritance during evolution. The updated BANK 2 class supports the old interfaces (PerfectBank and BankPlus), so any previous usage of BANK 2 objects through these interfaces is not affected by the change. After the update, BANK 2 objects can also be used through the SafeTrans interface. One needs to verify that the updated *upd* method satisfies the (inherited) conditions and the new invariant. This will be quite straight forward in this example.

We consider correctness of the updated code, and avoid complications such as run-time upgrades where new and old versions of the updated code are part of the running system. As before we assume type correctness. In general, the redefined class D (let us refer to it as $\hat{D}$) implements some interfaces, which may or may not be the same as for D. If $\hat{D}$ includes all interfaces of D, all type correct calls to D objects will be type correct and supported by $\hat{D}$ objects as well; and if the interface specifications are the same, global reasoning from interface specifications of D objects is not violated by replacing D objects by $\hat{D}$ objects.

Consider next the case that a class is modified by removing the support for an interface. In this case the statement $v := \mathbf{new}\ D$, becomes illegal when class D is modified so that it no longer supports the interface type of variable v. We may then change the statement to $v := \mathbf{new}\ B$ where B supports the interface. In general we may need a sequence of changes in order to obtain a desired resulting program, including changes to C and other classes using D. (Subclasses that inherit the interface clause of D may then explicitly add support for the interface, when desirable.)

The verification obligations caused by the redefinition consist of verifying $\vdash\ \hat{D}\ \mathbf{ok}$ and reverification of the subclasses of D since they may be affected by the change. We first mark the obligation $\vdash\ D\ \mathbf{ok}$, as well as all sub-obligations, as *pending*. And for each subclass D' we mark the obligation $\vdash\ D'\ \mathbf{ok}$, as well as all sub-obligations, as *pending*. Verification of $\vdash\ \hat{D}\ \mathbf{ok}$ is then done as defined above for the class resulting from the update, and the subclasses of D must be reverified. If an obligation depends on a pending sub-obligation, one should consider the latter first. Since subclasses may depend on classes defined earlier (as substantiated by Theorem 1 below), we reconsider the subclasses in the order defined. For a subclass D', the obligation $\vdash\ D'\ \mathbf{ok}$ should be marked as *pending* if the proof made use of a result from D, say $\vdash_{D,A} m(v)\ \mathbf{sat}\ [P,Q]$. For each such D result, it suffices to prove $\vdash_{\hat{D},A} m(v)\ \mathbf{sat}\ [P,Q]$. If all sub-obligations of $\vdash\ D'\ \mathbf{ok}$ can be reverified in this manner, the obligation $\vdash\ D'\ \mathbf{ok}$ is marked *correct*.

```
introduce interface SafeTrans { -- may append and check data,
                        -- but not change data
  Void append(Int x)
  Bool checkTrans(Int x) [true, return= (_←this.append(x) ∈ h)] }
```

```
introduce class SAFETRANS implements SafeTrans {List[Int] trans= empty;
  Void append (Int x) {trans:=(trans;x)}
  Bool checkTrans(Int x) {return x ∈ trans} }
```

```
update class BANK2 implements also SafeTrans inherits also SAFETRANS {
  Bool upd(Int x) {OLD:upd(x); SAFETRANS:append(x); return true}
  inv OLD:inv and sum(h)=add(trans)
  where add(empty)=0
        add(trans;x)=add(trans)+x }
```

Fig. 7. An update of Bank2 causing multiple inheritance.

The *state* of a proof obligation indicates whether it has been proved or not. We consider the states: *correct, incorrect, pending* . These express respectively that the obligation is verified, that the (old) proof is no longer valid, that verification remains to be done. As explained above, if a pending obligation can be verified or be reduced to a correct obligation, its state can be reset to *correct.* If a pending obligation cannot be verified, its state can be set to *incorrect.* In some cases it may be possible to reverify the obligation using additional specifications of inherited or called methods, but in general this may require human insight. Otherwise further modifications are needed.

An advantage of our approach is that violations in a class C caused by superclass modifications can be handled without changing the superclasses of C, called *Modification Independence*:

Theorem 1 (Modification Independence). *Assume that a class C is affected by a superclass modification such that some inherited superclass specifications are violated in C. Then C can be modified such that there is no violation.*

Proof. Let $[P, Q]$ be a violated m-specification. If this specification is inherited, we simply change C by not inheriting it and then the specification is no longer required in C. And if $[P, Q]$ is stated in C, we remove the specification. In case $[I, I]$ is then removed for an invariant I, we also remove the invariant from C, and remove any interface of C depending on the invariant. We repeat this process until all violations are removed.   □

This means that any undesired requirements due to modifications in a superclass can be removed. After removal one may add desired requirements and verify these requirements (modifying the class if needed). In this way one may reverify that the stated interfaces are satisfied. This gives full flexibility of properties during evolution, at the cost of reconsidering subclasses in case the modifications require changes in subclasses.

Our framework supports independence between different branches of a hierarchy, a property which is essential for flexible evolution. However, this kind of

Hierarchy Independence is non-trivial, especially in presence of multiple inheritance.

Theorem 2 (Hierarchy Independence).
Modification of a class C will only affect C and subclasses of C.

Proof. Let D be a class other than a subclass of C. The case when C is a subclass of D follows by the theorem above. Thus we may assume that C and D are hereditarily unrelated, but in the presence of multiple inheritance they may have common superclasses and common subclasses. By our healthiness condition on the binding strategy, a late-bound call in D cannot bind to a method defined in C because the healthiness condition then requires that C and D are hereditarily related. And it cannot bind to a common subclass of C and D because we may assume that D is the executing object, and thus all late-bound calls will bind to a method defined in D or a superclass. Such a call may bind to a common superclass (of C and D), but by Theorem 1, this superclass is not affected by the change in C.

A static-bound call occurring in D may bind to superclass of D which may contain a late-bound call. However, our binding strategy ensures that this is call binds to a class above D due to the healthiness condition. Thus it cannot bind to C.   □

5.1   Reasoning in Presence of Unverified Classes

Our approach may result in some verified classes and some classes that are not yet verified. In this imperfect setting we may still reason about the overall system by using the following formulation of the global system invariant $I(H)$ over the global history H (i.e., the sequence of all events that have occurred so far in the total system):

$$I(H) \triangleq wf(H) \bigwedge_{\to o.\, \mathbf{new}\, C(\_)\in H} \bigwedge_{F\in C} I_F(H/o)_o^{\mathsf{this}}$$

where C is restricted to range over classes that are tagged *correct*, i.e., those satisfying $\vdash C\,\mathbf{ok}$. The last conjunction ranges over all interfaces F implemented by C. Here $wf(H)$ denotes the wellformedness predicate, expressing the **before** ordering between events, given in Sect. 3.

This global invariant captures the partial knowledge of the global history H given by the interface invariants of the objects appearing in the system (possibly dynamically generated) considering only objects of *correct* classes. This global reasoning rule essentially turns off the interface invariants for the non-correct classes.

Limitation: We assume type correctness since reverification of a modified class C will be preceded by type checking of the modified class and other existing classes using C in creation statements. Thus we consider only program changes that result in type correct programs. Removal of declarations of fields, methods, parameters, and variables is therefore only allowed when not in use. Secondly we do not consider changes in an interface I. This can be simulated by adding the new version of I as a separate interface, making changes wherever I (or a subinterface) is used, and then removing the original I when no longer referred to.

5.2   Examples of Software Changes on BANK

Assume now that class BANK is changed so that upd calls checkAvail, which returns true.

update class BANK **implements** PerfectBank {
  Bool checkAvail(Int x){**return** true} [true, **return**]
  Bool upd(Int x){Bool ok:=checkAvail(x);
   if ok **then** bal:=bal+x **fi**; **return** ok}
  [**inv**, bal=sum(**h**)+x **and return**=true] }

All other aspects of class BANK are kept unchanged, including all BANK specifications. Thus **inv** refers to the original invariant of BANK. Since checkAvail returns true, the verification of upd can be reused, and the other verification conditions of BANK are as before and need not be reverified. And the verification of the added local method checkAvail is trivial. Furthermore, the subclasses are not affected by this change. Thus the verification conditions caused by the class update are straightforward.

However, if class BANKPLUS is changed by redefining checkAvail(x) as in

  update class BANKPLUS {
   Bool checkAvail(Int x){**return** bal+x>0} }

the local late-bound call to upd($-x$) in the inherited method sub results in the value of $bal - x > 0$ to be returned from sub. Again verification conditions are straightforward. In contrast this could not be verified in the frameworks of [10,11].

Adding a side effect in checkAvail such as **if** $x < 0$ **then** $bal := bal - 1$ **fi** would destroy the BANK invariant, but not the BANKPLUS invariant. Then the former should be removed.

Consider next the following update of class BANK with a redefinition of sub:

   update class BANK { Bool sub(Nat x)
    { bal:=bal−x; **return** true} }

The new version of BANK inherits the old interface (PerfectBank), the methods add, bal, and upd, the old invariant, the old specification of sub (i.e., postcondition return $= true$). The proof obligations amount to first verifying that the redefined sub maintains the invariant and satisfies the postcondition. This is trivial. Secondly it must be verified that each subclass is still **ok**. As subclass BANKPLUS now may allow a negative balance, the BANKPLUS invariant $bal \geq 0$ cannot be verified (because it is incorrect). We may still do (limited) global invariant reasoning about a system containing BANKPLUS objects.

To solve this inconsistency in BANKPLUS, we may update this class by removing the support of interface BankPlus and removing the last conjunct of the invariant and the specification of sub, and then reverify. Alternatively, we may change BANKPLUS by redefining sub so that the old specifications can be reverified.

Finally, the redefinition of sub in Sect. 3.1 can be handled by removing interface PerfectBank in class BANK2 and checking/adjusting any usage of **new** BANK2 (as PerfectBank) in other classes.

6   Related Work

Formal notions of refinement have been used to reflect software development. A refinement is in general leading from a design with certain properties to a design which preserves these properties while adding more detail. In this way refinement is semantics-preserving [27]. Certain refinement logics support the addition of error values, thereby semantics is preserved as long as no errors appear. Banach et al. have argued for the need of refinement-like steps that go beyond the limitation of semantics-preserving development [2]. But their approach does not support analysis of program properties. Hu and Smith [12,13] consider verification of evolving Z specifications. However, they do not look at changes to classes that may affect global system properties.

In the setting of object-oriented programs with inheritance, behavioral subtyping is the most common reasoning approach, restricting subclasses to obey the super-class specifications [19]. This means that subclasses must preserve behavior. Lazy behavioral subtyping [8,9] relaxes this condition; only behavior that is needed to verify local calls in a superclass must be respected by a subclass redefining the method. This gives added flexibility, allowing a larger class of changes without breaking the requirements.

Interface abstraction allows reasoning about remote calls to rely on the declared interface of the callee. This means that changes in a (super)class implementation may be done as long as the stated interface support is respected, and as long as subclass reasoning is not affected. A calculus allowing changes to methods, (super)classes and interfaces is presented in [11], based on lazy behavioral subtyping. Program properties, represented by Hoare triples, are classified in two categories for each class C, representing the verified ones and the unresolved (unverified) ones, $\mathcal{U}(C)$. The set of verified properties of a given class C and method m is denoted $\mathcal{G}(C, m)$. When the set of unverified program properties is verified (i.e., $\mathcal{U}(C)$ is empty) the class is found to be correct in the sense that all pre/post method specifications are satisfied by the corresponding implementation in a class as well as those in interfaces supported by the class. Changes in code or specifications may affect both categories. However, a program requirement added to $\mathcal{U}(C)$ may be impossible to verify (in case the Hoare triple is not satisfied), and it will then remain in $\mathcal{U}(C)$, and there is no guarantee that this problem is detected.

The approach in [10] addresses transformation of classes and allow classes in the middle of a class hierarchy to be changed. Modifications are archived by means of update operations *modify* and *simplify*. The modify operations extend class definitions, allowing code such as new fields, method definitions, guarantees, and interfaces to be added to classes, and existing methods to be redefined. The simplify operation allows redundant methods to be removed from class definitions. The approach does not classify classes using $\mathcal{G}$ and $\mathcal{U}$ such as in [11], rather, for each update applied to a class, all verification work is done to methods affected by the update. However, any superclass requirements needed to handle local calls are imposed on subclasses, as in [11].

A number of works on asynchronously communicating concurrent objects, partly by the authors of this paper, consider certain forms of software and/or specification changes: The concept of dynamic software updates allows changes to (super)classes during run-time [16]. A challenge with run-time upgrades of distributed systems is the need to allow updates in a distributed manner, and thereby allowing coexistence of different versions of the software [1,16,25]. In contrast to these works, we are focusing on the reasoning aspects. Bannwart and Müller [3] consider program changes through refactoring, and show how to preserve external behavior for a class of non-trivial refactoring. However, they do not include changes that violate behaviors.

Another line of work considers proof reuse, including partial reuse of proofs of earlier verified properties. This may require some storage of proof outlines or non-trivial verification steps. This means that when a module is corrected, one may try to rerun previous proofs to alleviate the verification burden [24]. The notion of abstract method calls allows reuse of abstract proof outlines, for a fixed method body, while their instances may need further work when other methods or requirements are changed [4,14]. A related approach is the use of symbolic predicates to express requirements to general properties for a given program without knowing what the concrete are [6]. These approaches simplify the verification task of evolving programs. The amount of proof reuse can be balanced against the amount of automation. Efficiently automated proofs need not be reused while interactive proofs could benefit from reuse, if possible. Our approach is oriented towards a language with a high degree of automation of verification conditions, and proof reuse is therefore not our focus. A recent work by Ulewicz et al. [26] supports a tight integration of verification of unchanged behavior (regression verification) with that of changed behavior (delta verification); but unrestricted changes are not supported.

We build on results from [21] concerning (single) class inheritance. In contrast to that work, we consider here program changes and evolution, supporting *Modification Independence* (Theorem 1), and give a reasoning rule for partially reverified systems. In addition we provide here more fine-grained control of reused code, and a simplified treatment of (static and late-bound) local calls. Furthermore, while [21] assumes single class inheritance, we here extend the approach to *multiple inheritance*. This greatly improves flexibility since addition of superclasses during evolution allows an outdated inheritance hierarchy to be adjusted with minor class changes. Multiple inheritance has also been considered in [20], but not in the context of program evolution.

The present work is an extension of the framework presented in [22], providing more details and theoretical results supporting *Modification Independence* and *Hierarchy Independence*, and extending that framework and reasoning system to multiple inheritance. This requires the reasoning rules to use a double-indexed proof symbol, without complicating the practical applicability. Multiple inheritance has been criticized due to possible confusion between horizontal and vertical name conflicts. However, our language include qualification of inherited names by a superclass, which provides fine-grained control of used names, solving both horizontal and vertical name conflicts at the cost of awareness of which superclass inherit the relevant definition. And we insist on a healthy binding strategy, as also argued in [9] for the purpose of program reasoning. This limits undesired vertical name conflicts in the case of late binding. In addition, we allow static binding to allow reuse of code from superclasses in a way not affected by added or changed subclasses.

Moreover healthiness is essential in order to ensure *Hierarchy Independence* (Theorem 2) in the presence of multiple inheritance. This ensures that changes in a class will only affect subclasses. Without this property we could no longer claim to have a flexible evolution framework! The particular binding strategy used in our approach is based primarily on depth-first traversal of the superclass hierarchy, and secondarily on following superclasses left to right. This is similar to binding in the Perl language (apart from healthiness). This binding strategy is not the most commonly used, but it is advantageous in the setting of evolution, since adding a superclass at the end of a superclass list (somewhere in a hierarchy) will not affect the binding made in existing code. This simplifies the reverification needed for inherited code. The binding strategy also ensures that calls that have a binding before an added superclass also has a binding after the class change. (If inherited method differ in parameter types and numbers, we would need to index the method name by the parameter types.) These factors are advantageous from a pragmatic point of view.

The considered concurrency model is used by a number of languages supporting active objects, including Creol, ABS, Encore, Rebecca, and ASP/Proactive. The core language used here is avoiding the use of futures, in order to simplify the basic reasoning rules for method calls, as discussed in a recent paper [18].

7 Conclusion

We have introduced a framework for evolution of distributed systems, offering flexibility with respect to both changes of code and specifications. We support reverification of changed classes without requiring changes or reverification of (unchanged) superclasses, captured by *Hierarchy Independence* (Theorem 2). Specification violations in changed classes or affected subclasses can be solved modulo local changes in these classes, captured by *Modification Independence* (Theorem 1). In contrast to earlier work [22] we consider evolution in presence of multiple inheritance. We have argued that multiple inheritance is useful and powerful during evolution, and demonstrated this by an example (given in Fig. 7).

By adopting a healthy binding strategy, we control vertical name conflicts, and healthiness is needed for Hierarchy Independence.

We are avoiding inconsistencies that are inherent in frameworks building on behavioral subtyping/lazy behavioral subtyping. Flexibility with respect to reuse and inheritance, beyond the limitations of behavioral subtyping, requires that all objects are seen through an interface (interface abstraction). Our approach builds on the principle of the interface substitution (any object of interface F supports any superinterface of F as well) and the principle of behavioral interface subtyping, where each class must support its declared interfaces, but need not support interfaces of superclasses. This allows the class hierarchy to be used for code reuse while the interface hierarchy is used for behavioral reuse. In contrast to lazy behavioral subtyping, no superclass requirements are imposed on subclasses by the framework. This gives a more flexible framework for software modifications than those of [10, 11] since methods can be redefined without restrictions caused by superclasses. This means that we may deal with software changes that cannot be verified with approaches building on lazy behavioral subtyping. The Bank example demonstrated this.

In our framework, modifications to a class C lead to reverification of that class, and subclasses must be reconsidered when they (directly or indirectly) inherit modified parts of C, but superclasses need not be reverified. Other (i.e., hereditarily unrelated) classes are not affected unless some interfaces are removed from the implementation clause of C, in which case all $v := \mathbf{new}\ C$ statements must be reconsidered, ensuring C still supports the interface of o and if not, using another class. During reverification, proofs can be reused as much as possible, and further changes to the class and/or subclasses may be done as needed.

Our framework considers the setting of active, concurrent objects, for which Java code can be generated. We have demonstrated that Hoare style reasoning is quite simple for this setting, in the sense that reasoning is like sequential reasoning, with sequential effects on the history added. The handling of multiple inheritance implies a double indexing of the proof symbol for Hoare triples, which guides the generation of verification conditions without adding practical complications. Our language supports late-bound remote method calls, as well as static local calls and late-bound local calls. The notion of static local calls is needed in the framework to reduce verification conditions about late-bound local calls to verification conditions about static local calls. Our framework gives fine-grained control of reused code, where the handling of local calls, both late-bound and static ones, as well as suspension, is essential. Static local calls are also useful in programming, avoiding the fragile base class problem since the binding is fixed for such calls.

We have assumed type correct programs. Therefore removal of fields, methods, classes, and interfaces is only allowed when these are superfluous. We have not considered changes in interfaces, other than removal of superfluous interfaces. As mentioned the change of an interface could be simulated by introducing a new version of the interface, and by changing all usage of the old interface, and then removing it.

Our framework may be extended to reason about dynamic (run-time) class upgrades, assuming existing objects are upgraded in invariant states, as in Creol [16], where new calls run renewed code and suspended old calls run old code. The new invariant must imply the old invariant, and it must be verified that old methods maintain the new invariant. This ensures that the interleaving of new code and remaining old code is not harmful. The requirements to an upgraded class are strengthened by these requirements, whereas the requirements to subclasses are as described.

Acknowledgments. This work is supported by the *IoTSec* project, the Norwegian Research Council (No. 248113/O70), and by the *SCOTT* project, the European Leadership Joint Undertaking under EU H2020 (No. 737422).

References

1. Ajmani, S., Liskov, B., Shrira, L.: Modular software upgrades for distributed systems. In: Thomas, D. (ed.) ECOOP 2006. LNCS, vol. 4067, pp. 452–476. Springer, Heidelberg (2006). https://doi.org/10.1007/11785477_26
2. Banach, R., Poppleton, M., Jeske, C., Stepney, S.: Engineering and theoretical underpinnings of retrenchment. Sci. Comput. Program. **67**(2–3), 301–329 (2007)
3. Bannwart, F., Müller, P.: Changing programs correctly: refactoring with specifications. In: Misra, J., Nipkow, T., Sekerinski, E. (eds.) FM 2006. LNCS, vol. 4085, pp. 492–507. Springer, Heidelberg (2006). https://doi.org/10.1007/11813040_33
4. Bubel, R., et al.: Proof repositories for compositional verification of evolving software systems - managing change when proving software correct. Trans. Found. Mastering Change **1**, 130–156 (2016)
5. Clavel, M., et al.: Maude manual (version 2.4) (2008)
6. Din, C.C., Johnsen, E.B., Owe, O., Yu, I.C.: A modular reasoning system using uninterpreted predicates for code reuse. J. Logical Algebraic Methods Program. **95**, 82–102 (2018)
7. Din, C.C., Owe, O.: A sound and complete reasoning system for asynchronous communication with shared futures. J. Logical Algeb. Methods Program. **83**(5–6), 360–383 (2014)
8. Dovland, J., Johnsen, E.B., Owe, O., Steffen, M.: Lazy behavioral subtyping. J. Logic Algebraic Program. **79**(7), 578–607 (2010)
9. Dovland, J., Johnsen, E.B., Owe, O., Steffen, M.: Incremental reasoning with lazy behavioral subtyping for multiple inheritance. Sci. Comput. Program. **76**(10), 915–941 (2011)
10. Dovland, J., Johnsen, E.B., Owe, O., Yu, I.C.: A proof system for adaptable class hierarchies. J. Logical Algebraic Methods Program. **84**(1), 37–53 (2015)
11. Dovland, J., Johnsen, E.B., Yu, I.C.: Tracking behavioral constraints during object-oriented software evolution. In: Margaria, T., Steffen, B. (eds.) ISoLA 2012. LNCS, vol. 7609, pp. 253–268. Springer, Heidelberg (2012). https://doi.org/10.1007/978-3-642-34026-0_19
12. Fu, Z., Smith, G.: Towards more flexible development of Z specifications. In: 2nd IFIP/IEEE International Symposium on Theoretical Aspects of Software Engineering, pp. 281–288, June 2008
13. Fu, Z., Smith, G.: Property transformation under specification change. Front. Comput. Sci. China **5**(1), 1–13 (2011)

14. Hähnle, R., Schaefer, I., Bubel, R.: Reuse in software verification by abstract method calls. In: Bonacina, M.P. (ed.) CADE 2013. LNCS (LNAI), vol. 7898, pp. 300–314. Springer, Heidelberg (2013). https://doi.org/10.1007/978-3-642-38574-2_21

15. Johnsen, E.B., Owe, O.: An asynchronous communication model for distributed concurrent objects. Softw. Syst. Model. **6**(1), 35–58 (2007)

16. Johnsen, E.B., Owe, O., Simplot-Ryl, I.: A dynamic class construct for asynchronous concurrent objects. In: Steffen, M., Zavattaro, G. (eds.) FMOODS 2005. LNCS, vol. 3535, pp. 15–30. Springer, Heidelberg (2005). https://doi.org/10.1007/11494881_2

17. Johnsen, E.B., Owe, O., Yu, I.C.: Creol: a type-safe object-oriented model for distributed concurrent systems. Theoret. Comput. Sci. **365**(1–2), 23–66 (2006)

18. Karami, F., Owe, O., Ramezanifarkhani, T.: An evaluation of interaction paradigms for active objects. J. Logical Algebraic Methods Program. **103**, 154–183 (2019)

19. Liskov, B.H., Wing, J.M.: A behavioral notion of subtyping. ACM Trans. Program. Lang. Syst. **16**(6), 1811–1841 (1994)

20. Owe, O.: Verifiable programming of object-oriented and distributed systems. In: Petre, L., Sekerinski, E. (eds.) From Action System to Distributed Systems: The Refinement Approach, pp. 61–80. Taylor&Francis (2015)

21. Owe, O.: Reasoning about inheritance and unrestricted reuse in object-oriented concurrent systems. In: Ábrahám, E., Huisman, M. (eds.) IFM 2016. LNCS, vol. 9681, pp. 210–225. Springer, Cham (2016). https://doi.org/10.1007/978-3-319-33693-0_14

22. Owe, O., Lin, J.-C., Fazeldehkordi, E.: A flexible framework for program evolution and verification. In: 7th International Conference on Model-Driven Engineering and Software Development (Modelsward 2019), February 2019

23. Owe, O., Ryl, I.: On combining object orientation, openness and reliability. In: Proceedings of the Norwegian Informatics Conference (NIK 1999), Tapir, pp. 187–198, November 1999

24. Reif, W., Stenzel, K.: Reuse of proofs in software verification. In: Shyamasundar, R.K. (ed.) FSTTCS 1993. LNCS, vol. 761, pp. 284–293. Springer, Heidelberg (1993). https://doi.org/10.1007/3-540-57529-4_61

25. Seifzadeh, H., Abolhassani, H., Moshkenani, M.S.: A survey of dynamic software updating. J. Softw.: Evol. Process **25**(5), 535–568 (2013)

26. Ulewicz, S., et al.: A verification-supported evolution approach to assist software application engineers in industrial factory automation. In: 2016 IEEE International Symposium on Assembly and Manufacturing (ISAM), pp. 19–25, August 2016

27. Ward, M.P., Bennett, K.H.: Formal methods to aid the evolution of software. Int. J. Softw. Eng. Knowl. Eng. **05**(01), 25–47 (1995)

Classifying Approaches for Constructing Single Underlying Models

Johannes Meier[1]([⊠]), Christopher Werner[2], Heiko Klare[3][iD], Christian Tunjic[4],
Uwe Aßmann[2], Colin Atkinson[4][iD], Erik Burger[3][iD], Ralf Reussner[3][iD],
and Andreas Winter[1]

[1] Software Engineering Group, University of Oldenburg, Oldenburg, Germany
{meier,winter}@se.uni-oldenburg.de
[2] Software Technology Group, Technische Universität Dresden, Dresden, Germany
{christopher.werner,uwe.assmann}@tu-dresden.de
[3] Software Design and Quality Group, Karlsruhe Institute of Technology, Karlsruhe, Germany
{klare,burger,reussner}@kit.edu
[4] Software Engineering Group, University of Mannheim, Mannheim, Germany
{tunjic,atkinson}@informatik.uni-mannheim.de

Abstract. Multi-view environments for software development allow different views of a software system to be defined to cover the requirements of different stakeholders. One way of ensuring consistency of overlapping information often contained in such views is to project them "on demand" from a Single Underlying Model (SUM). However, there are several ways to construct and adapt such SUMs. This paper presents four archetypal approaches and analyses their advantages and disadvantages based on several new criteria. In addition, guidelines are presented for selecting a suitable SUM construction approach for a specific project.

Keywords: Projectional · SUM · Model consistency · Integration · Metamodeling · View-based

1 Introduction

The increasing complexity of modern software-intensive systems means that individual developers are no longer able to cope with every detail of their structure and functionality. *View-based software development* approaches are therefore useful for allowing individual aspects of a system to be considered independently by separate developers. However, the resulting fragmentation of system descriptions leads to *redundancies* and *dependencies* between the information shown in different views which are difficult to resolve manually. Therefore, automatic mechanisms are needed to ensure holistic consistency between views and the system they portray.

View-based approaches can be characterized as either *synthetic* or *projective* [16] based on the primary source of information for the views. Synthetic approaches distribute information about the system over all the separate views, whereas projective approaches centralize the description in a Single Underlying Model (SUM) [2]

© Springer Nature Switzerland AG 2020
S. Hammoudi et al. (Eds.): MODELSWARD 2019, CCIS 1161, pp. 350–375, 2020.
https://doi.org/10.1007/978-3-030-37873-8_15

from which views are *projected* when needed. As with all model-driven development approaches, a SUM is constructed in terms of instances of concepts defined in a meta-model, which we refer to as a Single Underlying MetaModel (SUMM). Many of the challenges faced in defining generic mechanisms for creating and synchronizing SUMs therefore need to be solved at the SUMM level.

This paper compares the advantages and disadvantages of different strategies for realizing SUM-based approaches to software engineering. The common feature of all projective approaches is that views are regarded as constructively correct, and thus inherently consistent with one another, as long as they agree with the SUM. The problem of maintaining inter-view consistency therefore becomes the problem of maintaining the internal consistency of the SUM and the correctness of the SUM-to-View projections. To describe the different approaches in a uniform way and analyze their pros and cons systematically, this paper classifies the different strategies for constructing SUM(M)s and identifies criteria for evaluating them. Four existing approaches for constructing SUM(M)s are then compared in terms of how they fulfill the identified criteria. Finally, the suitability of the approaches for different situations is analyzed based on the identified criteria. The presented results allow researchers to classify new approaches for SUM(M) construction and help developers select SUM-based approaches for their specific requirements based on the identified criteria.

After discussing related work in Sect. 2, the running example and terminology used in this paper are introduced in Sect. 3, followed by classification criteria for SUM approaches that are described in Sect. 4. The four SUM approaches OSM (Sect. 5), VITRUVIUS (Sect. 6), RSUM (Sect. 7), and MoCONSEMI (Sect. 8) are presented subsequently and are classified using the criteria in Sect. 9. In addition, this section describes guidelines for deciding when to choose each approach. Section 10 summarizes the findings of this paper.

2 Related Work

The explicit use of views or perspectives in software engineering can be traced back to the VOSE method in the early 1990s [9], which strongly advocated a synthetic approach to views given the state-of-the-art at the time. Most "view-based" software engineering methods that have emerged since then, such as the 4+1 model [20] or the Unified Process [22], assume that views are supported in a synthetic way, although this is usually not stated explicitly (the actual distinction between synthetic and projective approaches to views was first clearly articulated in the ISO 42010 standard [16]). To our knowledge, no general purpose software engineering method available today is based exclusively on the notion of projective views driven by a SUM. However, there are approaches that address the more specific problem of keeping multiple views on a database consistent [7], or that support a synthetic approach to modeling in a limited context like multi-paradigm modeling [28].

The discipline in which the idea of using views to provide different perspectives on large, complex systems is the most mature is Enterprise Architecture (EA) modeling, characterized by approaches such as Zachman [31] and TOGAF [12]. These all provide some kind of "viewpoint framework" defining the constellation of views available to stakeholders and the kind of "models" that should be used to portray them. Some, like RM-ODP [24], adopt an explicitly synthetic approach, while others such as Archi-Mate [15] and MEMO [10] make no commitment. However, again no EA modeling platform today explicitly advocates, or is oriented towards, the use of projective views.

Bruneliere et al. [4] conducted a systematic study of model view approaches and from it distilled a detailed feature model of the different capabilities they offer. However, they mainly focused on mechanisms and languages rather than fundamental architectural choices, and did not specifically consider the "synthetic versus projective" distinction of importance here. Atkinson and Tunjic [3], on the other hand, focused on exactly this distinction when they identified several fundamental design choices for realizing multi-view systems. However, they were concerned with the fundamental differences between SUM-based and non-SUM-based approaches rather than between individual SUM-based approaches. In contrast, in this paper we explicitly focus on four distinct SUM-based approaches.

Given the growing importance of projectional approaches, one goal of this paper is to support the evolution of SUM construction methods based on criteria to specify the conceptual solution space (Sect. 4.1).The aims is for developers to be able to use these criteria (Sect. 4.2) to help select a concrete SUM approach for a specific situation. Four existing SUM approaches are therefore classified in terms of the criteria characterizing the feasibility of projective, multi-view approaches and examples of how to design and apply SUM approaches are presented.

All four groups actively developing SUM-based approaches at the present time are contributing authors of this paper, which is an extension of a MODELSWARD2019 paper [25]. The main additions are the inclusion of a fourth SUM-based method (RSUM) in Sect. 7, and a new, independent set of "technical criteria" for classifying SUM approaches in Sect. 4.3. The explanation of the use of the different SUM approaches in the context of the running ongoing example is also extended and made more explicit. Finally, further insights about how the different SUM approaches can be combined, arising from an ongoing series of joint meetings, have been added to Sect. 9.5. The progress made in these meetings and VAO international workshops was continued at the International Workshop on View-based Software Engineering in September 2019 with further researchers.

3   Running Example and Terminology

In this section we introduce a running example of a highly simplified software development project in which requirements, architecture models and implementation (i.e. code units) need to be kept consistent. These three views are described by *languages* using metamodels that define the elements (e.g., classes, associations etc.) that can appear in models. Figure 1 sketches metamodels for the three views. Since this example is used to demonstrate all four SUM approaches, it is directly taken from the initial paper [25].

As shown in Fig. 1, *requirements* contain natural language sentences (package Req). The RequirementsSpecification consists of Requirements which are identified by a unique id and contain the corresponding natural language sentence as simple text, written by an author. Simplified *class diagrams* are used for

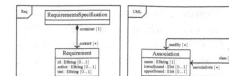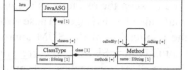

Fig. 1. Simplified metamodels for Requirements (left), Class Diagrams (middle), and Java source code (right), taken from [25].

the *architecture* and represent system modules as classes (package UML). Classes have a className, one or more unidirectional Associations and are collected in ClassDiagrams. The *implementation* is represented by simplified Java (package Java) and realizes the architecture and requirements. The JavaASG (Abstract Syntax Graph) contains ClassTypes with their name, which in turn contain Methods with their call relations.

These three languages describe different (but not necessarily all) facets of the system under development and thus represent three overlapping *viewtypes*. According to [11], a *viewtype* is the metamodel of a view, while a *view* is a model that projects information from another model (here: the SUM) for a specific purpose. Since all views share information about the system under development, they are semantically interconnected and contain *dependent information*, which requires updates of other views if one is changed. The interdependence of information can be explicitly defined in terms of *consistency rules* which define the relations that have to hold between instances of metamodels.

In the running example, two exemplary consistency rules can be found, which are directly taken from [25] – Consistency Rule 1, targeting redundant information which needs to be kept consistent, and Consistency Rule 2, controlling the way additional information is derived from other, already existing information. These two consistency rules are considered representative, because overlapping views usually contain redundant concepts or special interrelations.

Consistency Rule 1: Classes can be defined in the architecture view and in the implementation view. A class can be defined only in the implementation (Java.ClassType), or in both the implementation and the architecture (UML.Class) if it represents a module. In the latter case, the class has to be kept consistent in the implementation and architecture views (i.e. if it is renamed). Therefore, the implementation and architecture are only consistent if the architecture contains a subset of the classes in the implementation.

Consistency Rule 2: Since requirements define goals that the implementation should fulfill, the progress of the development project can be measured by counting the requirements that are supported by the current implementation. Therefore, Requirements must be linked to the implementing Methods. We thus require that each Method has to be automatically linked to those Requirements that contain the Method's name in their text. This *additional information* between the requirements and implementation has to be stored and kept consistent. Only these two consistency rules are considered to keep the example as simple as possible. However, in general many more rules could also be envisaged. These two consistency rules and three languages help to show the application of the SUM approaches in Sects. 5–8. *SUM approaches* specify conceptually how SUMs and corresponding SUMMs are constructed. *Platform specialists* design SUM approaches and implement supporting platforms. Sections 5–8 show how four such SUM platforms are applied to this running example. SUM approaches are applied by a *methodologist* who uses a SUM platform to construct a concrete SUM(M) fulfilling the needs of the particular multi-view-project [2].

Depending on the approach, the methodologist creates the SUMM either by reusing the existing metamodels in Fig. 1 or by defining a new metamodel from scratch. After that, the *developer* works with views projected from the SUM which is an instance of the SUMM developed by the methodologist. To provide views to cope with all the concerns of developers *new viewtypes* can be configured by the methodologist.

4   Classification Criteria

In order to classify SUM approaches, this section describes classification criteria grouped into three categories with the following objectives: *design criteria* which target the SUM construction process in Sect. 4.1, *selection criteria* which help users select an appropriate approach for the current application in Sect. 4.2, and *technical criteria* which focus on technical realization strategies to implement an already conceptually designed SUM approach in Sect. 4.3.

Because the first two criteria groups were already defined in the initial version of this paper, those definitions have been directly taken from [25] and repeated here. The extended criteria and their grouping represent the first new contribution of this paper. They are used to classify the four SUM approaches (Sects. 5.3, 6.3, 7.3, 8.3) and to compare them with each other (Sect. 9).

4.1   Design Criteria

Design criteria capture how a SUM is constructed independently of technical issues (Sect. 4.3). They describe the main conceptual design decisions for SUM approaches, which span the solution space of possible approaches from the problem perspective. They do not evaluate the quality of SUMs, but help *platform specialists* decide on the conceptual degrees of freedom when *designing a SUM approach*.

Criterion C1 (Construction Process) covers the *process* of creating a SUM(M) depending on the initial situation. In a *top-down* approach, a new SUM and SUMM are created from scratch. A *bottom-up* approach, on the other hand, starts with existing models and metamodels and combines them into a SUMM and initial SUM.

Criterion C2 (Pureness) relates to the absence of internal redundancy in the SUM under construction. An *essential* SUM is "completely free of any internal redundancy" [3] and dependencies by design. A *pragmatic* SUM contains redundant information (e.g., because it contains different metamodels that define concepts more than once) that has to be interrelated and kept consistent, and thus only behaves as if it is free of dependencies due to internal consistency preservation mechanisms. Pragmatic SUMs require additional information to wire the internal models together and thus involve more complex consistency rules than equivalent essential SUMs. In between these extremes, some initial redundancies could be resolved targeting a more essential SUM.

While **C1** focuses on the *starting point* of the SUM construction process, **C2** focuses on the *results*. Together they allow SUM approaches to be compared at a conceptual level, while the details of the approaches are designed individually.

4.2 Selection Criteria

When there are several concrete SUM approaches available, the selection criteria help to select the most appropriate SUM approach for a particular situation. These criteria reflect the conceptual preconditions and requirements that favor one concrete SUM approach over another for the application in hand. They therefore help *methodologists compare different SUM approaches* when selecting one to use for a particular project. For example, if many new viewtypes have to be defined on top of the SUM, an approach should be selected that eases the definition of new viewtypes (see following **E3**).

Criterion E1 (Metamodel Reusability) determines whether concepts to be represented in the SUMM are already available within predefined metamodels and should be reused in the new SUMM. If so, the SUM approach has to accommodate these legacy metamodels by combining them into an initial SUMM. This can either be done directly without additional work or indirectly by providing strategies for migrating the "legacy" metamodels into the SUMM ("easy"). The value "middle" indicates that some manual effort is required, while "hard" indicates no support from the approach. Since numerous languages, metamodels and tools with fixed viewtypes are usually already available, approaches fulfilling this criterion support their reuse. Reusing metamodels usually implies a bottom-up approach according to **C1**.

Criterion E2 (Model Reusability) establishes whether already existing artifacts (i.e., existing instances of the metamodels) need to be incorporated in an initial version of the SUM. If so, the SUM approach has to import these models. This can be done directly without additional work or indirectly using a strategy for migrating the legacy models into views or into the SUM by some kind of model-to-model transformations ("easy"). It requires the reuse of the corresponding initial metamodels according to **E1** and usually requires a bottom-up strategy according to **C1**. To reuse models they may have to be consistent according to the consistency relations between the integrated metamodels *before* they can be integrated into the SUM. This requires additional manual effort to ensure consistency beforehand ("middle"), in contrast to SUM approaches which offer strategies to handle inconsistent information *during* their integration into the SUM ("easy"). Existing artifacts developed without a consistency-preserving SUM approach usually do not initially fulfill the consistency relationships, which is why this criterion also checks whether those inconsistencies can be handled automatically during integration. The value "hard" indicates no support from the approach.

Criterion E3 (Viewtype Definability) focuses on the task of specifying new types of views on a SUMM for specific concerns (e.g., managing the traceability links from

Consistency Rule 2) whose instances can be used by developers to change the related information in the SUM. Supporting the definition of customized, role-specific viewtypes is an essential capability of view-based development approaches, so the level of difficulty involved has a strong impact on the usability of an approach. The degrees of difficulty depend on whether there are no redundancies ("easy") or all initial redundancies still exist ("hard") and how many models internally exist to query information from. This is because redundant and distributed information makes it harder to collect all relevant information and to propagate changes back into the SUM.

Criterion E4 (Language Evolvability) focuses on the task of maintaining the SUMM in the face of evolved language concepts represented in their metamodels, changed consistency rules, and the integration of new viewtypes. Changes in the metamodel can require corresponding changes in the model (i.e., model co-evolution [14]) as well as the creation or adaptation of consistency rules. Since languages are subject to change (e.g., new versions of Java are regularly introduced) the difficulty of updating the SUMM and its instances after evolution of the integration languages is a relevant criterion whose importance depends on the probability that languages will evolve. The degrees of difficulty, "easy", "middle", and "hard" depend on how many of the unchanged parts of the SUMM can be reused unchanged in the new SUMM version.

Criterion E5 (SUMM Reusability) focuses on the question of whether only a subset of the integrated metamodels and their consistency rules from one project can be reused to construct a SUMM for other projects, or if a SUMM can only be reused as a whole. Additionally, this criterion addresses the amount of effort involved in adding new metamodels to an already existing SUMM. Although this criterion does not target reuse at the model level, it is important since there are many software development projects that use slightly different languages or consistency rules, which need to be managed. The degrees of difficulty depend on whether each single part of the SUMM can be reused without any manual effort ("easy"), some manual effort is required with some restrictions ("middle") or the SUMM is non-reusable and unstructured ("hard").

4.3 Technical Design Decisions

Technical Design Decisions describe the degrees of freedom available in the technical realization of a single approach. These technical realization choices are orthogonal to the conceptual design decisions (Sect. 4.1) and the related conceptual selection criteria (Sect. 4.2) since they can be realized independently of the actual SUM approach used. In other words, they form degrees of freedom for realizing different technical aspects of a particular SUM approach after deciding on the design criteria. They help platform specialists identify and address technical challenges during implementation.

Criterion T1 (Configuration Languages) addresses the platform specialist's challenge of providing languages that can be used by methodologists to customize a SUM approach to the needs of the current project. In particular, languages to specify project-specific consistency rules are required that allow methodologists to tailor SUM approaches to different projects in different application domains. Methodologists need languages to consider and realize project-specific consistency rules, manipulate the SUM, define additional viewtypes and support additional needs of the developers.

Criterion T2 (Meta-Metamodel) addresses the issues of choosing a language to describe metamodels in the implementation of a SUM approach. This meta-metamodel defines the possible language elements available to methodologists to describe the SUMM and the viewtypes to be integrated.

5 Orthographic Software Modeling

Orthographic Software Modeling (OSM) is a view-based approach initially developed to support software development [2] using multiple perspectives. However, OSM can be applied to other domains like enterprise architecture modeling [27] in order to support methods like Zachman [31].

5.1 Design Objectives

The OSM approach is inspired by the orthographic projection technique used to visualize physical objects in CAD systems. OSM utilizes this principle to define "orthogonal" views on a system under development that present each stakeholder, such as software engineers, with the data he or she needs in a domain-specific notation. Stakeholders can only see and manipulate the system using the views, since the actual description of the system is stored in a SUM. The views are defined to be as "orthogonal" as possible using independent dimensions (i.e., concerns) ranging from behavioral properties and feature specifications to architectural composition. Ultimately, the system description in the SUM can be made formal enough to be automatically deployed and executed on appropriate platforms, thus allowing automatic redeployment on changes. To support the complete life-cycle of a system, ranging from requirements analysis to deployment, the internal structure of the SUM must support the storing of all required data in a clean and uniform way. The data in the SUM should thus be free from dependencies and capture all relationships between inner elements in a redundancy-free way using approaches like *Information Compression* and *Information Expansion* [3].

In order to use the OSM approach, an environment has to be developed which realizes its goals and principles. Both steps, the definition of the approach and the implementation of a framework which supports the concepts of the approach, are performed by a *platform specialist*. The work involves the development of a framework which can be customized for the used methodology (e.g., KobrA [1], MEMO [10], ArchiMate [15]) and the targeted domain (e.g., software engineering, enterprise architecture modeling). The configurations can be reused for projects in the same domain and the same methodology. [27] presents a metamodel which is used by the current prototype implementation to support the configuration of OSM environments. In particular, it facilitates the configuration of the SUMM and viewtypes, and their integration in a dimension-based view navigation approach using hyper-cubes of the kind used in OLAP [6] systems.

A software engineer, playing the role of a *methodologist*, performs the customization of the environment for a specific domain and methodology. In order to be able to configure and customize the environment according to the requirements, the methodologist must have knowledge of the involved domain and the OSM environment. In particular, he or she is responsible for defining the SUMM and the viewtypes in a way

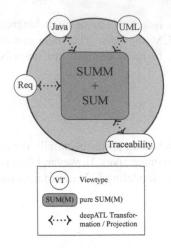

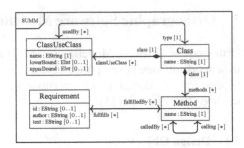

Fig. 2. SUM approach OSM.

Fig. 3. Exemplary metamodel for SUM in OSM (taken from [25]).

that adheres to the principles of redundancy-freeness and minimality. Defining a view-type involves the definition of a suitable metamodel as well as a model transformation that maps the concepts from the SUM to those in a view and vice versa. The resulting configuration can be stored in the tooling environment for reuse in other projects.

Once a complete configuration of an OSM environment has been defined by a *methodologist, developers* can use it to develop a specific system specification. To this end, either an empty SUM is created to start a project from scratch, or existing content is imported into the SUM using model-to-model transformations from external artifacts. When using the OSM platform to develop a system, developers are able to access views using the dimension-based view navigation approach and use them to see and update information from the SUM.

5.2 Application to the Running Example

Figure 3 shows an example of an OSM-oriented SUMM, corresponding to the information presented in Fig. 1. Since a fundamental tenet of the OSM approach is to have a *pure and optimized SUMM*, it is usually created manually from scratch based on the needed viewtypes and concerns of the involved stakeholders. Figure 3 is a reduced version of Fig. 1 in which all redundant information, and thus the correspondences that connect duplicate stores of data, have been manually removed. Thus, for example, the two equivalent elements ClassType and Class have been compressed into one concept Class in Fig. 3. This is possible because although the two concepts define their own properties for their own contexts, and use different names (i.e., name and className), they are in fact equivalent and can be combined. Both attributes are therefore mapped to the single attribute name in the SUMM. The two dependencies are distinct and are hence both added to the Class element: The first allows Classes to have Methods, while the second describes dependencies between two

`Classes` (Consistency Rule 1). Consistency Rule 2 is captured by a relationship between `Requirement` and `Method`, representing the fact that the requirement is being fulfilled by the method. In order to allow developers to create instances of the relationship, a new view can be defined containing at least the concepts `Requirement`, `Method` and the relationship between them. While Fig. 3 shows the integration of the 3 domains into a SUMM, Fig. 2 shows the arrangement of the viewtypes resulting from the integrated domains. Each viewtype is related by a one-to-one projection to the SUMM, or more precisely to the relevant concepts from the SUMM. The data structure shown in Fig. 3 is simpler than disparate representation in Fig. 1. This is achieved by unifying names for equivalent concepts (`ClassType` vs. `Class`) and using names with more meaning (`Association` vs. `ClassUseClass`). Although the SUMM is built from scratch in the presented example, in principle it is possible to import existing artifacts into the environment using model-to-model transformations.

5.3 Classification Based on the Criteria

In OSM the SUM is built following a *top-down* approach (**C1**) , based on the domain and applied methodology. Since the SUM is created from scratch, it can be constructed in an optimal way by avoiding any internal redundancies and dependencies, resulting in an *essential* SUM (**C2**) (see Table 1).

The **E1** selection criterion is only conceptually supported by the OSM approach ("hard") since engineers can always informally draw upon the information contained in existing metamodels when constructing the essential SUMM, either manually or by model-to-model transformations. However, this is not a formal part of the approach. The OSM approach supports the **E2** selection criterion in a semi-automatic way, i.e. by importing data from existing models into the newly constructed SUM using model transformations ("hard"). The models do not need to be initially consistent as long as the transformations are defined to generate consistent output. As the essential SUM provides an integrated and redundancy-free structure, the **E3** selection criterion can be easily fulfilled by the OSM approach ("easy"), since the information relevant for views is contained in one single artifact, the SUM. The **E4** selection criterion, related to model evolution, is supported quite well ("middle") by OSM's essential SUM principle, since it is free of redundant information but has to check that the changes keep the SUMM redundancy-free. However, the transformations that generate views from the SUM have to be updated manually to stay up-to-date with the SUMM changes. Finally, the **E5** selection criterion is supported by OSM, since a SUMM can easily be extended by adding new concepts directly into the existing structure where they are needed. However, redundancy-freeness must be preserved and when concepts are removed from the SUMM, related concepts have to be checked to ensure consistency ("middle").

The configuration of the current OSM prototype environment is realized using the ECORE modeling language (**T1**), which is used to define the dimension-based view-navigation feature of OSM. The SUMM and the view-types are defined using the PLM modeling language (**T2**), which supports the usage of multiple classification levels using ontologies, while the relationships between the SUMM and the view-types are defined using the DeepATL transformation language.

6 VITRUVIUS

The VITRUVIUS approach [18] is based on a so called *virtual SUMM (V-SUMM)*, which composes a SUMM of existing metamodels instead of creating it from scratch. Therefore, VITRUVIUS relies on pragmatic SUMMs that are defined in a bottom-up fashion.

6.1 Design Objectives

In the VITRUVIUS approach, the whole description of a system is encapsulated in a SUM, which may only be modified via projectional views. This conforms to the projectional SUM idea of the OSM approach. VITRUVIUS follows a pragmatic approach by composing a SUMM of existing metamodels that are coupled by Consistency Preservation Rules (CPRs), which specify how consistency of dependent information in instances of those metamodels is preserved after one of them is changed. The CPRs use and modify a trace model that contains so called *correspondences*, which reference model elements that have to be kept consistent. A set of metamodels with a set of CPRs constitutes a virtual SUMM (V-SUMM), while instances of them with an actual correspondence model are denoted as V-SUMs. These CPRs make dependencies between metamodels explicit and ensure that after modifications in one model, all other dependent models are updated consistently. A V-SUM operates *inductively*, i.e., it is always consistent before a modification and ensures that it is again consistent after modifications by executing the CPRs. As a consequence, a V-SUM behaves completely like an essential SUM in the OSM approach since it provides the same guarantees regarding consistency.

Consistency preservation in VITRUVIUS is performed in a delta-based manner. In other words, it tracks edit operations instead of comparing two models states like in state-based consistency preservation. This results in less information loss [8]. For example, a state-based approach cannot reliably distinguish the deletion and creation of an element from renaming it, whereas a delta-based approach tracks the actual operations. Specific languages have been developed that support the definition of such delta-based consistency preservation in the VITRUVIUS approach [17]. Consistency preservation in VITRUVIUS was first investigated on a case study of component-based architectures, Java code and code contracts [19].

The development of a framework such as VITRUVIUS first involves a *platform specialist* who defines the interface of a V-SUM, implements the logic for executing CPRs and defines or selects specific languages or at least an interface to define CPRs. The current implementation of the VITRUVIUS approach (http://vitruv.tools) based on Ecore contains a Java-based definition of V-SUMs and provides two languages for defining consistency preservation at different abstraction levels.

The *methodologist* selects metamodels and reuses or defines CPRs for those selected metamodels to define a V-SUMM. Finally, one or more *developers* can instantiate the V-SUMM, derive views according to existing or newly defined viewtypes, and perform modifications of them. A change recorder tracks modifications in a view and applies them to the V-SUM as a sequence of atomic change events (creation, deletion, insertion, removal or replacement). After each of these changes is applied, the responsible CPRs are executed to restore consistency, which results in an *inductively consistent* V-SUM.

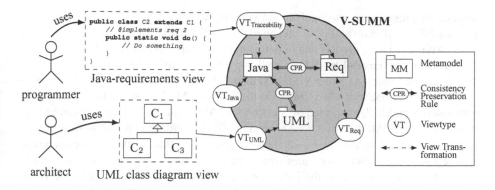

Fig. 4. Example V-SUMM in VITRUVIUS (extended version of Fig. 3 of [25]).

6.2 Application to the Running Example

We depict an exemplary V-SUMM for the metamodels from Fig. 1 in Fig. 4. It consists of the reused metamodels and a set of CPRs between them. For Consistency Rule 1 a CPR defines the creation of a Java class ClassType in reaction to the creation of a UML class Class. The methodologist is free to specify the expected behavior in the other direction, i.e., whether a UML class is created for each Java class or if the developer shall be asked what to do. Additionally, the rule propagates all changes on the name or className to the respective other model. The additional requirements traces in Consistency Rule 2 can be expressed by matching requirements and methods after adding or modifying methods as well as requirements, and by storing them as correspondences in the existing trace model. Alternatively, such links could be specified in an additional model, which is modified by a CPR whenever a requirement or method is changed.

Two types of projectional viewtypes can be defined on a V-SUMM. First, existing viewtypes for the existing metamodels, such as a textual editor for Java or a graphical editor for UML, can be reused. In Fig. 4, these viewtypes are VT_{Java}, VT_{UML} and VT_{Req}, which provide concrete syntaxes for the original metamodels from Fig. 1. Second, the methodologist and the developers can define additional viewtypes, which may combine information from different metamodels and their relations defined in the CPRs. Figure 4 contains $VT_{Traceability}$, which displays the trace information for Consistency Rule 2 by extracting information from Java and the requirements model, as well as from the correspondences generated by the CPRs. This viewtype could, as exemplarily sketched in Fig. 4, show the Java code with annotations attached to the methods that show the requirements they fulfill. Such viewtypes may combine information from multiple metamodels, which needs to be supported by an appropriate language. In VITRUVIUS, that can be expressed with the ModelJoin language [5].

6.3 Classification Regarding the Criteria

VITRUVIUS follows a *bottom-up* construction approach (**C1**) to build a *pragmatic* SUM (**C2**). This V-SUMM may contain redundancies, but keeps them consistent by explicit consistency preservation mechanisms. In general, VITRUVIUS provides good support for reusability and evolvability of metamodels and SUMMs, but requires considerable effort to reuse existing models and to define new viewtypes (see Table 1).

Metamodel Reusability (E1) is well supported ("easy"), because existing metamodels can be integrated into a V-SUMM as is without further effort. They serve as an unmodified component of a V-SUMM. On the contrary, **Model Reusability (E2)** is only moderately ("middle") supported by VITRUVIUS. Although existing models can be integrated into a V-SUM, they first need to be consistent according to the consistency rules, and second, have to be enriched with the correspondences that would have been created if the consistency preservation rules were executed during the creation of the models. This is necessary because of the inductive characteristics of the approach. **Viewtype Definability (E3)** is comparatively difficult ("hard") using VITRUVIUS, because information that is to be projected into a view is potentially spread across several models so that information has to be combined and aggregated. This may require high effort and especially high knowledge about the involved metamodels from the person who specifies a viewtype. To ease viewtype definition, VITRUVIUS provides the specialized ModelJoin language for defining viewtypes on several models.

One well supported feature is **Language Evolvability (E4)** ("easy"). Due to the integration of original metamodels into the V-SUMM, their evolution can be easily supported. Necessary adaptations after the evolution of a metamodels concern the defined CPRs, as well as defined viewtypes. Finally, **SUMM Reusability (E5)** is high ("easy"), because it is easy to add or remove single metamodels from the V-SUMM by just adding or removing the metamodels with associated CPRs. For that reason, the reuse of a subset of the metamodels in a V-SUMM is well supported and enables the reuse of parts of a V-SUMM in a different context and the combinations with other V-SUMMs.

Regarding technical design decisions, the configuration languages **(T1)** in VITRUVIUS consist of the declarative Mappings language and the imperative Reactions language for specifying CPRs, as well as the ModelJoin language for defining view types on several metamodels. All concepts of VITRUVIUS are designed for a meta-metamodel **(T2)** that conforms to the EMOF standard. This especially includes the Ecore metametamodel that is used for the current implementation of VITRUVIUS.

7   RSUM

The Role-based Single Underlying Model (RSUM, [30]) follows the same basic idea as the VITRUVIUS approach where several metamodels are kept consistent with consistency preservation rules. However, the metamodels are no longer regarded as separate, but can be reconnected and combined with new relations as visualized in Fig. 5.

7.1   Design Objectives

Regarding the design objectives, the RSUM approach differs only slightly from the VITRUVIUS approach and follows the projectional SUM idea, whereby all information is stored in a pragmatic SUM of different combined models. Additionally, only projectional views can be generated on this SUM. Compared to the VITRUVIUS approach,

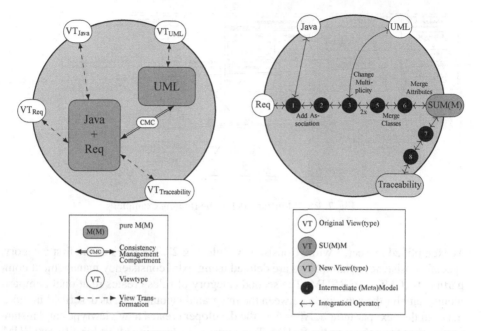

Fig. 5. SUM approach RSUM.

Fig. 6. SUM approach MoConseMI with Chain of Configured Operators to integrate Requirements, UML and Java, adapted from [25].

which works in the background with object-based programming, the RSUM approach uses role-based programming as introduced by Kühn *et al.* [21] in the form of the Compartment Role Object Model (CROM). The idea behind CROM is a new partition of elements into natural types, role types, and compartment types. Naturals describe fixed objects that play roles in compartments. A role adapts the behavior of a natural in a compartment and interacts with various other roles in it. The concept of compartments is used in the RSUM approach to explicitly describe consistency preservation rules (CPRs) and build relationships [29] between metamodel elements that blur the boundaries of the base metamodels. The compartments for consistency assurance follow an incremental approach and propagate all changes directly to the related elements. Such incremental direct propagation is also implemented between views and the RSUM, and back. It is planned to extend the change propagation with the use of transactions.

For the development of the RSUM framework, a *platform specialist* is required that provides the basic functionalities for the integration of new views, metamodels, models, and CPRs. The direct implementations can be automatically generated with Domain Specific Languages (DSLs), created by the *platform specialist*, and integrated into the framework. The current RSUM implementation uses CROM and is based on the SCala ROLes Language (SCROLL) [23], a role-based programming language in Scala.

The *methodologist* selects the needed metamodels and then defines all CPRs between these metamodels in predefined DSLs. Consistency rules differ in two classes,

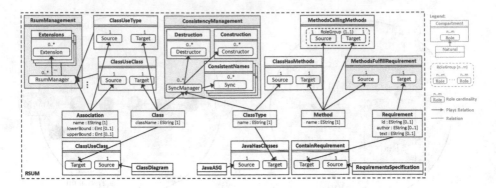

Fig. 7. RSUM metamodel of the running example.

as exemplified in Sect. 3 with "Consistency Rule 1 & 2". For rules of the first category, special consistency relationships are defined using extra consistency management compartments (CMCs) in RSUM. The second category of rules creates relational compartments that blur the separation between the integrated metamodels, as described in more detail in the next paragraph. After that, the developer creates new viewtypes and instantiates views from them on the RSUM. To minimize the learning effort for different SUM approaches, the RSUM approach uses the syntax of ModelJoin [5] to define viewtypes, which is used to generate view compartments with incremental change propagation to the RSUM. In the RSUM, consistency is automatically ensured by the defined CPRs.

7.2 Application to the Running Example

Figure 7 shows an RSUM at the metamodel level resulting from the running example in Fig. 1. The basic concept consists of separating all relations from the classes and managing them in extra relational compartments. This leads to a certain additional overhead but simplifies the administration of the elements in the RSUM and the views. Furthermore, they are automatically generated when integrating metamodels in the RSUM, whereby this design decision remains hidden from the developer. Figure 7 highlights three special compartments in grey that are not created by integrating metamodels. The RsumManagement compartment is the central component of the RSUM approach and manages the internal elements, the active and inactive views, and the extensions where currently only one extension for recording changes is preimplemented. The other two compartments serve to ensure consistency in RSUM and are only created when a consistency rule is defined and integrated. In this case, the ConsistencyManagement compartment (CMC) ensures consistency between the naturals Class and ClassType, defining what happens to the other element when deleting, inserting, or modifying one of these elements. This compartment is automatically generated after describing the CPRs from a *methodologist* in the predefined DSLs. The last highlighted compartment is the MethodsFulfillRequirement compartment, which represents a new relation between the naturals Method and Requirement. This compartment is created by a DSL and then integrated into the

RSUM. This new relation merges the requirements model with the Java source code model as shown on an abstract level in Fig. 5.

For the generation of views, projections can be generated on all relations (relational compartments) and naturals. In this approach, the views are implemented as compartments, which means that the elements in the RSUM only play roles in the views and therefore do not generate materialized views. The flexibility arising from the fact that roles can be played by other elements at instance level is a big advantage of the role concept and makes the approach useful.

7.3 Classification Regarding the Criteria

When considering the design criteria, the RSUM approach looks the same as the VIT-RUVIUS approach. It follows a *bottom-up* design approach **(C1)** to create a *pragmatic* SUM **(C2)** and does not resolve inconsistencies but provides consistency management through CPRs. If there are certain 1-to-1 mappings between model elements in the CPRs, it would be possible to merge them into one natural type. However, this leads to disadvantages in a language evolution step.

The reusability of metamodels **(E1)** is supported as the metamodels have no special dependencies in the RSUM and new ones can be added without much effort ("easy"). Regarding the reusability of models **(E2)**, it looks like the reusability of metamodels without the possibility to compare input models with existing instances ("middle"). Currently, (meta)models can be automatically integrated into RSUM as Ecore and XMI files. Since the definition of viewtypes **(E3)** requires knowledge of the integrated metamodels, this could lead to some problems ("middle"). If, however, enough knowledge of the underlying models is available or only predefined viewtypes of the *methodologist* are used, the use of ModelJoin no longer poses a problem. The evolution of languages **(E4)** is relatively easy due to the integration of metamodels ("middle"). However, not only the consistency compartments have to be modified, all additional relational compartments must be adapted. As in VITRUVIUS, the SUMM **(E5)** is easy to reuse since metamodels and consistency relationships can easily be integrated and removed because of the loosely coupling of all elements provide by the role concept.

Regarding the technical criteria, a DSL is used to generate the CPRs and also viewtypes are generated with ModelJoin queries **(T1)**. The management of the created elements is done by the `RsumManagement` compartment. In the background the RSUM approach works with the role-based programming language SCROLL on the CROM model, which is modeled with ECORE **(T2)**.

8   MoConseMI

MOdel CONSistency Ensured by Metamodel Integration (MOCONSEMI, [26]) combines the bottom-up reuse of existing (meta-)models with their operator-based improvement into one more essential SUM.

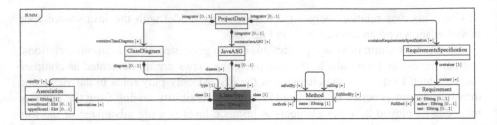

Fig. 8. SUMM with integrated Requirements, Class Diagrams and Java (taken from [25]).

8.1   Design Objectives

MOCONSEMI is a SUM approach which starts with existing initial models and conforming metamodels (exemplarily shown in Fig. 1) and creates a SUM(M) as suggested by [2]. In practice, many models and metamodels already exist in the form of DSLs and tools with fixed data schemas. To reuse them, these initial models and metamodels are integrated and kept in sync as views of the SUM. To achieve this, the initial models and conforming metamodels have to be transformed into the final SUM and conforming SUMM. Therefore, the required transformations have to target *models and metamodels together*.

After creating the initial SUM(M) as the output of the executed transformations with the initial (meta)models as input, the initial models have to be kept consistent with respect to changes made by the developer in the SUM. Therefore, the transformations have to be executable in an inverse direction from the SUM to the initial models, as well as in a forward direction. The last main design objective of MOCONSEMI is that the required transformations are reusable in different projects, not only in software engineering projects.

To fulfill these design objectives, MOCONSEMI uses *operators* which divide the whole transformation between initial models and the SUM into chains of small and reusable parts. Each operator does a small change on the current metamodel (e.g., adds a new association) controlled by metamodel decisions (e.g., multiplicities, source and target class of the new association). To achieve the required model co-evolution [14], the operator also changes the current model to keep it consistent with the changed metamodel. Degrees of freedom in the model-co-evolution process are influenced by model decisions, which allow consistency rules to be fulfilled (e.g., specify, when new links should be added, or if at all). The concatenation of several operators builds the whole transformation between initial models and SUM. Additionally, the operators can be used to define new viewtypes on top of the SUMM. The required backward executability of operators is attained by combining each operator with an inverse operator, e.g., `DeleteAssociation` for `AddAssociation`.

8.2   Application to the Running Example

The operators are developed once by the *platform specialist* and are provided as a reusable library (currently 23 operators including inverse ones). A supporting framework is under development using Java and a subset of Ecore, reusing parts of Eclipse EDapt [13], and extending some coupled operators [14] for the needs of MoCONSEMI.

The methodologist reuses the provided operators by combining them as chain of operators to describe the transformation between initial (meta-)models (Fig. 1) and SUM(M) (Fig. 8) in step-wise way as shown in Fig. 6 individually for each project. The methodologist uses the metamodel and model decisions to configure the operators to support the consistency rules for the current project.

The first step is to combine the initial models and metamodels for [Requirements], [Java] and [ClassDiagrams] only technically at ❶ and ❸. For this, the used EMF framework requires `ProjectData` and its compositions as container (Fig. 8).After that, Consistency Rule 2 is realized by the operator `AddAssociation` ❶→❷ as the first contentwise integration regarding traceability links between requirements and methods.It creates a new association between `Requirement` and `Method` whenever required and thereby enables traceability information to store. In the model, the operator adds links between some methods and requirements as configured by the methodologist to ensure that a method is linked with those requirements that contain the name of the method in their text.

Before fulfilling Consistency Rule 1, the operator `ChangeMultiplicity` is applied twice ❺ as a technical preparation. After that, `MergeClasses` ❺→❻ merges the two classes `Class` (from UML) and `ClassType` (from Java) into one single class in the metamodel representing data classes both in UML and Java at the same time. In the model, matching UML and Java instances are merged into each other, again controlled by a model decision, which was configured to identify matching instances when they have the same values for `Class.className` and `ClassType.name`. The motivation for this merging step is the unification of redundant information which ensures consistency and makes the resulting SUM more "essential". Finally, `MergeAttributes` merges the two redundantly name attributes. The last stable model and metamodel are used as the [SUM(M)]. The SUMM in Fig. 8 marks the changes done by the operators in red compared to the initial metamodels in Fig. 1.

Ultimately, MoCONSEMI "migrates" the initial (meta)models to view(type)s on the SUM(M). Therefore, the *developer* can change the initial models, the SUM and the newly defined views in the same way. To propagate the changes automatically into all other models in order to ensure their consistency, the operator chain is executed in forward and backward directions.

8.3   Classification Regarding the Criteria

Since MoCONSEMI starts with the initial (meta-)models, it is *bottom-up* regarding **C1** (see Table 1) and inherits all their initial redundancies. Because the operators can resolve redundancies in a step-wise way, pureness can be improved until, in the best case, a SUM(M) without any dependencies is attained **(C2)**.

Metamodel Reusability (E1) is well supported ("easy"), since the initial metamodels are used as the starting point of the operator chain. The same counts for the **Model Reusability (E2)** ("easy"), since even initial inconsistencies can be resolved by executing the operator chain in both directions. **Viewtype Definability (E3)** benefits by the

Table 1. Comparison of the four approaches regarding design criteria, selection criteria, and technical design decisions (extended version of Table 1 from [25]).

Criterion	OSM	VITRUVIUS	RSUM	MOCONSEMI
C1 Construction Process	top-down	bottom-up	bottom-up	bottom-up
C2 Pureness	essential	pragmatic	pragmatic	pragmatic → essential
E1 Metamodel Reusability	hard	easy	easy	easy
E2 Model Reusability	hard	middle	middle	easy
E3 Viewtype Definability	easy	hard	middle	middle
E4 Language Evolvability	middle	easy	middle	middle
E5 SUMM Reusability	middle	easy	easy	middle
T1 Configuration Languages	Ecore, DeepATL	Mappings/React., ModelJoin	RCs, ModelJoin	Bidirect. Operators
T2 Meta-Metamodel	PLM	Ecore	CROM	Ecore

explicit and integrated SUMM, since all information is collected and integrated inside one metamodel ("middle"). In contrast to OSM, the SUM(M) in MOCONSEMI might still contain redundant information, which makes the definition of new viewtypes harder, since the same information can be found at different places. The **Language Evolvability (E4)** in MOCONSEMI highly depends on the kind of change. Additional elements in the metamodels are directly added to the SUMM without any changes in the operator chain, while big refactorings in the metamodels require lots of changes in the operator chain ("middle"). **SUMM Reusability (E5)** is easy when adding new metamodels, because the existing chain of operators is lengthen by some more operators. Removing an already integrated metamodel requires all the operators which were needed for its integration to be removed or changed ("middle"). As a result, **E5** depends on the order of integrated initial (meta-)models ("middle").

Regarding technical design decisions, MOCONSEMI uses chains of operators as a configuration language which change metamodels and models together to create the initial SUM(M) and to keep all models consistent **(T1)** . The same operators allow new views to be defined. The current implementation supports a subset of ECore **(T2)** .

9   Discussion and Comparison of SUM Approaches

This section summarizes the classification of the four presented SUM approaches in Table 1 regarding the three groups of classification criteria. Each approach's classification is described in detail in its respective section, so this section contains a more abstract discussion about the dependencies of the criteria on each other. It also answers the general question of which approach fits best for which situation and why. We conclude this section with the idea of combining SUM approaches to create more flexible ones.

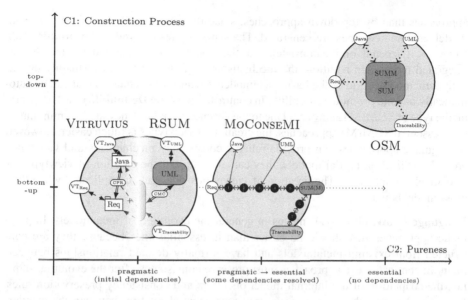

Fig. 9. Conceptual Classification of SUM Approaches.

9.1 Design Criteria

Design criteria form the foundation of every approach and therefore have considerable influence on the manifestation of the selection criteria and limit the technical implementation possibilities. Figure 9 shows the solution space spanned by the design criteria and the placement of the four presented approaches. Each approach can be distinguished as a *top-down or bottom-up* approach **(C1)**, whereby the decision to use existing models is considered as a starting point. Three of the presented approaches (VITRUVIUS, RSUM, and MOCONSEMI) follow a bottom-up approach while one (OSM) follows a top-down approach. The top-down variant has the advantage that a new model is created and can be adapted to the requirements of users. This facilitates the definition of new viewtypes and avoids redundancy. However, it offers no reuse opportunities and makes adaptation and evolution more difficult. Bottom-up approaches, on the other hand, offer increased reusability, but require more effort to manage the (meta)models.

The use of an *essential or pragmatic* SUM(M) approach **(C2)** is directly influenced by the decision whether a top-down or bottom-up approach is used **(C1)**. In a bottom-up approach, it is hard to achieve a SUM that is free of redundancy. The MOCONSEMI approach is the only one of the four approaches that offers a way of moving from a pragmatic to an essential SUM(M) by creating a redundancy-free SUM(M) bottom-up. In a top-down approach, redundancy can already be avoided by construction.

9.2 Selection Criteria

The selection criteria depend mainly on the underlying design criteria as mentioned in the previous section. **Metamodel Reusability (E1)** is better supported by bottom-up approaches than by top-down approaches, since they are already based on the meta-models and no new ones are generated. The same applies to **Model Reusability (E2)**. However, it depends on the consistency of the models to be integrated and the already integrated models. In addition, the mechanisms for reusability depend mainly on the automatic modification of the basic metamodels because only changes that can be auto-matically undone promote reusability. In contrast, **Viewtype Definability (E3)** depends on the type of SUM(M) approach. Due to the absence of redundancy and the minimality of an essential SUM(M) approaches, the creation of viewtypes is much easier. However, if pragmatic approaches can provide reliable consistency mechanisms and viewtypes are only defined on partial models, they can also support the creation of viewtypes in a relatively simple way. The creation of viewpoints only gets complicated when they cross model boundaries.

Language Evolvability (E4) means in general the evolution of metamodels. In prag-matic approaches this should be easier than in essential ones because they are con-structed from existing metamodels and have formally defined relationships between them. In contrast, these approaches must preserve consistency after the evolution steps, i.e., the adaptation of the internal model operators and consistency preservation rules. In essential approaches, there exists only a conceptual relation between the existing artifacts and the SUMM, i.e., a manual adaptation of the new metamodel must be done to ensure redundancy-freeness and minimality that leads to high effort and error prone-ness. **SUMM Reusability (E5)** does not have much to do with criteria E1-E4, since it is about adding and removing single metamodel elements in the SUMM. Pragmatic and essential approaches achieve this in a different way. Pragmatic approaches facilitate the simple addition and removal of metamodels, as the structure of the original metamodels still exist separately and the change operations are performed on the abstract metalevel. In contrast, essential approaches make it easy to fine-tune metamodels to project needs, since the manipulation of the essential SUMM is possible at the level of individual model elements. The existence of only one model without dependencies removes the clear boundaries between the starting metamodels.

The application of the selection criteria highlights the general differences between the four SUM approaches. None of the presented criteria is fulfilled by one approach best, i.e., each approach has its pros and cons regarding all considered criteria. In gen-eral, each selection criteria can be realized in a simple way if the corresponding design criteria is selected, or in complex way using a lot of boilerplate code if a different (non-corresponding) design criteria is selected. From the correlation of design and selection criteria, dependencies can also be determined within the selection criteria. The list of criteria presented here cannot be considered complete and it is unclear whether these are the most important criteria for selecting a SUM approach. However, the criteria can be used as an initial indicator of which approach would be best, since relevant situations such as the evolution and reusability of metamodels and other points are covered.

9.3   Technical Design Decisions

The technical design decisions (**T1** and **T2**) are independent of the two categories described before, since the implementation of each approach depends on the preferred

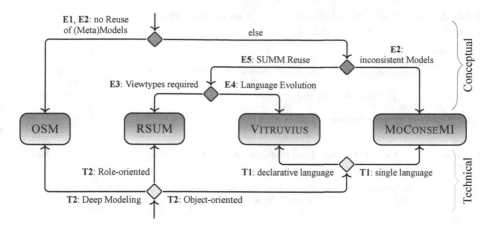

Fig. 10. Process for selecting SUM Approaches.

languages but could be done with different technical choices. The current implementations for each of the four approaches are presented here, all of which are constantly evolving. The used **Configuration Languages (T1)** apply the generic approaches to specific application projects. These configuration languages contain transformation languages to manage the consistency in, and the integration of models into, the SUM. In addition, they imply query languages to realize initial and new view(type)s on top of the SUM. If we consider the **Meta-Metamodel (T2)** of the four approaches they cover the complete space between object-oriented modeling via role-oriented modeling to deep modelling, which show that each technology allows the realization of SUM approaches.

9.4   Process for Approach Selection

After describing the overall differences between the four SUM approaches regarding the different criteria, in this section we describe a process for selecting a SUM approach, as illustrated in Fig. 10. This process considers the choice of an approach from a technical and a conceptual point of view.

From a conceptual point of view the main question is about the existence and degree of reuse of legacy tools or metamodels (**E1** and **E2**). If there are no tools or metamodels to reuse, the *top-down* OSM approach fits most because it defines a new metamodels without redundancy that can avoid dependencies to external tool vendors. In addition, OSM provides a simple viewtype definition strategy (**E3**). If the reusability of (meta-)models or viewtypes is important, *bottom-up* approaches (**C1**) like VITRUVIUS, RSUM, or MOCONSEMI are a better choice. These approaches are compatible to existing tools or even to complete development environments and facilitate integration without remodeling models. When the models have inconsistencies, MOCONSEMI is best because the models contained therein do not have to be conform to any specific consistency rules and can be initially adapted. If the reusability of the SUMM (**E5**) is more important, VITRUVIUS or RSUM are the most appropriate. These approaches allow the modular definition of consistency relationships and the reusability of these and the

Table 2. Main advantages and disadvantages of approaches with exemplary application areas (extended version of Table 2 from [25]).

	OSM	VITRUVIUS	RSUM	MOCONSEMI
Advantages	Easy Viewtype Definition	Reuse of Metamodels/Tools	Reuse of Models + Metamodels	Reuse of Models + Metamodels
	No Dependencies to Legacy Tools	Modular Views	Modular Views	Easy + incremental Integration
Disadvantages	No Support for Existing Artifacts	Difficult Reuse of Models	Overhead for role-modeling and programming	No Modularity
Exemplary Application Areas	No Reuse of (Meta-)Models	Reuse of Metamodels	Reuse of (Meta-)Models	Reuse of (Meta-)Models
	New Domain Description Language	Combination of Existing Standards for new Projects	Runtime adaptation and integration of (Meta-)Models	Software Re-Engineering Activities

(meta-)models across projects. VITRUVIUS and RSUM differ in the complexity of view definition (**E3**) (use RSUM) and language evolution (**E4**) (use VITRUVIUS).

If the selection of a SUM approach is based on technical specifications, the question of the implementation paradigm (**T2**) arises first. The OSM prototype implementation currently uses deep modeling for the implementation, whereby RSUM is based on the role-based programming paradigm. In contrast, the approaches MOCONSEMI and VITRUVIUS use object orientation. One important difference between VITRUVIUS and MOCONSEMI is the type of configuration languages (**T1**) supported. VITRUVIUS uses multiple declarative languages in while MOCONSEMI only uses a single language.

In summary, the guideline in Fig. 10 offers a decision-making aid for selecting the most suitable SUM approach from a technical or conceptual point of view. In addition, Table 2 summarizes the main advantages and disadvantages of the four SUM approaches.

9.5　Combination of SUM Approaches

As well as selecting a single SUM approach (Sect. 9.4), there can sometimes also be advantages in combining several SUM approaches. Since SUMs can be accessed by well defined views, their provided viewtypes can be used to merge several SUMs into a single unified SUM. If an essential SUM was defined to support the modeling of a specific aspect of a system using the OSM approach, it could be combined with other already existing metamodels in pragmatic SUMs using the VITRUVIUS, RSUM or MOCONSEMI approach.

A similar strategy helps to ease the construction of pragmatic SUMs. If several (meta-)models are combined, pragmatic SUMs can become incomprehensible because of the growing number of interrelations between the (meta-)models. Instead, combining only small numbers of metamodels into a pragmatic SUM and hierarchically composing these pragmatic SUM into larger SUMs reduces the complexity of each individual SUM and improves their reusability. For example, it may be reasonable to combine highly related metamodels, such as object-oriented programming languages and UML class diagrams, into one SUM, which is equivalent to create an essential SUM, and to combine that SUM with other, less related metamodels instead of combining them all together. Nevertheless, this currently only represents a conceptual possibility and its feasibility and applicability have to be further investigated in future work.

10 Conclusion

Larger and more complex systems require mechanisms to ensure holistic consistency during system development. This paper presents uniform terminology and a criteria catalog for the classification of approaches that use a SUM-based approach as a solution to the consistency problem. These are then used to define a set of guidelines that can be used to select which one of the four presented SUM approaches, OSM, VITRUVIUS, RSUM, and MOCONSEMI, is the most suitable for a particular project. To this end, the selection of an approach can be considered either from a technical point of view based on the programming paradigm or from a conceptual point of view based on the selection criteria including metamodel reusability and viewtype definability.

The four presented approaches cover the entire solution space available at the present time. The OSM approach describes a *top-down* approach where a *pure* SUM is created without redundancies. On the other hand, the RSUM and VITRUVIUS approaches are based on *pragmatic* SUMs that take a *bottom-up* approach to keep multiple models consistent through defined relationships. MOCONSEMI also introduces a *bottom-up* approach, but can move between *pragmatic* and *essential* SUMs since redundant information can be removed. We are not currently aware of an implementation of a pragmatic top-down approach.

OSM is regarded as the initiator of the initial SUM idea, where models are only views of an entire model and are projected from it by transformations. RSUM, VITRUVIUS, and MOCONSEMI are concrete strategies for constructing a pragmatic implementation, since the use of a single, redundancy-free model has some disadvantages as described in the discussion.

References

1. Atkinson, C.: Component-Based Product Line Engineering with UML. Addison-Wesley, Boston (2002)
2. Atkinson, C., Stoll, D., Bostan, P.: Orthographic software modeling: a practical approach to view-based development. In: Maciaszek, L.A., González-Pérez, C., Jablonski, S. (eds.) ENASE 2008. CCIS, vol. 69, pp. 206–219. Springer, Heidelberg (2010). https://doi.org/10.1007/978-3-642-14819-4_15
3. Atkinson, C., Tunjic, C., Moller, T.: Fundamental realization strategies for multi-view specification environments. In: 19th International Enterprise Distributed Object Computing Conference, pp. 40–49. IEEE (2015)
4. Bruneliere, H., Burger, E., Cabot, J., Wimmer, M.: A feature-based survey of model view approaches. Softw. Syst. Model. **9764**, 138–155 (2017)
5. Burger, E., Henß, J., Küster, M., Kruse, S., Happe, L.: View-based model-driven software development with ModelJoin. Softw. Syst. Model. **15**(2), 472–496 (2014)
6. Codd, E., Codd, S., Salley, C.: Providing OLAP (On-line Analytical Processing) to User-Analysts: An IT Mandate. Codd & Associates, Manchester (1993)

7. Dayal, U., Bernstein, P.A.: On the updatability of network views–extending relational view theory to the network model. Inf. Syst. **7**(1), 29–46 (1982)
8. Diskin, Z., Xiong, Y., Czarnecki, K., Ehrig, H., Hermann, F., Orejas, F.: From state- to delta-based bidirectional model transformations: the symmetric case. In: Whittle, J., Clark, T., Kühne, T. (eds.) MODELS 2011. LNCS, vol. 6981, pp. 304–318. Springer, Heidelberg (2011). https://doi.org/10.1007/978-3-642-24485-8_22
9. Finkelstein, A., Kramer, J., Nuseibeh, B., Finkelstein, L., Goedicke, M.: Viewpoints: a framework for integrating multiple perspectives in system development. Int. J. Softw. Eng. Knowl. Eng. **2**(1), 31–57 (1992)
10. Frank, U.: Multi-perspective enterprise modeling (MEMO) - conceptual framework and modeling languages. In: Hawaii International Conference on System Sciences (HICSS), pp. 72–81 (2002)
11. Goldschmidt, T., Becker, S., Burger, E.: Towards a tool-oriented taxonomy of view- based modelling. In: Proceedings of the Modellierung 2012. GI-Edition – Lecture Notes in Informatics (LNI), pp. 59–74. GI e.V. (2012)
12. Haren, V.: TOGAF Version 9.1. Van Haren Publishing, Zaltbommel (2011)
13. Herrmannsdoerfer, M.: COPE – a workbench for the coupled evolution of metamodels and models. In: Malloy, B., Staab, S., van den Brand, M. (eds.) SLE 2010. LNCS, vol. 6563, pp. 286–295. Springer, Heidelberg (2011). https://doi.org/10.1007/978-3-642-19440-5_18
14. Herrmannsdoerfer, M., Vermolen, S.D., Wachsmuth, G.: An extensive catalog of operators for the coupled evolution of metamodels and models. In: Malloy, B., Staab, S., van den Brand, M. (eds.) SLE 2010. LNCS, vol. 6563, pp. 163–182. Springer, Heidelberg (2011). https://doi.org/10.1007/978-3-642-19440-5_10
15. Iacob, M., Jonkers, D.H., Lankhorst, M., Proper, E., Quartel, D.D.: ArchiMate 2.0 Specification: The Open Group (2012). http://doc.utwente.nl/82972/
16. ISO/IEC/IEEE: ISO/IEC/IEEE 42010:2011(E): Systems and Software Engineering - Architecture Description. International Organization for Standardization, Geneva, Switzerland (2011)
17. Kramer, M.E.: Specification languages for preserving consistency between models of different languages. Ph.D. thesis, Karlsruhe Institute of Technology (KIT) (2017)
18. Kramer, M.E., Burger, E., Langhammer, M.: View-centric engineering with synchronized heterogeneous models. In: Proceedings of the 1st Workshop on View-Based, Aspect-Oriented and Orthographic Software Modelling, VAO 2013, pp. 5:1–5:6. ACM (2013)
19. Kramer, M.E., Langhammer, M., Messinger, D., Seifermann, S., Burger, E.: Change- driven consistency for component code, architectural models, and contracts. In: 18th International ACM SIGSOFT Symposium on Component-Based Software Engineering, CBSE 2015, pp. 21–26. ACM (2015)
20. Kruchten, P.B.: The 4+1 view model of architecture. IEEE Softw. **12**(6), 42–50 (1995)
21. Kühn, T., Leuthäuser, M., Götz, S., Seidl, C., Aßmann, U.: A metamodel family for role-based modeling and programming languages. In: Combemale, B., Pearce, D.J., Barais, O., Vinju, J.J. (eds.) SLE 2014. LNCS, vol. 8706, pp. 141–160. Springer, Cham (2014). https://doi.org/10.1007/978-3-319-11245-9_8
22. Larman, C.: Applying UML and Patterns: An Introduction to Object-Oriented Analysis and Design and Iterative Development, 3rd edn. Prentice Hall, Upper Saddle River (2004)
23. Leuthäuser, M., Aßmann, U.: Enabling view-based programming with scroll: using roles and dynamic dispatch for establishing view-based programming. In: Joint MORSE/- VAO Workshop on Model-Driven Robot Software Engineering and View-based Software-Engineering, pp. 25–33. ACM (2015)
24. Linington, P.F., Milosvic, Z., Tanaka, A., Vallecillo, A.: Building Enterprise Systems with ODP. Chapman and Hall, London (2011)

25. Meier, J., et al.: Single underlying models for projectional, multi-view environments. In: 7th International Conference on Model-Driven Engineering and Software Development, pp. 119–130. SCITEPRESS - Science and Technology Publications (2019)
26. Meier, J., Winter, A.: Model consistency ensured by metamodel integration. In: 6th International Workshop on The Globalization of Modeling Languages, Co-Located with MODELS 2018 (2018)
27. Tunjic, C., Atkinson, C., Draheim, D.: Supporting the model-driven organization vision through deep, orthographic modeling. Enterp. Model. Inf. Syst. Archit.-Int. J. **13**(2), 1–39 (2018)
28. Vangheluwe, H., de Lara, J., Mosterman, P.J.: An introduction to multi-paradigm modelling and simulation. In: AIS'2002 Conference, pp. 9–20 (2002)
29. Werner, C., Schön, H., Kühn, T., Götz, S., Aßmann, U.: Role-based runtime model synchronization. In: 44th Euromicro Conference on Software Engineering and Advanced Applications (SEAA), pp. 306–313 (2018)
30. Werner, C., Aßmann, U.: Model synchronization with the role-oriented single underlying model. In: MODELS 2018 Workshops (2018)
31. Zachman, J.A.: A framework for information systems architecture. IBM Syst. J. **26**(3), 276–292 (1987)

TRILATERAL: A Model-Based Approach for Industrial CPS – Monitoring and Control

Markel Iglesias-Urkia[1](✉) [iD], Aitziber Iglesias[1] [iD], Beatriz López-Davalillo[1] [iD],
Santiago Charramendieta[1] [iD], Diego Casado-Mansilla[2] [iD], Goiuria Sagardui[3] [iD],
and Aitor Urbieta[1] [iD]

[1] Ikerlan Technology Research Centre, P⁰ J. M. Arizmendiarrieta, 2,
20500 Arrasate-Mondragón, Spain
{miglesias,aiglesias,blopezdavalillo,scharramendieta,aurbieta}@ikerlan.es
[2] Deusto Institute of Technology, University of Deusto, Av. Universidades, 24,
48007 Bilbao, Spain
dcasado@deusto.es
[3] Mondragon Unibertsitatea, Loramendi, 4, Apartado 23,
20500 Arrasate-Mondragón, Spain
gsagardui@mondragon.edu

Abstract. Internet of Things (IoT) devices are advanced embedded systems within a Cyber-Physical System (CPS) that require to be monitored and controlled. Such necessities are becoming increasingly common due to the advent of the Industry 4.0 among other smart deployments. A recurring issue in this field is that existing and new projects are reinventing the wheel by starting the development and deployment of IoT devices from scratch. To overcome such loss of efficiency in development, we propose to use Software Product Line (SPL) and Model-Based Engineering (MBE) since they seem promising in the literature in order to accelerate and ease the development software while reducing bugs and errors, and hence, costs. Additionally, a personalized solution is needed since not all Industrial CPSs (ICPSs) are composed by the same devices or use the same IoT communication protocols. Thus, we realized that a Domain Specific Language (DSL) along with a standard, will allow the user to graphically model the ICPS for this to be monitored and controlled. Therefore, this work presents TRILATERAL, a SPL Model Based tool that uses a Domain Specific Language (DSL) to allow users to graphically model ICPSs with a IEC 61850 based metamodel, a standard originally designed for electrical substations but that has also been used in other domains. TRILATERAL automatically generates an artifact in order to create a middleware between the ICPS and the monitoring system to monitor and control all the devices within the ICPS. This tool is designed, implemented and finally, validated with a real use case (catenary-free tram) where different lessons have been learned.

This article is an extended version of the conference paper in [12].

S. Hammoudi et al. (Eds.): MODELSWARD 2019, CCIS 1161, pp. 376–398, 2020.
https://doi.org/10.1007/978-3-030-37873-8_16

Keywords: Internet of Things (IoT) · Cyber-Physical System (CPS) · Domain Specific Language (DSL) · Software Product Line (SPL) · IEC 61850 · Model-Based Engineering (MBE)

1 Introduction

The Fourth Industrial Revolution, also named Industry 4.0 is playing a pivotal role in several industrial domains [13,24], such as Smart Grids, Smart Manufacturing and Smart Logistics. This paradigm joins the cyber and physical world in Cyber-Physical Systems (CPSs), allowing to interconnect all kind of devices of the industrial processes with the Internet of Things (IoT) [22]. CPSs integrate the cyber world of computation with the physical world of industrial processes. On the other hand, IoT devices are embedded devices that have connectivity, and when they are deployed on industrial scenarios, the requirements in terms of monitoring and control are usually more advanced than consumer systems [33]. Joining these embedded IoT devices with the IoT for network monitoring and control of the physical processes is what enables the Industry 4.0.

CPSs in industrial domains are usually named Industrial CPSs (ICPSs). Being able to monitor and control the ICPSs remotely is becoming essential, as it enables to perform automated analysis, facilitate decision making, and finally, detect anomalies. Thus, monitoring and controlling enables the transition of a traditional industrial system towards an ICPS in the context of Industry 4.0. ICPSs can have a high number of devices, and capturing data and being aware of their state during operation is essential [14]. In these scenarios, IoT communication protocols make the communication between the stakeholder and the ICPS possible. Each stakeholder has different needs, hence, monitoring/controlling systems and IoT communication protocols must be adapted [11].

ICPSs integrate different devices that can be classified into sensors, actuators and displays [13]. Therefore, considering the number of devices an ICPS can have, connecting to them to capture data and know what is happening in the ICPS during operation is important. That is why IoT communication protocols are needed, as they make the communication between the stakeholder and the ICPS possible. Notice that each stakeholder has different needs. Thus, in each case, the monitoring/controlling system and IoT communication protocols must be adapted to the stakeholder.

The adaptation of IoT communication protocols is based on the stakeholder's needs or the industrial environment. At the same time, the ICPSs usually are composed by different devices even if they are from the same industrial domain. As in industrial domains safety is of critical importance, reducing the complexity of the design, development, testing and validation can decrease development time and costs increasing code quality. Due to such commonalities and variability within the same domains and across the domains, a common solution for ICPSs can benefit from the System Product Line (SPL) paradigm. As Capilla et al. assert, applying SPL paradigm can improve productivity and reduce costs [6]. In a SPL, a common architecture is defined in which the user can configure the exposed variability. Hence, users can produce specific systems by reusing common elements and configuring the variability. Combining a Domain Specific Language (DSL) with a SPL enables the communication with stakeholders simplifying complex code [8]. A DSL provides a notation adapted to an application domain and it is based on the concepts and relevant characteristics of the domains [35]. With DSL, a system can be more flexible while providing a more immediate response to the stakeholder [23], and at the same time, SPL enables to produce specific systems reusing common elements and configuring variabilities.

Taking into account the need to use different IoT communication protocols to communicate the physical world with the virtual environment, we analyzed an international standard, IEC 61850 [34]. IEC 61850 is a standard defined by the International Electrotechnical Commission (IEC) to enable the modelling, control and monitoring of electrical substations. This standard defines a Basic Information Model, some services to interact with the model and recommendations for communication protocols, although it is open for the use of additional ones. This standard is divided in five parts, with specific parts for general specifications, configuration, model definition and communications, and testing. Although IEC 61850 was designed for electrical substations, at Ikerlan we have successfully use it in other use cases such as smart elevators, catenary-free trams and wind turbine farms as it is described on the following pages. Following the knowledge acquired from these projects, we came to the conclusion that it has become necessary to provide a common solution that is able to meet stakeholder's needs, both in terms of abstract device definition and the use of IoT communication protocols. TRILATERAL (sofTware pRoduct lIne based muLtidomain iot ArTifact gEneration for industRiAL cps) is our proposal for addressing this issue and it aims to become a tool to join IEC 61850, Industry 4.0 (including IoT and CPS), and SPL. TRILATERAL was conceived as a tool that follows Model Based Engineering (MBE) techniques, and using the IEC 61850 standard, SPL paradigm and a DSL, allows for a user to graphically configure IoT communication protocols (HTTP-REST, WS-SOAP and CoAP). With that configuration, TRILATERAL automatically generates the source code that allows to transmit data between the *cyber* and the *physics* part in order to monitor/control an ICPS.

This book chapter is the extension of a conference paper previously presented at Modelsward 2019 [12], which presents TRILATERAL, a tool to generate code automatically based on the IEC 61850 standard, with the previously presented but extended contributions: (1) problem statement; and (2) related literature. In addition, this book chapter introduces the following novel contributions: (3) the description of the implementation; (4) a general evaluation of TRILATERAL; and (5) application of TRILATERAL on a real use case, i.e., a catenary-free tram.

The rest of this chapter is organized as follows. The next chapter states the problem. Section 3 analyzes the related literature. Next, the used technological tools are explained, followed by the proposed design, i.e., TRILATERAL. In

Sect. 6, the implementation of TRILATERAL is explained and the next section provides a general evaluation of our proposal and a validation on a catenary-free tram use case. Finally, we conclude this book chapter in Sect. 8.

2 Problem Statement

Considering the domain analysis fulfilled in the previous work [13], we realized that different domains have common needs in terms of control and monitoring. This is due to the important role that Industry 4.0 is playing on different industrial domains.

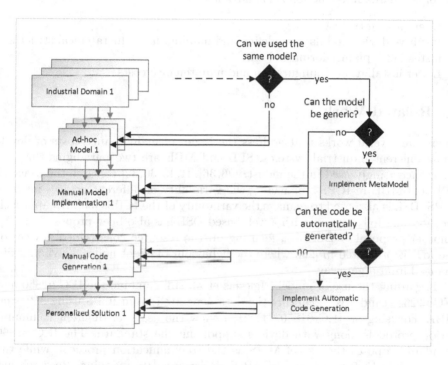

Fig. 1. Manual vs Automated processes.

As shown in Fig. 1, every ICPS is different, i.e., it is composed by different devices [14], that is why, if data from the devices needs to be captured, usually an ad-doc solution is required. As this solution is manual, the implementation process is error-prone [3,32]. This makes the implementation of every model costly (in terms of time, resources, etc.). Thus, taking into account that different industrial domains share requirements, *can the ICPS be represented by a base model?* If the model is not suitable, the model needs to be designed for each project. Otherwise, *can we generate a generic model?*, if so, a metamodel can be implemented, which can be used to describe a specific model instead of implementing the model manually. Finally, *can the code be generated automatically?*

If not, the source code needs to be manually written. Else, a code generator can be developed in order to automatically generate the source code and give a personalized solution from a common base.

Following the process presented in Fig. 1, our proposal is to choose a model that is valid for different industrial domain in order to create a metamodel. In this manner, personalized models that conform the metamodel can be configured, making the process less error-prone and reducing development cost. In order to give a solution, we believe that MBE and SPL are two promising paradigms to provide a solution. Additionally, using a DSL promotes effective communication with stakeholders which can help to give a personalized solution. Besides, the use of standards have the following advantages:

- Interoperability.
- Intuitive device and data modeling and naming, using hierarchical structure, instead of a plainly formatted one.
- Lower installation, configuration and maintenance costs.

3   Related Work

There are several works that address the issues of maintenance costs of developing different industrial systems. SPL and MBE are two paradigms that are being increasingly used in the industry [6,36]. [1,13,30,32] research the usage of SPL and MBE in ICPSs, managing the variability of different devices inside a ICPS. DSL is also used to manage the variability of the ICPSs [30]. An approach for modeling IoT systems with a web-based DSL has also been proposed in [31]. Another proposal of DSL use, focusing on the resource constrained devices of the IoT, is presented in [25], where the behaviour of client nodes is dynamically changed from a gateway.

Regarding the use of models, Iglesias et al. [13] combine the IEC 61850 and IEC 62264 standards to capture the data generated in an ICPS using SPL and MBE. Focusing on IEC 61850, [17,21] review the usage of different communication protocols along with devices supporting the standard. The IEC 61850 standard proposes the use of MMS as the communication protocol, while the related IEC 61400 proposes a SOAP Web-Services [10] mapping. Research has been done regarding the use of other protocols, i.e., CORBA [28], DDS [2,4], or a combination of both [5]. [26,27] are the first works considering a RESTful approach, using HTTP. A publish/subscribe paradigm based communication protocol has also been proposed using XMPP [9]. In order to reduce the overhead and communication capability requirements, CoAP has been the first specific IoT proposed to be used in combination with the IEC 61850 in [21,29].

To the best of our knowledge, TRILATERAL [12] is the first approach of using IEC 61580 as the basis for modelling a DSL and generate a framework capable of monitoring and controlling ICPSs. TRILATERAL does not only generate the base framework with the structure of the devices inside a ICPS, but also allows to configure the selected IoT communication protocol (e.g., HTTP-REST, WS-SOAP and CoAP) based on SPL and MBE.

4   Technological Overview

After reviewing the related literature, in this section we present and summarize the technical tools that we used for this project.

4.1   IEC 61850

As previously explained, the generic model used in this work is based on the IEC 61850 standard. This standard enables interoperability between Distributed Energy Resources of different manufacturers, allowing more flexibility on the electrical grid. This also allows to reduce the costs from design to operation and maintenance tasks, while enabling to select the solution with the best cost/benefit ratio for each case.

IEC 61850 uses two main building blocks to model the behaviour of intelligent electronic devices in an electrical substation, i.e., the Basic Information Model (BIM) and some Control Blocks (CB) for additional functions. The BIM models real world element information with a simple structure, marked in green in Fig. 2:

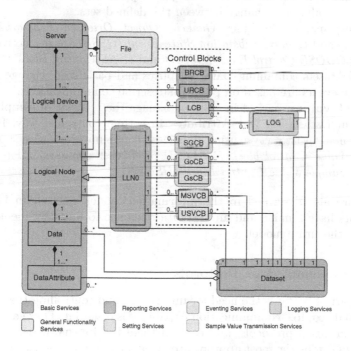

Fig. 2. The information model of the IEC 61850 standard (based on [12]). (Color figure online)

- *Server*: exposes the system to the outside and includes one or more Logical Devices (LDs).
- *Logical Device*: virtual representation of a real device, composed of one or more Logical Nodes (LNs).

- *Logical Node*: virtual abstraction application functionalities. All LDs have a special LN, *Logical Node Zero (LLN0)*, to represent data which is common for the entire LD.
- *Data*: physical world information, associated to a LN.
- *DataAttribute*: information piece of a Data, e.g., value, timestamp. The values of a DataAttribute are defined by a type.
- *Dataset*: group of existing Data and DataAttributes of a LD.

The CBs are the classes that allow to interact with the BIM, and are marked using different colors in Fig. 2, one color for each type of CB:

- **Reporting** marked in orange: *Buffered Report Control Blocks (BRCP)* and *Unbuffered Report Control Blocks (URCB)* define the generation of reports, the former ensures that the reports arrive to the destination while the latter works on a best effort basis.
- **Logging** marked in purple: *Log Control Block (LCB)* configures the creation of logs from Datasets, what to log and under which circumstances.
- **Configuration** marked in red: *Setting Group Control Block (SGCB)* groups settings and allows to change between the defined sets.
- **Eventing** marked in blue: *Generic Object Oriented Substation Event (GOOSE)* and *Generic Substation State Event (GSSE)* are respectively managed by *GOOSE Control Block (GoCB)* and *GSSE Control Block (GsCB)* to deliver Datasets containing DataAttributes and basic state change information. The events are based on publish-subscribe communications.
- **Sampled Values** marked in yellow: manage the transfer of sampled information in Datasets of DataAttributes in a time controlled way. It can be implemented in two ways: using multicast communication with a *Multicast Sample Value Control block (MSVCB)* or unicast communication with an *Unicast Sample Value Control Block (USCVB)*.

Files are also described in the information model, marked in black. All the elements have a name and an absolute reference to uniquely identify them throughout the entire model.

4.2   IoT Communication Protocols

A pivotal part of ICPSs is the need for monitoring and controlling their parameters, and to do so, IoT communication capability is essential. There are different IoT communication protocols, and each of them has its characteristics, hence, each of them can be the most appropriate one depending on the use case [15,17].

Among all the existing IoT communication protocols, in this work WS-SOAP, HTTP-REST and CoAP have been used. Although WS-SOAP and HTTP-REST are not strictly speaking IoT protocols, as they were not designed for resource constrained devices, they have been used historically on machine-to-machine (M2M) communications. M2M communications can be considered as the precursor of IoT, so in this work, we also refer to WS-SOAP and HTTP-REST as IoT communication protocols. There are more IoT protocols such as MQTT,

DDS or AMQP [18], and even though we did not use them in this project, the tool is prepared to include them if a use case that justifies their use arises.

HyperText Transfer Protocol (HTTP) is an application layer protocol that we used in two different forms in this work. On the one hand, in HTTP-REST, we follow the RESTful [7] architecture, using JSON as the resource representation format and using the CRUD (Create, Read, Update, Delete) methods, i.e., GET, PUT, POST and DELETE. On the other hand, HTTP can be used to encapsulate XML files on POST requests. This is the approach that follows WS-SOAP. The last protocol used in this work is CoAP [19,20]. CoAP is a lightweight protocol specially designed for IoT and resource constrained devices. It follows the RESTful architecture with GET, PUT, POST and DELETE methods and has a smaller headers than HTTP-REST. It is also capable of having pub-sub communication thanks to its Observe extension [16].

5   Solution Design: TRILATERAL

Considering the importance of monitoring ICPSs and that different IoT communication protocols exist to transfer the captured data we realized that a tool with configuration capabilities is a good starting point. The created tool will give configuration capabilities to different industrial domains that will allow to reduce costs in terms of development, test, etc.

Thus, we have developed a MBE tool, i.e., *SofTware pRoduct lIne based muLtidomain iot ArTifact gEneration for industRiAL cps* (TRILATERAL), using the SPL paradigm and DSL to make it easier for the user to graphically configure the IoT communication protocols in order to monitor/control a ICPS. The artifact is the framework responsible for establishing communication between the devices and the monitoring system. As a common solution is needed, a IEC 61850 based metamodel has been modeled, because it can be useful for different industrial domains.

With TRILATERAL, an IoT communication middleware is created to monitor/control devices within an ICPS. Although there is an interaction with the user to achieve the objective, note that if the stakeholder has its requirements and knows the real structure of its industrial domain, a part of the artifact

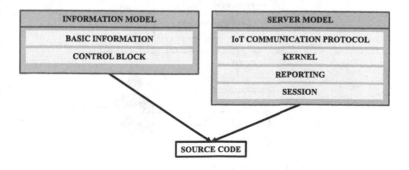

Fig. 3. TRILATERAL components.

(*IoT communication protocol* and *device data structure and logic*) can be generated through TRILATERAL, becoming the process faster and less error-prone.

TRILATERAL is divided into two parts: (1) the *server model* definition and (2) the *information model* definition. Both of them are configured by the user using the DSL. The former one, i.e., *server model* definition, is used for configuring the IoT communications (e.g., CoAP), and the logic of the device (e.g., when the data from the device needs to be transferred to the monitoring software system). The latter one is for configuring the ICPS structure where all the devices and the attributes which these devices are able to send, are specified based on IEC 61850 (Fig. 3).

In order to configure the *Information Model*, IEC 61850 is modeled. Thanks to it and the DSL, the intelligence of the electronic device can be configured. To do so, the BIM and CB of IEC 61850 need to be configured (see Sect. 4). The BIM defines the elements of the real world (Logical Device, Logical Node, Data, DataAttribute), i.e., the structure of the device within the ICPS to be monitored.

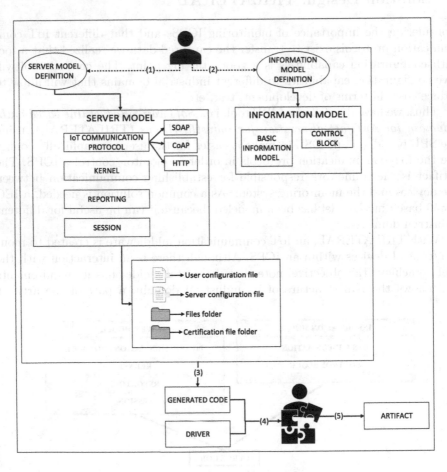

Fig. 4. TRILATERAL workflow.

The CBs are specialized classes to interact with the information model through some additional functionalities.

In the same manner, to configure the *Server Model*, the user needs to select and configure the communication protocol to use, the kernel, the reporting and also the session by using the DSL. Thanks to the DSL and the user collaboration, it is possible to automatically configure the server to communicate the *artifact* with an external monitoring system.

As shown in Fig. 4, the user first configures the *server model* by choosing the IoT communication protocol (step 1). More than one IoT communication protocol can be configured if required. Hence, the user must choose the protocol that best suits the ICPS. TRILATERAL provides three IoT communication protocols, i.e., SOAP, HTTP and CoAP. Thus, the user can configure the server according to the customer's needs. Figure 5 shows the feature model where the different options that the user has are presented in order to configure the *server model*.

Once the IoT communication protocol is chosen and the user has selected all the needed configurations, TRILATERAL automatically creates user and server configuration files where the user will enter the necessary information for the system to be adapted. Then, TRILATERAL automatically generates two directories: one for certificates, where all security certificates are stored; and another one where the files related to file management functionalities offered by the IEC 61850 standard are stored.

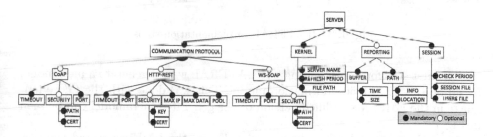

Fig. 5. Server definition feature model [12].

Thus, after the communication protocol is chosen, the user configures the *information model* based on IEC 61850 (step 2). Then, to configure the ICPS based on IEC 61850, the user configures the *BIM* and the *CBs* with TRILATERAL. Therefore, once the user configures the *server model* and the *information model*, TRILATERAL automatically generates the source code (*generated code*) using model-to-text (M2T) transformation (step 3). Thus, thanks to TRILATERAL, two parts of an *artifact* are automatically created (i.e., generated code).

After TRILATERAL generates the corresponding *generated code*, the user needs to introduce the corresponding driver (the connector that links the devices with the *information model*, connecting physical data with its virtual data model representation) and compiles the *generated code* with a specific driver (step 4). The driver and the device logic is different in each case, it depends on the device to control or monitor. Once the driver and the device logic are compiled with the *generated code*, some libraries and executables are created (step 5), i.e., *the artifact*.

In order to start monitoring or controlling the ICPS, the artifact needs to be deployed in a PC/machine within the ICPS. After its deployment, it is possible to communicate with the artifact from the outside using CRUD functionalities. Thus, thanks to TRILATERAL, we are able to create a middleware between the ICPS and the monitoring system to monitor and control all the devices within the ICPS.

6   Implementation

TRILATERAL is a graphical Eclipse plugin, developed with the Eclipse Modeling Framework[1], based on the *data model*. The *data model* is the tree structure of the ICPS that needs to be monitored and/or controlled. For the implementation of TRILATERAL, several steps were followed, as shown in Fig. 6. The main components are two: a tree view editor for the users to input the model of the system that they want to implement and a code generator.

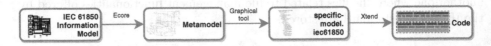

Fig. 6. TRILATERAL implementation steps.

The first step for implementing TRILATERAL was to generate a metamodel based on the IEC 61850 information model. This was done with the Ecore language in the EMF. A simplified version of the generated metamodel can be seen in Fig. 7.

Once the metamodel was defined with Ecore, the EMF generated the tree view editor. The tree view editor generates files with the .iec61850 extension, consistent with the name of the metamodel. The .iec61850 files are generated by the user, they define the model they want to implement. This files can also be opened as XML files.

In order to generate the code automatically, a code generator was implemented using Xtend. Xtend is the tool in EMF to make model-to-text transformation, in this case, the text is C++ code, divided in header (.h) and source (.cpp) files. The TRILATERAL code generator takes the .iec61850 file as input and generates all the needed source files, where some files are generated based on the model, while other are just copies of the needed framework, such as libraries.

Using the tree view editor, a user can choose between WS-SOAP, HTTP-REST or CoAP as the IoT communication protocol when creating the model.

---

[1]   https://www.eclipse.org/modeling/emf/.

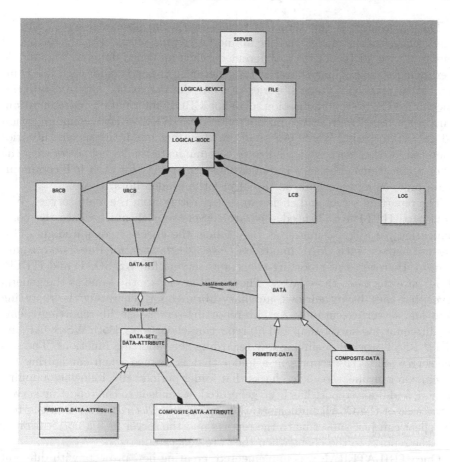

Fig. 7. Simplified version of the metamodel used in TRILATERAL.

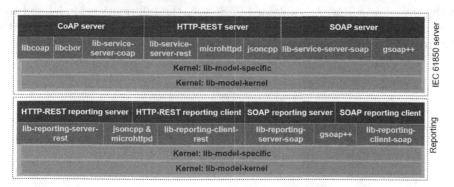

Fig. 8. Layers with the projects of the generated code.

More than one can also be included. The generated code composes several Eclipse projects in different layers, as can be seen in Fig. 8.

The lower level is the kernel of model, with the lib-model-kernel for the generic classes of the model, and the lib-model-*specific-model*, which is the model generated with TRILATERAL, different for each modelled domain. The middle layer includes the auxiliary libraries for generating the servers for each IoT communication protocol. These libraries are, on the one hand, external libraries (libcoap for CoAP communication, cbor for CBOR information representation, jsoncpp for JSON representation, microhttpd for HTTP-REST communication and gSOAP for using WS-SOAP) and, on the other hand, the specific libraries generated for this work, which allow to communicate the kernel layers with the server applications. The server applications are specific for each IoT communication protocol and are built on top of just the needed libraries.

The reporting server and clients work separately from the main servers. WS-SOAP and HTTP-REST need separate servers and clients because the communication paradigm changes, as they follow the client-server paradigm. This does not happen with CoAP due to its *Observe extension* for Pub/Sub communication. However, the reporting client and servers for WS-SOAP and HTTP-REST have the same three layers. The kernel layers are the same as the general server, but they have their own auxiliary libraries for generating the reporting client and server executables, i.e., lib-reporting-server-rest, lib-reporting-client-rest, lib-reporting-server-soap and lib-reporting-client-soap. Both WS-SOAP and HTTP-REST work in a similar way regarding the reporting functions. The service server stores the reports in a folder that is defined when configuring the system. On runtime, the client checks that folder periodically, following a polling method, and if any report has been generated, it sends it to the reporting server. In the case of the CoAP implementation, using the *Observe* extension, the regular client can just subscribe to the reports and the server uses a notification to send the reports to the client when they are generated.

Once TRILATERAL was implemented, creating new projects with different uses is quite trivial, as can be seen in Fig. 9. A user needs to describe the model in the tree view editor. As explained in Sect. 5, the Information Model and the Server Model are needed. TRILATERAL takes the .iec61850 file generated with the tree view editor and automatically generates the entire source code.

Fig. 9. Creating a ICPS artifact in TRILATERAL.

7 Evaluation and Validation

After explaining the implementation, in this section we evaluate TRILATERAL and validate the results with the concrete use of a catenary-free tram.

7.1   Evaluation

As explained in the previous section, the generated code is divided in different layers, and each layer has several projects. Table 1 shows the sizes that each library or executable has in KBs, and in with which communication protocol is needed.

Table 1. Libraries and apps need for introducing communication protocols to an artifact by TRILATERAL.

Protocol	KB	CoAP	HTTP	SOAP
app-reporting-client-rest	675.1		X	
app-reporting-client-soap	1600			X
app-reporting-server-rest	1300		X	
app-reporting-server-soap	1600			X
app-service-server-coap	9600	X		
app-service-server-rest	8200		X	
app-service-server-soap	9700			X
libenv.a	1200			X
libgsoap++.a	1600			X
libjsoncpp.a	2000		X	
libcoap.a	814.5	X		
libcbor.a	381.6	X		
libreporting-client-soap.a	2800			X
libreporting-server-soap.a	3000			X
libreporting-client-rest.a	2700		X	
libreporting-server-rest.a	2900		X	
libservice-server-rest.a	6900		X	
libservice-server-soap.a	7100			X
libservice-server-coap.a	6900	X		
libmodel-specific.a	?????	X	X	X
libmodel-kernel.a	25 700	X	X	X
Total	96 671.2	43 396.1	50 375.1	54 300
		45%	52%	56%

The projects starting with app-service-server-* are the final server executables for each protocol, while the ones starting with app-reporting-* are the executables for the reporting server and clients. Below that, there are the auxiliary external libraries needed. Next, the libraries to generate the server and reporting executables. The *libmodel-specific* library is very model dependant, as it is the description of the model itself, so its size is very variable (See Fig. 10). Finally, the kernel is common for all the implementations created with TRILATERAL.

Thanks to the modular design of TRILATERAL, selecting the IoT communication protocol in the tree view editor makes the created system optimized. Only the needed projects are included in the code, leading to a reduction in the range of 50% and 30% of the size, depending on the protocol, as can be seen in Fig. 10.

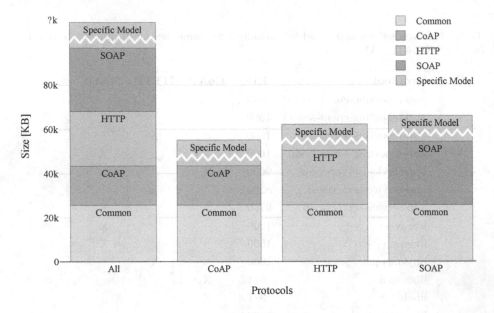

Fig. 10. Different protocol sizes.

7.2 Validation

To validate TRILATERAL, we selected the transport domain, where there are companies that focus on design, development and commissioning of trains and trams. Trams are a means of passenger transport that run on rails in urban areas. In this specific use case we are focused on a type of tram, i.e., catenary-free tram, which is a special type of tram being increasingly used in Europe. Its great advantage compared to a normal tram is that it does not need a catenary, making the necessary infrastructure simpler. In order to convert the catenary-free tram in a controlled environment for the citizens' safety, it is important to monitor different devices within the catenary-free tram, e.g., engine and brake status, battery health, etc. Depending on stakeholders' needs the quantity of wagons will be different and each wagon has its own characteristics as shown in Fig. 11.

Thus, catenary-free tram systems may have different parameters to monitor its state, ranging from critical parameters such as speed, direction or maintenance related information (e.g., state of the power source, break wear, etc.) to non critical systems such as information or multimedia features, or climate systems. In a regular wagon usually a battery controller is found, i.e., battery controller is the component that controls the entire energy system to make the tram

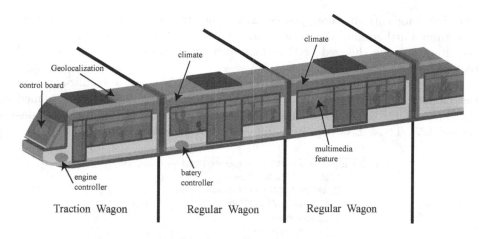

Fig. 11. Catenary-free tram partial Layout.

move from one place to another. This is composed of twelve different devices that are capable of sending more than 200 critical attributes or values. In addition to the energy manager, there are other components such as speed and resistance profiles, engine controller, braking motors, auxiliary loads, etc.

In addition to the quantity of devices within an catenary-free tram, two different peculiarities need to be taken into account. On the one hand, when the tram is moving the environment is mobile and can have power or connectivity limitations. On the other hand, the tram can bulk much more information when it is on a station or a stop. However, since a catenary-free tram has to follow a schedule, the time for bulking the data is limited, so the data transfer time must also be taken into account. Thus, depending on whether the tram is moving or in station the communication protocol to use will be different. Note that the quantity of information to bulk, the speed, etc. will be different, hence, it is necessary to adapt the system to multiple scenarios.

Therefore all catenary-free trams are not equal, i.e., catenary-free trams have different features depending on the city to be installed, the used mechanism, the route to be followed, etc. Because of that, each train will depend on the needs and requirements of the stakeholder. Note that this kind of trams work without catenary, this means that they need to collect energy to move forward and for this different techniques can be used. For example, in some kind of trams fast change accumulators are used, while others get energy from the rails themselves. Thus, even if both of them are related with energy, depending on the system the devices within the catenary-free tram are different. Non critical systems can also be installed in order to collect more information about the tram (e.g., multimedia feature), but these depends on the stakeholders' requirements.

Over time, elements that were considered non-critical can be considered critical, which can provoke to force updates in the devices in order to have more control about them. Additionally, time to time the tram can evolve, e.g., the stakeholder may want to introduce more devices into their tram in order to control more parameters of their catenary-free tram or a new wagon needs to be introduced for carrying more people. Thus, the structure of a tram can evolve over time. Furthermore, the devices can evolve, i.e., they can be damaged and therefore must be changed or they may even become obsolete over time and require replacement.

Figure 12 shows a screenshot of TRILATERAL's tree view editor, where the climate system of a tram is being described. There is a *Server* named *SERVER_NODE*. The *Server* has the *ClimateSystem_LD LD*, which includes several *LNs*. Those *LNs* then have different *Datas*, *Datasets* and *CBs*.

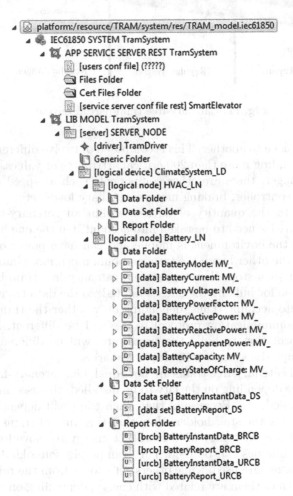

Fig. 12. Screenshot of TRILATERAL's tree view editor describing a catenary-free tram.

For the catenary-free tram use case, two different scenarios were defined: (1) when the tram is on route, or (2) when it is on a station. Depending on the scenario, the tram needs to communicate with the monitoring system with a different protocol. When the tram is on route, the CoAP protocol was used, because it is a mobile scenario where connectivity or power issues can occur.

For a tram on a station, HTTP was used, since the scenario is in a controlled environment, with no connectivity issues.

As explained in the previous subsection, the library file generated for the specific model is different for each described model. In this case, the library was named libmodel-tram.a, and its size is 11700 KBs.

After TRILATERAL was developed and validated with a real use case, we realized that even if the use case is related to a transport domain, the proposed solution can be used in any IoT environment (manufacturing, energy, etc.) that needs to be monitored/controlled remotely. IEC 61850 has proven useful outside the electrical substations. Also, it can be seen how beneficial the paradigms SPL and DSL can be. Even though many differentiated domains exist, a lot of them share similar requirements and many commonalities exist between them. In addition, although the DSL development was complex, once it was well designed and developed, the configuration of an IoT system becomes much simpler, mainly due to the use of a visual editor.

This has been proved internally, as we also implement other use cases from different domains. These other use cases are smart elevators for tall buildings with several elevators and wind farms, where wind power generates electricity using wind turbines. Table 2 summarizes the use cases, with the protocol used in each of them and the characteristics of the use case.

Table 2. IoT communication protocols for each use case characteristics.

Protocol	Use case		
	Wind farm	Smart elevator	Catenary-free tram
WS-SOAP		- Controlled environment - No connectivity/power issues	
HTTP-REST	- Remote location - Connectivity issues		Station - Controlled environment - Smaller header with big payloads
CoAP			On route - Mobile - Connectivity/Power issues

7.3 Lessons Learned

From these implementations, we learned the following lessons:

- The first and most important lesson is that development and deployment time has decreased drastically from previous similar projects. Using a generic model makes an ad-hoc model not necessary. This, along with removing manual tasks thanks to the automated source code and artifact generation, leads to a reduction of development time and costs. Not only that, but it also has the benefit of increasing the quality of the code and the delivered artifacts, making maintenance easier, thus, reducing engineering and maintenance costs.

– Even though the IEC 61850 is oriented to electrical substations, we learned that it can be applicable to other domains. We used TRILATERAL in domains that are not related to electrical substations, but are somewhat related to energy systems. However, the domains are diverse enough that they present different communication patterns (device-to-cloud systems and device-to-device systems). Therefore, we believe that TRILATERAL can be used in any IoT domain that requires remote monitoring and/or control, such as manufacturing, transport, etc.

– Using common blocks in different projects, the validation process of the system is improved. The kernel code is the same, and the libraries and server and client application also, with minimal changes. Hence, those parts are already tested and validated, so using them in a new scenario would not require to validate them again. This also helps in the maintenance of the code, as updates, bug correction, etc. would be developed once and deployed on all systems.

– Finally, thanks to this work, we can prove the benefits of the SPL paradigms in industrial domains. With similarities on requirements throughout the diverse domains, there are many commonalities in the solutions. Even though the development of TRILATERAL was complex, DSL have also proven their benefits, as creating a new system for a different use case is easy with TRILATERAL. The use of the visual tree editor is a big part of that. Thanks to the joint use of SPL and DSL, the development time has been decreased as stated in the first learned lesson. Hence, as a last learned lesson, we conclude that using SPL and DSL on industry is very beneficial.

As shown in Fig. 13, creating TRILATERAL has been more costly in terms of workforce time than creating a project from scratch. However, we expect that its application on different projects will have long term benefits. A Return

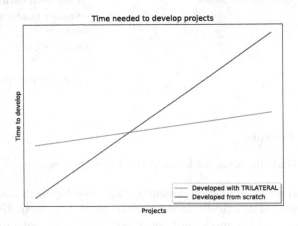

Fig. 13. General view of the time to develop projects from scratch versus projects implemented with TRILATERAL.

Of Investment (ROI) analysis is expected as a future work, when we get the corresponding data of the costs of different projects.

In summary, TRILATERAL has allowed Ikerlan to improve the engineering process of the development of ICPS, reducing time and costs but also improving the validation and maintenance tasks. Also, it has allowed to open a new opportunity to extend it to other IoT domains.

8   Conclusion

This book chapter extends the work presented in [12] with the previously presented but extended contributions: (1) problem statement; and (2) related literature. In addition, this article introduces the following novel contributions: (3) the description of the implementation; (4) a general evaluation of TRILATERAL; and (5) application of TRILATERAL on a real use case, i.e., a catenary-free tram. Hence, the design, implementation and evaluation of TRILATERAL are explained. TRILATERAL is a MBE SPL solution using IEC 61850 for configuring IoT communication protocols graphically. The presented tool makes it possible to define the data model of different ICPSs even if they belong to different industrial domains. This is possible due to the definition of a DSL which is integrated in the solution and the use of MBE and SPL, since a part of an artifact can be automatically created in order to monitor and control the industrial domain.

As concluded in the previous work, with IEC 61850 it is possible to model the architecture and requirements for the monitoring and control of ICPSs. In order to evaluate the usability of TRILATERAL an evaluation has been carried out in a catenary-free tram domain. With this evaluation, some additional conclusions have been achieved: (1) the development of a monitoring system of an ICPS is faster, less complex and less error prone, (2) the designed system is modular, which makes the artifact more lightweight, i.e., as explained in Sect. 7 with the modular system a reduction between 30 and 50% can be achieved in the evaluated domain. In addition, the use of standards provide: (3) greater flexibility by enabling interoperability, and (4) external connectivity functions to monitor and control ICPSs. The main disadvantage of this standard is that the interfaces and operator functions are not standardized.

Carrying this work out has provide some important lessons in the use of SPL paradigm and DSL in industrial domains where different ICPSs share similarities in requirements such as control and monitoring. We have learned how manual tasks can be removed, leading to common code maintenance, updates and bug fixes, while reducing engineering and maintenance costs. In addition, the importance of using already existing standards has been pointed out, which can lead to develop tools like TRILATERAL, and using them also outside of their original intended domain. IEC 61850 was originally designed for monitoring of electrical substations, but in this work it has also been used in other IoT use cases that require remote monitoring and control.

The main disadvantage of TRILATERAL which would be addressed in the future is the capability of adaptation, i.e., if the ICPS evolves, the artifact needs to be updated by the user (with TRILATERAL) but its deployment is manual. Some additional future lines are expected to be addressed in the short-medium term:

1. Apply TRILATERAL in other domains, such as Automated Warehouses or Press Machine domains.
2. Convert TRILATERAL into a Dynamic SPL (DSPL), regarding physical element changes (update, add or remove physical nodes).
3. Allow to remotely update the artifact in the ICPS, in this way we will be able to further reduce the maintenance costs.
4. Automatic *driver* generation, since TRILATERAL is able to generate two of the three parts (*IoT communication protocol*, and *device data structure and logic*) of the artifact leaving the driver out.
5. Create a user interface able to connect to the artifact using the corresponding IoT protocol in order to visualize the captured data using CRUD functionalities.

Acknowledgements. This work has received funding from the Electronic Component Systems for European Leadership Joint Undertaking under the MegaM@Rt2 project (Grant agreement No. 737494) in the EU Horizon 2020 program and the Basque Government through the Elkartek program under the TEKINTZE project (Grant agreement No. KK-2018/00104).

References

1. Ayala, I., Amor, M., Fuentes, L., Troya, J.M.: A software product line process to develop agents for the IoT. Sensors **15**(7), 15640–15660 (2015)
2. Bi, Y., Jiang, L., Wang, X.J., Cui, L.Z.: Mapping of IEC 61850 to data distribute service for digital substation communication. In: IEEE Power and Energy Society General Meeting, pp. 1–5 (2013)
3. Bougouffa, S., Meßmer, K., Cha, S., Trunzer, E., Vogel-Heuser, B.: Industry 4.0 interface for dynamic reconfiguration of an open lab size automated production system to allow remote community experiments. In: 2017 IEEE International Conference on Industrial Engineering and Engineering Management (IEEM), pp. 2058–2062, December 2017. https://doi.org/10.1109/IEEM.2017.8290254
4. Calvo, I., Garcia de Albéniz, O., Pérez, F.: A communication backbone for substation automation systems based on the OMG DDS standard. In: Przeglad Elektrotechniczny, vol. 88, pp. 146–150 (2012)
5. Calvo, I., García De Albéniz, O., Noguero, A., Pérez, F.: Towards a modular and scalable design for the communications of electrical protection relays. In: IECON Proceedings (Industrial Electronics Conference), pp. 2511–2516 (2009)
6. Capilla, R., Bosch, J., Trinidad, P., Ruiz-Cortés, A., Hinchey, M.: An overview of dynamic software product line architectures and techniques: observations from research and industry. J. Syst. Softw. **91**, 3–23 (2014)
7. Fielding, R.T.: REST: Architectural Styles and the Design of Network-based Software Architectures. Doctoral dissertation, University of California, Irvine (2000)
8. Fowler, M.: Domain-Specific Languages. The Addison-Wesley signature series, Addison-Wesley (2011). http://vig.pearsoned.com/store/product/1,1207,store-12521_isbn-0321712943,00.html

9. Hussain, S.M.S., Aftab, M.A., Ali, I.: IEC 61850 modeling of dSTATCOM and XMPP communication for reactive power management in microgrids. IEEE Syst. J. **12**(4), 1–11 (2018)

10. IEC TC-88: Wind energy generation systems - part 25–4: Communications for monitoring and control of wind power plants - mapping to communication profile (2016)

11. Iglesias, A., Arellano, C., Yue, T., Ali, S., Sagardui, G.: Model- based personalized visualization system for monitoring evolving industrial cyber-physical system. In: Accepted for Publishing in 25th Asia-Pacific Software Engineering Conference, APSEC 2018 (2018)

12. Iglesias, A., Iglesias-Urkia, M., López-Davalillo, B., Charramendieta, S., Urbieta, A.: Trilateral: software product line based multidomain iot artifact generation for industrial cps. In: Proceedings of the 7th International Conference on Model-Driven Engineering and Software Development, MODELSWARD, INSTICC, vol. 1, pp. 64–73. SciTePress (2019). https://doi.org/10.5220/0007343500640073

13. Iglesias, A., Lu, H., Arellano, C., Yue, T., Ali, S., Sagardui, G.: Product line engineering of monitoring functionality in industrial cyber-physical systems: a domain analysis. In: Proceedings of the 21st International Systems and Software Product Line Conference, SPLC 2017, vol. A, pp. 195–204 (2017)

14. Iglesias, A., Sagardui, G., Arellano, C.: Industrial cyber-physical system evolution detection and alert generation. Appl. Sci. **9**(8), 1586 (2019). https://doi.org/10.3390/app9081586. http://www.mdpi.com/2076-3417/9/8/1586

15. Iglesias-Urkia, M., Casado-Mansilla, D., Mayer, S., Bilbao, J., Urbieta, A.: Integrating electrical substations within the IoT using IEC 61850, CoAP and CBOR. IEEE Internet of Things J. pp. 1–1 (2019). https://doi.org/10.1109/JIOT.2019.2903344

16. Iglesias-Urkia, M., Casado-Mansilla, D., Mayer, S., Urbieta, A.: Enhanced publish/subscribe in CoAP: describing advanced subscription mechanisms for the observe extension. In: ACM International Conference Proceeding Series. Association for Computing Machinery (2018). https://doi.org/10.1145/3277593.3277594

17. Iglesias-Urkia, M., Casado-Mansilla, D., Mayer, S., Urbieta, A.: Validation of a CoAP to IEC 61850 mapping and benchmarking vs http-rest and ws-soap. In: IEEE International Conference on Emerging Technologies and Factory Automation, ETFA, vol. 2018-September, pp. 1015–1022 (2018). https://doi.org/10.1109/ETFA.2018.8502624

18. Iglesias-Urkia, M., Orive, A., Barcelo, M., Moran, A., Bilbao, J., Urbieta, A.: Towards a lightweight protocol for industry 4.0: An implementation based benchmark. In: Proceedings of the 2017 IEEE International Workshop of Electronics, Control, Measurement, Signals and their Application to Mechatronics, ECMSM 2017. Institute of Electrical and Electronics Engineers Inc. (2017). https://doi.org/10.1109/ECMSM.2017.7945894

19. Iglesias-Urkia, M., Orive, A., Urbieta, A.: Analysis of CoAP implementations for industrial internet of things: a survey. Proc. Comput. Sci. **109**, 188–195 (2017). https://doi.org/10.1016/j.procs.2017.05.323

20. Iglesias-Urkia, M., Orive, A., Urbieta, A., Casado-Mansilla, D.: Analysis of CoAP implementations for industrial Internet of Things: a survey. J. Ambient Intell. Hum. Comput. **10**(7), 1–14 (2018). https://doi.org/10.1007/s12652-018-0729-z

21. Iglesias-Urkia, M., Urbieta, A., Parra, J., Casado-Mansilla, D.: IEC 61850 meets CoAP: towards the integration of smart grids and IoT standards. In: ACM International Conference Proceeding Series. Association for Computing Machinery (2017). https://doi.org/10.1145/3131542.3131545

22. Kagermann, H., Helbig, J., Hellinger, A., Wahlster, W.: Recommendations for Implementing the Strategic Initiative INDUSTRIE 4.0: Securing the Future of German Manufacturing Industry; Final Report of the Industrie 4.0 Working Group. Forschungsunion (2013). https://books.google.es/books?id=AsfOoAEACAAJ
23. Kelly, S., Tolvanen, J.: Domain-Specific Modeling - Enabling Full Code Generation. Wiley, Hoboken (2008). http://eu.wiley.com/WileyCDA/WileyTitle/productCd-0470036664.html
24. Leitão, P., Colombo, A.W., Karnouskos, S.: Industrial automation based on cyber-physical systems technologies: prototype implementations and challenges. Comput. Ind. **81**, 11–25 (2016)
25. Negash, B., Westerlund, T., Rahmani, A., Liljeberg, P., Tenhunen, H.: Dos-il: a domain specific internet of things language for resource constrained devices. Proc. Comput. Sci. **109**, 416–423 (2017). https://doi.org/10.1016/j.procs.2017.05.411
26. Parra, J.: Restful Framework for Collaborative Internet of Things Based on IEC 61850. Ph.D. thesis, Universidad del País Vasco - Euskal Herriko Unibertsitatea (UPV/EHU) (2016)
27. Pedersen, A.B., Hauksson, E.B., Andersen, P.B., Poulsen, B., Træholt, C., Gantenbein, D.: Facilitating a generic communication interface to distributed energy resources: mapping IEC 61850 to RESTful services. In: 2010 First IEEE International Conference on Smart Grid Communications (SmartGridComm), pp. 61–66 (2010)
28. Sanz, R., Clavijo, J.A., Segarra, M.J., de Antonio, A., Alonso, M.: CORBA-based substation automation systems. In: Proceedings of IEEE Conference on Control Applications (2001)
29. Shin, I.J., Song, B.K., Eom, D.S.: International Electronical Committee (IEC) 61850 mapping with constrained application protocol (CoAP) in smart grids based European telecommunications standard institute machine-to-machine (M2M) environment. Energies **10**(3), 393 (2017)
30. Sinnhofer, A.D., et al.: Combining business process variability and software variability using traceable links. In: Shishkov, B. (ed.) BMSD 2017. LNBIP, vol. 309, pp. 67–86. Springer, Cham (2018). https://doi.org/10.1007/978-3-319-78428-1_4
31. Sneps-Sneppe, M., Namiot, D.: On web-based domain-specific language for Internet of Things. In: International Congress on Ultra Modern Telecommunications and Control Systems and Workshops, vol. 2016-January, pp. 287–292. IEEE Computer Society (2016). https://doi.org/10.1109/ICUMT.2015.7382444
32. Tang, H., Li, D., Wang, S., Dong, Z.: CASOA: an architecture for agent-based manufacturing system in the context of industry 4.0. IEEE Access **6**, 12746–12754 (2018)
33. Tao, F., Zuo, Y., Xu, L.D., Zhang, L.: IoT-based intelligent perception and access of manufacturing resource toward cloud manufacturing. IEEE Trans. Ind. Inform. **10**(2), 1547–1557 (2014)
34. TC-57, I.: Communication networks and systems in substations - part 7–1: Basic communication structure for substation and feeder equipment - principles and models (2003)
35. Van Deursen, A., Klint, P.: Domain-specific language design requires feature descriptions. J. Comput. Inf. Technol. **10**(1), 1–17 (2002)
36. Young, B., Cheatwood, J., Peterson, T., Flores, R., Clements, P.C.: Product line engineering meets model based engineering in the defense and automotive industries. In: Proceedings of the 21st International Systems and Software Product Line Conference, SPLC 2017, vol. A, pp. 175–179 (2017)

Author Index

Author Index

Printed in the United States
By Bookmasters